I0446096

Florida's American Heritage River

UNIVERSITY PRESS OF FLORIDA

Florida A&M University, Tallahassee

Florida Atlantic University, Boca Raton

Florida Gulf Coast University, Ft. Myers

Florida International University, Miami

Florida State University, Tallahassee

New College of Florida, Sarasota

University of Central Florida, Orlando

University of Florida, Gainesville

University of North Florida, Jacksonville

University of South Florida, Tampa

University of West Florida, Pensacola

The Melbourne artist Spence Guerin likes to work on location using carefully selected materials that are meant to last. He painted *Managed Marsh* at the Goodwin Waterfowl Management Area along the St. Johns River Marsh near the river's headwaters southwest of Melbourne. This portion of the reclaimed marsh is "managed" as a waterfowl habitat. "When I was a kid," Guerin recalls, "the area looked much as it does in the painting. That was before the marsh was ditched, drained, farmed, and subdivided. Now, to have natural native marsh we have to manage it. There are some ironies here."[1] *Managed Marsh* was created over a period of months during 1999–2000. Guerin works slowly. "I work on paintings until they seem to have a satisfying sense of solid reality to them," he says. "The continuous flow of changing conditions throughout the work session—that may extend over weeks or months or even years—offers endless visual opportunities for enriching and strengthening the painting. . . . Long-term paintings . . . encompass the passage of time and become a kind of celebration of time and life, the cycle of life and death, and the organized chaos of nature at work."[2]

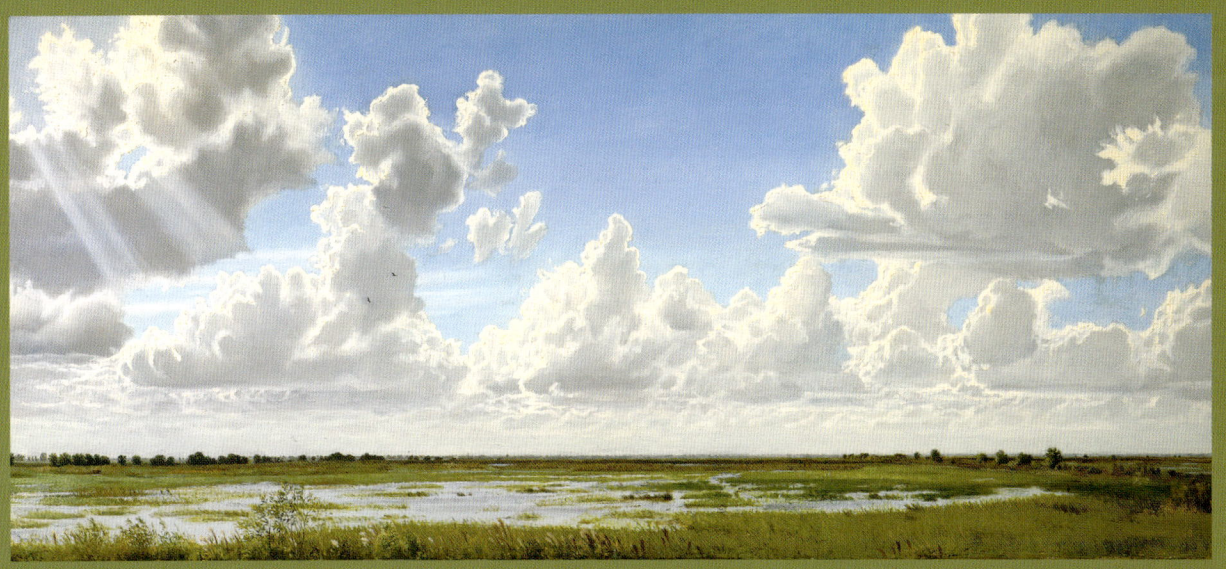

Spence Guerin. *Managed Marsh*, 1999–2000. Oil on linen, 16 × 36 in. Courtesy of the artist.

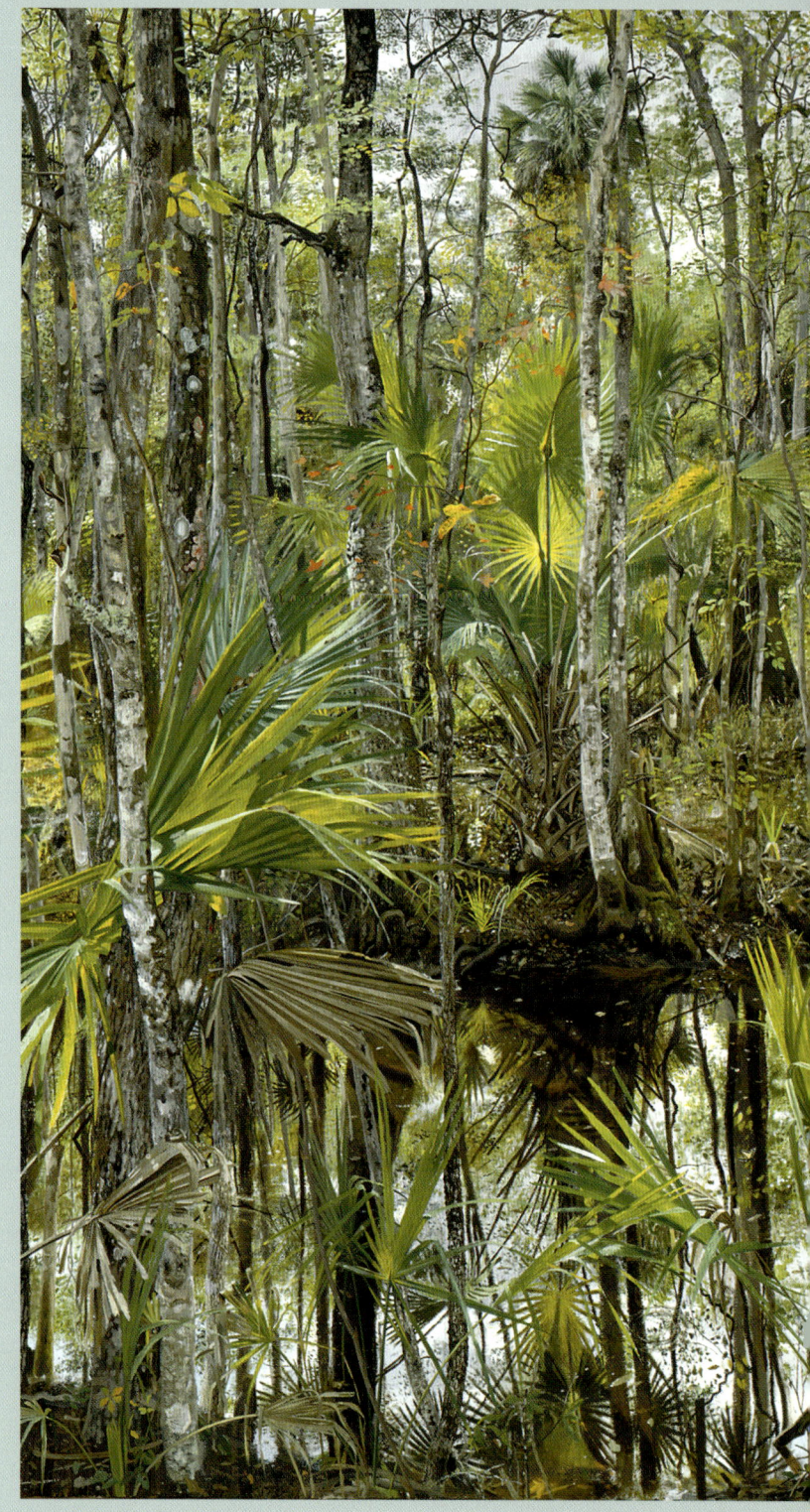

University
Press of
Florida

Gainesville
Tallahassee
Tampa
Boca Raton
Pensacola
Orlando
Miami
Jacksonville
Ft. Myers
Sarasota

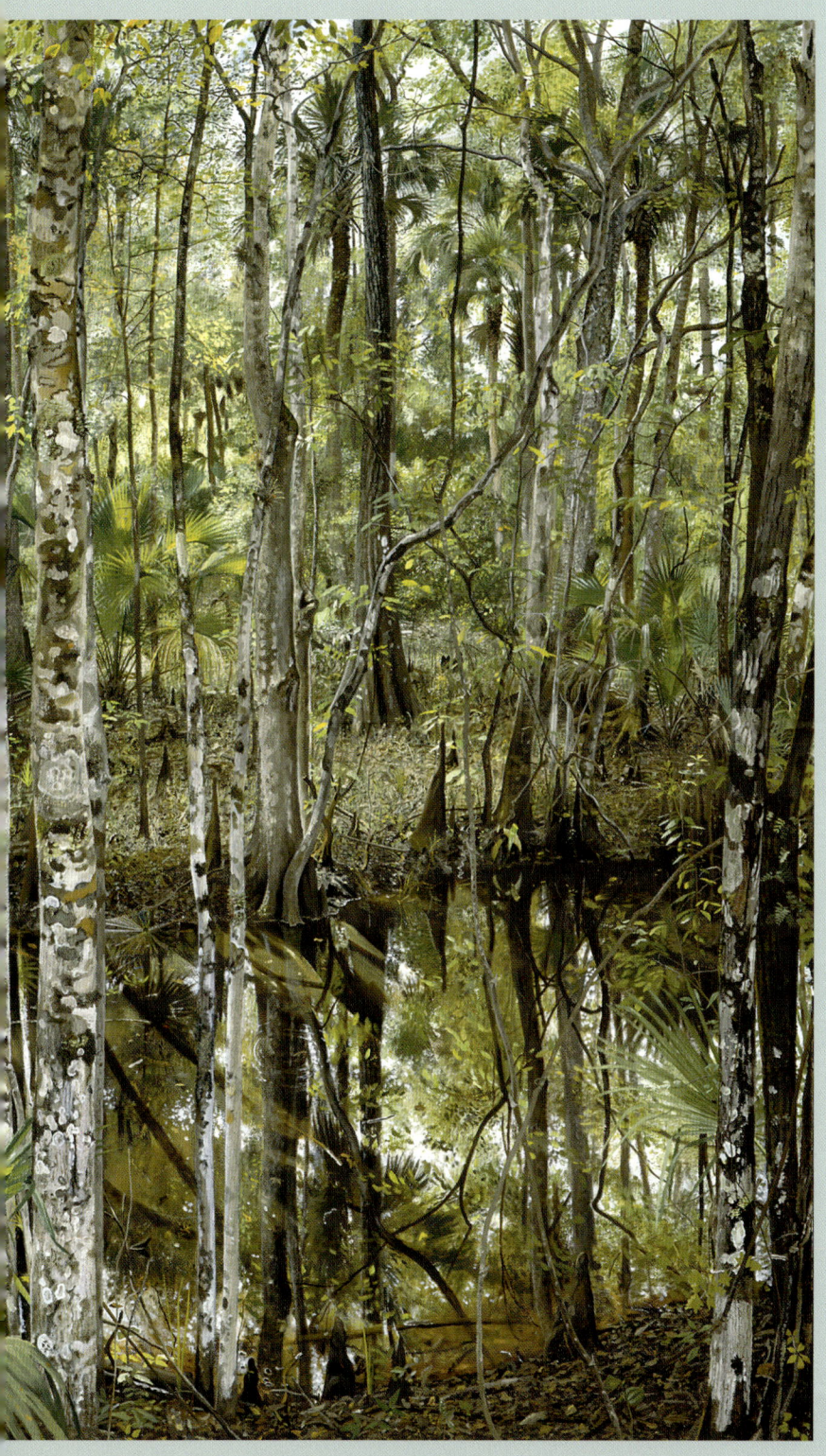

Florida's American Heritage River Images from the St. Johns Region

Mallory M. O'Connor
and Gary Monroe

Introduction by Bill Belleville

Painting on previous page: Spence Guerin. *Tootoosahatchee*, 1991–94. Oil on linen, 48 × 60 in. Courtesy of the artist.

Copyright 2009 by Mallory M. O'Connor and Gary Monroe
Printed in China on acid-free paper
All rights reserved

14 13 12 11 10 09   6 5 4 3 2 1

Library of Congress Cataloging-in-Publication Data
O'Connor, Mallory McCane.
Florida's American Heritage River : images from the St. Johns region / Mallory M. O'Connor and Gary Monroe.
p. cm.
Includes bibliographical references and index.
ISBN 978-0-8130-3352-5 (alk. paper)
1. Saint Johns River Region (Fla.)—In art.
2. Art, American. 3. Cultural landscapes—Florida. I. Monroe, Gary. II. American Heritage Rivers Initiative (U.S.) III. Title.
N8214.5.U6O28 2009
704.9′4997591—dc22   2008052379

The University Press of Florida is the scholarly publishing agency for the State University System of Florida, comprising Florida A&M University, Florida Atlantic University, Florida Gulf Coast University, Florida International University, Florida State University, New College of Florida, University of Central Florida, University of Florida, University of North Florida, University of South Florida, and University of West Florida.

University Press of Florida
15 Northwest 15th Street
Gainesville, FL 32611-2079
http://www.upf.com

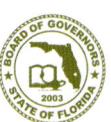

The New England landscape painter Martin Johnson Heade arrived in Florida in 1883. Heade's Florida experience, like that of many of his contemporaries, began with a boat ride down the St. Johns River, and he returned to the river again and again for inspiration.[3] His work was greatly influenced by the romantic landscapes of Frederic Church, and his preference for capturing the effects of light at transitional times of day made the lush landscape along the St. Johns especially attractive to the artist. Many of his most important paintings were views of what was then considered the exotic and romantic environment of the river and its surrounding area.

Paintings like this one by Heade present viewers with a vision of paradise that pre-dates the disappointing realities of crowded beaches and thoughtless development. To surrender to the allure of these images is to leave reality behind and enter the world of the imagination, the realm of myth. And it is through myth that we can best appreciate the impact that artists have had on the development of Florida's visual mythology—a mythology in which the St. Johns River has played a major role.

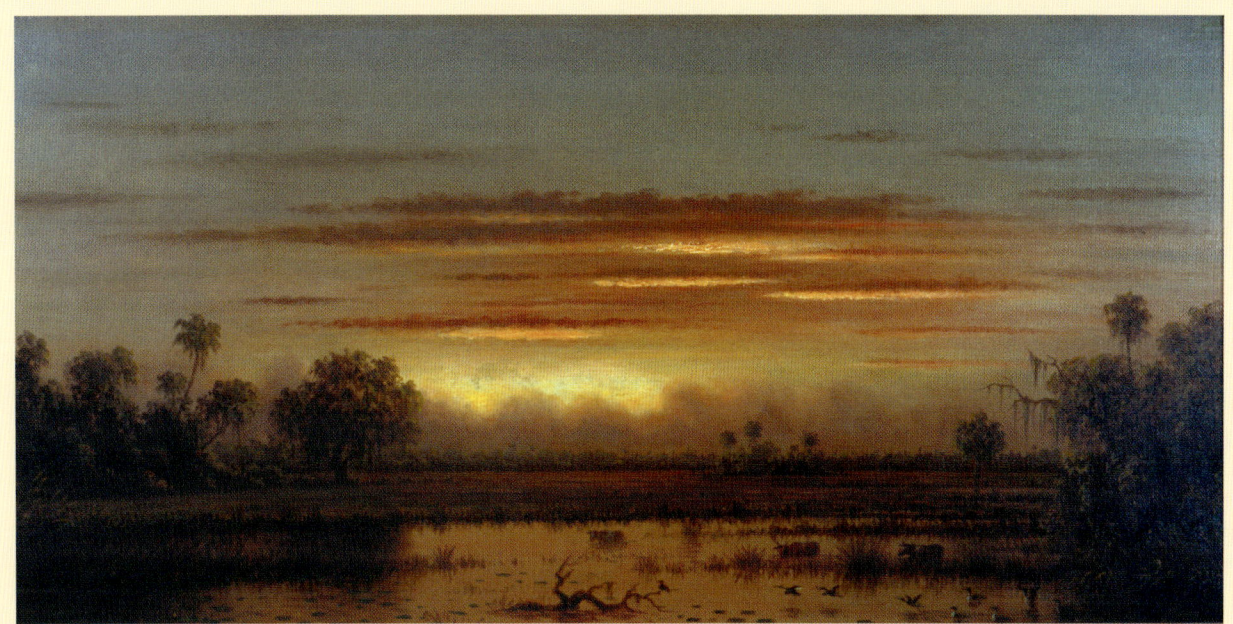

Most of the world's great civilizations grew up around rivers, and few forces have so clearly shaped the destiny of human populations.
—Michael Specter, "The Last Drop"

Martin Johnson Heade. *The St. Johns River*, ca. 1890. Oil on canvas, 13 × 26 in. The Cummer Museum of Art and Gardens, Jacksonville, Florida.

Contents

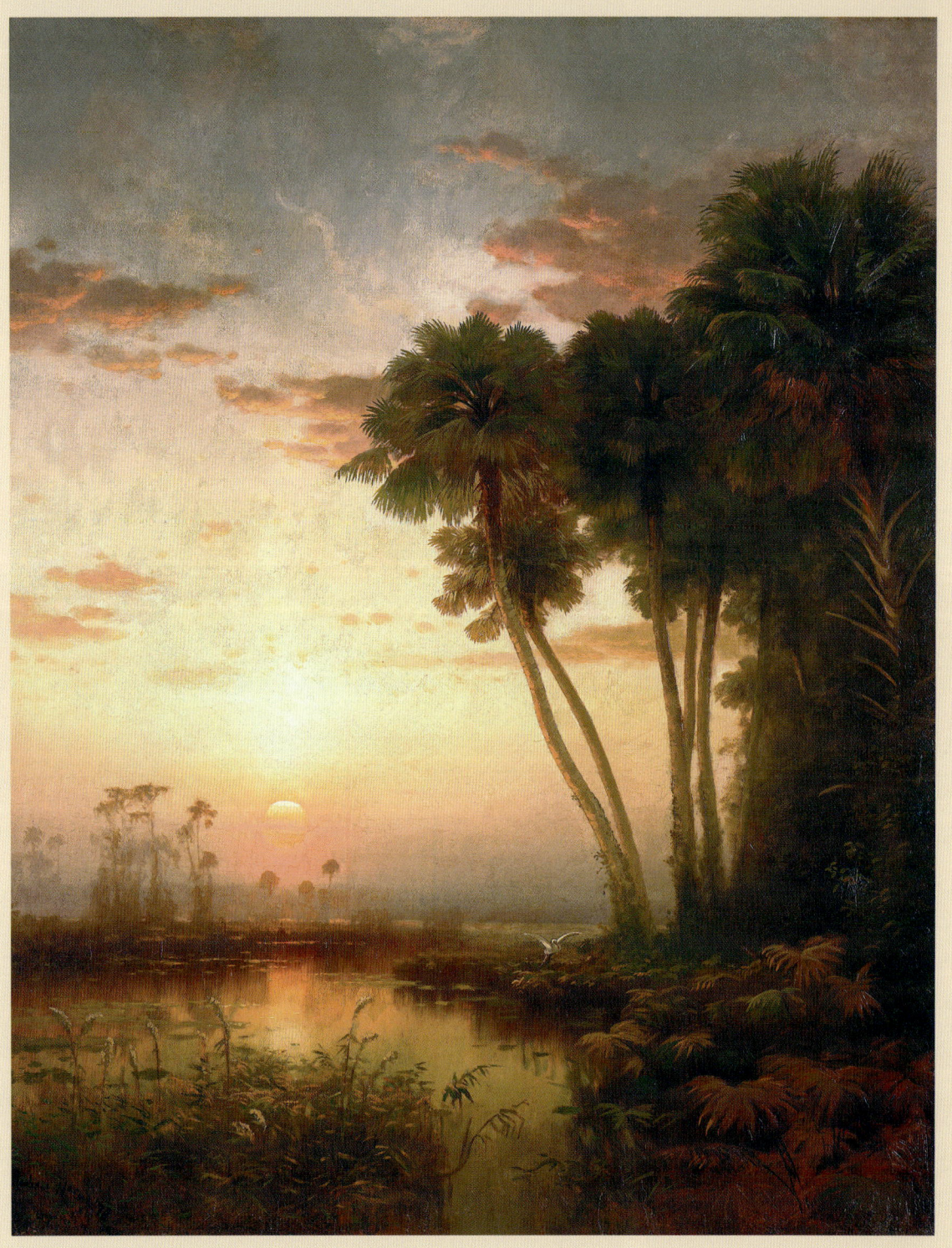

Preface and Acknowledgments

ARTISTS HAVE ALWAYS BEEN ATTRACTED TO WATER. Maybe it's the magic of reflected light that draws them. Or perhaps it's the alchemical challenge of trying to capture the essence of that boundary between water and land, between solid and liquid—the place where opposites meet and mingle. With approximately 12,000 miles of rivers and streams, 7,700 lakes, and nearly 700 springs, Florida has in abundance those very elements so prized by generations of artists. And great artists have always known that when cultural memory demands documentation, a picture can indeed be worth a thousand words.

The ecological, historical, and cultural characteristics of the St. Johns River combine to make it one of America's most unique waterways. For over ten thousand years, people have lived, worked, traveled, and dreamed on or alongside the St. Johns, and its recorded history is among the oldest in North America. Because of the river's cultural and historic significance, the St. Johns was officially designated an American Heritage River in 1998, one of fourteen rivers nationwide to receive this recognition. The designation provided a unique opportunity to mount an extensive exploration of the river's cultural, ecological, and historic role in Florida's development and to focus attention on the need for historic and cultural preservation, economic revitalization, and natural resource and environmental protection. This book is the result of that exploration.

In order to adequately examine the historical and ecological significance of the river, we had first to determine the extent of the river's impact on the region. It soon became clear that it was impossible to separate the river itself from its surrounding environment. The river was not only a stream of water that moved from south to north along a 310-mile route, it was also the tributaries that joined with it along the way, the canals that siphoned

Plate 1. (*facing*) George Herbert McCord. *The St. Johns River Sunset*, 1878. Oil on canvas, 34 × 26 in. The Ogden Museum of Southern Art, University of New Orleans, New Orleans.

off its water, the springs that replenished it, and the adjacent lakes, marshes, and streams that made up the complex system that nurtured the river and affected it in many different ways. We needed to explore the entire St. Johns drainage basin—also known as the watershed—if we were going to understand the true significance of the river.

The St. Johns River Water Management District covers a fifteen-county area that is bordered on the east by the Atlantic Ocean and reaches as far south as Indian River County, as far north as the Florida-Georgia border, and as far west as western Alachua County. The area includes all three of the St. Johns major drainage basins—the Upper Basin, where the river forms in the marshes of Indian River and Brevard Counties (see frontispiece); the Middle Basin of Central Florida, where the river widens into a string of lakes and also draws from the rivers, lakes, and springs to the west (see plates 3 and 4); and the Lower Basin, which runs from southern Putnam County to the river's mouth, where it empties into the Atlantic Ocean (see plate 5). To fully explore the visual history of the river, we included all fifteen counties and the major tributaries of the St. Johns in our exploration.

The images included in this book were selected from hundreds of pictures that frame the St. Johns River region in a myriad of different ways. Some echo the chants and songs of the earliest human inhabitants who relied on the river and its bounty for their very survival. Others mirror the development of human activity as people came and went and came again over the centuries. Some speak of the advent of industry, of advances in transportation, of the fertility of the river basin and the agriculture that was nourished by its water, of the struggle for territory and wealth, of the cadence of cultural evolution and diversity that changed the course of history but not the river's never-ending flow.

We began our search in summer 2001 after a conversation about the many different ways that people have viewed the St. Johns region. How did the sportsman's view differ from that of the environmentalist? Or the hydrologist's from that of the artist? And of all of those from that of the developer? What do people see when they look at a river, a lake, a canal, a marsh? How have their views changed over time? Do images mirror culture or do they create culture? We set out on a mission of exploration and discovery.

The images were out there—thousands of them. We found them in antique shops and art galleries, in books and magazines and pamphlets, in private collections and public places, in fish camps and flea markets and, of course, on the Internet. Some of our selections represent the "fine art" tradition of artists such as Thomas Moran or Martin Johnson Heade; others were created by anonymous craftsmen or eccentric self-taught "visionaries." Some of the objects are ancient; others were completed within the past year.

More than mirroring culture, the work of the artists represented in this book mirrors environments, both physical and ideological. These artists have responded to both a sense of place and a sense of cultural identity, and those factors have determined the style and content of their creations. Rather than write a history of the St. Johns region and then look for pictures to use as illustrations, we decided to use the images, artifacts, and objects that we found as a point of departure and see what they could tell us. The narrative is, then, informed by the images. Each image has a story to tell. Our job was to put those stories into the larger historical context of the river valley region and to examine the ways in which the *place,* the river region, has affected the development of human culture.

We don't pretend that we have told every story—we invite further investigation and discovery—but of the hundreds of images that we encountered, we have selected 202 that we believe best represent the diverse ways that people have interacted with their liquid muse over the past ten thousand years. These pictures tell a thousand stories. The river has heard them all.

Over the past five years, we were assisted in our work by many wonderful friends, colleagues, museum professionals, and, of course, the artists themselves; however, there are a few we would like to mention with special thanks. Bill Belleville was a voice of inspiration for our project, and it was his book *River of Lakes* that gave us the idea for an illustrated journey along the St. Johns. Murray Laurie was also involved with the manuscript almost from the beginning and has offered her insights, expertise, and encouragement throughout the life of the project. Likewise, Arlene Fradkin lent her able criticism of the archaeological section of the manuscript and advised us on content, and Elsbeth Gordon contributed images of Florida colonial architecture.

Collectors were very gracious and shared with us so many gems from their holdings. Special thanks to Sam and Robbie Vickers, Danny and Tracy McKenna, Dick and Yvonne Punnett, John Herrmann, Tommy Vincent, David La Cagnina, Larry Wilson, David and Susan White, Bob Harper, and Joseph and Faith Tiberio. Likewise, cultural institutions provided images and expertise. Our thanks to Alicia Clarke (Sanford Museum), Karen Jacobs (Museum of Seminole County History), Charlotte Porter, Kathleen Deagan, Darcie McMahon, and Donna Rhul (Florida Museum of Natural History), Tom Baskett (Volusia County Historian), Bill Dreggors (West Volusia Historical Society), Suzi Preston (Volusia County Schools), Scott Mitchell (Silver River Museum), Steve Spect (Silver Springs), the Matheson Museum, Alecto Historical Editions, the American Philosophical Society, and the Florida Humanities Council.

Finally, many thanks to our respective spouses—John and Teresa—for their patience and input during the very long time that we pursued our dream of collaborating on a book about the history of the St. Johns. They deserve a medal for bravery in the face of chaos. Our gratitude goes out to all of those who helped us and who believed in the significance of what we were attempting to accomplish.

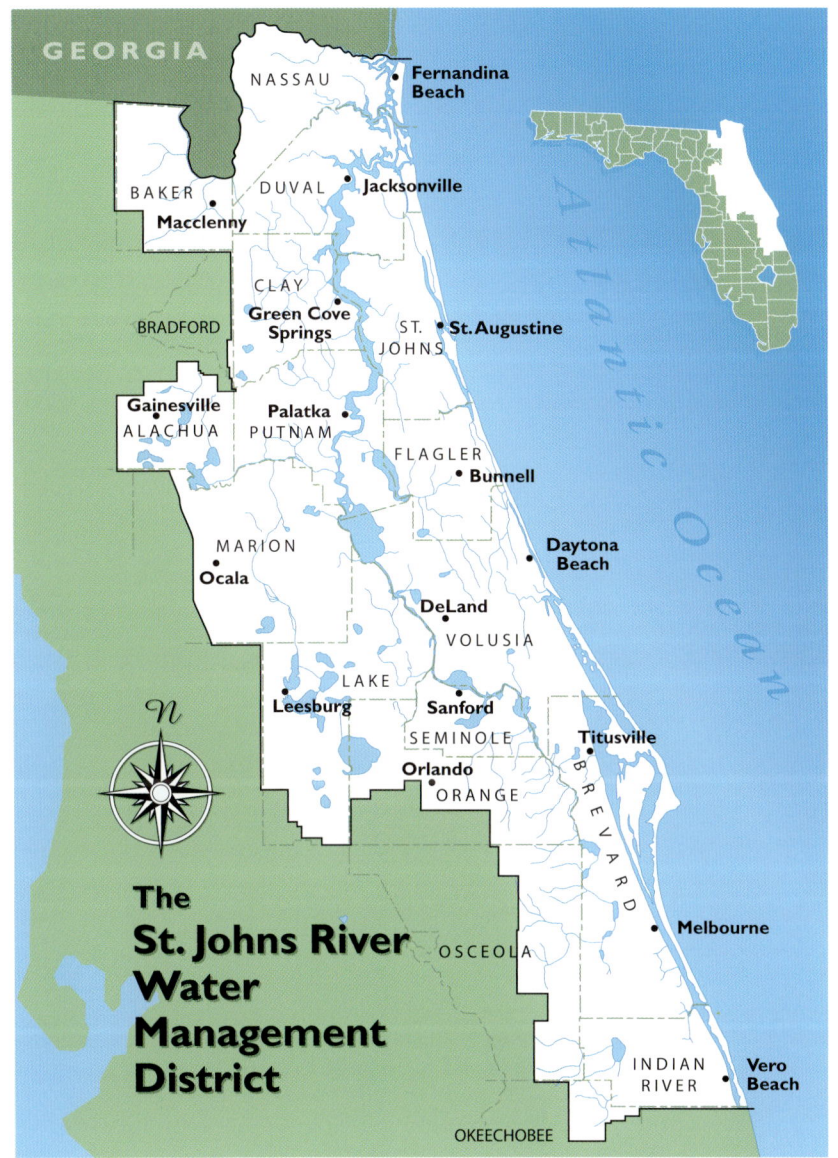

GEORGIA

NASSAU
• Fernandina Beach

DUVAL
• Jacksonville

BAKER
• Macclenny

CLAY
Green Cove Springs

BRADFORD

ST. JOHNS
• St. Augustine

Gainesville
ALACHUA

Palatka
PUTNAM

FLAGLER
• Bunnell

MARION
• Ocala

Daytona Beach

DeLand
VOLUSIA

LAKE
Leesburg

Sanford
SEMINOLE

Titusville

Orlando
ORANGE

B R E V A R D

Atlantic Ocean

n

The
St. Johns River Water Management District

OSCEOLA

Melbourne

OKEECHOBEE

INDIAN RIVER
Vero Beach

Plate 2. Map of the fifteen counties that make up the St. Johns River watershed. Courtesy of the St. Johns River Water Management District, Palatka, Florida.

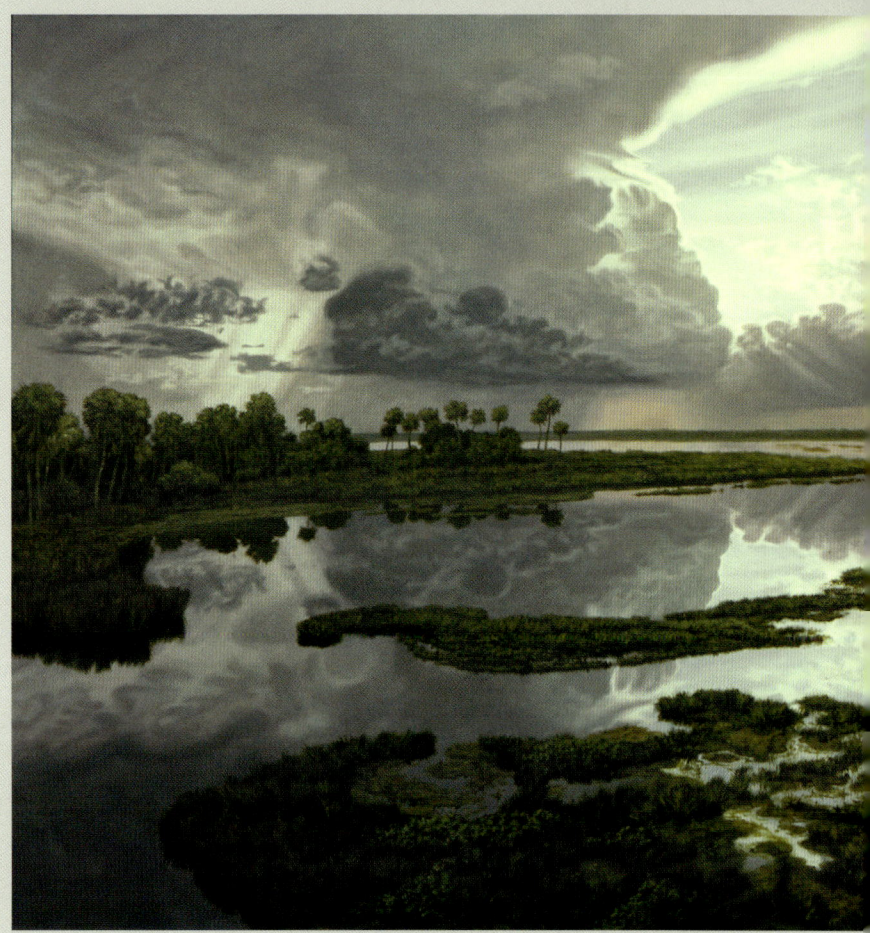

Hansen Mulford has devoted most of his career as an artist to painting landscapes of the Florida wilderness. He has chosen subjects from the high dunes of Ponte Vedra to the mangrove flats of Florida Bay. Another favorite locale has been the St. Johns River because of its beauty, its varied terrain, and its many unspoiled stretches. Mulford is attracted to the seemingly limitless space that recedes to wide low horizons, to an expanse that is dominated by the sky. Water and sky are important elements in his work; the tangle of forest and river grasses bordering the horizon adds complexity to the compositions. Viewers of Hansen Mulford's paintings are apt to experience the images as a kind of quiet meditation about existence. This is in keeping with the values of nineteenth-century landscape painting, which have maintained their distance from twentieth-century aesthetics.

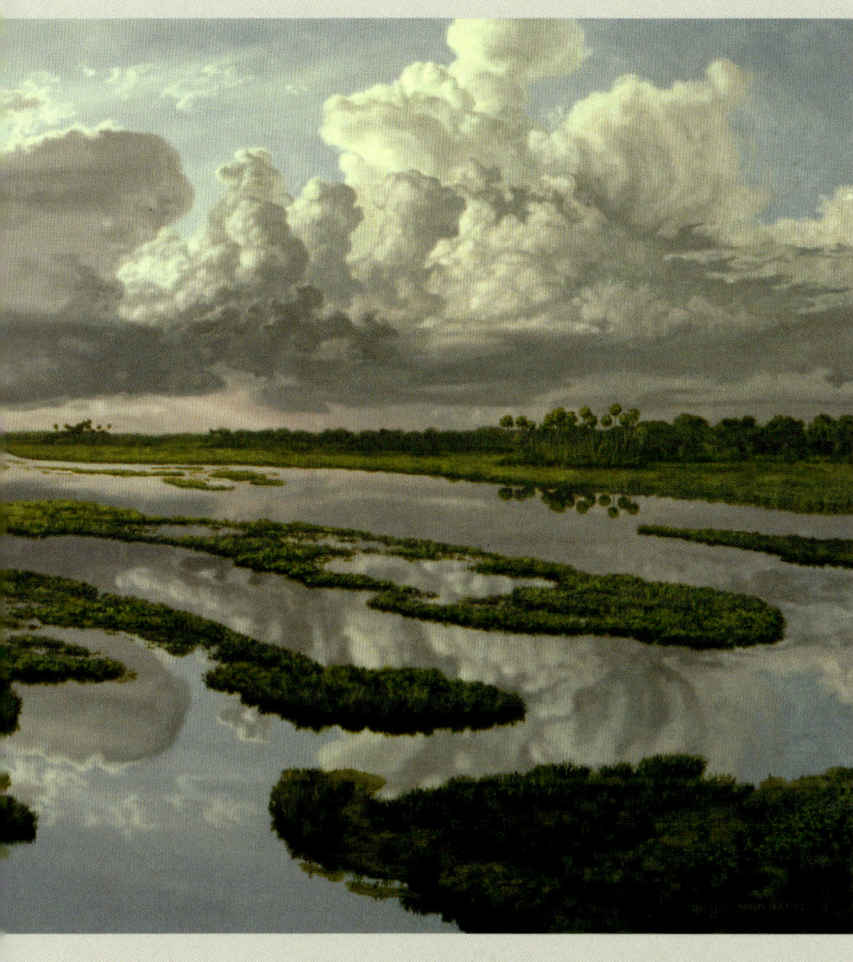

Plate 3. Hansen Mulford. *Storm Approaching over the St. Johns River*, 1984. Oil on canvas, 40 × 84 in. Collection of Michael A. Mennello.

The Hudson River school of artists and their successors, whom Mulford admires, reveled in the awe-inspiring vastness of the land. Mulford acknowledges debts to such nineteenth-century American painters as Frederic Church and Martin Johnson Heade. "When I began painting in Florida I looked for models, sources to start from. There is relatively little of visual interest in Florida's topography, but the sky is exciting to watch. I found in the American Luminist painters a way to approach the romantic drama of Florida's sky."[4]

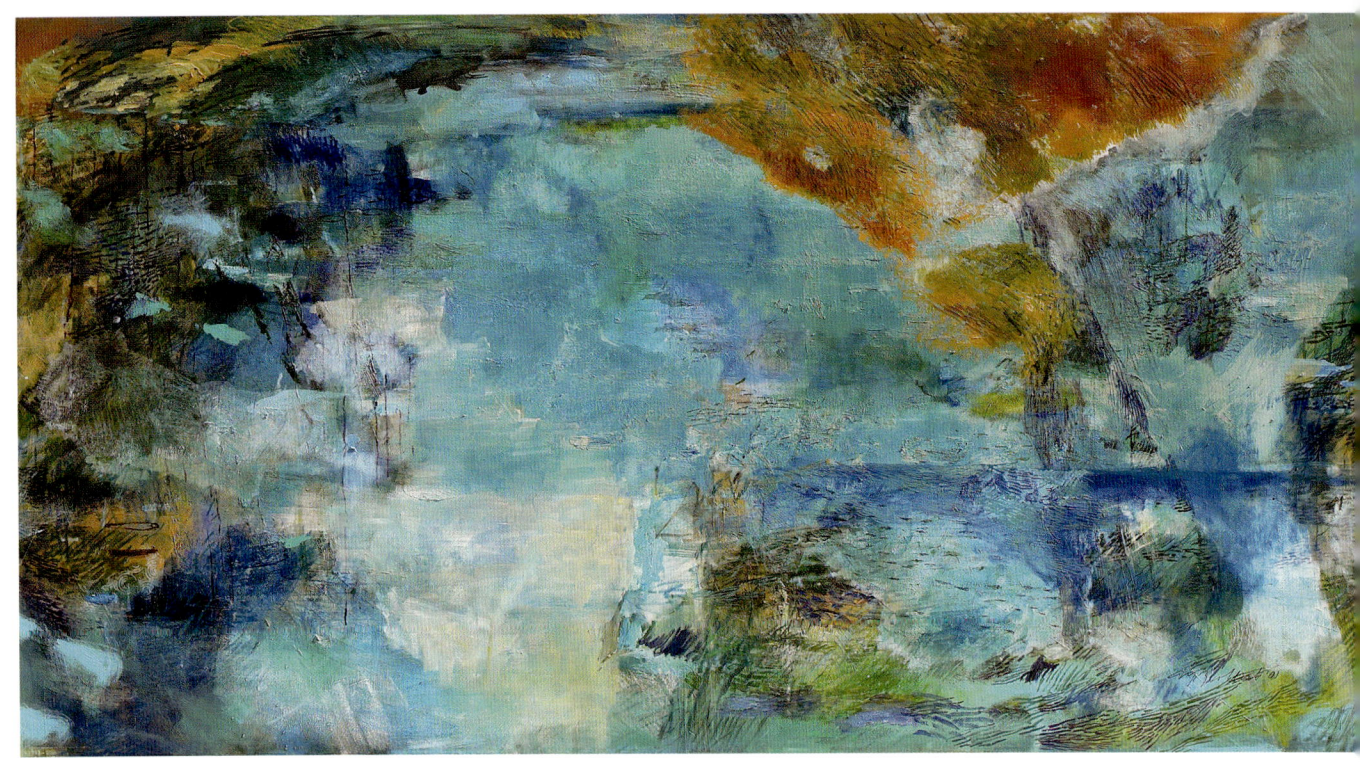

Plate 4. Margaret Ross Tolbert. *Beyond Blue Springs*, 2001. Oil and mixed media on canvas, 72 × 144 in. Collection of the Volusia County Courthouse/Funded by the Art in State Buildings Program.

The story of art in the twentieth century has mirrored the rapid urbanization and mechanization of Western culture—developments that led a generation of creative spirits away from the Muse of the natural world and into the cold, hard steel and glass canyons of contemporary urban life. Modern art was birthed at the German Bauhaus and grew to maturity in the urban centers of Europe and America. In the "less is more" world of modernism, the organic sensuality of nature came to be considered archaic and untidy. This mind-set produced a critical climate that condemned representations of nature as sentimental and outdated.

Yet, when they are exposed to the idyllic and mysterious vestiges of wild nature, contemporary artists such as Gainesville's Margaret Tolbert have found themselves drawn into the rich, voluptuous body of the Old Goddess, Gaia herself. Although she was trained in the modern abstract tradition, Tolbert grew up surrounded by pockets of still-pristine wilderness and has sought out archetypal scenes that invite the viewer to abandon the hard ecology of the urban landscape and descend with her into the mysterious and timeless world of the Florida aquifer.

In her series of "Springs" paintings—done mostly at spots visited by the eighteenth-century artist-naturalist William Bartram himself—Tolbert demonstrates that a contemporary artist can create art that is true both to twenty-first-century esthetics and the geographic environment that has inspired and nurtured Floridians, both native and adopted, for the past ten thousand years.

In order to fully experience her subject, Tolbert literally immerses herself in it, diving into the depths of the springs, turning her vision of the world inside out. The surface of the painting is made up of layers of transparent color. Diagonal shafts of light slice through tiers of blue, and white bubbles shimmer as they rise in the whirling water. In describing her "Springs" paintings, Tolbert often relies on poetry:

> Enter; a blue city, inside a
> Wildly vaulted upside down space;
> Brilliant dust streams to the surface from a dark vent far below.
> In the colored world a gar hovers, a bowfin hides
> In waving grasses, then dragon-like, unfurls to a new recess;
> Shadows of schools of mullet ink the grasses,
> A net of diamond minnows spans the blue and distant void
> Between plants and mirrored surface, the water's sky.
> —Margaret Ross Tolbert

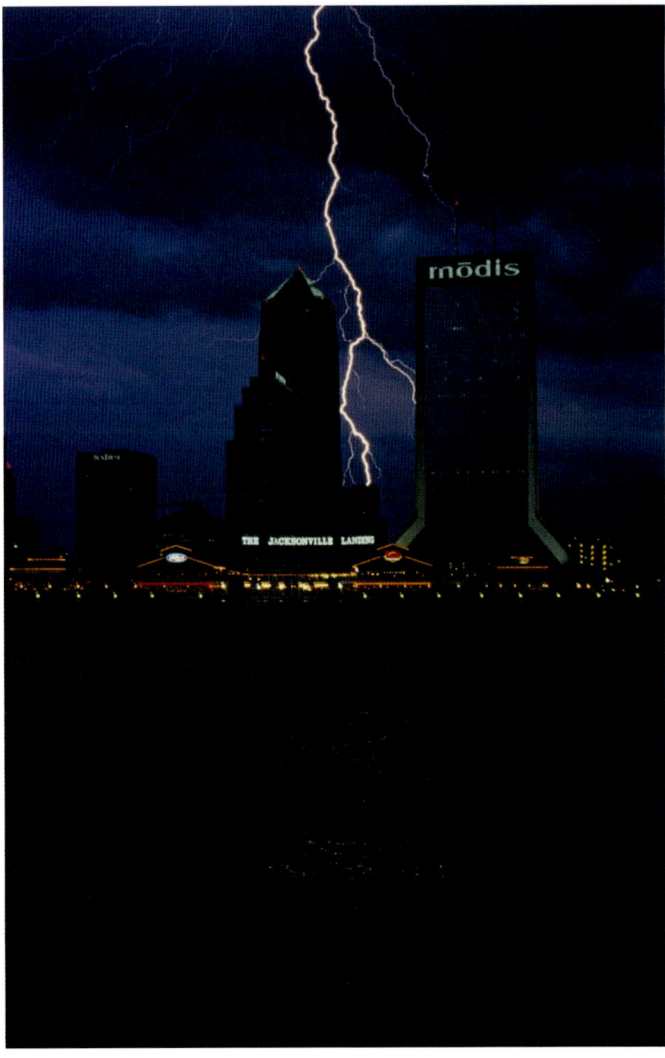

Plate 5. James Johnson. "Lightning Striking the MODIS Building," n.d. Color photograph. Courtesy of the artist.

The Jacksonville photographer James Johnson appreciates the drama of the urban landscape, and he frequently focuses on the landmarks that characterize the power and allure of the contemporary man-made environment—the steel towers rearing toward heaven, the spans of bridges glowing like strings of jewels, the mythic power of architecture to encompass a vision of structure and stability. Yet he also acknowledges the power of nature to challenge man's arrogance. In this remarkable photograph of the Jacksonville skyline as viewed from the St. Johns River, Johnson unites heaven and earth—nature and man—as a bolt of lightning connects the towering MODIS building with the threatening sky above.

Florida's American Heritage River

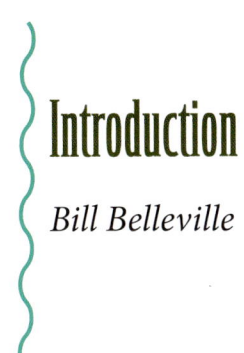

Introduction

Bill Belleville

THERE ARE BEARS IN THE WOODS TODAY. I know because I see their tracks in the soft white sugar sand, the sign of an ancient animal on an ancient dune, miles from the sea. It is *Ursus americanus floridanus*, a subspecies of the black bear, and it is unique to Florida.

I look closely and see the pads of the feet are big and full. Except for the claw marks, which cut into the sand, the tracks might almost be cartoonish, as if left by a giant, precious toy bear come to life.

But if black bears are precious—in fact, they're threatened with extinction in Florida—they are not toys. They are big, wild animals that need a lot of landscape to roam. When their territory is fragmented, the animals still lumber across these man-made boundaries, just as they've been doing long before we started building roads and Golden Arches. The native pre-Columbian tribes and, later, the Creeks who would become Seminoles hunted this bear on the peninsula. So did the white settlers who followed.

Bears range for the same reasons we do—for food, comfort, and, when the need arises, a warm body. They especially range at the swampy edges of the St. Johns River and along the sandy scarps that define the low valley of the river basin. The St. Johns is both a habitat and a natural corridor for bears, and they wade its swamps and swim its waters to get where they want to be. There are more Florida bears packed together in the basin of the Ocala-Wekiva Corridor of the St. Johns than anywhere else.

About a half million acres of land have been set aside as a riverine buffer along much of this historic 310-mile-long river, from its headwaters near Lake Okeechobee to its oceanic confluence east of Jacksonville. Thousands more acres are protected inside national forests and wildlife refuges and inside state and county parks and preserves. Though civilization increasingly

This St. Johns becomes a river of infinite potential, a place to indulge myths, to evoke shards of timeless magic, to search for the natural realities that are sublime instead of merely virtual and safe. After all, this is a river where dreams have been chased through the early morning mist for centuries . . . from inside the heart-pine log dugouts of the earliest Paleoindians to the sleek polymer hulls of the most modern canoeist and boater.

—Bill Belleville, *River of Lakes*

pushes in on all sides, there is still enough wilderness left in the St. Johns basin to accommodate the bears.

Like people and their art, the bears who live here have been changed by the experience, shaped into something different from their counterparts back on the continent. In this way, the bear can be seen as a metaphor for how culture has been configured to adapt to our singular Florida realities. We are warm, wet, a little strange. The St. Johns itself—once marketed as the "Nile of the Americas" because it is exotic and flows north—has a persona all its own. Historically, it has been an aquatic superhighway funneling people into the interior of a soggy predredged peninsula where there were few dependable roads. For this reason, the history of the river has been closely aligned with the history of the state itself.

Ironically, when railroads and, later, highways were built, the utility of the river suffered, its prestige waned. By the middle of the twentieth century, most river towns had turned their back on the St. Johns. Once a conveyor of myth and opportunity, the St. Johns became a glorified ditch to transport wastewater. Many wetlands had been drained and converted to farm- and pastureland, especially in the headwaters. Then federal clean-water laws began to take effect. By the early 1970s, biologists with the regional Water Management District began quietly working on plans that would re-create the wetlands and creeks that once had birthed the river. State land-acquisition programs bought wooded shoreline to keep its swamps intact, storing and filtering water. The St. Johns River would have a second chance.

Today the woods on the trail around me are luxuriant and alive—the oaks have dropped chubby acorns, cinnamon ferns have sent up new fiddleheads, and berries are thick on the saw palmettos. As if to celebrate the advent of this bruin bacchanal, wildflowers are raging—the bright purple rods of blazing star, the carnival frill of the passionflower, the cerulean blue of the celestial lily.

Last night it rained, and the tracks I see now are so new they must have been made just a few hours—or perhaps minutes—ago. Scat, which appears in great blue-black piles of berries and nuts on the trail, seems just as fresh. I look closely at the trunks of young longleaf pines for other signs, and soon they appear: Bark has been stripped off several trees, as if a bear has stood on its hind legs and reached up as far as it could. On one bare trunk, claw marks have been left behind, the signature of a male marking his turf. Pine resin still trickles from the gashes. Collectively, you can think of these signs as the art of the bear, an oeuvre that was being created long before a river craftsman shaped the first stone point and clay pot, before the landscape painter first touched brush to canvas.

I have been searching for bears for twenty years along the St. Johns. As searches tend to do, this quest has taken me to places I never intended to go, introducing me to an authentic wilderness where I thought there was none. After all, Florida is an odd, discordant state where most tourists are lured into believing that no reality exists except in contrived theme parks or on replenished faux beaches, seen from a patio over pink-umbrella drinks.

Where there is no such development, wet forest and marshlands may stretch out for miles, as they do around the St. Johns River. When I first ventured deep into this relic of the wild Florida landscape, I did so in this 8,840-square-mile river valley because that is where I live. Like other artistically minded souls—from artists to writers to musicians—I was moved enough by the experience to want to memorialize it in my own craft. Certainly this north-flowing river has been used longer by Europeans than any other in North America, beginning with a French colony at Fort Caroline near Jacksonville in 1564. It is a river that still has lots of stories to tell. Some of those stories can be read and understood through the art left behind—and from the art still being created.

During my own explorations, I "traveled" with a naturalist guide, one of the best there ever was. His name is William "Billy" Bartram, and in his *Travels* (published in 1791), he convinced me of the magic hidden here. Although he roamed the American Southeast in his journeys, he seemed most infatuated with the St. Johns and its gothic, vine-hung mystique.

During most of his explorations, Bartram sailed and rowed up and down this "grand and noble San Juan," sleeping on "couches" of Spanish moss under the canopies of massive live oaks and magnolias. He not only made two extensive journeys upstream—one all the way into labyrinthine Puzzle Lake—he also lived for two years on the river near Picolata, trying without much success to run a small indigo plantation there.

Despite his challenges, Bartram's spirit seemed indomitable. His child-like enthusiasm has become a fine antidote to our modern world-weariness:

"How happily situated is this retired spot of earth!" he wrote after a night on Drayton Island. "What an Elysium it is!"[1] All plants and animals fascinated him as he thought them to be no lower or higher than humans in the entire scale of life. He grieved once after killing a bear, and thought the carnivorous *Drosera* to be a "sportive vegetable."

The Orlando artist Jackson Walker is best known for his renderings of military subjects. In *The Forlorn Hope of Fort King Road,* he chronicles the events of the Dade Massacre, and in the *Wrath of the Privateers*, he recalls the 1586 raid on Spanish St. Augustine by Sir Francis Drake. But his knowledge of Florida history and his knack for storytelling compelled Walker to paint the *The Flower Hunter*, a depiction of the gentle William Bartram as he paddled his solitary vessel along the St. Johns River. As to how he acquired his nickname, Bartram wrote in his *Travels*:

> We were welcomed to the town, [Cuscowilla near present-day Micanopy, Florida] and conducted by the young men and maidens to the chief's house. . . . The chief, who is called the Cowkeeper, attended by several ancient men, came to us and in a very free and sociable manner, shook our hands. . . . After the usual compliments and inquiries relative to our adventures . . . the chief trader informed the Cowkeeper, in the presence of his council or attendants, the purport of our business, with which he expressed his satisfaction. He was then informed what the nature of my errand was, and he received me with complaisance, giving me unlimited permission to travel over the country . . . and saluting me by the name of Puc Puggy, or the Flower Hunter, recommending me to the friendship and protection of his people.[2]

For this painting of William Bartram, Walker traversed the St. Johns' riverbanks to see what had washed up, what the explorer himself might have seen, stepped over, or drawn. These objects become foreground details in his painting. Walker wants the viewer to "look out for fifty miles but also to see clearly and in detail, objects in the foreground."[3] With the flair of a Dutch master, he dramatizes a scene to create a historical record, a method more emotionally provocative than fastidiously accurate. Walker arranges the facts of his compositions to achieve monumental acclaim, even in the most sublime activities and settings. The solitary explorer Bartram coasts along with Nature. Following the river's classical curve, the viewer is drawn to the light, where a rainbow might otherwise appear.[4]

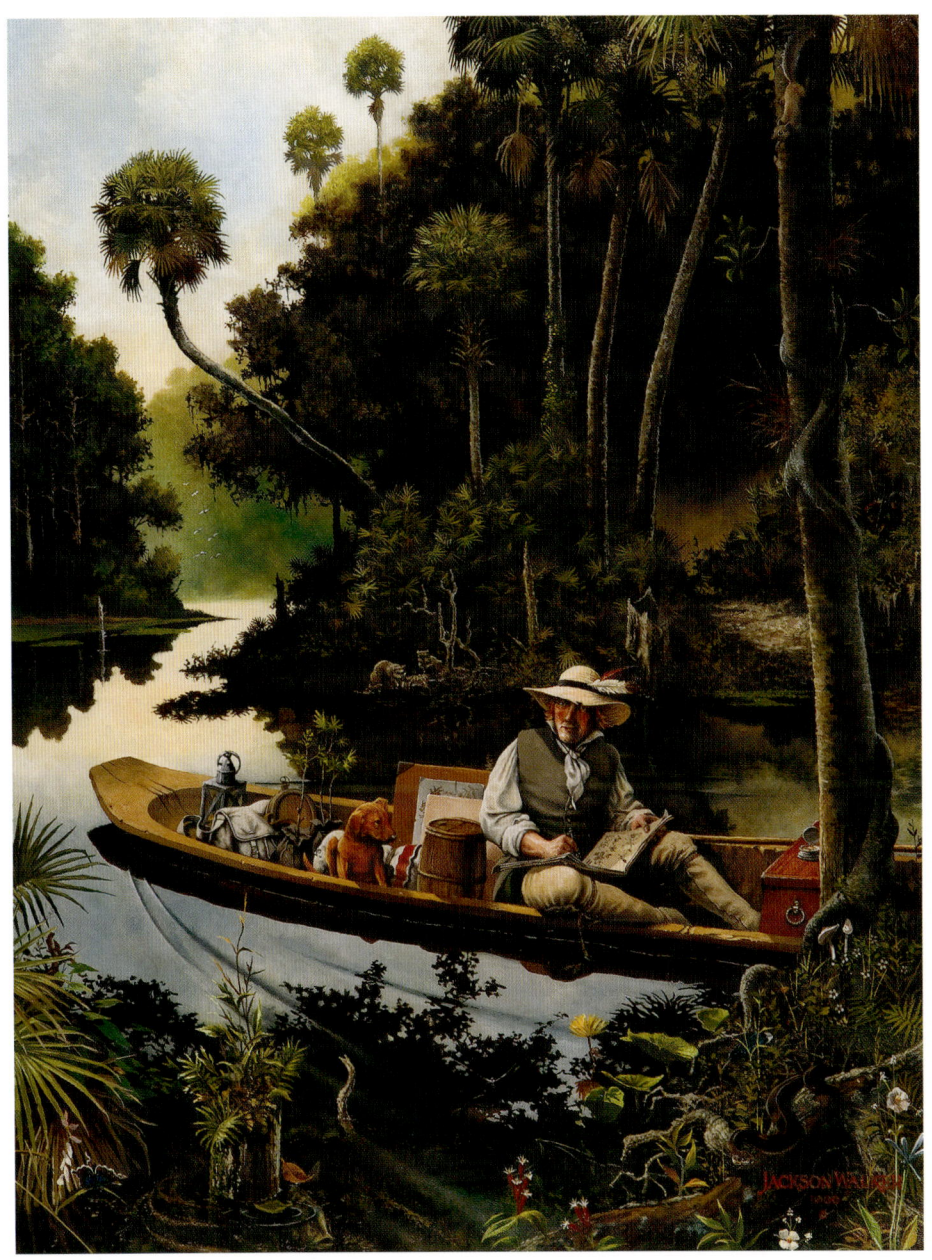

About this painting, Walker writes, "It is my intention to present a view of a moment in time within the bounds of historical reality and to tell this tale in a dramatic and colorful portrayal."[5] In *The Flower Hunter*, Walker captures both the mysterious and awe-inspiring mood of the primordial forest and the solitary courage of Puc Puggy as he explores the beautiful and terrifying wilderness.

Plate 6. Jackson Walker. *The Flower Hunter*, 2000. Oil on canvas, 60 × 48 in. From the Legendary Florida Collection of The Museum of Florida Art, DeLand, Florida. Photo by Tariq Gilbran.

The Flower Hunter is one of sixteen paintings from the artist's Legendary Florida collection, all of which are in the permanent collection of the Museum of Florida Art, DeLand, Florida.

~~~~~~

BEFORE THE NATURALIST-ARTIST returned home to Philadelphia for good, the St. Johns had taken him into a wilderness that not even the fierce conquistadors had been able to fully penetrate. Bartram's charmingly baroque illustrations and narrative in *Travels* simmers with his guileless affection for the river and all that lived in and around it. As such, he left me with the clear idea that a god—in whatever form we know him or her—can be found in the details of wild places. Later, others would absorb *Travels* and be forever influenced by his notion of communing with the wild landscape, instead of simply exploiting it.

Bartram wrote lovingly of emerging *Ephemera* (mayflies) and the coloration of Carolina paroquets, of "tygers" (panthers) and bumblebees and the distinct snorkel-like snout of soft-shell turtles. Plants, which grew in great profusion in the temperate-tropical habitat mix of the St. Johns, fascinated him. He drew them and collected them and named them. "Perhaps there is not any part of creation," he wrote, "which exhibits a more glorious display of the Almighty hand, than the vegetable world, such a variety of pleasing scenes, ever changing throughout the seasons."[6] The Seminoles called the gentle explorer "Puc Puggy," the Flower Hunter.

Nonetheless, for much of the rest of the world, the natural Florida has remained woefully unknown. As the historian Gary Mormino notes, by the end of World War II, Florida was the least populated state east of the Mississippi. Much of its interior—waterlogged wetlands or arid scrub—was being overlooked in favor of the balmy coasts, where most of the newcomers settled. In a 1921 map of Florida by the U.S. Geological Survey, the Upper St. Johns River rises out of Lake Washington. Lake Sawgrass and the true navigational headwaters of Lake Hellen Blazes—which are south of Washington—are not even mapped.

Even as the state began its modern land boom in the 1970s and tourism became its major source of income, few visitors—and few new residents—bothered to consider the nuances that characteristically defined the authentic natural Florida. It was much easier to indulge in the theme-park interpretation, where all was safe and sanitized and nothing would bite, nibble, or otherwise threaten one's safety. And, after all, wasn't it easier to go on a regularly scheduled Jungle Cruise than to wait for days in a swamp to have a real encounter with Florida? As the Italian philosopher-author Umberto Eco has noted, Americans like their reality validated for them, with experiences at least twice-removed from the core event itself. A state park—even one with magnificent springs such as Blue along the St. Johns—couldn't compete with the themed corporate theater that dramatically manipulated and enfenced wilderness and place. As the John Sayles film *Sunshine State* pointed out, Florida to most was "nature on a leash."

And so by the end of the twentieth century, the river that had once been regarded as the "Nile of the Americas" had lost its luster, its artistic legacies undefined to all but an enterprising few willing to learn just how compelling—and influential—this Florida river had once been. If the artists and craftsmen who considered the St. Johns River over time also indulged in mythic and Romantic interpretation, they did so from a vision that bored into the core of the river experience itself rather than one that orbited in a safe marketing distance from it. Ultimately, it was the artists who kept the knowledge of the river close to their hearts, sustaining the secrets that are still available to us today.

And so that is what this book is about: The secrets of the river, and the heartfelt connections that first brought them to tangible form. In an age in which we put so much unbridled faith in technology, it is worth remembering the spirit of the river and how it has enlivened, inspired, and animated us over time.

What is special about this river and why? The St. Johns is more than a mainstem of a channel that can be traced from one point to another on a map. There are hundreds of miles of water in the larger gestalt of this system, including tributaries, spring runs, sloughs, and "dead rivers"—which are only dead navigationally, not ecologically. And the land that cradles this system is just as vital—whether we call it a basin, a valley, or a watershed. It is land that has been defined by the river. This basin both captures rainfall inside porous sandhills and scrub and filters it as it runs down into the limestone aquifer below. Or it sends rain coursing over the sloping terrain, into swamps and marshes that hold the river—not unlike the way the unconscious holds forgotten memories and dreams, waiting for special moments to release them back into the light.

If we break our river quest down to the core, we find that its essence is, of course, water—an element that has shaped culture in Florida from the very first moment humans stepped foot on this ancient sea bottom. When they arrived over ten thousand years ago, the peninsula was dry, and nearly twice as large as it is today. Few modern rivers or springs flowed as they do now, and these nomadic Paleo-Indians encamped around limestone catchments on prairies and at mouths of coastal rivers, the latter of which are now inundated with the sea. Some of these catchments were inside what is now the watershed of our river.

As the glaciers began to retreat, the climate warmed, and water from the shallow seas was drawn up into the sky. The great hydrological cycle that sets Florida decidedly apart from other global deserts on this same latitude began to stir. Freshwater springs, charged by the new rain seeping into the soft sea rock upland, begin to flow. Swamps and marsh were birthed, and rivers snaked through their lush and moist topography. The vast everglade of shallow water and plants and limestone south of Lake Okeechobee took form, revealing what the Spanish would one day map as the "Lagoon of the Sacred Spirit." Just to the north of Okeechobee, the St. Johns begins to create itself in prehistoric rills and spring runs, a giant Etch-a-Sketch drawing with only some of the lines intact.

By 5,000 BC, millions of years after most of the North American continent had fashioned itself into mountains and valleys, the St. Johns finally took the shape and substance of what it is today, spreading out into a prehistoric lagoon basin. This new river was verdant and biologically diverse, one colossal organic marketplace of fish and game. At last it had stabilized enough to offer sanctuary, to allow time for mythology to arise from the connection between people and place. Nomadic hunters could settle on the banks of the St. Johns, build midden mounds from freshwater snails and animal bones and sand, and even grow crops. Tools, points, and pottery could become finer, more sophisticated, and tribal cultures and their art more complex. Leaders could evolve into chiefs and shamans, powerful men who could mediate with the forces of nature—especially the powers we moderns would one day call hydrology. These dynamics happened everywhere here, of course, but the St. Johns seemed most richly imbued with all of these treasures.

Perhaps more than any single place on our continent, the new wet landscape of Florida was occupied almost as quickly as it had been formed. It was if the water-driven terrain and its people grew together, the environment shaping culture as quickly as it shaped itself.

But this is Florida, and water does odd things here. Most rivers in North America surge down from tectonically molded mountains and hills to the east, west, and south, headed for the sea. But the St. Johns rises from its vast rain-fed saw-grass marsh and trickles slowly to the north, picking up momentum along the way as it is augmented by springs and tributaries and the gradual but ponderous energy of slope. It does so because the land remembers its oceanic origins: ancient coastlines and terraces, now abandoned by the seashore, have become escarpments, often identified as bluffs and rolling hills.

This St. Johns sits inside of a valley that has been created by scarps to the east and west. But its defining scarp—the one that sends it flowing north—splays across the saw-grass prairie north of Okeechobee. It is a 27-foot-high ridge, one so subtle and recondite that it is revealed less by visual ground-truthing than by a careful study of topographic maps. Rain falling to the north of this natural ridge becomes part of the St. Johns system, beginning its slow but sure movement northward to the sea.

But this valley of inches sometimes stutters, and when it does, the river inside it dilates itself into broad, shallow lakes. Often the channel flows through the middle of the lake, as it does with Lakes George and Harney; but sometimes it only nicks off the edge, as in the case of Lakes Jesup and Beresford. The Creeks, in recognition of this, called it Welaka: River of Lakes.

But this is also a river in which prehistoric salt water, once captured in the deepest recesses of the aquifer, seeps up through some of its springs and sandy lake bottoms. This characteristic influences ecology, stretching the oceanic reach far beyond the push of the tides. The only breeding population of southern stingrays of any North American river lives in the St. Johns because of this, and many other saltwater species—such as Atlantic needlefish, pipefish, and blue crabs—are found throughout much of the river.

Finally, we have a long waterway that is bisected by two climatic zones—

warm temperate to the north and subtropic to the south. Between its salt-water determination and its mix of climate, our river becomes one of the most biologically diverse in all of North America. No wonder it has drawn people to it since its very beginnings.

We must add to this matrix the strange and peculiar condition of Florida itself, in which our sunny, rain-rich state hosts a slew of exotic non-native plants and animals simply because it can. At this point in time, the names of the new flora and fauna in the St. Johns basin are reminiscent of some odd children's storybook, full of languages from other countries. Tropical fish hobbyists, bored or frustrated with one Amazonic or African fish or another, toss their woebegone miniatures into the river system, where, often, the fish thrive. Among many others, the pacu—a less lethal cousin of the piranha—lives here now, as does the clown knifefish and the Amazon suckermouth armored catfish. As an algae-eater in a fish tank, the little catfish is quite docile, but loose in the St. Johns it grows large, crowding out native fish and harassing the gentle manatees by chomping algae off their backs. The non-native plants are just as bothersome, with air potato vines and wild taro and Chinese tallow choking the landscape above, and the prolific hydrilla doing so below. At the surface is the water hyacinth, which at once bears a lovely lavender bloom and grows so fast it can actually clog navigation.

Despite its singularity, in our modern, go-fast Florida world, the river shares little of the name-recognition celebrity that has characterized, say, the Everglades or the Suwannee. Nonetheless, the St. Johns has bitten off the largest chunk of literary and cultural history in Florida. Or, as the authors of the wonderfully florid *The St. Johns: A Parade of Diversities* observed in 1943: "Upon no other river in the U.S. have white men lived for so long a while, or so variously . . . this a pageant of strange persons passing, with Time as their drum major, beside its broad brown waters."[7]

Certainly, we have lost much: the panthers that once roamed the Ockla-waha's shores; the great green shoals of Carolina paroquets (see plate 7); the gigantic ivory-billed woodpecker; the immense first-growth virgin cypress. But we still have much left. And so, then, the art portrayed in this book can be viewed both aesthetically and historically. In some ways, it reminds us of what we have lost; in others, it reminds us of what still endures. Finally, it sometimes reminds us of what artists want it most to be—what they imagine, envision, dream.

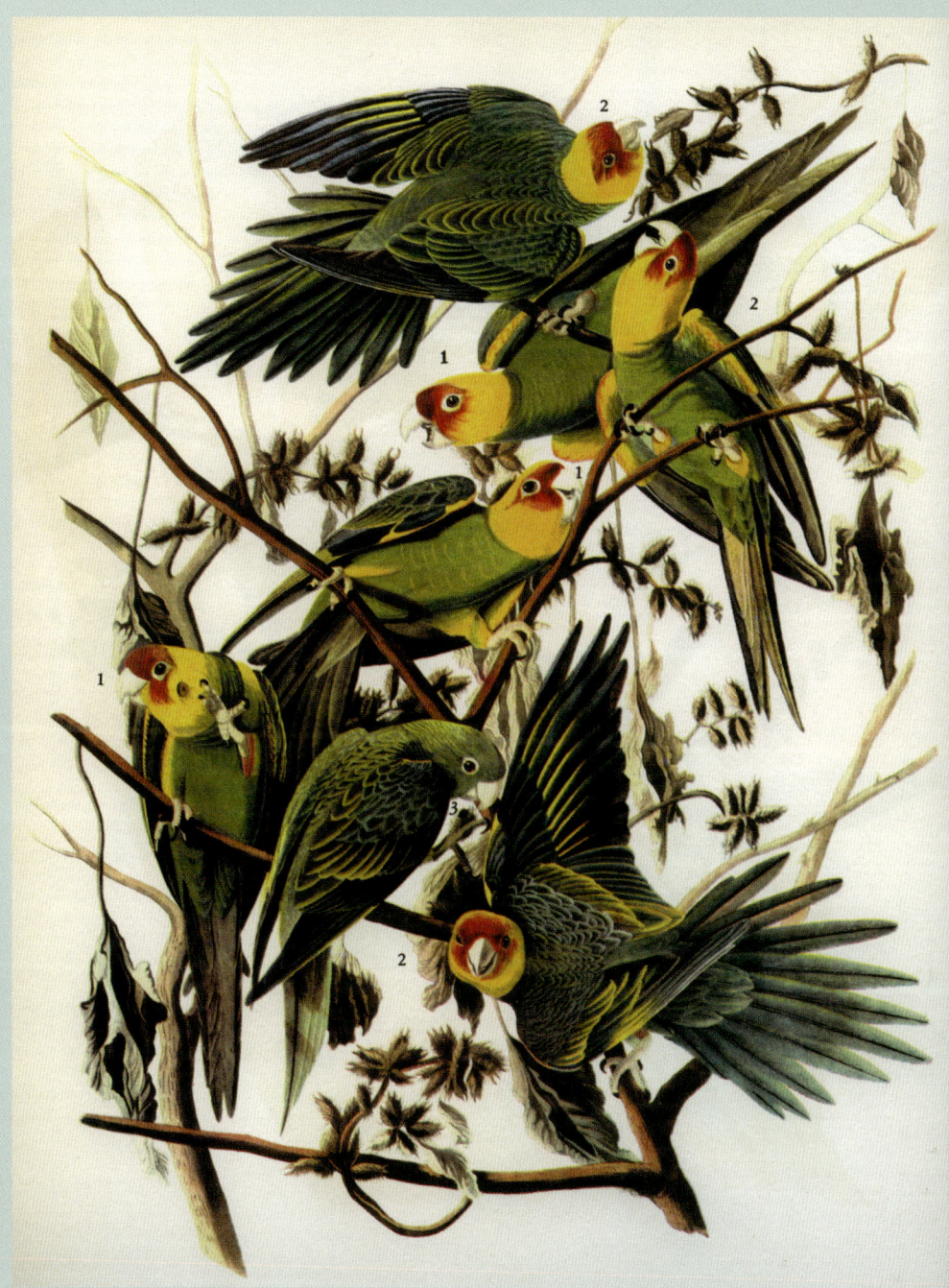

John James Audubon's painting *Carolina Paroquet* depicts the only parrot found in eastern North America. Once plentiful in the eastern United States, the Carolina paroquet was hunted to extinction. It was last sighted in 1904.

Plate 7. Johns James Audubon. *Carolina Paroquet*. Plate 26 from *The Birds of America* (1832). Courtesy Department of Special Collections, George A. Smathers Library, University of Florida, Gainesville.

The Greek philosopher Heraclites once observed that you can never step twice into the same river. The reason is obvious—water around your legs, even in a slow-moving blackwater river like the St. Johns, will have long moved downstream during any subsequent visits. Yet if the waters have flowed to the sea in real life, the art itself has not. It remains with us, reminding us of a landscape, a bioregion, a single moment in time. It reminds us most of all of a spirit with the capacity to reach inside and touch our soul.

Bartram understood the promise this grid work of nature had—still has, even today—to hold mystery close to its heart. Unlike open savannas or mountains, you cannot see very far at all in a jungle, and every cypress trunk, every vine-clogged pathway, every bend in the river conceals a new discovery. In contrast with the geological drama of continental mountains and valleys, this is a territory woven into the folds of biological nuance.

For Bartram and other like-minded visitors, the St. Johns was a natural cathedral—a place where we "learn wisdom and understanding in the economy of nature, and [to] be seriously attentive to the divine monitor within." So it is, too, with the art that has been created along its shores, its tributaries, in its watershed. We have been gifted by the memorials of this art that remain. As for modern practitioners, we are simply grateful that they have cared enough to know the St. Johns, and have come away inspired. Like others before them, they have looked hard and long at the river system. But they have also had the courage to look within, to convey their subjective impressions of water and light. Sometimes, in a moment of whimsy, they invented an idiosyncratic geegaw—a TV table, a mileage meter, a sign—that celebrates a vernacular vision of the river.

As for me, I am deeply appreciative that the sensibilities of coauthors O'Connor and Monroe are rich, informed, and devoted, or they would not have committed to this collection with such passion. And so I am grateful not just for their own respective river voyages of discovery. I am also grateful for each twist of clay, each dash of oil paint, each individualistic artifact that has somehow outlasted the ravages of time. To celebrate the art of the St. Johns is to celebrate life itself, to revel in the spirit of water and the remembrance of its capacity to lay itself down on our souls.

It is that continuum that allows us context and understanding. In its greatest moment, this continuum may even gift us with a shard or two of wisdom—perhaps even an ethic that demands sustainability, conservation, and preservation of the river system. And for that, we should all be grateful that we again have the chance to become informed by the grace of nature and place. "I do not know," the author Marjorie Kinnan Rawlings once wrote, "how one can live without some small place of enchantment to turn to."[8] We hope this collection will reveal the many variants of this enchantment, and that, in the long haul, we will all be better for it.

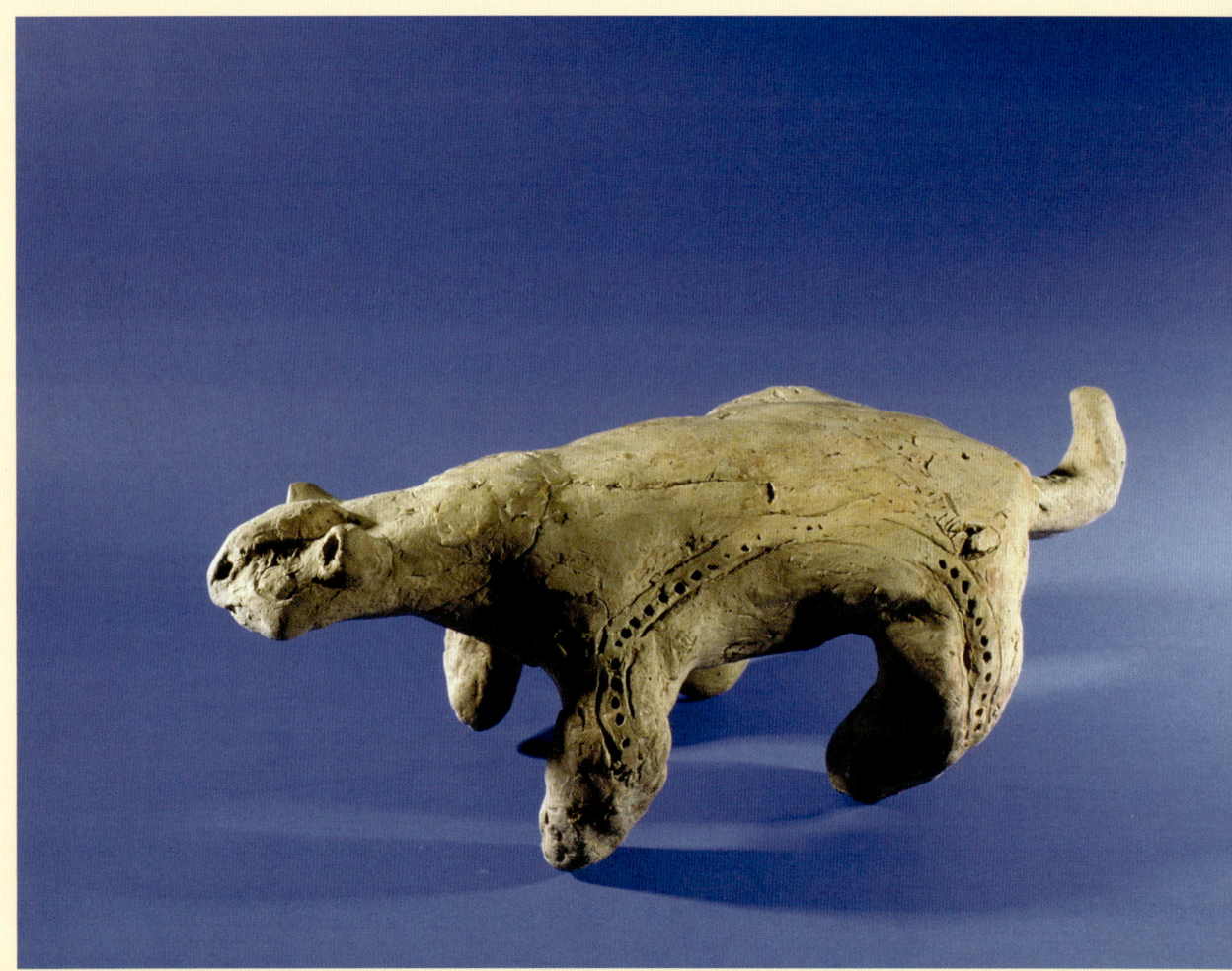

Plate 8. Feline figure, Lake County,
Florida, Late Prehistoric. Ceramic, 4⅓ ×
11¾ in. National Museum of the American
Indian, New York. Photo by Roy Craven.
Courtesy of Barbara Purdy.

1 } First along the River

CULTURE HAS ALWAYS PRECEDED the written words needed to record it, and for the first ten thousand years, visual objects alone must tell the story of those early people who lived and worked and loved and dreamed along the St. Johns River and its tributaries. There are no written accounts left by these ancient people—no diaries, letters, reports, or records that can fill in the blanks in our mind's eye—only the tangible objects themselves, such as the small ceramic sculpture created by the ancient inhabitants who lived along the river's edge for ten millennia before the arrival of the Europeans (see plate 8).

The archaeological record indicates that diverse populations and cultural traditions characterized the St. Johns River region over the past ten thousand years. As time passed, the immigrants settled in villages, made pottery, and built large burial mounds. They traded with other indigenous people in the Southeast; this interaction resulted in their adopting various cultural traits.

As St. Johns society evolved, so did its social, political, and religious organizations, which became more complex over time. Still, because of the abundant resources in the region, a general hunting-gathering-fishing subsistence pattern persisted throughout the pre-Columbian period with a primary reliance on the river's plant and animal resources. In time, agriculture was practiced, but it likely played a secondary role in the overall economy.

Archaeological sites along the river consist predominately of freshwater shell middens, essentially refuse heaps, and sand mounds that were intentionally built by the Indians. Portions of several sites, such as the Early Archaic period Windover site located in Brevard County near Titusville, contain wet deposits that resulted in the extraordinary preservation of archaeological remains, including items made of typically perishable materi-

The Native Peoples who inhabited Florida prior to the arrival of the Europeans in the sixteenth century created exquisite works of art in wood, bone, shell, and ceramics. . . . Most art historians do not believe that the twentieth century concept of "art for art's sake" is valid for pre-industrial societies. The objects . . . were probably made in order to objectify the relationships of people to the natural and supernatural worlds . . . to honor and appease the gods, to pay homage to the ancestors, to aid the dead in their journey into the next world, to indicate status, to adorn the body, and for utilitarian purposes to deal with everyday survival.
—Barbara Purdy, *Indian Art of Ancient Florida*

als like wood and plant fibers. Among the other significant and best-known archaeological sites in the St. Johns River valley are the shell middens at Tick Island and Hontoon Island in Volusia County and the mounds at Mt. Royal in Putnam County.

It was not until the nineteenth century that scientific excavations were first conducted in the St. Johns region. Jeffries Wyman, curator at Harvard University's Peabody Museum, excavated shell middens along the St. Johns River in the 1860s. Clarence Moore, a wealthy Philadelphian, journeyed along the river as well as other waterways in Florida in his steam-powered houseboat, the *Gopher*, visiting and excavating archaeological sites in the late nineteenth and early twentieth centuries.

With the advent of modern archaeology in the second half of the twentieth century, many more archaeologists explored the river and its surrounding basin. These explorations continue to the present day. Because of these efforts, a cultural chronology has been established for the region as a whole and for local variations within the area.

Climate and location have always been a part of Florida's allure—its geography and environment are distinctive. When Indian people first arrived in the region, the newcomers found a glacierless garden filled with exotic flora and fauna. Because sea levels were lower at that time, Florida's land mass was larger. The climate was also drier and colder than that of today. But an amazing number of Ice Age animals flourished in the region, making it especially attractive for the Paleoindian hunters who relied on large game to meet their needs. The extensive grasslands were home to bison and mammoths while mastodons, tapirs, and giant ground sloths foraged in the woods and marshes. Like the animals they hunted, the early people had to seek out freshwater sources in order to live and prosper. Many of these waterholes became part of springs and rivers as the water levels rose. The St. Johns basin is full of artifacts that detail how these early people lived. Archaeologists seeking to piece together the story of these early inhabitants often search out the ancient waterholes to look for clues. Contemporary artists are now collaborating with archaeologists to produce images of scenes that no longer exist and of people who have been dead for thousands of years. Using as much evidence as they can find, artists are bringing the past to life, creating a pictorial record through their paintings and drawings of Florida's First People.

This painting by Florida artist Dean Quigley portrays Florida during the Paleoindian period (12,000–6,000 BC). Mastodons, a giant ground sloth, and other ancient inhabitants of the region are gathered around a water-hole. Quigley used fossil remains and archaeological records to re-create this scene, combining his artistic skills with documented evidence to create a unique blend of art and archaeology and give the viewer a glimpse into a world that we could otherwise only imagine.

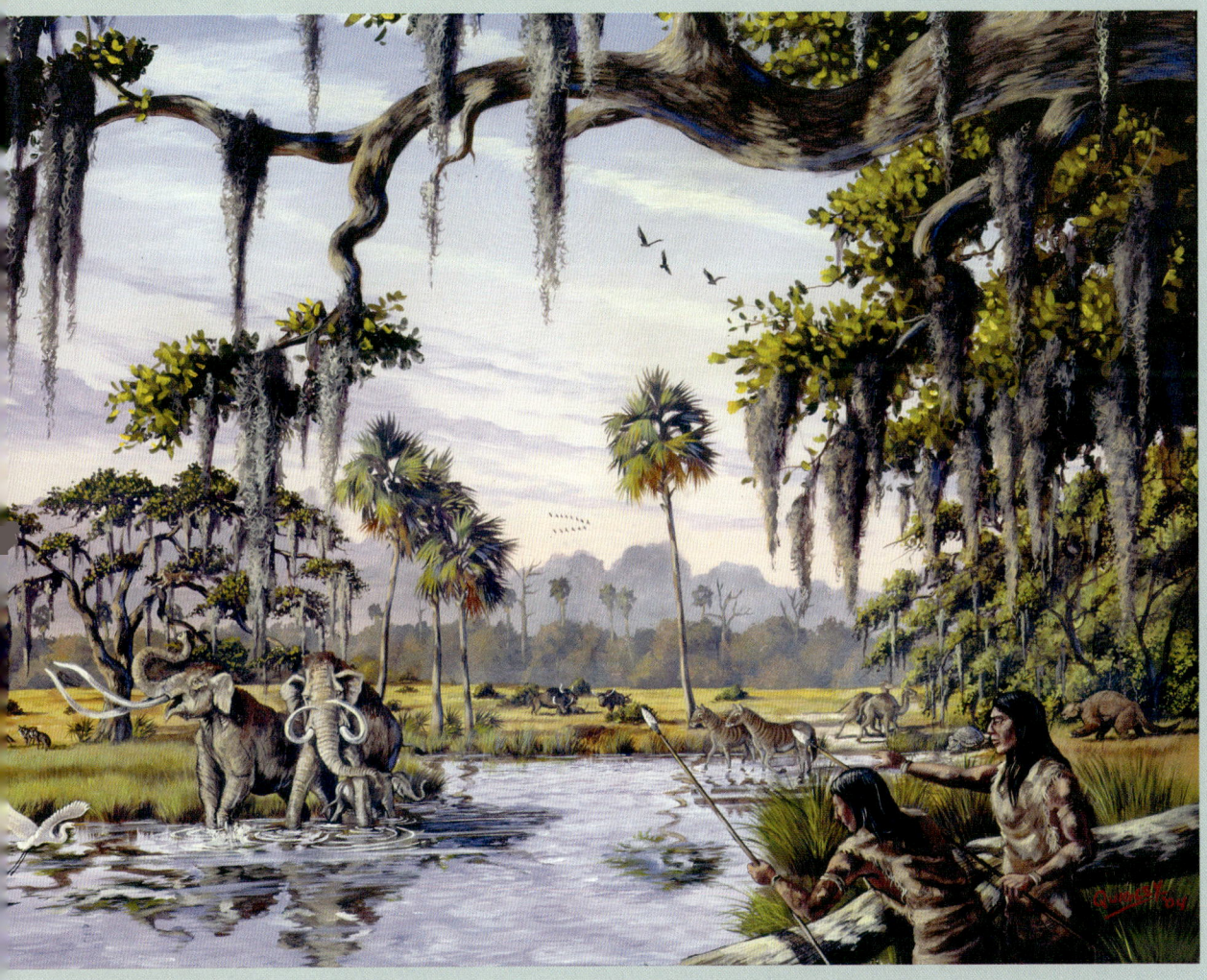

Plate 9. Dean Quigley. *Pleistocene Waterhole*, n.d. Acrylic on canvas, 40 × 30 in. Courtesy of the artist.

It has been said that a building developer is an archaeologist's best friend but also his worst enemy.[1] The reason for this is that the earth-moving equipment used to clear the land often dislodges undiscovered Indian burial grounds where human skeletons and the grave goods that accompanied the burials were preserved in water-saturated deposits that have kept the materials from deteriorating. A case in point is the Windover site, an Early Archaic period (6,000–5,000 BC) site located in present-day Brevard County.

"In 1982, a heavy equipment operator named Steve Vanderjagt stared into the bucket of his backhoe. The round objects protruding from the black muck were not rocks. They were human skulls, and they didn't look very old."[2] A team of archaeologists from Florida State University was called in. Lab tests indicated that the bones were at least seven thousand years old.

Because most of the human remains and the accompanying artifacts were submerged in peat, they were amazingly well preserved. But recovering the material presented significant challenges. A labor force made up of FSU teachers, students, and volunteers from the community of Titusville participated in the recovery effort. Weeks of pumping were required to lower the water level so that the site could be excavated. It was worth the effort—the bones and other material found at the site represented some of the oldest intact human remains discovered in the country. The recovered material included eighty-six pieces of hand-woven fabric and twine, tools made from antler and bone, pollen and seeds that helped identify the food the people used and—perhaps most astonishing—a child's skull that still contained enough brain tissue to provide the identification of human DNA.[3]

The fibers that the Indians used in their weaving were difficult to identify but appear to be similar to palm-leaf fiber.[4] Both sabal palm and saw palmetto grew in the region, and both have the type of long, straight fibers that would have made them a likely choice for the ancient weavers. The fibers were apparently processed and made into twine that could then be used to produce the fabric. According to Robin Brown, thirty-seven of the burial sites at Windover contained hand-woven fabrics that were used to wrap the bodies of the dead in preparation for burial. This photograph by the Windover site photographer Richard Brunck clearly shows impressions of the ribs and humerus of the interred body (see plate 10).

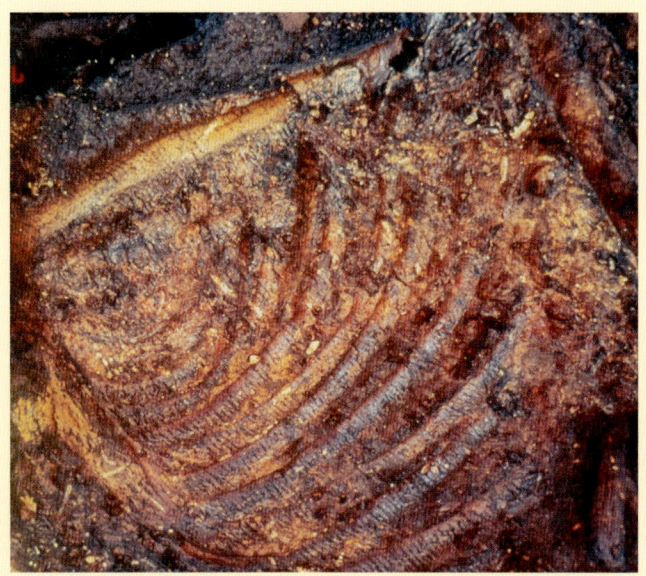

Plate 10. Preserved woven fabric from the Windover, Florida, site, ca. 6000–5500 BC. Photo by Richard Brunck. Courtesy of Glen Doran.

FLORIDA'S EARLIEST INHABITANTS were drawn to the St. Johns River and other waterways for several reasons—the plentiful food supply, the abundance of freshwater, the climate made moderate by proximity to a body of water. The St. Johns was particularly attractive because it also provided access to three hundred miles of the region's interior. Indeed, until the building of the railroad in the late 1800s, the St. Johns River was the interstate highway for north-south travel and trade. Robin Brown writes: "The dugout canoe that evolved to ply Florida waters could go places otherwise impossible to reach. It required only a few inches of water to float, its streamlined shape was easy to paddle or pole, and it slipped quietly over water weeds and through cattails and rushes. In addition, the canoe carried loads that, on an overland trek, would burden many people."[5] Most dugout canoes were made of hard yellow pine. Not only were these pines abundant, but the high resin content of their logs burned very readily. Since controlled fire was used by the Indians to burn away the inside of the logs, these trees were a vital natural resource. After burning, the charred wood was scraped away to form the canoe.[6]

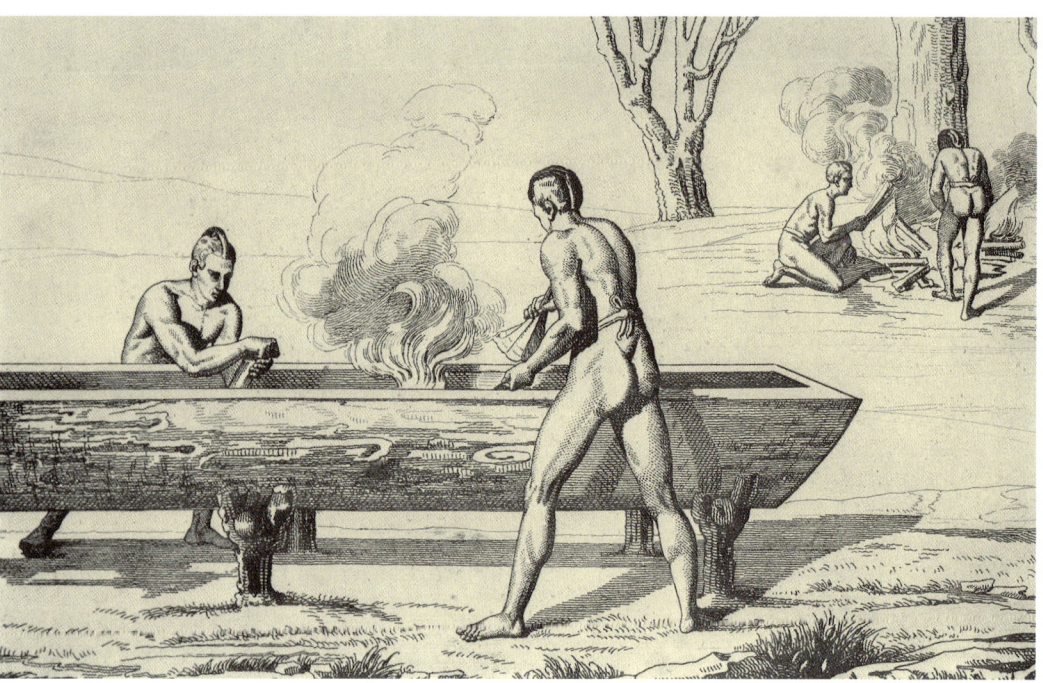

Plate 11. Anonymous. *Timucuan Men Building a Canoe*, late sixteenth century. Photocopy courtesy of State Archives of Florida.

The charring process used to construct the canoes is illustrated in this picture of Timucuan men building a canoe. Thomas Hariot described the process as follows:

"The way they [the Indians] build their boats . . . is very wonderful. For although they completely lack any iron tools such as we use, they can make boats as good as ours. And these boats are seaworthy enough to take them sailing or fishing wherever they want to go. First they choose a tall, thick tree the size required for the boat's frame. Then they light a fire close to its roots. . . . When the tree is almost burnt through, they make a good fire to cause it to fall. . . . The tree is raised upon a platform built on forked posts at a height convenient for working. The bark is stripped off with sharp shells; the inner length of the trunk is kept for the bottom of the boat. A fire is made all along the length of the trunk, and when it has burned sufficiently it is quenched and the charred wood scraped away with shells. Then they build a new fire, burn out another piece, and so on, sometimes burning and sometimes scraping, until the boat has a good bottom. Thus God has endowed these savages with enough reason to make the things they need."[7]

In spring of 1999, Eastside High School teacher Steve Everett and a group of his environmental science students stumbled across an unanticipated treasure while hiking along the edge of Newnans Lake, one of several lakes connected to the St. Johns watershed in Alachua County near Gainesville, Florida. One of the students noticed the outline of what appeared to be a large canoe. Digging around the outline revealed an ancient dugout, one of approximately one hundred Indian dugouts that were found nearby; it was the largest single discovery of Indian canoes ever recorded in North America. Radiocarbon dating of wood samples revealed that the canoes were up to five thousand years old. The ancient dugouts ranged in length from fifteen to thirty-one feet, and all but one was formed from pine trees that are common in the area.[8]

The Newnans Lake canoes are similar to other prehistoric canoes found throughout the Southeast, although several of the Newnans canoes included a "'thwart' or bulkhead [that created] a partition between sections of the boat. . . . In general, the ends of the canoes were blunted or slightly rounded, though some had distinctive overhanging platforms."[9] Robin Brown, in his book *Florida's First People*, remarks that canoes "more suited to rough water have been found on the Atlantic Coast, the St. Johns River, and large lakes. The front extends upward and outward into a platformed prow, and some have a V-shaped bow beneath a jutting platform."[10]

Experts have not agreed on why so many canoes were found at one location. Was Newnans Lake the site of an Indian canoe factory? Did discarded dugouts simply accumulate here as new models were made to replace them? Perhaps our answer is found in the fact that the Seminole Indians, who once lived in the area, called Newnans Lake "Pithlachocco," which means "where the boats were made."

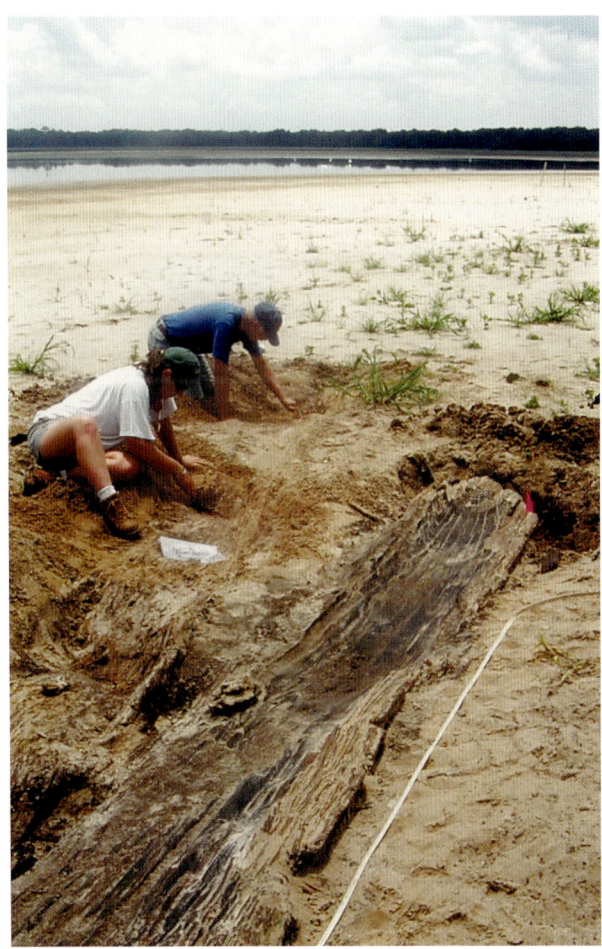

Plate 12. Prehistoric canoes found at Newnans Lake, Alachua County, Fla. Photograph courtesy of the Florida Division of Historical Resources.

Early Florida Indians traded with each other on a regular basis. Otter and alligator skins, shells, beads, food, tools, and weapons were included among the commodities that supported the economy of early people. Almost all of the trade was conducted via the waterways that served as the main transportation routes of the Native people.

Trade was not only regional. Archaeological evidence points to a far-flung trade network that provided raw materials and finished products to areas throughout eastern North America. Robin Brown writes: "During the Archaic Period . . . (6,000 to 1,000 BC), inland Floridians along the St. Johns River boiled their food in large Gulf coast whelk shells and shaped wood with tools made from Atlantic whelk shells. Five thousand years ago, people living in an Archaic village in Kentucky were wearing beads made from marine shells and drinking from vessels made of whelk shells. . . . All of these marine items were bartered and they can be traced up the continent, fanning outward from the rivers that formed the trade routes of aboriginal America. Gulf coast shells and the beautiful objects made from them made their way as far west as Oklahoma and as far north as Wisconsin."[11]

One of the most significant Indian sites in Florida is the Mount Royal site located on the St. Johns River between Palatka and Lake George in western Putnam County. Mount Royal had a long history of Indian occupation dating back several thousand years and was one of the most important trade and ceremonial centers in pre-Columbian America. The mound was explored by the artist-naturalist William Bartram when he visited the area in 1774. He described it as "a magnificent Indian mount . . . [with] a noble Indian highway, which led from the great mount, in a straight line, three quarters of a mile . . . [to] an oblong artificial lake."[12]

Art often reflects the artist's environment. Imagine yourself living along the St. Johns River in 5,000 BC. Imagine the environment—the pristine pools of water, the mist rising from the river, the boiling springs, the myriad creatures. These were a people who were embedded in nature, who lived their lives in intimate contact with the natural world around them. The joyful, vibrant decorations that they carefully incised on their tools and ornaments suggest their delight in the beauty and dynamic energy of the world that surrounded them and provided for all their needs. The river was the thread that held their world together.

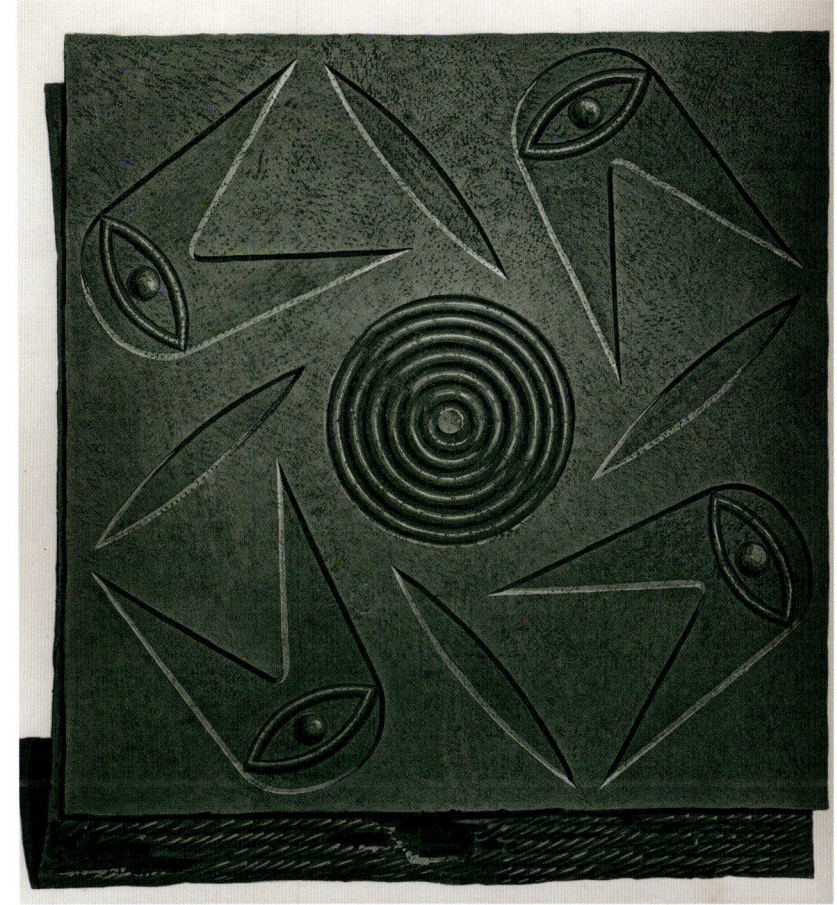

Plate 13. Copper breastplate from the Mt. Royal site, Putnam County, Fla., ca. AD 1400. Photo courtesy of the Smithsonian Institution, Washington, D.C.

The copper breastplate illustrated here was one of several ceremonial objects found at Mount Royal. The plate was discovered by the archaeologist Clarence Moore when he visited the Mount Royal site in the 1890s. The copper plate likely dated from sometime after AD 1200 when influences from the Mississippian culture (AD 1000–1600) entered the region. It is inscribed with the "forked eye" motif, a symbol found throughout the region on objects associated with the Southeastern Ceremonial Complex. Objects made from copper were widely distributed through trade networks, and decorated copper objects similar to the one found at Mount Royal were also discovered in burial sites in Georgia and Oklahoma. The large number of copper objects found at Mount Royal indicates that it was a wealthy and important community.[13]

These hairpins, found in a site on Tick Island in Volusia County, date from somewhere between 4,000 BC and AD 800, a time known by archaeologists as the Middle Archaic period. Like many other objects found in Indian graves, the pins are made from deer bones and are decorated with intricate geometric patterns that were incised on the bones. Similar patterns have been found on ceramic objects from the same area. The incised patterns include zigzags, dots, wavy lines, spirals, and an image that suggests a sun symbol. Patterns often appear in bands or are separated from each other by unincised areas. Universally, the spiral has often been associated with water, and wavy lines with waves. The incised patterns seen on the Tick Island hairpins suggest water droplets, eel grass, whirlpools, bubbles, and the sun—all familiar images to a people for whom the river was a way of life.

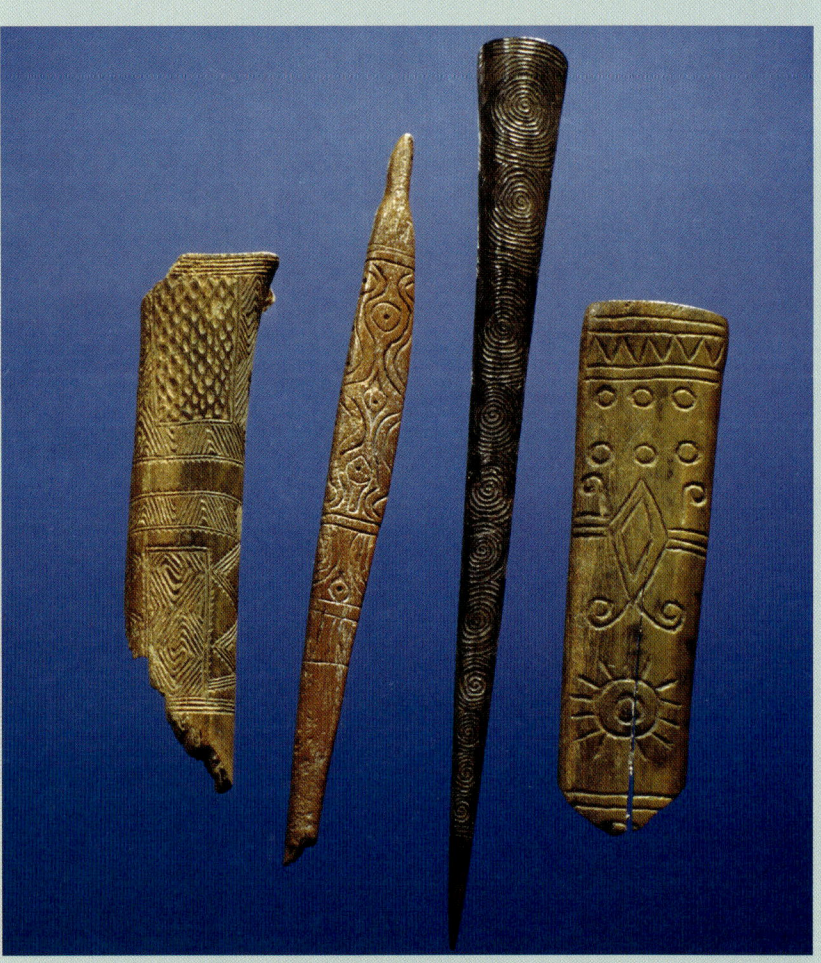

Plate 14. Hairpins, Tick Island Site, Volusia County, ca. 4000 BC–AD 800. Incised bone, 6⅝ × ¾ in. Private collection. Photo by Roy Craven. Courtesy of Barbara Purdy.

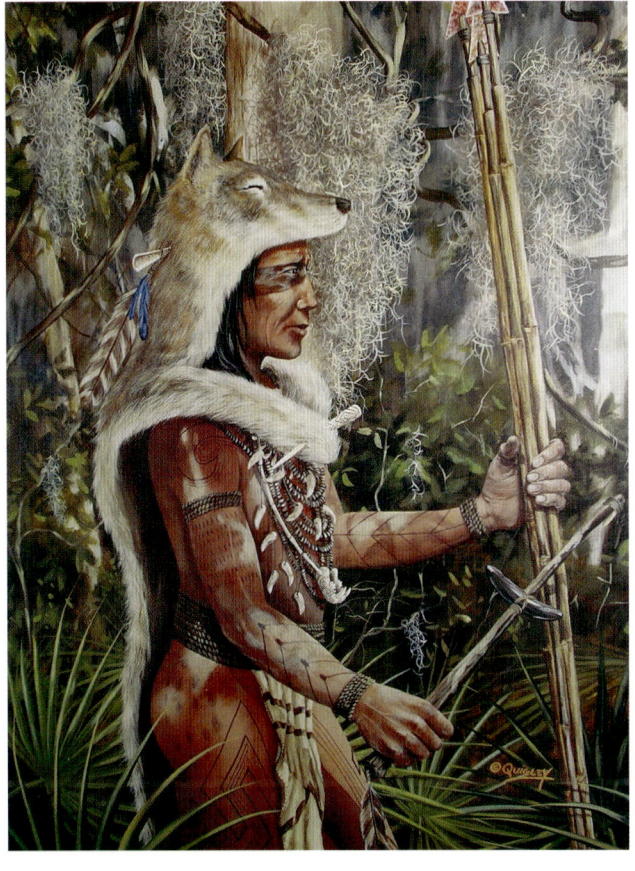

Plate 15. Dean Quigley. *Wolf Seeker*, n.d. Acrylic on canvas, 40 × 30 in. Courtesy of the artist.

This painting by Dean Quigley depicts a Florida Indian wearing a costume made from materials found at the archaeological site on Tick Island in Volusia County.[14] Among the 175 burials recovered there, a few showed graphic evidence of violence—Newnan and Hillsboro projectile points were found imbedded in the vertebrae of one particular individual. Other artifacts that were found at the burial sites included drilled and polished manatee rib bones, incised deer bone points and awls, drilled alligator teeth, ornaments of shell and stone, and an intricately incised and drilled set of wolf jaws. The drilled wolf jaws, probably worn as a symbol of rank or status within the Indian community, suggest that the individual in the grave was of some stature in his tribe. Wearing the hide and jaws of such a powerful predator may have heightened the respect and authority he held among his people; perhaps it also invoked the sympathetic spirit of the wolf. Quigley's painting clearly shows the use of decorated shell pins, which were also found among the grave goods at the Tick Island site.

Hontoon Island, located in the same area as Tick Island, is another archaeologically significant site on the St. Johns River. Human occupation of the island dates from the Early Archaic period, and the Indians continued to live on the island for several thousand years before the arrival of the Europeans. The island still has two large shell mounds that date from the Archaic era. Long after the Indians had disappeared from the area, settlers moved onto the island to fish, farm, and raise cattle. A boatyard and a fish-packing house were also built on the island. In more recent times, the island was a pioneer homestead, a boatyard, a commercial fishing center, and a cattle ranch. The state purchased the 1,650-acre island for use as a state park in 1967.[15]

Today, visitors enjoy solitude and tranquility as they look across the river, while the light shimmers off the water or rakes across the treetops. They may take delight in the cypress knees at the end of the trail. They may look past the tangles of tree limbs and vegetation living under forest light, out to Hontoon Lagoon. Some visiting fishermen may try to lure largemouth bass with live shiners, or catch bluegills with earthworms and crickets. Fishermen know that speckled perch enjoy live minnows while earthworms at the river bottom attract channel catfish. Other visitors hike nature trails through pine flatwoods at the park's higher elevations; some walk the palm and oak hammocks to the cypress swamps and marshes. Astute hikers might take note of the two shell middens created by the shells of snails gathered from the shallows of the river by Native Americans.

Larry Moore worked as a graphic designer after graduating from the University of Florida in 1979, only to become disenchanted with the business. Soon he picked up an easel and "began painting outdoors before I knew what plein air was." He left the design profession in 1983 to become a full-time landscapist. Having grown up in Cocoa Beach, water and scrub imagery is in his blood so now he seeks out places that speak of Old Florida, such as Hontoon Island State Park.

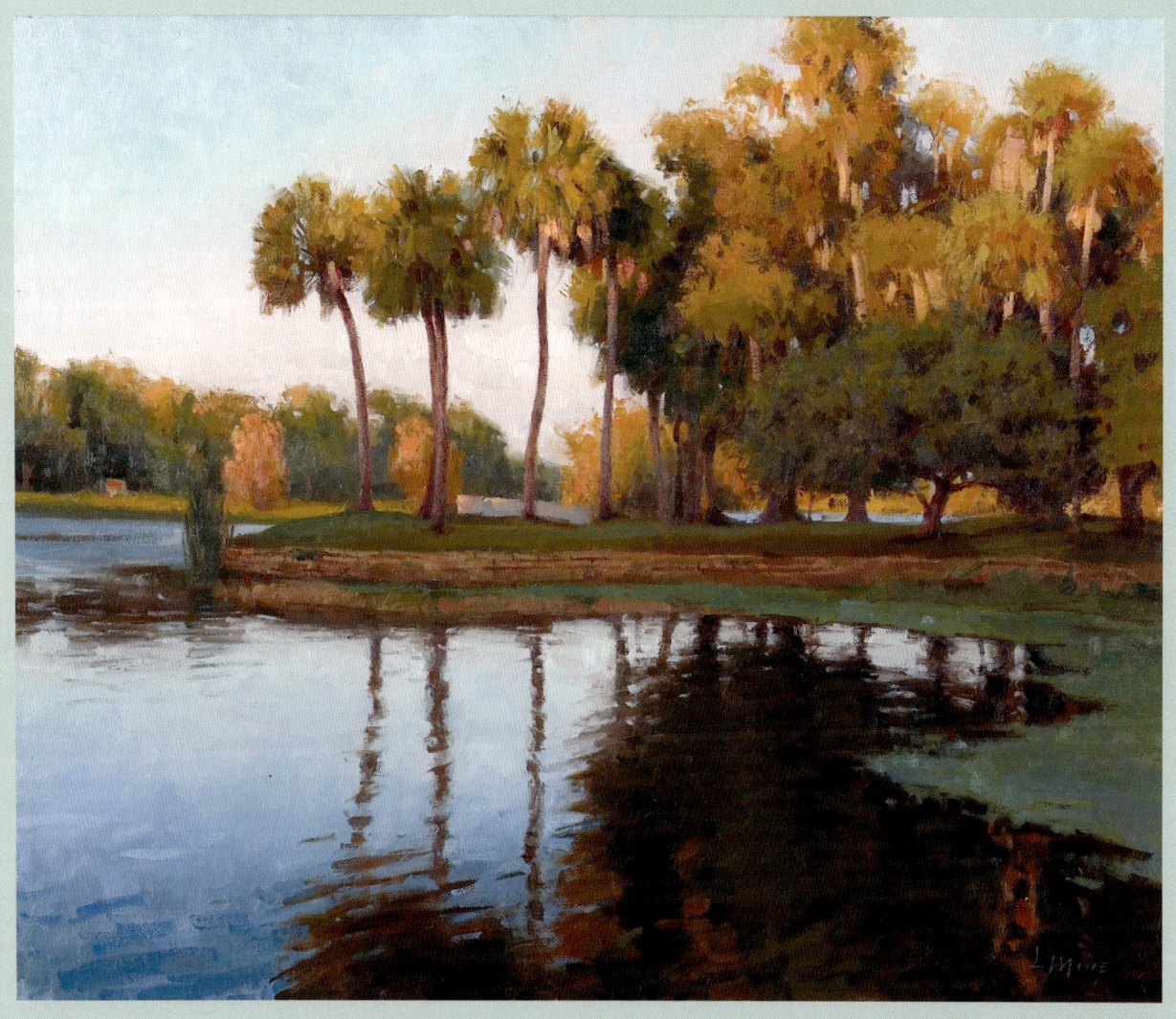

The viewpoint of this painting by Moore is from the landing where people can board the small public ferry that takes them across a broad expanse of the St. Johns River to Hontoon Island. It was at the landing that the artist, like many others, sensed something wonderful and went about capturing this sensation. After some contemplation, Moore "found an angle where the scene lined up" for him to practice his on-site "shorthand," a style dependant on a cool palette and broad brushstrokes "to communicate as much as possible with as little as possible."[16]

Plate 16. Larry Moore. *Evening on Hontoon Island*, 2006. Oil on canvas, 24 × 60 in. Courtesy of the artist.

Woodcarving was likely a widespread art form for Florida's Native people. Unfortunately, wood is not a very durable material and does not last long in a subtropical environment. The best examples of wood sculptures—mostly in the form of masks, plaques, and sculptures—have been retrieved from ponds, lakes, or rivers where the mud preserved the wood from the effects of insects and climate.

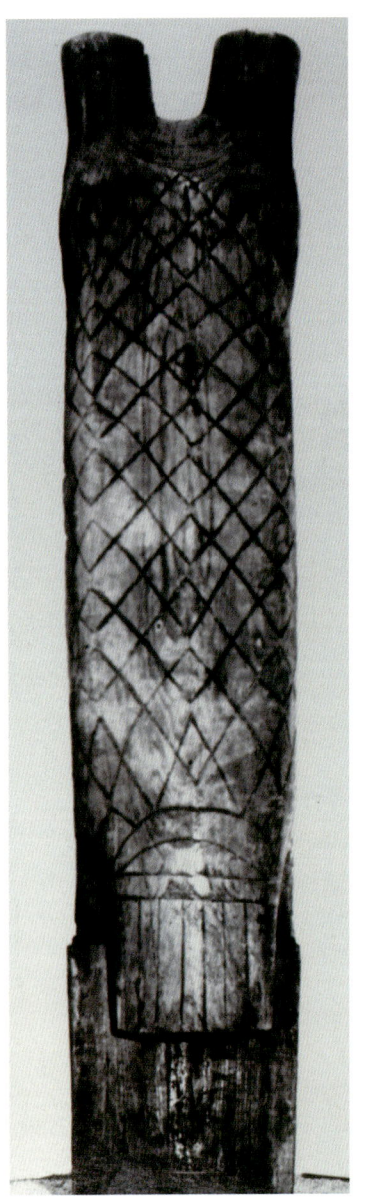

One major piece of wood sculpture was discovered in 1955 when a drag-line operator pulled a large wooden totem out of the St. Johns River near Hontoon Island. The totem—probably a charnel (or funeral) house guardian and not a clan totem such as those found in the Pacific Northwest—represents a great horned owl. At over six feet tall, it is the largest prehistoric wood sculpture found in the Western Hemisphere. A radiocarbon date of AD 1200–1300 was obtained from a sample of the carving. The back of the owl was carved to depict feathers (see plate 17).

A second wooden sculpture found nearby is smaller than the owl, but is so stylistically similar that some scholars believe it may have been done by the same artist or at least at the same time (see plate 18).[17] Both pieces are made of pine, and the details and design elements are nearly identical. This carving appears to represent an otter holding a fish. The exact function of the two pieces is unknown, but the only other place in Florida where similar large wood carvings have been discovered is in the Lake Okeechobee basin, where large wooden sculptures of birds and animals were apparently associated with mortuary activities among the Glades Indians.

Plate 17. Owl effigy (*back view*), Thursby Midden, Volusia County, ca. AD 1200. Heart pine, 75 in. (*h*). Fort Caroline National Memorial Museum, Jacksonville, Florida. Photo courtesy of Barbara Purdy.

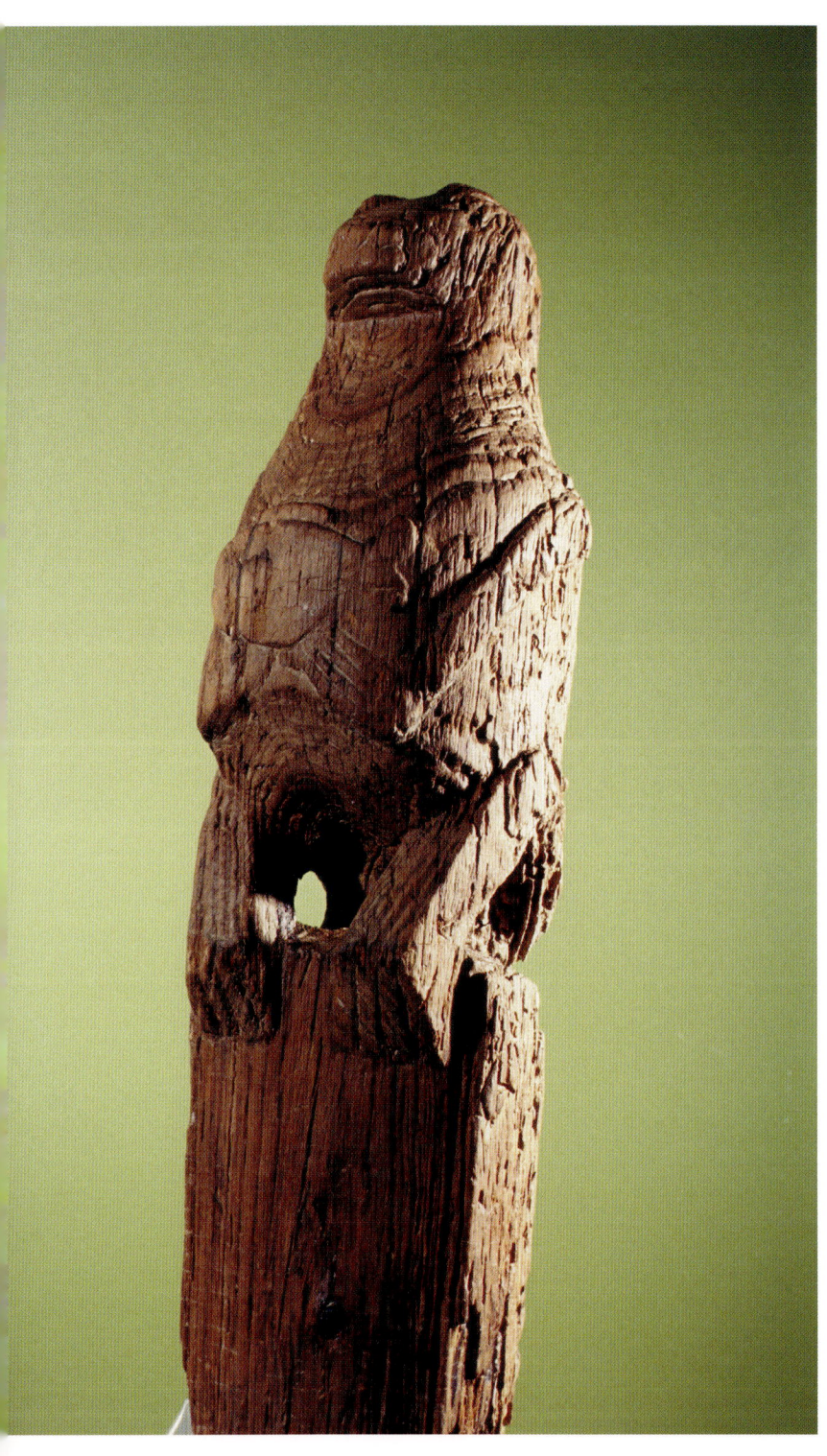

Plate 18. Otter holding a fish, Thursby Midden, Volusia County, ca. AD 1200. Pine, 27½ in. (*h*). Bureau of Archaeological Research, Tallahassee. Photo by Roy Craven. Courtesy of Barbara Purdy.

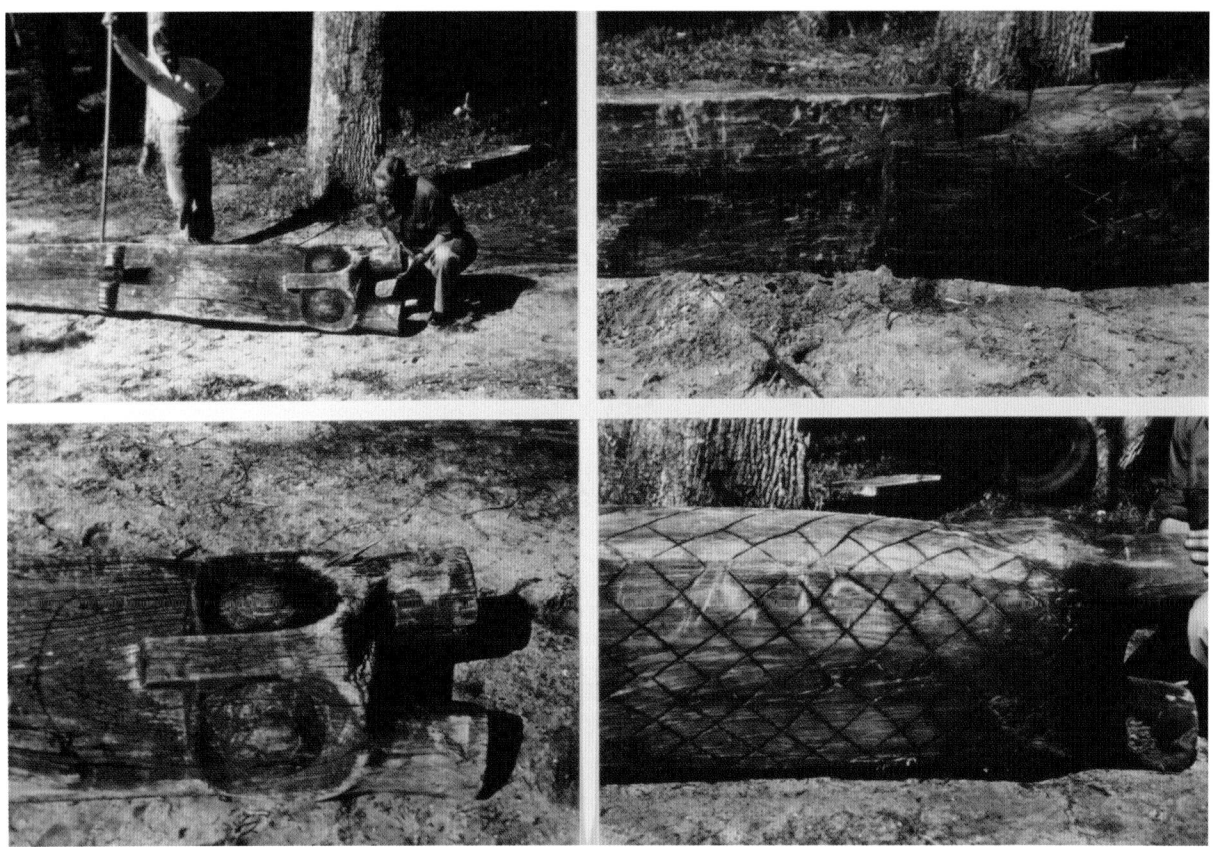

Plate 19. Workers recovering the owl totem from the river. Photo courtesy of Barbara Purdy.

Bill Belleville, the author of *River of Lakes*, writes: "Despite the diligent work of the archaeologists, no single artifact they uncovered was as spectacular as the totems, which were more or less blundered upon during river bottom dredging. The owl came up during the digging of a canal in 1955 near where the mainland parking lot for the park is today; a pelican emerged in 1978 after a barge repairing an underwater utility cable snagged what workers thought was a muddy log in the river. When the log revealed itself as a pelican, divers then searched the bottom and found another wooden icon, an otter-like animal holding a fish."[18]

Fired clay pottery first appeared in Florida around 2000 BC along the St. Johns River. In fact, according to the Florida Indian expert Robin Brown, the St. Johns River valley is likely one of the sites in eastern North America where pottery was invented. Using palm fiber or Spanish moss as tempering agents to hold the clay together, early Florida potters made simple, un-decorated ceramic vessels for cooking and storing. Later potters used sand as a tempering agent to create stronger, less porous pottery.[19]

More sophisticated religious practices led to the development of special-ized pottery such as this ceramic vase molded into the form of a crouch-ing human. This effigy vase, as it is called by anthropologists, is an ex-ample of ceramics that may have been used by the Indians for rituals and ceremonies.

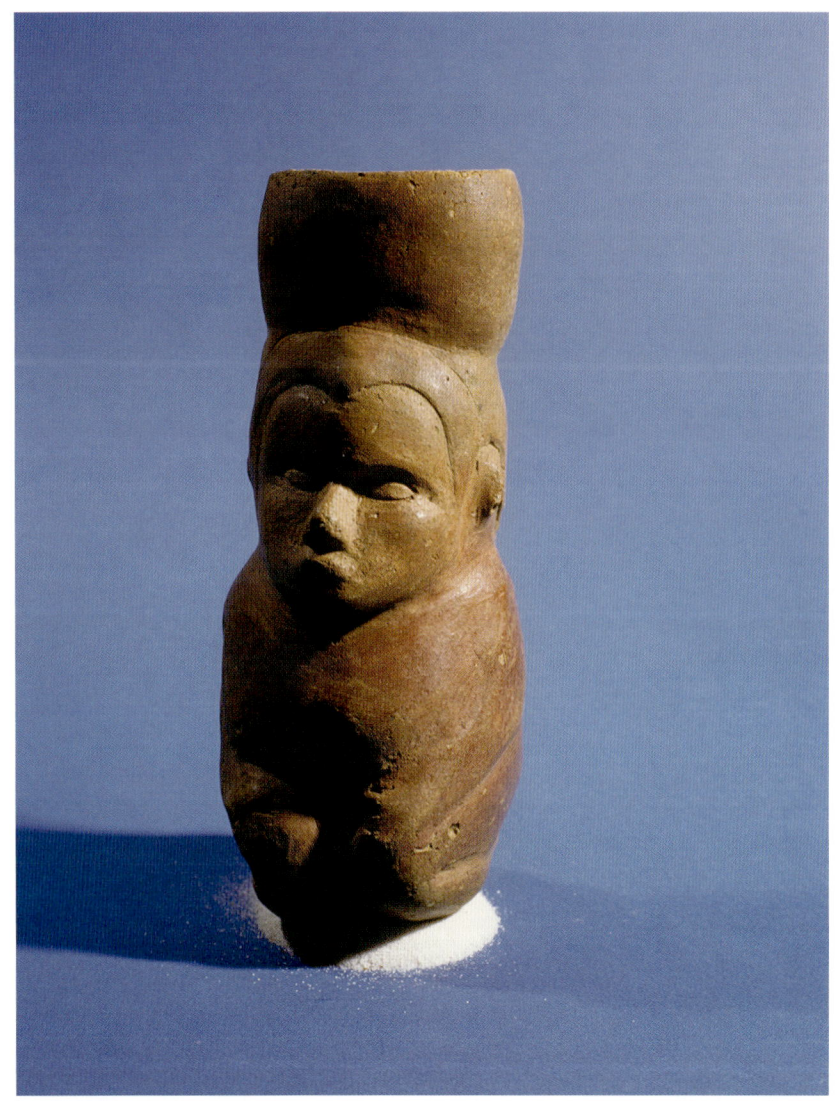

Plate 20. Human effigy figure, mound near Jacksonville, ca. AD 250– 800. 9½ in. (*h*). Private Collection. Photo by Roy Craven. Courtesy of Barbara Purdy.

Some of the earliest-known pottery in Florida is called Orange Pottery after the place near Melbourne where it was first found. This type of ceramic ware was hand-molded rather than coiled. Coiled construction appeared around 1,000 BC, about the same time that sand replaced fiber as the tempering agent.

The Natives who lived in loosely allied village groups located along Florida's east coast from Fort Pierce northward to Cape Canaveral and inland to the St. Johns River in Brevard County were known as the Ais Indians. Their culture was a southern variant of the St. Johns culture. Ais village remains have been found along the coast and in the marshy headwaters of the St. Johns. Geographically, these settlements were located outside the main region of foreign influence, but their inhabitants encountered the Spanish and other Europeans who were survivors of the shipwrecks that often occurred along the coast. The area contains a large number of sites that have yielded both Indian and Spanish artifacts including Ais pottery. The pottery made by the Ais Indians at the time of European contact was a mix of St. Johns ware and sand-tempered ceramic—a distinctive tradition that was different from that of the Timucuan and Mayaca regions to the north and those of south Florida.[20]

The Orlando artist Maury Hurt's painting *Ais Woman Decorating a Pot* shows a woman seated in a sandy landscape. She is holding a piece of pottery, and other pots are grouped around her. Although inspired by the Ais culture, Hurt says that his painting is based less on archaeological facts than on "an intense interest in primitive and archaic art, with an emphasis given to animals, human-animal relationships, and the basic and utilitarian aspects of prehistoric and primitive life . . . at times integrating surrealistic elements into the paintings.

"My interest in these people [the Ais Indians] arose from finding a pottery fragment on one of my outings on the St. Johns River. Among the sites and shell middens that I have explored along the St. Johns River, I have found many potshards that have a black clay base, with a rich red ochre layer over the top. Although I have never found examples of Ais pottery with designs, it may have been that some creative individual integrated [them} . . . into their pots. . . . I have taken the liberty to portray the woman in the painting not just as an Ais but also as an innovator."[21]

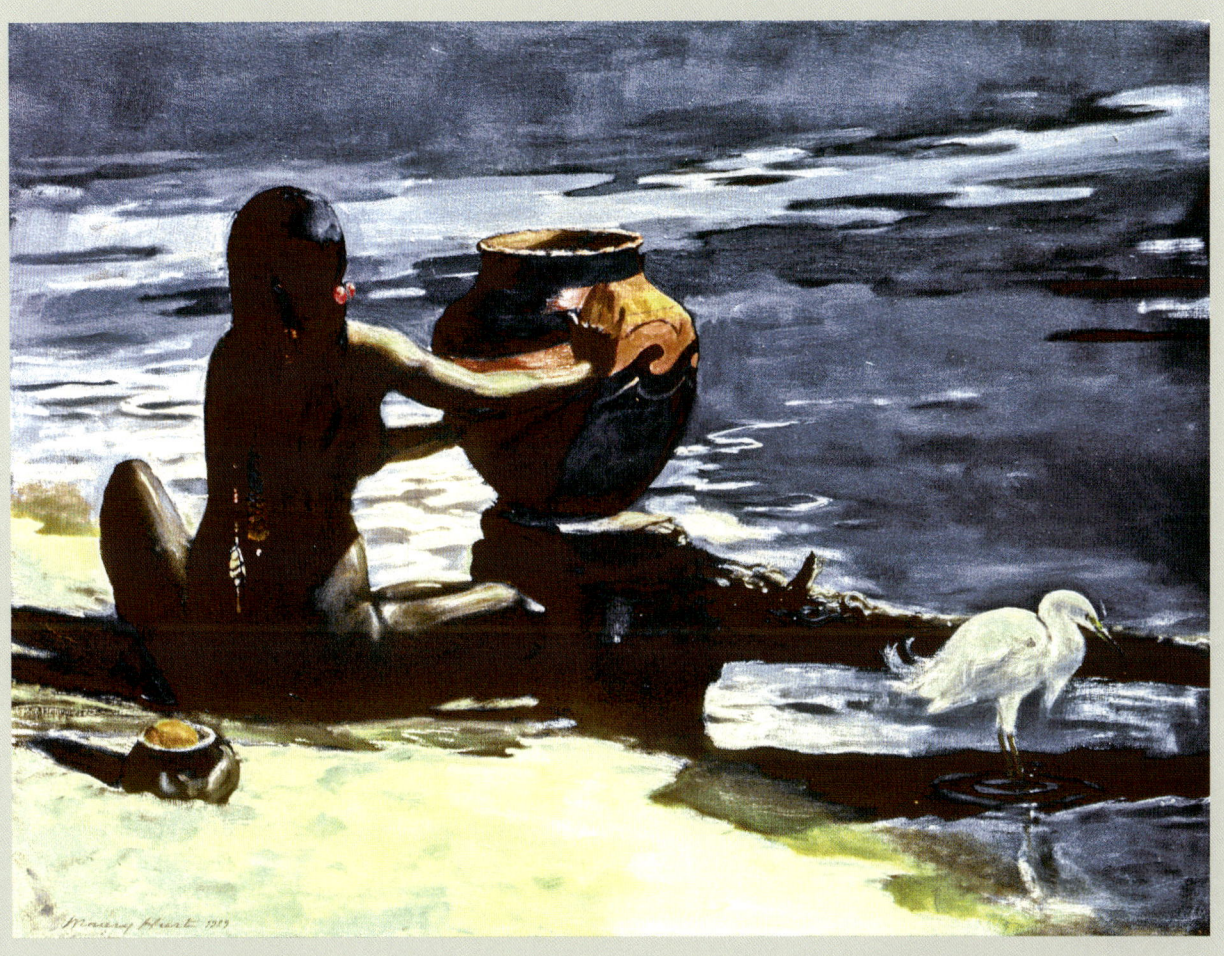

Plate 21. Maury Hurt. *Ais Woman Decorating a Pot*, 1988. Oil on canvas, 30 × 40 in. Collection of Mr. and Mrs. Robert Benton.

Of the Timucua—here along the St. Johns for at least 4,000 years before the Europeans arrived—we know at least shards of their language. Of their words, there were five different ones for trust, six for virtue. But there was only one root word for water. Dew, rainfall, pond, river, lake, lagoon: it is all ibi. . . . Ibi, a liquid god that rendered this once-arid sandbar and savanna luxuriant, that made it a jungle, warm, wet and wildly productive.

—Bill Belleville, *Florida's Deep Blue Destiny*

WHEN THE EUROPEANS began to arrive in the sixteenth century, they encountered the descendants of the St. Johns people, especially the Timucuan groups who lived along and near the St. Johns River and its tributaries. Archaeologists have identified several cultural groups that occupied the region. Analysis of linguistic patterns indicates that most of the St. Johns basin was populated by groups that spoke variants of the Timucuan language. The territory of the Timucuan-speakers ranged from mid-Georgia southward along the river valley to below Daytona Beach and inland across north Florida to the Aucilla River and southward through the central Florida lakes district to the Marion-Lake county line south of Ocala. The Mayaca and Jororo of the Upper St. Johns valley as well as the Surruque of the Cape Canaveral area may also have been Timucuan-speakers.[22]

The word "timucua" likely comes from the Indian word *thimogona,* which referred to a group of Indians who lived upstream from where the French first encountered Florida's indigenous people. The French and later the Spanish used this word to refer to these people. Later scholars applied the name to the entire group of Timucuan-speakers, which was divided into subgroups that included the Saturiwa, Utina, Potano, Edelano, and Acuera. Each of these groups had leaders who formed alliances with one another to maintain control of their territories and to fight intruders. Although they shared the same language and had developed similar cultural traits, the various groups did not consider themselves to be one people; rather, their allegiance was to their local and regional leaders. "It is probable that none of the Timucuan speakers ever referred to themselves as 'Timucuans.'"[23]

The Tallahassee artist Sally Boswell worked with the Museum of Florida History in Tallahassee to re-create images of the Timucuan Indians who lived in north Florida along the St. Johns River before the arrival of the Europeans (see plate 22). Using archaeological research, Boswell strives to make her scenes as authentic as possible. Here, she gives us a view of a typical Timucuan village. The conical buildings on the bluff are Indian dwellings. The large structure on the opposite shore is an earthen mound topped by a ceremonial structure. The accounts of early European explorers described Timucuan villages and also mention the impressive dugout canoes that the Indians used to carry people and cargo along the river.[24]

For over ten millennia, the Timucua and their ancestors lived throughout the St. Johns watershed. They inhabited the biggest territory—much of north Florida and parts of south Georgia and westward to Alachua and Marion Counties—and their population was the largest—estimated at 150,000 at the time of contact—of any of the native people encountered by the Europeans.[25] Archaeological sites throughout the region attest to their presence and their culture while later French and Spanish documents bear witness to both their accomplishments and their demise. The archaeologist Jerald Milanich writes: "By the early 1760s the indigenous population of Florida, once numbering in the hundreds of thousands, was reduced to almost nothing. Handfuls of individuals . . . were taken to Cuba when Spanish population withdrew from Florida in 1763. . . . For the Florida Indians it was the end of time."[26]

Plate 22. Sally Boswell. *Timucuan Village on the St. Johns near Deland c. 1450*, 1995. Acrylic on canvas. State of Florida Collection, Tallahassee, Florida.

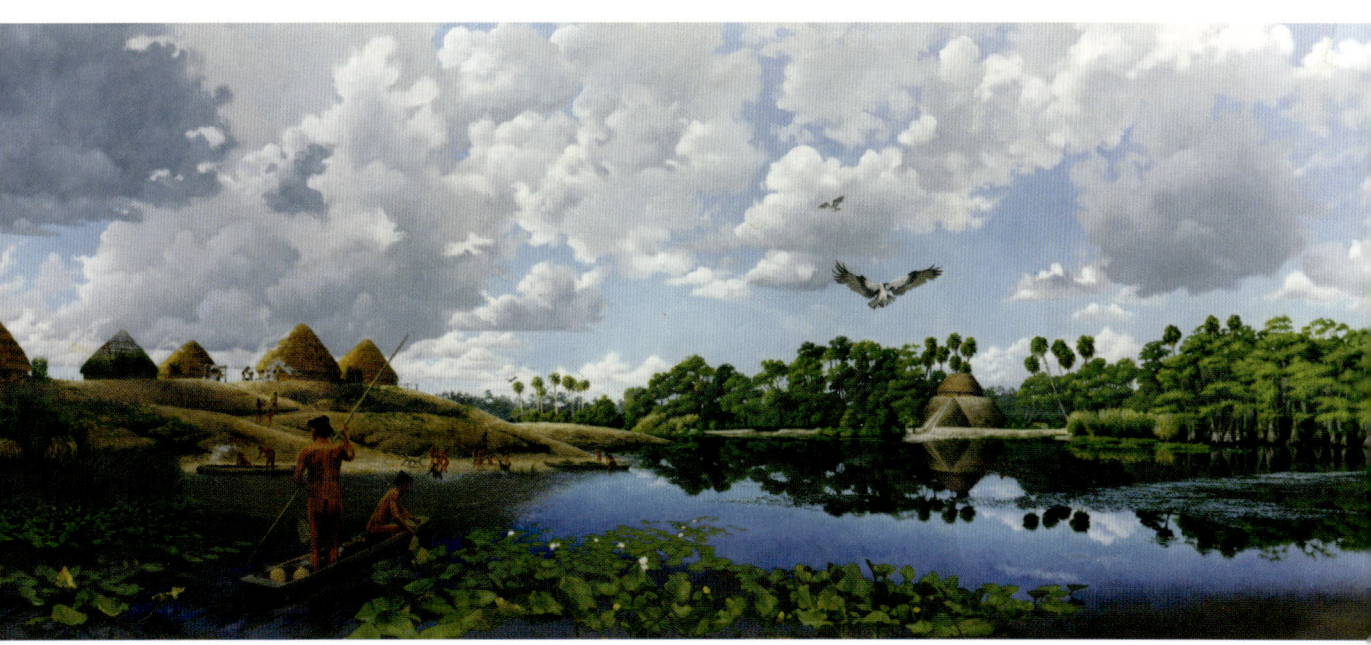

2 The Fourth Part of the World

The part of the Earth that nowadays we call the fourth part of the world, or America, or the West Indies was unknown to the ancients because it was so far away. Similarly all the islands of the West and the Fortunate isles were only discovered by men of our own day, although some would say that they were discovered in the time of Augustus Caesar and that Virgil mentions them in the sixth book of his Aeneid. Where he says that there was a land beyond the stars and the voyage of that year and the sun, where Atlas the sky carrier supports the Pole on his shoulders. However, it is easy to see that he did not mean this land. No one at all of his time had ever heard of it, nor had anyone for more than one thousand years to come.

—René de Laudonnière, *L'Histoire notable de la Floride* (1586)

THE FIRST EUROPEAN ACCOUNTS of the land and people of the St. Johns River area were written in 1562 with the arrival of an expedition of French Protestants headed by Captain Jean Ribaut, a devout Calvinist who came to the New World under the sponsorship of the Huguenot Admiral Gaspard de Coligny. Coligny hoped to establish a French colony where the Protestant Huguenots could practice their religion free from persecution. René de Laudonnière, a member of a distinguished French family and an experienced sea captain, was chosen to be second in command. On February 18, 1562, Ribaut, Laudonnière, and a contingent of sailors and colonists sailed from Havre-de-Grace in three ships. Two and a half months later, Ribaut sighted the coast of Florida and made landfall near present-day St. Augustine. He named the place Cape Francois in honor of the kingdom of France.[1] Laudonnière later reported that Captain Ribaut "viewed the coast all along with an inspeakable pleasure of the odoriferous smell and bewtye of the same."[2]

A second French expedition, headed this time by René de Laudonnière, left for the New World in April 1564. Laudonnière had recruited soldiers, sailors, and artisans—approximately three hundred men and four women—with hopes of starting a permanent settlement. The prospective settlers reached the coast of Florida in June and cast anchor at the mouth of what they called the River May, now the St. Johns River. They were immediately greeted by an enthusiastic group of Indians led by Athore, the son of Chief Satouriona.[3] Among Laudonnière's recruits was the cartographer and artist Jacques Le Moyne de Morgues.

When they arrived on the shores of the New World, European artists brought with them the tools of their trade—paper, ink, pigments—with which to create their images, but the local environment had an enormous impact on their creations. They observed unfamiliar animals, exotic natives, strange flowers and trees, and tried to capture these curiosities in ink and watercolor. However, tied as they were to their own European cultural assumptions—the product of *their* native environment—their pictures often revealed more about the artists than they did about the subjects, while the monuments they created, from Ribaut's Column to the Castillo de San Marcos, reflected not only European aesthetics but also the European obsession with dominance, authority, and control.

As part of his responsibility as artist and cartographer, Le Moyne created a series of paintings of the Timucuan Indians of the north Florida area. Painted either on the spot at Fort Caroline, near present-day Jacksonville, or, more likely, back in England, where Le Moyne lived after his return to Europe in 1565, these paintings later became a model for European artists who wanted to create images of the inhabitants of the New World.[4]

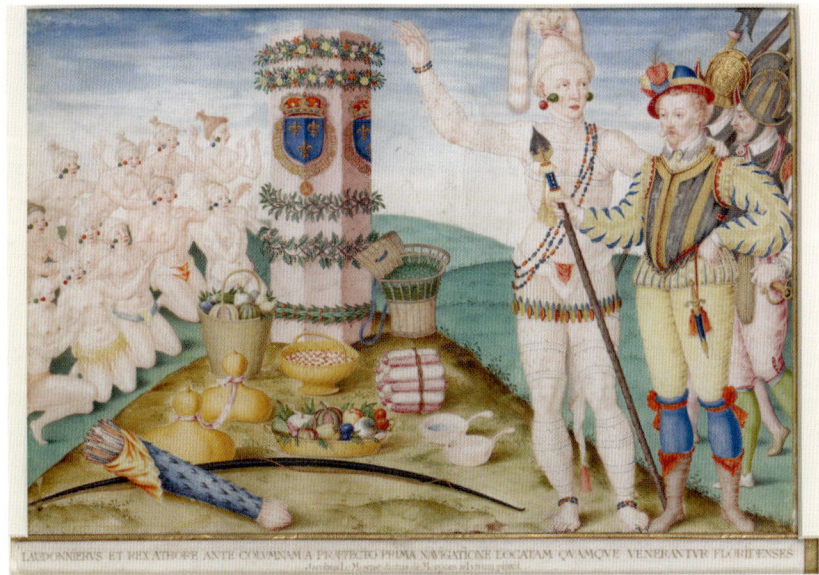

Plate 23. Attributed to Jacques Le Moyne. *René de Laudonnière and the Chief, Athore, at Ribaut's Column*, ca. 1564. Gouache and metallic pigments on velum, 7 × 10¼ in. Courtesy of the New York Public Library.

This gouache painting done on vellum, now in the collection of the New York Public Library, is said by some scholars to be the only known surviving original of the paintings of the New World done by Jacques Le Moyne.[5] The painting purports to illustrate the French commander René de Laudonnière and Athore, a chief of the Timucuan Indians, standing before a column engraved with the arms of the king of France that had been erected by Jean Ribaut, leader of the first French expedition to Florida, several years before.

Despite his close observation of nature, Le Moyne was working under the influence of the European artistic tradition, and his figures are exaggerated in design. His record of the offerings that surround the base of the column—fruits, vegetables, and flowers—are likely more accurate and give the viewer a clue as to the bounty available to the local population. Le Moyne's Timucua are painted a strange shade of pink and he shows them bowing before the column as if in awe of the power of France.[6]

In a narrative attributed to Jacques Le Moyne, the adventurous artist tells us: "Many rivers were explored before the French decided that the River May was the best for a settlement. They sailed upstream until they came to the neighborhood of a certain hill [now called St. Johns Bluff], where they chose a spot which seemed to be . . . suitable . . . and so pleasant that those which are melancholicke would be inforced to change their humour. . . . Next day, at dawn, they offered prayers to God and gave thanks for their happy arrival; then they all went briskly to work. First they marked out a triangular outline on the ground; then they began to dig the earth, to make fences of brushwood, and to build the wall. Each man was so busy with spade, saw, ax or some other tool, and all toiled so hard that the work progressed rapidly."[7]

According to the historian Charles Bennett in his introduction to *Three Voyages*, the Timucuan chief, Satouriona, took great interest in the building of Fort Caroline. Reportedly he "took measurements of the walls. Then, 'seeing that the earth was being taken from the ditch and formed into a rampart' he asked what purpose it served. Advised that the earthworks were to protect the settlers, he said he would like to see the work completed and responded to Laudonnière's request for help by sending 'eighty of his strongest men.'"[8] Laudonnière reported that "'the Indians worked hard, some bringing palmetto leaves, and others weaving them together. In this way the order of their chief was carried out.'"[9]

Theodore de Bry, a Flemish engraver, is said to have been especially indebted to Le Moyne's work as inspiration for his own drawings of New World people. According to de Bry, he was fortunate enough to acquire Le Moyne's narrative of his Florida adventures along with a portfolio of his art works after the artist's death in 1588. De Bry had the manuscript translated into Latin, made engravings from the art works, and had the whole manuscript published in 1591. The fact that all but one of Le Moyne's original paintings have disappeared, and even that one is suspect, leads some scholars to wonder if de Bry didn't use other sources, including the accounts of explorers such as André Thevet, John White, and Hans Staden, in creating his images.[10]

Whatever his sources, it's clear that de Bry did not have direct access to his subjects, and so, although they provide a fascinating interpretation of early European encounters with the inhabitants of the Southeast, the engravings are not as accurate as the work of artists who made their images directly from life.[11]

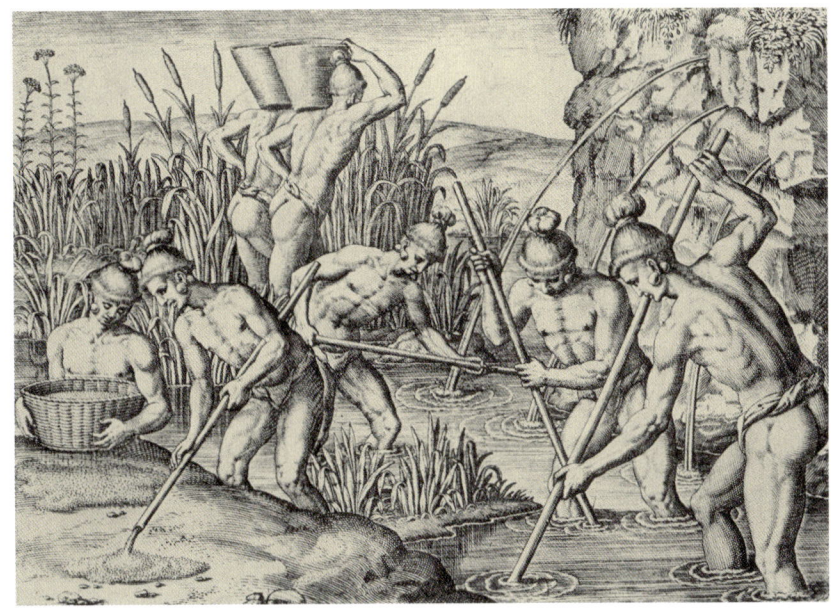

Plate 24. Theodore de Bry. *How They [the Indians] Collected Gold in the Rivers Flowing from the Apalatci Mountains.* Engraving for his volume on Florida printed in 1591, 6 × 8¼ in. Photocopy courtesy of the State Archives of Florida.

In this engraving, de Bry shows us a scene of Native Americans hard at work supposedly collecting gold from a river. De Bry is said to have based his image on the following passage in Le Moyne's narrative, *Brevis narrato eorum quae in Florida Americae*: "A long way from our fort [Fort Caroline] are the Appalachian Mountains. There . . . three great rivers rise, and in the sands of these a great deal of gold, silver, and brass is found. The natives dig ditches in these streams, into which the sand brought by the current falls because of its weight. Little by little they collect the precious metals and bring them down the River May [the St. Johns], which empties into the sea. The Spaniards use the wealth thus obtained to great advantage."[12]

According to Charles Bennett in *Laudonnière and Fort Caroline*, "The principal source of domestic gold . . . prior to the California gold rush . . . was in the Georgia and North Carolina section of the Appalachian Mountains,"[13] and the Native people were apparently aware of this resource. Gemstones were also found in the same region. The French carpenter Nicolas Le Challeux, a survivor of the Spanish attack on Fort Caroline, recalled in his memoirs that the lure of gold was used to recruit men to serve under Jean Ribaut: "Men were persuaded by these promises . . . (believing they would be made rich by this voyage because of the gold), and came in legions to the town where the muster for the voyage was held."[14] While both the narrative and the artwork may be questioned, what is true is that the French were highly motivated in their efforts by their competition with the Spanish for land and wealth in the New World and that the myth of El Dorado was a powerful inducement for their actions.

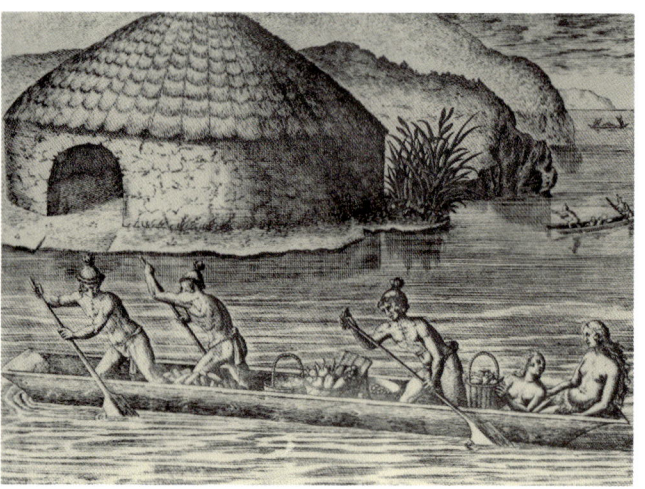

Plate 25. Theodore de Bry. *Storing Their Crops in the Public Grainery*. Engraving, 1591, 6 × 8¼ in. Photocopy courtesy of the State Archives of Florida.

The interaction of the Native Floridians with the St. Johns River was a frequent subject of de Bry's imagery. This engraving is based on Laudonnière's description of the way the Indians stored their harvest: "In this part of the region there were a great number of islands where they [the Indian] harvested a variety of fruits twice a year. These were loaded into their dugouts and taken home for storage. Their storehouses were wide and low, built of stones and earth with roofs of thickly laid palm leaves and soft soil. These kinds of huts were usually built near the river. . . . They also left other produce there from time to time or took food away when they needed it without worrying about their neighbors stealing from them."[15]

In June 1565, Pedro Menéndez de Avilés was dispatched from Cadiz, Spain, with a contingent of soldiers, sailors, and settlers. Wary of the French intrusion into north Florida, Menéndez was given the charge by the Spanish Crown of establishing a colony that could secure the land for Spain. Landing on Florida's northern coast on September 8, 1565, Menéndez took formal possession of all of Florida, placing the land and its people under the authority of King Philip II. He established a fort on land provided to him by the leader of the local Timucuan Indians and founded what was to be the first permanent European settlement in the New World, St. Augustine.

This painting by Dean Quigley depicts the initial encounter between the Timucuan Indians and the Spanish.

Plate 26. Dean Quigley. *The Arrival of the Spanish*, n.d. Acrylic on canvas, 30 × 40 in. Courtesy of the artist.

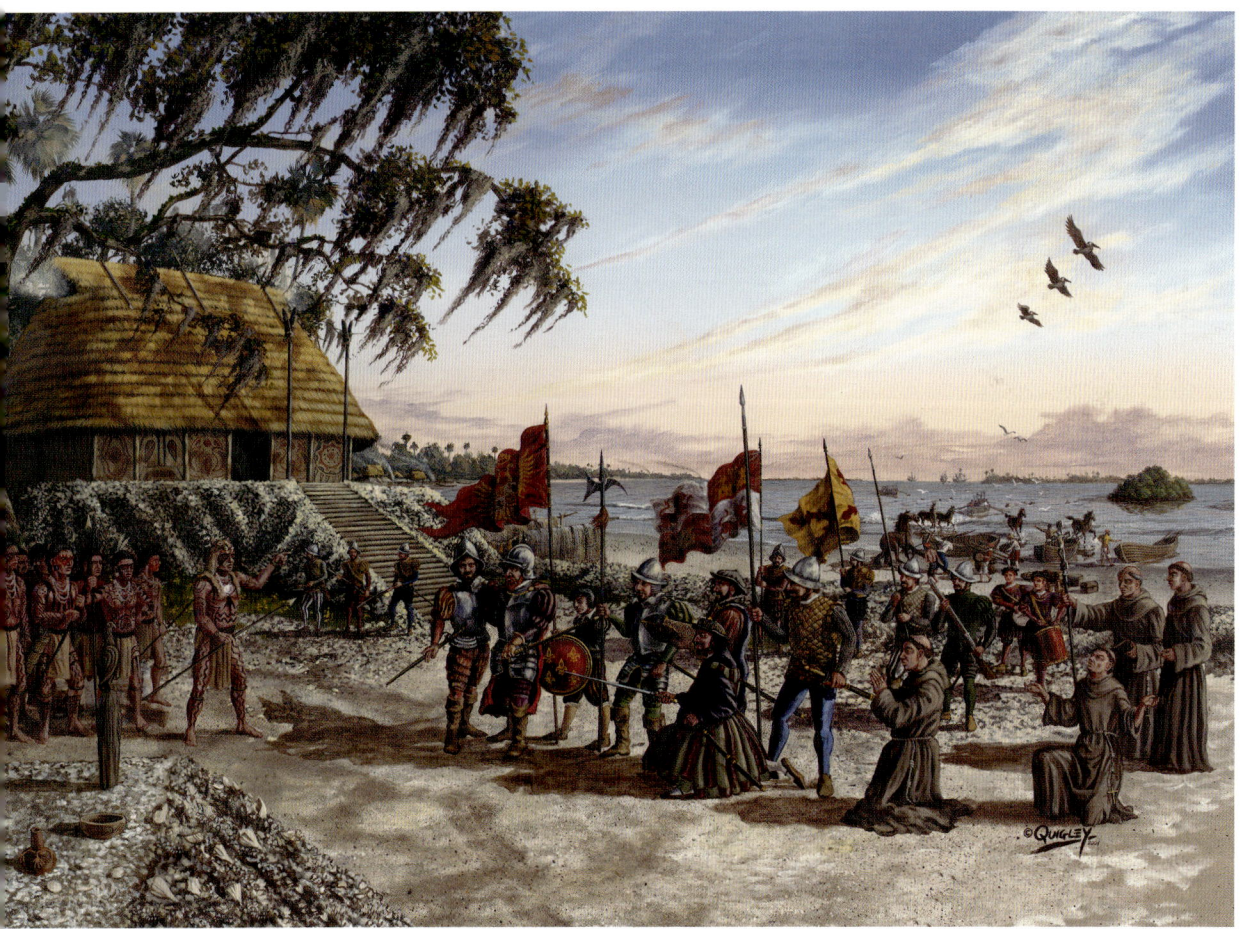

Menéndez was soon under attack by a French contingent under the command of Jean Ribaut who had recently established Fort Caroline on the St. Johns River near present-day Jacksonville. Against the advice of Laudonnière, Ribaut decided to sail against the Spanish fleet to head off an attack on Fort Caroline. Unfortunately for the French, a large storm—perhaps a hurricane—wrecked their fleet, and the Spanish seized the opportunity to attack the poorly defended fort. Left with only a small contingent of defenders, Fort Caroline fell to the Spanish attack in less than an hour. Of the 240 Frenchmen who were guarding the fort, 132 were killed. The Spanish did not lose a single man. Laudonnière, along with the artist Jacques Le Moyne, managed to escape. After wandering in the forest, the survivors finally made their way to two French ships that were lying at anchor and managed to obtain safe passage back to Europe.

Thus the French colony at Fort Caroline ceased to be. The Spanish renamed the captured fort San Mateo. They soon erected two blockhouses on the north and south sides of the St. Johns River to protect their new fort. Menéndez wrote to Philip II, the Spanish king, "in the future Florida will be of little expense, and will pay Your Majesty much money, and will be of more value to Spain than New Spain or even Peru, and it may be said that this country is but a suburb of Spain, for it does not take more than forty days' sailing to come here."[16]

The French, however, had their revenge. Enraged by Menéndez's massacre of the Ribaut expedition, Dominique de Gourgues, a French Catholic, vowed to get even. In August 1567, he left France with three ships and sailed to Florida. With the help of their Timucuan allies, the Frenchmen attacked Fort San Mateo in April 1568. After burning the two blockhouses and routing the Spanish, they destroyed the fort and left the captured Spaniards hanging from trees.[17] Both the French and the Spanish had failed in their attempt to establish and hold a strategic position that guarded the entrance to the St. Johns River.

Spanish Catholics hoped that in addition to obtaining productive colonies and enhancing Spain's wealth, they would also be able to convert the indigenous population of the New World to the Catholic faith. Missionary efforts began almost as soon as the first Spaniard set foot in Florida and continued for the next two centuries.

While many people are familiar with the missions of California, most of which date from the eighteenth century, few are aware that there were once Florida missions that bore the names of Santa Cruz, San Diego, and San Francisco. A combination of politics and climate conspired to obliterate the mission villages that once bore witness to the Spanish presence in La Florida. Our knowledge of the Florida missions comes from archaeological excavations and from historical documents that tell the story of the lost enclaves.

The first Spanish mission to be established in Florida was Nombre de Dios, founded at St. Augustine in 1565 by the priests who accompanied Pedro Menéndez's expedition. Jesuit missionaries soon followed, but it was the Franciscans, who arrived in 1573, who enjoyed the greatest success in establishing the Florida mission system. Eventually, some twenty-six thousand Christianized Indians lived in and around the missions.

One of the most successful missionaries assigned to Florida was Fr. Francisco Pareja, a Franciscan missionary who arrived in St. Augustine in 1595. He spent the next thirty-one years working to convert the Timucua to the Catholic faith. As part of his missionary activities, Fr. Pareja wrote a grammar of the Timucuan language that was published in Mexico in 1614.

Mission San Juan del Puerto, founded in 1587, was located on the western shore of San Juan Island, later known as Fort George Island, at the mouth of the river the French had named the River May and the Spanish had renamed the San Mateo. The mission eventually became so well known that in time the river itself became known as the San Juan. It was from his headquarters at mission San Juan that Fr. Pareja set off on long journeys throughout the region to carry his message to the Indian people. Charles Bennett, in his book *Twelve on the River St. Johns*, writes: "Pareja's superior, Fr. Luis Geronimo de Ore, [wrote,] 'In the beginning, the Indians offered him many affronts but he overcame them all with much patience and perseverance by abiding in their midst, teaching them the law of Christ and defending them from the molestation of the Spanish soldiers.'"[18]

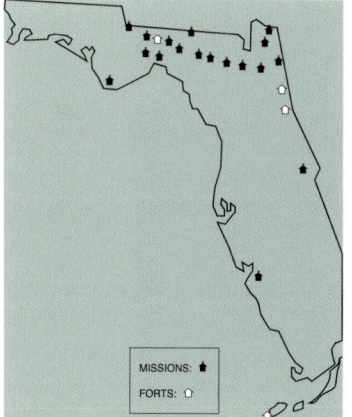

Little today remains of the more than one hundred Spanish mission settlements that once dotted the Florida landscape from the Atlantic Ocean west to the Aucilla River (near present-day Tallahassee) and south along the St. Johns to Lake George.

Plate 27. Map of the Spanish missions in the St. Johns region.

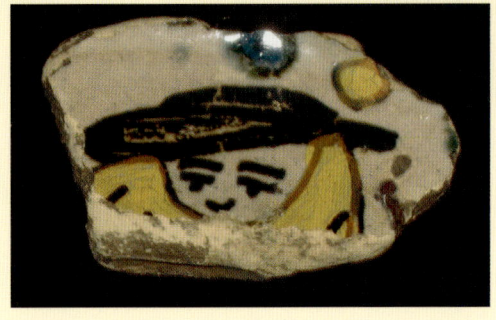

Plate 28. Anonymous. Majolica fragment showing a priest, found at the San Juan del Puerto mission site, sixteenth century. Florida Museum of Natural History Anthropology Division, Gainesville.

This sixteenth-century majolica fragment, now in the collection of the Florida Museum of Natural History, shows the image of a priest wearing a typical wide-brimmed hat. The piece was found at the site of the San Juan mission on Fort George Island.

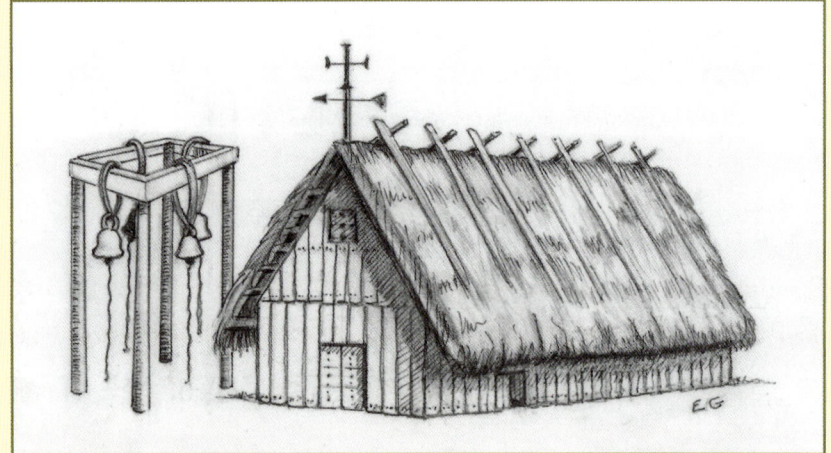

Plate 29. Elsbeth Gordon. *Parish Church, Nuestra Senora de los Remedios, c. 1572*, 2002. Graphite on paper. Courtesy of the artist.

Since none of the original Spanish missions are still standing, images of them are necessarily speculative. However, pictures such as this are based on recent archaeological evidence and probably come close to reconstructing the look of Florida mission architecture. The architectural historian Elsbeth Gordon writes: "All the buildings . . . had pole frames set directly in the ground and covered with palm thatch. . . . The European-style church and friary were rectangular and gabled, built with hewn timbers and hardware. The chief's house and the Timucuan council house were round, built with poles and cordage from plants and animals."[19] Gordon used her architectural knowledge to compile this image.

The Spanish missions were eventually destroyed by the English under the leadership of James Moore of South Carolina. Moore led raiding parties into Florida in the early 1700s that succeeded in wiping out the missions, the missionaries, and what was left of the converts. According to Elsbeth Gordon, "Jonathan Dickinson stopped at the mission [San Juan] in 1696 and described its location in the middle of the island as having a church, a friary, a corn house, and a large council house."[20] The San Juan mission was burned by the English raiders, but was rebuilt only to be abandoned when the British gained control of Florida in 1763. Gordon notes that when John Bartram visited the San Juan site in 1765, he reported that the mission was once "a fine settlement with cedar posts still standing on each side of their fine straight avenues."[21] However, Florida's humid climate then proceeded to bury the remnants of the buildings under layers of foliage and decay.

Gordon points out that the early Florida mission buildings were the result of a collaboration between the Spanish and the indigenous Indian people: "Pedro Menéndez made his historic campsite in 1565 in a preexisting Timucuan village, and where a Timucuan building became his headquarters. The conversion of an Indian building marked the beginning of more than a century of collaboration in construction, during which Indian labor and building practices were largely responsible for the successes of the Spanish Franciscan missions that stretched across Florida's wilderness."[22]

The church at San Luis was roofed with palm thatch, which was typically used for Indian structures, while the walls were constructed of vertical planks—a Spanish practice. Thus the sixteenth-century Spanish buildings were a hybrid of Indian and European architectural elements.

In addition to the missions located along the St. Johns River and elsewhere to the west, Spanish archives record three missions along the Ocklawaha River in Marion County, a major tributary of the St. Johns. The earliest mission in the area, San Blas de Avino, operated from about 1609 until 1620. It was replaced by two missions, San Lucia de Acuera and San Luis de Ocale, that operated from the 1620s to 1656.[23] According to John Hann, a historian at the San Luis Archaeological and Historic Site in Tallahassee, all of the early Florida missions were established in existing Indian villages, eliminating the need for a policy of *congregacion*, or forced relocation, which was used in California. "Because soldiers did not accompany the friars and because friars had no herds of cattle or supplies of maize or other foodstuffs to attract natives to settle at a point the friars found desirable, the religious had no choice but to go where the natives were living, beginning usually with the village of the head chief of a district."[24]

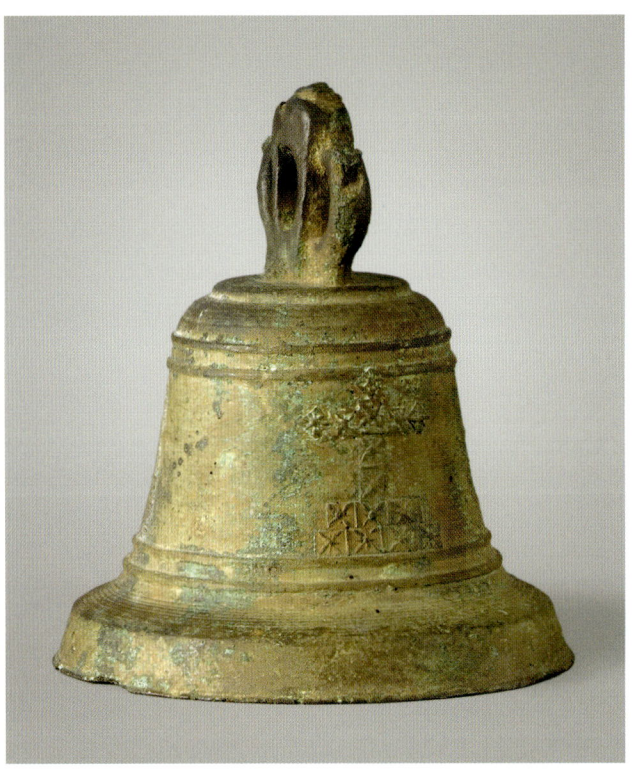

Plate 30. Spanish mission bell, ca. 1620–56. Bronze, 12 × 11⅛ × 11⅛ in. Silver River Museum Collection. Photo by Scott Mitchum. Courtesy of the Silver River Museum, Ocala, Florida.

This cast bronze Spanish mission bell dates from about 1620 to 1656, and was found by Ben Waller while he was diving in the Ocklawaha River in the 1960s. It was encrusted, but upon cleaning, a prominent cross was revealed. It is believed to be from the mission San Luis de Ocale. Presumably from Spain, it also may have been made in the New World settlements of Cuba or Mexico. It was likely brought up the river to Connor Landing, which was northeast of Ocala. "That bell rang mass for close to forty years. The bell is a tremendous symbol of the intermingling, and clash, of old world Catholicism and Native American agrarian peasants—two groups who couldn't be more different," says Scott Mitchell, director of the Silver River Museum near Ocala, Florida.[25]

The number of Timucuan missions peaked in the mid-1600s at twenty-one despite a drop in the Native population. According to John Hann, the number of baptized Christian Indians stood at around thirty thousand in 1635, but declined over the next twenty-five years due to waves of epidemics of measles and smallpox that killed thousands.[26]

The missionary process, according to the archaeologist Jerald Milanich, was essential to the goal of colonialism—"creating profits by manipulating the land and its people."[27] While the stated goal of the mission's developers was to bring Christianity to the heathen Indians, the mission system also provided a way to build a labor force that could be used to expand the Spanish presence in the region. Nearly all of early Florida's manual labor was supplied by mission Indians; labor quotas and the conscription of people to serve on labor gangs were organized by the mission villages. Further, the mission system helped to acculturate the Natives into the rudiments of European farming, animal husbandry, carpentry, weaving, and reading and writing.

According to Milanich, "Conquistadors, missionaries, and entrepreneurs went hand-in-hand to conquer the lands and people of the Americas. All were, in part, responsible for the decimation of the native populations served by the missions. In Florida and Georgia that decimation was total . . . except for small groups of refugees who fled La Florida in the early eighteenth century."[28]

However, the Spanish left behind a legacy of art, architecture, and decorative arts that survives to the present day.

3 { The Conquistador's Gift
Cattle, Horses, and Citrus

The first working rancho in La Florida started operation in 1605 near the settlement of St. Augustine. Franciscan friars and Spanish rancheros established the first cattle and horse herds primarily with Andalusian livestock descended from those brought a hundred years before by Spanish conquistadores. During the 18th century, Indians became the most important stock raisers in Florida. And during the 20-year British occupation prior to the American Revolution, a number of British planters started cattle herds, particularly along the St. Johns River Valley.

—Joe A. Akerman Jr., *America's First Cowmen*

THREE OF THE MOST ENDURING GIFTS left behind by Florida's Spanish settlers were cattle, horses, and citrus trees—all were imported to the New World by early Spanish colonists, and all would become mainstays of the Florida economy that have lasted to the present day. The development and growth of these industries have been documented by generations of artists, and the stories—and legends—of cattle- and horse-raising and citrus cultivation are a wonderful and rowdy component of Florida's folk mythology.

Little today remains of the more than one hundred Spanish mission settlements that once dotted the Florida landscape from the Atlantic Ocean west to the Aucilla River (near present-day Tallahassee) and south along the St. Johns to Lake George.

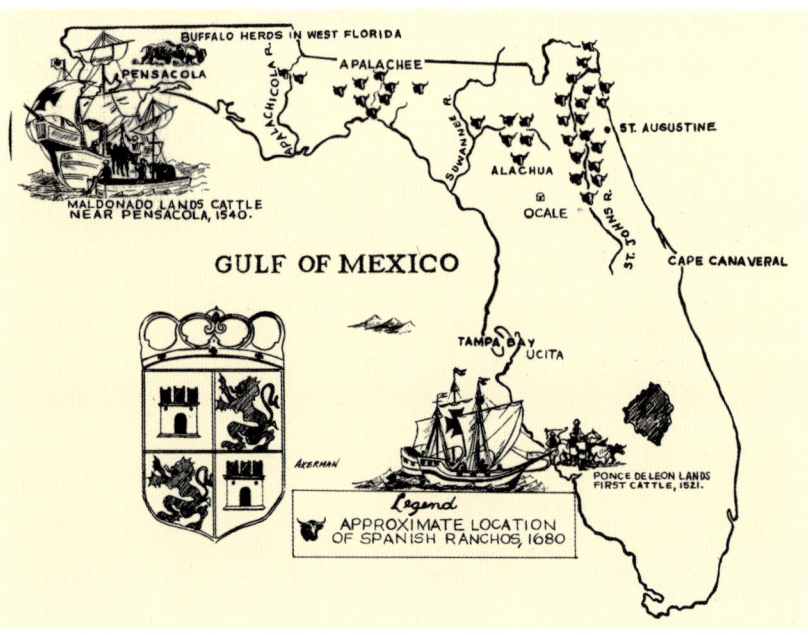

Plate 31. Joe Akerman Jr. Map showing Spanish cattle ranches in the seventeenth century. Courtesy of the artist.

Part of the Spanish plan to colonize Florida was to establish large ranches, or haciendas, throughout the region. The ranches served two important purposes—to maintain direct Spanish control of large tracts of land and to provide agricultural products for the growing community of St. Augustine. Spanish ranchers followed the missions into the valley of the St. Johns River, establishing their haciendas along the river near Picolata and further inland in the Orange Lake basin near present-day Gainesville. These were the first cattle ranches in North America. "No other part of the country had cattle until the Pilgrims brought more in 1624."[1] As the Indian population declined due to the ongoing spread of European diseases, the Spanish met with little resistance to the appropriation of lands formerly inhabited by the Indians.[2]

One of the most successful ranches was located in southern Alachua County, an area formerly inhabited by the Potano Indians, a branch of the Timucua. According to John Hann, the Potano region "had some of the best natural pastures in Florida, characterized by treeless, seasonally flooded savannahs such as Paynes Prairie," where the La Chua Hacienda was established.[3] The ranch was owned by the Menéndez-Marquez family, who were related to Pedro Menéndez de Avilés, the founder of St. Augustine.

The mission *rancheros* provided food, work animals, and raw materials such as hides and tallow that met the needs of the growing Spanish settlements. The remaining Indians often tended to the livestock, leading eventually to a new lifestyle for the Native American—cattle ranching. According to the ranch historian Joe Akerman Jr., persons born in Florida to Spanish parents were known as "criollas." Many criolla men worked as vaqueros, or cowboys, on the ranches, and they often came into conflict with the Indians, who were by that time also raising cattle. These confrontations were probably the first fights between "cowboys and Indians" in North America.[4]

Even though the Spanish were eventually expelled and replaced—first by the British and later by American settlers—the bloodlines of the cattle and the Andalusian horses that were brought to Florida by the Spanish remained embedded in the Florida landscape. William Bartram wrote enthusiastically about the "innumerable droves of cattle; the lordly bull, lowing cow and sleek capricious heifer"[5] that grazed on the Alachua Savanna. Bartram once met with Seminole Chief Cowkeeper and his family at the Indian village of Cuscowilla, near present-day Micanopy. By the time of Bartram's visit, Cowkeeper's tribe had become quite prosperous from its ranching, and Cuscowilla had evolved into the largest town in northern Florida.

During the three Seminole Wars (1813–58), the Seminole Indian settlements were largely destroyed. After the end of hostilities, the remaining Indians were forcibly removed from the area, and their large herds of cattle and horses were left behind to fend once again for themselves. New settlers came into the region and took over the remnants of the earlier herds, joining them with their own herds, which they brought with them from the Carolinas and Georgia.

As the settlers moved south along the St. Johns River valley, cattle ranching became a major industry in the region east of the St. Johns River and in the St. Johns Marsh where the river's headwaters are located. Many settlers lived at first in north central Florida; later they moved farther south looking for cheaper land. They were also attracted to a cattle ford that was located south of Lake Poinsett and to the great expanse of good pastureland in the region.[6]

Plate 32. Anonymous. *Two Florida Cowmen*. From *Illustrated London News*, March 26, 1892. Courtesy of the Matheson Museum, Gainesville, Florida.

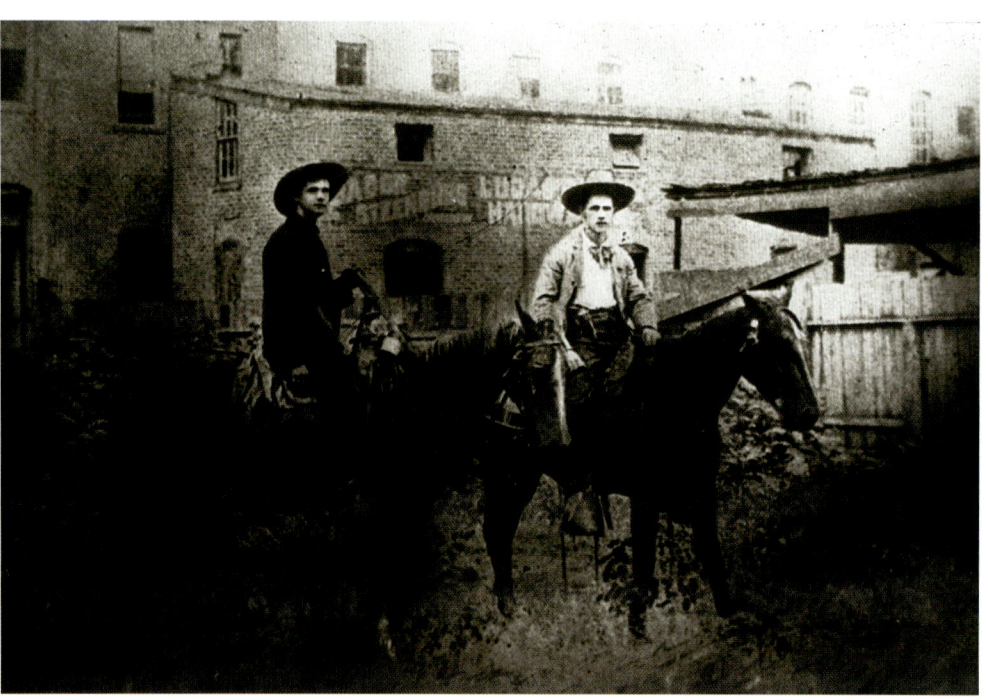

In the late 1800s, purebred beef and dairy breeds from northern Europe were brought into Florida. However, these imports didn't fare well in Florida's climate, and they soon died out. In the 1930s, the heartier Brahman cattle were introduced, which significantly changed the genetic makeup of the Florida herds. Crossing the hardy Cracker cows with other breeds became popular, and eventually the pure Cracker cattle were nearly bred into extinction; by the late 1960s, only a handful remained. Fortunately, thanks to the members of the Florida Cracker Cattle Association, with the cooperation of some descendents of the pioneer families, a small herd of the original stock was preserved.[7] This herd became the basis for the introduction of purebred Cracker cattle into preserves such as the Paynes Prairie State Preserve near Gainesville and Lake Kissimmee State Park, where the breed is thriving.

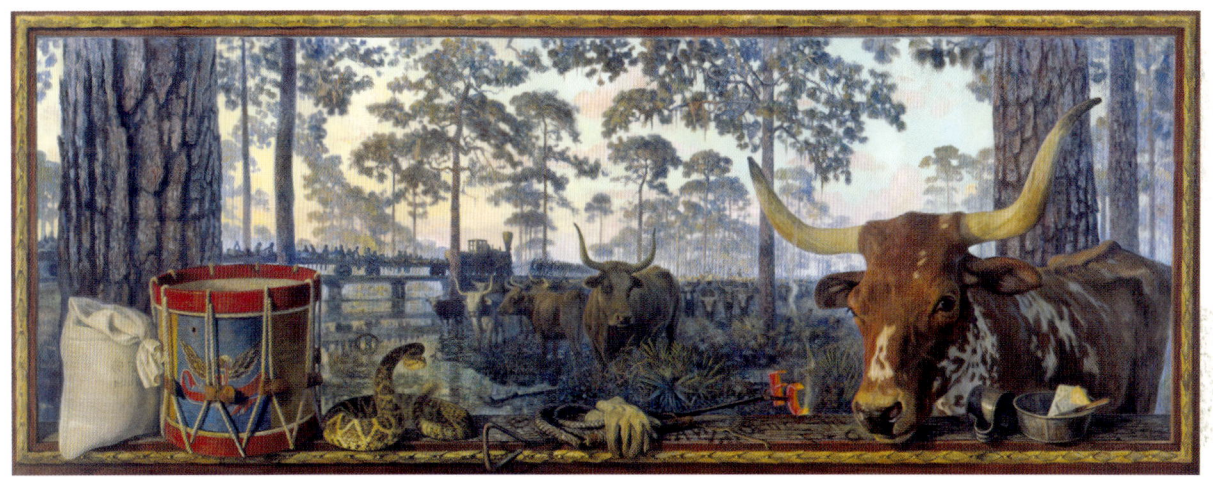

Christopher Still is a native Floridian who studied art at the Pennsylvania Academy of Fine Arts and anatomy at the Jefferson Medical School in Philadelphia. After spending time in Italy, the artist returned to Tampa Bay in 1986 to explore his home state with his art. His paintings are in numerous collections, including the Florida Governor's Mansion and the Smithsonian Institution. The work illustrated here shows Cracker cows from *Reflecting on Ocean Pond*, one of ten murals commissioned by the Florida House of Representatives and executed by Still in the House Chambers in Tallahassee during 2001–3.

Plate 33. Christopher Still. *Reflecting on Ocean Pond*, 2002. Oil on linen, 48 × 120 in. One of ten paintings by Still commissioned by the Florida House of Representatives, Tallahassee.

The origins of the word "Cracker" are as colorful as the people to whom the term was applied. According to Dana Ste. Claire, author of *Cracker: The Cracker Culture in Florida History*, the term was originally applied to a class of people rather than a character trait. He believes that the name originated with the coastal gentry in the late 1700s to describe the Scots-Irish frontiersmen of the rural South. "During the 1760s," Ste. Claire writes, "the term identified loosely organized gangs of horse thieves, counterfeiters, and slave-nappers—surely one of the first criminal syndicates in America."[8]

Edward King, a travel writer who visited Florida from the North in the mid-1800s, described the Cracker cowboys he met as "quick to anger, vindictive when rage is protracted and becomes a feud, and generous and noble in their rough hospitality. They live the most undesirable lives . . . subsist on hog and hominy, and drink the meanest whiskey."[9] As Ronald W. Haase, the author of *Classic Cracker*, remarked, "The first-generation Florida Cracker was not a pillar of society."[10]

It is worth noting that King was a northerner whose biases had been sharpened by the recent hostilities between North and South. If King found the Cracker cowmen a wild bunch, they likely found him to be an obnoxious Yankee. Life on the Florida frontier was by necessity a rough-and-tumble affair, but as the artist and Cracker historian Regina Briskey points out: "I'm sure there were many individuals who appeared and behaved [badly], but there were also many intelligent, cleanly dressed, law-abiding cowmen who were family men, church-goers, and pillars of their respective communities. The fact is everybody had some cows. The cattle ran without fences. Periodically, they would be gathered, marked, branded and driven to market. Everyone helped out. There were big ranchers and small ones and they didn't *all* look or behave like [the infamous Cracker roughneck] Bone Mizell!"[11]

By the twentieth century, the term "Cracker" had been turned into a positive epithet to describe the folksy, backwoodsy Florida of yesterday, a term of affection meant to conjure up images from *The Yearling* and *Doc Hollywood*. Today, many Floridians refer to themselves with pride as Crackers. Additionally, the term has been used to describe a style of down-home cooking—a kind of Anglo soul food—as well as an indigenous style of architecture especially suited to Florida's hot, humid climate. Cracker literature, Cracker music, and Cracker heritage have all been celebrated and recognized as an important part of Florida's history.

A little-known fact is the contribution of African Americans to the development of Florida's cattle industry. The African refugees who escaped enslavement in Georgia and South Carolina and settled in Spanish Florida were skilled workers who entered various occupations. Some became soldiers in the Spanish militia, often serving as scouts or interpreters. Others practiced blacksmithing, carpentry, and weapons manufacture. Black women opened bakeries or sold commodities such as honey.[12]

One other occupation open to the black immigrants was cattle ranching. Beef was an important food source for the Spanish colony, and many of the black residents became cowmen. One of the few Spanish cattle ranches that survived the English attacks of the mid-1700s was that of Diego de Espinosa, a mulatto entrepreneur who operated a large ranch north of St. Augustine between the St. Johns and the Matanzas rivers. Aware of the English threat, Espinosa fortified his isolated ranch so well that it became known as "Fort Diego."[13]

Another famous African American cattleman was Lawrence Silas. According to Joe Akerman, Silas was the son of an ex-slave who started out working for white ranchers and eventually built his own cattle business.[14] Akerman quotes Silas as saying: "I went into the cattle business just like my father did. Bought a cow or two at a time, sold my *he's* and put the money into *she's*. Sarah, my wife, she took in sewing and kept the house going while I put all that I could rake or scrape into cows. Finally we came to have quite a few."[15]

In 1942, when he was fifty-five, Silas was interviewed by the writer/folklorist Zora Neale Hurston for an article that appeared in the *Saturday Evening Post*. Hurston had this to say about the cowman: "Considering that Florida is in Dixie, it will sound like poker playing at a prayer meeting when you read that Lawrence Silas, Negro, is one of the important men of the cow country. But that is the word with the bark on it. The cattlemen in the state have a name for him, and it is good. . . . They do not tell you about his thousands of head of cattle, his fifty-odd miles of fence, or his chunky bank account. They like more to tell you about his character and his skill."[16]

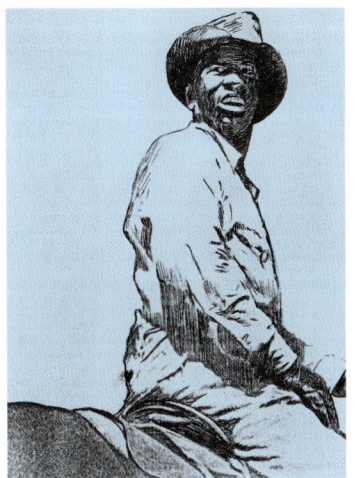

Plate 34. Joe A. Akerman Jr. *Sketch of Lawrence Silas (Based on a photograph)*. Graphite on paper. Courtesy of the artist.

Today, a cattle ranch in Florida bears little resemblance to its earliest predecessors. These days the ranches often walk a fine line between working ranches and picturesque "theme parks." Denise Wolf, a freelance writer who came to Florida from Illinois, visited the Adams Ranch, located on the upper reaches of the St. Johns Marsh, and found herself surrounded by "anhingas, egrets, hawks, herons, roseate spoonbills, sandhill cranes and wood storks"[17] as well as fifty thousand citrus trees and, of course, cattle. Like some other ranches, the Adams Ranch provides tours of their 60,000-acre operation. On her visit, Wolf discovered that Florida is still "the ninth largest cattle-producing state in the nation. But," she continues, "the real story at the Adams Ranch is the wildlife, and there are few places in Florida where you'll have more access to nature's bounty. . . . The Adams Ranch is a working example of nature's balance at its best."[18]

The artist Sean Sexton is a third-generation Florida rancher who lives, works, and paints on his land. Sexton's grandfather, Waldo Sexton, founded the ranch in the 1940s in what used to be the Indian River citrus region of southern Brevard County. If the Sextons are relative newcomers, they have nevertheless established themselves within the colorful and historic cattle culture of the region.

Sexton received a bachelor's degree in animal science from the University of Florida, Gainesville. While pursuing that degree, he also studied art at Santa Fe Community College, where he met artists Lennie Kesl and Norman Jensen, who became his mentors. In 1979, he returned home "and began my life's work as a cattleman and artist, working out with my father terms by which I might have time to paint in the course of my week. This arrangement has prevailed ever since. . . . I paint on Tuesdays and Thursdays except in the Fall when I have to stop painting to plant ryegrass for our cows to graze all winter. I generally make up the lost time in the Fall in the longer days of Summer when there seems to be so much more opportunity for both art and ranch work. I am a real advocate of working outside, en plein air, and rely upon the infusion of energy that comes from natural light. . . . [T]he 'Cow-bidness' is very conducive to art, provides me with a fabulous life and rich material . . . both visually and metaphorically."[19]

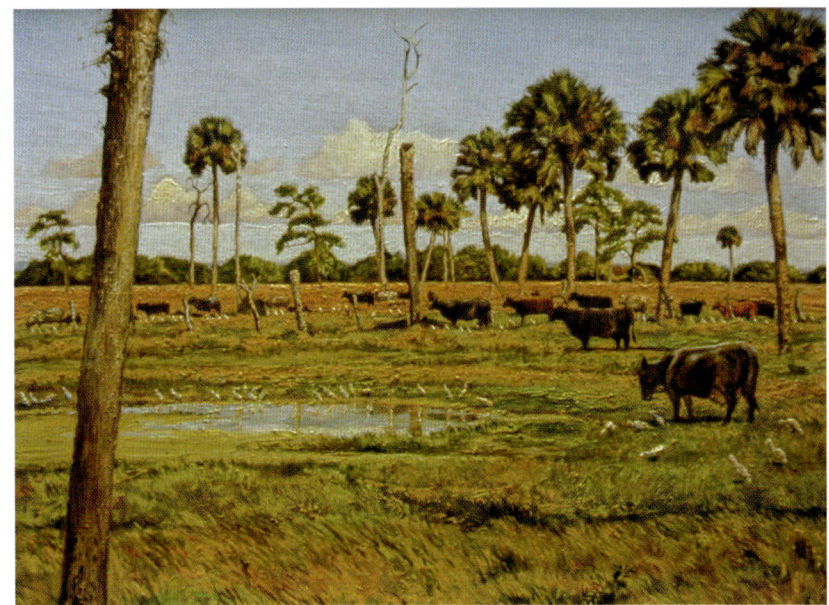

In this painting Sexton's images are evenly divided between his two passions—art and the ranchland he calls home.

Although Florida has become best known for its beaches and theme parks, more than 5.5 million acres of land is still used as pasture for cattle and horses, and Florida remains one of the most important cattle states in the country. Florida ranchers do not, however, raise "finished beef." Instead, most raise calves that are shipped to the Midwest, where they are grain-fed until ready for market. Florida ranchers breed and raise the best type of calves—ones that gain weight well and have a body frame that is built to yield top-quality meat, and modern ranches still sprawl over the countryside in and around the St. Johns River valley.[20]

Plate 35. Sean Sexton, *Pastorale*, 2001. Oil on Masonite, 22 × 30 in. Courtesy of the artist.

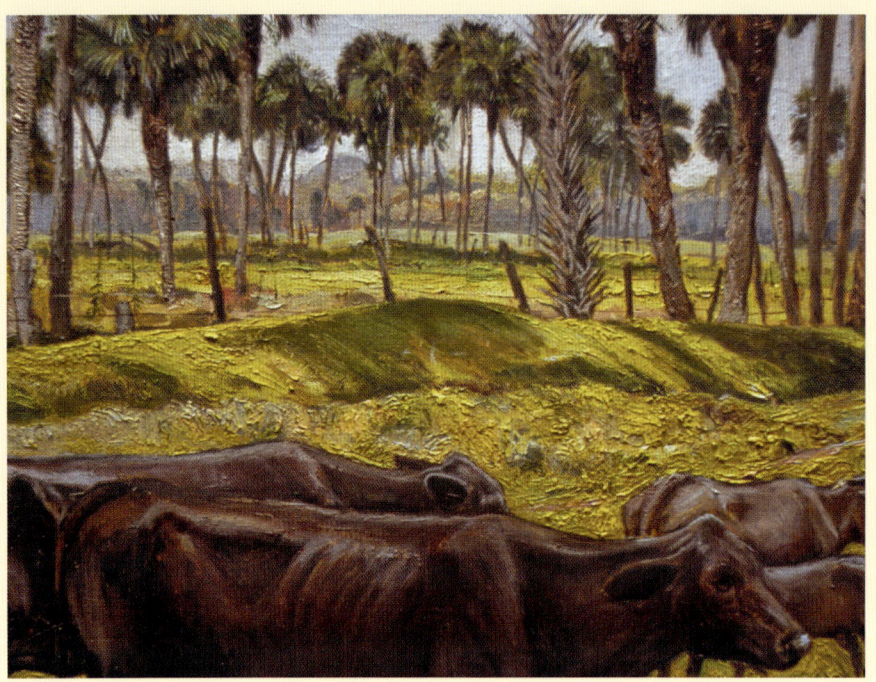

Plate 36. Sean Sexton. *Late Winter Condition*, 2004. Oil on canvas board, 9 × 12 in. Courtesy of the artist.

In this painting, Sexton depicts a herd of cattle at the end of winter standing in the noonday sun. Sexton explains: "Their condition is due to the fact that their calves, which were born in the Fall of the year, have been nursing them all winter, and in essence 'pulling' their body condition down. It is subtle, but the landscape in the background mimics the condition of the cows—the grass is short and the land seems a bit bare-boned as well." Kurt Piazza, in a catalogue essay on Sexton's work, remarks: "Sean's personal experience as both an agriculturalist and steward of his family's cattle ranch imbues his work with an extraordinary perspective of the modern world and its link to an agrarian past. . . . [He] is a painter guided by his unique circumstances and his emblematic subject matter continues to convey the relevance of a bygone era."[21]

The most valuable tool of the Cracker cowhunter, besides his rawhide whip, was the Spanish horse. In his book *Cracker*, the historian Dana Ste. Claire writes: "Their ponies, too, had bloodlines going back to the Andalusian breeds of the Spanish conquistadores. Called 'marshtackies,' these small horses were favored by cowmen for their smooth ride, durability and quick maneuverability, and were well adapted to the Florida wilderness."[22] The Frenchman Francis de Castleman, who traveled in Florida in 1837, described the "Florida horses" as being "small, long-haired and bright-eyed, lively, stubborn and as wild as the Indians themselves."[23]

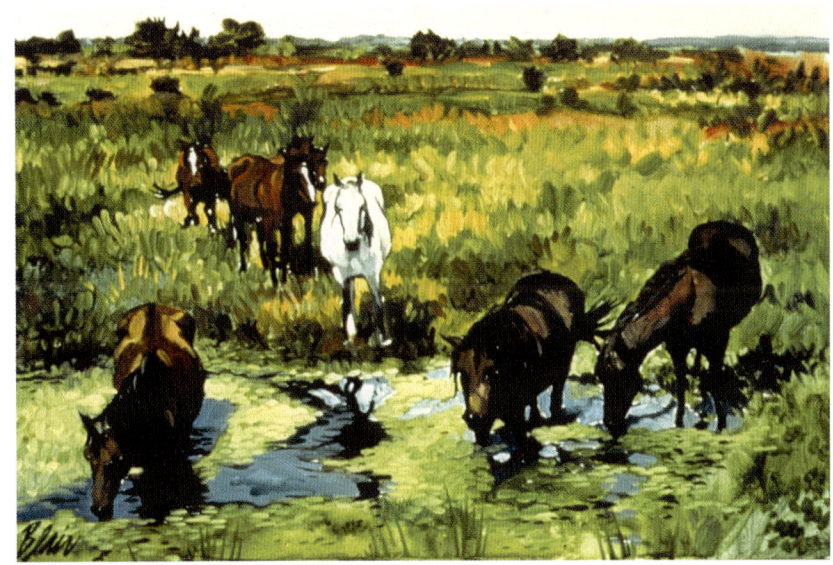

Plate 37. Eleanor Blair. *Spanish Horses on the Prairie*, 1994. Oil on canvas. Private collection.

Eleanor Blair is a Florida artist who specializes in landscapes, but she has also painted still lifes, interiors, and scenes that recall Florida's history and culture. In 1985, a herd of Spanish horses was introduced on the Paynes Prairie State Preserve near Micanopy, Florida. The horses, left to roam free throughout the 20,000-acre preserve, have prospered, with the herd growing and new foals arriving every year. Blair depicts the herd approaching a waterhole on the prairie. Like their Andalusian forebears, many of the Paynes Prairie horses are brown when born, but slowly turn white as they age. However, all solid colors are now found in this breed, including grey.[24]

While the general public might be surprised to learn that Florida produced the first American cowboys, it immediately recognizes oranges as the symbol that has long defined Florida, and in the early years, the St. Johns River valley was the heartland of the citrus industry. Helen Kohen, an art historian and former art critic for the *Miami Herald*, points out that "of all blooms celebrated in Florida, the state named for flowers, none has done more to define it, build it, and sell it than the orange blossom. . . . The orange is Florida, and it made Florida, providing an authentic Fountain of Youth with its vitamin highs, supplying the legendary gold that the state's explorers and settlers lusted after. . . . The first advertised land sales [in Florida] were for orange groves, and the first sales pitches for those Edenic gardens employed a quasi-religious vocabulary consistent with the offering of paradise."[25]

Citrus fruits were brought to America in the earliest years of Spanish exploration—first by Christopher Columbus in 1493 and later by Ponce de León, who planted the first orange trees in Florida around St. Augustine in the early sixteenth century. By the late eighteenth century, citrus trees could be found growing wild throughout many of Florida's forests, and cultivated orange groves were located along the St. Johns River and around Tampa. When he visited the valley of the St. Johns region in the 1770s, William Bartram remarked many times on the groves of orange trees that dotted the wilderness landscape, and he correctly credited the Spanish for bringing citrus cultivation to the region.

There are many different legends about the origin of citrus fruits, but most researchers agree that they probably originated in Southeast Asia around 4,000 BC. The earliest written references to oranges are to be found in ancient Chinese manuscripts dating back to 2,200 BC. It is believed that the word "orange" may be derived from Sanskrit.[26]

The spread of citrus fruits from Asia to Europe was slow. Early varieties of the fruit were bitter—probably inedible—and were used mainly for their ornamental value. By the fourth century BC, citrus had reached Greece, where it was hailed as "the Golden Citron from the garden of Hesperides" and was said to have been the wedding gift to Zeus and Hera from Tellus, goddess of the Earth.[27]

Florida's sandy soil and subtropical climate were found to be ideal for citrus production, but for the first three centuries after the introduction of citrus to the region, commercial production was confined to areas near the coast because the only available means of transportation was by water.

Despite the inherent problems of climate, irrigation, and transportation, citrus pioneers moved into the interior of the state and southward along the St. Johns River valley following the sandy ridge that runs parallel to the river for some three hundred miles. The trees left by the Spanish missionaries and those planted by the Indians proved that the land was ideally suited for growing citrus, and groves were established throughout the region.

Following the Civil War, annual commercial citrus production reached 1 million boxes; it climbed to more than 5 million by 1893. Many northerners—attracted by Florida's climate and the prospect of a lucrative business venture—considered taking up citrus production in the Sunshine State. Mark Derr, in *Some Kind of Paradise*, points out that, "Between 1874 and 1877, Florida growers imported 200 million oranges, trees, and cuttings worth $2 million. . . . In 1880, approximately sixty varieties of oranges were under cultivation."[28]

In 1867, Harriet Beecher Stowe purchased an orange grove on the St. Johns River near Mandarin. Although she had in her best-known book, *Uncle Tom's Cabin,* vigorously condemned the South for its institution of slavery—President Abraham Lincoln is said to have called her "the little lady who caused this great war"—Stowe quickly succumbed to the charms of life on the banks of the St. Johns. Over the next two decades she was not only a regular winter visitor, but she also became one of the first writers to enthusiastically promote Florida as a tourist destination in the many articles she wrote for northern magazines.

The Florida experience also prompted the author to write a new book, a series of sketches titled *Palmetto Leaves*. According to Mary Graff, in her introduction to the 1968 facsimile edition of the book published by the University Press of Florida, Stowe's orange-growing operation was a great success: "Orange crates headed for northern markets carried proof that Stowe's name was getting top billing in the bold stenciled letters: 'Oranges from Harriet Beecher Stowe, Mandarin, Florida.'"[29]

In a letter dated March 25, 1872, Stowe wrote: "What a bouquet of sweets is an orange tree! Merely as a flowering-tree, it is worth having, if for nothing else. We call the time of their budding the week of pearls. How beautiful, how almost miraculous, the leaping-forth of these pearls to gem the green leaves! The fragrance has a stimulating effect on our nerves—a sort of dreamy intoxication. The air, now, is full of it. Under the trees the white shell-petals drift, bearing perfume."[30]

Stowe, always ready to sing the praises of her adopted home along the St. Johns, wrote in *Palmetto Leaves*: "A gentleman propounds to us the following inquiry: 'Apart from the danger of frosts, what is the prospect of certainty in the orange crop? Is it a steady one?' We have made diligent inquiry from old, experienced cultivators, and from those who have collected the traditions of orange-growing; and the results seem to be, that, apart from the danger of frost, the orange-crop is the most steady and certain of any known fruit."[31]

Mrs. Stowe was well advised to mention the problem of frost to the inquiring gentleman, because not many years later—in the winters of 1894–95 and 1896–97—twin killer frosts all but wiped out the citrus industry in Florida. Most of the state's citrus trees were damaged or destroyed. Although many of the trees in the Indian River region recovered, the crop did not return to substantial commercial importance for more than a decade.

According to the historian Jerrell Shofner, Florida's readmission to the Union and the attendant problems following the Civil War "affected both black and white farmers for decades . . . and left a bitter legacy."[32] The result was a decline in the cotton industry that had dominated the prewar economy, but a rise in other agricultural endeavors including citrus.

The American poet and newspaper editor William Cullen Bryant traveled to Florida in 1873. During his visit, Bryant wrote a report to the *New York Evening Post* that described the city of Palatka as "largely still a forest," but remarked that Jacksonville was "thriving, with four thousand people and two new hotels, with orange trees growing everywhere."[33]

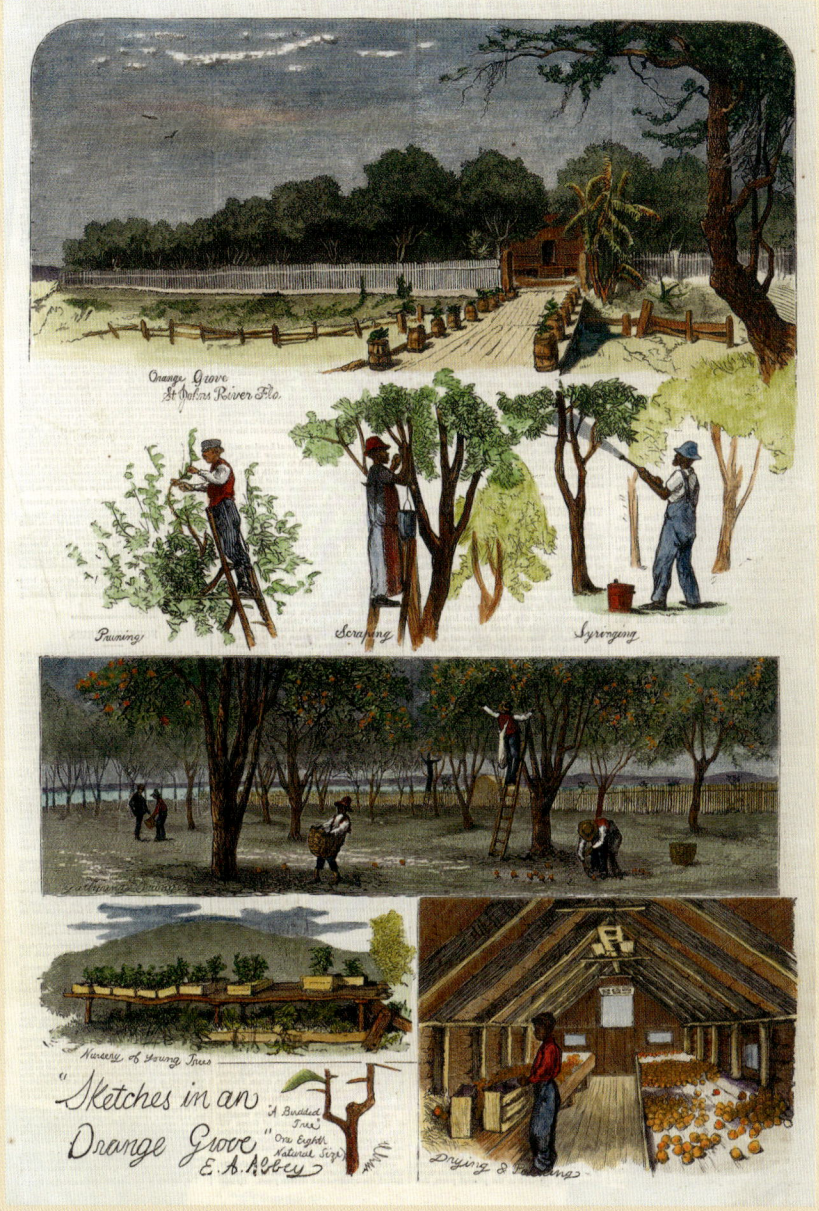

Plate 38. Edwin Austin Abbey. *Sketches in an Orange Grove*, 1875. Woodcut, 14½ × 8¾ in. From *Harper's Weekly*, February 20, 1875. Courtesy of the Matheson Museum, Gainesville, Florida.

The self-taught artist Edwin Austin Abbey, who studied wood engraving and worked for *Harper's Weekly*, made this illustration of the steps necessary for orange cultivation that was published in the February 1875 edition of *Harper's Weekly*. He included the process of growing, picking, and packing in his illustration.

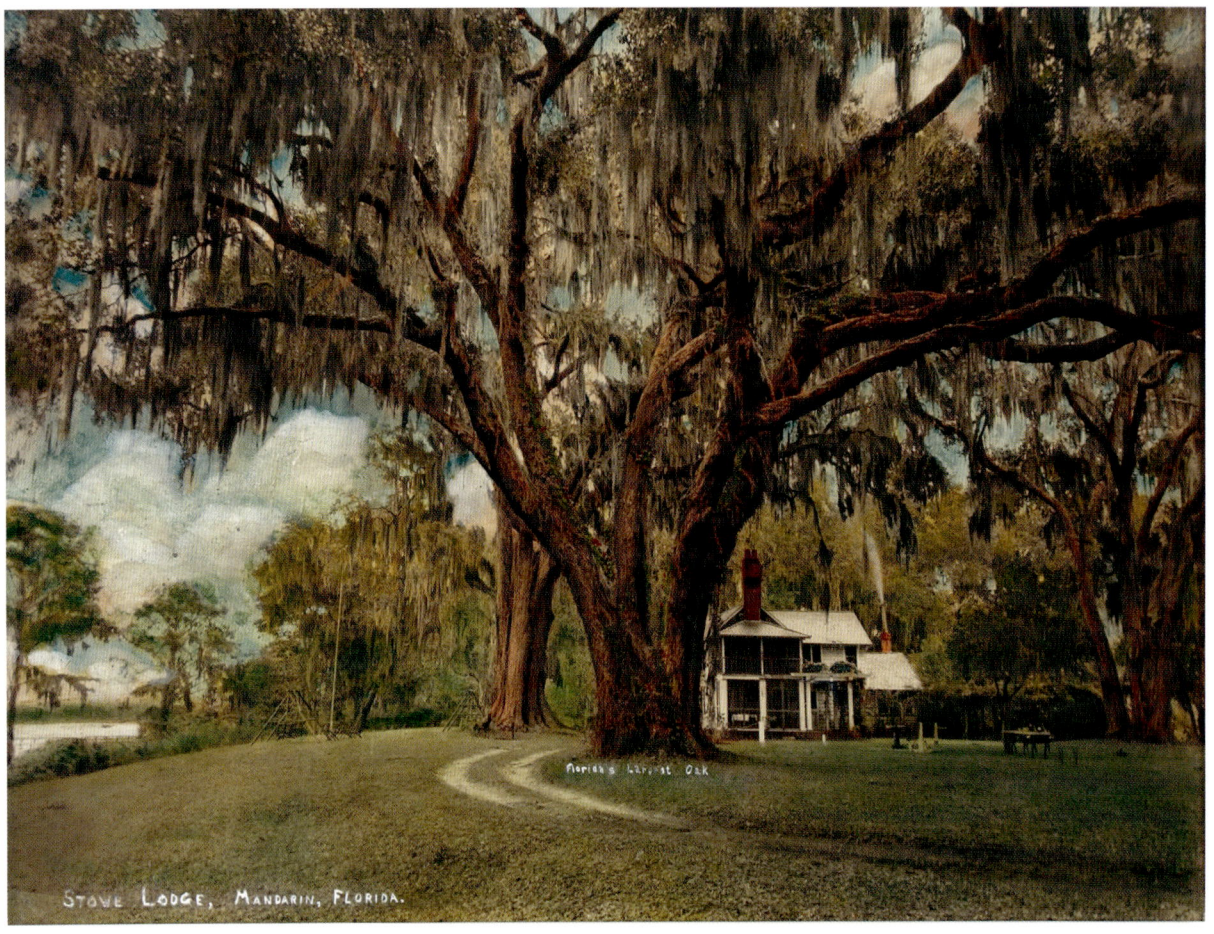

STOWE LODGE, MANDARIN, FLORIDA.

Plate 39. Anonymous. *Stowe Lodge.* Hand-colored photograph, 19 × 14 in. Collection of John C. Herrmann.

Mandarin, the location of the Florida home owned by Harriett Beecher Stowe, lies on the east side of the St. Johns River south of Jacksonville at a point where the banks are five miles apart. The town was named for a variety of orange that was introduced from China. Besides the renowned orange grove that surrounded her house, "Stowe Lodge" was built in the shade of one of the largest live oak trees in the area. Sidney Lanier commented on the tree when he wrote his travel book on Florida: "Her house is a brown cottage, near the shore, nearly obscured by foliage. It is not nearly so imposing as her Tree—a magnificent king that overhangs her roof with a noble crown."[34] Soon, Stowe Lodge would become the most photographed residence in the community.

Old Mandarin is more phantasmal than most of Jacksonville artist Jim Draper's works, illustrating lessons learned. His energetic but controlled brushwork renders his birds as Spirit guides. They, like his land, depend not merely on replication but on drama, and verge on the surreal. "The goose, who, along with my other feathered or cold blooded characters, are the viewer's guides into a mysterious world. I chose these characters because of their transcendent properties. Birds, especially water birds, are at home in multiple elements, earth, wind, and water. Amphibious reptiles breathe oxygen and that makes them our relatives, yet they are comfortable in the world of the fishes. The rooster, on the other hand is afforded wings and longer legs, but has been doomed to suffer our earthly existence, having the power to fly only short distances. So the rooster, especially that kind of Bantam rooster, finds himself in situations where he has to fight his way out."[35]

Hidden beneath this image of domesticity lies the artist's angst—the bountiful wilds were corrupted so that man could no longer live in harmony with nature. Draper can no longer, in good conscience, describe "ancient Florida," a veritable Eden in which man is part of the ecosystem and plays his dramatic role with dignity. Instead Draper feels that, "The Europeans, a stinking lot of filthy sailors, spend their lives seeking adventure and carnal pleasure in order to appease an arbitrary pantheon of higher powers, nobles, royalty, the church, a Christ and a vengeful father who is Hell-bent on his chosen people devouring every speck of decency in the world in order to do him homage."[36] Thus begins Draper's version of a civilized "new Florida," whose linear attitude toward time dooms one's future. While Draper feels that the ancient world has the opportunity to be renewed each day, each month, each spring, the disconnect with nature he describes scratches at the surfaces of his seemingly bucolic images.

But all the plants featured in the pre-Raphaelite cartouche *Old Mandarin*, framing the goose as if in a fairy tale, are imported. They are non-native, as is the goose. The goose, compared to the native birds that once covered the skies from horizon to horizon, seems a little mean, "slightly stupid, full of himself, like a modern-day politician or CEO of a major corporation. He lives in a fantasy world of his own designing. He lives on gaudy high-maintenance fruits and flowers. He is domesticated."[37] Draper's narrative suggests that we have cut down Eden to plant a garden, which we do a poor job at maintaining.

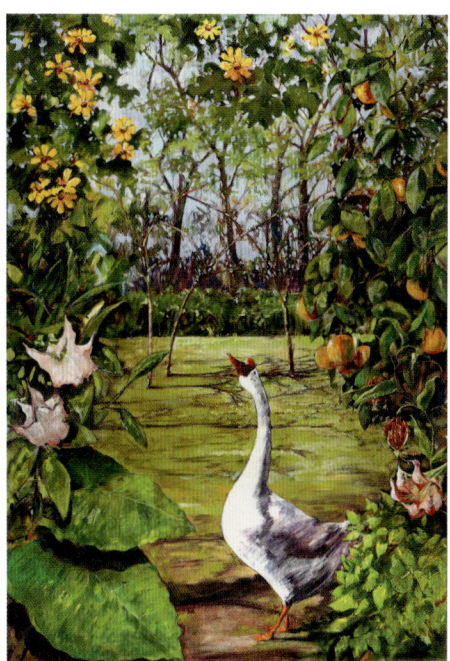

Plate 40. Jim Draper. *Old Mandarin*, 2005. Acrylic on canvas, 84 × 60 in. Courtesy of the artist.

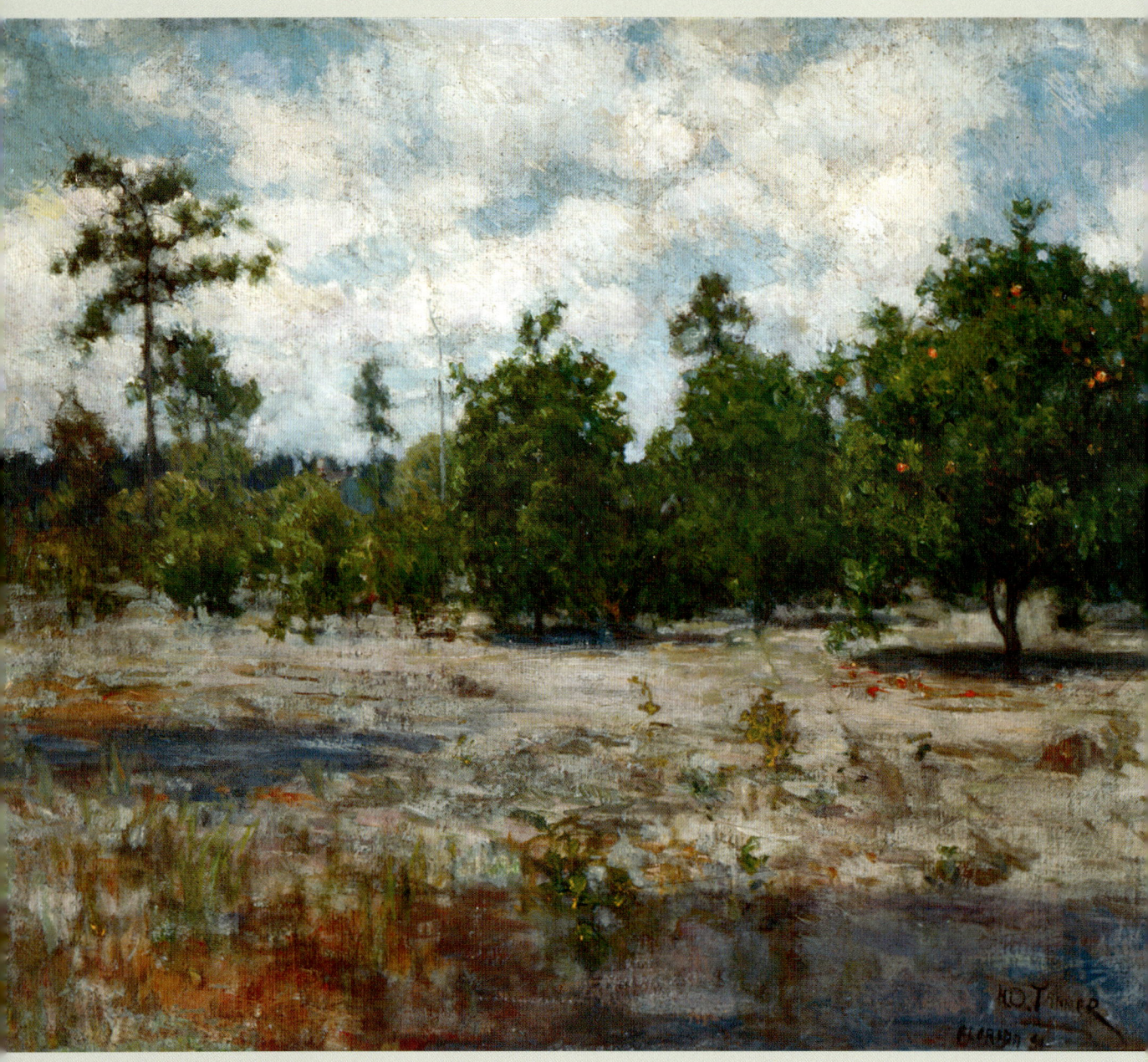

Plate 41. Henry Ossawa Tanner. *Florida*, 1894. Oil on canvas, 18½ × 22½ in. Walter O. Evans Collection of African-American Art.

Like many other artists of his time, Henry Ossawa Tanner associated Florida with the orange groves that in 1894 were still widespread across the state, although the freezes of 1890–91 had already destroyed the groves in the northernmost part of the state. Oranges had become synonymous with Florida. Gary Mormino writes: "The lordly orange . . . held a divine place in the Florida dreamscape. . . .The concentration and ubiquity of orange trees pervaded the landscape and popular culture. Each spring the aroma of billions of orange blossoms saturated the nostrils, wafting through every crevice . . . the orange was the state's most pervasive symbol, bringing together visions of health, sunshine and fertility."[38] This image of a Florida orange grove, painted by Tanner in 1894, clearly shows the influence of the impressionists in its broad brushstrokes and diffused light.

According to the author F. W. James, Henry Ossawa Tanner (1859–1937) was the first African American artist to win international fame.[39] He was born in Pittsburgh, Pennsylvania, but moved to Philadelphia when he was five years old. His father, who was a teacher and minister, later became a bishop in the African Methodist Episcopal Church. Tanner's mother was a former slave; his grandmother had sent her daughter north to Pittsburgh through the Underground Railroad. At age thirteen, Henry Tanner decided to become an artist. Although his father disapproved of the idea, Tanner was eventually allowed to attend the renowned Pennsylvania Academy of Fine Arts, where he studied under Thomas Eakins. He later moved to Paris, where he was influenced by the impressionist painters and also studied at the Academié Julian.[40] Because of chronic health problems, Tanner spent time in Florida and in the mountains of North Carolina. In both locales, he made drawings and sketches of the local scenery and people. He later incorporated them into subjects for his paintings.

The first African American elected to full membership in the National Academy of Design, Tanner enjoyed unprecedented success in his profession. He is best known for his religious paintings and his images of rural African American life, but for the sake of his career he spent most of his life in France, where he divided his time between Paris and a farm in Normandy. According to a biography of Tanner found on the Web site *African-American History through the Arts*: "In his later years, Tanner was a symbol of hope and inspiration for African American leaders and young black artists, many of whom visited him in Paris prior to his death in 1937."[41]

Loudon U. Dodge was an illustrator and publisher in Rochester, New York, who rendered in various forms, from frameable prints to view books, which were collections of popular souvenir pictures. *Illustrated Florida* consists of nineteen chromolithographed prints that each measures 4¾ × 7½ in. and slides into a black cloth-covered sheath to constitute a portfolio of scenes along the St. Johns River; an additional print is affixed to the front of the box. On the back is the seller's label: Ashmead Bros., Publishers & Stationers, Jacksonville.

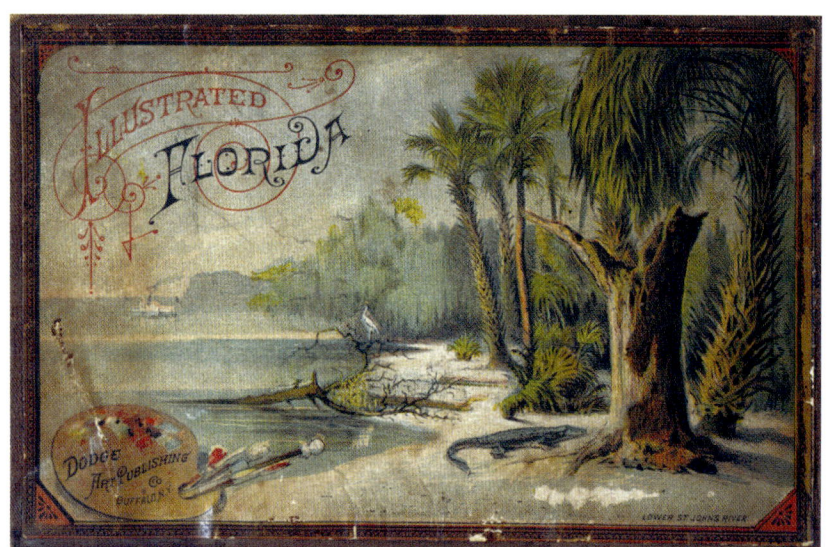

Plate 42. Loudon U. Dodge. Illustration from *Illustrated Florida*, ca. 1882. Chromolithographed print, 4¾ × 7½ in. Dodge Art Publishing Company. Courtesy of Gary and Teresa Monroe.

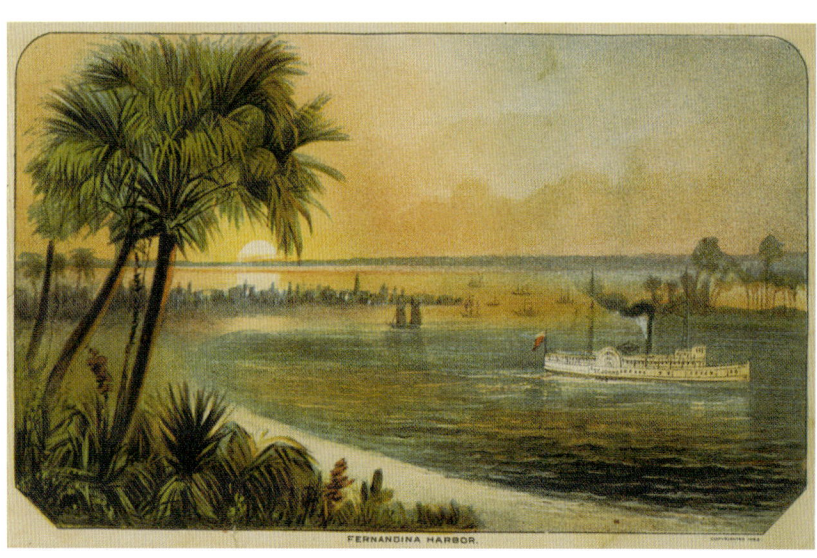

Plate 43. Loudon U. Dodge. Illustration from *Illustrated Florida*, ca. 1882. Chromolithographed print, 4¾ × 7½ in. Dodge Art Publishing Company. Courtesy of Gary and Teresa Monroe.

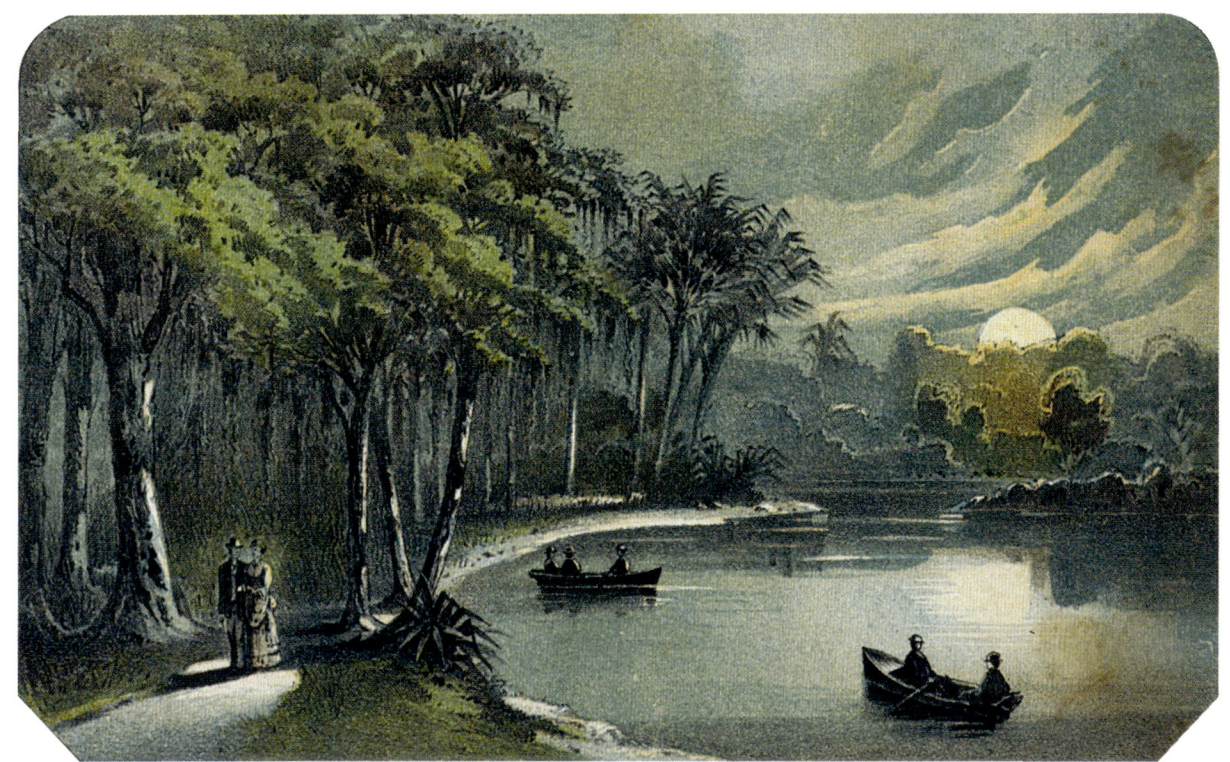

The Dodge Art Publishing Company, whose tag line reads "Publishers of Illustrated Resorts," copyrighted the piece in 1882. The paintings are not signed, but since the credit on a large print, "Orange Grove, Florida," with a copyright date of 1880, is tagged "Sketched from Nature by L. U. Dodge, Rochester, NY," it is safe to assume that Dodge painted the pieces for *Illustrated Florida* that possess the same style and technique as that piece and others.

A couple of images are of sites near the river, while two others represent ideas: "the sunny land of fruits and flora" and "way down in Dixie." The rest identify with precision what is most germane to river locales.

Dodge's style bordered on the primitive. His work has a certain charm, with its penchant for bright colors. There are not many examples of his artwork to be found. His primary occupation, according to the city directories of Buffalo and Rochester, was as a lithographer. He was never listed as an artist per se. L. U. Dodge died on March 28, 1887, at age forty-nine.

Plate 44. Loudon U. Dodge. Illustration from *Illustrated Florida*, ca. 1882. Chromolithographed print, 4¾ × 7½ in. Dodge Art Publishing Company. Courtesy of Gary and Teresa Monroe.

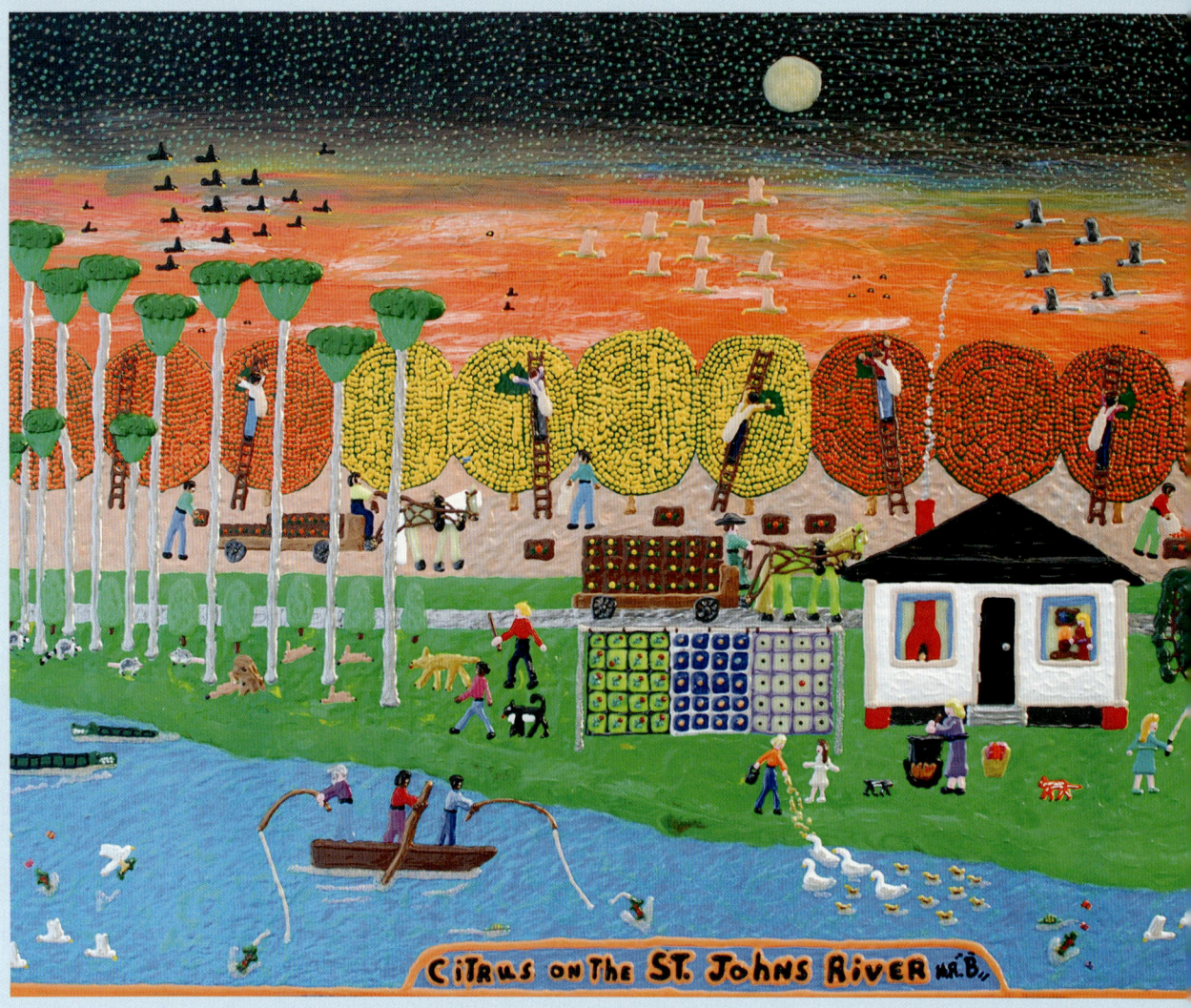

Citrus on the ST. Johns River MR.B.

Plate 45. Jack Beverland. *Citrus on the St. Johns River*, 2008. Dimensional fabric paint on board, 24 × 36 in. Courtesy of the artist.

In his painting *Citrus on the St. Johns River*, Mr. B shows workers busy harvesting oranges and lemons from trees loaded with fruit. An orange sunset glows behind the grove, reinforcing the color of the fruit, and in the foreground a turquoise river suggests the irrigation that helps the crops thrive. He usually includes himself in each painting but assumes different personas. He may be a black man with a grey beard, or a younger blond man smoking a pipe. And sometimes he dons Native American costumes. Regardless of who's on watch, all paintings are signed "Mr. B."

Jack Beverland, better known to art lovers as "Mr. B," is a nationally recognized self-taught folk artist who began painting in 1991 as a therapeutic activity following a series of traumatic experiences. Ousted from his middle-management career with a major Florida-based grocery store chain in 1990 at age fifty-two, he experienced feelings of "worthlessness, shame, confusion, depression and suicide."[42] He even contemplated the assassination of the corporate executives he held responsible for his "forced early retirement." He credits his brother Jerry for helping him rise above the horror that he was living. Jerry suggested that painting might help resolve his deep-seated anger.

Mr. B's first paintings were simple and moralistic and had titles such as *Drowning* and *Alone*. More recently, his work has become less desperate and more orthodox. Using dimensional fabric paint, he creates a unique variety of human and animal figures within a lush voluptuously tropical environment.

Mr. B says that these days he has his life pretty well under control, but admits to still feeling "a little off-center." When he takes a break from painting, he finds comfort in the garden at his Citrus Park home, where he has planted a tropical-like jungle to further distance himself from the cruel world. Perhaps, like Marjorie Rawlings, Mr. B finds solace among the "jade-green leaves" of his personal paradise.

Today, more than 169,000 acres of citrus are grown in the St. Johns River basin. Despite the ongoing problem of periodic freezes (major freezes occurred in 1962 and again in 1984), oranges have continued to be an important part of Florida's economy. In 1972–73, the orange crop reached an all-time high of 175 million boxes.[43] Since then, the overall output has decreased mainly because of grove lands being sold to developers. Central Florida in particular has witnessed unrestrained construction, especially after the coming of Disney World in the early 1970s. Many ranchers and farmers have been willing to sell their land, and thousands of acres of groves and pastures have been converted into apartments, housing developments, and strip malls. As Mark Derr points out in *Some Kind of Paradise*: "the loss of farms could produce ecological benefits of greater value than the lost crops—providing the acreage was restored to natural conditions and not converted into golf-course-centered subdivisions. Restoration of native vegetation would improve the quality and quantity of surface and ground water by removing major polluters and users and re-creating conditions ideal for water purification and aquifer recharge."[44]

Unfortunately, in most instances the removal of the trees has been quickly followed by rampant "development." Thomas Cook, in a 2005 article for the Central Florida Heritage Foundation, writes: "Time was when you couldn't drive a mile through Central Florida without passing an orange grove. . . . Thousands of acres of groves dotted the land and for nearly one hundred years those groves provided the lion's share of agricultural revenues for Central Florida. . . . Today, instead of citrus, visitors that ride the elevator to the top of the Citrus Tower look out on a seemingly endless view of houses in what are colloquially known as the bedroom communities of the metro-Orlando area."[45] Mormino concludes: "Symbolically, the last orange grove on Orange Avenue [in Orange County] was bulldozed in 1977 and replaced by a supermarket; more ominously, the last commercial groves on the Orange Blossom Trail [were] sold in 2003."[46]

4 { A Parade of Diversities

Colonization and Conflict

CULTURAL PLURALISM—the existence side by side of diverse ethnic groups—is one of the great themes of American history, and nowhere is this phenomenon more apparent than in Florida. Over the past five hundred years, the St. Johns region has seen an amazing parade of human culture—Timucuan hunters, Spanish explorers, French settlers, English planters, African workers, American frontiersmen, and Seminole, Greek, Russian, and Caribbean immigrants, and the list goes on and on. Claimed by France, Spain, England, and the United States, Florida has been a battleground where cultures clashed and new alliances were born. Suited by climate and geography to a variety of uses, the St. Johns River valley region has supported maize and melons, cattle and oranges, cotton and cane as well as a vast inventory of indigenous and imported flora and fauna. If diversity is an important component of a vital and robust organism, then Florida must be a healthy place indeed.

To adequately address each and every ethnic group and cultural efflorescence that has illuminated the river's history would in itself make a lengthy manuscript, and so we have selected a handful of examples from the early years of immigration and settlement that will provide a taste of the enormous smorgasbord of cultural offerings and a glimpse into the richness of the river's heritage.

Although the Spanish were the first to successfully establish a presence in Florida, their influence would falter as new arrivals—especially the English—began to challenge their claim to the region. By the mid-1700s, Britain, France, and Spain were all vying for control of the St. Johns River valley. James Moore, the British governor of what would soon be South Carolina, led a raid into Florida, taking back several thousand head of cattle and horses to sell to settlers in the Carolinas and Georgia. In 1763, the conflict known as the French and Indian War ended with the Treaty of

Florida had a variegated population during the British period. Many English migrated from the north. Most numerous were blacks, of whom the great majority were slaves. . . . In the towns a visitor could find, alongside proper officials and merchants, large numbers of unruly soldiers and sailors, and alongside bathhouses and bookstores, bawdy houses and taverns. A great many languages were heard: English . . . Mandingo, Muskogee, Hitchiti, Cherokee, Catalan, Greek, French, German, Spanish, Italian, and Sicilian.
—Michael Gannon, *Florida: A Short History*

Paris. At this time, Florida was given to England while Spain regained control of Cuba. By this time, the Spanish haciendas had all but disappeared. When William Bartram explored the region in 1774, he mentioned only "vestiges of the old Spanish plantations and dwellings; [such] as fence posts and wooden pillars of their houses."[1]

If the Spanish were the first to become landed gentry by establishing large haciendas along the "mission trail" during the First Spanish Period (1565–1763), it was the British who widened the scope of settlement by turning the St. Johns River valley into a commercially successful agricultural empire. Whereas the Spanish had done little to colonize their holdings during the two hundred years of their occupation, the British aggressively encouraged settlement and actively sought to wrest control of the interior of the state from the Indians.[2] Using African slaves as laborers, huge tracts were cleared and put into production.

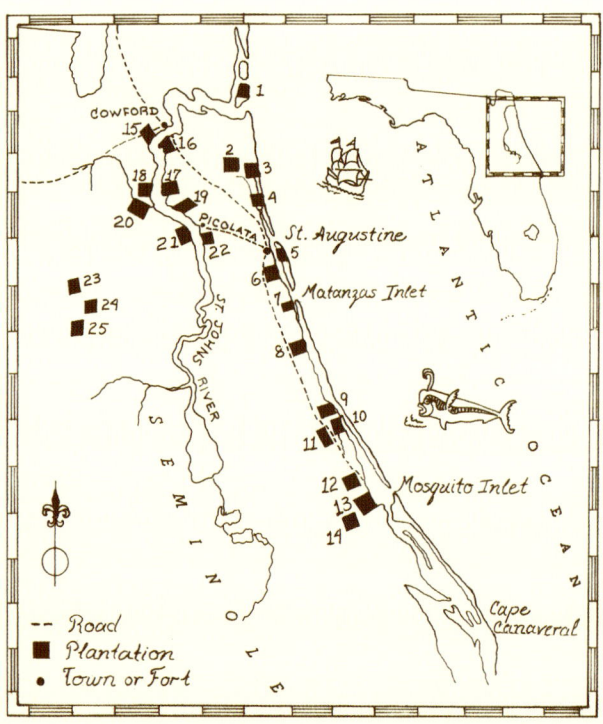

Plate 46. Elsbeth Gordon. *Map of Spanish Haciendas and English Plantations along the St. Johns River*, ca. 2002. Courtesy of the artist.

During the colonial period, Spanish ranchos, or haciendas, and English plantations were established throughout the St. Johns River region and the adjacent bays and estuaries. This map by Elsbeth Gordon indicates the location of the major settlements.

1. Kingsley Plantation (1797)
2. Hacienda San Diego (1703)
3. Mt. Pleasant (1780)
4. Grant's Villa (1768)
5. Vergell (1763)
6. Bella Vista (1765)
7. Forbes Plantation (ca. 1770)
8. Bulow plantation (1820)
9. Rosetta (1765)
10. Mt. Oswald (1764)
11. Swamp Settlement (1770)
12. Dunlawton (1804)
13. New Smyrna Plantation (1767)
14. Ambrose Hull, Cruger, and Depeyster Plantation (1801)
15. San Juan Nepomuceno (1792)
16. Beauckerk's Bluff (ca. 1769)
17. New Switzerland (1771)
18. Hibernia (1785)
19. Mt. Hope (1776)
20. Toyn's Plantation (1768)
21. Franco Ligarroa Hacienda (late 1600s)
22. Sanchez Risar Hacienda (late 1600s)
23. Hacienda La Chua (1620s)
24. Pilgrimage Plantation (1820)
25. Cuscowilla (ca. 1750).

James Grant was appointed governor of the new British territory in late 1763. Arriving in St. Augustine, he found a disorderly garrison town populated mostly by soldiers who had occupied the city in July of that year. One visitor commented that in St. Augustine "luxury and debauchery reigned." Apparently, Governor Grant approved for he wrote to a friend in his native Scotland, "There is not so gay a town in America as this is at present, the people are Music and Dancing mad."[3] During Grant's first year in office, he and his houseguests are reported to have consumed "236 gallons of rum, 216 bottles of wine, 1,200 bottles of claret, and 519 bottles of port."[4] Despite his penchant for indulgence, Grant would later be remembered primarily as an indigo producer and a promoter of commercial agriculture based on the labor of African slaves.

Apparently, Grant did not originally intend to become a serious planter. He considered his land holdings to be more recreational than avocational, but he soon realized that in order to stimulate development and encourage British immigration to the area he needed to demonstrate the profitability of agricultural operations. In July 1763, only days after he had been appointed governor of the territory, he tried to persuade the Board of Trade to prohibit land grants to absentee speculators. His advice was disregarded, however, and absentee landholders, based mostly in England and Scotland, were granted tracts of ten thousand to twenty thousand acres.

Grant continued to lobby to attract settlers. He tried to find individuals among the applicants who were qualified to successfully manage large agricultural operations. He believed that plantations could be profitable only if the right crops were planted. On his own land, he experimented with wine grapes, West Indian cotton, coffee, and mulberry bushes for producing silk, but he finally settled on two crops—rice and indigo—that he believed to be best suited to the climate. Grant also maintained that African slaves were by far the most suited to the rigors of agricultural work in the hot, humid climate of East Florida. "Africans," he wrote, "are the only people equipped to work in warm climates."[5]

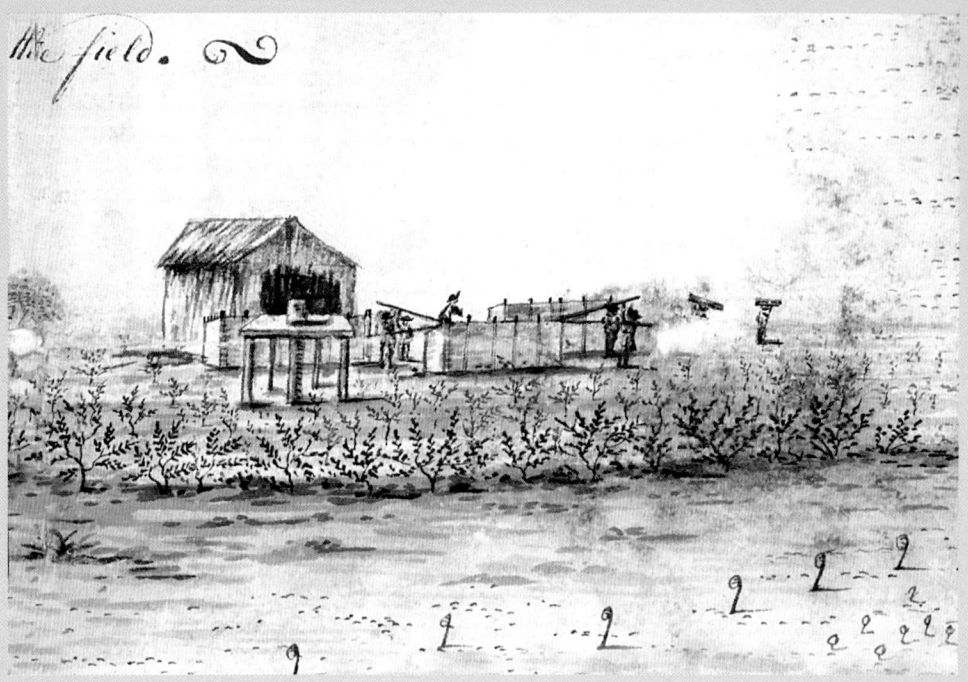

the field.

Plate 47. Joseph Purcell. *Indigo Works,*
detail from A Plan of Beauclerk's Bluff
Plantation on the east side of ye River St.
Johns, 1771. Public Records Office, PRO:
MPD2. Photocopy courtesy of the State
Archives of Florida.

The indigo plant (*indigofera tinctoria*) was one of the plants documented by both the Bartrams and André Michaux while they were in Florida. It was in high demand for use as a dye. This drawing by Joseph Purcell shows the indigo production process as it was practiced at the Beauclerk's Bluff Plantation located on the St. Johns River opposite today's Naval Air Station. Purcell's sketch shows the pump platform, indigo vats, a curing house, and slaves bringing the plants and processing them in the vats. Purcell indicated on the drawing that it was made from an actual survey of the plantation done in 1771.

The building of St. Peter's Church in St. Augustine is an example of the multicultural blend that resulted from the changing demographics of the region. In 1572, the Spanish built a small wooden church, Nuestra Senora de la Soledad, in St. Augustine. Over the years, it was enlarged to include a hermitage and a hospital. In the early 1700s, the church was rebuilt in stone and a bell tower was added. Shortly after the British took control of Florida of 1763, they set to work to transform La Soledad into an Anglican church, which they named St. Peter's.[6]

The plan of St. Peter's Church was influenced by Anglican architecture, especially the design of the tower-steeple, but the remodel retained part of the preexisting Spanish construction. The result was a hybrid architectural style that adapted the needs of an Anglican congregation to the original Spanish church. When completed, the steeple of St. Peter's was the tallest landmark on the St. Augustine skyline.[7]

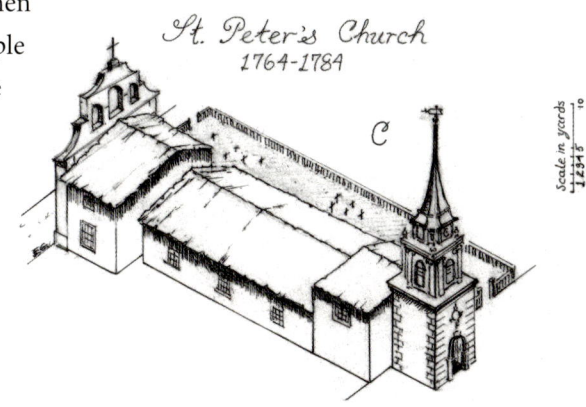

Plate 48. Elsbeth Gordon and C. Tingley. *St. Peter's Church, St. Augustine, 1764–1784*, 2002. Graphite on paper. Courtesy of the artists.

One British gentleman, Denys Rolle, had a very different take on the value of labor—he saw it as a means to salvation. A philanthropist and member of the British Parliament, Rolle established a large plantation on the river just north of the village of San Mateo in 1765. His utopian dream was to rehabilitate petty criminals by relocating them to America to learn the value and rewards of hard physical labor. To that end, he populated his community, which he named Charlotta after the wife of King George III, with "forty prostitutes, pickpockets, and beggars from the slums of London" to reform them through his work program.[8]

It was both an altruistic vision and a colossal failure. His "colonists" were not farmers, and the demanding labor combined with less than elegant accommodations and uncomfortable health problems soon resulted in the disappearance of his labor force. The lack of law enforcement gave Rolle no way to stop the runaways who turned up in Georgia, South Carolina, and St. Augustine, where most probably reclaimed their former careers. Rolle had little choice but to substitute African slaves to provide the labor he needed to keep his plantation in operation. Eventually, he purchased close to eighty thousand acres in the area and successfully produced rice, corn, beef, and lumber. When Spain reacquired Florida in 1783, he was forced to give up his land and flee to the Bahamas with his slaves.[9]

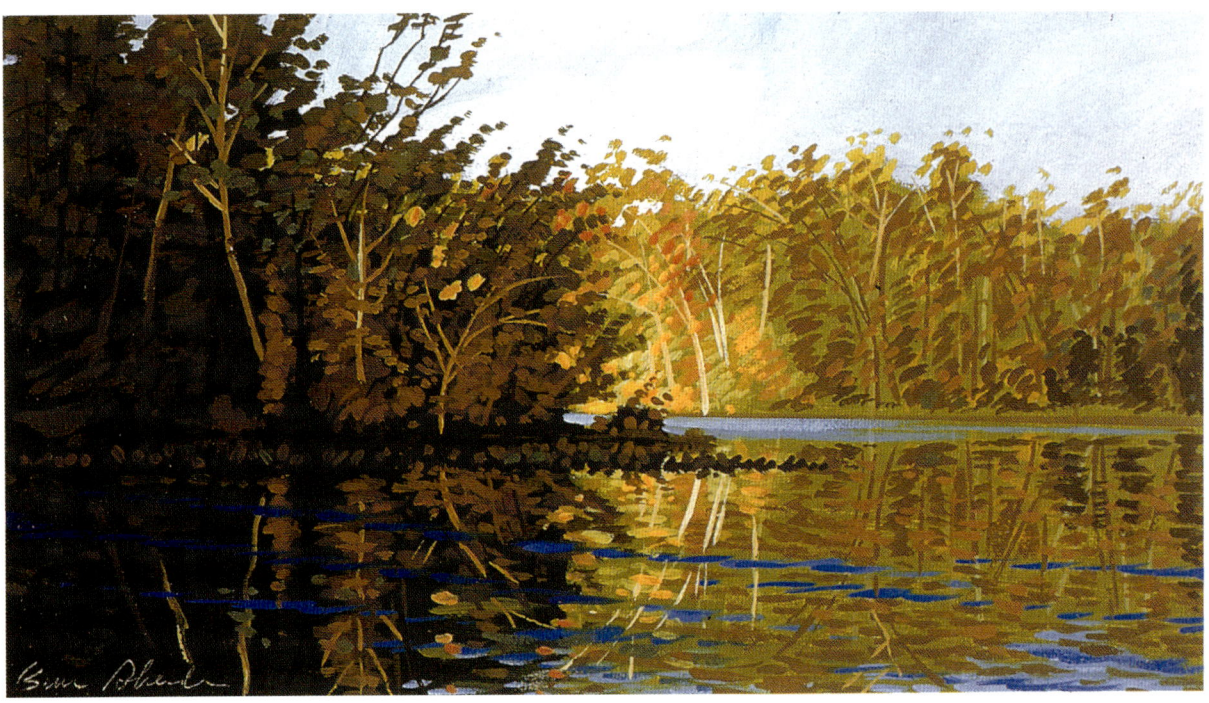

Plate 49. Gene Roberds. *Murphy's Creek*, 1993. Oil on canvas, 7⅞ × 14 in. The Debbie Geiger and George Percy Collection, Tallahassee, Florida.

This painting by the Palatka artist Gene Roberds depicts a location close to U.S. Highway 17 south of Palatka near where Rollestown once stood. The combination of water, trees, and reflections creates a complex pattern of light and dark, sky and water. Roberds calls his work "a little impressionistic, a little expressionistic, but mostly fabrications of abstract brushstrokes."[10] Although he is not an environmentalist per se, Roberds is very concerned about the future of Florida. "I feel strongly about the documentary aspect of painting these areas that may not be there much longer," he says.[11] As Denys Rolle discovered, today's vision might not last past tomorrow.

The story of the Minorcan presence in Florida is a tale fraught with violence, injustice, and hardship. It rivals the drama of the Jamestown and Plymouth settlements while it provides a glimpse into the hardships faced by the settlers who found themselves in a new, strange land and who had to depend on their own courage and cunning to survive. Although the Minorcan settlements were located primarily along the Atlantic coast—first at New Smyrna and later at St. Augustine—they often ventured into the interior, where they plied their fisherman's trade along the St. Johns and in the surrounding lakes and streams.

The story begins in 1763 during the British period of Florida's history. Hoping to encourage settlement of their new holdings, the British government offered attractive terms to prospective settlers looking for land. A Scottish physician, Dr. Andrew Turnbull, seized the opportunity. Realizing that settlers used to the cool English climate would likely find the heat and humidity of Florida intimidating, Turnbull followed the advice of his Greek wife and recruited 1,403 colonists from Italy, Greece, and Minorca to undertake the challenge of founding a new settlement on the land he had acquired on the Ponce de Leon inlet near present-day Daytona. He called his colony New Smyrna after the birthplace of his wife.[12]

Almost at once the colony ran into problems. A supply ship was wrecked before it reached Florida, and 148 of the would-be colonists died during the voyage to the New World. When the survivors finally arrived, they were dismayed to find themselves in a mangrove swamp. The land had not been cleared, and they were instructed not to gather, hunt, or fish. They struggled to build shelters while they faced alligators, hostile Indians, and their worst enemy, the mosquitoes that brought an epidemic of malaria to the colony. During the first year, 450 colonists died.[13]

Despite these problems, the settlers persisted in their efforts. All had signed letters of indenture with Turnbull that provided for their discharge from service after a specified period of time. Additionally, they were promised that Turnbull would give them a small plot of land. However, when the more skilled colonists, such as blacksmiths and carpenters, completed their indenture and asked for their land, they were imprisoned and made to sign new indentures. According to the Web site Rootsweb.com, colonists who were deemed not to be working to capacity were beaten or chained to logs in their fields. Turnbull used his overseers to enforce his judgments, and the penalties were often severe. In spite of this—or perhaps because of it—by 1777 New Smyrna was the most profitable indigo plantation in North America.[14]

The story of the Minorcans' liberation had all of the elements of legend. When, in 1777, a group of Englishmen from St. Augustine visited New Smyrna, a young boy overheard them say that if the colonists knew their rights they wouldn't submit to such virtual slavery. According to the story, the boy told his mother, who relayed the news to other colonists. On March 25, 1777, three of the settlers got permission to go to the coast to hunt for

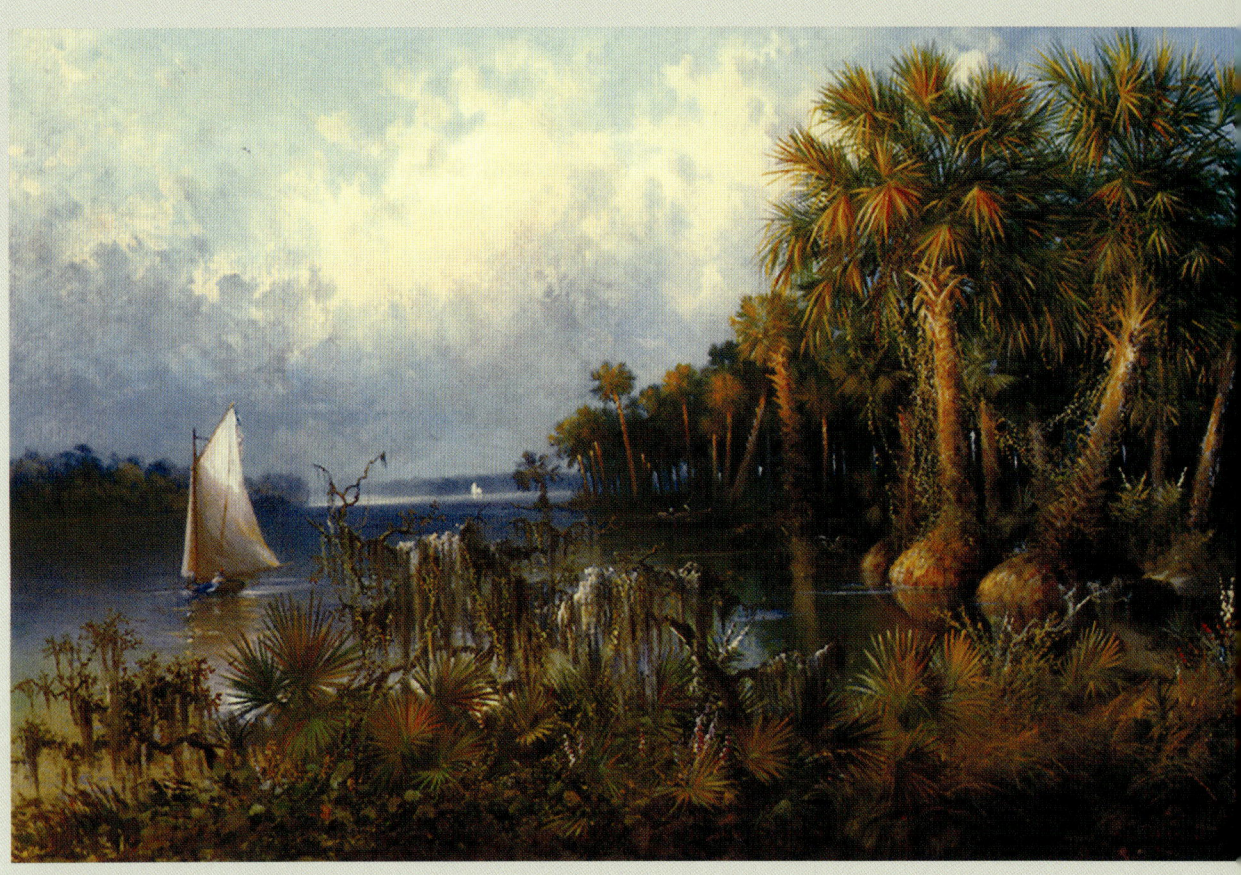

Plate 50. Christian Eisele. *View of the St. Johns*, 1875. Oil on canvas, 30 × 50 in. Sam and Robbie Vickers Florida Collection.

This painting by Christian Eisele titled *View of the St. Johns* depicts a boat sailing the St. Johns River near Jacksonville. According to the art historian Gary Libby, the design of the boat and sail are distinctively Minorcan.[15] Little is known about the artist, but Libby suggests that he may have been "one of the many accomplished European artists who came to America to paint the 'new frontier,' including Florida, during the nineteenth century."[16] Eisele lavished a great deal of attention on his depiction of the exotic flora and fauna of the region. The painting includes "Spanish moss, scrub oak, Palmetto palms, coral beans, native opuntia cactus, sawgrass, yucca and smilax" along with a great blue heron.[17]

turtles. Instead of a hunting trip, they headed for St. Augustine where they met with Governor Tonyn. Distressed by their story, the governor promised to investigate. "A number of factors came into play; the conditions at New Smyrna, the need for men to protect Florida because of the outbreak of the American Revolution, and antagonism between Tonyn and Turnbull, led Governor Tonyn to liberate the New Smyrna colonists. During May and June 1777 most of the colonists migrated to St. Augustine and by July 1777 Turnbull's attorneys had set all the colonists free. In the ten years of its existence 964 colonists died at New Smyrna."[18]

As Florida reverted to Spanish control and was later acquired by the United States, the Minorcans became the core population of St. Augustine, settling into an area next to the city gates, now part of the restored area. According to the art historian James Murphy, in the 1800s members of the Minorcan community were considered "exotic and romantic by the increasing numbers of tourists visiting the city."[19]

Contrary to popular belief, the first Africans to arrive in the Americas were not slaves. Instead, they were black sailors, soldiers, and settlers who came from Spain rather than from Africa. One of the sailors who served on Columbus's flagship, the *Santa Maria*, was a black man named Juan las Canarias.[20]

According to Kathleen Deagan and Darcie MacMahon of the University of Florida's Museum of Natural History, "slaves" and "Africans" were not synonymous in fifteenth-century Spain, where there were enslaved people of all races—mostly prisoners of war who had been captured by the Muslims during the Moorish invasion.[21] The laws governing slaves in Spain, and later in the Spanish colonies, were not based on race but rather were a consequence of war or refusal to accept the conqueror's religion. Slaves could buy their freedom and sue their masters for mistreatment. After 1492, the Spanish code was established in America wherever the Spanish settled.

The first slaves to make the long crossing to America were not Africans but Caribbean Indians who had been enslaved by Columbus and sent to the court of King Ferdinand in 1495 and returned to America as servants. As the native Indians' numbers were reduced through warfare and illnesses such as smallpox that were brought from Europe by the invaders, an acute labor shortage developed. By the 1520s, the Indian population of the Caribbean was nearly extinct. As a consequence of the disappearance of the Indians, millions of Africans were enslaved and brought by force to the Americas.[22] When the English began to establish large plantations in the Southeast in the 1700s, they too began to import African slaves to work their large land holdings. English law was, however, much less lenient than the Spanish code with regard to the treatment and rights of slaves. As Deagan and MacMahon write: "By the 1550s in the Americas, black skin came to be associated with hard physical labor. Social attitudes and controls quickly developed to institutionalize this idea, and this is perhaps the most devastating legacy of the encounter for black Americans."[23]

Although they established missions and cattle ranches in the region, Spanish settlements remained few and far between and much of the land remained unexplored wilderness. This made it a very attractive place to hide for the slaves who ran away from the large plantations that had been established in Georgia and South Carolina. In 1738, black refugees who had escaped from English-owned plantations to the north established Fort Mose a few miles north of St. Augustine. The fort became the first free black community in North America.[24]

During the same period, a number of Creek Indians from Georgia and Alabama were moving into Florida. As both groups tried to survive in their new surroundings, they began to join forces. Many African Americans intermarried with Seminoles, and a new people was born: the Black Seminoles. By the early 1700s, there were more than 100,000 Black Seminoles living in Florida. As had been the case earlier, the Black Seminoles often served as interpreters between the Indians and the whites. As former slaves, they knew the English language and the customs and habits of their former owners.[25]

Despite its role as a bulwark against English intrusion into north Florida, Fort Mose was not destined to last. When Florida was given to the English in the Treaty of Paris, Fort Mose was abandoned as an African American community and, along with the other inhabitants of the Spanish colony, the black families fled to Cuba. The fort itself, however, was occupied by the British during their twenty-year rule and was used as a military outpost by the Spanish when they regained control of Florida in 1784. It was finally destroyed and abandoned in 1812.[26]

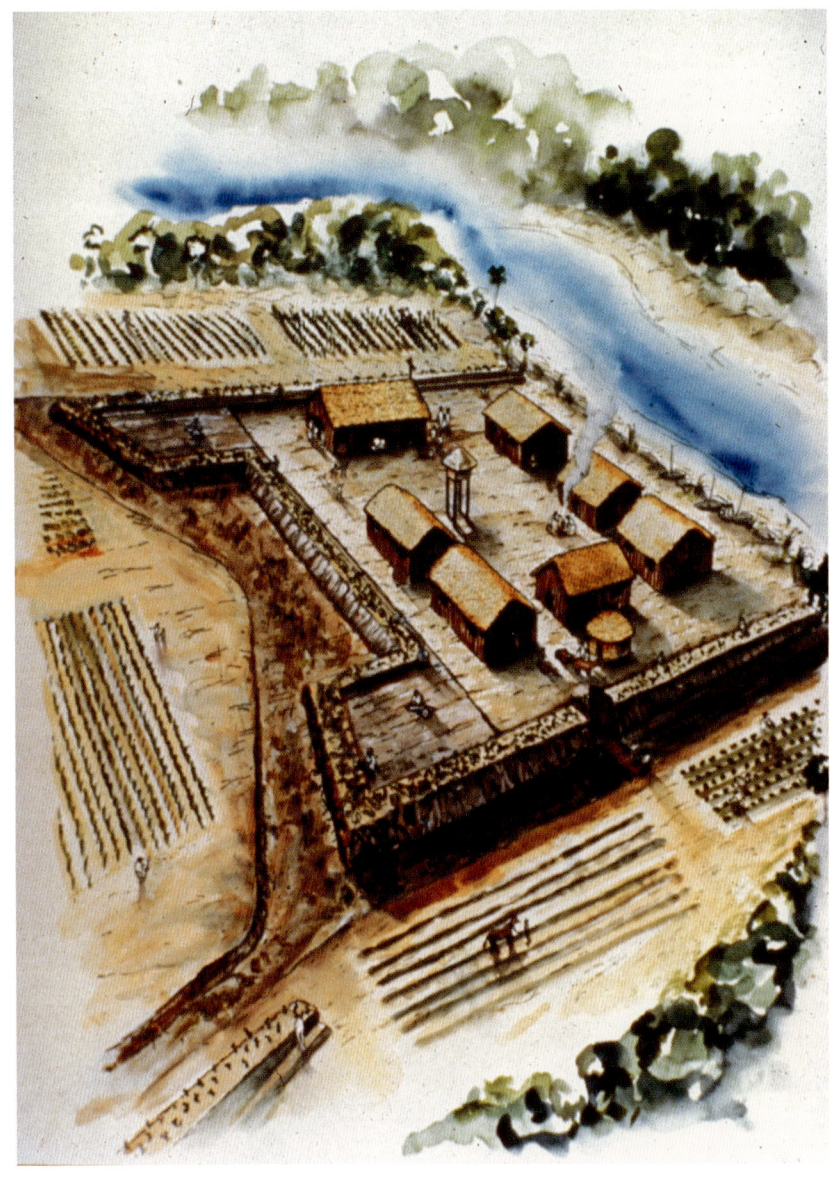

Plate 51. *Reconstruction of Ft. Mose*. Watercolor on paper. Reproduced courtesy of the Florida Museum of Natural History, Gainesville.

This reconstructed image of Fort Mose gives us a good idea of what the fort originally looked like.

In 1806, an African teenager who had been abducted from her native village in Senegal and shipped across the Atlantic to be sold into slavery arrived at the port of Havana, Cuba. Her name was Anta Majigeen Njaay, and she was thirteen years old.[27] On the day that Anta was exhibited for sale, a planter from Spanish Florida, Zephaniah Kingsley, was in the crowd. Kingsley, who had been born in Bristol, England, was reared in Charleston, South Carolina, where his father had become a successful merchant. The family had been forced to leave Charleston in 1782 because of their support for the British during the American Revolution. Young Kingsley returned to Charleston in 1793 and then moved to East Florida that had been retaken by the Spanish under the treaty ending the American Revolution. When he left Havana in October 1806, Kingsley brought with him the girl from Senegal that he had purchased at the slave auction.[28]

The exact nature of the relationship between Kingsley and Anta has always remained obscure. Kingsley claimed that he had first seen Anta in Africa, where he in fact had traveled in 1805. He further stated in his will that they were married, which was "celebrated and solemnized by her native African custom, although never celebrated according to the forms of Christian usage."[29] Whatever the legal definition of their relationship, Kingsley would ever after refer to her as his wife, and he lived openly with her and their children for the rest of his life.

Anta, now referred to as Anna, lived at Kingsley's Laurel Grove plantation located on Doctor's Lake, an inlet of the St. Johns River, for the next five years. Here she found herself surrounded by orange groves, cotton fields, and plots of land for corn and vegetables. There were slave's quarters, barns, carpentry shops, and a host of other outbuildings that made the plantation more a self-sufficient village than a simple farm. Huge reserves of pine forests and wetlands were available for future expansion.

Anna soon became the manager of the Kingsley household, and Kingsley was quoted as saying that "her managerial abilities rivaled his own."[30] On March 4, 1811, Kingsley formally emancipated Anna and the three children he had fathered. Anna remained at Laurel Grove for one more year, but in 1812 she and her children moved across the river, and she established a home of her own at Mandarin, where she had been granted five acres by the Spanish government.[31] She acquired twelve slaves to help run the operation and built a two-story house. Her independence, however, was short-lived. In 1813, during the Patriot's War, she set fire to the house to keep it from falling into the hands of marauding soldiers. Laurel Grove was also destroyed.[32]

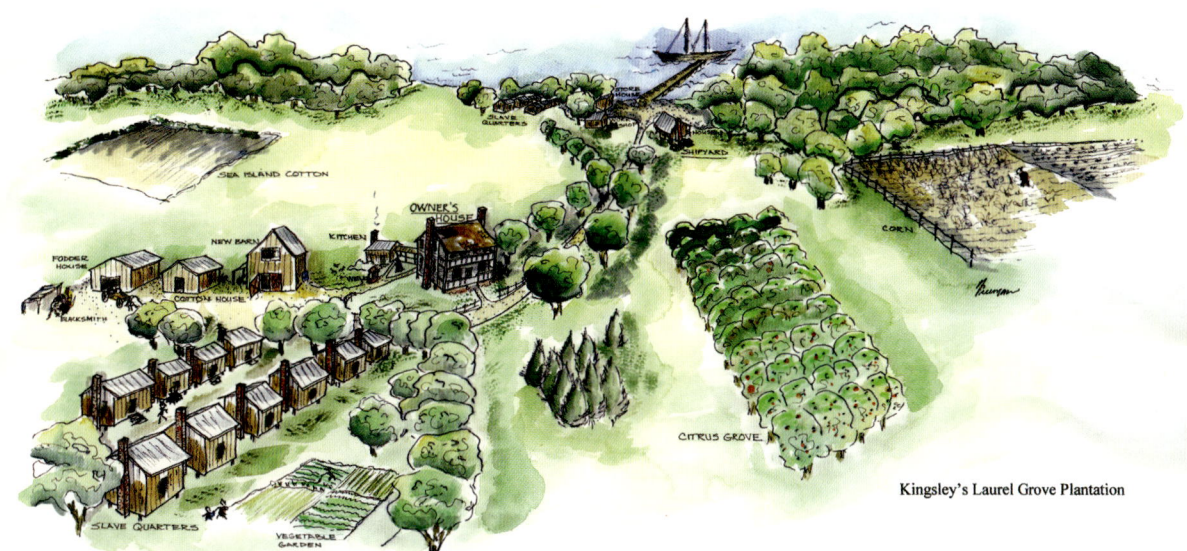

Kingsley's Laurel Grove Plantation

This sketch of Laurel Grove by Nancy Freeman gives an idea of the grand design of the estate.

Plate 52. Nancy Freeman. *Artist's Conception of Laurel Grove Plantation, 1812,* n.d. Drawing. Courtesy of the artist.

In 1814, Kingsley and Anna were reunited and moved north to Fort George Island, where they first rented and then bought a plantation from a wealthy Georgia planter, John McIntosh, who had been using the Fort George land as a timber plantation. Here, Anna and Kingsley built an even more impressive operation that included citrus groves and fields of cotton and sugar cane. Anna continued to play a major role in the day-to-day operations of the plantation and served as manager when her husband was away on business. She gave birth to one additional son in 1824. By that time, East Florida had become a territory of the United States and the additional security and stability brought about by the transition prompted Zephaniah to purchase additional plantations.

The Kingsley family grew and prospered, eventually acquiring property in Haiti, where Anna and Zephaniah took up residence in 1836. Following her husband's death in 1843, Anna returned to Florida, where she purchased a 22-acre farm on the east bank of the St. Johns River north of the growing town of Jacksonville. The estates of her daughters and their husbands were nearby. Although the Civil War disrupted the peace of Anna's last years, she was able to spend the final years of her life at the estate of her daughter Mary, where she died in July 1870, at the age of seventy-seven.[33]

The Kingsley Plantation, seen here in a drawing by Nancy Freeman, was bought by the State of Florida in 1955. Today the main residence, along with several outbuildings, has been restored and is part of the Timucuan Ecological and Historical Preserve. The plantation is maintained by the National Park Service and is open to the public.

Plate 53. Nancy Freeman. *Artist's Conception of the Kingsley Plantation,* n.d. Drawing. Courtesy of the artist.

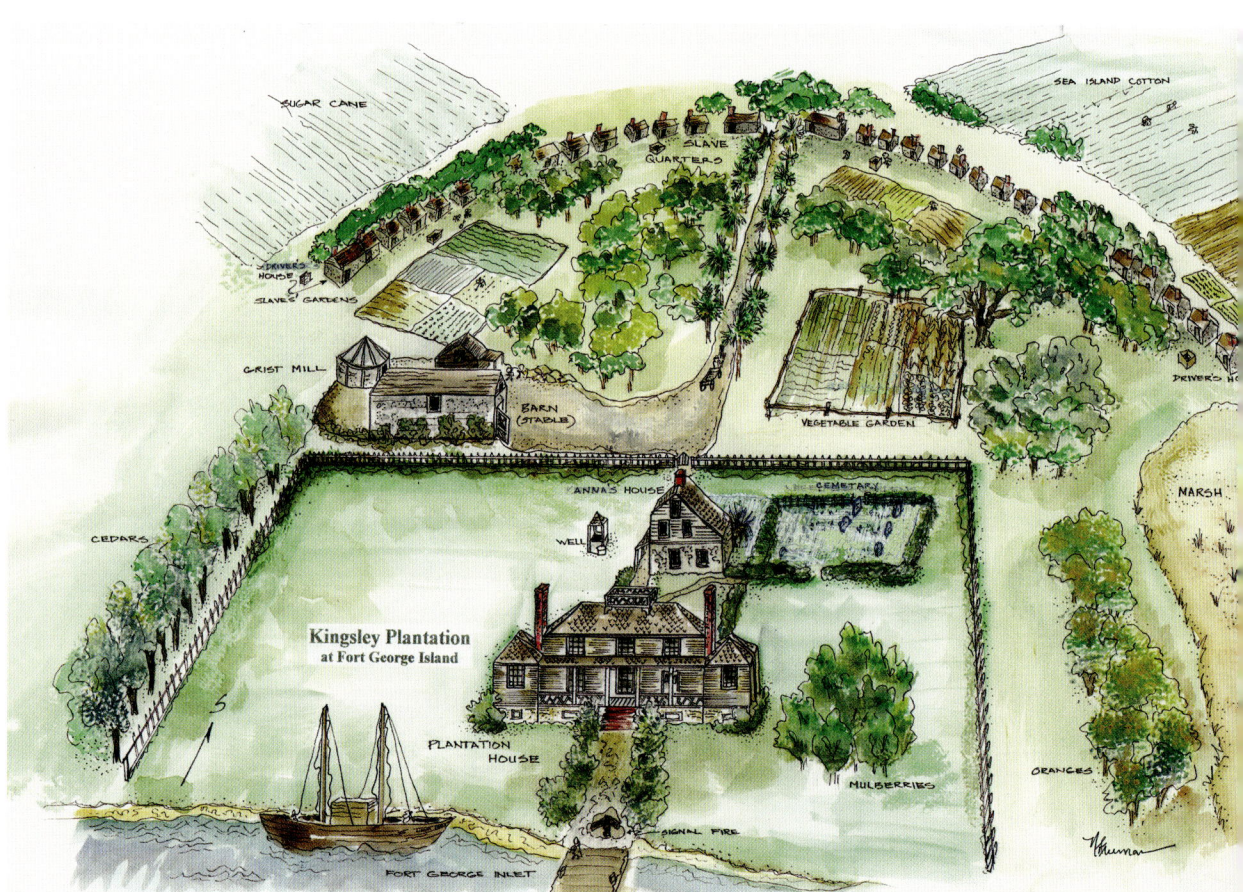

It is interesting that when Harriet Beecher Stowe, the author of *Uncle Tom's Cabin*, moved to Florida in 1867 she established her son Frederick at Laurel Grove. Ironically—or perhaps in a serendipitous example of poetic justice—Laurel Grove had originally been developed and managed by Anna Kingsley, Zephaniah Kingsley's Senegalese wife. As an outspoken abolitionist whose writings had helped launch the Civil War, Stowe must have wondered at the curious link that connected her family to the property of a former slave.

When the Spanish ceded Florida to the British in exchange for Havana in 1763 as part of the treaty that ended the French and Indian War, many Spaniards left for Cuba, taking with them the remnants of the Timucuan Indians who had been largely wiped out by two centuries of disease, displacement, and warfare. By the end of 1764, Florida's indigenous people were essentially gone.

This population vacuum was, however, soon filled by an influx of Lower Creek Indians from Georgia and Alabama. These newcomers, encouraged by the abandoned fields and orchards that had been vacated by the Spaniards and the mission Indians, found northern Florida well suited to their needs. They also took over the feral herds of cattle and horses left over from Spanish ranching operations. When he visited the Alachua Savanna in 1774, William Bartram reported meeting the Seminole Chief Cowkeeper, whose herds of Spanish cattle and horses roamed the prairie in large numbers. By the time the Spanish retook Florida under the Second Treaty of Paris in 1783, the Lower Creeks had established themselves in both the Tallahassee area and in and around Paynes Prairie in southwestern Alachua County. Both areas had been the site of major Spanish ranching and mission operations.

The Spanish officials were happy to have the Creeks in the area. The collapse of the mission system had left colonists without a native presence to aid them against the growing British threat in the Carolinas and Georgia. According to Theodore Morris in his book *Florida's Lost Tribes*: "One term used by the Spaniards to refer to the Florida Creeks was *cimarrones*, a word used throughout the Americas by the Spaniards for non-Christian Indians living apart from Spanish settlements. . . . As pronounced by the Creeks, ci-marr-on-e became se-mi-no-les. Over the next few decades, as the Florida

Creeks began to act and be independent of the Creek settlements they had left behind, they began to develop a new identity: they were Seminole Indians."[34]

Even though they had developed a new and distinctive life style, the Seminole retained many of their Creek customs. They played the traditional stickball game, smoked the calumet or pipe, drank black drink in purification rituals, and celebrated the Busk or Green Corn to welcome the new crop of corn, an important staple in their diet.[35]

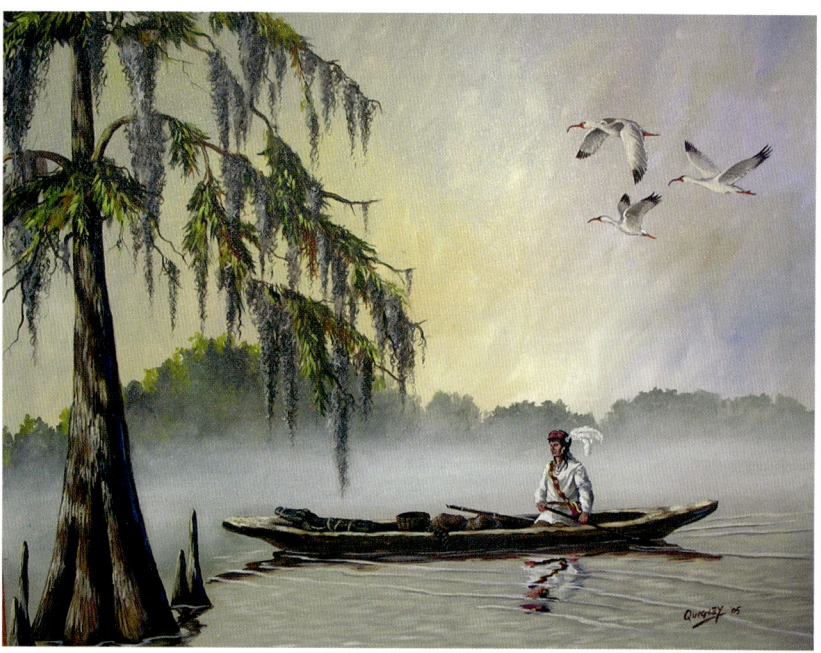

Plate 54. Dean Quigley. *Seminole Hunter in a Dugout Canoe*, n.d. Acrylic on canvas, 30 × 40 in. Courtesy of the artist.

In this painting, *Seminole Hunter in a Dugout Canoe,* the artist Dean Quigley portrays the Indian hunter returning from a trip, his canoe filled with his catch—including a large alligator.

Their roots in Creek culture can also be seen in Seminole art, especially in their beadwork, which relies on a rich combination of plant and abstract motifs and the use of black backgrounds to bring out the contrasting bright colors. As in many Native cultures, the decorative beadwork that appears on leggings, sashes, and carrying cases, or bandolier bags, was the work of Indian women. According to Maybelle Mann, author of *Art in Florida, 1564–1945*: "Women made the clothing in which the beadwork decoration was the culture's primary form of artistic expression. Later, particularly after the introduction of the sewing machine, women also developed the patchwork clothing that is now recognized as a great artistic accomplishment."[36] Patchwork clothing is still being produced by the Seminole and Miccosukee people of south Florida today.

Seminole art historian Dorothy Downs believes that the decorations found on this Seminole bandolier bag have specific significance. The stylized animal tracks seen on the bag are those of a raccoon while the leaves interspersed with the tracks are from a "raccoon tree." According to Downs's Seminole friends, the leaves were used to concoct a tea that was used as a cure for "raccoon disease"—what we call insomnia—which caused dark circles to form around the eyes of the patient.[37]

Plate 55. Seminole bandolier bag, ca. 1850. Blue/red cotton cloth, blue/white glass beads, 30½ × 19¾ in. Courtesy of the Anthropology Division of the Florida Museum of Natural History, FLMNH Cat. No. E603; photo by Roy Stanyard.

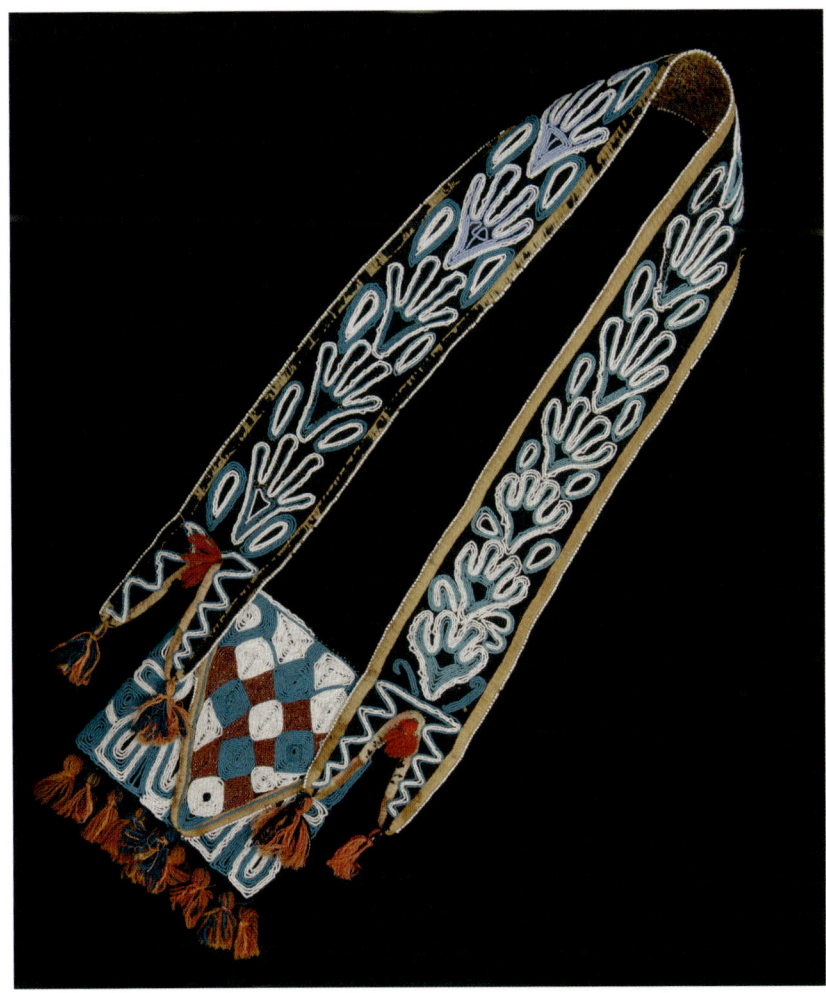

According to the historian Michael Gannon, the history of the Florida Seminole can be divided into two periods: the migration of the Creeks into Florida (1716–67) and the era of prosperity under British and Spanish rule prior to the transfer of power to the United States (1767–1821).[38] During the early years, the Indians retained much of their Creek culture—square ground towns were presided over by chiefs such as Cowkeeper, the ancient ball game was still played, and the black drink ceremony was still practiced. However, as more and more non-Indians migrated into Florida, tensions between Indians and settlers began to rise, culminating in campaigns into Florida from Georgia to challenge Seminole control. In 1812, King Payne, Cowkeeper's successor, was mortally wounded in a skirmish with Col. Daniel Newnan of the Georgia militia near Paynes Prairie in Alachua County.

The period between 1813 and 1858 were years of almost constant turmoil as Spaniards, Anglos, African Americans, and Seminoles vied for control of the Florida peninsula. Even though Florida had been returned to Spanish control following the American Revolution, Spain's hold on the region continued to weaken due to constant border disputes with Georgia, a lack of effective governmental control and eventually the intervention of American military forces during the War of 1812. When Col. Edmund Gaines moved to attack the Seminole village of Fowltown in November 1817, the First Seminole War broke out. Gaines burned the town and killed five Indians. In retaliation, the Indians opened fire on a boat coming up the Flint River, killing thirty-seven soldiers as well as several women and children. U.S. Secretary of War John C. Calhoun ordered General Andrew Jackson to subdue the Indians. In March 1818, Jackson brought 4,800 troops to Florida and easily advanced against the 1,300 Seminole and Black Seminole defenders. Jackson is reported to have written that his campaign's purpose was "to chastise a savage foe, [who] combined with a lawless band of negro brigands . . . [were] carrying on a cruel and unprovoked war against the citizens of the United States."[39]

Spain finally conceded ownership of the region, and Florida became a territory of the United States in 1821. Andrew Jackson, who had already secured his reputation as an Indian fighter and military leader, was installed as the first military governor of the territory. He resigned after just three months, but he had "issued ordinances and established precedents that would begin the Americanization of Florida."[40]

However, relations between the Seminoles and the settlers continued to worsen during the early years of American control as white intruders drove the Florida Indians off lands they had occupied for more than a century. Slave raiders harassed the Indians and their black neighbors, the Treaty of Moultrie Creek (1823) attempted to confine the Seminole to a reservation south of Ocala, and the American government pressed for removal of the Indians to Oklahoma. The Second Seminole War erupted in 1835 in opposition to the relocation policy. Led by Osceola, the son of a white father and a Creek mother, the Indian resistance resulted in the longest and most costly Indian war in U.S. history.

In 1837, a cease-fire led to a meeting between Osceola and Lt. Col. William Harney at Fort Mellon near present-day Sanford. The Indian forces, nearly 2,500 strong, camped along the St. Johns River at Lake Monroe. In a show of cordiality, Osceola organized a game of lacrosse, perhaps to give the American officers and men a glimpse of Indian prowess.

According to Jean Parker Waterbury in a 1982 article for *El Escribano* (vol. 19): "Although the Americans believed the Seminoles would shortly move, as agreed, to Fort Brooke [near Tampa] for transfer to the west, they stayed on . . . scheming to avoid deportation. Before long their supposed compliance with the terms of the Armistice became untenable. On June 2 [1837], Osceola and a small band of warriors appeared at Fort Brooke, [rescued the Indians held there] . . . and melted into the Florida wilderness."[41]

Captain John Rogers Vinton, a West Point graduate, was also a skilled artist. When he encountered Osceola at the meeting at Lake Harney, he used the opportunity to make a sketch of the Indian leader. Vinton would later use the sketch to make several portraits of Osceola. Osceola was captured later that year in St. Augustine, tricked by a white flag of truce into surrendering. He spent his final days imprisoned in South Carolina, where he posed for several artists including George Catlin, but apparently only John Rogers Vinton persuaded the Seminole warrior to "sit" for a portrait while he was still at liberty. Vinton depicted the Indian leader dressed in full regalia looking out at Lake Monroe.

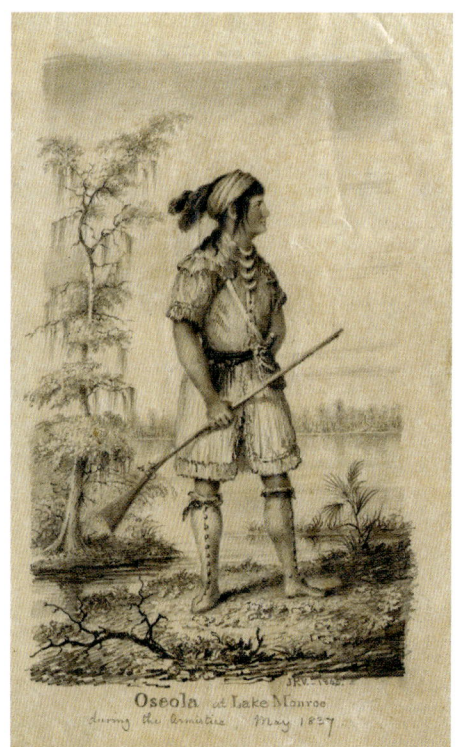

Plate 56. John Rogers Vinton. Sketch for *Osceola at Lake Monroe*, 1837. Graphite on paper, 10 × 13 in. Courtesy of the Special Collections, University of Miami Libraries, Coral Gables, Florida.

Osceola died in prison in 1838; his request to be buried in Florida was denied. Following his burial, someone placed a stone on his grave that read "Oceola [*sic*], Patriot and Warrior."[42]

In late 1835, Seminole war parties led by King Philip, a Seminole chief, began to raid plantations located along the coast east of the St. Johns. One of the plantations destroyed by the Indian raids was the Cruger and Depeyster Plantation in New Smyrna Beach. Built in 1830 by two New York investors, Henry Cruger and William Depeyster, the plantation was operated by Thomas Stamps, a South Carolina sugar planter. According to the art historian Gary Libby: "On Christmas Day 1835, armed Seminoles were observed by settlers in New Smyrna Beach who evacuated to the Col. Dummett House at Mt. Pleasant. After the Seminoles burned New Smyrna Beach and the plantation, Col. Dummett led the survivors north to Bulow Plantation near Ormond beach, where they waited for a military escort to St. Augustine."[43]

Also during the Second Seminole War, King Philip and his son, Coacoochee, or Wildcat, camped in the area now known as Osceola Fish Camp, located on Lake Harney near Geneva. The army referred to the area as King Philipstown after King Philip, who was the leader of the Miccosukee Seminole band. Coacoochee, who disagreed with his father's decision to leave Florida, was captured along with Osceola in October 1837 and imprisoned at Fort Marion. He later escaped and became the war chief most respected by the U.S. Army after Osceola's death.

In 1916, the Tidewater Cypress Company established a mill town on the same spot, naming the town Osceola after the Seminole warrior. Home to two hundred people, the town continued to thrive until the cypress industry declined and the town was abandoned. The fish camp is all that remains. However, a large Indian shell mound still stands in the area. The clam and mussel shells that make up the mound were discarded by the original Indian inhabitants over centuries of time. Pottery shards identify at least two prehistoric Indian groups who once lived in the area—the Orange culture (1450–1250 BC) and the St. Johns culture (AD 800–1300).

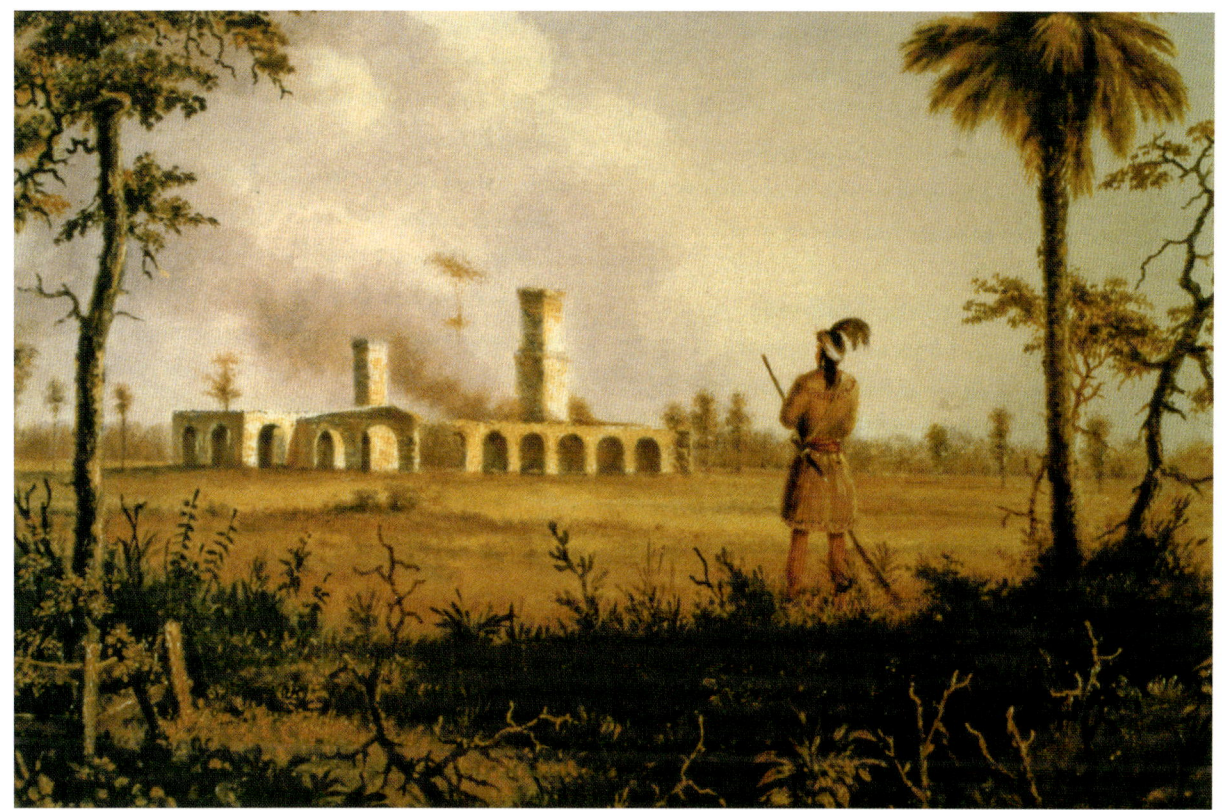

Plate 57. John Rogers Vinton. *The Ruins of the Sugar House*, 1843. Oil on canvas, 11 × 16 in. Sam and Robbie Vickers Florida Collection.

According to the art historian Gary Libby, Vinton "frames the important event [the burning of the plantation] with dark oaks and a single palm accurately rendered in effective chiaroscuro. The dense, dark undergrowth is seen in stark contrast to the bright and hotly painted scene of the plantation in ruins and on fire observed by the Seminole warrior, a representative of the forces of destruction. In many ways, Vinton's painting participates in the nineteenth century romantic dialogue, placing forces of good and evil in opposition to each other in specific historic incidents."[44]

There are so many more stories to tell—of the Greek community in St. Augustine, the Russian colony in Orlando, the Puerto Rican enclaves of central Florida. All along the river corridor are vibrant reminders of the Crackers and Criollos, Indians and Italians, Swedish and Irish, Japanese and Jews who have contributed to the rich texture of Florida's grand patchwork of cultures.

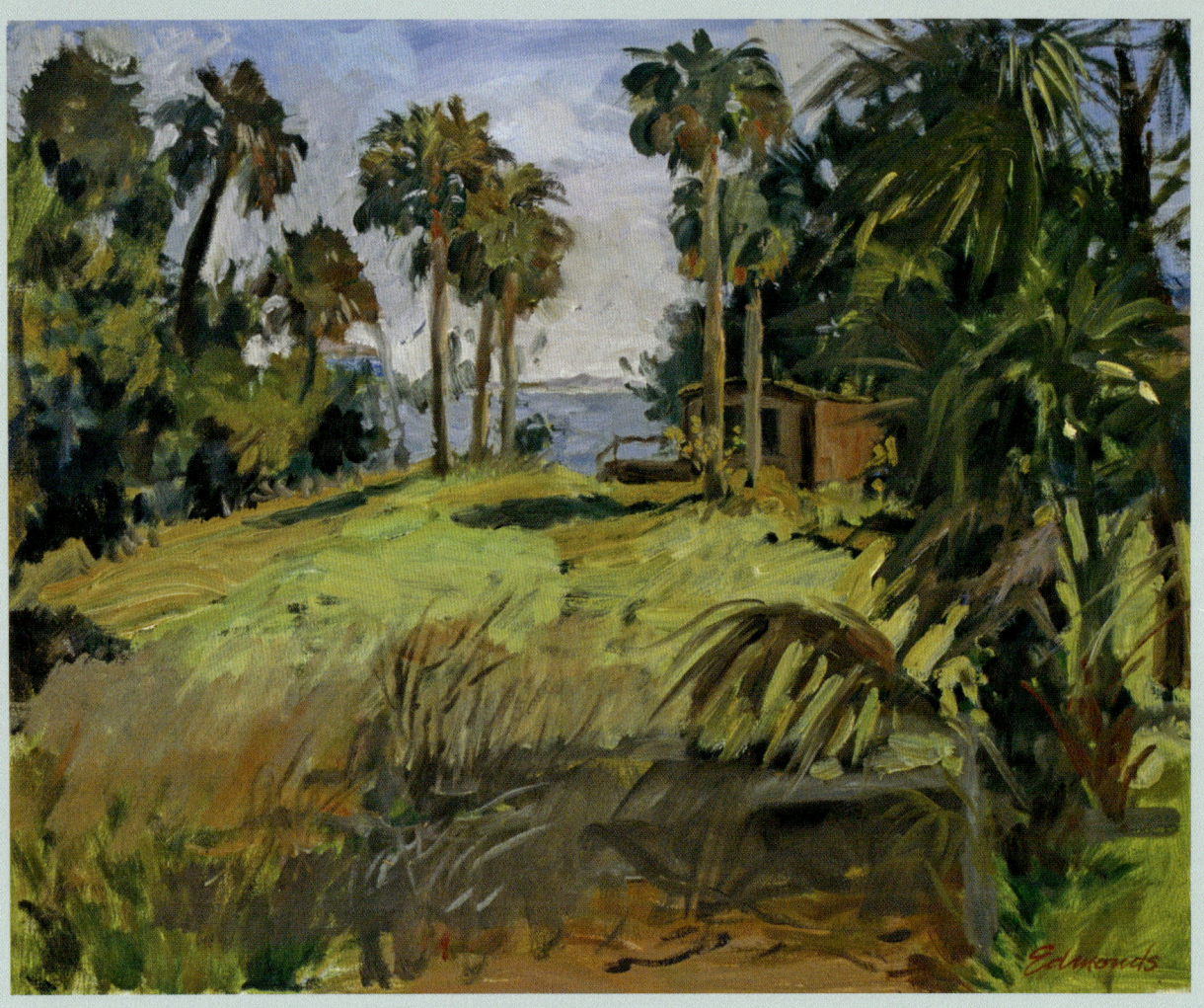

Plate 58. Cynthia Edmonds. *King Philips-town—Osceola Fishcamp*, 2006. Oil on canvas. Private Collection.

The Winter Park artist Cynthia Edmonds painted this view of *King Philips-town—Osceola Fishcamp* in 2006. She has been painting scenes along the St. Johns River for the past five years and has a special interest in places that are connected to Florida's history. Edmonds writes: "Since I first started [the series] . . . much of the land along the river has been cleared for new development. The old way of life on the river is disappearing fast. Few of the old fishing cabins and charming marinas remain. Now large homes are replacing the 'Old Florida' and I have to drive farther to find the pristine wilderness."[45]

5 { Artist-Naturalists in *La Florida*

For more than four hundred years, the St. Johns River corridor has been a naturalist's paradise. It is not difficult to understand why artist-naturalists have found the area to be a mecca for exploration and discovery. From the time of European infiltration until the present day, artists, botanists, and zoologists have sketched, pressed, painted, photographed, and videotaped almost every inch of the region. New wonders are still being discovered, whether they are the bones or fossils of ancient megafauna or tiny living plants and animals that simply have managed to remain out of sight for all these centuries until some adventurer catches sight of them.

Using art to illuminate nature is an ancient human activity, dating back to the drawings of deer, bison, and horses created by Paleolithic artists on the walls of caves thousands of years ago. We don't know exactly what motivated these early artists to create images of animals. Perhaps it was because of their implicit reliance on those creatures for their survival; or maybe it was their way of interacting with the beautiful and terrible chaos of the wild nature that surrounded them. What we do know is that from the very beginning of human culture, images of the plants and animals with which we share this planet have reflected our tireless and constant investigation of the natural world.

For artist-naturalists, the allure of the St. Johns River has been irresistible. "Faunally speaking," wrote the modern naturalist Archie Carr, "the St. Johns River is an extraordinary stream, like no other in America."[1] Blessed with a 310-mile length, a streambed that wanders from marsh to pond to creek to lake to miles-wide channel, a climate that ranges from subtropical in the southern region to warm temperate in the north, a mix of fresh-

To the rough, practical Northern mind, Florida is a land of dreams, a strange country full of surprises, an intangible sort of place, where at first nothing is believed to be real and where finally everything is considered possible.
—David Leon Chandler, *Henry Flagler*

water and salt water and input from numerous springs, sand boils, and tributaries, the St. Johns boasts an amazing array of diversity. Bill Belleville writes: "The sheer variety of plants and animals—which skyrocket when an environment is wet and warm like this one—is further hot-wired by the odd salt-fresh mix. The river itself is home to some 183 species of fish. . . . If you take this singular, diverse riverine environment and populate it with endangered wildlife—like wood storks and bald eagles and manatees— then chunk in some endemic plants and animals found nowhere else on earth, you have one long, winding natural corridor where most anything is possible."[2]

Early European visitors to the New World were filled with wonder as they observed unfamiliar animals, exotic Natives, strange flowers and trees. According to Susan Scott Parrish in *American Curiosity*, the investigation of America's natural resources was an integral part of the transformation among European intellectuals from an attitude of "wonder at the preternatural and a belief in magic, demonism, and providential monsters" to "curiosity about God's stable and orderly creation."[3] In other words, the contribution of American explorers, botanists, and naturalists played a huge role in the development of the European Enlightenment. "Various people in the Americas participated not only in the creation of material prosperity in Europe through their labors with American natural resources but also in the creation of an empirically based and hence locally divergent and complex type of nature-knowledge. . . . The specimens that tacked eastward across the Atlantic . . . were a major material source, from 1492 onward, for the development of botany, pharmacology, zoology, paleontology, geology, and ethnology, among other sciences."[4]

Initial reports about the New World, such as the letters of Columbus, were received with enthusiasm in Europe, but interest lagged when the explorers did not find streets paved with gold and treasure chests of gemstones. The factual reports of men such as Jacques Cartier failed to arouse the interest of the populace. More than dry facts were needed to kindle the European public's imagination and stimulate their interest in "curiosities." Illustrations helped whet the European appetite for new and marvelous things, and European artists often tried to capture these curiosities in drawings and paintings. However, tied as they were to their own European cultural assumptions—the product of *their* native environment—their pictures often reveal more about them than about their subjects.

One pioneering anthropologist cum travel writer, the Franciscan friar André Thevet, realized that exaggeration and hyperbole would sell more copy than boring realism. Born around 1516 in the French town of Angoulême, Thevet was a world traveler in a time when the sphere was expanding exponentially. Before becoming royal historiographer and "guardian of the royal cabinet of curiosities" for the French court, Thevet had visited Italy, Spain, Egypt, and North Africa. Shortly thereafter, Thevet published his *Cosmographie de Levant,* which explored the people, places, flora, and fauna of the region.

His one voyage to the New World came as part of the Durand de Villegagnon expedition to South America in 1550. His participation in this adventure made him an instant authority on the region's flora, fauna, and human inhabitants, even though ill-health forced his return to France after only a few weeks in Brazil. While his studies of the region stake a claim for his part in the development of anthropology, these scholarly pursuits were not the reason for his popularity in sixteenth-century France. Fabulous stories and exotic specimens were what his contemporaries wanted, and Thevet was happy to oblige, even if it meant conjuring up words and images based on the descriptions of other travelers and not on creatures and events he had personally seen. His two major works—*Singularitez de la france antarctique* (1558) and *Cosmograpjie universelle* (1575)—are filled with far-fetched tales and astonishingly inaccurate images. Nevertheless, he succeeded in arousing the curiosity of his European audience and stimulating later and more exacting explorations.

Thevet was among the first to use the new technique of engraving to provide illustrations for his text. For two centuries thereafter, European editors borrowed from his works to illustrate new travel reports, thus perpetuating Thevet's embellished mythology.[5] According to Elsa Conrad, while today, Thevet is seen "largely as a compiler and editor of experiences that belonged to others," his work remains useful to those studying the first European encounters with the New World, and his books, "with their extensive descriptions and lavish illustrations, give a broad picture of the extent of the historical and geographical knowledge of the sixteenth century."[6]

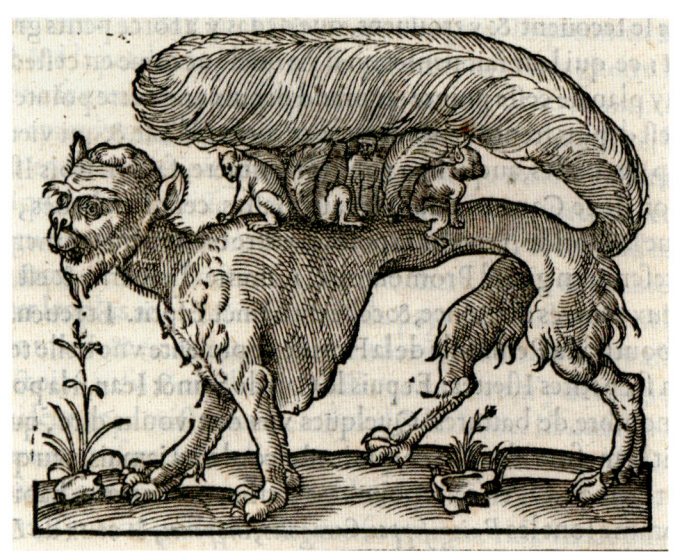

This engraving from the *Cosmographie* is likely based on earlier descriptions of an animal that was described by Pietro Martire d'Anghiera, chaplain to the court of Ferdinand and Isabella of Spain, as a "monstrous beast with a snowte lyke a foxe, a tayle lyke a marmasette, eares lyke a batte, handes lyke a man, and feete lyke an ape, bearing her whelpes aboute with her in an outwarde bellye much lyke unto a great bagge or purse."[7] In Thevet's text, a similar creature is described as "a rapacious beast living on the river banks near Fort Caroline" [present-day Jacksonville]; this strangely elongated creature sports a bearded gargoyle's head, a plumed tail and feet with wicked-looking talons."[8] The subject, according to Charles Bennett, is a common opossum. So why is the creature demonized?

Plate 59. André Thevet. *Succarath.* Woodcut illustration for *Cosmographie Universelle* (Paris, 1575). Courtesy of Special Collections, The Newberry Library, Chicago, Illinois.

The opossum, a marsupial, was not known in Europe until one was brought back to Spain by Vincent Pinzón, master of the *Pinta*, in 1492. Thus, the creature was seen as a novelty, possibly even a preternatural monster. Parrish writes, "Martire, trying to understand and explain what this American creature is . . . takes parts from familiar animals, from the human and from the artificial . . . and joins them to account for and physically approximate this new creature."[9] Parrish further contends that "a general European fascination for the non-natural characterized the period from 1500 to 1650,"[10] a period when European exploration brought the Old World into contact with all manner of new and fabulous flora and fauna from Asia, Africa, and the Americas. Over a period of two and a half centuries, these collections formed the basis for the development of modern scientific inquiry. "By the end of the seventeenth century, natural history had turned toward systemizing the abiding and rational text of creation and redeeming the anomalous through the clarifying tools of dissection, numeracy, mechanical analysis, and universal nomenclature."[11] European naturalists were well on their way to accepting Martire's exhortation to "feede their myndes."

IT IS IN THE WRITINGS OF WILLIAM BARTRAM that we find one of the clearest examples of the changes that had taken place in the understanding of natural history by the late eighteenth century, two hundred years after Thevet's quasi-supernatural reportage. By the mid-1700s, London had become the self-proclaimed center of the New Science—a science based on empirical observation and rational inquiry. Members of the Royal Society of London for Improving Natural Knowledge were not willing to publicly acknowledge their debt to the colonial naturalists who were key to the development of European natural history, but they were not shy about requesting specimens, funding explorations, or encouraging inquiry. Susan Parrish writes: "The [Royal] Society . . . functioned mainly as a clearinghouse for information, a center of a global correspondence network, [and] a printer of books. . . . [They solicited information from many sources including] "the collecting work and testimonies of African slaves, freed blacks, and Indians" as well as educated colonial men and women.[12]

Born in Philadelphia in 1739, William Bartram was a homegrown American colonist and America's first native-born artist-naturalist.[13] He learned botany from his father, John, who instilled in him a love of the wilderness and a curiosity that verged on obsession. He was also singled out by his father from among his eight siblings to receive a formal education.

William is a transitional figure in the history of natural science writing. His roots were grounded in the European Enlightenment, but his view of nature as a grand and sublime expression of God's handiwork linked him to the Romantic movement of the early nineteenth century. His passionate rhetoric displayed an "awareness, knowledge and discourse . . . affected by specific ecologies."[14] One only need compare the attitudes of John Bartram and his son William to understand the watershed that separates the anthrocentrist classicism of the eighteenth century from the Transcendentalist Romanticism of the nineteenth.

When John Bartram visited the St. Johns River in 1764 on a reconnaissance mission for his patron, King George V of England, he looked primarily for resources to exploit.[15] As botanist to the king, it was his job to explore Florida, recently acquired from Spain, and to report on the natural resources that might be useful to Britain. A product of the eighteenth-century Enlightenment, John Bartram appreciated the importance of cat-

The shores of this great river San Juan are very level and shoal, extending, in some places, a mile or two into the river, betwixt the high land and the clear waters of the river, which is so level, as to be covered not above a foot or two deep with water, and at a little distance appears as a green meadow, having water-grass and other amphibious vegetables growing in the oozy bottom, and floating on the water.

—William Bartram, *Travels*, 1791

egories, of dividing the natural world into an orderly hierarchy that could be observed in sequence. He was also aware that as a colonial naturalist he was under scrutiny from his European counterparts, and he wished to be as prudent and careful as possible in his scholarship. William, on the other hand, was introduced by his tutor, Charles Thomson, to William Hogarth's *Analysis of Beauty* and to Edmund Burke's thoughts on the "sublime," instilling in him a way of looking at nature that that was quite different from his father's.[16]

Thus when John's son William returned to Florida in 1774, instead of visualizing board feet and ship's stores, he turned his poet's eye on the astonishing beauty and inspirational magnificence of the natural environment. When William viewed the forest along the banks of the "noble San Juan" he saw "an enchanting little forest . . . partly encircled by a deep creek, a branch of the river, that has its source in the high forests of the main. . . . I penetrated the grove, and afterwards entered some almost unlimited savannas and plains, which were absolutely enchanting; they had been lately burnt by the Indian hunters, and had just now recovered their vernal verdure and gaiety. . . . How happily situated is this retired spot on earth! What an Elysium it is! . . . Seduced by these sublime enchanting scenes of primitive nature, and these visions of terrestrial happiness, I had roved far from Cedar Point."[17]

The purpose of William's trip, which was sponsored by the English physician John Fothergill, was similar to his father's earlier venture—to provide prospects and specimens for commercial production and horticultural investigation. Nevertheless, the younger Bartram's journal reaffirms his utter delight and fascination with the natural environment and his deeply spiritual commitment to the world of Nature. It is also important to keep in mind that William's major book, *Travels*, was written following the American Revolution, a period that saw the development of a distinctly American identity and a new attitude toward European empiricism. William was in a position to take more chances with his narrative than were earlier writers, to exalt in the American landscape and to relish a new sense of freedom from past restraints.

Because of his florid style and his boundless enthusiasm, Bartram has frequently been portrayed, as he was in Cabell and Hanna's *Parade of*

Diversities, as a hopelessly sensitive and romantic free spirit wandering the Florida wilds like a lost flower child. But his sensitivity to the beauty of nature and his powerful emotions do not necessarily translate into a lack of courage or physical weakness as is obvious to those who have read Bartram's *Travels*. Mark Derr, in *Some Kind of Paradise*, puts it this way: "One does not have to abide the myth of poor, sensitive, effete Billy Bartram to recognize in the man a unique consciousness. . . . At the start of *Travels* Bartram professed his animism: 'If we bestow but a very little attention to the economy of the animal creation, we shall find manifest examples of premeditation, perseverance, resolution, and consummate artifice, in order to effect their purpose.' Plants also exhibited volition and premeditation. All of creation deserved human respect, and Bartram gave it, mourning a rattlesnake, refusing to kill sandhill cranes because, though excellent food, they were so marvelous singing on the wing. As an old man, the Traveler, as he was sometimes known, kept a pet opossum and a crow that often perched on his shoulder or accompanied him to his garden. His pantheism led him to observe and record as few had before him and no one could after."[18]

Ashton Nichols, in *Romantic Natural Histories*, also points out that Bartram was part of a "pervasive paradigm shift, away from a nature that was static and unchanging toward a nature characterized by dynamic links among all living things."[19] Whereas the reduction of the natural world to a mechanical model during the Enlightenment period brought about what some scholars have called "the disenchantment of the world," Bartram, as the first post-Enlightenment nature writer, appreciated and perhaps internalized "indigenous and Afro-American beliefs in the potency of nature and the efficacy of the invisible world" that he encountered as part of his "American experience."[20]

William Bartram's talent as an artist was recognized early on. Encouraged by his father to draw from nature, William worked hard to make his illustrations true to life. In a letter written to his friend and mentor Peter Collinson in 1753, John referred to William as "my little botanist" and further mentioned that "Botany and drawing are his [William's] darling delight."[21] According to Sandra Sammons in *John and William Bartram: Travelers in Early America*, William also profited from the many friends of his father who visited the Bartram's Philadelphia home such as Benjamin

Tab. I

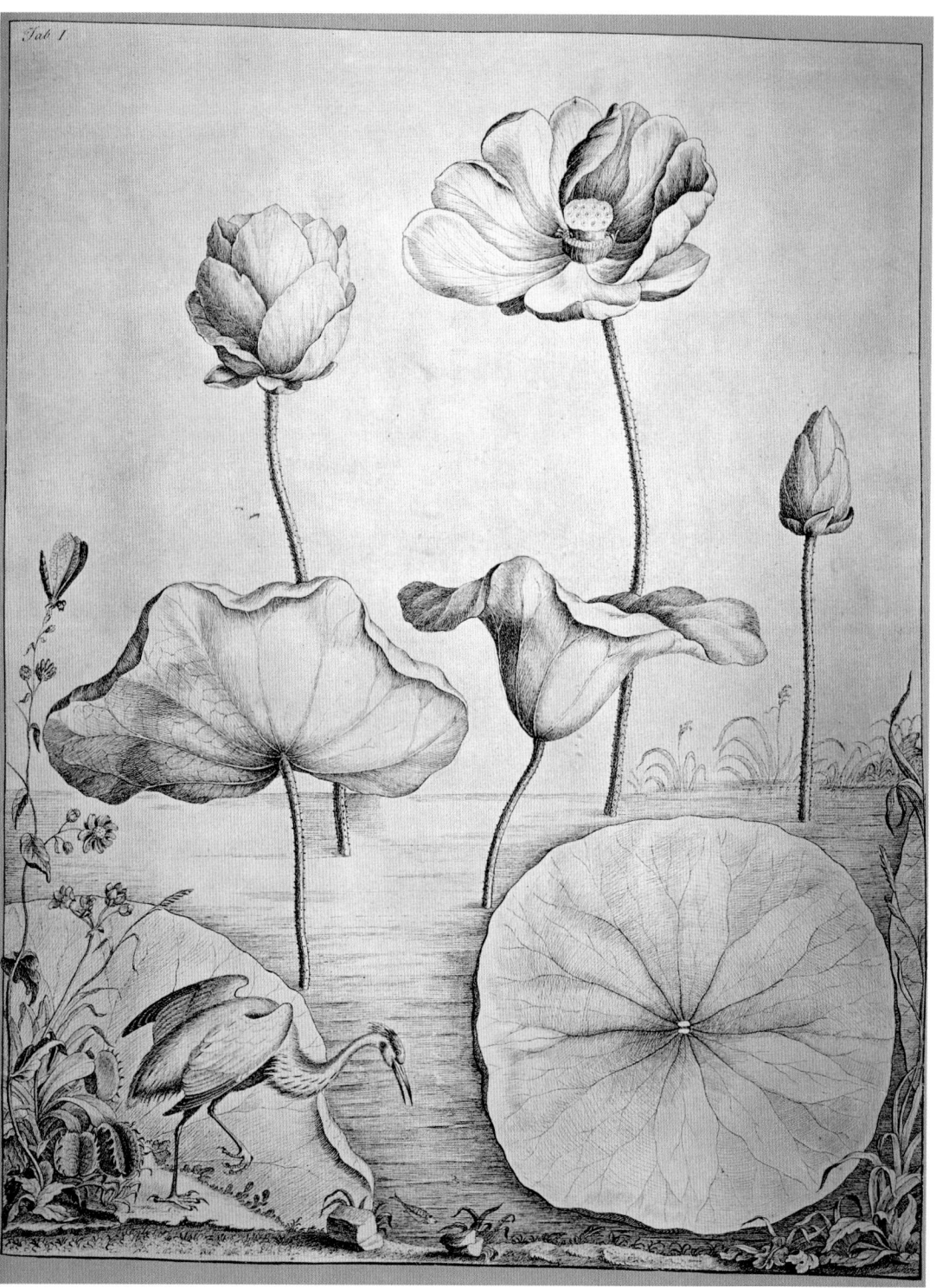

Franklin and from the works that he saw by artist-naturalists such as Mark Catesby and George Edwards, whose paintings of wildlife captured William's imagination.[22]

Most of Bartram's illustrations were done originally in pen and ink, which made corrections difficult. The drawings are also very meticulous, although they sometimes take as much "poetic license" as does Bartram's vivid narrative. Thomas Slaughter goes so far as to label them "surrealistic" since they combine "William's various ways of seeing into an extraordinary vision from the South, from his past, from nowhere to represent everything that he knows, that he saw, that's still alive in his head."[23] In his drawing *Colocasia*, for example, Bartram characteristically combines several subjects into one tableau that includes an American lotus, Venus flytrap, and great blue heron. Bartram frequently depicted several species on a single page, often paying little attention to the comparative size of his images. Slaughter points out that the enormous blossoms of the lotus tower over a bird that is "all out of proportion to the gigantic plants. . . . A dragonfly perches on a flower, which is perhaps the next meal of the Venus flytrap in the lower left corner; next in nature's consuming plan is the crane, which stalks a small fish that, in turn, is searching for plant life to eat."[24] We are drawn into Bartram's intense, almost voyeuristic observations. It is as if he is determined in his art—as in his writing—to reveal to us the true extent of the complexity, and yet the oneness, of the natural world.

About the American lotus, Bartram wrote in *Travels* that he viewed a lagoon that "presents a very singular and diverting scene, a delusive green wavy plain of *Nymphaea Nelumbo*, the surface of the water is overspread with its round, floating leaves, while these are shadowed by a forest of umbrageous leaves with gay flowers, waving to and fro on flexible stems, three or four feet high."[25] Bartram goes on to say that he had observed the lotus "along the Eastern shores of this continent, . . . particularly in a large pond or lake near Cape Fear river in North Carolina . . . and all over East Florida."[26]

Plate 60. (*facing*) William Bartram. *Colocosia (Lotus and Blue Heron)*, ca. 1774. Ink on paper. Courtesy of the George Smathers Library Digital Collection, University of Florida.

John Moran's photographs have documented many beautiful places throughout north central Florida. As a staff photographer for the *Gainesville Sun*, Moran produced numerous shots of the lakes, springs, and rivers and documented scenes that reached a wide audience. More recently, Moran has been working on his photography full-time and has written a book, *Journal of Light*, in which he talks about his photography and the stories behind the images. When, following a rise in water levels on Paynes Prairie, large portions of the basin burst into bloom with thousands of yellow lotuses, Moran grabbed his camera and headed for the savanna.

About his photograph "American Lotus," Moran wrote:

A year after the highest water levels in decades, receding water levels on Paynes Prairie yielded conditions ideal for an unusually profuse blossoming of American lotuses. Between Interstate 75 and U.S. 441, tens of thousands of the spectacular 10-inch flowers arose in unison to create a brightly colored mosaic on the land.

In the week before my visit to see the flowers, half a dozen people sought me out to urge me to get to the prairie with my cameras. Finally I arrive, and I'm not disappointed. Diving in, I'm awash in a sea of yellow and green, adrift in countless acres of impossible beauty. Where to begin my task of making pictures? I pause, and recall advice received years ago. Before you focus your camera, you must first focus yourself.

I switch to a close-up lens on my camera and become visually intimate with a single lotus blossom, standing inches away from its sweetly scented ring of undulating stamens, punctuated by a large, conical pistil. It's all so sexual, right out here in front of God and all those tourists bound for Orlando. I'm reminded of Carolus Linnaeus, the 18th-century Swedish naturalist regarded as the father of modern botany, who observed that, "The genitalia of plants we regard with delight; of animals with abomination; and of ourselves with strange thoughts."

The picture looks great in the viewfinder. A perfect summer sky smiles down on a thousand perfect flowers. But I've seen this picture a hundred times before, and on this day I'm looking for something a little different. It's time to refocus.

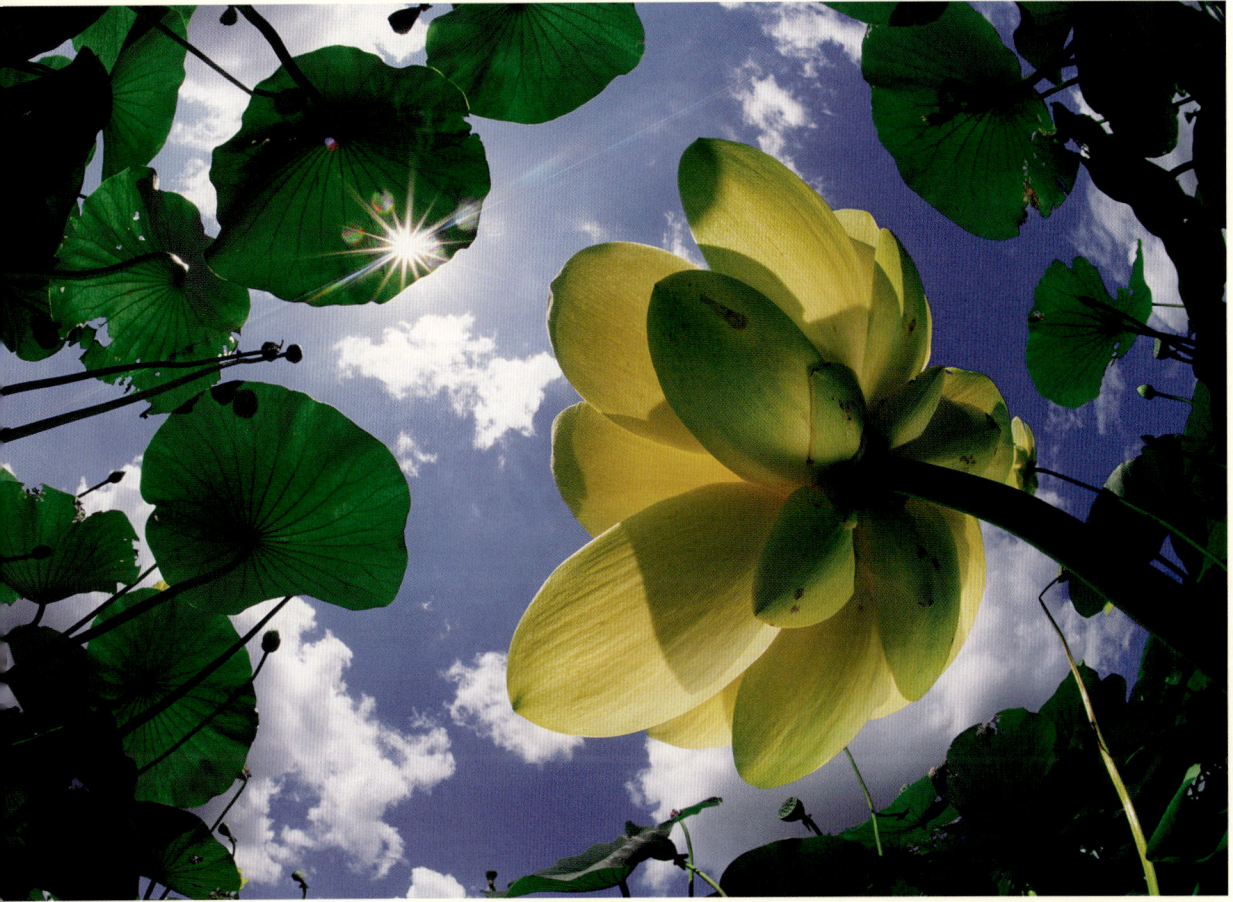

Something crawls across my sandaled foot and is gone. What, I wonder, does this flower show look like to the critters down there in the muck of the marsh? Soon I'm on my belly, crawling through a damp forest of spongy lotus stalks and spent flower petals.

Three feet overhead, a canopy of circular leaves shades my aimless wander. Finding an opening, I roll onto my back, and settle into the warm, fecund mud of Paynes Prairie. Gazing skyward, I reach for my camera and marvel at the snail's-eye view of the world that comes into focus.

The photograph was made with a 16mm full-frame fisheye lens on Fujichrome Velvia slide film. An aperture of f/22 provided extreme depth of field, and also produced a 14-point starburst pattern to the sun. A flexible silver fabric reflector provided fill-sunlight to the underside of the flower.[27]

Plate 61. John Moran. "American Lotus, Paynes Prairie State Preserve," 1999. Photograph. Courtesy of the artist.

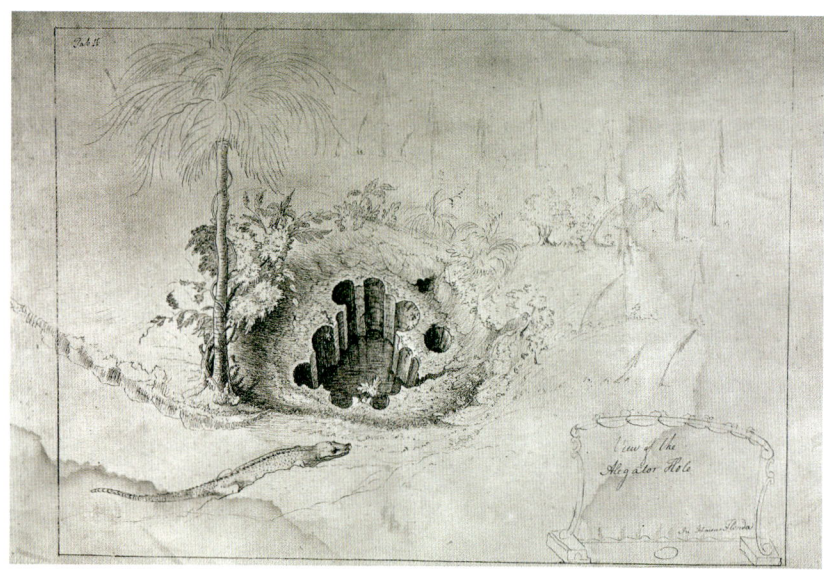

Plate 62. William Bartram. *View of a Gator Hole*, ca. 1774. Pen and ink on paper. Natural History Museum, London. Courtesy of the George Smathers Library Digital Collection, University of Florida.

Not surprisingly, Bartram was enthralled by the alligators that he encountered nearly everywhere along the St. Johns River and throughout the region. In his *Travels*, he returned to the topic again and again, his curiosity always trumping his fear of the dangerous reptiles. Even after describing his terror at the frequent attacks of the "monsters," Bartram refused to give up his investigation of their habits. "I now employed my time to the very best advantage in paddling close along shore," he writes, "but could not forbear looking now and then behind me, and presently perceived one of them coming up again. The water of the river hereabouts was shoal and very clear; the monster came up with the usual roar and menaces, and passed close by the side of my boat, when I could distinctly see a young brood of alligators, to the number of one hundred or more, following after her in a long train."[28]

Bartram goes on to describe the alligator's nest. "Still keeping close along shore, on turning a point of projection of the river bank, at once I beheld a great number of hillocks or small pyramids, resembling hay-cocks, ranged like an encampment along the banks. They stood fifteen or twenty yards distant from the water. I knew them to be the nests of the crocodile, having had a description of them before. . . . These nests being so great a curiosity to me, I was determined at all events immediately to land and examine them."[29]

In his drawing, *View of a Gator Hole*, Bartram depicts a "sink hole," a geological formation found in Florida in which the collapse of porous limestone has created a round crater that fills with water from the aquifer. Bartram called the formation an "Alligator Hole," noting that it was "lately formed by an extraordinary eruption or jet of water; it is one of those vast circular sinks, . . . it is about sixty yards over, and the surface of the water six or seven feet below the rim of the funnel or bason; the water is transparent, cool and pleasant to drink, and well stored with fish; a very large alligator at present is lord or chief."[30] Bartram's drawing attests to his determination to document his discoveries despite his trepidation.

One of the most celebrated and controversial descriptions recounted by William Bartram in his *Travels* was the famous alligator battle that he witnessed on Lake Dexter at the entrance to Mud Creek. While a number of his American contemporaries doubted the veracity of his description and thought he had exaggerated his account, European poets and writers, moved by the Romantic passion of his writing, were delighted with his rhapsodic narrative. The vivid account of the battle goes beyond prose—it verges on poetry.

> Behold him rushing forth from the flags and reeds. His enormous body swells. His plaited tail brandished high, floats upon the lake. The waters like a cataract descend from his opening jaws. Clouds of smoke issue from his dilated nostrils. The earth trembles with his thunder. When immediately from the opposite coast of the lagoon, emerges from the deep his rival champion. They suddenly dart upon each other. The boiling surface of the lake marks their rapid course, and a terrific conflict commences. They now sink to the bottom folded together in horrid wreaths. The water becomes thick and discoloured. Again they rise, their jaws clap together, reechoing through the deep surrounding forests. Again they sink, when the contest ends at the muddy bottom of the lake, and the vanquished makes a hazardous escape, hiding himself in the muddy turbulent waters and sedge on a distant shore. The proud victor exulting returns to the place of action. The shores and forests resound his dreadful roar, together with the triumphing shouts of the plaited tribes around, witnesses of the horrid combat.[31]

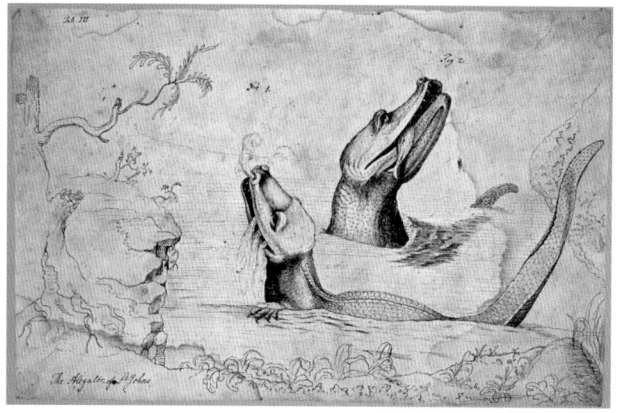

In his drawing of the "alegator," Bartram shows one beast grasping a fish in its jaws while a second reptile snorts clouds of steam from its nose. The Bartram scholar Thomas Slaughter writes: "Make no mistake about it, William's alligators are monsters on a heroic scale. His drawing [of the alligators] resembles medieval representations of the dragons battled by St. George more than the photos of modern naturalists."[32]

Plate 63. William Bartram. *The Alegator of the St. Johns*, ca. 1774. Pen and ink on paper. Natural History Museum, London. Courtesy of the George Smathers Library Digital Collection, University of Florida.

"I'm an image junkie," admits the Gainesville artist Hope White. "I'm happiest when I'm looking at images or making them."[33] White grew up in California and then spent time in Rome, where she had the opportunity to study the grand artworks in the Italian collections. "I thought it was all profoundly wonderful," she recalls, "and I started drawing from the sculptures." After her time in Europe, she moved to Oklahoma and then to New York City, where she began to work on her art in earnest. She began as a sculptor and still is attracted to it—especially relief sculpture, which allows her to explore the organic forms that she loves. "I love anything that has to do with water," says White. "If I hadn't been an artist, I might have been a biologist. Still, I don't feel that my images have to be biologically correct. I like to take an organic shape and play with it, alter the form a bit."[34]

White believes that it is the fanciful character of William Bartram's drawings that drew her to create her *Homage to William Bartram*. "I've always been fascinated by his drawings," she says. "They are so compelling. It was natural for me to try to re-create the alligator piece—the dragons of the St. Johns. I related to that. Dragons are part of the unknown, the unconscious."[35]

Homage is a mixed media work that combines relief sculpture with a painted base. While the relief is based on Bartram's *Alegator*, the painting was done from a photograph that White took on a boat trip on the St. Marys River. "The St. Marys looks primordial, but it is really quite polluted. I wanted to juxtapose the mythic St. Johns from Bartram's time with the reality of today's conditions."[36] White cast the relief of the alligators

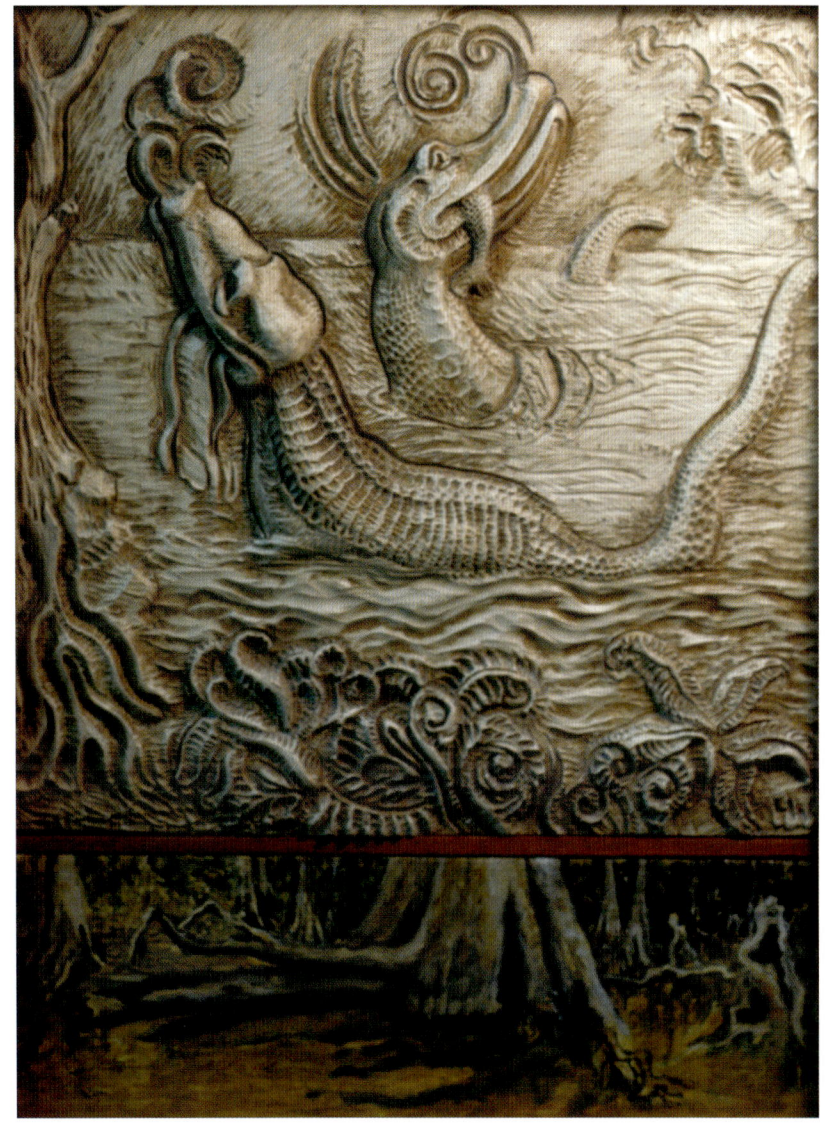

Plate 64. Hope White. *Homage to William Bartram*, 2002. Mixed media, 15 × 12 in. Private collection.

in hydrocal using a latex mold. The painting portion of the piece is oil on board. She enjoys working in mixed media because it parallels the webs and layers that she sees in nature. "The recognition of natural patterns is at the heart of my artistic exploration," says White. "Nature is always elegant in its economy, repeating certain forms and patterns, modifying and adapting them to meet the needs of a dynamic environment. But underlying all the modifications and adaptations is a hidden unity. Discovering the hidden patterns in nature and how they unify all things is my focus and my fascination."[37]

"To me," writes the Florida artist Reed Pedlow, "the alligator is a symbol, on several levels, of the profound ongoing conflict between man and nature and of my own personal struggle to understand my relationship to nature and my past. Having spent most of my childhood in rural Florida, my earliest memories are of the 'wilds' of the South—the dark swamps and blackwater rivers and lakes teeming with alligators and other wild creatures."[38]

Plate 65. Reed Pedlow. *Up the Creek*, **1993. Acrylic on canvas. Courtesy of the artist.**

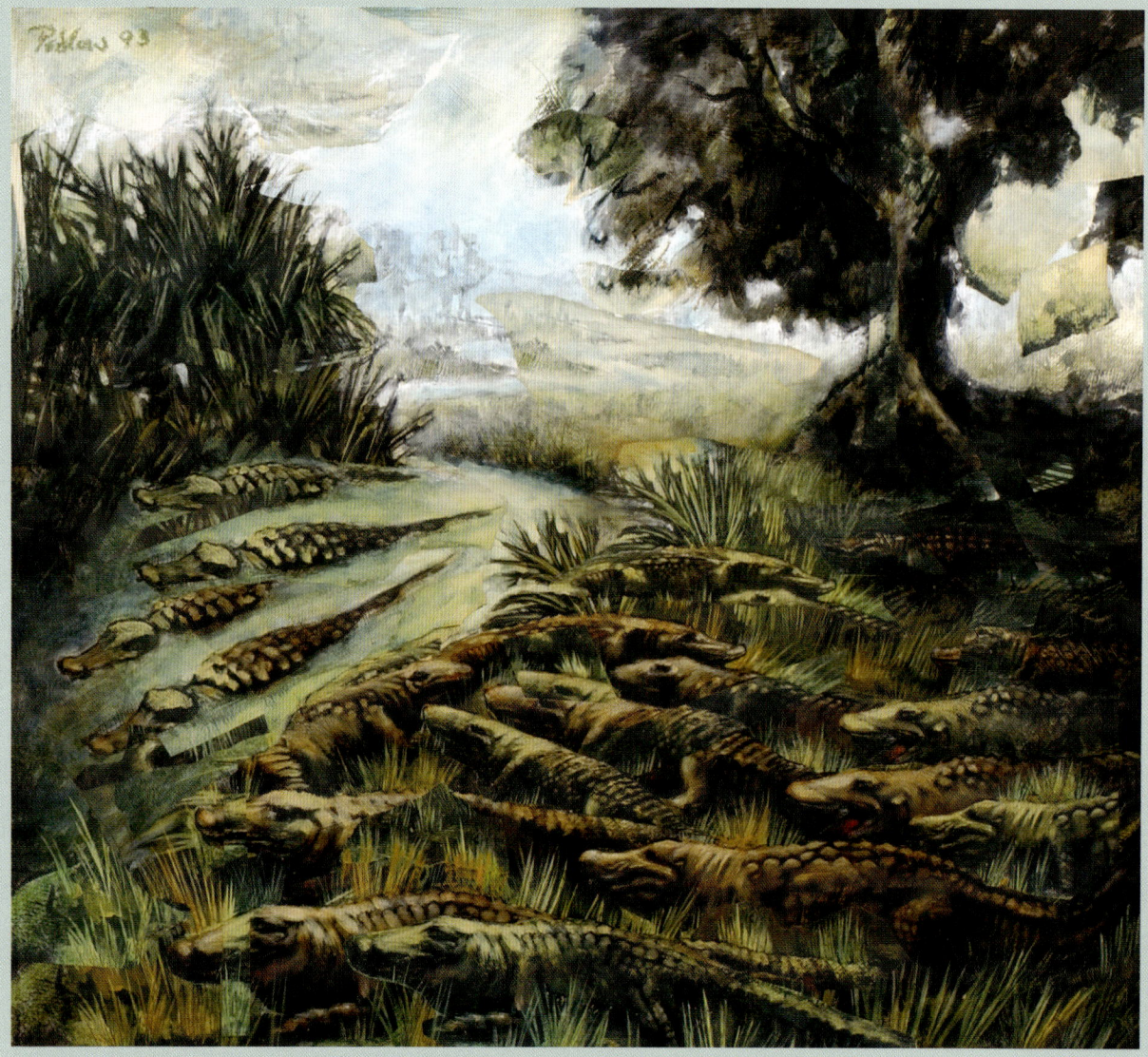

Reed Pedlow received his B.A. from Goddard College, Vermont, where he was a teaching assistant in the drawing and painting program. He has worked as an illustrator and graphic artist for many years and has shown his paintings throughout Florida as well as in Washington, D.C., Maryland, and Virginia.

In *Up the Creek*, Pedlow depicts a scene that might have come right out of Bartram's description of a "prodigious assemblage of crocodiles" that he witnessed during his travels along the St. Johns: "The river . . . from shore to shore, and perhaps near half a mile above and below me, appeared to be one solid bank of fish, of various kinds, pushing through this narrow pass of the St. Juan's into a little lake, on their return down river, and that the alligators were in such incredible numbers, and so close together from shore to shore, that it would have been easy to have walked across on their heads, had the animals been harmless."[39]

Once valued for its skin, by the 1950s the Florida alligator had been harvested to the brink of extinction. In the 1960s and 1970s, a new public awareness and the resulting environmental laws led to a rebound of alligator populations. Hailed as one of the great environmental success stories of our time, alligators continued to resurge for several decades only to be confronted by a similarly rapid rise in human population growth. Today there are an estimated 2 million alligators squeezed into an increasingly fragmented habitat. With Florida's human population approaching 18 million, confrontations between people and alligators are no longer rare.[40]

"As an adult," Pedlow writes, "I am saddened to see many of the very places that symbolized the mystery and spirituality of nature irreparable altered by human influence. As a delicate and unique landscape overburdened with accelerating population growth, Florida in many ways epitomizes the conflict between man and nature. The alligator is the hallmark of this struggle. My painting is an expression of my attempt to come to grips with this ongoing conflict."[41]

William Bartram was also enthralled with another Florida phenomenon, the "loud, sonorous, watchful savanna cranes."[42] The annual migration of this spectacular bird, which Bartram described as a "stately bird about six feet in length from the toes to the extremity of the beak when extended,"[43] brings thousands of them to the area around Orange Lake and Paynes Prairie—Bartram's Great Alachua Savanna. Around five thousand to seven thousand sandhill cranes spend November through February of each year in the region. With their distinctive gray plumage and red crowns, the cranes are a familiar sight as they fly in squadronlike formations, circling grandly above the marsh. Familiar too is their plaintive call, exotic yet strangely primitive, that can build to a raucous crescendo when the cranes are alarmed.

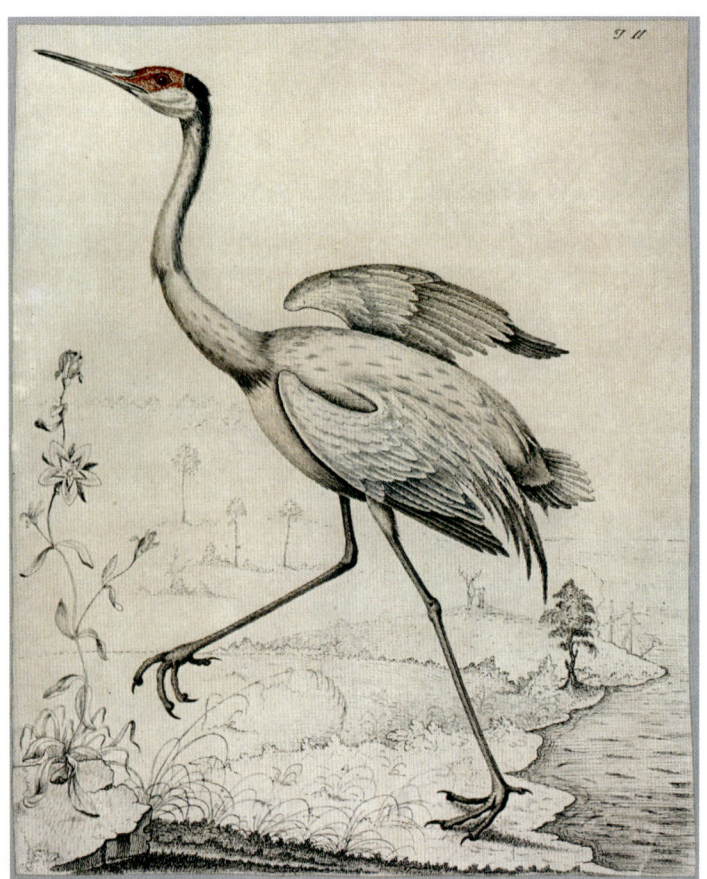

This drawing by Bartram of a "wattoola," the Indian name for the crane, depicts the crane in motion and possibly was inspired by Bartram's encounter with two cranes guarding their nest near the Alachua Savanna: "The wary, sharpsighted crane, circumspectly observed our progress. We saw a female of them sitting on her nest, and the male, her mate, watchfully traversing backwards and forwards, at a small distance; they suffered us to approach near them before they arose, when they spread their wings, running and tipping the ground with their feet some time; and then mounted aloft, soaring round and round over the nest."[44]

Plate 66. William Bartram. *Wattoola or Crane*, ca. 1774. Ink on paper. Courtesy of the George Smathers Library Digital Collection, University of Florida.

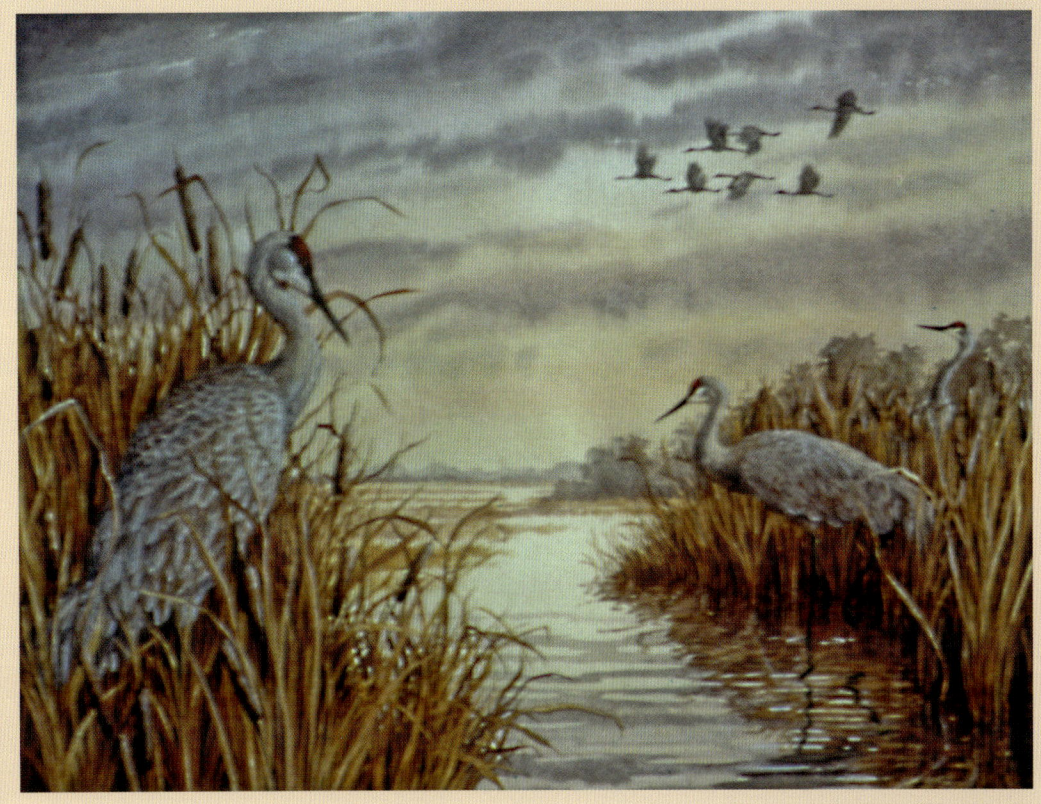

The artist Kate Barnes, who lives in Cross Creek, Florida, is a graduate of the Cleveland Art Institute. The influence of four years of study in Japan is reflected in the delicate, asymmetrical style of her Florida images. Her work is included in private and corporate collections in the United States, Japan, Australia, and throughout Europe. Barnes, a past member of the Alachua County Commission, has been active in local politics as an advocate for environmental protection. Her knowledge of local history and her interest in the unique character of north Florida's small communities has permeated her paintings, giving them a feeling of nostalgia. Her watercolor painting *Sandhill Cranes on Paynes Prairie* is infused with the dusky light and muted palette of a north Florida autumn.

Plate 67. Kate Barnes. *Sandhill Cranes on Paynes Prairie*, 1982. Watercolor on paper, 22 × 30 in. Courtesy of the artist.

Bartram's lively drawings, combined with his effusive narrative, provide us with an inspired vision of what Florida in general and the St. Johns River region in particular looked and felt like over two hundred years ago. Together, he and his father documented over 320 new plants and sent samples to their English patrons, a prodigious feat that earned them both a place in the annals of American natural history.

Titian Ramsey Peale, the youngest son of Charles Wilson Peale, the founder of America's first museum, was only seventeen years old when he embarked on a trip to Florida to explore the wilderness described by William Bartram in his *Travels*. Indeed, young Titian brought a copy of *Travels* with him to read on the trip.[45] He left Philadelphia on Christmas Day 1817 with his friend George Ord, a zoologist, and sailed to Savannah, Georgia, where they were joined by William Maclure, a wealthy geologist, and Thomas Say, a naturalist and the great-nephew of William Bartram. According to Say, it was Maclure's idea to follow in "the track of Bartram,"[46] and the four men planned to do just that. However, they were thwarted by Spanish authorities and reports of hostile Indians and had to cut short their adventure and return to Philadelphia. In a letter to his friend John Melsheimer, Say concluded that their "voyage of discovery was rendered abortive."[47]

Despite the fact that they were unable to stay as long as they hoped or to truly "follow Bartram's track," they were able to sail up the St. Johns River as far as Picolata, and Titian, who was an enthusiastic sportsman, was able to shoot a number of birds to use as specimens for his illustrations. An account of his Florida adventure, written after his return by either his second wife, Lucy, or his grandson, Lincoln, describes some of his experiences on the St. Johns. He reported seeing numerous "Porpoises," fishing pelicans and whooping cranes and mentions several times the "little Egret," which he calls a "Snowy Heron," likely a snowy egret. He also mentioned seeing the ruins of plantations along the river, many of them "deserted or burned," but one with a fine grove of orange trees, "upwards of five hundred trees, many of them almost breaking with their load of fruit."[48] The party marveled at the beauty of the Florida wilderness, reporting that "from the north end of Fort George Island where there is a high range of hills covered with Live Oak, they enjoyed the finest prospect they had ever seen in Florida—a wide expanse of Sea, besides the nearer islands, lakes and lagoons." Another fine view was enjoyed "from St. Johns Bluff the highest front of land yet seen," but they reported that "it was here the town of St. John was to have been built, nothing however was to be seen but two poor huts."[49]

After returning to Philadelphia, Peale went on to a somewhat uneven career—he accompanied Stephen Long's expedition to the Rocky Mountains in 1819–20, traveled to Florida again in 1824, spent three years, 1829–32, traveling from Maine to Columbia, and joined the first U.S. expedition to the South Seas in 1838. Early successes—he illustrated insects for Thomas Say's publications and contributed to Alexander Wilson's *American Ornithology*—were followed by devastating troubles. The family's museum in Philadelphia closed, and Peale's second wife and his daughter both died. After several traumatic years, Titian Peale took a job at the Patent Office in Washington, D.C., where he spent the rest of his career.

Although he never regained his position as a successful naturalist and illustrator, he did continue to make contributions to that profession. He developed a lithographic process for printing scientific illustrations, took up the new hobby of photography, and proved himself a competent artist in a series of oil paintings.

Plate 68. Titian Ramsey Peale. *Glossy Ibis, Red-breasted Snipe and Pectoral Sandpiper.* Plate B-23 from Bonaparte's Supplement to Alexander Wilson's *American Ornithology* (Philadelphia, 1825). Courtesy of the George Smathers Library Digital Collection, University of Florida.

Titian Peale's illustration is typical of several of the images he drew for the supplement to Wilson's book. Peale often groups together birds whose habitat is similar, but the details of the surrounding environment remain sketchy. Of the ten plates that he drew for the Bonaparte supplement, only plate B-9, *Wild Turkey, male and female*, provides specific details of the surrounding habitat. Because of the generic character of the background, *Three Birds* could represent any area of the bird's range, which included Florida and the Caribbean. The specimen was, however, likely collected in Florida during one of the two trips that Peale made to the area.

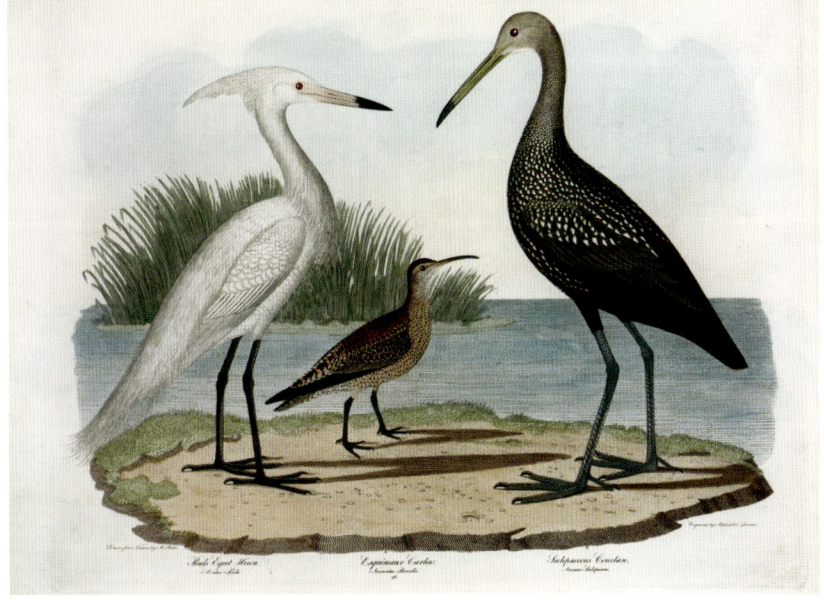

Not many hours after we had crossed the [sand] bar, we perceived the star-like glimmer of the light in the great lantern at the entrance of the St. John's River. This was before daylight; and, as the crossing of the sand-banks or bars, which occur at the mouths of all streams of this peninsula is difficult, and can be accomplished only when the tide is up, one of the guns was fired as a signal for the government pilot. The good man, it seemed, was unwilling to leave his couch, but a second gun brought him in his canoe alongside. The depth of the channel was barely sufficient. My eyes, however, were not directed toward the waters, but on high, where flew some thousands of snowy Pelicans, which had fled affrighted from their resting grounds. How beautifully they performed their broad gyrations, and how matchless, after a while, was the marshalling of their files as they flew past us.
—John James Audubon,
Ornithological Biography, 1834

JOHN JAMES AUDUBON is best known for his monumental work *The Birds of America*. The book contains 1,065 bird portraits reproduced from the original artwork by copper-plate engravings. It was published in Edinburgh and London between 1826 and 1838. The complete work, published in four huge leather-bound volumes, sold in England for 182 pounds, in America for $1,000.[50] A later work, *Ornithological Biography*, was issued between 1832 and 1839 and contained over three thousand text pages. This massive work contains "the life histories and detailed accounts of the habits of all the birds depicted in *The Birds of America*."[51]

Audubon's life story has been so romanticized that it is sometimes difficult to distinguish fact from fiction. He was born out of wedlock in the West Indies and was sent to France for his education. At eighteen, he came to America to manage his father's estate near Philadelphia, but left after a quarrel with the estate's overseer. Over the next few years he drifted from one failed enterprise to another, got married, and developed an interest in natural history. He began painting birds using a new technique of sketching recently killed birds rather than working from stuffed specimens. Audubon stated, "The birds, almost all of them, were killed by myself, after I had examined their motions and habits . . . and were regularly drawn on the spot where I procured them."[52] Like his predecessor William Bartram, Audubon proved to be a dismal failure as a businessman, but he distinguished himself as an artist, a scientist and an intrepid traveler who popularized the study of nature—especially birds—at a time when most of his contemporaries looked at the wilderness and its inhabitants as "nuisances."

In 1826, mired in one frustrating defeat after another, Audubon sailed for England to try to find a publisher for his *Birds of America*. Three years later he returned victorious. Taking his wife and family back to England with him, he set to work on the *Ornithological Biography*, a separate volume that would complement *The Birds of America*. In 1831, he traveled to Florida, promising to go farther down the peninsula than any of his naturalist predecessors. Because he had won coveted membership in London's Royal Society, he was able to obtain U.S. permission to travel on a government cutter, the *Spark*, which regularly patrolled Florida's wilderness rivers. Once aboard and sailing up the St. Johns, Audubon did not find Florida to his liking. "I have been deceived most shamefully about the Floridas," he wrote to his wife. "My account of what I have or shall see of Florida will be far, very far, from corroborating the flowery saying of Mr. Barton [Bartram]."[53] In his journal, he wrote: "The river [the St. Johns] did not seem to me equal in beauty to the fair Ohio; the shores in many places are low and swampy. . . . Fully one hundred miles from the mouth of the river . . . the fog was so thick that neither of the shores could be seen and yet the river was not a mile in breadth. The 'blind mosquitoes' covered every object, even the cabin, and so wonderfully abundant were these tormentors, that they more than once fairly extinguished the candles whilst I was writing my journal."[54]

He later described the St. Johns area as a place where "all that is not mud, mud, mud is sand, sand, sand; where the fruit is so sour that it is not eatable; and where in place of singing birds and golden fishes you have . . . alligators, snakes, and scorpions."[55]

In what seems to us today to be a terrible and excessive slaughter of wildlife, Audubon often speaks of shooting "30 or 40" birds before getting the right specimen for his model while clearly taking great pride in his marksmanship as did Titian Peale before him. It's important to recall that, in the early 1800s, naturalists had no camera, no binoculars, no camcorder—in short no way to get a good close look at their subject other than shooting it. The alternative was to use the stuffed birds favored by those Audubon termed "closet ornithologists." Hunting was also the cultural norm in the 1800s and a quite socially acceptable, if not required, behavior for a gentleman adventurer. Audubon wrote in his *Biography*: "I may here tell you that all the roosting places of the Anhinga which I have seen were over the water, either on the shore in the midst of some stagnant pool; and this situation they seemed to select because there they can enjoy the first gladdening rays of the morning sun, or bask in the blaze of its noontime splendor, and also observe with greater ease the approach of their enemies, as they betake themselves to it after feeding, and remain there until hunger urges them to fly off. There, trusting to the extraordinary keenness of their beautiful bright eyes in spying the marauding sons of the forest, or the not less dangerous enthusiast, who, probably like yourself, would venture through mud and slime up to his very neck, to get within rifle shot of a bird so remarkable in form and manner, the Anhingas, or 'Grecian Ladies' stand erect, with their wings and tail fully or partially spread out in the sunshine, whilst their long slender necks and heads are thrown as it were in every direction by the most curious and sudden jerks and bendings."[56]

After leaving Florida, Audubon spent time in Canada studying migrating birds. He also made a trip to Missouri to collect material for his next book, *The Viviparous Quadrupeds of North America*. While continuing to work on the production of his books, he lived out his last years in New York City at a woodland estate he purchased in 1842. He died there in 1851.

Despite his dislike of the region, Audubon did find abundant birdlife to observe, and he produced some exquisite paintings based on his Florida misadventures. However, of the numerous examples that he illustrated, only one bird is shown specifically along the St. Johns River—the glossy ibis (*Ibis falcinellus*). In his *Ornithological Biography*, Audubon noted: "The Glossy Ibis is of exceedingly rare occurrence in the United States, where it appears only at long and irregular intervals, like a wanderer who has lost his way. . . . Its flight resembles that of its companion, the White Ibis, and it is probable that it feeds on the same kind of crustaceous animals, and breeds on low bushes in the same great association as that species. . . . I have given the figure of a male bird in superb plumage, procured in Florida, near a woodcutter's cabin, a view of which is also given."[57]

Unlike his predecessor Titian Peale, Audubon has included more details of the surrounding area in his depiction of the glossy ibis. He shows the ibis on the bank of a river. On the opposite bank are a woodcutter's cabin and several outbuildings. According to his notes, Audubon recollects that the bird was painted from one he procured when he visited a group of woodcutters along the St. Johns and so the woodcutter's cabin was included in the background of the finished painting. Audubon's story "The Lost One," which chronicles a tale told to him by a Florida woodcutter, is an accurate reflection of the woodlands near the St. Johns and along the banks of the river. In addition to including more details, Audubon also depicts his ibis in a dramatic pose that activates the composition and brings the subject alive.

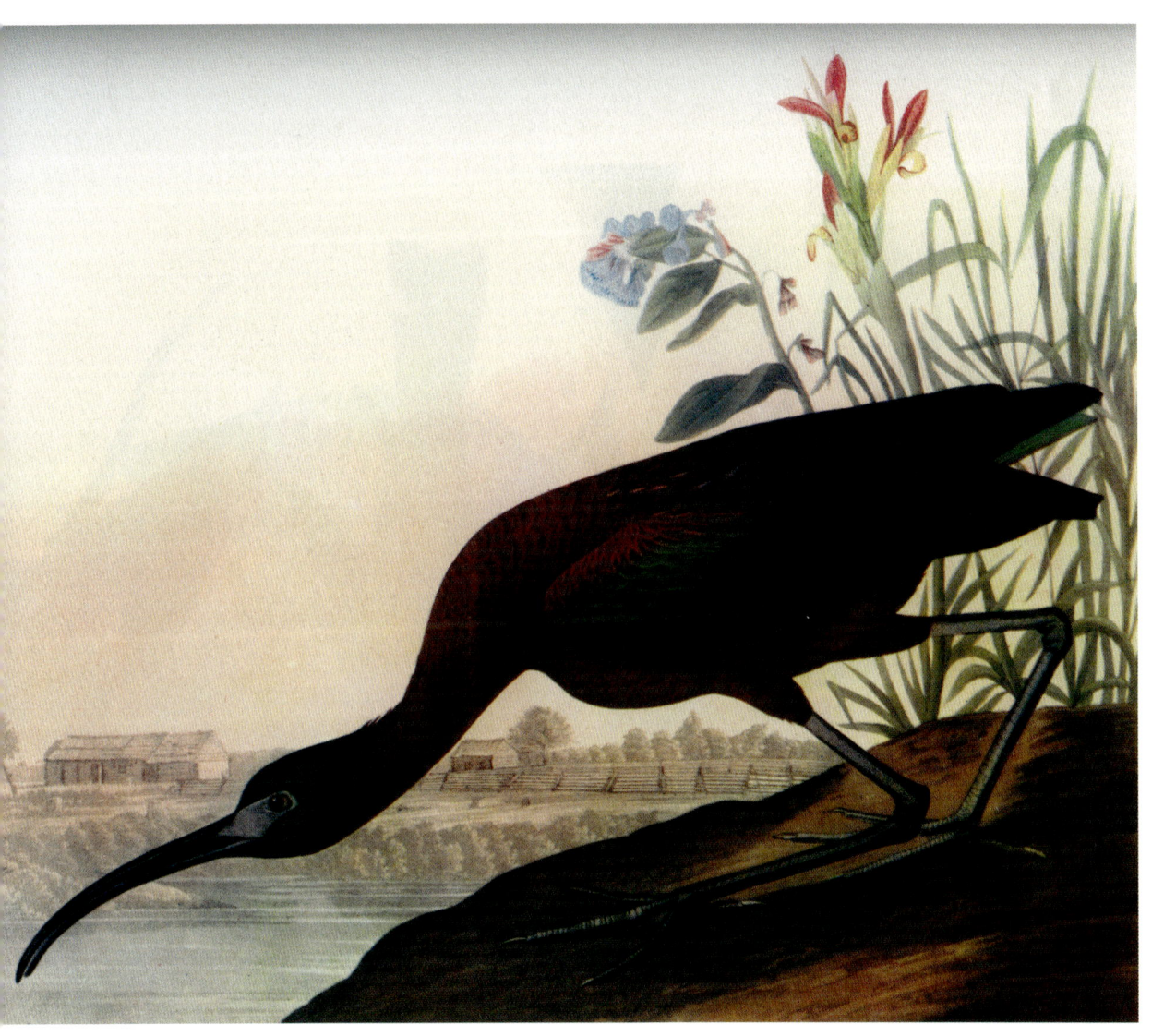

Plate 69. John James Audubon. *Glossy Ibis,*
1832. Plate 387 from *The Birds of America*
(London).

On a warm summer day in [1563], an English slave ship stopped to take on fresh water upriver and found a colony of [French] soldiers, which, despite the abundance of fish and game in the surrounding woods, was not doing so well. Englishman John Sparke, who recorded the visit, seemed dumbfounded that the French were not able to sustain themselves from a natural bounty "with commodities . . . more than are yet known to any man." After reporting a rich inventory of flora and fauna, Sparke casually mentioned he also saw a strange animal at the edge of the river Mai [the St. Johns], quenching its thirst. It was, said Sparke, "a beast with one horn, which, coming to the river to drink, putteth the same into the water before he drinketh." By Sparke's description, it was a unicorn.

—Bill Belleville, *River of Lakes*

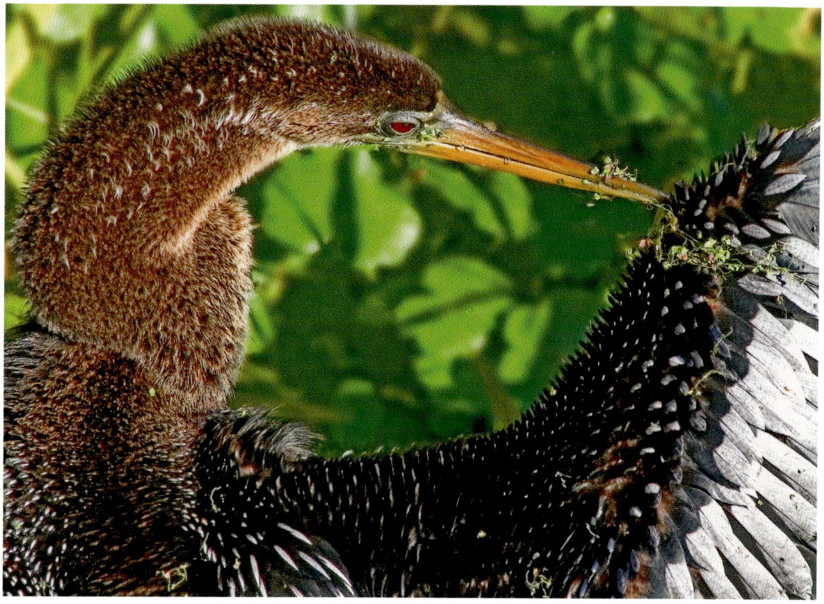

Plate 70. Dominick Martino. "Preening Anhinga," 2006. Photograph. Courtesy of the artist.

Dominick Martino is a wildlife photographer who spends many hours each week photographing the birds and animals of north central Florida. One of his favorite spots to find his quarry is at the Paynes Prairie State Preserve in southern Alachua County. This photo of a preening anhinga was taken along the banks of Lake Wauberg, where anhingas are often seen perched in the trees, wings outstretched to dry in the warm Florida sun. Martino has the great advantage of having modern photographic equipment and can go "hunting" with his camera instead of a rifle. He has photographed hundreds of birds in the St. Johns watershed along with numerous other wildlife subjects.

The naturalist's love affair with the St. Johns basin has been an ongoing romance that has not yet ended. Artists such as John Moran, Reed Pedlow, Dominick Martino, and Kate Barnes are still captivated by the magical diversity and beauty of the natural flora and fauna of the region. It is still a place where "everything is considered possible."

6 { A Sportsmen's Paradise

Fishing, Hunting, and Recreation in the St. Johns Region

FISHING HAS BEEN A FLORIDA OBSESSION since the first humans arrived over ten thousand years ago. With more than seven thousand miles of freshwater shoreline, it's easy to understand why fishing has always been an important component of Florida's culture whether for sport or for a livelihood. When Florida became increasingly accessible to sports enthusiasts during the steamboat era, fishermen came from all over to participate in their favorite pastime. Businesses sprang up along the waterways to cater to the needs and fantasies of the sportsmen.

The St. Johns River is home to about 170 kinds of fish, 55 of which are freshwater species. Because the river is a mix of fresh- and salt water, many fish have adapted to both environments. The northern edge of Lake George marks the boundary between the freshwater moving north from the marshes and the salty tidal flow that reaches inland for 110 miles. Although largemouth bass are the most frequently mentioned sports fish to be found in the river, it is also home to bluegill and bream, mangrove snapper and redfish, and saltwater mullet, along with a host of lesser-known varieties.

The popularity of the St. Johns as a fishing mecca pre-dates the arrival of the Europeans by thousands of years. Throughout the region, the Native population used the resources of the river as a source of food. The bones of fish and the shells of fresh- and saltwater mollusks can be found in every Indian mound and midden. The techniques used by the Indians to trap fish were varied and included, in addition to baited lines, spears, harpoons, and weirs—or traps—which were constructed in the middle of the river where the current would direct the fish into the barricade.

In late December 1958, . . . I visited my sister in Rockledge, Florida [and] . . . planned a fishing trip on the St. Johns River. I departed the boat ramp as the sun began to appear on the horizon. One hour later, I hooked and landed a seven-pound largemouth bass. I had hooked the bass, but it was I who really got hooked. I decided that I wanted to live near this magnificent river.
Leroy Wright, *Saving the St. Johns River*

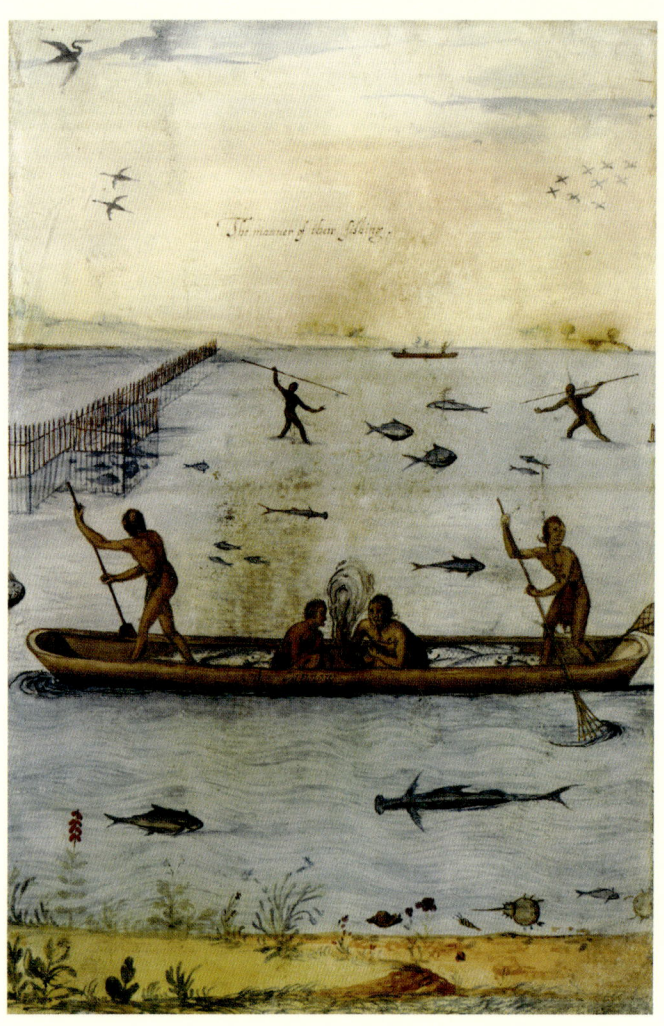

The manner of their fishing.

Plate 71. John White. *Indians Fishing*, 1585. Watercolor on paper, 13 × 9¼ in. British Museum, London.

The English explorer and artist John White's watercolor of Indians fishing shows a weir, or trap, made of upright poles. In the background, two Indians use spears to hunt their quarry. The dugout canoe in the foreground is filled with harvested fish. An interesting detail is the two Indians in the dugout's center who have gathered around a fire. Several ancient dugouts found in Florida have circular burned area in their bottoms, which almost certainly resulted from the practice of carrying fire—possibly for night fishing or for cooking the fish while traveling. According to Robin Brown, the fires were built in the canoe bottoms in circular enclosures filled with sand or in basins of clay.[1] White's painting depicts several varieties of fish including gar, bream, and catfish. Bones of these fish have been found at numerous midden sites along the St. Johns River.

White was sent in 1587 by Sir Walter Raleigh to act as governor of a colony of English settlers on Chesapeake Bay. During the time he spent in America, White made a number of sketches of the southeastern Algonkians who lived nearby, documenting the people, their villages, and their customs. He also made drawings of the local plants and animals. He took these sketches back to England with him, where he worked up more detailed paintings based on his notes. Theodore de Bry may have used White's paintings as models for many of his own engravings of the New World Indians. Thomas Hariot, a friend of Sir Walter Raleigh who stayed for a year in the Virginia Colony, published these illustrations in 1590 in a book titled *A Brief and True Report of the New Found Land of Virginia*.

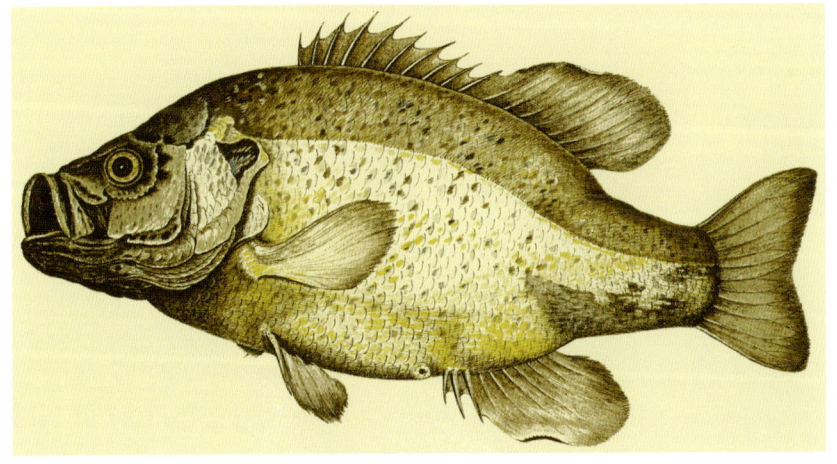

Plate 72. William Bartram. *Great Yellow Bream, called Old Wife of the St. Johns*, ca. 1774. Ink and watercolor on paper. Original in the British Museum. Courtesy of Alecto Historical Editions, London.

This drawing by William Bartram of a great yellow bream was likely done near Lake Dexter in western Volusia County northwest of present-day DeLand. Bartram was enchanted with the beauty of the yellow bream, which he also called the "sun fish." He described it in great detail in his *Travels*: "What a most beautiful creature is this fish before me! Gliding to and fro, and figuring in the still clear waters, with his orient attendants and associates: the yellow bream or sun fish. . . . He is a fish of prodigious strength and activity . . . a warrior in a gilded coat of mail; and gives no rest or quarter to small fish, which he preys upon. They are delicious food and in great abundance."[2]

The community of Enterprise is one of the oldest interior towns along the St. Johns. Cornelius Taylor, a cousin of president Zachary Taylor, led a group of five families and about twenty-five single men to this wilderness outpost in 1841. At that time, St. Augustine—some one hundred miles to the north—was said to be the nearest white settlement. Because of continued problems with the Seminole Indians, the settlers constructed a fort. In 1843, Taylor was elected to the Territorial Legislature, and he successfully introduced a law naming Enterprise the county seat of what was then "Mosquito County."[3]

Prior to 1858, when the Seminoles were finally driven from the area, few steamboats on the St. Johns attempted to navigate the river south of Palatka. A pioneer in luring adventurous travelers farther south was a Vermont native, Captain Jacob Brock, who came to Florida in the 1840s. An astute businessman, Brock foresaw the potential for a tourist mecca in the little-known area around Lake Monroe. In the early 1850s, he built Brock House near the settlement of Enterprise. It soon became a haven for sportsmen who came to fish, hunt, and relax at the exotic wilderness lodge. He had already established a steamship line that ran two boats, the *Darlington* and the *Hattie Brock*, from Jacksonville to Enterprise. Building the hotel on Lake Monroe allowed him to control a large part of the growing tourist trade.

Enterprise was "the southernmost outpost of civilization," according to James Sterling, who wrote *Letters from the Slave States*. At this time, it was truly America's Playground. South Florida was not yet in Flagler's sights. Brock House was part of the adventure found here. The two-and-a-half story, 110-foot-long Brock House stood broadside to the lake. Its open porch overlooked the long wharf of the terminus where wooden tracks facilitated the transportation of goods to and from the steamers. Beyond this point lay the vast Lake Monroe.

A trip from Jacksonville to Brock House required spending the night in Palatka so that the boat captains could traverse the narrow and crooked Upper St. Johns River by daylight. Snakes slithered onboard from hanging moss, alligators got entangled in paddle wheels, and tree branches as sturdy as baseball bats swatted the ship. Nevertheless, the otherwise lovely nine-dollar ride, perfumed by the surrounding orange groves from Jacksonville through the yet-untamed wilds, was fascinating to adventurous travelers.

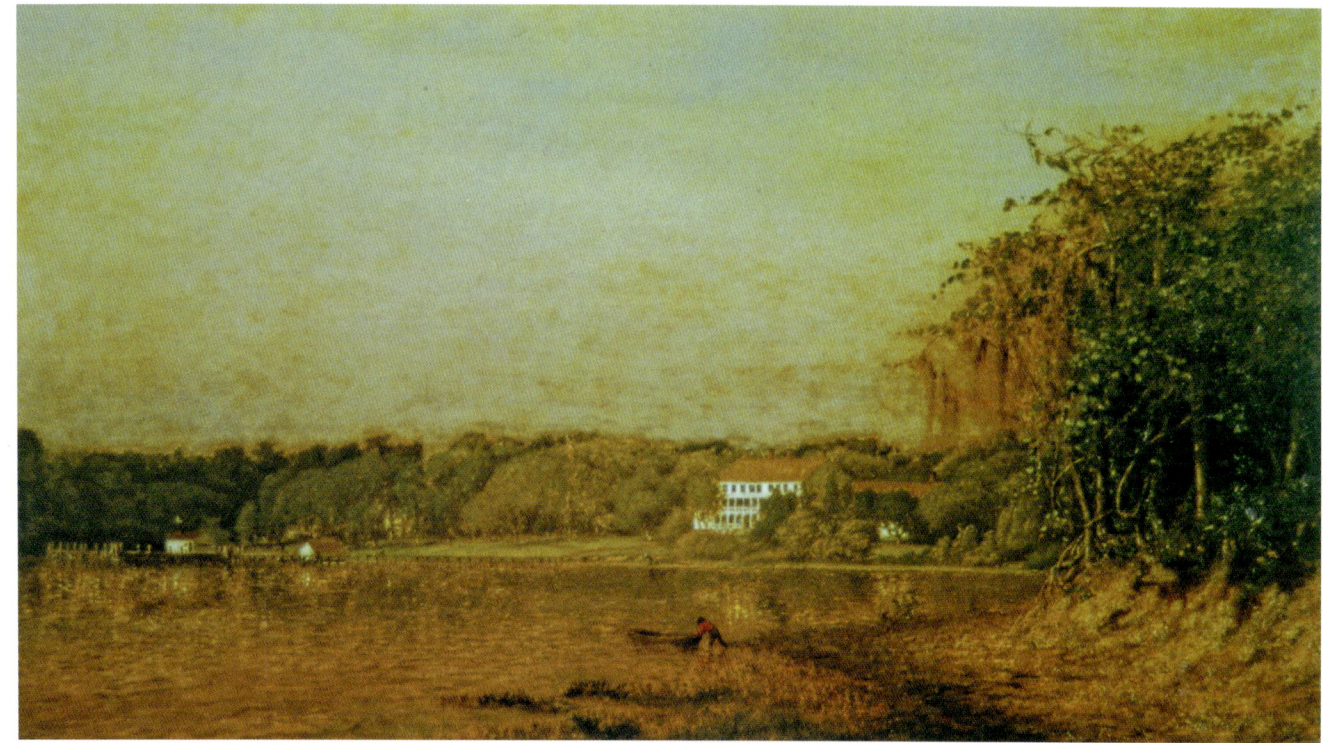

Alexander Wyant, who had been born in Ohio but moved to New York to study painting with his mentor, George Inness, traveled to Florida in the 1870s to paint the scenery. His *Enterprise at Lake Monroe* depicts the famous Brock House grandly situated on the edge of the lake, framed by moss-covered trees.

Filled to capacity, the remote but comfortable refuge was a sportsman's paradise. The *St. Augustine Examiner*, in its August 21, 1867, issue, printed a writer's testimony praising the Brock House as "a fine hotel commanding an extensive use of scenery, unsurpassed in Italy."[4] The room rate of $3.50 per day, the beautifully wild and fragrant landscape, and the dinner fare, which included venison and fish caught within a mile of the hotel, attracted many visitors. Brock House guests could also hunt deer, quail, and turkey; boat along the river to Lake Harney; and frolic at the sulfur-laden Green Spring. The esteemed guests, including presidents, artists, and tycoons, might take with them a lunch or snack box that was provided by the hotel.

Plate 73. Alexander Wyant. *Enterprise at Lake Monroe*, 1871. Oil on canvas, 15 × 27 in. Sam and Robbie Vickers Florida Collection.

It is easy to imagine Brock House guests having their food prepared as they readied to walk to the spring, down the north shore of Lake Monroe. They could take a small boat into the lake to fish, or book a day trip on a small steamer that was designed to traverse the St. Johns River above Lake Monroe. Perhaps they would even pack a lunch for the boat ride returning them to their northbound train or oceangoing steamer in Jacksonville, having ended their winter sojourn to Florida's semi-tropical wilds.

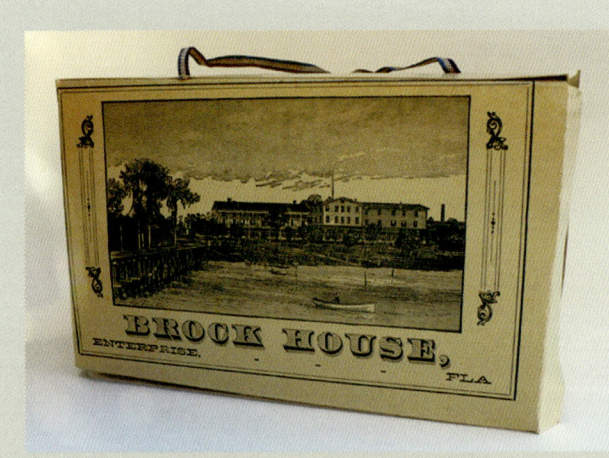

Plate 74. Brock House lunch box, n.d. Photolithography on card stock, 4¼ × 2⅜ in. Robert Gair Manufacturer, New York. Courtesy of Gary and Teresa Monroe.

The Volusia County historian Tom Baskett observes: "The Brock House lunch box turned out to be a souvenir for St. Johns River tourists hoping to capture their Florida adventure. It also worked as an advertising piece, and was produced by a pioneer mass-packager, Robert Gair. Most of all, this box figured in the Brock House experience itself—guests conveniently exploring Florida's semi-tropical wilds away from the inn. With prepared lunches in hand, visitors could take various day excursions that helped make this Enterprise hotel famous."[5] This seemingly inconsequential but functional box, sporting what would become an iconic line drawing of the Brock House, depicts the perfect Florida moment of yesteryear. It contrasts a civilized, safe environment and the gentility of the inn with the primordial darkness of the junglelike natural environment accented by gators and snakes.

Winslow Homer has become one America's most beloved artists. Because he was also an avid fisherman, a number of his finest works were inspired by his adventures along the St. Johns and its tributaries. He was born in Boston in February 1836, where he became interested in art and trained as an illustrator at the lithography shop of John Bufford. In 1859, at age twenty-three, he moved to New York, where he rented a studio and began to work as a freelance illustrator for *Harper's Weekly*. He continued his art education at the National Academy of Design, but made frequent trips on assignment for *Harper's*—he covered the inauguration of President Abraham Lincoln in 1861 and was one of the magazine's major illustrators during the Civil War.

In December 1885, he made his first trip to Florida, where he stayed three months visiting Jacksonville, Tampa, and the Florida Keys. He also visited the Brock House at Enterprise on Lake Monroe. On this and later trips to Enterprise, Homer gathered material for a number of angling paintings. Many of the Florida paintings show fishermen in small boats. Nicolai Cikovsky Jr., curator of American Art at the National Gallery of Art in Washington, writes, "At their best, these watercolors are notable for their fluid washes and delicate harmonies of color."[6]

This painting, now in the Museum of Fine Arts, Boston, has been appraised as one of the most successful of the St. Johns series. Patti Hannaway, in *Winslow Homer in the Tropics*, writes: "The beauty of the lagoon is disturbed only by the two men in the boat, one whose fishing line is pulled taut by a catch. In the background the trees are densely hung with Spanish moss—the foreground water is filled with shimmering, rippled reflections. . . . The expressive color scheme is warmly tropical. Even the grays are alive."[7]

Plate 75. Winslow Homer. *Thornhill Bar (Florida)*, 1886. Watercolor over graphite pencil on paper, 14 × 20 in. The Museum of Fine Arts, Boston. Gift of Mrs. R. B. Osgood, 39.620.

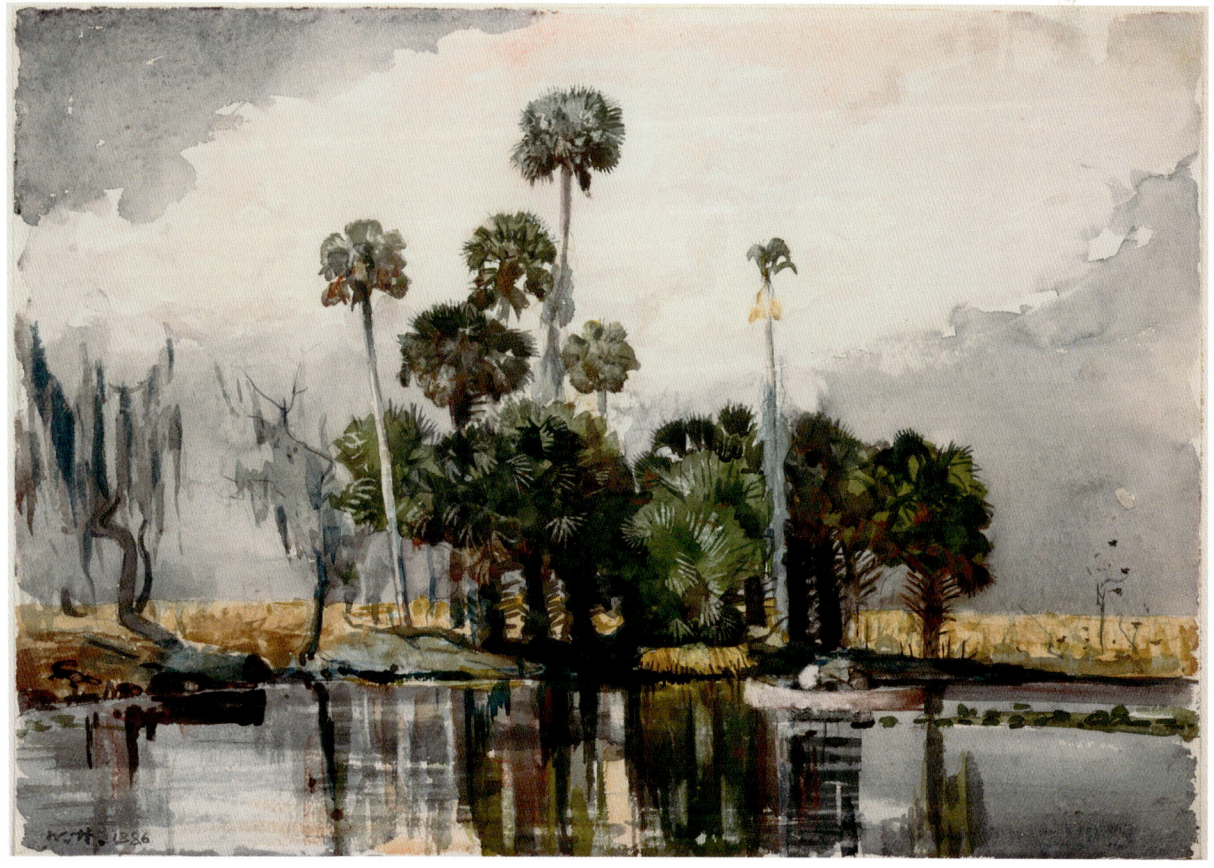

Each winter, American shad migrate more than two hundred miles up-stream from the Atlantic Ocean to beyond Lake Harney, which lies half in Volusia County and half in Seminole. North of the lake, sports anglers fish for shad downstream to the mouth of Lake Jesup, casting from shore or trolling from boats. Bill Belleville, who has been among the shad fishermen, writes: "Shad do this [migrate to spawn] in other rivers along the eastern seaboard; but they always begin their migration the earliest in Florida, in this river [the St. Johns]. Each individual shad, some say, is trying to return to the exact spot where it was first born, genetically encoded to find that place of refuge where it knows its spawn will be safe. It is natural selection at work, a seasonal celebration of its own survival. . . . These shad journey here in a single-minded pursuit, seldom letting mortal needs like hunger stand in their way. . . . The shad that are freshest from the ocean not only run hard when hooked but also jump often, the blue iridescence of the sea still flashing from their bodies with each brave leap."[8]

Plate 76. Anonymous. *Shad Fishing in Florida*. From *Harper's Weekly*, vol. 29, p. 204. Courtesy of the Matheson Museum, Gainesville, Florida.

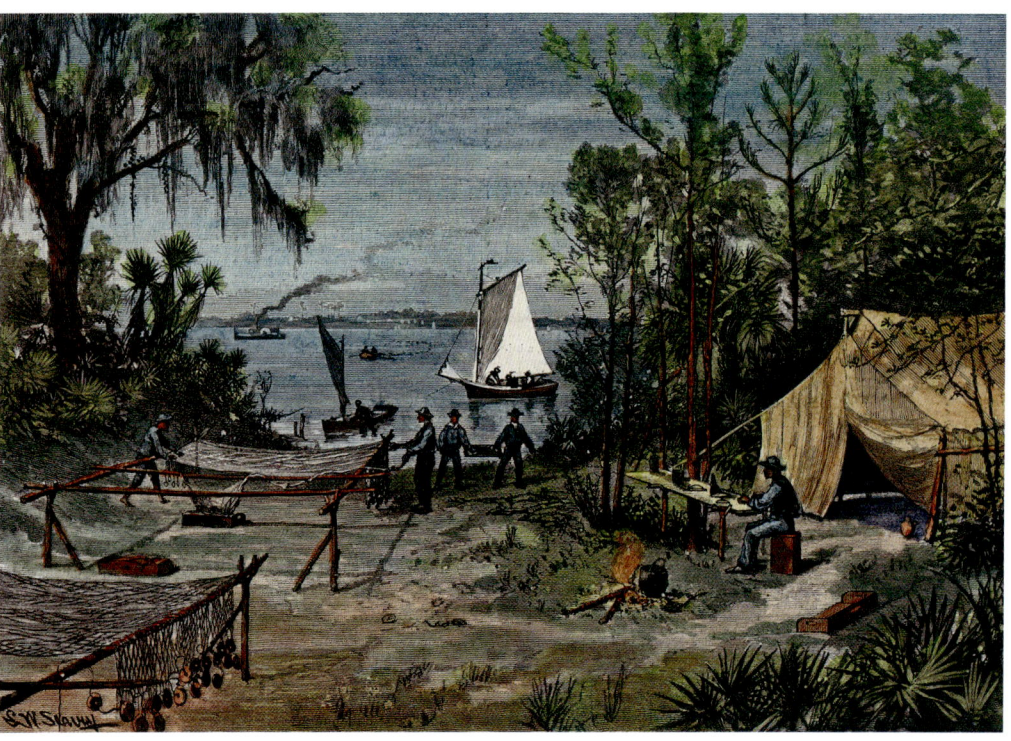

This illustration from *Harper's Weekly* depicts shad fishermen on the St. Johns in the 1890s.

In 1881, following the death of his mother, seven-year-old Frederick Frieseke was taken by his father to live in Jacksonville. The family stayed only four years, but the experience made an indelible impression on the youngster. Forty years later, after living all his adult life in France, Frieseke began a series of watercolors representing life along the St. Johns as he remembered it. He used the paintings to illustrate a charming memoir titled *Uneventful Reminiscences.*

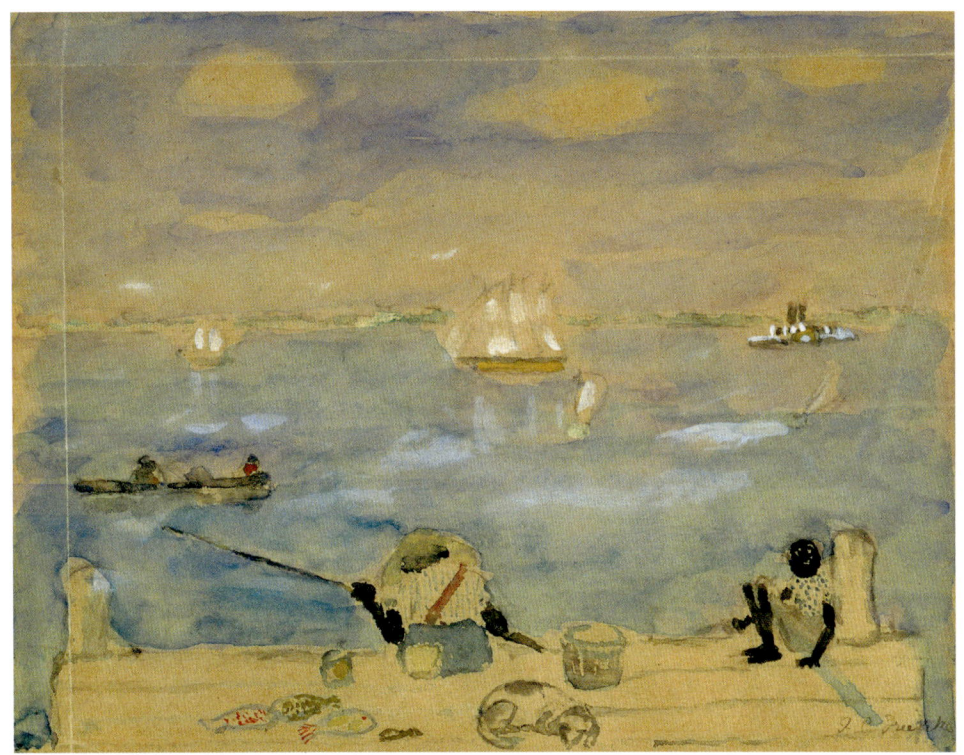

In this painting, *Fishing from the Jetty,* Frederick Frieseke recalls one of those limpid, shadowy days when the air is heavy as damp silk and the river reflects the dark bellies of clouds laden with moisture. "This was a favorite spot of mine," Frieseke wrote in his memoir. "While I quietly fished with a hand line, I would keep my eyes open for wildlife in the jungle opposite. Once an otter swam the river. Moccasins and alligators were no longer a novelty. . . . In the deep clear water the fish, spotted fish, red fish, striped fish, black, blue, impossible fish. I liked that country. It still enchants me, though I have never returned."[9]

Plate 77. Frederick Frieseke. *Fishing from the Jetty*, ca. 1921. Watercolor on paper, 7½ × 12 in. The Cummer Museum of Art and Gardens, Jacksonville, Florida.

In the spring of 1937, at age sixty-three, Frieseke wrote to his dealer, Robert Macbeth: "To be sure, at my age I had hoped my next change would be direct to Heaven, but if needs must—curiously you speak of Florida and I have had Florida on my mind as the only place in America that would tempt me, though I should find it sadly changed. . . . However, the idea appeals strongly to me."[10] Two years later, on the eve of the Second World War, Frieseke was making preparations to move to Florida when he suddenly died. One can only wonder how he would have reacted to seeing, after nearly sixty years, a place that had so touched his heart.

FISH CAMPS ARE NOTHING NEW. For thousands of years the Indians created temporary housing along the shores of lakes and rivers to take advantage of the local resources. The water teemed with fish, and animals were drawn to the area to drink. Fishing and hunting lodges were natural additions to Florida's watery landscape.

Modern fish camps sprang up along the St. Johns River as settlers moved into the region and began to exploit the local resources as their Indian predecessors had done. According to Jack Montrose, author of *Tales from a Florida Fish Camp,* the early camps were kept as simple as possible—"four walls, a floor, and a roof were enough." Montrose also points out that "remote hard-to-reach locations were preferred, lending an air of mystery."[11] The camps were initially built on state-owned land to avoid altercations with local ranchers. In addition to providing a camping spot for fishermen, the shelters were also used by boaters escaping a storm or forced to hold up until daytime if their boat broke down. Each camp was named, usually with a colorful and easily remembered tag such as Sugar Shack, Gator Den, and Two Story.[12] Besides fish, the camps also provided an opportunity to observe—or hunt—local wildlife. The swamps and estuaries were filled with birds, otters, gators, and snakes. They were also filled with mosquitoes, but that didn't deter the generations of outdoor enthusiasts who frequented the camps over the years.

Lone Cabbage Fish Camp is one of dozens of camps along the river. Roger Bull described the locale in the *Florida Times-Union*: "The river widens into lakes often down here . . . dry ground is rare and the river zigs and zags. . . . Coming north out of Lake Winder, as the water narrowed back to

I pass a series of fish camps and marinas on the river's easterly shore, a thriving cottage industry to service boaters and sport anglers, modern evidence of the environment continuing to shape culture, just as it did for the Timucua. In this particular culture, giant largemouth bass are portrayed ferociously. In signs, on souvenirs, and on murals, the predatory fish usually fires itself up from the water like a Triton missile, purple rubber worm lure in the crook of a mouth the size of a small cavern.

—Bill Belleville, *River of Lakes*

the river, the gators gathered. You are never long between alligator sightings, particularly in the Upper Basin. . . . A few fishermen were out there in their boats, working the edges of the lake. But the gators outnumbered them. The fishermen had come down from the boat ramp on Florida 520, which runs west from Cocoa Beach and Cocoa. Lone Cabbage Fish Camp sits on the banks there. Back when Norman Early bought the place in 1973, his customers were mostly locals who came out to fish. But it's mostly tourists these days. They take the airboat rides and eat in his restaurant."[13]

In the Upper River region around Blue Cypress Lake and Lake Hellen Blazes, the "river" is more often a marsh. One of the best ways to get around in this area is by airboat. These sledlike vehicles are powered by aircraft engines that make them so noisy that you can literally hear them a mile away. They prowl the channels, canals, and marshes, zooming over the shallow water and tall grass with ease, buzzing like giant bumblebees. They have become a tourist attraction in themselves.

The fish camp buildings are decorated with lively murals that provide just the right ambience—rustic charm and unschooled enthusiasm. Gators lie in the reeds alongside the lake, palm trees line the shore, and a huge Florida sun sinks majestically into the marsh, spilling rays of light across the turquoise water. It captures pure Florida nostalgia.

Lone Cabbage, like other camps I will find on the river, is becoming gentrified, with just enough good-ole-boy feel left to make it seem authentic; especially to northern tourists looking for tastes of the real Florida after mind-numbing doses of virtual reality at nearby Disney World. Airboat rides along the upper river have become a cottage industry, mixing doses of thrill-ride elation with exposure to a primitive environment. Gators—and the ornamental residue of gators—help sweeten the deal, making this a Mr. Toad's Wild Ride with real bumps and real cold-blooded reptiles.
—Bill Belleville, *River of Lakes*

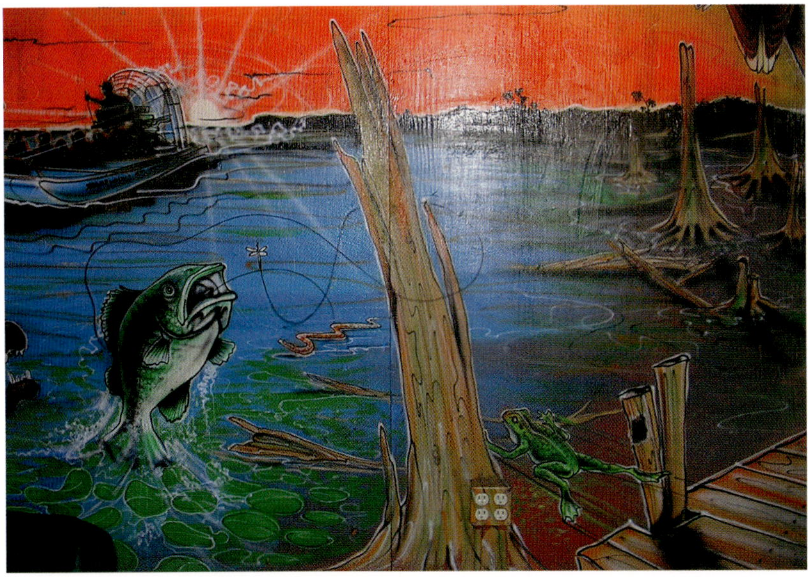

Plate 78. Anonymous. *Airboat Rides*. Lone Cabbage Fish Camp mural. Photo courtesy of Murray Laurie.

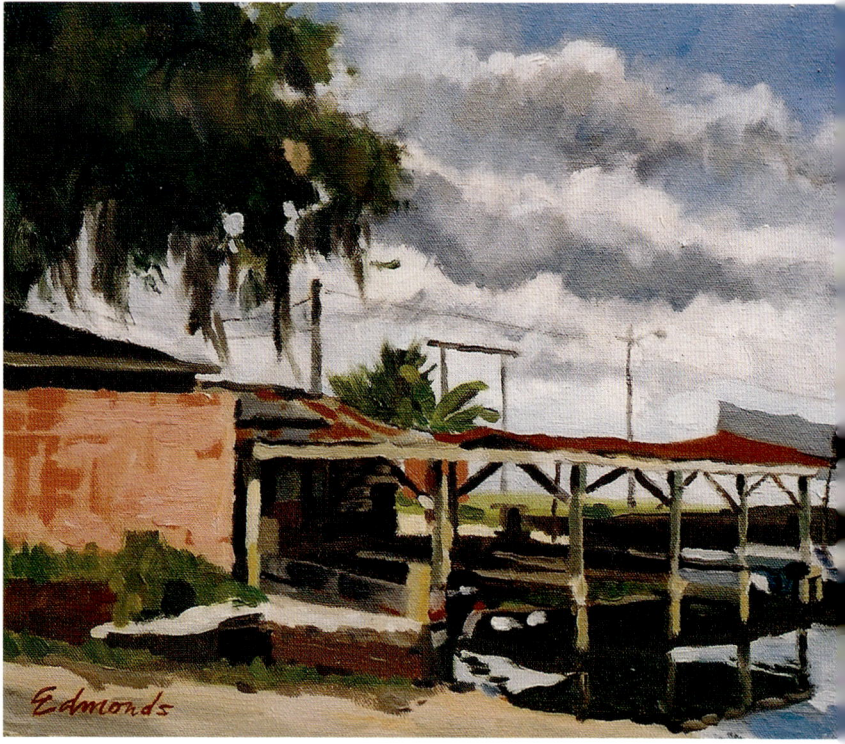

Plate 79. Cynthia Edmonds. *Black Hammock Marina, Lake Jessup*, n.d. Oil on canvas. Collection of Ray and Jennifer Kennedy.

This painting by Cynthia Edmonds captures the dilapidated charm of Black Hammock Marina on Lake Jesup, a popular spot for area fishermen. In the twentieth century, the lure of Florida as a fishing destination continued to grow, with dozens of smaller camps and marinas replacing the elaborate, large hotels of the Gilded Age. Unfortunately, the popularity of the St. Johns as a fishing paradise has also led to environmental problems such as habitat destruction, water pollution, and overfishing. As the twenty-first century opens, the traditional and picturesque Cracker fish camps may themselves soon be a dying breed headed for extinction.

Orange City, located between Sanford and DeLand, was once the home of Indians who lived along the St. Johns River, subsisting on the fish and freshwater snails that were abundant in the region. A mound formed by the accumulation of centuries of snail shells served as the foundation for the area's first permanent home, the 1872 Thursby House, now preserved as a museum in the Blue Spring State Park.[14]

Today, however, Orange City has lost its small-town flavor to rampant growth and development. Gone are the Fire Department benefits where chicken perlu was cooked in large wash pots, the same kind of tubs that the elderly women used for making lye soap. Today Mrs. Culp, the town's telephone operator, doesn't have to call each of the volunteers to report a fire from the switchboard in her home. No longer do baseball games, talent shows, or Lions Club performances—such as the "Womanless Wedding" skit, in which men would dress in drag and other zany costumes—provide community entertainment.

But the most lasting source of good clean fun was found at Blue Springs. Children would walk from surrounding towns for the day to swim and frolic amidst nature, oblivious to alligators, bears, and snakes. Blue Springs offered great fishing then, too. The varieties that are plentiful there today— including tilapia, armored catfish and garfish—were absent some fifty years ago, when bass, bream, saltwater mullet, and foot-long catfish made for tasty dinners. The bottom of the run, from the swimming deck to the river, was black, covered with catfish and, in season, blue crabs. In the St. Johns proper, the bottom-feeders were at least twice the size of those found else-where, and blue crabs were easily caught by hand lines. But commercial fish-ermen using large traps had depleted these delicacies by the mid-1980s.

When a passerby grabbed a painting out of a trash bin at a DeLand thrift shop, he didn't know what he had. No reason why he would have recognized the signature—A. E. Allen—but since palm trees were central to the composition, he thought that it might make a good addition to the DeLand House, a city-run history museum. Like most of Allen's paintings, it is a landscape—this one tropical. Although Anna Elizabeth Allen isn't a household name, she is a painter of some note. Ms. Allen had worked in Florida and in Turners Falls, Massachusetts, the two places she had called home. She arrived for the first time in Orange City with her frail mother and her sister Ruth in 1911.

Only ten of her Florida paintings have come to light, mostly through the efforts of Harley Strickland, a native Orange City resident and president of its historical society. There is no doubt that there are other paintings. He re-members seeing her "house full of azalea paintings" that mirrored the plants in front of the family home when he was a child. There she taught painting while Ruth gave piano lessons. The home served as a kindergarten, so "the Allen girls" had a steady stream of students, both children and adults.[15]

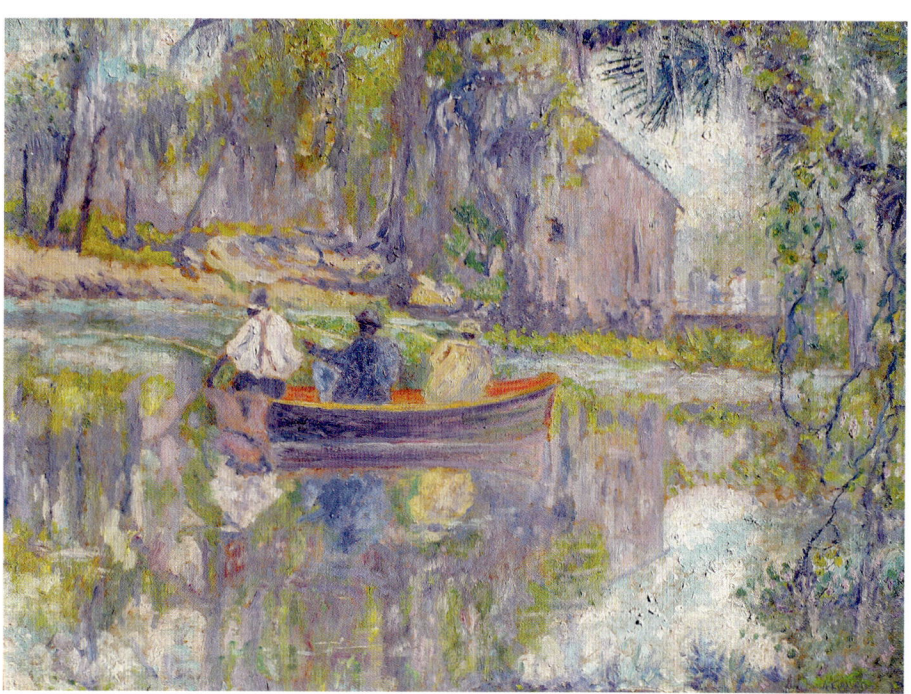

Plate 80. Anna E. Allen. *Fishermen at Blue Springs*, n.d. Oil on board, 22 × 29¾ in. Courtesy of Gary and Teresa Monroe.

It is likely that the three black men fishing in the rowboat in Allen's painting were afloat by the old boathouse, along the run at the mouth of the spring. This would have been adjacent to Shell Cottages, rental units that were on the south side of the spring's mouth until the 1960s, when the state acquired Blue Springs. It is also likely that the men would have rented the boat at the concession stand. They would have been too poor to have owned one, reasons historian Strickland. In all likelihood, the men did not put in downriver at Lake Beresford because it is just too far away to walk.

Strickland points out that the image pre-dates the 1950s and Jim Crow laws, "when battle lines were drawn," because until then blacks were as welcome at the springs as anyone. He imagines that the outing would have been on a Saturday afternoon, when most people were not working. Sunday was reserved for church and family; weekdays meant work. Blacks were often fieldworkers who may have had to be ready at 4:30 a.m. to be transported up to the citrus groves in the Lake George area. These fishermen would likely not have launched at Highlands because it was more of a club or fishing camp. They probably would not have had a boat to drop off at Lake Monroe. Fishing along the shore was a common activity for area blacks then, as it is today.

Little is known about J. E. Baker. In fact, some art collectors in central Florida wonder if he ever existed. As the story goes, charming little paintings depicting aspects of African American family life began appearing by the millennium. There were few clues to reveal much about the artist, and less with which to substantiate any claims. The common belief was that Baker was a black man who lived in or near Titusville and painted during the late 1920s and early 1930s. It was thought that his paintings had hung in a gas station in Mims and then, decades ago, when the place closed, had vanished—only to resurface in the mid-1990s.

The plot thickens: Florida folk art aficionados recognized two kinds of Baker paintings. One looked old, consistent with the dates noted on the paintings. The other kind of paintings, similarly conceived and dated, was more finely rendered. Although both kinds were encased in aged frames, they looked brand-new. There was little reason to think that someone would be painting these today; why would someone find the motherlode and make banal copies of interesting artwork?

An elderly, disheveled white man sold the paintings out of his beat-up station wagon, and rather inexpensively. He claimed to know nothing about the artist, other than what was noted on the paintings: name, date, and description.

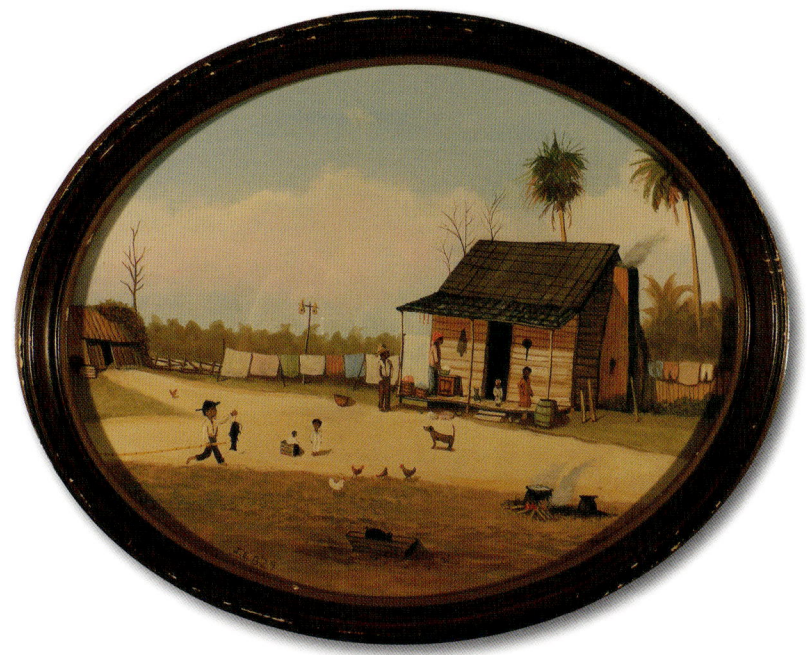

Plate 81. J. E. Baker (pseudonym). *Untitled*, ca. 1994. Watercolor on paper, 10⅜ × 13¼ in. oval. Courtesy of Gary and Teresa Monroe.

But investigation yields a sobering story. None of these charming paintings are authentic, at least not within the realm of vintage folk art, which was how they were peddled. It turns out the old peddler had fallen on hard times and painted the pictures himself to look charmingly old. He had used earlier examples of southern imagery, such as the paintings of William Aiken Walker, to add authenticity. He now had saleable art, replete with old frames, wavy glass, and square nails. However, he couldn't tell his antique dealer friends the truth, especially after selling the first few paintings, because he had been in that business himself.

Although his fears were generally sound, they didn't necessarily fit with contemporary thought about propriety, or even authorship. One might now contextualize the artwork as appropriated imagery, digested and transformed into something new—perhaps authentic contemporary folk art. His anonymity might have appealed to people's unfettered tastes. Signing them with a pseudonym and using an early date doesn't amount to a sin; it simply located the imagery, if not the art, in its time. Ultimately, J. E. Baker paintings were simulacra, or counterfeits, that gained something in the translation. Had the dispirited old man just created the work and signed it as his own, he likely would have gotten himself out of debt.

Benjamin Perry Vincent plied the St. Johns River at Sanford and started the Vincent Fish Market in 1890, which the family operated for three generations. At the original fish house, the daily catch of catfish, mullet, white shad, perch, bream, herring, trout, and black bass was brought in from the river, cleaned, and shipped in barrels to northern markets. Fishermen might have even trapped blue crabs; this in the dry seasons, when less freshwater pushes in from the headwaters to the south, so salt species migrate farther upstream. Then fishing along the river's lakes—Monroe, Jesup, and Harney—played a major role in the economy along with citrus, until successive freezes in the 1890s. Later, the local economy was driven by row crops—mainly celery, as Sanford was once dubbed the "Celery Capital of the World."

Benjamin's son James E. Vincent relocated the fish market a few blocks inland, behind the family home. In the late 1940s, James's son William Vincent Sr. moved the business into town, where he focused on the retail market. By then laws governing commercial fishing changed and sportfishing had become more popular; both factors contributed to the depletion of fish. Netters were put out of business, and fishermen resorted to using trotlines, which were baited long lines stretched along the river bottom. Commercial fishermen went to the coasts, bringing back saltwater varieties like grouper and red snapper. The family-owned seafood business was inextricably changing, to be lost to aqua farmers who could steadily supply seafood to restaurants that offer fixed menus. When fish were scarce at Vincent's Fish Market, folks would still come for southern hospitality that abounded there.

Bill Vincent didn't post his business's name on the storefront; no sign hung outside. At this point, he still operated the Vincent Seafood Market, but now he "held court." People would come to chat about the good old days and maybe buy fish from the smokehouse. Said area businessman Brian Schanel: "One day I looked back there and it looked like the whole courthouse was there. Those days are gone."[16] Where fish once may have lain on ice, more and more historical artifacts were displayed. "Locals brought him photographs and memorabilia which he collected and displayed until he had the town's largest history collection," points out Alicia Clark, director of the Sanford Museum.[17] In fact, as Vincent began to consider closing the business, there were more interesting things in the place than fresh fish, making the place more a museum than a market.

Alicia Clark explains: "Several years after Mr. Vincent's death, the market was given to the Sanford Museum. Among the objects found inside was this sign."[18] It was likely made in the late 1950s or early 1960s, as 1963 was the last year that letters were used in phone numbers there. Several of these signs were propped inside the store, looking like a school of fish, serving as a surrogate for the dwindling real thing. Tommy Vincent recalls how his father created his bold and beautiful signs: "Dad got a big red snapper, laid it out on a big old board, and traced it around, and cut it out."[19] Only this one remains.

Plate 82. William Vincent. Fish market sign, ca. 1975. House paint on wood with metal, 12¾ × 33¾ in. Courtesy of the Sanford Museum, Sanford, Florida.

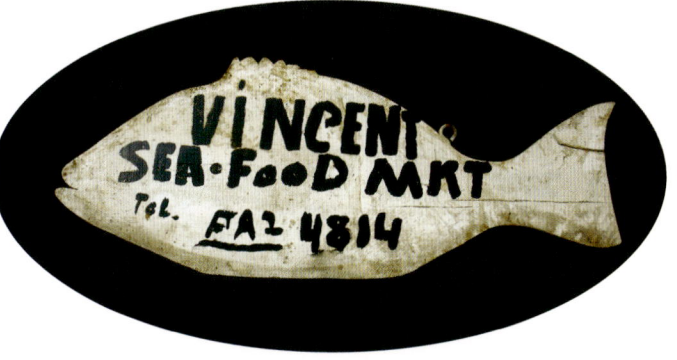

"I have drawn and painted since my first memories. It's just part of me," says the DeLand artist Tim Peterson. "My older brother subscribed to outdoor sporting magazines. My favorite was *Sports Afield*—especially the front cover art. I would study the art very carefully. Some of the best outdoor sporting magazine artists during the 1960s were Robert Abbet, George Luther Schelling, John Scott and Clark Bronson. I was highly influenced by their treatment of landscape.[20]

Originally from California's Central Valley, Peterson has made Florida his home for the past twenty-five years. For the last ten of those years, he has been painting the Florida landscape plein air, working on the spot instead of relying on photographs. Photographs did not convey the subtleties, like the depth of shadows, and color qualities, that he sought.

Hawkinsville Landing is the kind of place that Peterson seeks out. "It says fishing without having to show a boatload of fishermen," he says. "When my boat slides quietly up to a spot [like this], it becomes my own private place for an afternoon."[21] Near Crows Bluff, Hawkinsville Landing is located in an area known as a "high bank," one of only a handful of places along the low and swampy riverbank that could be used as a landing for the paddle-wheel steamboats that plied the river in the late 1800s and early 1900s. During that period, steamers frequently docked at Crows Bluff while the Hawkinsville site was used as a shipyard and lumber-loading dock. Peterson notes: "The exact location of the painting had narrow gauge railroad tracks running down to the water. The Cummer Lumber Company cut down giant cypress trees throughout the area and dragged the trees to the rail line. The railroad cars were backed into the river until the logs floated. The logs were then pulled by boat to the lumber mill a short distance to the south."[22]

With a keen interest in local history, Peterson was also fascinated to hear another story about the Landing. According to the current owner of the property, Hawkinsville Landing was attacked and destroyed during the Civil War. "The Yankees came south on the river and were beaten back at Crows Bluff, but a second larger assault resulted in the burning of the town of Hawkinsville and the destruction of the landing. All able-bodied men in the surrounding area who didn't hide in the swamps were rounded up and taken to Hilton Head. Those who survived starvation and yellow fever were released a full year after the end of the war. They had a long walk—some two hundred miles—to get back home."[23]

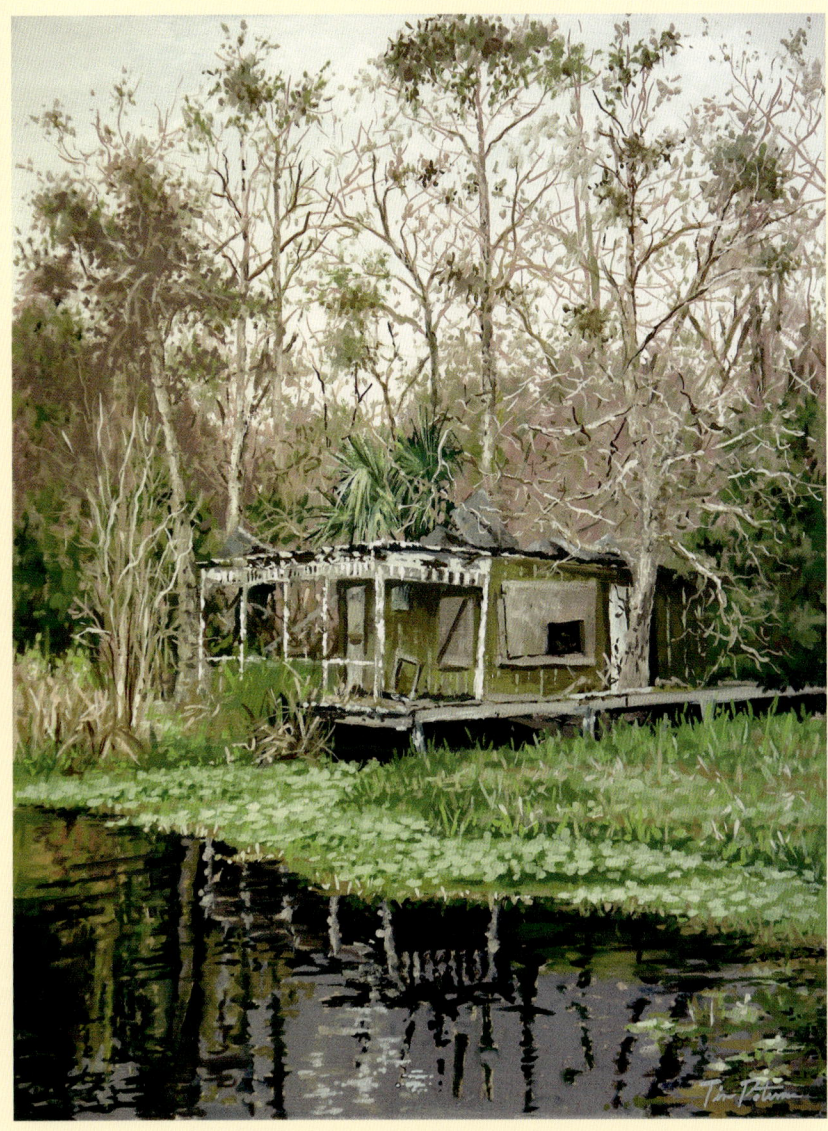

Plate 83. Tim Peterson. *Hawkinsville Landing*, 2007. Oil on linen, 18 × 24 in. Private collection.

Today, as depicted in Peterson's painting *Hawkinsville Landing*, there's not much left of the original Landing—only a dilapidated fish shack to mark the once bustling site. The current owner of the property—a serious history buff—has a collection of Civil War mementoes that preserve the history of the spot. In addition to the historic significance of the site, Peterson was attracted by the serenity of the setting and by the reflections he saw in the still water of the river. "I can sit and study water reflections for hours and be thoroughly entertained," says Peterson. "Freshwater reflections have always fascinated me."[24]

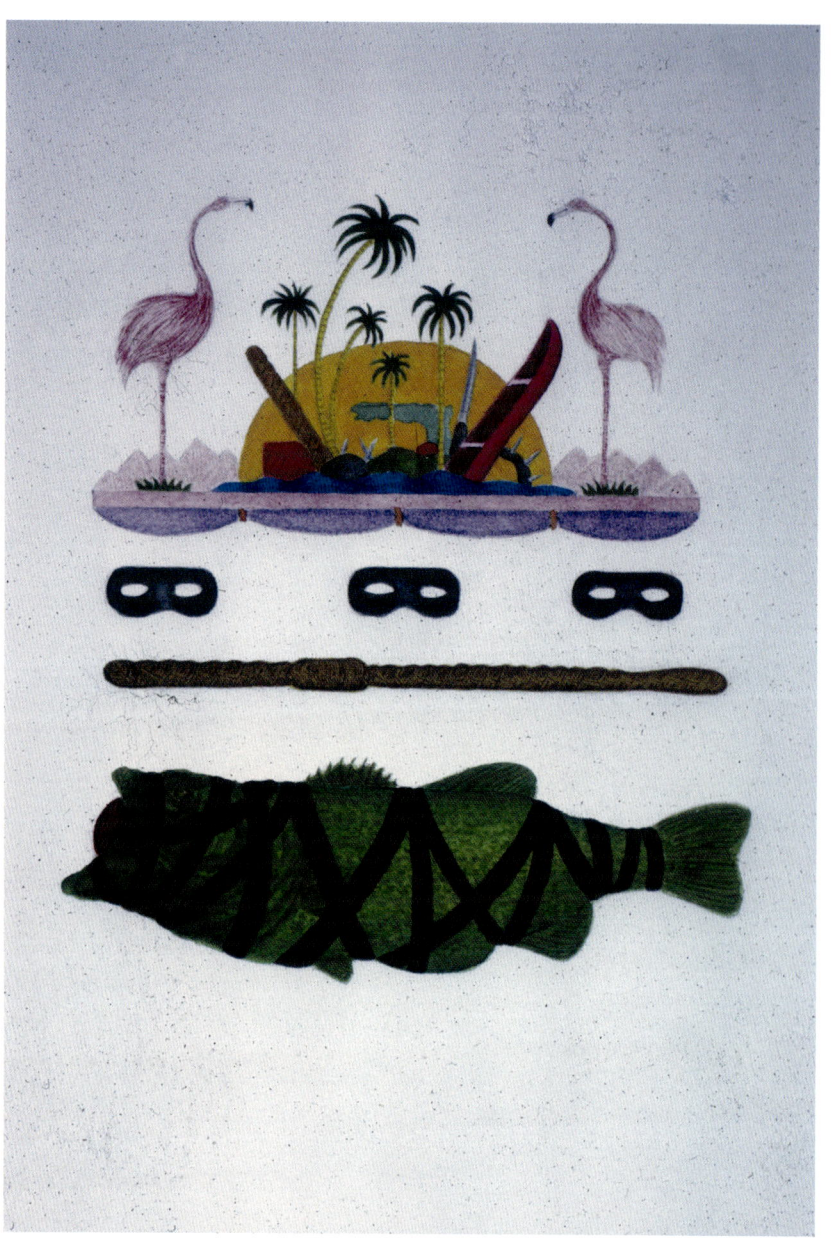

Plate 84. Nathan Ruiz [Nate Shiner]. *The Thrill'a in Tuscawilla*, 1975. Watercolor on paper, 16 × 12 in. Collection of Larry Wilson.

Nate Shiner came to Gainesville in 1973 to teach art at the University of Florida. Born in Vallejo, California, in 1944, he studied art at California State University, Sacramento, where he received a B.A. in sculpture in 1968 and a M.A. in painting in 1971. Before moving to Florida, he taught art at Sacramento City College and also participated in a series of group exhibitions culminating in three exhibitions at the Whitney Museum of American Art, New York, in 1972 and 1973. Although he maintained his connection with the New York City art world through his close friend Marcia Tucker, the founding director of the New Museum of Contemporary Art, New York, Shiner's move to Florida marked the beginning of a period of personal introspection and the development of several new approaches to his work.

However, his appreciation of Florida's climate was a bit slow to mature. His first reaction to the local environment was written shortly after his arrival in Gainesville. "Oh Lordy, I got them rain-soaked, swamp water, humidity'n alligator bite blues," he wrote in 1973. "These were the first words uttered by me after coming out of a coma which was the result of stepping into a time tunnel and experiencing a warp eight on the slump scale. This place is so far out in the woods I'm sure if I had a show here it would be reviewed by *Field and Stream*."[25] Later, as he delved ever more deeply into a study of the local culture, he began to celebrate the opportunity to explore his new environment. One way he became better acquainted with Florida was through fishing.

From the early California works influenced by cartoons and pop culture to the late portraits that reflected New York City's edgy and violent cityscape, Shiner's paintings always reflected his surroundings. In Florida, he began to paint flamingoes and palm trees, shells and lotus flowers, oranges and fish.

The Thrill'a in Tuscowilla documents a successful fishing trip to Tuscowilla Prairie, located in northern Marion County, with his friend and fellow artist Bill Oelrich. Characteristically, Shiner gave the painting to Bill as a memento of their adventure. The painting was later acquired by another of Nate's friends, Larry Wilson. The tableau of the flamingoes standing before a sinking canoe and the setting sun was a theme that Shiner had used in a large sculpture titled *Florida Environment: Flamingo Farm*. The masks that appear in the painting were also frequently found in his work. Why is the fish bound? Only Nate could answer that, and he's not talkin.'

In May 1982, the year after he left Florida for a brief stay in Tennessee, Shiner wrote the following reminiscence about his Florida fishing experience: "No doubt about it, Florida is the bass capital of the United States. Oh, you can catch bass in Tennessee but the method and means and results are not the same. Let me explain. First of all, and one of the most important [things] for me, is the environment. The fishing environment here [in Tennessee] is very impersonal. It's man-made and monstrous in size. Consequently, it is very difficult to become intimate with your surroundings. The threat is not from nature, but from one's own boredom with the mega-monochromatic lake. The structure is totally different: no grass, no pads, no reeds, no cattails, no rushes, no duckweed, no hyacinths, no algae, no scum. . . . My wee wings, moss hoppers, snagless sallys, bang-o-lures and buzzers are collecting dust in the bottom of my tackle box."[26]

Shiner's friend Marcia Tucker wrote: "Nate's work was very much like him—unpredictable, contradictory, funny, elusive, colorful, irreverent and unfashionable. [He] had an incredible facility with whatever he put his hand to. . . . It seemed that whatever he touched immediately became deliciously seductive. He was an innate colorist, a draughtsman of superb skill, and a remarkable technician with wood, metal, enamel and watercolor. . . . He liked to make beautiful pictures out of grotesque subjects and grotesqueries from things the rest of us would find appealing and familiar. . . . His work meant more to him than anything else and he incorporated into it every passion, every obsession, everything he learned and cared about. Just as he avoided predictability in his life, he avoided it in his art."[27] Nate Shiner died February 7, 1984, in New York City. He was thirty-nine years old.

Like fishing, hunting has a very long tradition in Florida beginning with the Paleo-Indian hunters who tracked mammoth and mastodon across the tundra of the Pleistocene peninsula. Their beautifully crafted weapons that date from the end of the last ice age have been found in many archaeological sites throughout the state. Later, Archaic Indians hunted for small game among the sandy ridges and developing hardwood hammocks. By the time the Europeans arrived, the Timucua and their Indian neighbors were busy hunting deer and other wild game along the St. Johns and its tributaries. In later centuries, hunting lodges became a preferred destination for the rich and famous.

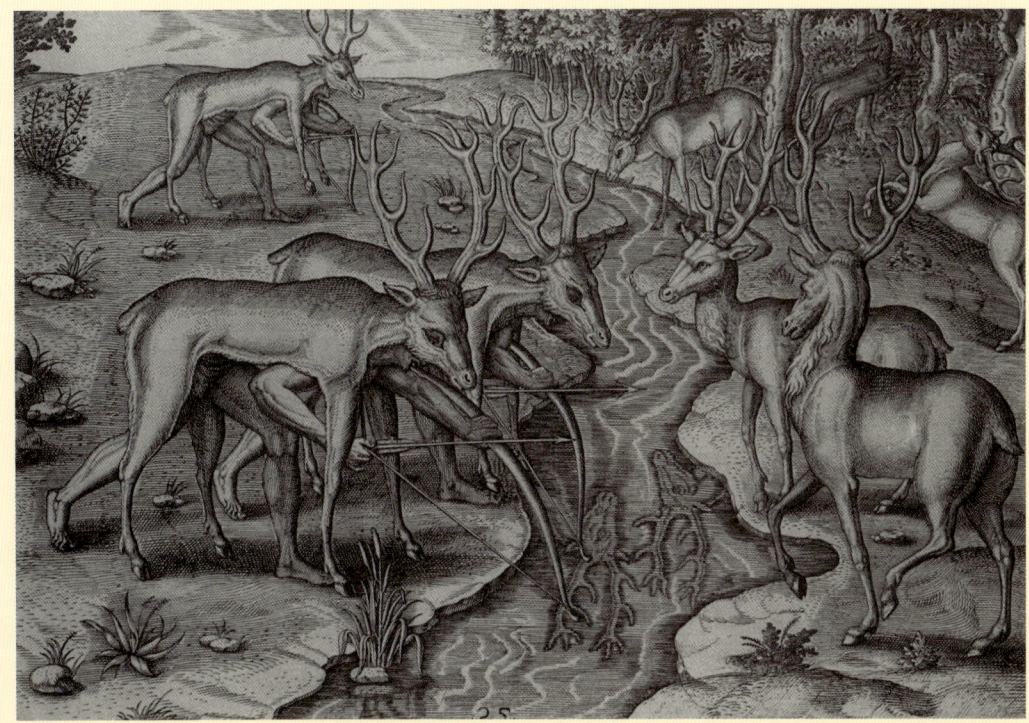

This engraving by Theodore de Bry demonstrates the method used by the Timucuan Indians to hunt deer. The caption reads:

Plate 85. Theodore de Bry. *How the Indians Hunt Deer*, 1591. Engraving. Photocopy courtesy of the State Archives of Florida.

> The Indians hunt deer in a way we have never seen before. They hide themselves in the skin of very large deer which they have killed some time before. They place the animal's head upon their own head, looking through the eye-holes as through a mask. In this disguise they approach the deer without frightening them. They choose the time when the animals come to drink at the river, shooting them easily with bow and arrow. To protect their left forearm from the bowstring, they usually wear a strip of bark. And they prepare the deerskins without any iron instruments, using only shells, in a surprisingly expert way. I do not believe any European could do this better.[28]

"DeBary Hall doesn't always seem to be about Florida," points out the Volusia County historian Tom Baskett. This observation is also true about much of the state throughout its history. It has always been a fantasyland, a paradisiacal place for people to reinvent themselves or simply to rejuvenate themselves far from their everyday lives. The steamy, abundant, and fecund semitropical wilds, suggesting promises of health and wealth and even immortality, offered hedonistic delights. This pleasure principle was hard at work at DeBary Hall.

DeBary Hall ("hall" is the British term for the main building of an estate) was a retreat and hunting lodge complete with stables, gun- and greenhouses, and workers' quarters, among other outbuildings. Those who came were invited guests of Frederick deBary. DeBary built the Victorian house on a ridge in the Florida frontier, near Enterprise, a mile from Lake Monroe on the St. Johns River in 1871.

Frederick deBary, a Belgian-German merchant who had made Manhattan his primary residence, was an importer of French wines and champagne. A gentleman farmer and entrepreneur, he tried orange growing and running a steamboat line. The guests at his home were the well-heeled of the Gilded Age—post–Civil War Union officers, captains of industry, and politicians. Nellie Augusta Hayes, a niece of Adolphe deBary (Frederick's son), assisted her mother as a hostess at DeBary Hall during the winter seasons. She recalled seeing General William T. Sherman (after the Civil War, of course) and other prominent people. Most revealing is Hayes's observation that, "The deBarys, father and son, were men of charm and distinction and their guests came from far and near because their hospitality was internationally known."[29]

After the Civil War, plantations throughout north Florida were converted into quail-hunting preserves. Hunting wagons were used by those who enjoyed high-style sportsmanship. This hunting wagon, which is still kept at DeBary Hall, reveals the status of its users. Made in Valdosta, Georgia, by the South Georgia Buggy Company in the late nineteenth century, "it is part of a key leisure and land-use story in Georgia and Florida," points out the historian Tom Baskett.[30]

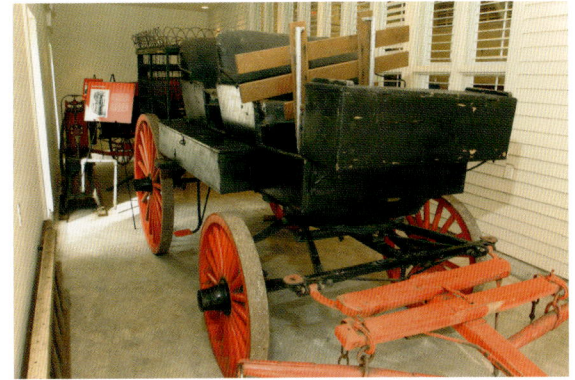

Plate 86. Hunting wagon at DeBary Hall. Late nineteenth/early twentieth century. Wood and steel, 70½ × 135 in. Courtesy of DeBary Hall and Volusia County government, Florida. Photo by Jeff Crumbley.

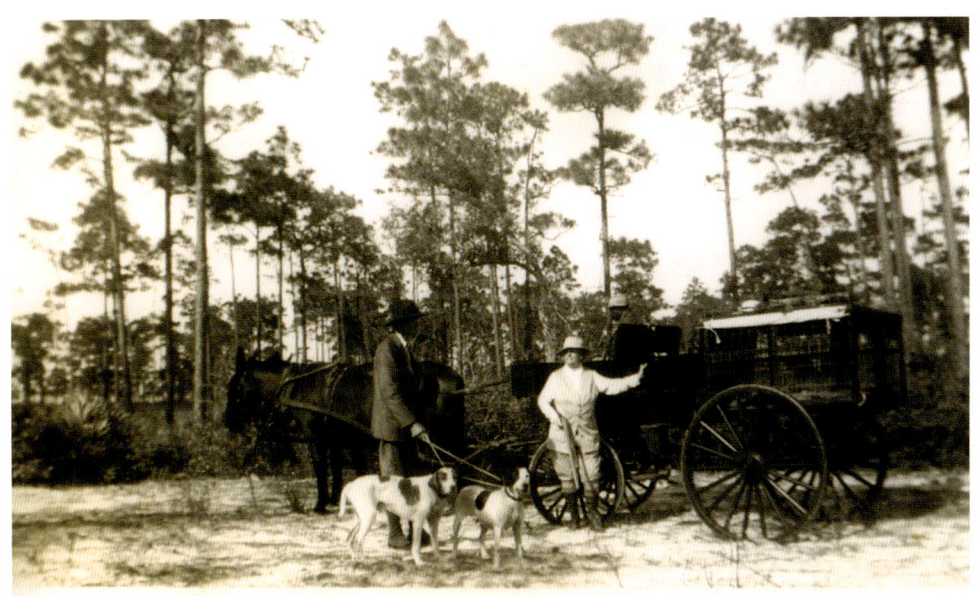

Plate 87. Photo of wagon in use, ca. 1920. Silverpoint. Courtesy of DeBary Hall Historic Site/Lyon Collection, Volusia County government, Florida.

Dog handlers and "flushers," whose job it was to drive birds out of the brush or flank them for the convenience of the shooters, were employed. This was stylized hunting, facilitated by hunting wagons that could carry sportsmen, their shotguns, bird dogs, and any game that the party shot. Before the hunt, dogs were readied while breakfast was served; picnic lunches were prepared for the guests. Servants opened the cart's gun box for the hunters and cages for the dogs. The wagon would embark across the pinelands, its wide steel-rimmed wheels designed to traverse the sandy soil easily. One could even take aim and shoot without leaving the wagon.

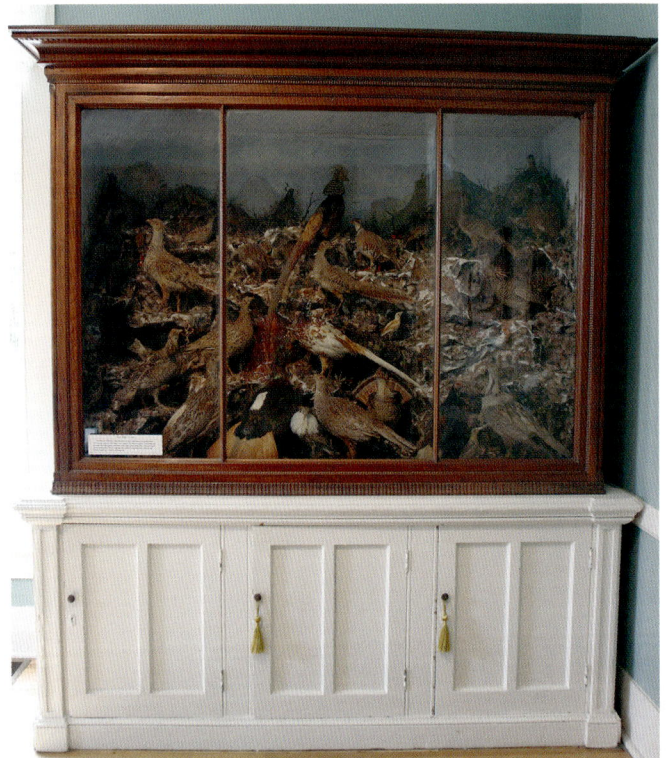
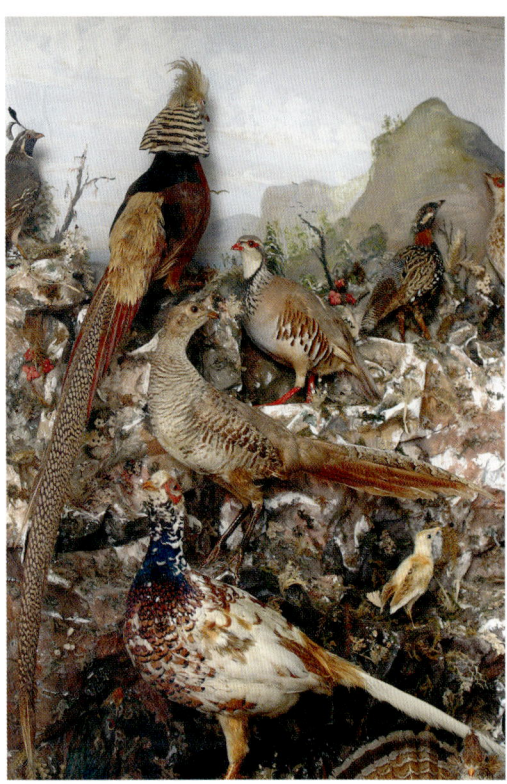

Plate 88. Vintage photo and detail of Victorian bird display at DeBary Hall, late nineteenth century. Wood, glass, and mounted birds, 62 × 87½ × 28 in. Courtesy of DeBary Hall and Volusia County government. Photo by Jeff Crumbley.

Victorians were keen collectors, and mounted birds were favorite keepsakes. Frederick deBary's display is noteworthy for what it is and isn't: it is a charming array of birds, but only the snipe and woodcock are native to the Upper St. Johns region. Some of the species are not found in Florida or even the United States but are from as far away as China.

The game birds may have provided a kind of visual aphrodisiac, whetting the appetites of the deBarys' mannered guests who came by invitation to enjoy his six thousand acres. How deBary acquired the non-native specimens in the case is unclear, according to Tom Baskett. But he notes that exotic birds were available to wealthy Victorians.[31] Frederick deBary had the perfect local contact: Henry Patrick Gradick, a Confederate veteran and orange grower at Geneva, Florida, south of DeBary Hall, and an avocational taxidermist. According to descendants of Gradick, this avid outdoorsman stuffed and sold birds, and he likely created Frederick deBary's remarkable game bird display.

Probably constructed in the early 1880s, the walnut display case is 60 inches tall, 78 inches wide, and 28 inches deep and holds thirty-one birds with at least four mounts missing. This is a large number of birds for a relatively small area. The display itself is interesting, too: the birds have a decorative presence, emphasizing them as trophies, which are especially appealing to hunters. It certainly is not an academic presentation geared for the zoologist; it is more folk art than ornithological explication, and as much Victorian as it is Florida "folk"–related. Grassland birds are perched on plateaus set in the mountainous terrain, as this likely gave the creative taxidermist places to position the birds in consideration of the overall composition. The painted background is also clever: a face inconspicuously blends into a mountainside on the left panel for no apparent reason other than adding some whimsy to the piece.

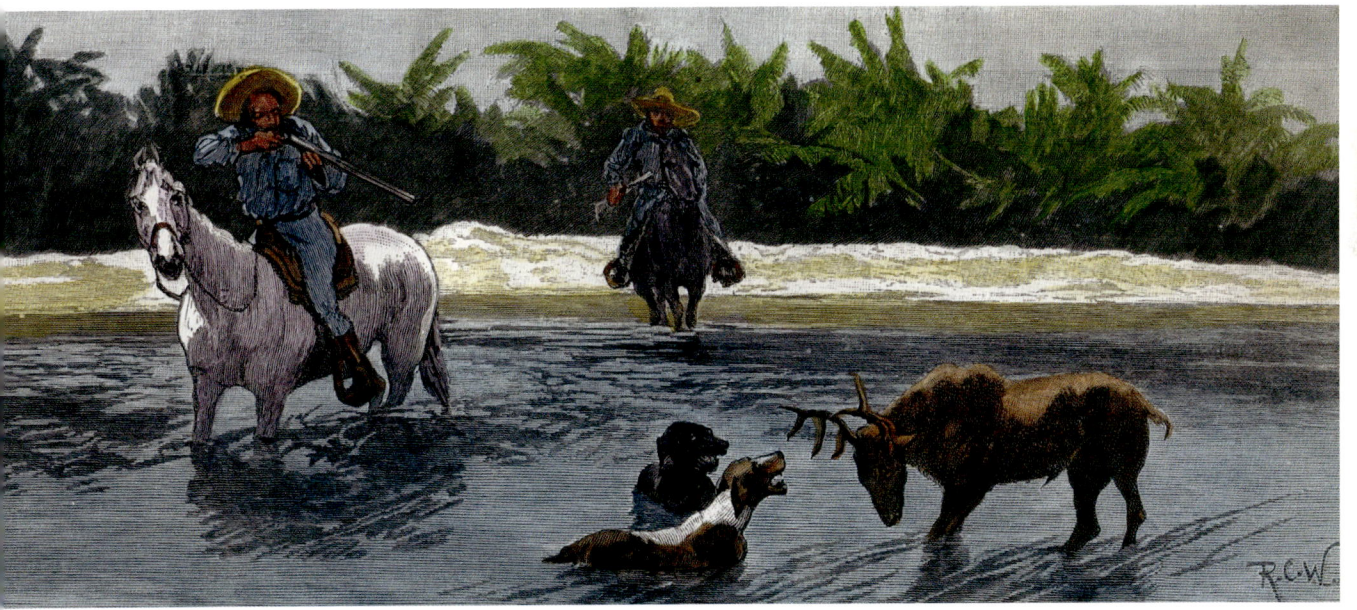

Plate 89. Anonymous. *Florida Deer Hunters*. From *Illustrated London News*, March 26, 1892. Courtesy of the Matheson Museum, Gainesville, Florida.

Besides fishing and hunting, the St. Johns River region has also been simply a source of recreation and enjoyment for generations of Floridians. The river and its tributaries offer delightful opportunities for canoeing and kayaking while the springs attract divers from all over the world. And who has not enjoyed a restful afternoon relaxing on the riverbank watching the water flow past and perhaps enjoying a memorable picnic lunch?

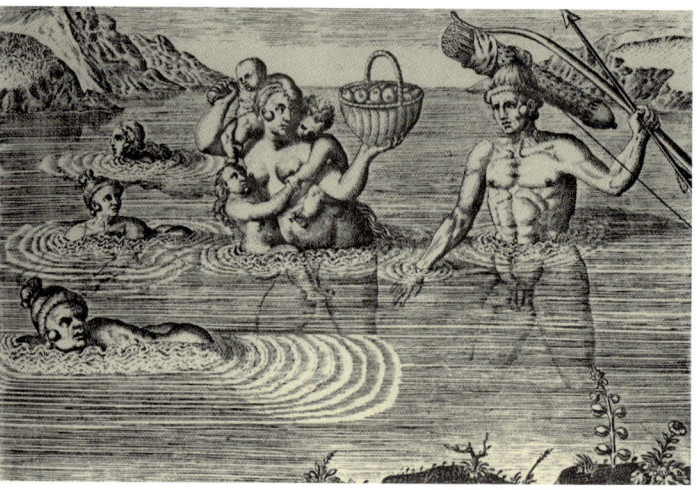

Plate 90. Theodore de Bry. *Floridians Crossing over to an Island on a Pleasure Trip*, 1591. Engraving. Photocopy courtesy of the State Archives of Florida.

If we are to believe this picture, the St. Johns River has long been a magnet for recreation for here we see an Indian family wading through the water on their way to a picnic. Laudonnière's description reads: "The country has many delightful islands, lying in shallow rivers of clear, pure water, running no more than breast high. When the natives wish to go to one of the islands to enjoy themselves, they swim skillfully across the rivers or, if they have young children with them, they wade. The mother takes with her three of her children, the smallest one on her shoulder, while the two others cling to her arms. She also carries fruit and provisions for the trip in a basket."[32]

Wendy Beeson's watercolor portrays a scene that she describes as being "on the St. Johns River next to Georgetown. This man and his helper dive for artifacts off Drayton Island."[33] Beeson lives in Satsuma, a few miles north of Lake George. Many of her paintings depict the St. Johns and the surrounding area. These are not typical landscape paintings. History and landmarks abound in her work, and there is something intensely personal to be found as well. A viewer might even believe that the plants and animals depicted are intimate friends of hers. Ghosts of famous people emerge from the jungle canopy, old houses line the river's shore, and even the skyscrapers of Jacksonville take on an unexpected animation.

In her Drayton Island painting, Beeson gives us a world of myriad details—structures and docks, signs and banners, boats and wildlife. The painting teems with life—human, plant, and animal. Trees and ferns and cattails and palms vie for attention; a heron stands watching the spectacle; boats roar past. In the foreground, a snorkeler wades awkwardly toward the shore, grasping his trident. The banner, the boat, and the oddly costumed figure are almost reminiscent of images of the Europeans landing on the virgin shore of the New World. Leaving civilization behind on the opposite shore, the artifact hunter enters the wilderness. In this painting, the past is tied to present in one seamless moment.

Plate 91. Wendy Beeson. *Drayton Island Delights*, **2000. Watercolor on paper. Courtesy of the artist.**

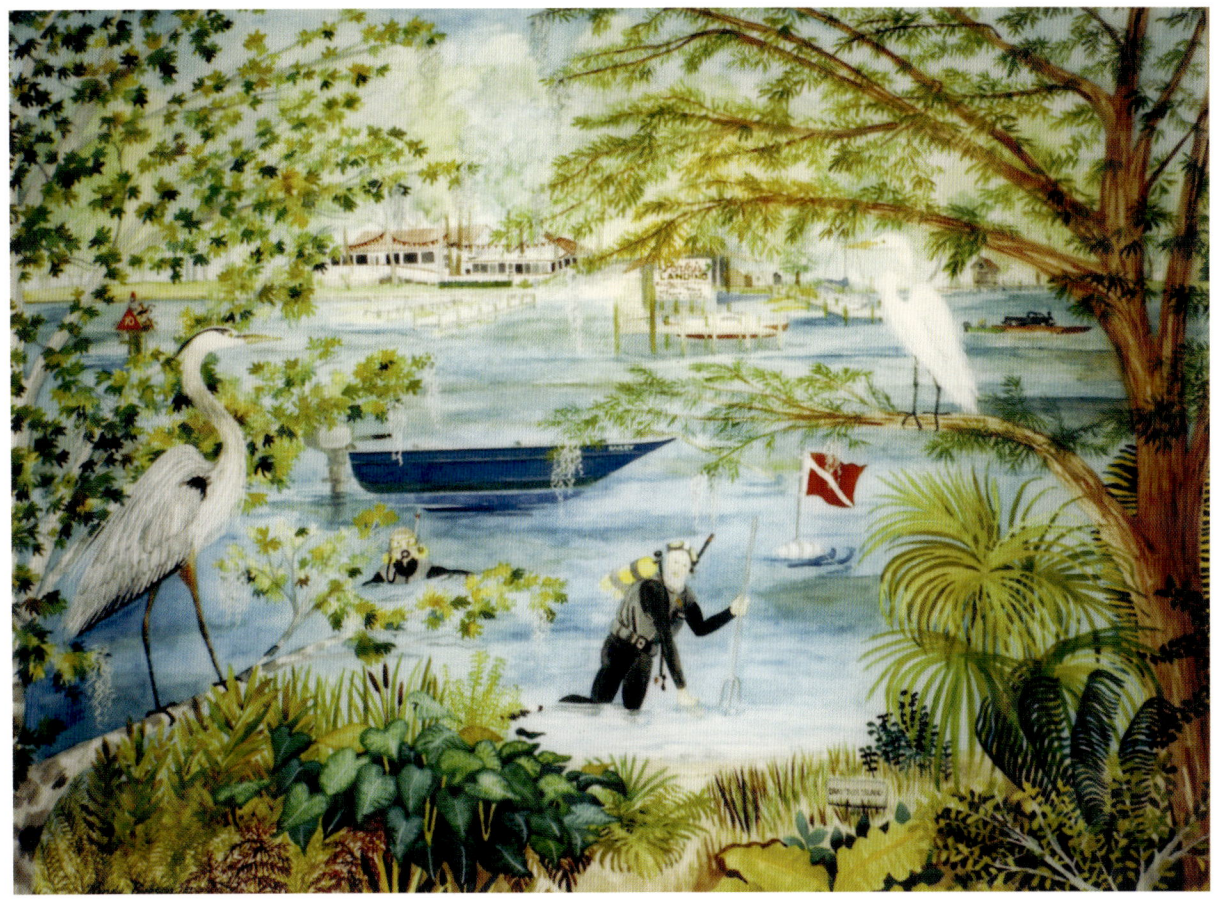

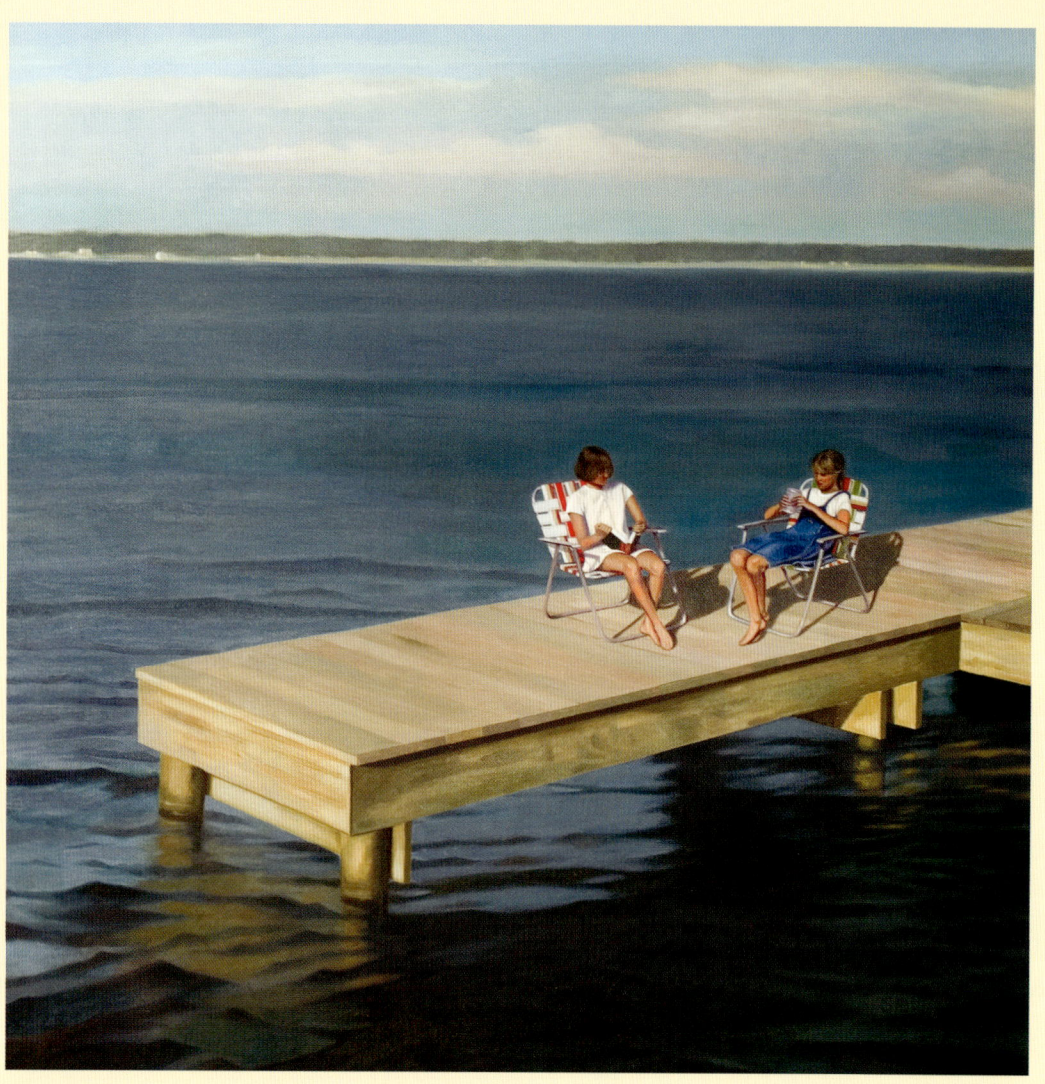

Plate 92. James Freeman. *A Day on the St. Johns River,* 1996. Acrylic on canvas, 36 × 36 in. Courtesy of the artist.

James Freeman's vision of river recreation is more relaxed. Two women sit in folding chairs on the wooden dock, taking in the sun and the scenery. The blue-green water surrounds them. Sunlight glints on the lazy ripples. The distant horizon indicates the breadth of the river and dramatizes the isolation of the figures. In the still heat, one can almost feel the intensity of the sunlight beating down on the water. Freeman's image has become iconic—a fully contemporary scene that we have seen again and again, as common today as it was to the traveler on the steamboat a hundred years ago.

7 { Treasures of Welaka

IT IS IN THE MIDDLE BASIN that the St. Johns truly earns its Indian name—Welaka, River of Lakes. Between the Econlockhatchee River at the southern end and the Ocklawaha at the northern end of the basin, there are over a dozen places where the "river" becomes a "lake." Lake Monroe is as far south as large boats can go on the St. Johns, which explains why Sanford is the southernmost town of any size on the river.

Rather than actually flowing into the string of lakes, the St. Johns instead dilates itself into a broad, shallow body of water. Without defined banks to contain it, the river flows outward and covers the available land. But there remains a central core, a channel that inches northward, intent on reaching the distant sea. Over the years, many artists have sought to capture the unique character of the Middle Basin region. Here are some of their stories.

The Econlockhatchee River—so named by the Seminole by piecing together the Creek words *ekana* for earth, *laiki* for mound, and *hatchee* for river or creek—arises thirty-six miles to the west of the St. Johns and follows a serpentine path through the marshland east of Orlando before joining the larger river north of Puzzle Lake. One of three major tributaries of the St. Johns—along with the Wekiva and the Ocklawaha—the Econlockhatchee, or Econ as it's usually called, is a blackwater river colored by the tannic acids that dissolve in the water from decaying leaves and wood. The surrounding marsh is a rich oasis for abundant wildlife that includes turtles, deer, wild turkey, sandhill cranes, and otters.

From the Seminoles came a version of a word first used to describe the St. Johns, Welaka—a corruption of Ylacco. It was said to mean "river of lakes". . . . There is another, lesser-known interpretation of Ylacco. For me it fits just as well, for it wanders into poetry: It hath its own way, is alone contrary to every other.
—Bill Belleville, *River of Lakes*

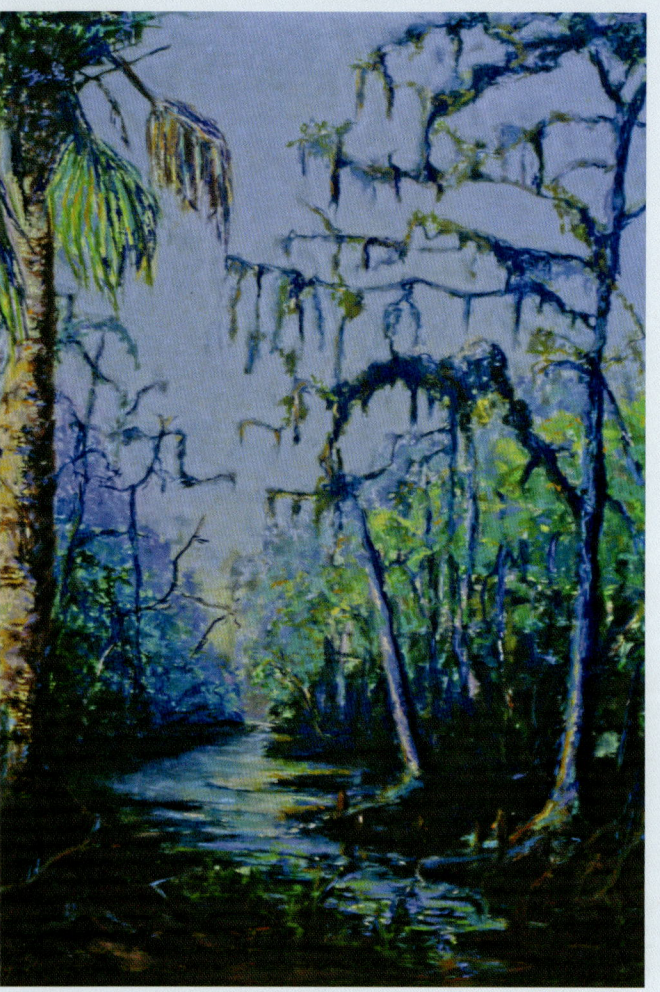

Bettye Reagan lives in Lake Mary, a western suburb of Sanford. A Florida native, she studied art at the Loch Haven Art Center in Orlando and at Seminole Community College. Her pastels are mostly landscapes done on-site near her home. "Using color and light to create mood and feeling is my ultimate goal," she says. "The ideas for my figure paintings evolve from every-day activities I have experienced."[1] In this pastel of the Econ River, Reagan captures the softness of the marshy landscape as the sun sinks behind layered clouds and the moss turns silver in the dusky light. There is a mood of melancholy in the painting that is not lightened by the after-glow of the sunset or its smoldering reflection.

Plate 93. Bettye Reagan. *Econ*, n.d. Pastel on paper, 19 × 26 in. Courtesy of the artist.

West of Melbourne, the grassy lands south of Lake Jesup increase toward the St. Johns River's source to become vast swamps. During the rainy season, many of the pastures and hammocks are submerged, but Jordan Slough, like nearby tributaries, maintains its snaking form. Locals point out that manatees swim this far upriver, and when the water rises they eat the grass off the submerged bank. They will tell a visitor that fifteen miles either way from that point in the St. Johns River is one of the few places in the world where there are freshwater stingrays. Although they are farther away, only the St. Johns River stingrays live year-round in freshwater. Many people might think this a fanciful folk tale, but the pioneering naturalist William Bartram noted "the dreaded stingaree" in Florida springs in the 1700s.

The formal organization of his paintings is an important concern to the Orlando artist Hansen Mulford. He begins by taking photographs and culls these, splicing them together to create panoramic maquettes. Elements in the compositions are added, altered, or deleted to create rhythms of line and shape that direct the eye through the depicted space, giving the viewer a sense of underlying order. New information is fabricated. Clouds and people appear out of nowhere. This strategy is perhaps most evident in the juxtapositions of sky and land. Each comes from different sources, and they are selectively paired to pull the overall composition together.

A moodiness, a stillness or aloneness, is present in Mulford's paintings, a result of his early attraction to Edward Hopper. His art is less a document than an experience in which one is "fighting the rush of time, the end of life."[2] Mulford does not intend these paintings to be casual impressions of a lovely vista or a document of a specific locale; rather he sees them as an attempt to capture the sense of wonder the artist felt while there: "My goal is to fix what is transient and create an idealized vision of the scene."[3]

Plate 94. Hansen Mulford. *River of Grasses*, 1989. Oil on canvas, 14 × 24 in. Collection of Sherry French.

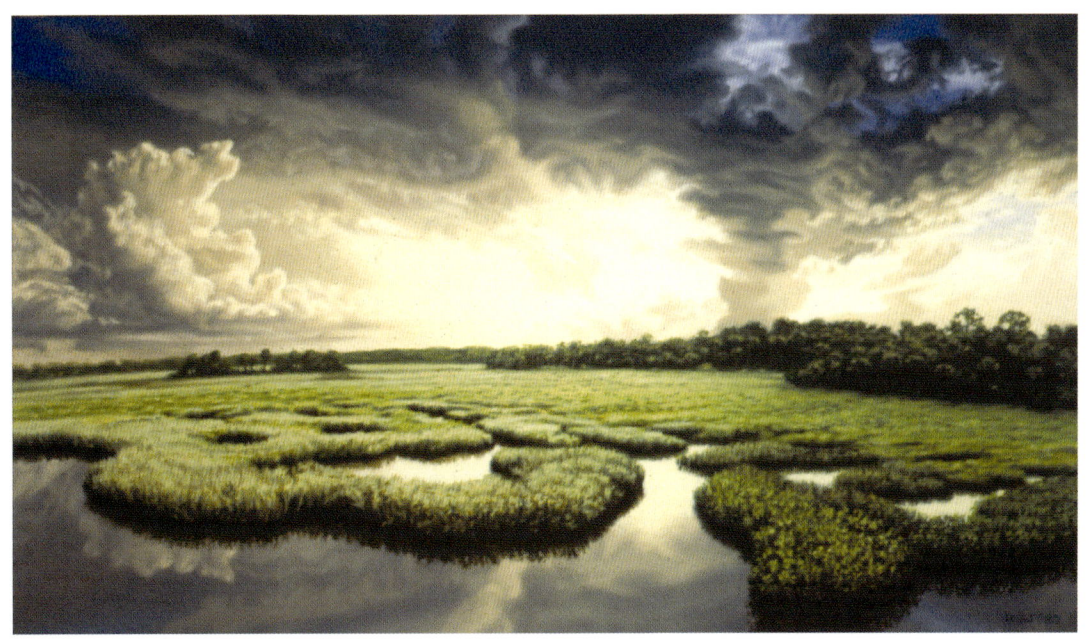

Kevin McNamara talks about his paintings in terms of "painterly realism" that is achieved through an impressionistic approach to light, color, and space while exacting a formal resolve to experience. His interest is not in pure realism, as this feat of verisimilitude would lack emotion for him. His goal is to spark responses from viewers similar to those that the scene aroused in him. To do this, McNamara approaches a scene to find its most interesting composition at a time of day when the light has most to offer in terms of atmosphere or drama. The tranquility in his work is achieved by control over the perspective, close attention to color temperatures and tonal values, and a vigorous application of paint. His brushstrokes harmonize on the canvas as well as in the eye. Consequently his colors flow to appear gentler and softer than they do with the impressionists' riotous canvasses. This makes even the bright morning Florida sun palatable, as evidenced in *River's Bend*.

To capture the crisp early morning winter light, McNamara left his home in Geneva as the sun rose and drove east on Highway 46. He turned north on an unimpressive road and drove past brush to a turn in the road. Suddenly homes appeared, most likely weekend getaways for Orlando residents or winter retreats for northerners.

McNamara parked at the road's end and opened a gate; then he entered Jordan's Cove, a remnant of primordial Florida south of Lake Harney. After following a winding path through thick native vegetation, he set up his easel. This gave him a view across Cow Island. He was taken by how the sun's angled rays made the place shimmer, and he set about capturing this quality on canvas. Later, he learned that there had been a fish camp and bait store on the site where fishermen stored their boats until 1940, when the land began to be used for cattle raising.

According to Bill Belleville, this section of the river is historically important for yet another reason. Some geologists believe that this part of the river may be older than the Upper River by as much as 3 million years: "With the basin of the upper river still inundated by the sea, the headwaters for this westerly offset [of the river] would have originated somewhere east of present-day Sanford."[4]

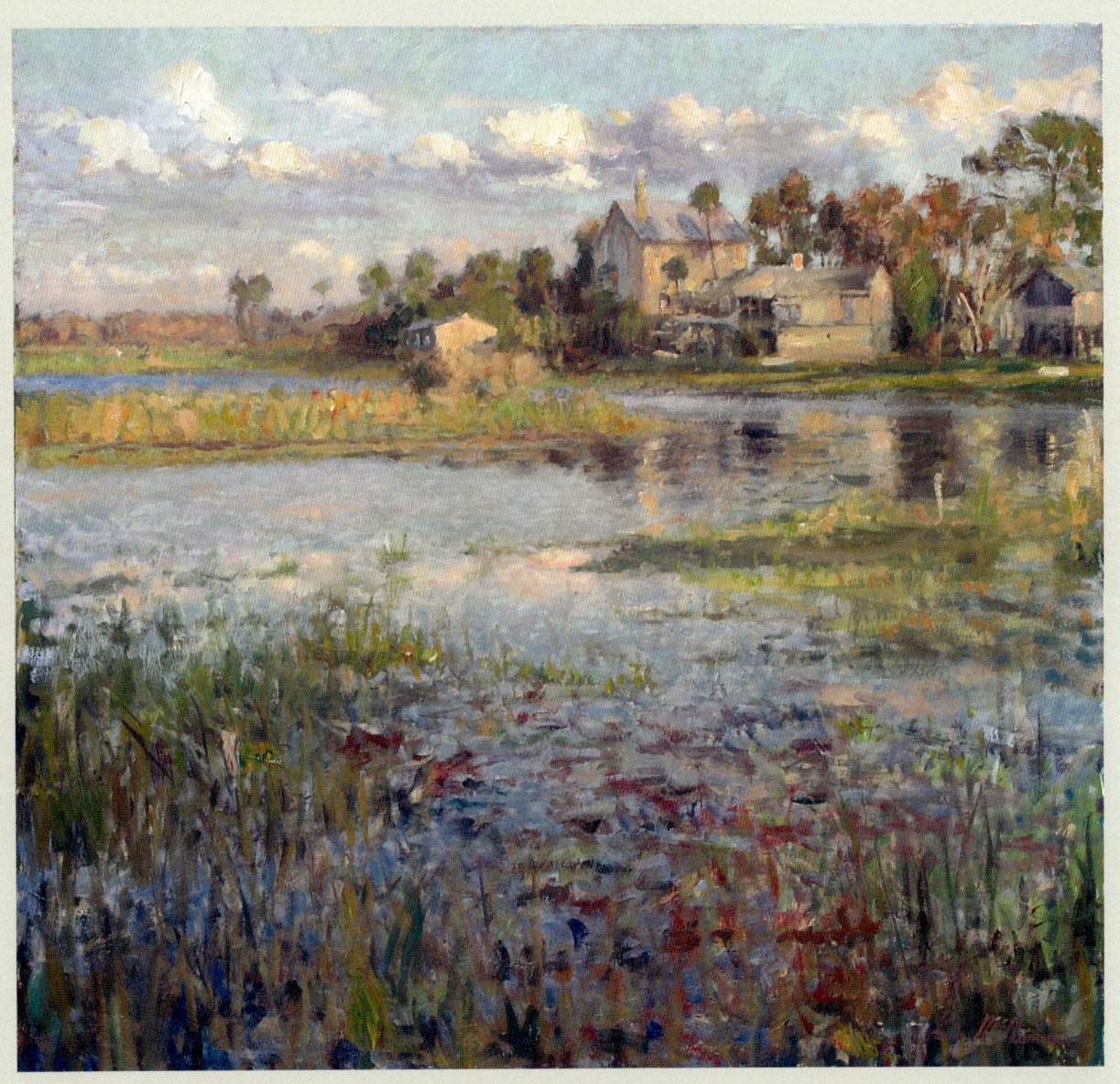

Plate 95. Kevin McNamara. *River's Bend*, 2006. Oil on canvas, 36 × 38 in. Courtesy of the artist.

Lake Jesup, once an easily navigable body of water with four busy steamboat landings, was connected to the St. Johns by natural passageways that allowed the water to circulate and keep the lake clear and flowing. According to Bill Belleville, all that changed in the 1930s when a navigational canal and causeway, built by the Army Corps of Engineers, short-circuited the lake's connection to the river.[5] More recently, leakage from septic tanks, fertilizer runoff, and a new expressway have all contributed to the degradation of the lake. Advocates for restoration continue to battle for recognition for their cause. Meanwhile the lake suffers with nine feet of bottom muck that has accumulated from years of neglect and abuse.

Despite the impact of environmental mistreatment, the lake, now more of a marsh, has its share of wildlife. Wading birds nest in the reeds, and alligators abound in the shallow water. "Although at a crossroads in its existence today," writes Bill Belleville, "Jesup was healthy enough in its prehistory to have been an oasis for all manner of life. In 1987 a local homeowner dug a pit near the shore and discovered the bones of a now extinct giant ground sloth, a relic of the Pleistocene epoch. Deeper in the pit were the bones of an ancient whale which likely swam through the deep saltwater channel that today is the basin of the St. Johns."[6] Lake Jesup is only one example of how thoughtless development and its unintended consequences have impacted the natural ecosystem of the river and interrupted a process that had worked so successfully for thousands of years.

Mullet Lake, one of several small lakes scattered between Lake Harney and Lake Jesup, was named for the silvery, blunt-nosed marine fish that can be found in tidal creeks and lagoons not far from the sea.[7] In times of extended drought, Mullet Lake is totally disconnected from the St. Johns and reforms itself into a series of small pools that are fed by an upwelling of brackish water—an inland salt marsh.

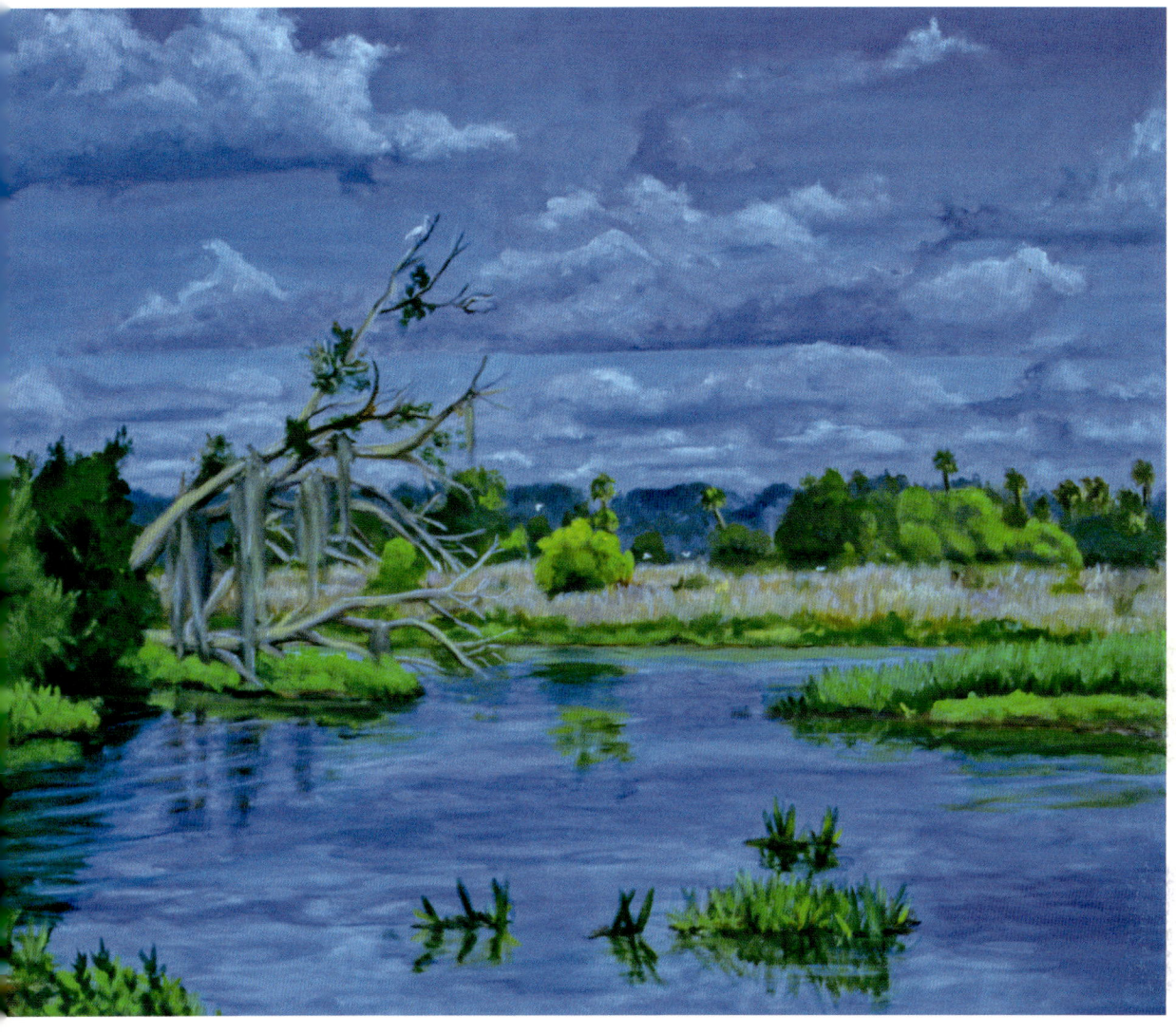

The warm waters of the lake are especially attractive for mullet and also attract huge numbers of wading birds. In this painting, the Winter Park artist Brenda Hofreiter depicts a familiar scene of white herons using a dead tree as an overlook from which to watch for the schools of minnows that will make a tasty meal.

Plate 96. Brenda Hofreiter. *White Heron—Mullet Lake*, n.d. Oil on canvas, 22 × 28 in. Courtesy of the artist.

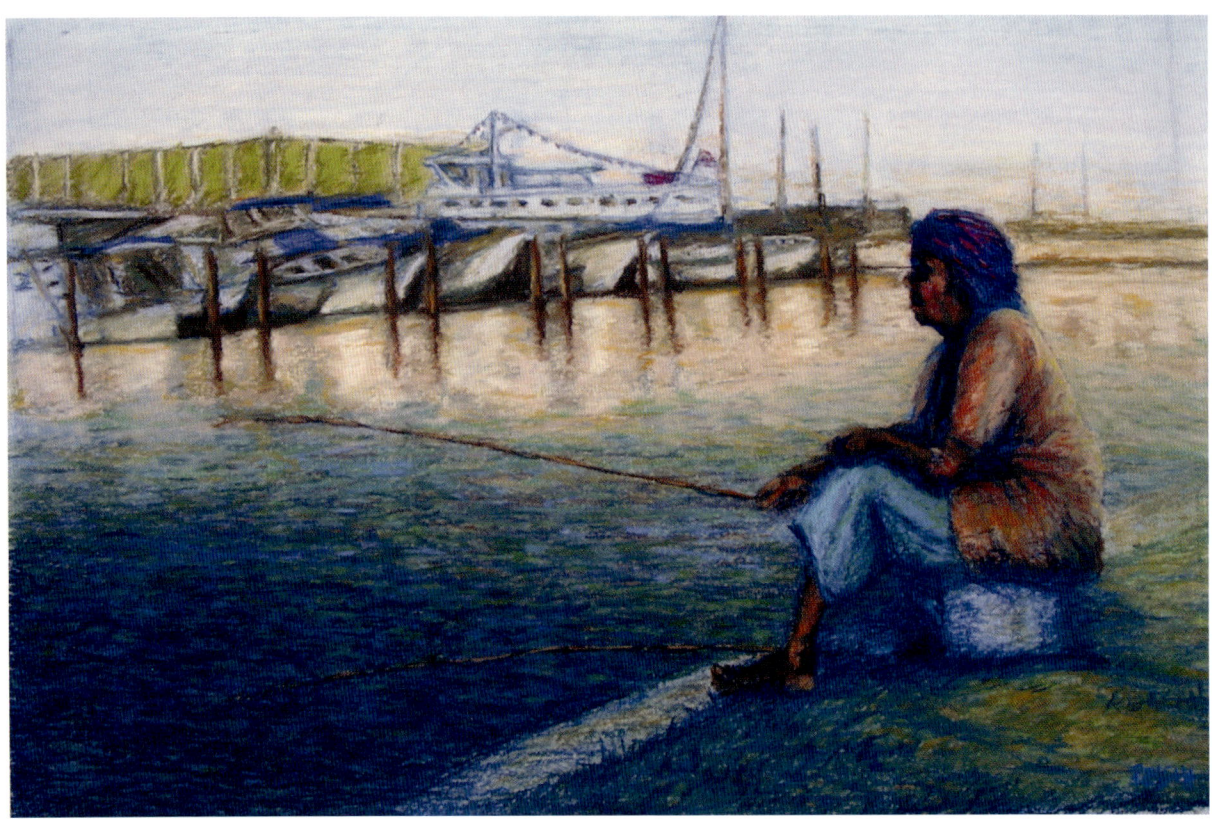

Plate 97. Bettye Reagan. *Fishing Lake Monroe*, n.d. Pastel on paper, 16 × 24 in. Courtesy of the artist.

Fishing Lake Monroe is another good example of Bettye Reagan's pastel "paintings." The solitary figure sitting on the water's edge seems lost in quiet thought, separated from the crowded dock seen across the lake. It might be early morning or late afternoon—the light is softened by the humid atmosphere and the shimmer of light reflected off the water's surface. The mood of reverie is unbroken. You can almost hear the slow slap of water against the pier and the distant cries of birds or perhaps muffled music from a radio somewhere on the distant dock.

Because it was once the southern hub of the St. Johns steamboat traffic, Sanford initially seemed destined for greatness. Located on the south shore of Lake Monroe, the town grew from a trading post in the 1830s to a 12,000-acre citrus empire in the 1870s to a tourist destination that advertised itself as "A Real Playground Where the Mound-Builders Lived."[8] Tourists flocked to the "Gateway to South Florida" while local agriculture flourished and busy wharves facilitated the loading of winter vegetables onto boats headed for northern markets.

But the bubble burst. By the 1920s, large-scale agriculture was moving south and the tourists were disappearing, lured to the southern beaches now accessible by rail and highway. Bill Belleville writes, "On the north side of the river, [the town of] Enterprise floundered, the Brock House was torn down, and, on the south side, the city of Sanford finally went into bankruptcy."[9] Today, Sanford is a quiet community of about forty thousand that, like most of the surrounding towns, is being reinvented as a bedroom community for the exploding city of Orlando.

John Mitchell, a true river rat, lived in and around Sanford from 1922 until his death in 1987. He was the kind of guy who, when he sliced his hand while cleaning fish, would have his wife, Kathleen, sew it with thread, put a glove on it, and return to filleting. His wife bore two daughters, Susan and Christine. Susan remembers "spending days on the river bank. Daddy would be running his trotline and momma would be cooking over an open fire." In spite of growing up in a house without plumbing or electricity, without a television or telephone, but with kerosene lamps, a wood-burning stove and an outhouse, her romantic view is probably accurate.

In the mid-1970s, soon after the girls had grown and moved away, John and Kathleen, whom he called "Pooh Bear," retreated to Uncle Tom's Island, near Sanford, to live in a tent. Then they moved to Buzzards' Roost, a grassy island in the Upper River near Osteen. A friend gave them a worn-out houseboat, which J. D., as he was called, ran ashore. The river soon entered the hull, bringing silt and sea life along. "The river," he had said, "is the only running water I have."[10]

Expelled from grade school for having ridden a donkey down the middle of the school hallway, he returned to school decades later. Then he attended the School for the Blind in Daytona Beach: John Mitchell was legally blind. He fell off a wagon when he was a child, hitting the back of his head on a rock. His optical nerves dried-up, taking his sight. He didn't learn to write his own name until he was forty-two. Still, he could shoot a gun with accuracy and navigate the river, where he eked out a living fishing and guiding sportfishermen.

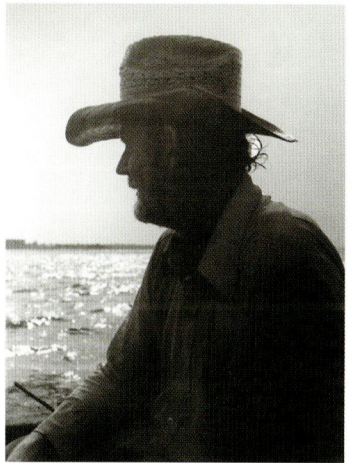

Plate 98. Bill Vincent Jr. Photo of J. D. Mitchell, ca. 1974. Gelatin silver print, 7 × 5¾ in. Courtesy of Tommy Vincent.

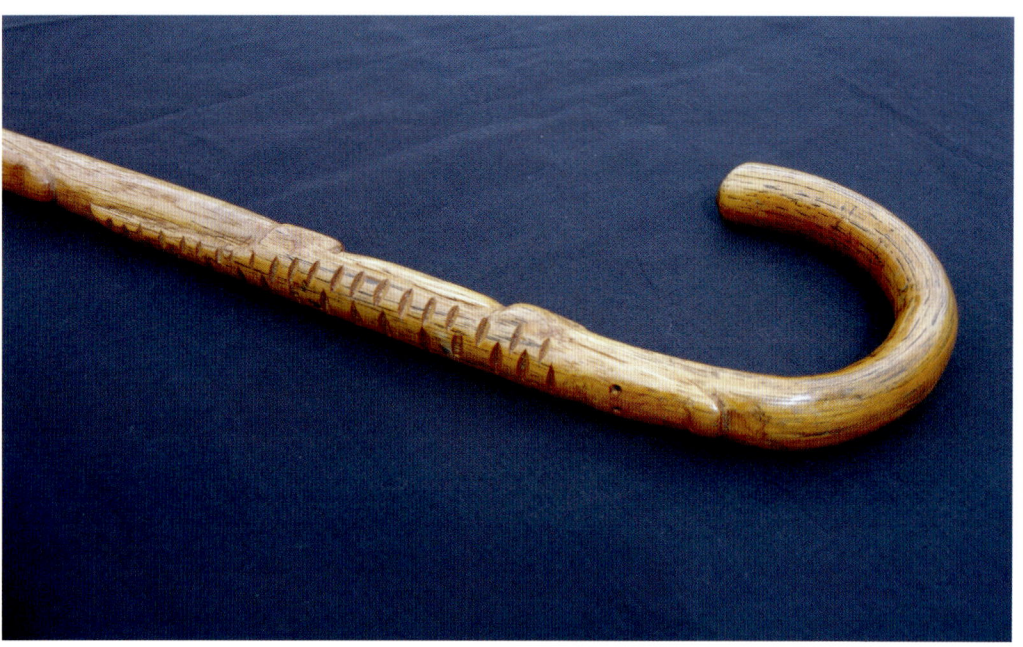

Plate 99. J. D. Mitchell. *Untitled* (walking stick), n.d. Wood, 37 × 1 × 1 in. Courtesy of Tommy Vincent.

J. D. whittled away the hours. He crafted alligators, sometimes on the shafts of canes; he carved a family of armadillos and miniature rocking chairs that "you could just touch and they'd rock back and forth," remembers Christine. He carved a set of large dentures for a dentist's office. He carved a ball and chain from a 4" × 4" × 6' shaft of wood. In the marshes, he carved alligators and squirrels on trees. He carved on scrap wood with whatever knives were on hand. He neither signed nor notched the finished pieces; once completed, he gave them away. This carved walking stick is characteristic of Mitchell's eccentric style.

Mitchell "was kind and generous, but that old man was a mess, flat out a mess," remembers Christine, saying he was given to too much drinking, which inflamed his temper. But when times on the river got tough, when fishing was slack or a fellow fisherman took ill, others "helped out just like you were family. I remember daddy filling up a crocker sack [burlap bag] with staples like dry beans, peas, rice, sugar, coffee, flour, meal, lard, and a piece of fatback or salt pork, with penny-pieces of candy for the kids. We would take it to the family and you didn't worry about it being paid back cause that's the way it was, you helped each other," writes Christine.[11]

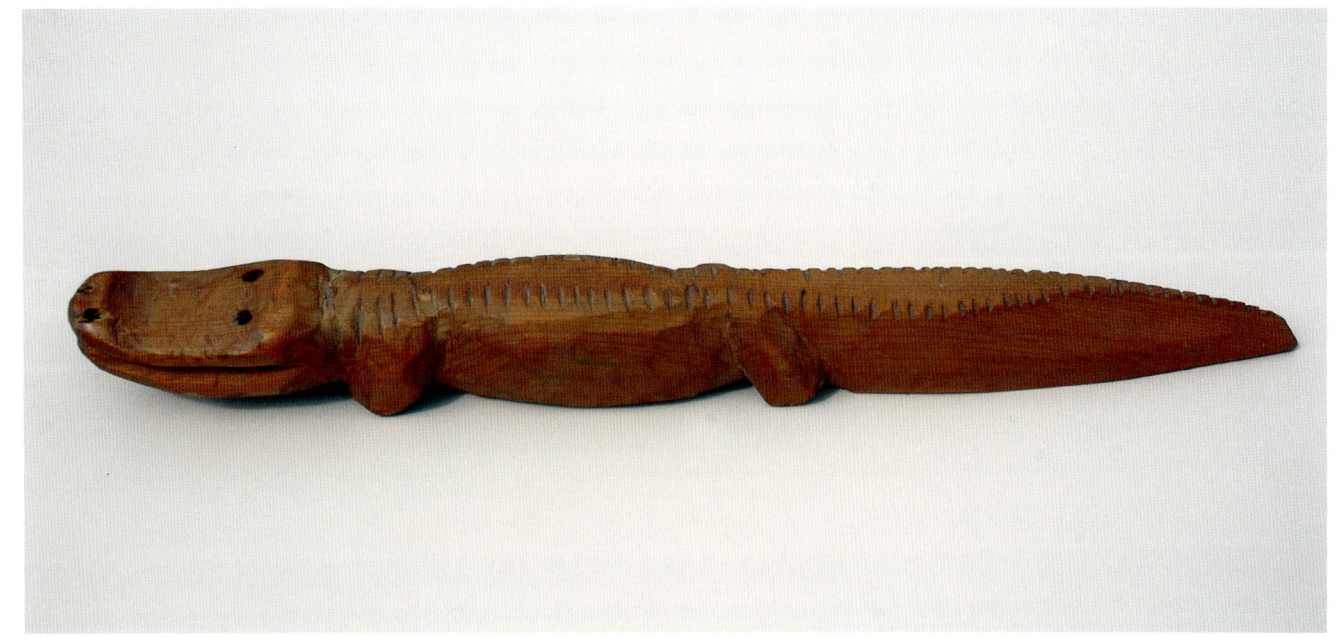

When times got really bad for J. D., he resorted to alligator hunting. Christine describes an outing: "Daddy took me with him so I could bail out the boat cause it leaked so bad you either bailed or sank. Daddy sharpened a hatchet that he made; so sharp he could cut the hair off his arm. Then he took a cypress pole and put a large steel hook in the end of it and made a very long gaff hook and reached up and in a gator cave until he hooked the gator, then he pulled him out and buried the ax in the gator's head, between the eyes. Then he would drag him up on the bank and skin him. He would roll the hide up in a wet crocker and take it home and pour a lot of boxes of salt on it to preserve it until he sold it."[12]

John Mitchell loved the river that defined him; he knew it, worked it, and was at home on it. One can envision J. D. "running his boat up and down the river and yodeling and singing, dipping his hat into the spray from the outboard motor for a drink of water," happy in his environment.

Plate 100. J. D. Mitchell. *Untitled* (alligator), n.d. Wood, 14½ × 1½ in. Courtesy of Tommy Vincent.

Carl Knickerbocker refers to his art as "Suburban Primitive" or "Naïve Pop." The former carries with it the weight of his sociopolitical observations while the other points downstream from his mission of actualization—to place style above substance. Although he blends folk forms with pop influence—including a touch of graffiti—his art is content-driven. The style may seem primitive, but the ideas come from his refined observations and/or from the proverbial child within.

Knickerbocker lives in the country near Orlando. Gated communities have sprung up where orange groves once scented the air, but Knickerbocker's cottage lies on sixteen pristine acres of unspoiled Florida wilderness—a perfect setting for the artist to conceptualize his paintings. His colors are bright. His figures are cartoonish, making them accessible to his audience. Among his icons are alligators, ladders, cars, blue and green dogs, Mickey Mouse ears, and flying saucers. Yet his art is serious, simultaneously entertaining and enlightening, while transforming the prosaic into visual poetry.

"My job," says Knickerbocker, "is to get people's attention. I'm competing for people's eyes, and there's a lot of competition out there."[13] He has painted at sites throughout the Orlando area, sometimes working in front of a "live audience." This painting of the Osteen Bridge uses a flattened "map" of the St. Johns River as a serpentine element to hold the composition together. Palms sprout like green torches along the water's edge, and a huge blue alligator approaches the bridge with mouth agape. A startled bird stands like a totem with wings outspread, and above the bridge floats a metallic saucer (or is it a gigantic eye?). The evidence of his intellect is cleverly concealed behind his humor.

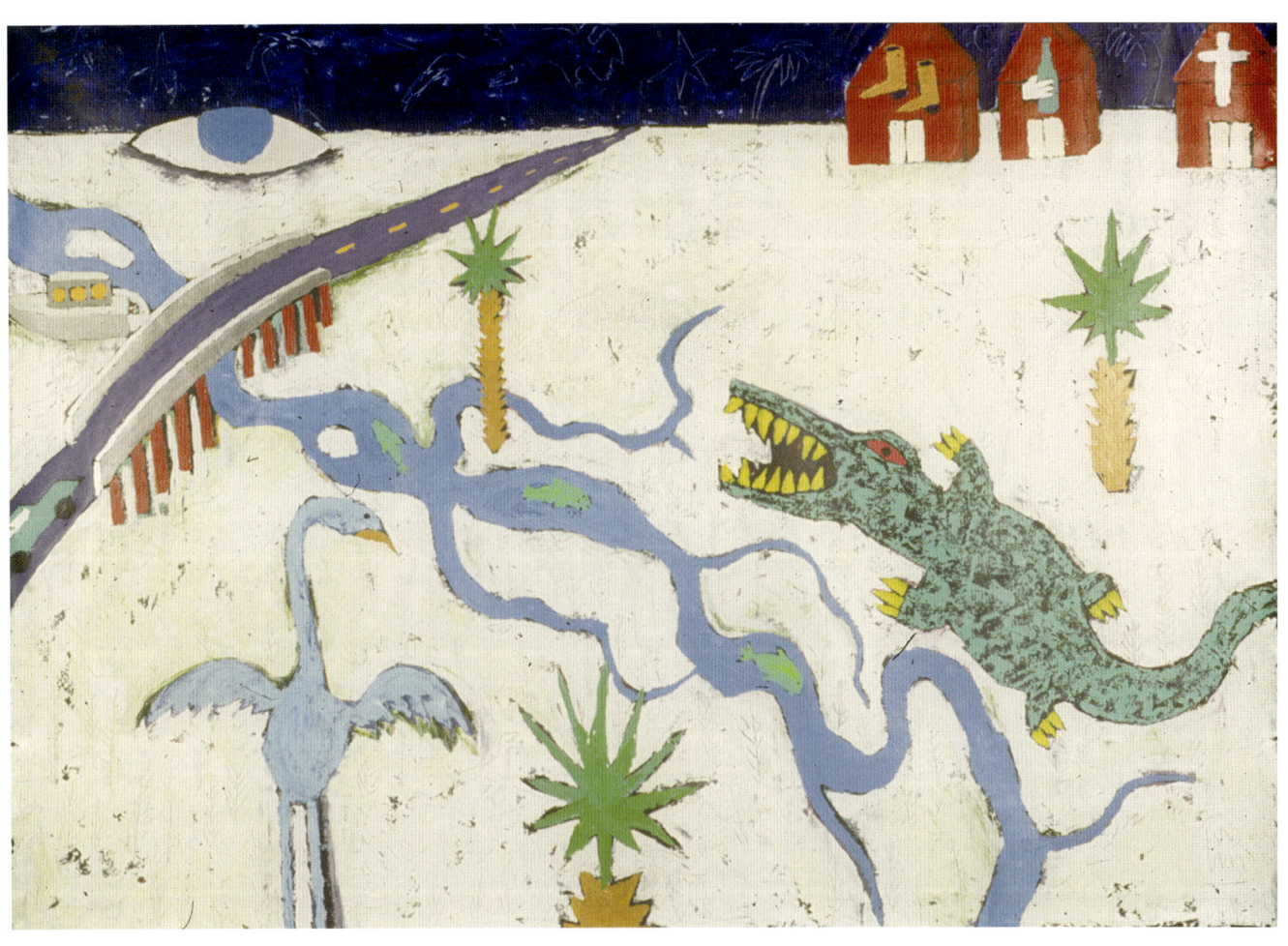

Plate 101. Carl Knickerbocker. *Osteen Bridge*, 1998. Acrylic on canvas, 84 × 129 in. Courtesy of the artist.

Edmund Stowe was born in Mt. Dora on August 30, 1894, and died one hundred years later in a nursing home in Sanford, not far from the house that he had built on the banks of the St. Johns River in Indian Mound. He traveled to every state but kept returning to Sanford, where he lived in that same house for fifty years. Once permanently settled in Sanford, he farmed, focusing on celery, then the region's bumper crop. He painted as a teenager, but it wasn't until he approached retirement, at about age fifty, that Stowe began painting in earnest. His interest was certain: "I don't paint anything with blood in it."[14]

E. B. Stowe advised, "You should paint the things of which you know most. So I paint Florida scenery."[15] Most of the scenery that he cared to paint were views of the St. Johns River. Although his technique was as traditional as his compositions, he was content knowing that his canvases both captured something elemental about Florida and delighted his patrons, mostly locals who knew less about art than about what they liked. The quintessential regionalist did not care about critical acclaim, but he was concerned about his environment. The *Orlando Sentinel* writer Wendy Spirduso points out Stowe "can tell you which plants freeze in the winter and where the river goes from here, why the clouds are flat on the bottom and how this world changes every day to form a different picture."[16]

When he wasn't painting, Stowe was teaching in the glass-enclosed studio on the second floor of his home. He taught as many as four days a week with six students or fewer in each class. But the artist was usually painting for his own satisfaction and selling the framed works soon after they were completed.

Reasonably priced at sixty dollars for a 24 × 30 in. canvas in the late 1970s, the price was calculated at eight cents per square inch. Of Stowe's estimated five thousand paintings, 1,700 were commissioned by the owner of a string of Holiday Inns at Daytona Beach; Stowe took almost three years to complete this project. For these paintings, the artist said: "I set up a ladder horizontally in the garage and put nine canvases on it. Then I put a chair with wheels in front of the ladder. I'd roll up and down and put in nine palm trees and nine skies and nine roads."[17]

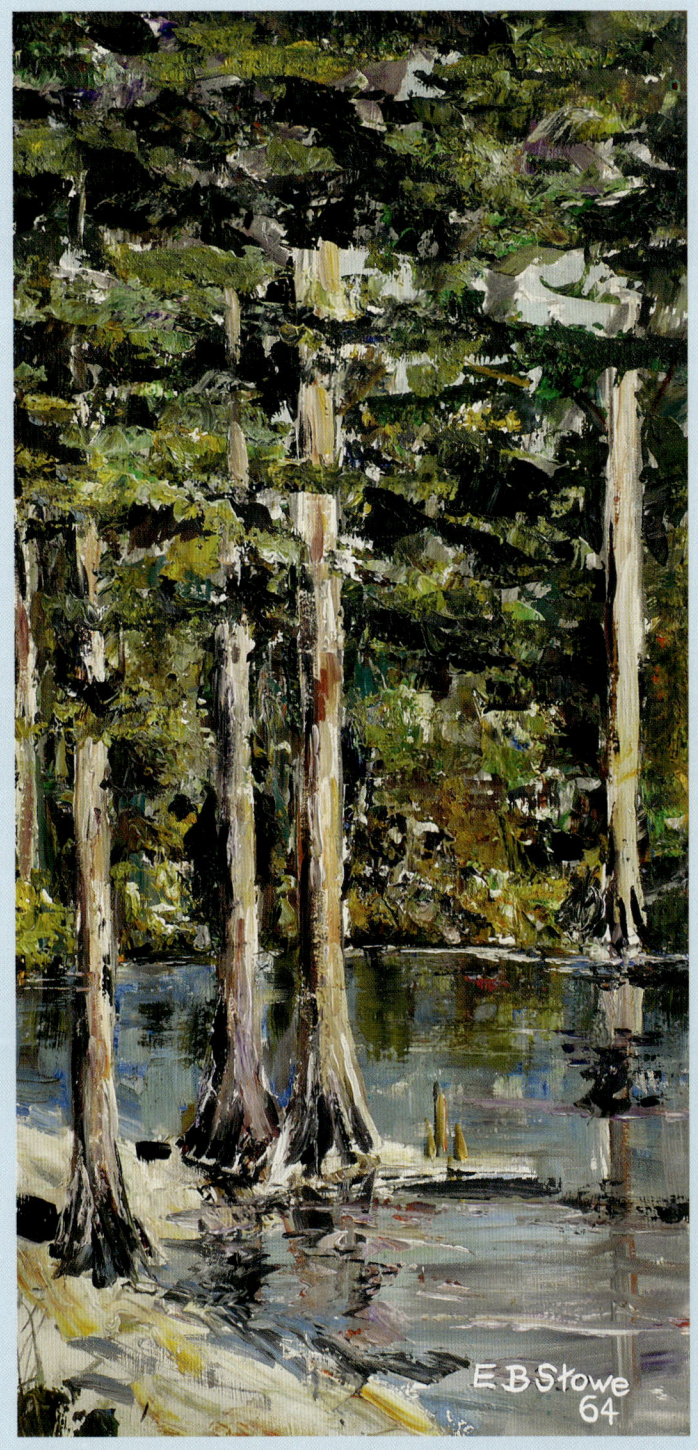

Plate 102. Edmund B. Stowe. *Untitled*, 1964. Oil on board, 29⁹⁄₁₆ × 14⁹⁄₁₆ in. Courtesy of Gary and Teresa Monroe.

Dreamers and schemers built Florida, and few dreams were more inspired than Jim Terwilleger's dream-causeway across Lake Monroe. Terwilleger, the owner of Sanford's Miracle Concrete Company, was selling his product across the 9,400-acre lake for massive home building in the Mackle brothers' planned community of Deltona. He explained that driving the proposed causeway would be more cost-effective than driving the long haul around the sweeping curves of the lake's southern shoreline. It was an idea that would have expanded Sanford northward, and it would prove an economic boon to Sanford once the new community took hold, with families taking the causeway to shop and dine there.

Terwilleger commissioned the Sanford artist E. B. Stowe to paint a picture of his dream. A Seminole County commissioner approached the Volusia County Commission in 1968 with the proposal to seek cofinancing of the $5.5 million project. Even though the causeway would be self-sustaining in six years from funds collected as tolls, the Volusia County Commission gave the proposal a cool reception. Of course, the five hundred signatures of citizens from Deltona and neighboring DeBary expressing opposition to the plan did not help either. These same people had countered the proposed widening of Highway 17/92 to four lanes, which would have eased any inconvenience of driving the scenic route around the lake. Ultimately, the proposal for the causeway never reached the State Road Board for further consideration.

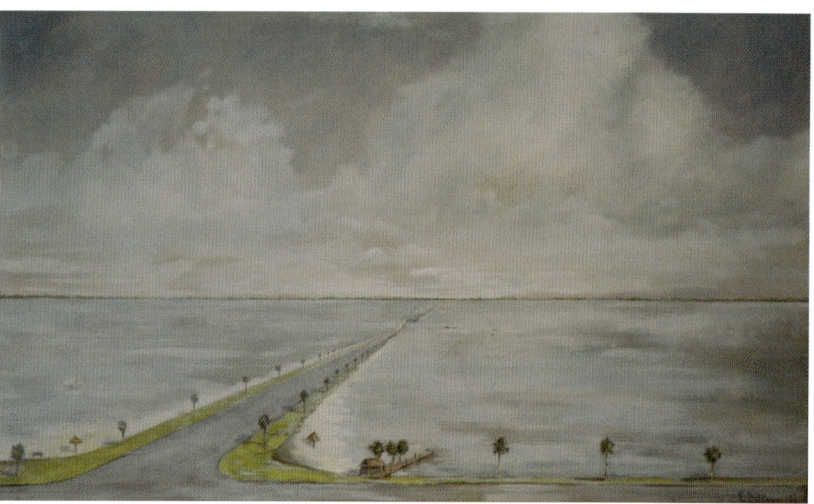

Plate 103. Edmund B. Stowe. *Proposed Bridge across Lake Monroe*, 1967. Oil on canvas, 35½ × 65½ in. Courtesy of the Museum of Seminole County History.

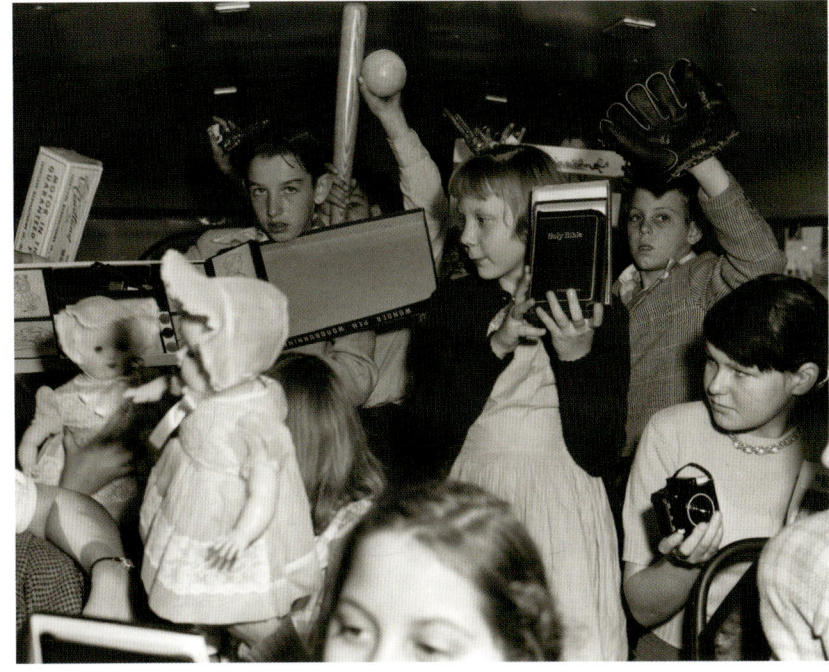

Plate 104. Anonymous. "Methodist Children's Home," n.d. Silver gelatin print, 8 × 10 in. Courtesy of the United Methodist Children's Home.

The Florida United Methodist Children's Home, a faith-based charity, was founded in 1908 on the banks of Lake Monroe in the town of Enterprise. In its beautiful 100-acre campus—the former site of the famed Brock House from the river's glory days as Florida's capital of Gilded Age tourism—abused, abandoned, neglected, or dependent children are well cared for in accord with the Children's Home charter Statement of Purpose:

> Here we propose, by the help of God and the cooperation of all good people, to found a noble Christian institution for the relief, education, and training of destitute, fatherless and motherless children, who may look for us for help.[18]

The statement, although having served and guided the institution, is sterile in light of the reality of the Children's Home: No more than ten residents live in each of the twelve cottages on the elegant campus; a cottage resident-therapist resides in each one. A spiritual influence is an integral part of all their programs and services, which physical and mental health professionals as well as educational and recreational experts who work on campus avail with love and care that these unfortunate youths might otherwise not have experienced. The photographs, though, cannot reveal more

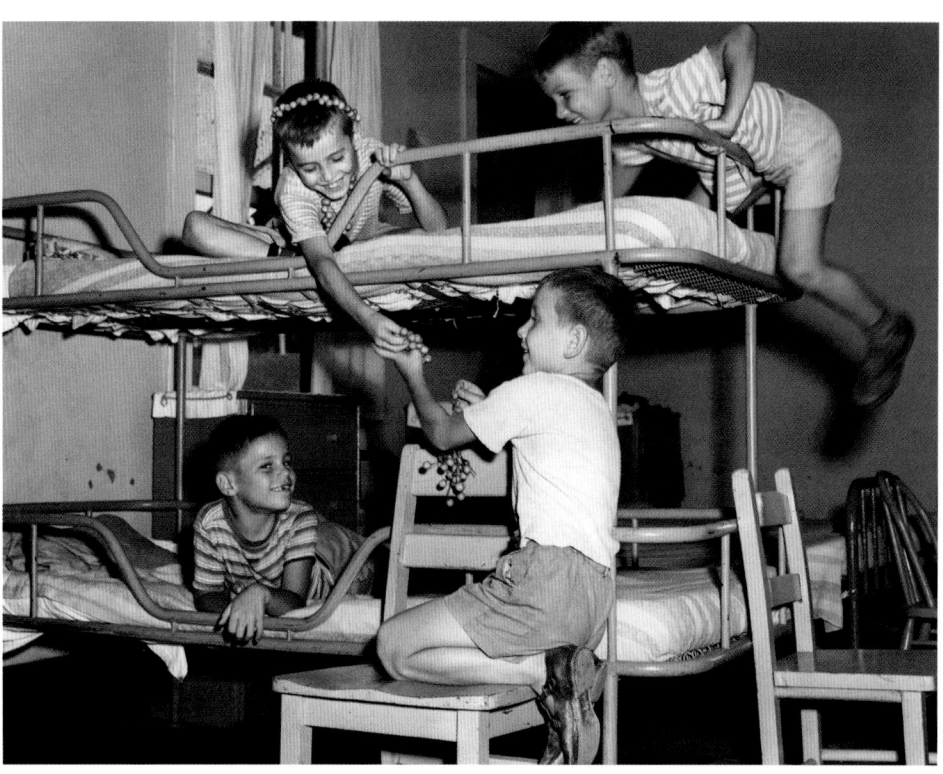

Plate 105. Anonymous. "Methodist Children's Home," n.d. Silver gelatin print, 8 × 10 in. Courtesy of the United Methodist Children's Home.

than these facts: the superintendent was called "Dad," and adults return to the home decades later for reunions in appreciation. The first two orphans, a brother and sister, came from Lakeland by horse and carriage to the western banks of Lake Monroe, at Sanford, where they were put on a rented rowboat and rowed by the minister of the First Methodist Church of Lakeland across the wide waters to their home in Enterprise, a children's boarding house that became the Florida Methodist Orphanage.

Photographs do not narrate, although they possess the aura of narrative; no photograph has a beginning, middle, and end. It might be argued that photographs are the story's climax, but they offer no resolve. Rather, the images are suspended in space; theirs is a case of suspended animation, and the best photographs are dramatically animated. John Szarkowski offers a key to understand the paradox of the photograph: "To quote out of context is the essence of the photographer's craft."[19] The photograph is its own reality, plucked from time and space and represented anew, a new reality whose relationship to its subject is not objective, didactic, or linear, but inferred.

The inferred narratives' meanings are malleable, meaning different things to different people.

Interpretations vary, but photographs are convincing because of their apparent fidelity to fact, if only for their surface description. After all, the camera only records surfaces convincingly. Beauty may be skin deep, but it is compelling. As photographs suggest realities and the viewers tell their stories, lending their own beliefs, realities, meanings, or endings, the power of photography lies in this empowerment of the viewer-consumer, who is offered a cornucopia of truths from which to question, confirm, or delight in the pleasures of seeing, knowing, and, above all, thinking.

In the hands of the best photographers, those who are attuned to the camera and the world they are searching and serving—as is the case with these untitled, uncaptioned, undated, and uncredited photographs of orphans at the Methodist Children's Home—we are convinced that the people in the photographs speak for themselves, in their native tongues. It seems that, as an intermediary, an unbiased photographer employed a disinterested machine-camera to simply record what was there, the simple truth. In truth, believability is the crux of photographic imagery—the photograph is an illusion.

These images do testify to the high ideals of the orphanage. Believable and compelling, they appear to have been made by a professional or advanced amateur photographer with both skill and insight.

Plate 106 (*left*) **and 107** (*right*). **Anonymous. "Methodist Children's Home," n.d. Silver gelatin print, 8 × 10 in. Courtesy of the United Methodist Children's Home.**

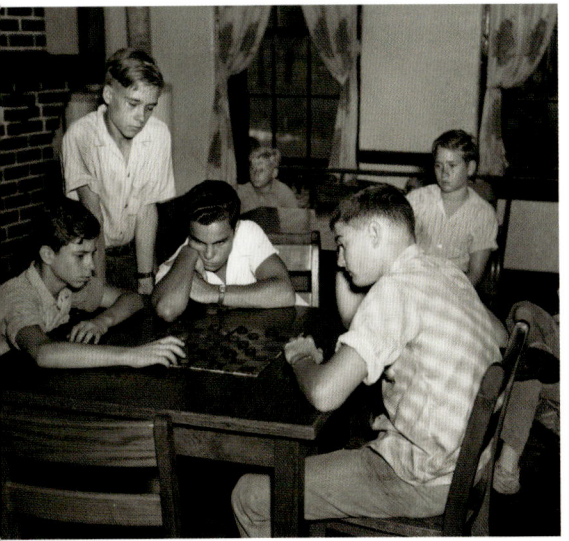

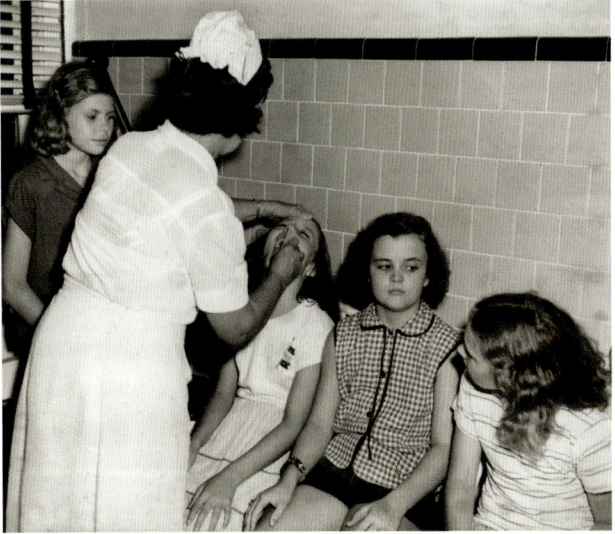

Between Lake Monroe and Lake George, the topography of the river basin changes noticeably—the banks are higher, the river narrower. This part of the river is fed by numerous artesian springs—bursts of water pushed upward by the pressure of the water itself as it seeps into the underground caverns that feed the Florida aquifer. It is in this area that the Wekiva River joins the St. Johns in its slow journey toward the sea.

The name "Wekiva" comes from a Creek Indian word meaning "spring of water," and nine major springs feed into the Wekiva.[20] Indian mounds along the river's banks have helped archaeologists determine that people lived here as early as 2000 BC. The surrounding forests support a large number of Florida black bears along with deer and other types of wildlife, including ospreys, hawks, waterbirds. and even a small band of rhesus monkeys that, according to local legend, were introduced to the area for the filming of Tarzan movies in the 1920s and 1930s.[21]

Bill Belleville calls the Wekiva "a microcosm of the entire St. Johns. . . . An area of biological transition where the range of temperate zone plants meets and overlaps the margin of tropical ones." The result is a region of tremendous biodiversity that supports 178 species of birds and dozens of exotic plants.[22]

The Orlando-based artist Tom Sadler grew up amid natural surroundings that looked similar to the imagery that would distinguish his mature artistic works. While drawing and sketching in his youth, he developed an affinity for the landscape in month-long camping trips across the continent. Encouraged by a high school art teacher to pursue art in college, he earned his bachelor's degree in fine arts at Auburn University but found true mentorship under the guidance of Jack Dempsey, a professor from the University of Alabama. Sadler says that when he began painting with oils while under Dempsey's tutelage, it was "like a light bulb going on"—a fair analogy for an artist whose paintings would be distinguished by the play of light.

For his thesis exhibition, Sadler illustrated the story of the pirate Blackbeard. "My work wasn't wild enough to go abstract," he says in reference to the topical explorations in the then-contemporary art world.[23] Besides, he was attracted to the sublime beauty of works by such artists as Inness, Church, Bierstadt, Corot, and Monet. He finally set the stage for his artistic foray when he docked his sailboat at Vero Beach after having navigated around Florida.

Occasionally the artist positions himself so that his point of view includes a city skyline on the horizon, just off in the distance enough to remind patrons that times are changing. His renderings often emphasize a nostalgia to which viewers could fall prey. His sense of realism is admittedly "Romantic"; he knows that it is to a landscape painter's advantage to cherish the natural wilds from a vantage point with good-quality light. "What can be a great composition at one time of the day, might not have the appeal under different light," he points out. Should the actual composition not be ideal, he "may move a palm tree."[24]

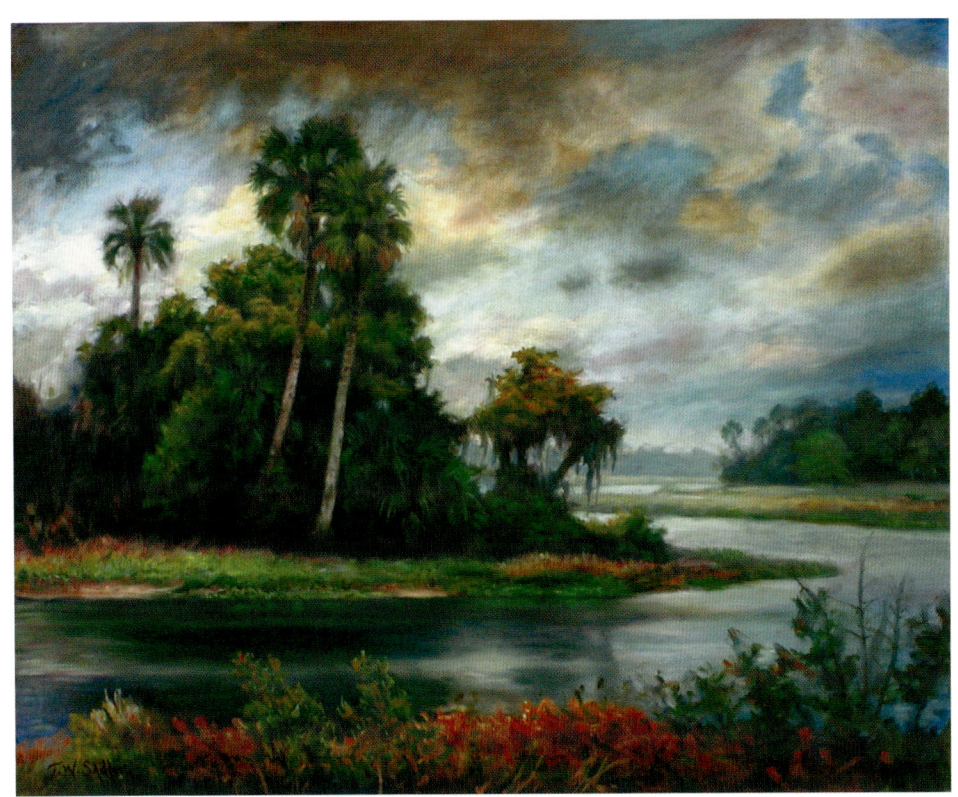

This painting by Tom Sadler of the St. Johns River was inspired by a scene off S.R. 46 south of Sanford. It depicts the river at the point where it becomes navigable and begins to reveal itself as a waterway rather than a marsh.

Plate 108. Tom Sadler. *Wekiva Palms*, 2006. Oil on linen, 46 × 60 in. Courtesy of the artist.

When Sadler settled in Orlando in 1983, he quickly established himself as a viable landscape artist. His paintings soon adorned law firms' offices, and commissions followed. Realizing that the "Old World" charm of his paintings appeared most pronounced beneath track lights, he opted for gallery representation over outdoor art shows. He realized too that site-specific paintings appealed to his clients, so he focused his efforts on the immediate surroundings, emphasizing the "timeless" qualities of the Wekiva River.

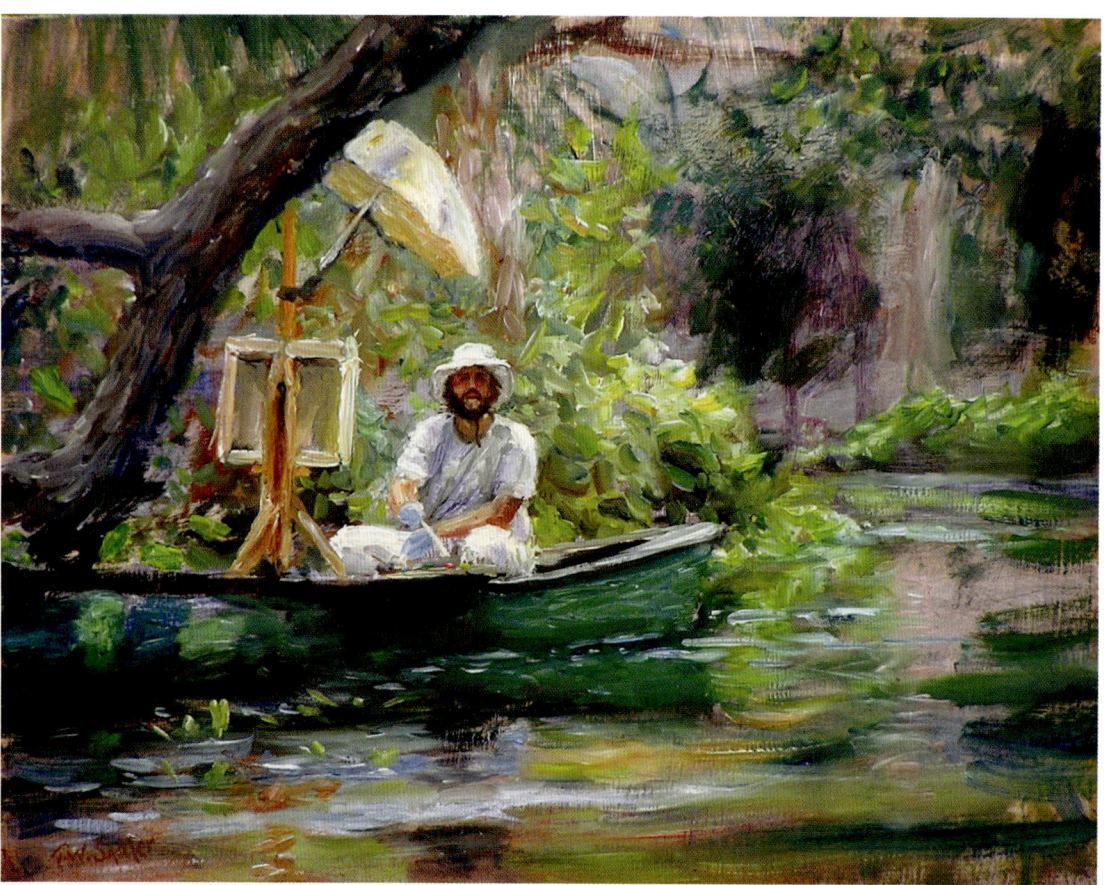

Plate 109. Tom Sadler. *Artist at Work*, 2008. Oil on panel, 10 × 13 in. Courtesy of the artist.

This painting, titled *Artist at Work*, brings to mind images made famous by Manet, Monet, and other impressionist painters, who loved to go out on the river together to work from landscapes *en plein aire*. Of this painting, Sadler recalls: "Several artist friends of mine set out to paint either from the canoe or along the banks of the Wekiva River. They included Kevin McNamara, Bernie Martin, Mitch Kolbe and myself. We paddled downstream each in our own canoe which we had loaded down with our painting easels and gear. Painting directly from the canoe is a great way to appreciate and study the river first-hand."[25]

Sadler begins each canvas by either making a small study "to capture color and light from life" or by taking a photograph; sometimes he does both. As he paints, he employs the technique of glazing, in which layers of transparent paints add depth to the image. Working this way is slow, so at any time there may be fifteen paintings in process. Although a skilled technician, Sadler understands that an artist is "always selecting what to bring out, [that the process of perception] is subconscious."[26] And he knows that it is best to paint "what comes from the heart, what you love." He knows when a piece is complete; at that point, he wants to keep it for himself. However, that is when the painting is ready for the gallery.

Jim Draper felt uncomfortable as a child growing up in rural Mississippi—out of place, even. His youthful artistic aspirations were not at one with the place; the first painting to stir his consciousness was of "Jesus knocking at the door." It was, if nothing else, his sentient knowledge of the land that would inspire him throughout his career as a landscapist. His awkward beginnings left him with a profound sense of metaphor that overtook any need to paint realistically. His experiences at graduate school seemed at odds with his calling. There, his coursework emphasized abstract expressionism with a dose of conceptualism. However, this may have actually fed his need to explore his place and himself, and to express each simultaneously through painting.

Draper recalls traveling from "the bleakness of home to the southern coast," and suddenly seeing palm trees and feeling elated: "Things just got better. You knew you were in a better place," he recalls.[27] Certainly he was in a better state of mind. Draper eventually would paint his *Healing Palms*; its images were elevated to that of Byzantine iconography with a tropical flair. His trees were symbolic; palms regenerate under the worst circumstances, offering a metaphor for personal transcendence.

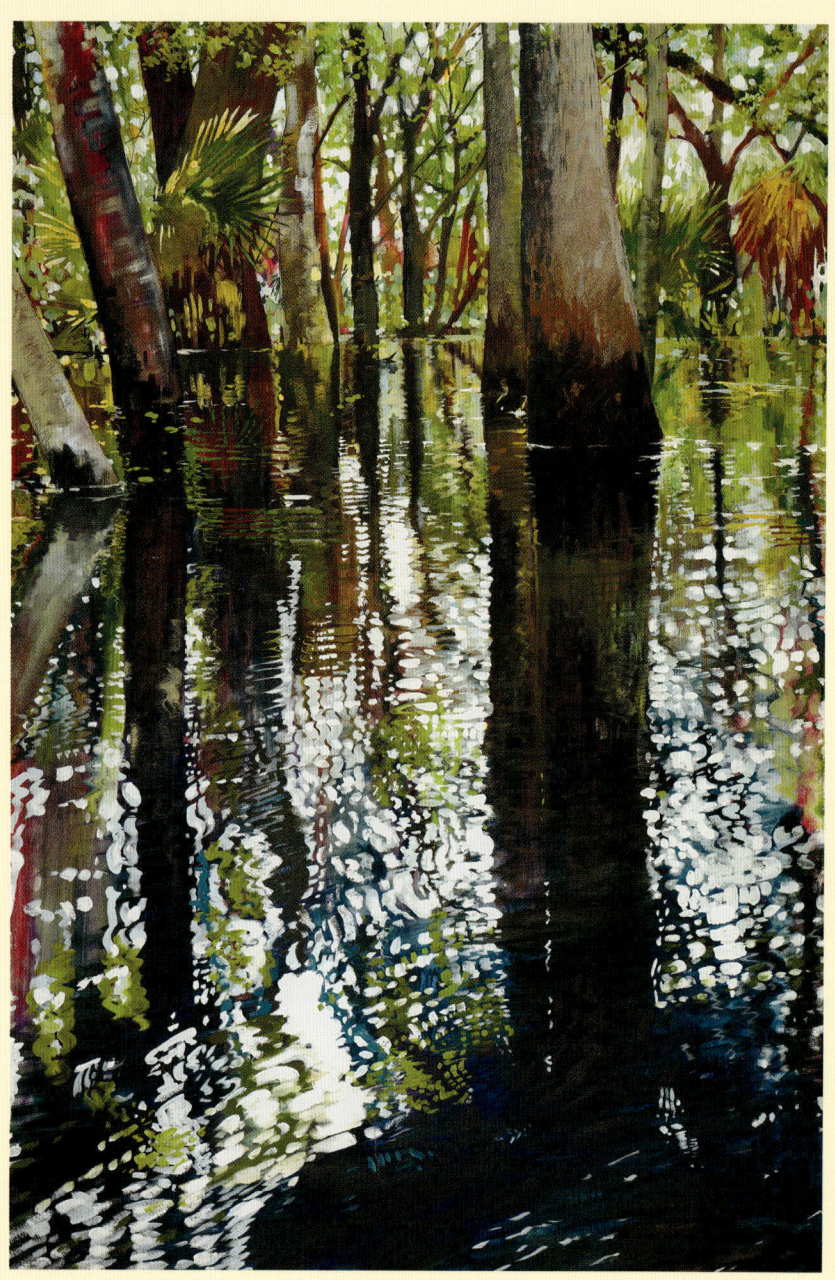

Plate 110. Jim Draper. *Wekiva Reflections*, 2006. Oil on canvas, 60 × 40 in. Courtesy of the artist.

It was the uniqueness of Florida that brought out the best in Jim Draper's work. Springs here are so very clear; looking at their water causes disorientation, a feeling of vertigo. The river's blackwater reflections are equally unsettling, creating a luminosity that is unlike anything else. "A blackness that's not black," like dark tea, a result of tannic acids.

Draper's comment about "an oddness for *the artist* not in his element" reveals something about what drives him to metaphoric responses. The color and scale of his work elevates nature above worldly concerns. That his palms "take abuse and rebound" is inspirational; that his birds are elevated beyond a general treatment suggests that mankind can also rise above the mundane. Draper's paintings are visual lessons taken from nature. For him it is more personal: "My mind is wild. I swim with the gators and play chess with rattlesnakes. I crawl finger and toe through the marsh and the muck and eat snails and wild berries and take all that stuff, the mud and the juice, and thin it with syrup from sap and paint it all into a picture."[28]

The town of DeLand was founded in 1876 by Henry A. DeLand, whose interest in trees added a natural charm to the village that is still evident today. DeLand is home to Stetson University, named for its benefactor John B. Stetson. The first law school in Florida opened at Stetson in 1900.[29] Over the years, DeLand has nourished the spirits of a number of artists while the beauty of the surrounding area has inspired their work.

"Artist Harry Fluhart, whose handsome paintings in the Claredon lobby have been so much admired, has opened his studio on Grandview Avenue," according to the *Daytona Gazette-News* of January 28, 1911. Fluhart, who had wintered in the resort beachside town with his wife, became a well-established artist through his allegorical paintings, historical images, and, mostly, his regional landscapes. Having had artist-parents, Fluhart spent his whole life in the studio, surrounded with art. He studied in Munich and Paris, and taught at Knox and Earlham colleges before coming to DeLand, where he taught at Stetson University from 1915 to 1935, when his health began to fail. He passed away three years later.

In *Stetson University: The First 100 Years*, Gilbert Lycan remembers Fluhart for his "beautiful and entrancing Florida landscapes."[30] He also recounts a troubling tale. The trustee Edward Solomon had purchased a number of Fluhart's paintings for the university, and additional paintings were purchased from Fluhart each year. Eventually, more than a hundred of Fluhart's paintings were stacked on the floor along the walls in Holmes Hall. Stetson students took the opportunity to carry at least one hundred of these away for themselves. A few paintings were left after the plundering free-for-all because they were hung in offices throughout the campus.

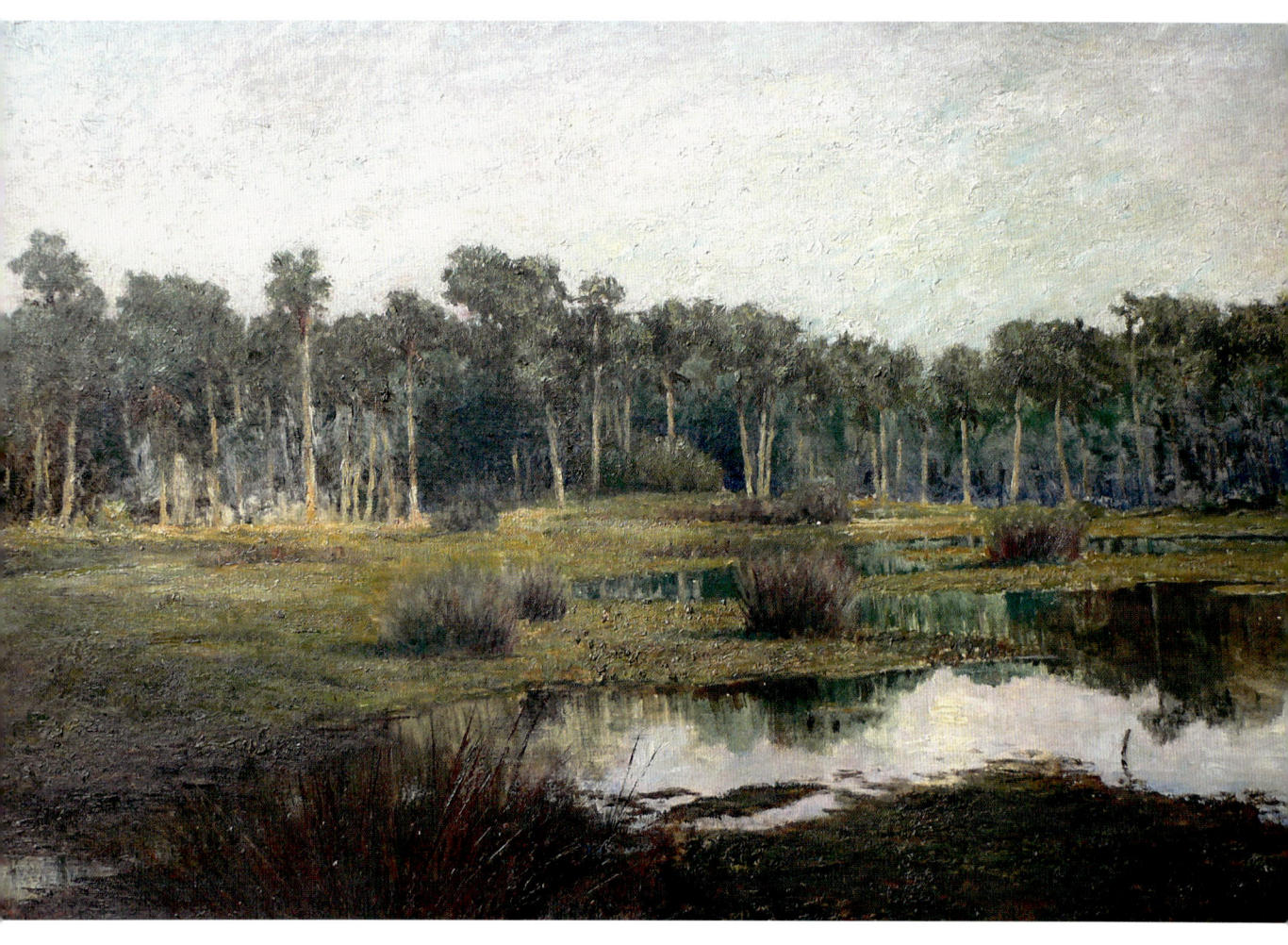

Plate 111. Henry Fluhart. *Untitled*, n.d. Oil on canvas, 23¼ × 37³⁄₁₆ in. Courtesy of Stetson University, DeLand, Florida.

The subject in this painting, like the others in the collection of Stetson University, is unidentified. At first, it looks like a view across of Lake Woodruff, but as Bill Belleville points out, "it would have to be very low water for those reeds (bulrush, etc.) to be poking up out of the bottom of the lake inside of it. Just don't think it gets that low there mainly because Ponce DeLeón spring and a few other small springs can keep that lake cooking."[31] Belleville agrees with the folk historian Bill Dreggors, who believes the topography to be of the Upper River, below Lake Monroe. It could be any of that very braided section between Lake Monroe and the mouth to Lake Jesup. But, as Belleville points out, "farther south than that, the shoreline is dominated with low marsh grasses, sometimes studded with old sable palm hammocks, like at the mouth of the Econ [the Econlockhatchee River]."[32]

When Trish Thompson says, "Painting is primary," she means that the action of painting and the resulting artifact are more important than the subject matter. Where other artists employ their craft to distinguish a subject, hers is a process in which she "creates chaos and then goes about resolving it" in pictorial terms. Thompson's terms are largely formal, as she knows well that the thing depicted is not the thing itself, that ultimately a painting is self-referential . . . otherwise the image becomes sentimental. Yet it is sentimentality that compels her to paint by the bridges that cross the St. Johns River at DeLand and Astor.

Thompson's oeuvre is characterized by investigations into process-oriented square panels that teeter between intellectual posits about the nature of art and an abstraction that implies nature itself. She plays her own game by approaching her panels without preconceived notions; she doesn't know how a final piece will evolve. To tantalize the process, sometimes she will paint with her left hand, abandoning her right-handedness. She will turn a work in progress upside down, and use unconventional tools such as brayers and styluses to gouge at the surface. She will also employ joint compound and sand, along with acrylics, to create her paintings.

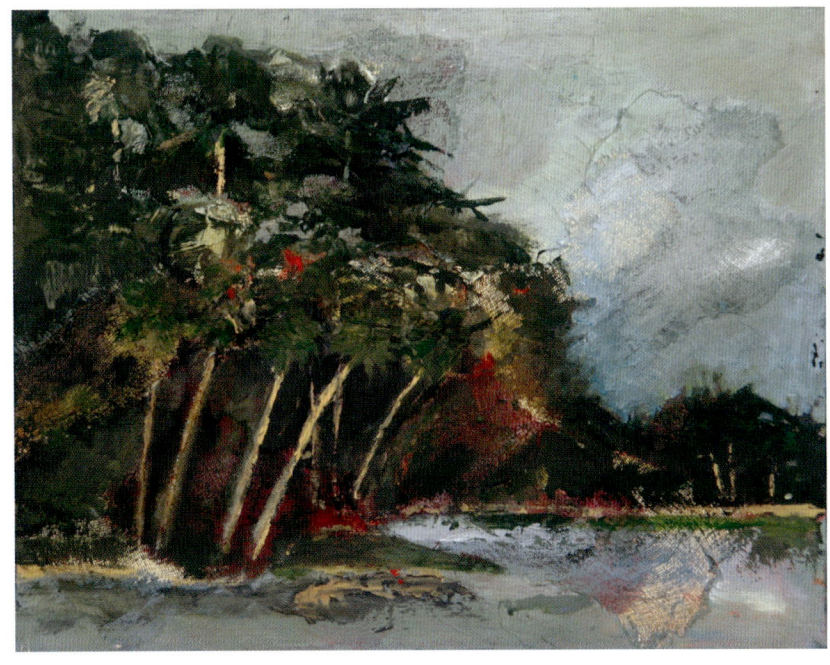

Plate 112. Trish Thompson. *St. Johns East Bank, S of 44*, 2006. Acrylic on canvas, 11 × 14 in. Courtesy of the artist.

Thompson's investigation is aesthetic; she is an artist who explores the meaning and the possibility of art primarily for art's sake. Nevertheless, another side emerges when she is painting privately, as if her pieces were journal entries. These meditations are also personally constructed but from a very different place, further removed from the art world from which she has developed her more structured artistic interests.

Thompson grew up in Panama City, along the Gulf of Mexico. But she gravitated to the rivers throughout north and central parts of the state. To her they were like roads from one place to another, signifying destination and travel. "Like a one-way railway," she analogizes. During her youth, Thompson's family would meet at a remote campground in west Florida and play along the riverbanks. She found these sites to be intimate, places to have fun. She developed a strong affinity to a waning way of life by floating along with the current in inner tubes and taking in the varied life forms that swim beneath the water and those that create a sanctuary along the banks.

Plate 113. Trish Thompson. *View from Beresford Lady, St. Johns*, 2006. Acrylic on wood panel, 11 × 14 in. Courtesy of the artist.

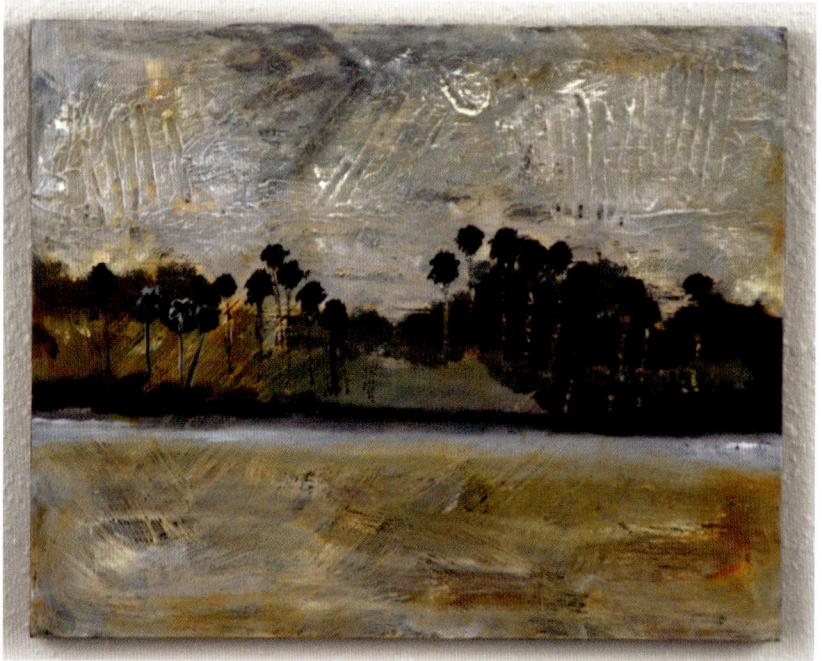

Unlike her more formal investigations, Thompson doesn't exhibit the unpretentious but evocative images of particular places to which she comes for rest and, sometimes, to paint.

With enviable drafting ability, Pam Griesinger has long painted narrative figure studies that are generally large and bold angst-ridden images. But she has seasoned, and today she tempers her art with "spontaneous" images of the central Florida landscape, especially those nearby her home in Volusia County. In 1980, she was first drawn to Lake Woodruff, a wilderness preserve that offers wondrously varied views as well as refuge for wildlife.

Vulnerability and the cycles of life have long driven her art, and at Lake Woodruff Griesinger's work is at its most personal and perhaps most piqued for intangible qualities of the landscape offer both solitude and the means to realize her connection to nature. Her jaunts to the preserve are less about making art than about reflection. "It's just a space where I feel at home. It feels sane and normal in a world that isn't," she offers. "I love to watch it all, from sunrise to sunset . . . the changing of the guard, with critters coming and going."[33]

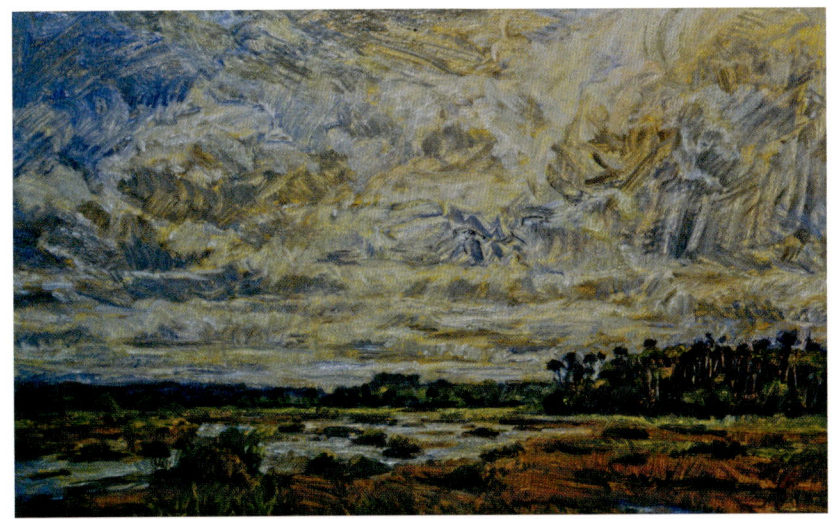

Plate 114. Pam Griesinger. *Lake Woodruff Diary 11-3-03*, 2003. Oil on board, 9 × 15 in. Courtesy of the artist.

Pam Griesinger considers the small paintings she creates on-site not as specific records but rather as pages from a diary; her response to time and place. Nothing is planned, and certainly no formal strategies enter her mind. The rules are simple: She hikes about with all she'll need in a backpack, stopping at spots that compel her, places that are as likely to be as meditative as they are beautiful. She "just starts to paint by throwing down red paint or green or whatever, depending on my mood and paint into it."[34]

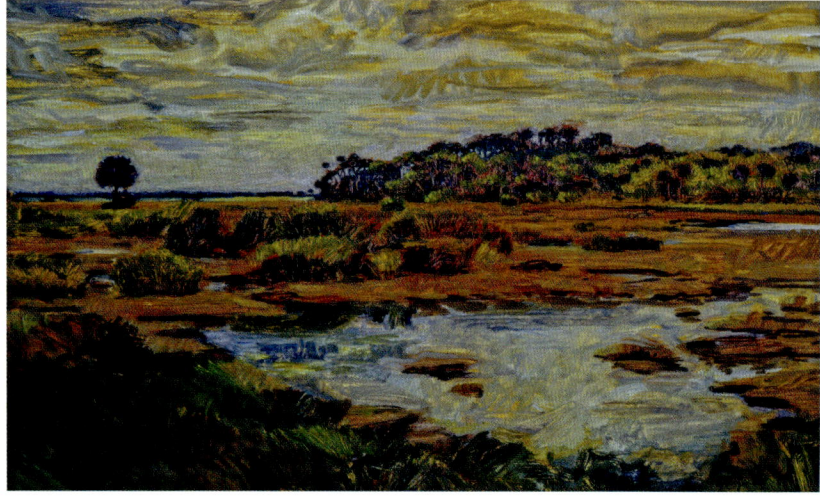

Plate 115. Pam Griesinger. *Lake Woodruff Diary 3-6-04*, 2004. Oil on board, 9 × 15 in. Courtesy of the artist.

There is a sense of channeling in Griesinger's experience-based approach. Griesinger's intuitions help her along; she has little interest in laboring over details that would consume these works. She does not objectify the landscape; she creates poetry for the eyes.

Griesinger spends a half hour to four hours on each of these paintings, until her fascination ends and self-consciousness sets in. This forces her to contend with her sensations and facilitates her departure from mere recording. These landscapes are not studies. They are not about the time of day or split seconds of changing light that inspire other artists who attempt to reveal God's domain. In Griesinger's art, the physical world gives way to the sublime; we travel along with nature, and "peace and quiet become more and more important" as we accept our mortality.[35]

WHEN THE BRITISH occupied Florida in 1763, an enterprising trader named James Spalding opened two outposts along the river to serve the needs of new settlers and travelers. The Lower Store was located near present-day Palatka while the Upper Store stood near the town of Astor. The Bartrams (John and William) visited both stores during their 1765 visit to Florida, and when William returned alone in 1774, he relied on the Spalding stores for supplies and used them as bases for his exploration of the area. He stayed for several months at the Upper Store, where he sorted through his specimens and made notes on his discoveries.[36]

During the Second Seminole War (1835–42), a fort was built on the site to protect the military operations on the river. Union troops occupied the fort during the Civil War until Confederate Captain J. J. Dickison captured it in 1864.[37] Following the war, the town of Astor grew up on land that was bought by William Astor, the grandson of John Jacob Astor. Astor built a railroad to haul the fruit that he grew on the 12,000-acre estate. The town prospered until the freezes wiped out the citrus groves. With the end of the steamboat era, the town faded into oblivion. Today, Astor is a small village, but its location still makes it desirable.

Cultural heritage activities are primary functions of the Pioneer Settlement for the Creative Arts of Barberville, not far from Astor in rural Volusia County. Barberville, formerly called Midway, was a major stopping area for travelers between the St. Johns River and the ocean. Housed in the former Central School of Barberville (ca. 1919), the Settlement began amassing regional historically significant buildings, and a historical "village" emerged. The setting includes the Pierson Railroad Depot (ca. 1885), Astor Bridgekeeper's House (ca. 1926), Turpentine Comm./Store (early 1900s), Turpentine Still (ca. 1924), Pottery Shed (1920s), Lewis Log Cabin (ca. 1875), Midway United Methodist Church (ca. 1890), Huntington Post Office (ca. 1885), Quarters House (1920s), The *Pastime* touring boat (ca. 1910), and the Joseph Underhill House, ca. 1879, "which is believed to be Volusia County's oldest existing brick home. Its bricks were made on site from clay found nearby."[38]

Workshops were established to encourage schoolchildren's active participation in forgotten folkways, which led to asking Steve Vrooman to help rebuild a steam engine. Next he rebuilt a spinning wheel and loom. Simultaneously, the retiree became a design weaver. Consistent with the facility's programming, he gave demonstrations to visiting children on fieldtrips; all the while his passion and his skill grew. Because a fifth-grade teacher wanted her class to spend an entire day with Mr. Vrooman at the weaving station, he had to come up with something different and engaging to fill the time. Having heard of women making sun catchers from old bread wrappers, he thought about those nonbiodegradable plastic bags that stream from grocery and big-box stores only to overflow cupboards and clog landfills.

Soon he devised a plan to recycle these ecologically damaging products into functional beach mats; after all, he was in Florida. In fact, he tells the children that they'll be weaving an indigenous material—Florida tumbleweed! Replacing rags with plastic, he figured out a way to cut and tie the bags together so that they would endure the weaving process. Soon schoolchildren were bringing bags to cut, tie, and weave into beach mats that could easily be toted, hosed off, and reused. He and the children then began separating the bags by colors. Each store had its own colors: Wal-Mart used blue bags but later switched to white, and Winn-Dixie and Publix had brown bags while their text colors differed.

Eighty to one hundred bags were used to create the finished products: eventually these evolved from beach mats to throw rugs. They are no longer white or brown; now they are vibrant with well-considered colors. Many are woven with keen design sensibilities. Some are even two-sided. Schoolchildren have become artisans, having a good time while producing hundreds of rugs, learning a nondigital craft, and helping to protect the environment. The rugs are popular with visitors to Pioneer Settlement; their sales in its country stores have generated thousands of dollars that fund programming.

Plate 116. Rug woven from plastic bags, 2008. Photo by Jason Sweeters. Courtesy of Steve Vrooman.

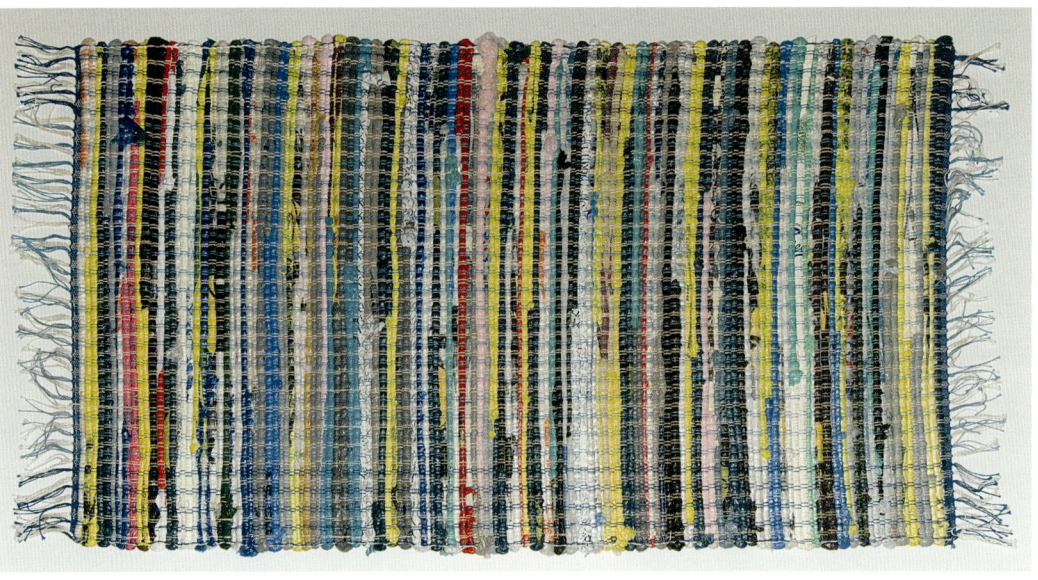

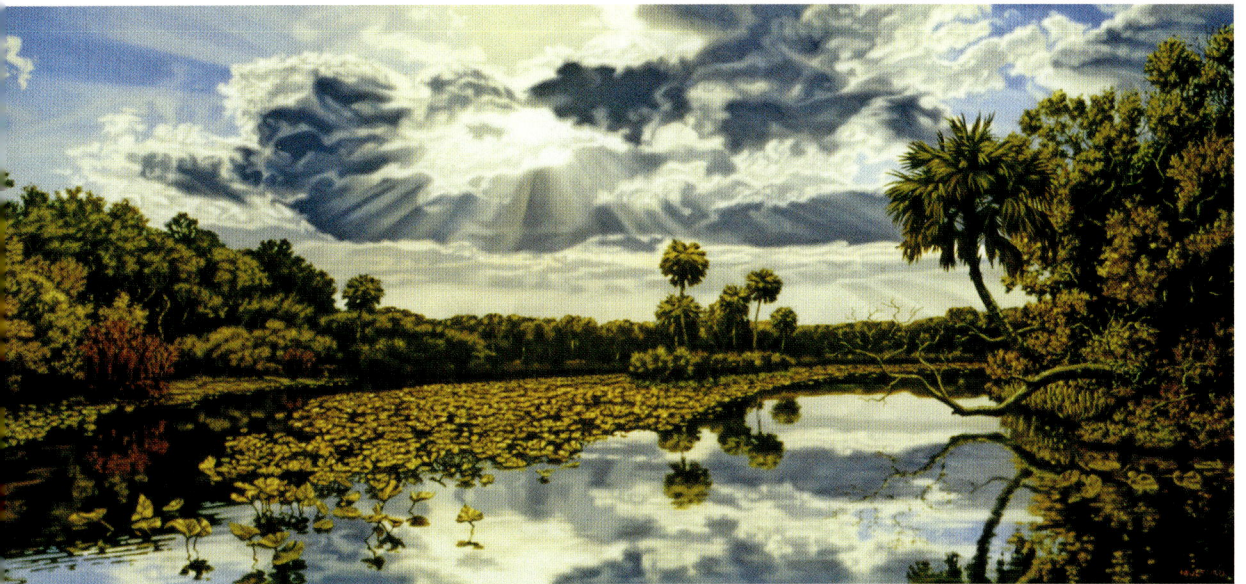

In this painting, the Orlando artist Hansen Mulford depicts Alexander Springs run as it follows its fifteen-mile-long path from its origins deep in the forest to its union with the St. Johns.

Plate 117. Hansen Mulford. *Alexander Springs Run*, n.d. Oil on canvas, 30 × 60 in. Collection of the University of South Florida Eye Institute, Tampa, Florida.

Alexander Springs, a popular recreation destination, is located in the Ocala National Forest near Astor. A first-magnitude spring, it has the largest flow of any natural spring on U.S. government land.[39] Bill Belleville has dived into the spring basin, "where white sand lies on the sides of the limestone walls like snow on a mountain cliff."[40]

After Lake Okeechobee, Lake George—at seventy-two square miles—is the largest lake in Florida. According to the naturalist Bill Belleville, the elongated bowl of the lake's bottom was likely scooped out of the sea floor at a time prior to Florida's emergence as a peninsula.[41] Named for England's King George III when Florida was still under British rule, it is, says Belleville, "the last great expanse of wildness on the middle river."[42] On the lake's western shore lies the 430,000-acre Ocala National Forest, home to abundant wildlife and numerous developed recreational sites. Bald eagles and black bears are abundantly evident in the region—indeed, Lake George has been historically noted for its many types of birds.

The tales of trouble on Lake George are the stuff of legend. Almost anyone who has encountered this massive body of water has a tale to tell. In 1774, Billy Bartram had an impressive encounter with the lake that he called "a little ocean."[43] "I cannot entirely suppress my apprehensions of danger," Bartram wrote. "My vessel at once diminished to a nut-shell on the swelling seas. . . . Soon after entering the lake, the wind blew so briskly from the west, with thunder-clouds gathering upon the horizon, that we were obliged to seek shelter from the approaching tempest."[44]

Marjorie Rawlings and her companion Dessie Smith had a similar experience when they crossed Lake George in a small boat 150 years later. Although a former steamboat captain advised them to cross with care and to hug the western shore, the adventurous Ms. Rawlings struck out across the lake's expansive middle and was soon caught in a "frothing, whitecapped sea which it took them almost two and a half hours to navigate."[45]

Bill Belleville had a similar adventure when he traveled across the lake in his journey of discovery along the St. Johns River's 310-mile length. "As I launch my own crossing," Belleville writes, "it is a bright, cheery spring day with a sky full of puffy cumulus. . . . Lake George appears before me as a great pussycat of a lake, a flat mirror that sparkles from one horizon to the next."[46] However, it wasn't long before "it appears that the sleeping pussycat of a lake is waking up and is a bit grumpy to boot. A strong wind is now blowing toward me from the opposite end of Lake George, delivering watery tannin hills with it that hiss with spindrift. In no time, Bartram's little ocean becomes just that, with baby whitecaps metamorphosing into large, angry waves that crash repeatedly into the bow, splashing over onto the deck. The boat lists at a dangerous steep angle, drawers slams open and shut, glasses crash onto the floor, and I stagger at the wheel like a drunken sailor, holding on for dear life. . . . I look anxiously for a shoreline and see none, just acres and acres of whitecaps and waves."[47] Although all four adventurers survived their ordeal, they came away with an enhanced appreciation of the lake's notorious power.

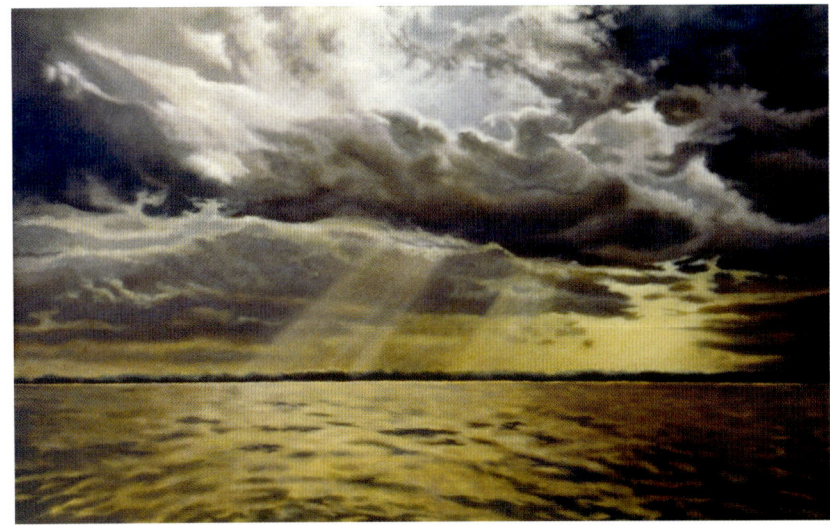

Plate 118. Sydney McKenna. *Trouble Brewing on Lake George*, n.d. Oil on canvas, 25 × 40 in. Courtesy of the artist.

Sydney McKenna was well aware of the stories about the lake's capricious nature when she painted this painting aptly titled *Trouble Brewing on Lake George*. The clouds are gathering, the waves rising, and the shoreline is receding into the distance. The painting takes on Romantic overtones that hint at the power of nature and man's insignificance, even today, in the face of the awesome uncontrolled elements.

Originally from Santa Monica, California, McKenna has made Florida her home since 1964. From interior farm country to coastal wetlands, the common thread found in her work is the bright sun and the humidity produced by the abundance of water. These elements, she says, produce an "atmosphere and architecture that is specific to Florida."[48] "My work is primarily about evaporation," McKenna notes, "and how it blurs the line between what we see and what we don't see; the physical and the spiritual. In the humid air of the South, evaporation is an ever-present condition that often underscores the 'oneness' of our environment. At times, an environmental 'statement' emerges as I work to show the interaction between air and water in Florida."[49] McKenna's Lake George painting fuses light and water to convey a sense of drama and redemption.

North of Lake George, the entrance to the Ocklawaha River is guarded by the town of Welaka, named for the original Seminole word for the St. Johns River itself—River of Lakes. The town sits atop a bluff on the east side of the river. According to Bill Belleville, the poet Sidney Lanier described Welaka as the site of an old pre-Columbian Indian village. Later, Spanish settlers built their own town on the same location. Belleville notes, "Like other steamboat landings, it once had ambitious promise, and now it has something else, the endangered taste of Old Florida."[50]

In 1989, David La Cagnina bought a house on the St. Johns River near Welaka. His work kept him traveling during the week, but on weekends he loved the quiet of the river and enjoyed the plants and creatures that surrounded his house. Elephant ear and staghorn ferns grew in abundance while water creatures of all kinds—turtles, gators, herons, ospreys—were constant visitors.[51]

David had spent much of his life working with his father, Henry La Cagnina, a talented artist who in addition to painting in oil, enamel, and watercolor was equally skilled as a furniture designer and sculptor. Born in 1909 in Brooklyn, New York, Henry studied art at Cooper Union Art School and the Phoenix Art Institute. In the 1930s, Henry was the youngest of thirteen artists who settled in Key West as part of a WPA program to advertise the Florida Keys as a tourist destination and art colony. Later, he designed and developed furniture for major national and international companies.

In 1969, Henry and David opened an art gallery in Stuart, Florida. Henry worked on his projects while David handled the business details. Later, father and son ran galleries in Naples, Florida, and in Hobe Sound. By 1980, however, Henry was ready to retire, and David moved on to other ventures. Henry relocated to Mississippi, but when David moved to Welaka in 1989, Henry became a frequent visitor, often staying several weeks at a time.

In the 1950s, Henry La Cagnina had carved several wood doors for clients in South Florida—one was featured in the magazine *Town and Country*—and he decided to carve a door for David's Welaka house. David remembered his father asking, "What do you want on here [the door]?" and David replied that he wanted the beautiful things that he saw surrounding his home. "He just started carving," David recalled. "He did the bird first and then the other plants and animals—he didn't do any preparatory drawings. He never did. He always just worked straight from his head."[52]

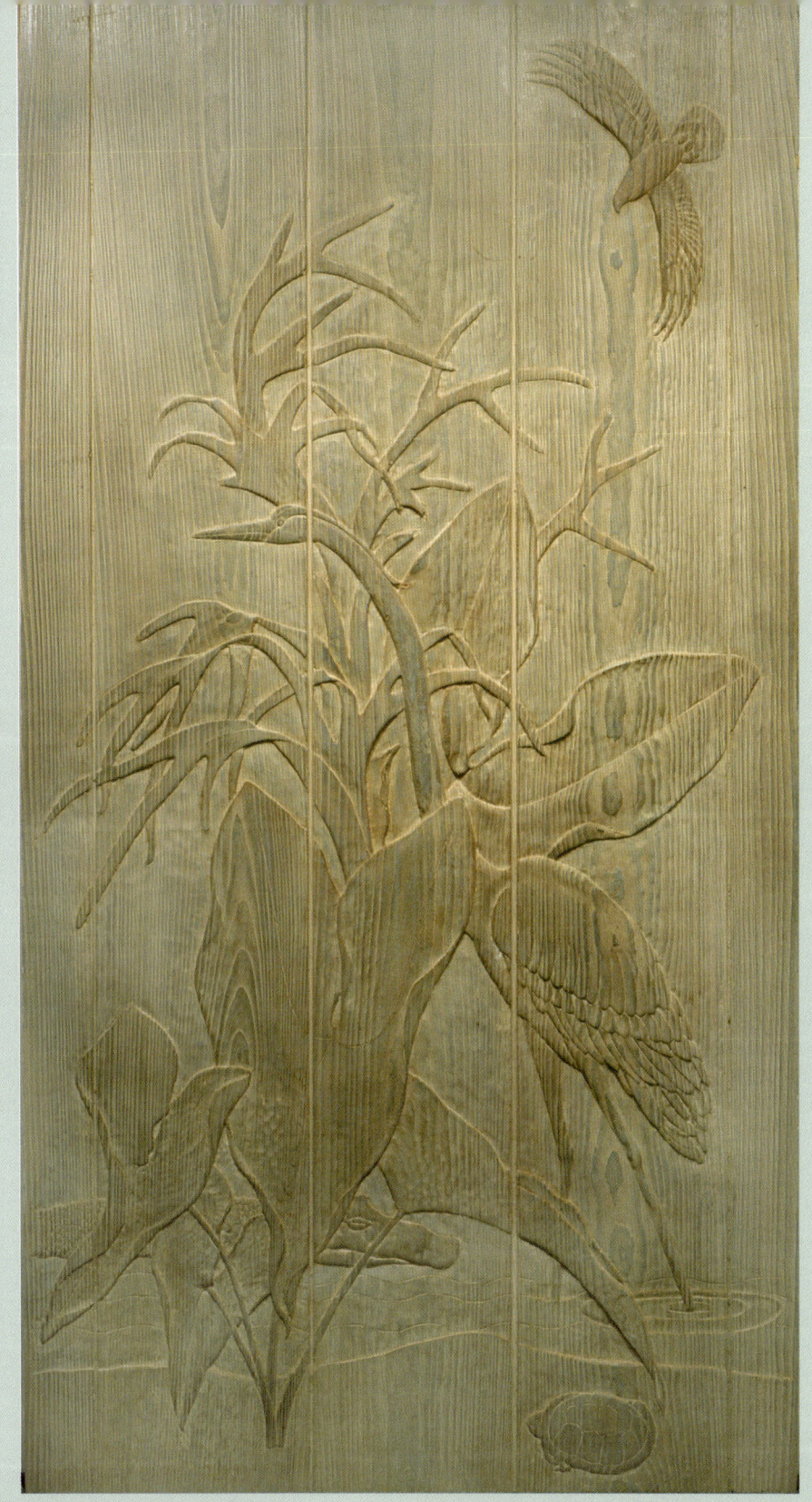

Plate 119. Henry La Cagnina. *St. Johns River Door*, ca. 1993. Wood, 80 × 36 in. Courtesy of David La Cagnina.

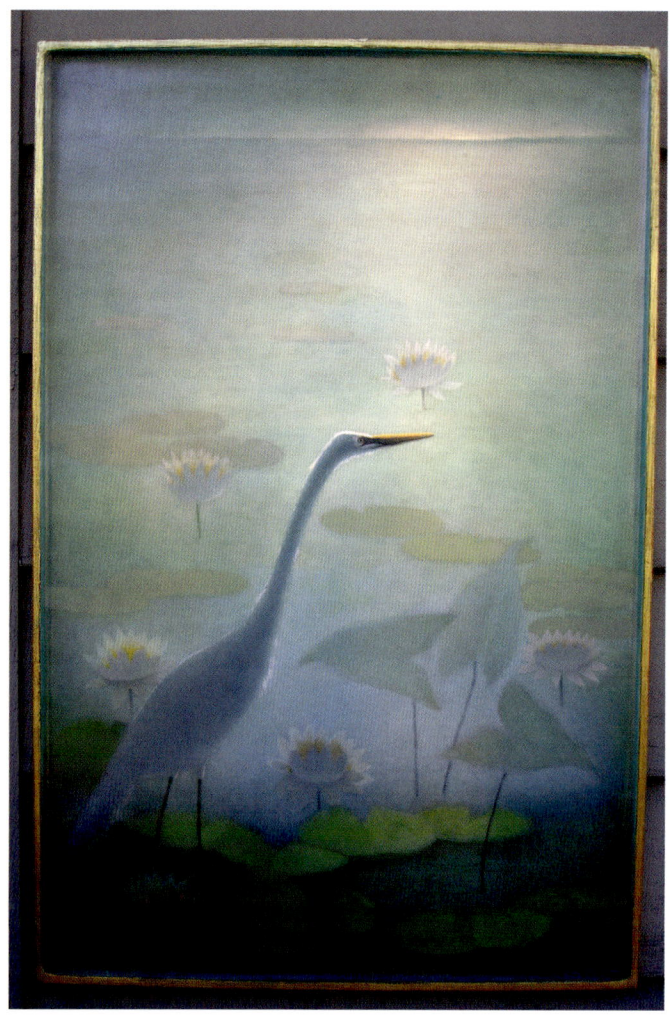

Plate 120. Henry La Cagnina. *Dawn*, 1988. Oil on canvas. Courtesy of David La Cagnina.

After several years, David moved on, resettling in Highlands, North Carolina, where his father continued to visit and to work on his art. Often, the images that Henry had seen in Florida cropped up in his art—flowers and ferns, waterbirds and fish. In this painting, done in 1988 in Mississippi, Henry looked back at the images he had seen along the St. Johns and re-created an egret standing in a pool of water surrounded by beautiful lilies. The image has the clarity of a suddenly remembered dream that captures in one glimpse an iconic Florida scene. The images and memories of Florida stayed with Henry and continued to influence his work until his death in 2003 at the age of ninety-four.

The Welaka Maritime Museum is the embodiment of the vision of two men—Richard and Rand Speas. Richard Speas, who grew up near the shores of Lake Michigan, always loved boats but was never able to afford to buy one. So, in 1962 he designed and built a 62-foot square-rigger that he named *Andante*. He was so pleased with his accomplishment that he moved onboard and, with his wife and five children, headed for the Virgin Islands. Later, he moved to Pompano, where he and his son Rand went into business building and restoring boats. By 1988, Richard had retired and moved to New York State while Rand had opened his own shop in Welaka—the Welaka Landing Wood Boat Building Company, an airy, open facility with a grand view of the St. Johns River.

During his stay in New York, Richard began to create vases that were made from the scraps of wood left over from his boat-building activities. When he returned to Florida several years ago, he continued to make vases and also joined forces with Rand to establish the Maritime Museum a few blocks away from Rand's shop. The museum now houses an assortment of the boats that Richard has built and those that Rand has restored, including historically significant boats that were used both for commercial and recreational use on the St. Johns River.

Richard Speas has also continued to create the wooden vases that are on display in the museum. Many of the vases are quite large—the biggest is nine feet tall and was constructed of more than forty thousand pieces of wood. The vase pictured here is made of mahogany and decorated with carvings that resemble eel grass. Father and son are hoping to expand the museum that also includes a collection of historic photographs of the Welaka area and local maritime memorabilia.

Plate 121. Richard Speas. *Untitled*. Vase. Mahogany, 62 in. (*h*). Courtesy of the artist.

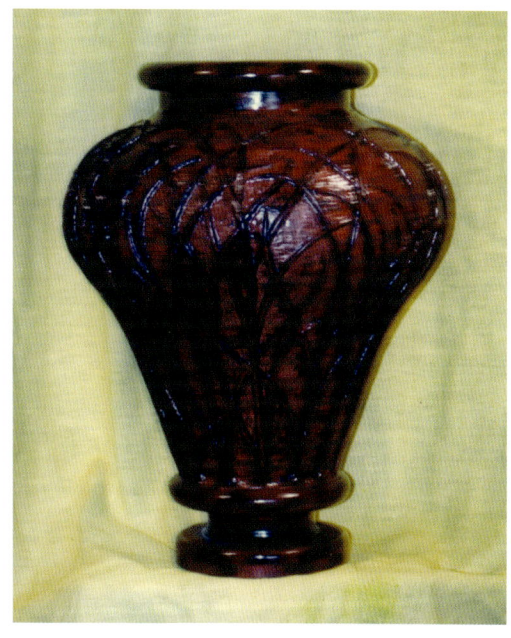

8 { Searching for Paradise

Tourism in the River Region

What though Welaka's name this
    changing world has lost?
I'll sing of thee, St. Johns, and of thy
    glories boast . . .
Thy current moves, like Time, with
    long imprisoned souls
Who mark how much their life, like
    thine, has tides and shoals;
And tough procrastination is of
    Time the thief,
Full well we know, to those thus
    bound, Time brings relief . . .
And that is why, St. Johns, I sing
    of thee,
Calling to friends up north, "Come
    down and see!"
—Solon Robinson, *The Glories of
the St. Johns*

WHEN DOES A "TRAVELER" BECOME A "TOURIST?" William Bartram, the intrepid Quaker who explored the St. Johns region in the 1770s, called the narrative of his adventures *Travels*. A century later, more than twenty-five thousand people were visiting the Florida peninsula each year. They came for a variety of reasons—for recreation, for adventure, or to search out a mild climate that would cure their illnesses. Two distinct social groups formed as a result of this pattern: the year-round inhabitants and the "visitors."

The nineteenth-century "visitors" tended to be city folk, a class of people with the resources and the time to take a leisurely trip on Florida's storied waterways. Northerners and midwesterners predominated in the St. Johns region. They viewed the native population with the same degree of lurid fascination that they gave to the alligators and rattlesnakes—living evidence of the survival of primordial creatures in a "modern" world. The "natives" had little in common with the winter residents, and inevitably there was friction between the groups. As Mark Derr points out in *Some Kind of Paradise*, stereotypes were created on both sides—"the slothful Cracker, the shiftless Negro . . . and the naïve, stupid and profligate Yankee."[1]

But as tourism increased, so did the opportunities for the natives to make money by catering to their haughty visitors. Wealthy investors and government officials soon also began to see the potential of a "tourist industry." Marketing efforts promoted Florida's charms—its balmy climate, its beautiful scenery, its exotic flora and fauna. Many visitors ended up buying property in the state and became winter residents. The growing tourist trade was one of extremes: "flush winters and barren summers."[2]

Edward King, a nineteenth-century travel writer, contributed to the growing interest in the South. His 1875 book *The Great South* laid the groundwork for renewed interest in that region following the Civil War, and Florida had a special appeal. The drawings by J. Wells Champney that illustrated the book provided a romanticized vision to accompany King's "enthusiasm for the attractions of the southern landscape."[3] About the St. Johns River, King wrote: "For its whole length of four hundred [*sic*] miles, it affords glimpses of perfect beauty. . . . The very irregularity is delightful, the decay is charming, the solitude is picturesque."[4]

While early travelers to the St. Johns region, such as William Bartram, were intent on exploring an unknown wilderness, later visitors came looking for adventure and excitement in an exotic setting. Increasingly, Florida became a popular "vacation destination." Gail Davidson, in "Landscape Icons, Tourism, and Land Development in the Northeast," points out that "as incomes grew and working people had more leisure hours, scenic touring became accessible to middle-class as well as wealthy Americans."[5] She also contends that the paintings of artists such as Winslow Homer and Thomas Moran "reflect how closely at times their choice of geographic subject matter paralleled the burgeoning tourist and land-development industries" and also "enticed vacationers to these areas."[6]

Steamboating in Florida began around 1830. Jacksonville and Palatka became the major ports of call along the St. Johns and also the major shipbuilding locations. Palatka had already established itself as a center of the logging industry. After the disruption of the Civil War and Reconstruction, the town resumed its position as a hub of the lucrative steamboat tourist trade. By the 1880s, at least one hundred boats, both stern-wheelers and side-wheelers, traveled the St. Johns River and its tributaries carrying supplies, mail, cargo, and, of course, tourists.

In *Steamboating on the St. Johns*, Edward Mueller writes: "The steamboat era in Florida lasted just over a century and during that time they were plentiful. The first steamboats started to serve the sparse Florida settlements in the 1820s. A few were still to be found in the 1920s."[7] Although the St. Johns was the primary route for steamboats, smaller crafts plied the shallow channels of the Ocklawaha as well as the Suwannee, the Apalachicola, and the Kissimmee.

According to Mueller, "The first steamboat to visit Florida's east coast was the *George Washington*, an adventurous side-wheeler of 1827 vintage, built at Charleston [South Carolina]. The *George Washington* is alleged to have reached Jacksonville, then a settlement of a few hundred souls on the St. Johns, on May 18 or 19, 1829, while on an excursion from Savannah."[8]

Direct service from Charleston to Jacksonville began in 1851, and business continued to increase until the advent of the Civil War. Although steamboats continued their regular runs for several months after the start of hostilities, the Federal blockade soon cut all service.

Following the war, boat traffic resumed, peaking in the 1880s with the DeBary-Baya Merchants Line emerging as the most successful fleet. However, passenger traffic fell off sharply in the early 1890s with the coming of the railroad, but the "workaday fleets, the harbor craft, tugboats and ferries continued to serve for a number of years," with some still in use today.[9]

Although the heyday of steamboat transport has long passed, an 1835 article in the *Jacksonville Courier* gives us the flavor of what these boats meant to the people of that era: "Steamer *Florida* arrived at our wharves last evening from Savannah on her way to Picolata. We are glad to see her gliding up and down our river. It seems to give life to everything. The merchants move with quicker step, the planter looks around and hastens the preparations of his crop and dreams of other sections which send such streams of activity to enliven his prosaic life. . . . Individuals feel its influence, the community feels it, and the streams of life course their way with quicker pulsation through the veins of society."[10]

This hand-colored postcard, *Boating through Tropical Scenery on the St. Johns River, Florida*, by an anonymous artist, was published by S. H. Kress

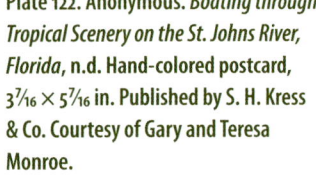

Plate 122. Anonymous. *Boating through Tropical Scenery on the St. Johns River, Florida*, n.d. Hand-colored postcard, 3⁷⁄₁₆ × 5⁷⁄₁₆ in. Published by S. H. Kress & Co. Courtesy of Gary and Teresa Monroe.

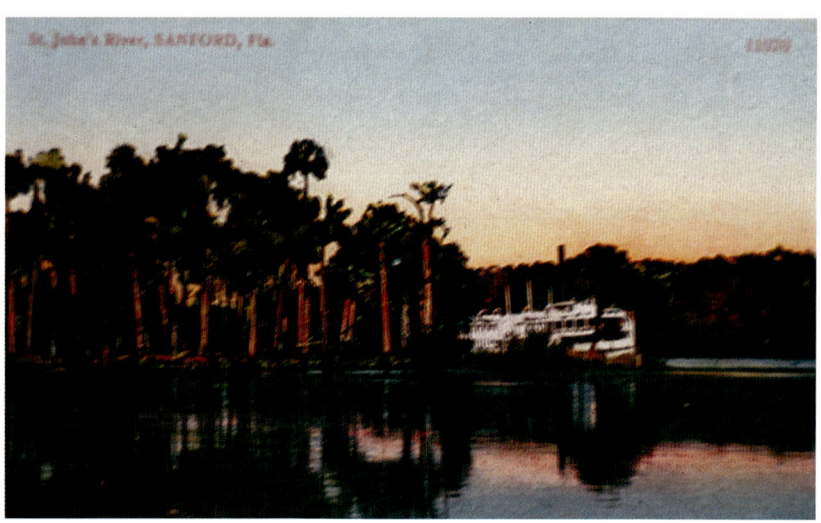

and Company as an advertisement for the various ports of call along the river. A travel tract from the same time advertised Jacksonville as "the Mecca of every health or pleasure seeking pilgrim"[11] and also took the reader on a tour of Palatka, the Ocklawaha, and the state's citrus-growing region, which at that time was largely in northeastern Florida.

Nineteenth-century landscape painters, inspired by the Transcendentalists' philosophy of Divine nature, recognized the benefits they might derive from participating in the public's appetite for picturesque scenes. Plying their craft, they pioneered the movement to explore, celebrate, and ultimately to protect the beauty and integrity of the American wilderness. For many, such as Frederic Church and Thomas Moran, it became their passion to find a way to convey their concerns to the rich and powerful. One way to accomplish this was to tie preservation to tourism. By providing picturesque images of America's epic landscape, these artists built an audience eager to see for themselves the grandeur depicted in paintings of places such as the Grand Canyon, Yellowstone, and Yosemite. Gail Davidson, in *Tourism and the American Landscape*, writes: "Painters recorded, romanticized, edited and sometimes embellished iconic views that dovetailed with the nationalistic currents of the time such as manifest destiny, abolition, pastoral nostalgia and anti-urbanism. Their drawings and paintings, disseminated via exhibitions, reproductive prints, illustrated publications, and deluxe 'coffee table' guidebooks, stimulated the burgeoning tourist industry, created a national market for landscapes, and established artists' careers."[12] This body of artistic work also helped to persuade the government of the United States that places of great natural beauty and historic significance should be preserved as part of a heritage shared by all Americans, thus paving the way for the development of the national park system.

Thomas Moran was a key player in the "Great American Landscape" pageant. His panoramic views of *The Grand Canyon of the Yellowstone* (1872) and *The Chasm of the Colorado* (1873) were both sold to the U.S. Department of the Interior through a special act of Congress. His visits to Florida in 1877–78 also resulted in a series of paintings to introduce the public to the exotic charm of the Florida wilderness. Moran captured the iconic Florida image that has continued to seduce and enchant viewers for over a century.

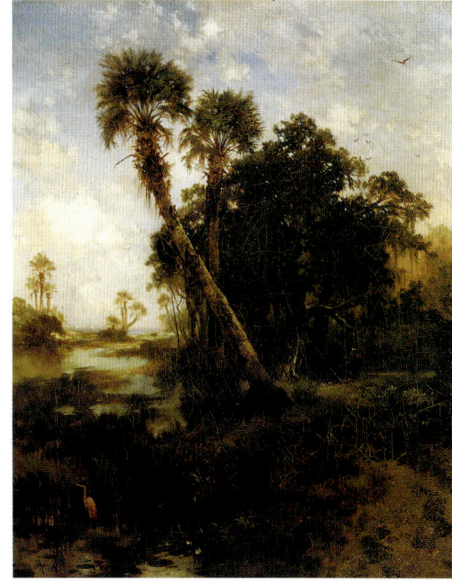

Plate 123. Thomas Moran. *Florida Landscape (Saint Johns River)*, 1877. Oil on canvas, 21 × 17 in. The Museum of Fine Arts, St. Petersburg, Florida.

When Martin Johnson Heade arrived in Florida from New England in 1883, he explored the St. Johns River by steamer and then took the popular side trip up the Ocklawaha River to Ocala before traveling to St. Augustine. Although he had spent much of his life moving from one place to another—he had wandered throughout the Northeast, the Midwest, and the South and also made trips to Europe and South America—in Florida, Heade seemed to finally have found his "home" for he soon bought a house and settled in with his young wife, Elizabeth.[13]

Meanwhile, the railroad baron and developer Henry Morrison Flagler was busy with his own plans for the future. Eager to establish St. Augustine as a tourist destination and cultural mecca, Flagler had built a group of art studios in his grand resort hotel, the Ponce de León, that he intended to make available to artists in order to establish an artist colony in the city. Heade was an early recruit and was quick to recognize the potential of Flagler's vision. Indeed, Flagler would become an important patron of Heade's work during the next two decades.

Born in rural Pennsylvania in 1819, Heade studied with the Quaker folk artist Edward Hicks. Upon returning from his European travels in the 1840s, he moved to New York, where he painted landscapes in the Hudson River school style. According to the art historian Erik Robinson, Heade's work was "distinctive in his use of the light of sunrise and sunset to create rich, colorful effects and create moods of nostalgia and reverie."[14] While living in New York, Martin Johnson Heade had shared a studio with the Romantic landscape painter Frederic Edwin Church.

In addition to the more traditional landscape subjects of seashores and picturesque mountain scenes that occupied the attention of most landscape painters, several of Heade's early paintings, such as the 1882 *Haystacks on the Newburyport Marshes*, show that the artist had already developed a taste for the unusual beauty of marshlands. An avid sportsman, Heade had spent a great deal of time in the northeastern marshes hunting and fishing, and the subtle beauty and mysterious charm of swampy areas was not lost on him. Thus, unlike some other northern landscape painters, Heade was not dismayed by Florida's flat topography; he did not need lofty peaks or rushing cataracts to stimulate his imagination. The glow of the sunset on quiet pools of water, the luminous wafts of morning mist, the subtle tones of marsh grass—these were enough to capture his eye and his skill. In Florida, he became, in essence, a painter of wetlands.

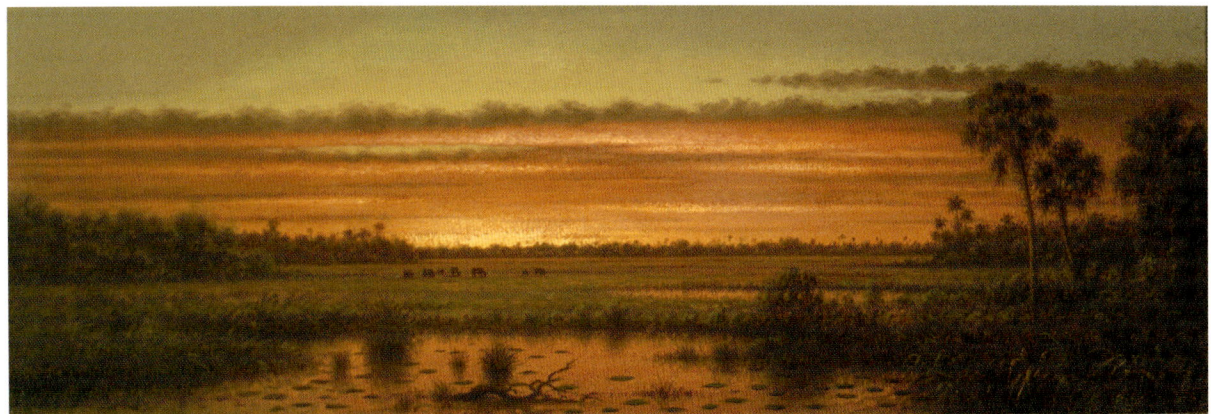

Plate 124. Martin Johnson Heade. *Sunset: Tropical Marshes, Florida*, ca. 1887. Oil on canvas, 12 × 36 in. The Charles Hosmer Morse Museum of American Art, Winter Park, Florida. © The Charles Hosmer Morse Foundation, Inc.

In this painting, *Sunset, Tropical Marshes, Florida*, by Martin Johnson Heade, we see nature as the source of divine inspiration. Painted around 1887, it depicts the St. Johns River near its mouth. One of several late nineteenth-century artists referred to as the Luminist school of landscape painters, Heade gives us a sublime portrait of Florida at its best—the radiant sun, the delicate clouds, the iridescent reflections, the exotic vegetation. The late nineteenth-century writer Abbie Brooks, in describing the St. Johns, wrote that "the [river] appears overspread with a kind of semi-transparent mist through which the sun shines with a nimbus of golden sheen that fills the air and sky. Imagination could not paint the River of Life more beautiful."[15]

Heade's earnings from selling his art to Henry Flagler and the tourists who flocked to Flagler's hotel enabled the artist to establish a solid career in St. Augustine, where he enjoyed a pleasant and moderately prosperous lifestyle. Heade died in St. Augustine at the age of eighty-five and was buried in Brooklyn, New York.

According to her biographer, Deborah Pollack, Laura Woodward is one of Florida's best-kept secrets. "Laura Woodward was Florida's most important woman artist of the nineteenth century, no question about it," Pollack states.[16] "It was a treasure for Florida to have her promoting the state by exhibiting her paintings all over the country."[17]

Laura Woodward was born in Mount Hope in upstate New York in 1834. An 1860 census listed her as still living at her parents' home, but following the Civil War she moved to Brooklyn, where she studied at the Brooklyn Academy of Design.[18] Influenced by artists of the Hudson River school, Woodward traveled throughout New England and the mid-Atlantic states, sketching the scenery and painting landscapes that sought to capture the special mood of the place. By 1872, Woodward was living in Manhattan, where she met a number of serious artists—among them the Luminist painter Martin Johnson Heade—and began to exhibit her work around town, including at the National Academy of Design.[19]

In the 1880s, Woodward began spending her winters in Florida—first in St. Augustine and later in Palm Beach. She became one of several artists who received encouragement and help from the railroad baron Henry Flagler. In Palm Beach, she took a studio in Flagler's opulent new Royal Poinciana Hotel. "She was Palm Beach's first professional artist," Pollack states.[20] Just as she had in earlier years, Woodward roamed the countryside, even though the Florida wilderness was very different from that of New England. In a 1924 interview with the *Palm Beach Times* columnist Frances Gillmor, Woodward says: "There were footpaths through the jungle . . . and I explored every one, I knew every foot of it. I even knew the times when it would make pictures, the times when the shadows and the sun would be just right. In the north, I could paint outdoors only in the summer. . . . Here, however, I could paint all the year round."[21]

Plate 125. Laura Woodward. *Afterglow: View of the St. Johns River*, ca. 1890. Oil on canvas. Collection of Robert and Alicia A. Harper.

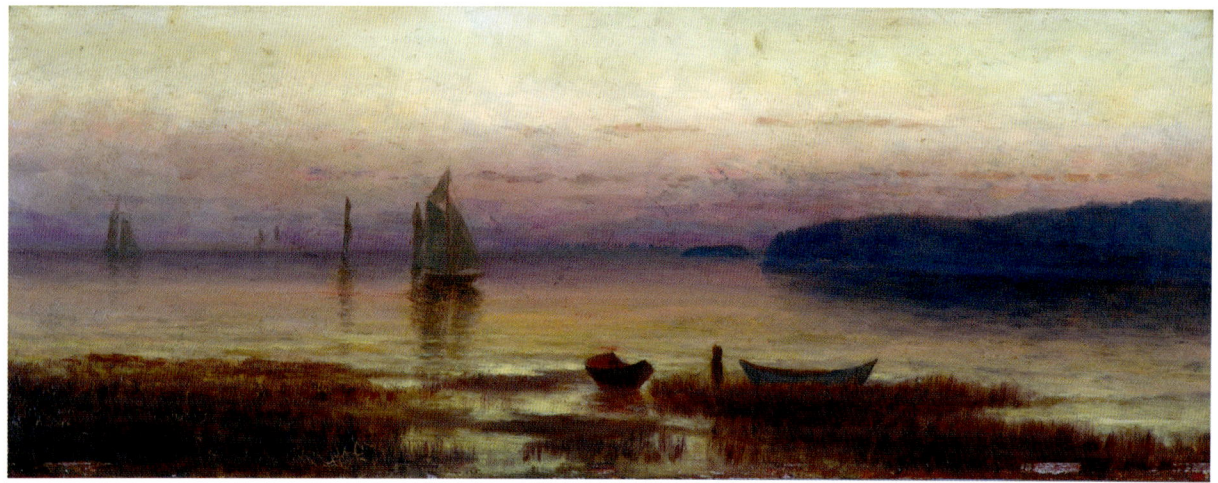

In her far-ranging rambles, Woodward visited sites along the St. Johns River as well as the Tomoka wilderness region near Ormond Beach and the interior of Florida along the Ocklawaha. In *Afterglow: View of the St. Johns River,* Woodward depicts a scene along the St. Johns River at that magical moment between sunset and dusk. Painted around 1890, it is, according the Deborah Pollack, "an early example of what would become known as her 'afterglow' paintings. She was highly praised for that kind of painting—just after sunset. It was one of the reasons she was so appreciated in Florida."[22]

~~~~~~

IF A CENTURY AGO you had decided to take a steamboat up the St. Johns River to visit the wild interior of Florida, you would have followed the river's winding course until you got to the 100-mile marker. At that point, if you wanted a truly exotic wilderness experience, you would have turned right into the magical and exotic world of the Ocklawaha River, the river that the poet Sidney Lanier described as "the sweetest waterlane in the world." According to the poet, it was "a lane clean to travel along for there is never a speck of dust in it save the blue dust and gold dust which the wind blows out of the flags and lilies . . . as if God had turned into water and trees the recollection of some meditative ramble through the lonely seclusions of His own soul."[23]

According to Bill Belleville, the Ocklawaha River is fed by twenty artesian springs and is one of the oldest continuously flowing rivers in Florida. Peats, mucks, and freshwater marls have been analyzed from the Ocklawaha floodplain and found to be nearly seventeen thousand years old. "From this," writes Belleville, "we know that the Ocklawaha was behaving like a river long before the St. Johns, most likely sluicing its way from its headwater lakes inside a separate and more ancient marine lagoon basin."[24] Scattered along the banks of the river are twenty-four pre-Columbian Indian mounds and middens and the wrecks of nineteenth-century steamboats. Rare fish such as the Lake Eustis pupfish, the bluenose shiner, the rainwater killifish and the tessellated darter also make the Ocklawaha their home. Belleville also claims there is "a striking visual illusion at work on the Ocklawaha. When the surface of the water moves, it doesn't so much ripple or splash. Rather, it seems to melt into thick ebony folds, dark mercury taking its time to get where it needs to go, swirling in slow motion around the cypress knees at the river's edge."[25]

Suddenly we found ourselves on the banks of the Ocklawaha River. . . . Thick forests of tall cypress, live oak and palmetto fringed it; huge vines twisted among and interlaced the trees, jungles of unfamiliar growths, bright oftentimes with native flowers, while below and overhead was draped with the eternal Spanish moss. The celebrated river moves slowly, but is very deep. . . . It seemed to have sinister shadows on its bosom, and along its course are so many dark bays and coves where the deadly water snake breeds that one scarcely knew where the channel lay.
—Lynn Tew Sprague, *An Easter Outing in Florida,* 1901

Margaret H. Watts has been painting the Ocklawaha basin since 1953, when her family moved to Ocala from New Jersey. She studied painting with Sabina Gonzales, a mural painter, as well as with the pastel artist Daniel Greene and the muralist John Briggs. She works in a number of media including watercolor, pastel, oil, and acrylic, but her inspiration is the world of nature and the incomparable beauty of the area around her Ocala home. As part of her commitment to giving back to the community, Watts has painted a number of murals in the Ocala area as well as a series of works for the Queen of Peace Catholic Church in Ocala.[26]

Plate 126. Margaret Watts. *The Ocklawaha River from Colby's Landing,* n.d. Pastel on paper. Private collection.

In this painting, *The Ocklawaha River from Colby's Landing,* Margaret Watts concentrates on the mysterious darkness of the river and the way it reflects the surrounding forest. Blackwater rivers, because of their dark color, are especially reflective, acting almost like a mirror while hiding their depths in shadow. This effect is quite evident in Watt's painting, which was done along the river north of State Road 40.

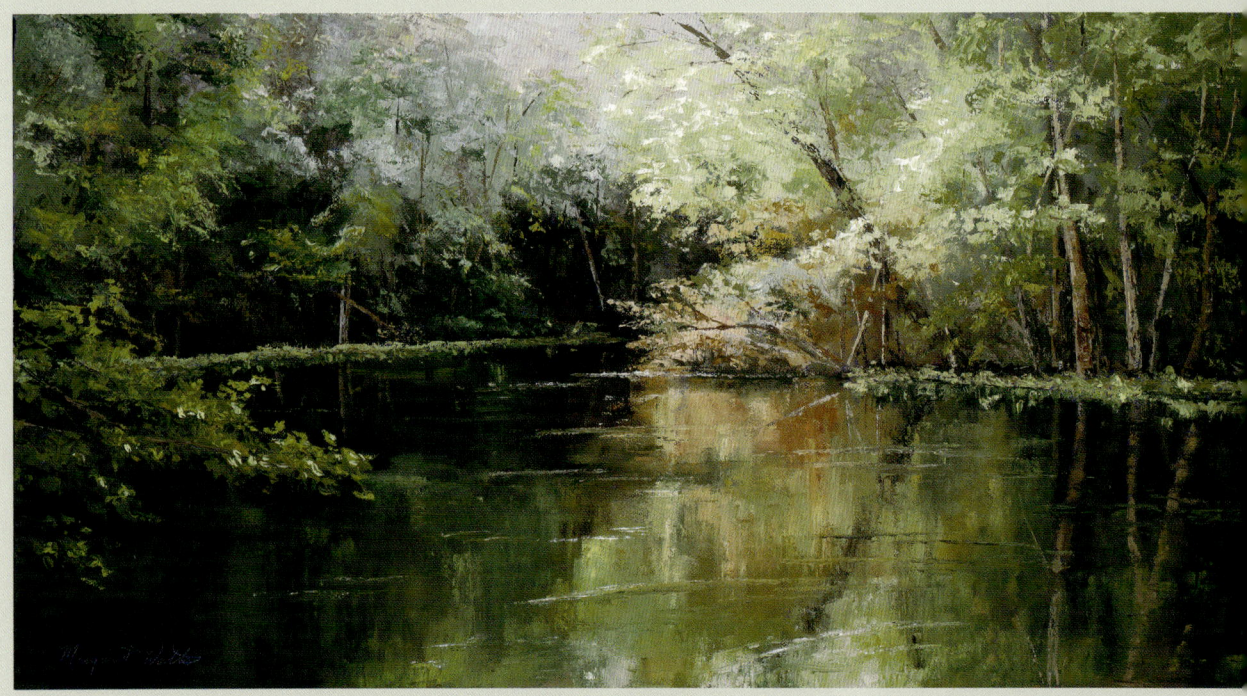

Tourists have always sought adventure. The best vacations combine the stimulation of a change of scenery with the luxury of relaxation, exotic food, and novel experiences. "Consumers," writes the Italian philosopher Umberto Eco, "want to be thrilled not only by the guarantee of the Good but also by the shudder of the Bad."[27] Florida did not disappoint. If the thrill of the exotic—tinged with a hint of danger—was to your liking, a trip into the primordial jungle of interior Florida was just the ticket.

Several steamboat lines began operating on the St. Johns River just before the Civil War, when Hubbard L. Hart was contracted to carry mail from Palatka to Silver Springs. But during the war many of these boats ran supplies for the Confederacy. The riverboat boom happened later and peaked in the 1880s.

During the riverboat's heyday, tourists would board for their adventurous tour in Jacksonville and be transported upriver to Palatka, then the hub of riverboat traffic. There they would board a smaller boat with a shallow draft, one that could navigate the tight bends of the Ocklawaha River.

While the St. Johns was the most celebrated steamboat "highway," smaller craft with shallow drafts, narrow hulls, and covered paddle wheels were constructed that could navigate the constricted channels of scenic tributaries like the Ocklawaha, carrying people and cargo deep into Florida's interior.

The riverboat scholar Edward Mueller points out that, although the river itself was extraordinarily beautiful, "Ocklawaha River vessels were by no means pretty craft. Because of the unusual nature of the river, its torturous bends, its shallow water, its snags and obstructions, the type of craft arrived at looked like a not-yet-completed houseboat erected on a rowboat shaped hull."[28]

The *Okeehumkee* was built in 1873 in Hart's East Palatka shipyard, and named after a legendary Indian chief whose name was consistently misspelled. A 1930s Smithsonian report described the boat's construction: Yellow pine was used for the keel and stern while planking, beams, floors, decks, frames and ceilings were fashioned with cypress. Bitts and stems were of oak, while galvanized spikes and bolts fastened the steamer. The recessed paddle wheel was 10.5 feet in diameter and 3.5 feet wide. The one-foot ten-inch draft allowed the 84-foot-long unaesthetic but "substantial and active" boat to navigate the beautiful river.[29]

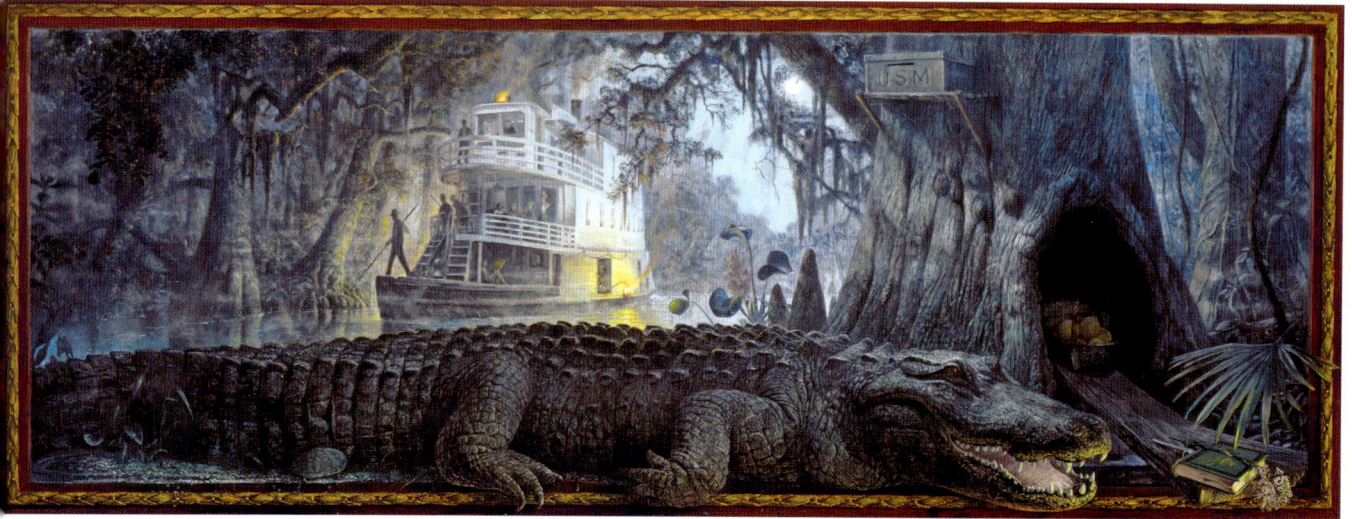

Plate 127. Christopher Still. *The Okeehum-kee on the Ocklawaha River*, 2002. Oil on linen, 48 × 126 in. One of ten paintings by Still commissioned for the Florida House of Representatives, Tallahassee.

In this painting by Christopher Still, we see the image of the *Okeehumkee*, purported to be "the longest serving steamboat on the Ocklawaha route."[30] The Ocklawaha River runs for 120 miles from Lake Apopka in central Florida to the St. Johns River south of Palatka. The steamers were given romantic names to make them more enticing to tourists. At night, bonfires were built on the decks of the steamers so passengers could view the scenery and wildlife in the flickering firelight.

In their search for adventure and "sport," many Florida tourists decimated the shores of the waterways as they passed, stripping them of flowers and clearing them of wildlife. A favorite pastime was shooting at birds and animals as the boat passed by. One outraged traveler described the experience for an article that was published in *Harper's New Monthly Magazine* in October 1870. "On the bow of the boat, indeed all over the boat, wicked people had stationed themselves with all sorts of firearms, firing at every helpless creature they could see. One of these bore especially the marks of imbecility in face and form. He sat in the extreme bow of the boat, and blazed away at everything at one time. . . . And so, all the way up and down the river these men sat there and fired at the beautiful birds which by the thousands inhabit the riverbank and swamps. . . . The cowardly fellows shot all day long. If the officers of the boat can not stop this mean business, the game laws of the State ought to."[31]

By the late 1870s, game populations along the middle St. Johns and its tributaries were so depleted that some of the ships' captains took matters into their own hands to stop the slaughter, but the "sportsmen" simply went farther inland to search for game. Mark Derr writes: "The hunts became adventures, subject to the vagaries of weather, of transportation, the whim of guides, the lack of accommodations, and the threat of illness or injury from poisonous snakes, animals, and their own guns. Wherever they traveled, the hunters and fishermen left a trail of spoiled meat. Like their counterparts in the American West who were laying waste the herds of bison and antelope, the flocks of passenger pigeons, these Florida sportsmen cared primarily for blood."[32]

This illustration published in *Harper's Weekly* shows passengers shooting at alligators from their boat. There were no laws prohibiting the number of alligators the sportsmen could "harvest," and so thousands of the reptiles were destroyed for profit and/or sport.

Plate 128. Anonymous. *Shooting Alligators.* From *Harper's Weekly,* October 3, 1874. Courtesy of the Matheson Museum, Gainesville, Florida.

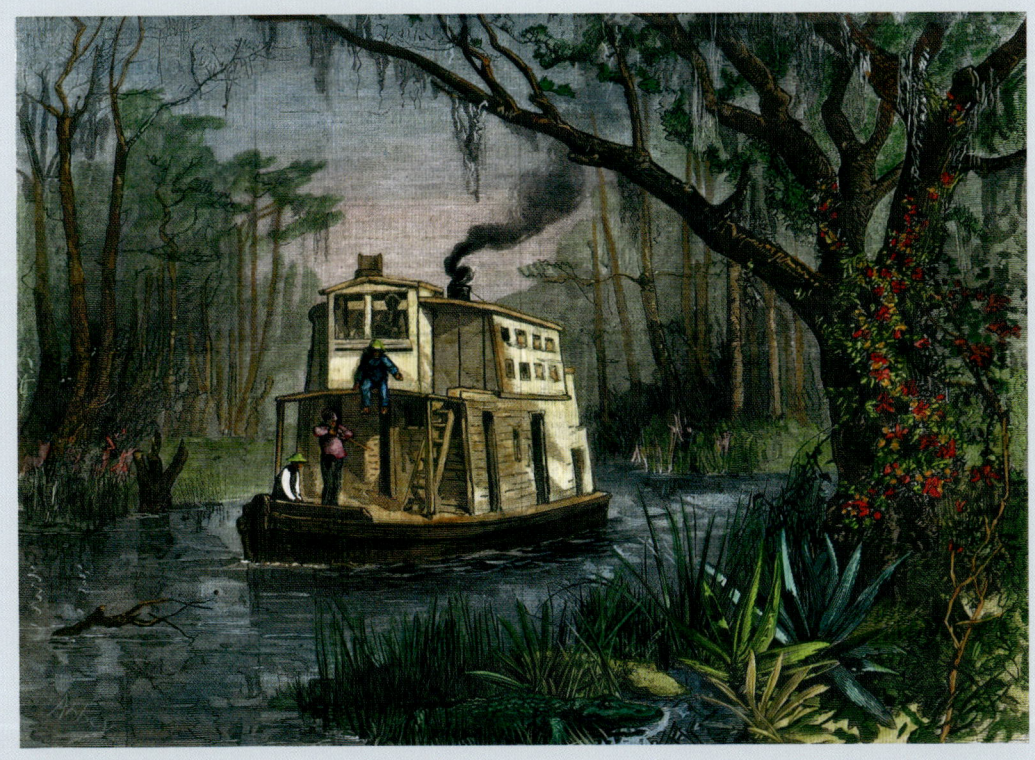

Before rubber alligators and cheap T-shirts became staples at gas stations along every Interstate exit and in Florida tourist traps at every beachside town, before metal, bone, and orangewood mementoes that were crafted in the United States and Europe were replaced by plastic ones that were made in Japan and constituted acceptable keepsakes from a vacation to the Sunshine State, a few stores during the golden age of Florida tourism purveyed better merchandise, objects not just stamped Florida but that were indigenously Floridian. Osky's was a primary dealer of Florida curiosities and souvenirs. Headquartered in Jacksonville, the store boasted housing "the

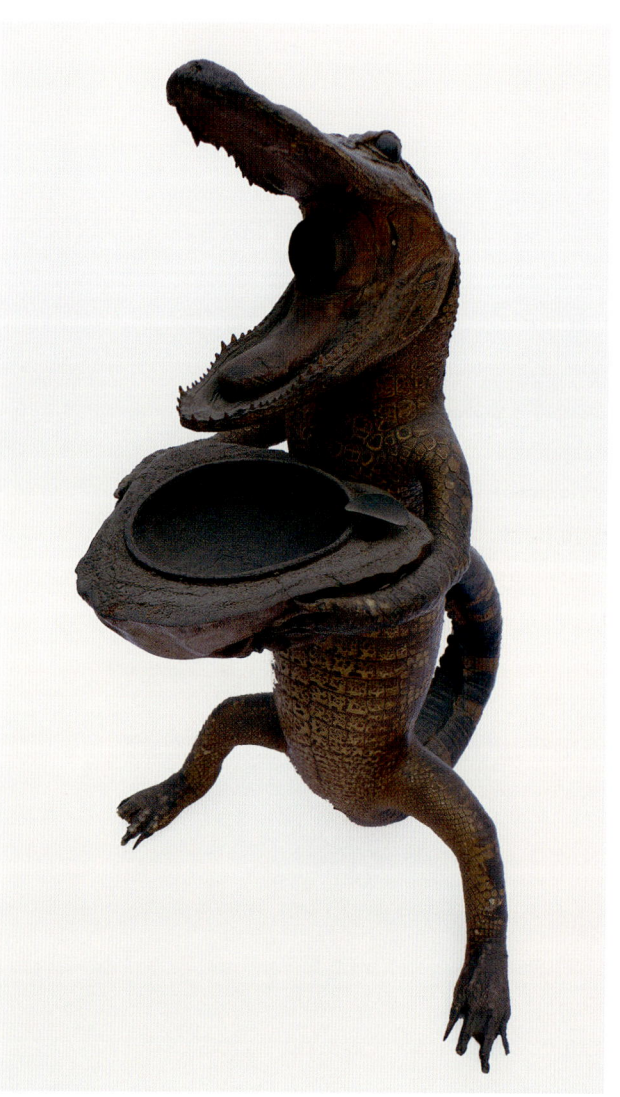

Plate 129. Anonymous. *Alligator Lamp*, ca. 1900. Mounted alligator, coconut, light-bulb socket, 22 × 14⅝ in. Dan and Tracy McKenna Collection.

largest live alligator in captivity on free exhibition." They also had plenty of dead ones that were sold by the foot.

Osky's offered a wide array of souvenirs including handbags and suitcases, alligator tooth jewelry, canes with gators carved into the handles, corkscrews, pens, pipes, while usually sporting a alligator motif, as well as napkin rings, ink stands, and necklaces fashioned from shells. Alligator eggs were available, too.

Live foot-long gators were fifty cents each in 1903; gators 2 feet to 6 feet cost one dollar each; an 8-foot gator went for two dollars, while a ten-footer cost three dollars. These came with directions for their care, and with the warning that they could be shipped but at the purchaser's risk. No live alligator would be sent C.O.D. Ever-popular stuffed alligators were available, too. An eighteen-inch gator cost one dollar, while two-feet- to five-feet-long ones went for one dollar per foot; a six-foot to eight-foot gator cost $1.50 per foot. These were available mounted. A gator wrapped around a shell that served as an ashtray cost $1.25. Stuffed alligators mounted in crawling positions or upright, which were designed for use as card receivers and umbrella stands and the like, were also available. Some were further embellished. The one pictured here holds half a coconut shell in which is set an ashtray, while an electric socket placed into the gator's throat houses a light bulb.

Between hunting and commercial harvesting, the alligator population has varied and at times approached extinction. Regulations failed to stop their decimation, but federal laws established in 1970 succeeded, and the alligator population rebounded. After the millennium, it was estimated that a startling number of gators lived in Florida's lakes, ponds, rivers, marshes, swamps, and canals, wherever there was water—1 million of them.

Born in 1838, Harry Fenn produced the first illustrated gift books in the United States, and found fame with his sketches from his travels. Fenn came to this country in 1857 ostensibly to see Niagara Falls. He married in 1862, and the next year went to Italy. During his time in America, he was employed as a wood engraver, and he illustrated early dime novel covers— popular books about western adventures, working-girl narratives, and detective stories aimed at youthful, working-class audiences. This work may have planted the seeds for Fenn's sense of imagery.

Upon returning to the United States in 1864, he illustrated John Greenleaf Whittier's *Snow Bound and Ballads of New England*. He ventured out west in 1870 to gather material for his landmark two-volume book set *Picturesque America*. Published in 1872, it was edited by William Cullen Bryant and included sketches by James Smillie, Alfred Waud, Thomas Moran, and others. Fenn then traveled in Europe to make sketches for *Picturesque Europe*, and spent two winters in the Middle East sketching for *Picturesque Palestine, Sinai and Egypt*. By then a renowned illustrator, Fenn returned to the United States in 1881 and opened a studio in New York City.

Picturesque America, also referred to as *The Land We Live In*, was marketed as "The most Magnificent Illustrated Work ever produced in America." Chapters were reprinted as folios, each one highlighting a different region.

In *A Florida Swamp* (plate 130), Harry Fenn shows a nearly primordial Florida, a place more haunting than quaint. The cross-hatching of the black-and-white ink lines that form the images enhances this quality. It is, therefore, not surprising that these plates were often cut from the folios, and artists were hired to color them by hand. The results were liberating. Suddenly the graphic newspaperlike pictures were transformed in to subtle works of art, and handsomely framed.

Dick Punnett, an expert on Florida artists and photographers, considers Fenn to be "the number-one guy that illustrated the St. Johns River," because he was among the earliest, predating the surge of fine artists who followed Henry Flagler into the state as his railroad unraveled southward along the Atlantic coast. Punnett points out that Fenn was set apart by his seemingly endless energy, that "he was all over the map."[33]

Later in life, Harry Fenn concentrated on painting with watercolors. He was a member of the New York Watercolor Club, the Society of Illustrators, and the Salmagundi Club, and was a founder of the American Watercolor Society. He exhibited at the National Academy of Design in 1864 and at various times at the Brooklyn Art Association between 1864 and 1885. He exhibited at the Columbian Expo in Chicago in 1893, where he was awarded a medal.

Fenn's illustrations are often packed with information. "He stuck every-thing in there—birds, dogs, chicken, ducks, snakes, alligators—in the same scene," points out Dick Punnett.[34] This adds to the images' conveyance of a remote and untamed place where the tropics slip away, but the landscape is not quite that of, say, Deep Georgia. Fenn's interior Florida is particularly foreign and mysterious, not as exotic as how Florida would soon be rep-resented, but as intrepid explorers might describe it, "not for the faint at heart."

In her second novel, *Dred: A Tale of the Dismal Swamp*, Harriet Beecher Stowe conveys a sense of menace that seems to lurk among the "deliri-ous exuberance of vegetation, of that darkly struggling, wildly vegetating swamp of human souls . . . cut off . . . from the usages and improvements of cultivated life."[35] Fenn's image *Awaiting Decomposition* echoes Stowe's dark vision.

Plate 130 (*left*), Harry Fenn. *A Florida Swamp*, ca. 1872. Engraving, 8³⁄₁₆ × 5⅛ in. Plate 131 (*right*), Harry Fenn. *Waiting for Decomposition*, ca. 1872. Engraving, 8³⁄₁₆ × 5⅛ in. From *Picturesque America*, ed. William Cullen Bryant.

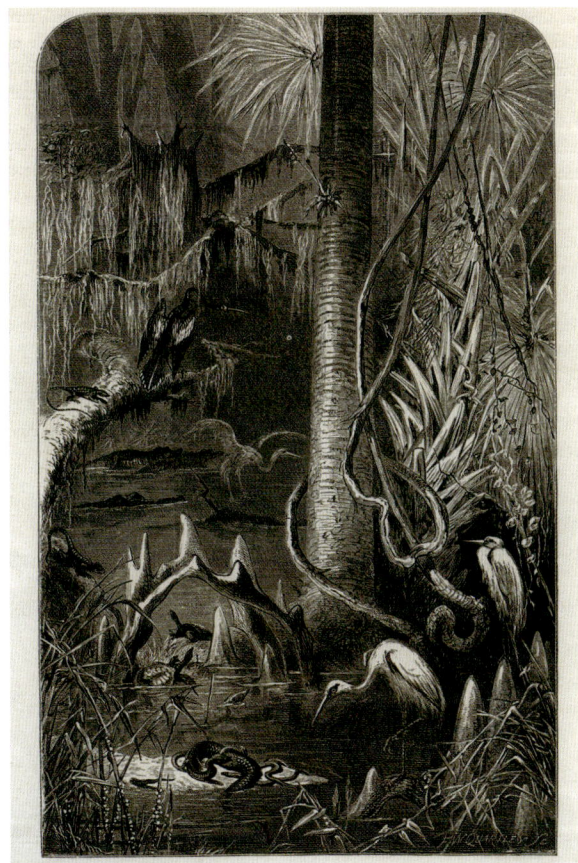

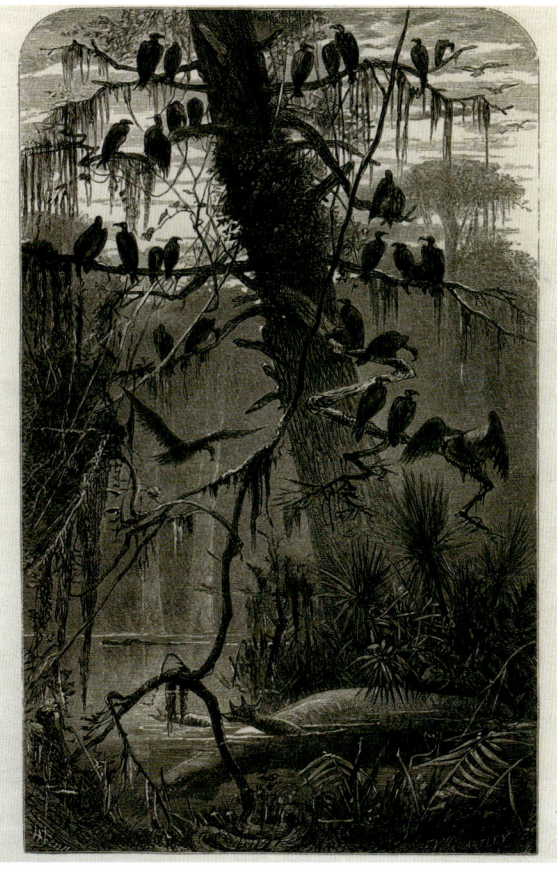

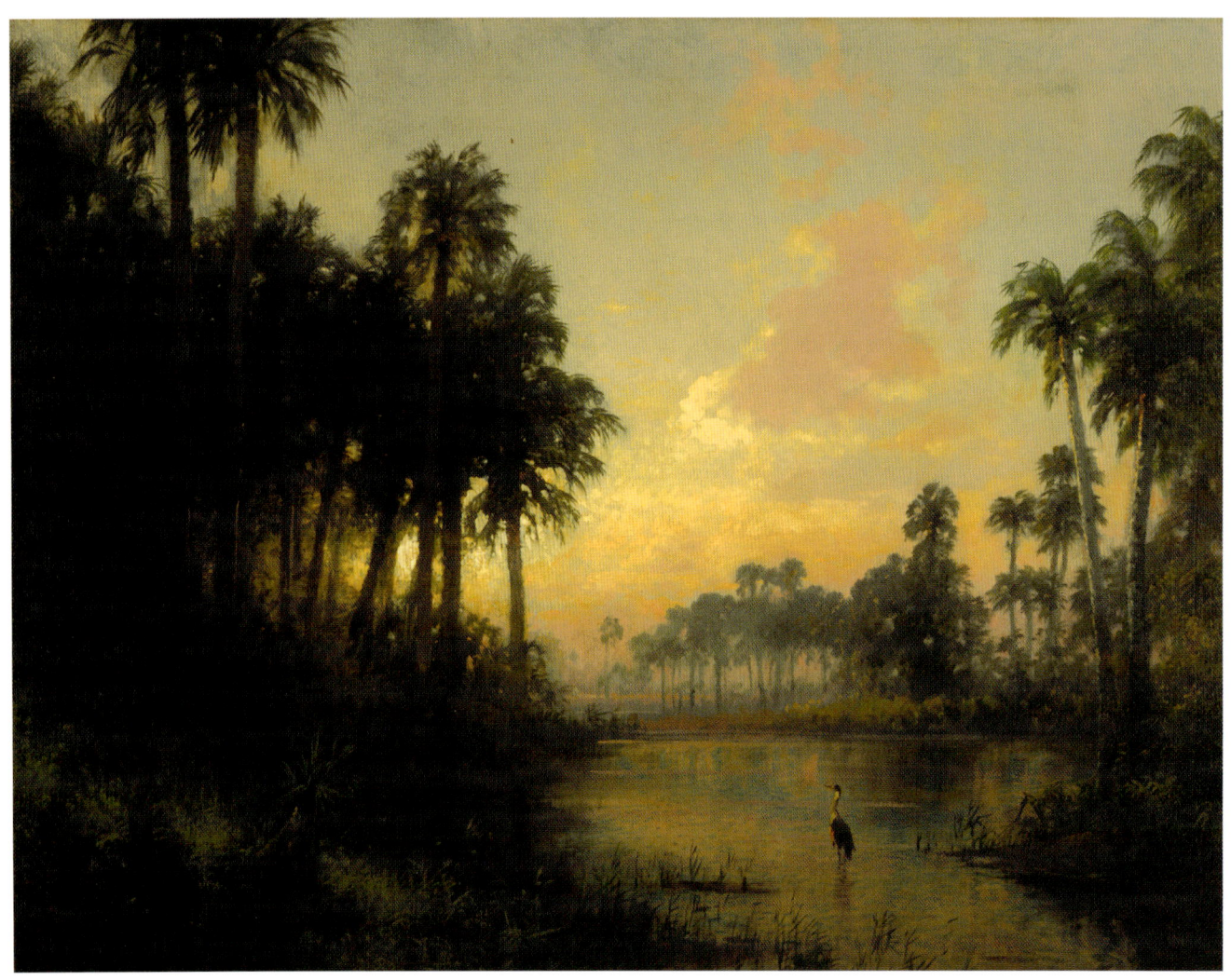

Plate 132. Herman Herzog. *Landscape with Heron*, ca. 1900. Oil on canvas. The Samuel P. Harn Museum of Art, Gainesville, Florida. Gift of David and Maryanne Cofrin.

Like Joseph Conrad's *Heart of Darkness*, Herman Herzog's *Landscape with Heron* whispers to us of a hidden world that lurks beneath the dark pools of water or under the heavy forest canopy. David Miller writes: "For centuries, the swamp had been seen as an emblem of evil, as a land of the dead. . . . In the 1860s it was repeatedly linked to a dawning sense of unconscious life which to the . . . Victorian middle class seemed increasingly alluring."[36]

In this painting by Herzog, the marshy terrain has taken on a shadowy persona, as though we are truly descending into "the heart of darkness."

What in bright daylight seemed merely exotic, in twilight's gloom becomes mysterious, even sinister. One visitor, writing about his trip for the *New York Daily Times* in March 1853, said: "Between the points of land, and under the large trees, how dark and heavy the shadows! How still and black the pools of water! Dark and deep enough for Zenobia. You shiver and look away to where the sunlight lingers."[37]

Born in Bremen, Germany, in 1832, Herman Herzog studied painting at the Dusseldorf Academy and trained privately with the Norwegian landscape artist Hans Gude. According to the art historian Roberta Favis, his work was also influenced by the German philosopher and naturalist Alexander von Humboldt.[38] He enjoyed success early in his career and had an enviable list of patrons that included Queen Victoria and the emperor of Russia. In the late 1860s, in protest over the German unification under Prussian rule, Herzog immigrated to the United States and established himself in Philadelphia. For the next sixty years, until his death in 1932 at age one hundred, Herzog traveled throughout the United States seeking the wild, primordial landscapes that were his inspiration.

Herzog was trained in the European tradition of landscape painting that infiltrated the United States during the nineteenth century through the work of artists like Thomas Cole and William Morris Hunt. In the late 1800s and early 1900s, Herzog was a frequent visitor to Alachua County—his son was an early faculty member of what would soon become the University of Florida. Herzog's Florida paintings usually followed the familiar formula of pastoral scenes painted with Romantic overtones, but like other artists who arrived in the tropical South, Herzog found himself confronted by a landscape that was often more primordial than pastoral. Like his predecessor Martin Johnson Heade, Herzog seemed attracted to the brooding and untamed mystery of the swamp.

The development of photography in the late nineteenth century allowed the general public to gain access to the acquisition of a wide assortment of visual images—something that would have been impossible in previous times. Photographs were inexpensive, easily duplicated, and widely accessible; now "pictures" were available to everyday people. As the tourist industry grew and flourished, photographs played an ever-increasing role in advertising by making images of exotic places available to a growing and receptive audience. One of the most successful photographers working in Florida in the early years of the twentieth century was William James Harris.

Harris was born in England in 1868. His family immigrated to America in 1870 and settled in Wilkes-Barre, Pennsylvania. Harris learned the photographic trade, and at age twenty he set up a studio in his parents' home and began operating his first photography business. By 1890, he began to travel widely in order to capture new images for his growing audience. In 1893, he traveled to the World's Columbian Exposition in Chicago, where he photographed George Ferris's new invention—the Ferris wheel. In a stroke of promotional genius, Harris donated two thousand photos of the wheel to the Ferris Wheel Company, each of which included his name and address. This action helped to expand his business considerably.[39]

It was also at the exposition that Harris first saw what would become a major trend in American life—postcards. In 1898, Congress passed legislation authorizing the manufacture of "private mailing cards." What began as a novelty soon became a huge business. As the antiques expert Michael Ivankovich points out, "the telephone was not yet commonplace and postcards soon became a primary means of casual communication."[40]

Also in 1898, Harris moved to St. Augustine where he opened the Acme View Company. In addition to selling cameras and equipment, he offered free instruction to budding photographers. He traveled throughout Florida photographing what was fast becoming one of America's most popular tourist destinations.

Having established himself as a well-known black-and-white photographer, Harris began to experiment with hand-tinted photos, which were becoming increasingly popular. His most successful pictures were from the Adirondack region and from Florida. His hand-colored prints soon replaced his postcard business as his primary source of income. He specialized in exterior scenes, especially tinted landscapes that looked very similar to the paintings of the Romantic landscapists of the previous century such as Heade and Moran. His best-selling works were reproduced using the photogravure process and then individually hand-colored. The results were dramatic and lushly colored scenes that could almost pass for paintings.

This hand-tinted photo was taken somewhere along the Ocklawaha River. Harris sometimes manipulated his photos—borrowing and merging parts of different photos to construct the image he had in mind. He also was known to "improve" the natural setting by using artificial props. Ivankovich writes: "One interesting story about Harris relates to several of his pictures that feature an egret standing in the Florida water. Apparently for the sake of simplicity, Harris carried a 'stuffed' egret as part of his photographic equipment, presumably because it was easier to shoot a still bird for effect rather than a live, uncontrollable bird. He was also known to carry a stuffed alligator for effect as well."[41]

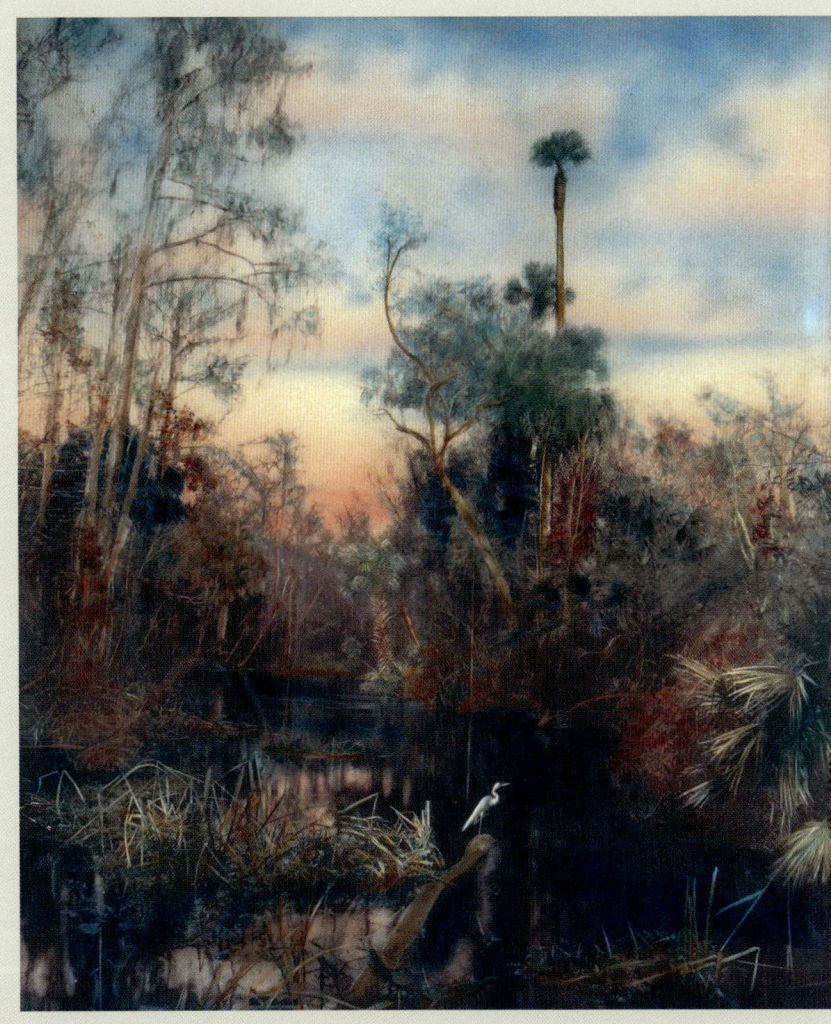

Plate 133. William James Harris. *The Ocklawaha*, 1915. Hand-colored photogravure, 13 × 16 in. Collection of John C. Herrmann.

Harris enjoyed a long and active career in his adopted city of St. Augustine. He was a member of the St. Augustine Historical Society, serving as its business manager and head curator. When he died in 1940, he left behind a large body of photographic images that helped fuel the imagination of the public and feed their interest in Florida as a tourist destination and place of mystery and adventure. As Michael Ivankovich writes: "His [Harris's] photographic works certainly helped popularize Florida more than any other photographer of his time."[42]

Silver Springs, which lies at the western end of the Ocklawaha River in Marion County east of Ocala, has always been Florida's most famous spring attraction. The Spanish were probably the first non-native visitors to marvel at the spring's amazing features. At the bottom of the spring lies the wreckage of a cypress boat thought to be of Spanish origin, indicating a European presence there from four hundred years ago. Not far away, inside an enormous underwater cave, lie the fossilized bones of Pleistocene beasts, undisturbed for ten thousand years.

Tourism to Silver Springs gained momentum when entrepreneur Hubbard Hart won a land grant from the state to dredge the Ocklawaha River to permit the passage of small steamers. In the 1870s, the state's first Republican governor, Harrison Reed, awarded Hart a charter for constructing a cross-peninsula canal, but the project was ultimately abandoned. Nevertheless, the idea of a cross-Florida canal, first envisioned by Pedro Menéndez de Avilés, proved to be an enduring fantasy for developers and politicians alike.

Passengers on Hart's famed boats would see the wondrous flora and fauna along the riverbanks and become ever enchanted as they went deeper into Florida's primeval interior. Sightseers became explorers as the boat captains deftly maneuvered their way upriver, carefully avoiding tree branches that threatened to whack passengers. The journey was more important than the destination, even as they traversed up the Silver River into the basin at the headwaters of Silver Springs, where they could swim, picnic, and ride in a small flat-bottom rowboat to peer beneath the water's surface. The water there was so clear that distant objects some fifty feet deep looked to be inches away.

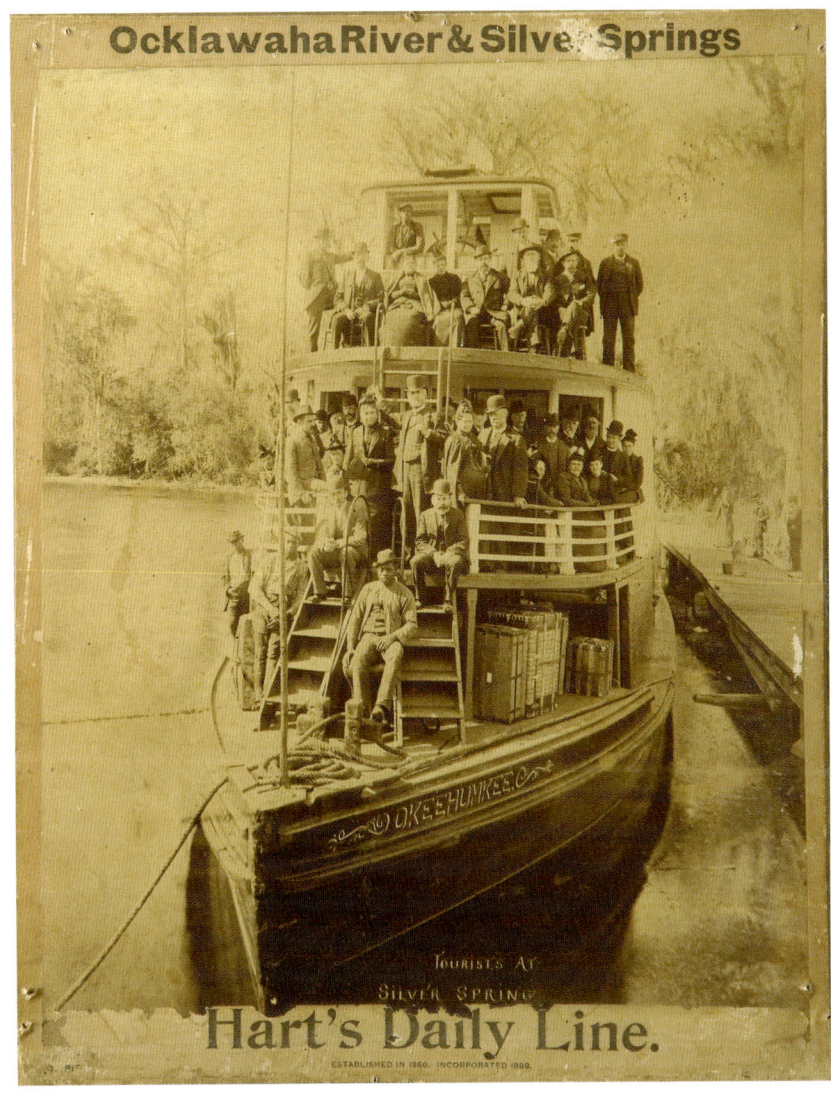

Besides the *Okeehumkee*, seen in this circa 1890 photograph of tourists onboard, other famous Hart Line steamers included the *Griffin*, *Astatula*, *Silver Springs*, *Osceola*, and *Hiawatha*. Although riverboat traffic slowed with the railroad's southward expansion, it was halted altogether by the advent of the automobile, which transported the "tin can" tourists of the 1920s.

Plate 134. Anonymous. *Okeehumkee*, ca. 1890. Hart Line advertisement. Albumen print, 13½ × 10 in. Courtesy of Silver River Museum. Photo courtesy of Scott Mitchum.

Olive Commons's exquisite jewelry is emblematic of the St. Johns River's timeless beauty. Her dime-sized porcelains contain the essence of the waterways in surprising detail: tranquil scenes dotted with moss-laden oaks, palms, and pines cast under pastel sunrises and magical sunsets, sometimes including a small boat. "The St. Johns River seemed to flow out of her paintbrush," said Larry Roberts, premier collector of souvenirs from Florida's Golden Age.[43]

In 1908, the Commons family settled near Sanford. Their house reportedly offered views of the river from nearly every window. Mr. Commons began planting groves of orange trees and was the first to commercially grow lima beans. Mrs. Commons painted a scene on a medallion to give to a friend. To rave reviews, she mounted others as jewelry for gifts, and her pastime became a lucrative souvenir business.

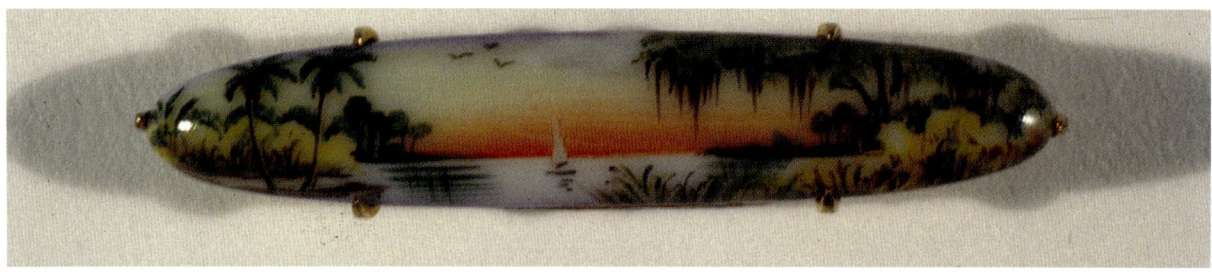

Plate 135. Olive Commons. *Untitled* (brooch), ca. 1918. Paint on porcelain, ⁷⁄₁₆ × 2 × ¼ in. Courtesy of Gary and Teresa Monroe.

In the mid-1920s the Commons family moved to Miami's Coconut Grove, where Olive opened the House of Commons. There she introduced her Platinum Palm Ware, using her own technique of painting with platinum on china, making thousands of ornamental plates and bowls along with her jewelry into the early 1960s.

"Cameonas" was the name Commons gave to her tiny hand-painted Florida scenes on china mounted as jewelry, earrings, pins, and brooches. Each miniature was fired twice to ensure permanence and achieve a rich tonal range, and no two pieces were alike. She was given the "Highest Award of Merit" medal at the 1939 New York World's Fair for her "Platinum Palm Ware." During her banner years, it is believed that she made two thousand pieces that went, from Florida, all over the world.

Although there are numerous examples of rhapsodic descriptions of Florida's natural beauty and exemplary climate penned by visitors over the centuries, Florida's appeal was not universally appreciated. Harriet Beecher Stowe, who moved to Florida after the Civil War, was an enthusiastic promoter of her adopted home, but she nevertheless warned her readers not to have unrealistic expectations. "Now, tourists and travelers generally come with their heads full of certain romantic ideas of waving palms, orange groves, flowers, and fruit all bursting forth in tropical abundance," she wrote in *Palmetto Leaves*, "and, in consequence, they go throughout Florida with disappointment at every step. . . . In point of fact, they find, in approaching Florida, a dead sandy level, with patches behind them of rough coarse grass, and tall pine-trees, whose tops are so far in the air that they seem to cast no shade, and a little scrubby underbrush. . . . We caution everybody coming to Florida, Don't hope for too much."[44]

One of the earliest Europeans to visit Florida was a sixty-year-old carpenter from France, Nicolas Le Challeux, who arrived in 1565 as a member of the René de Laudonnière expedition. After staying in the New World a few short months, he returned home, where he wrote a history of his adventure and also wrote several poems. One of the poems, titled "Octet," was written on his arrival in his hometown of Dieppe.

> Who wants to go to Florida?
> Let him go where I have been,
> Returning gaunt and empty,
> Collapsing from weakness,
> The only benefit I have brought back,
> Is one good white stick in my hand,
> But I am safe and sound, not disheartened,
> Let's eat: I'm starving!
> —*Nicolas Le Challeux, 1566*

9 { Tourism Continued

Trains, Planes, and Automobiles

If you have never given Florida particular thought, perhaps it's in the back of your mind as a sunny peninsula covered stem to stern with waving coconut palms, and populated with bathing girls, rich tourists and race horses.
—George and Jane Dusenbury, *How to Retire to Florida*, 1947

"FUN IN THE SUN" HAS BEEN the mantra of Florida tourism for over a century. But beaches, bathers, and outdoor activities became the stereotype of tourism only in the post-steamboat days as the focus of the tourist trade shifted from the St. Johns River and its tributaries, made accessible by the steamboat, to the Florida coast, newly accessible by train and automobile. Flagler's railroad opened south Florida to development, and by the 1930s, images of palm trees and bathing beauties had replaced those of steamboats venturing deep into exotic jungles as a tourism marketing ploy.

Prior to the building of the east coast railroad, getting to St. Augustine from Jacksonville required a forty-three-mile trip up the St. Johns River to Tocoi, and then an unattractive 14-mile trek in a tramway horse-car or, later, in a train across the flatlands and scrub. This St. Johns Railroad route operated from 1870 to 1895. It was replaced when Flagler's Florida East Coast Railroad built a bridge over the St. Johns River that led directly to St. Augustine.

Henry Flagler built or bought hotels for the very wealthy at towns and cities as his trains came south along the Atlantic coast, knowing that Florida would become the perfect winter retreat. Engulfed in Old World charm reminiscent of the Spanish era in the 1500s, guests at St. Augustine hotels could luxuriate in steam baths and indoor pools. Flagler built the Ponce de Leon (now Flagler College) and the Alcazar (now the Lightner Museum). He also bought the Cordova (now the Casa Monica). These three grand hotels faced one another on the plaza of the Ancient City. He also purchased the San Mateo, a hotel just beyond the city gates adjacent to the Castillo de San Marcos.

Flagler was in Palm Beach during 1894, where bellhops at his new Royal Poinciana Hotel were expected to deliver messages on bicycle through the structure's three miles of hallways. A crippling freeze late that year brought Flagler to Miami, and his trains arrived at Biscayne Bay in 1896 because Miami seemed "freeze proof," while ice formed at the Royal Poinciana on the shores of Lake Worth sixty miles north. So, while building the exclusive Palm Beach Inn in 1896 (renamed the Breakers Hotel in 1901) on the Atlantic Ocean, he built the amenity-laden Royal Palm Hotel, which opened in 1897 at the mouth of the Miami River, near what would become downtown Miami, which until that year was unincorporated. Flagler's march southward spelled the end of river traffic.

Henry Plant, a wealthy investor from Connecticut, was also in the railroad business. He built a railway from Jacksonville to Tampa that opened a cross-state swath of the Florida peninsula to development. In 1921, George Graham Currie, a poet who was also the mayor of West Palm Beach, wrote a sly verse about an imagined meeting between the two tycoons, Flagler and Plant.

> In Jacksonville station once, Flagler met Plant
> Each on his way south for a wintertime jaunt;
> Said Plant unto Flagler in jocular speech:
> "Where, sir, can you tell, is the place called Palm Beach?"
> Then Flagler retorted most woefully loud:
> "If you're really in earnest, sir, 'follow the crowd.'"
> —*George Graham Currie, 1921*

Plate 136. Anonymous. *St. Augustine Fan*, n.d. Mixed media, 13 ⅞ × ¾ × 1¼ in. Collection of Dan and Tracy McKenna.

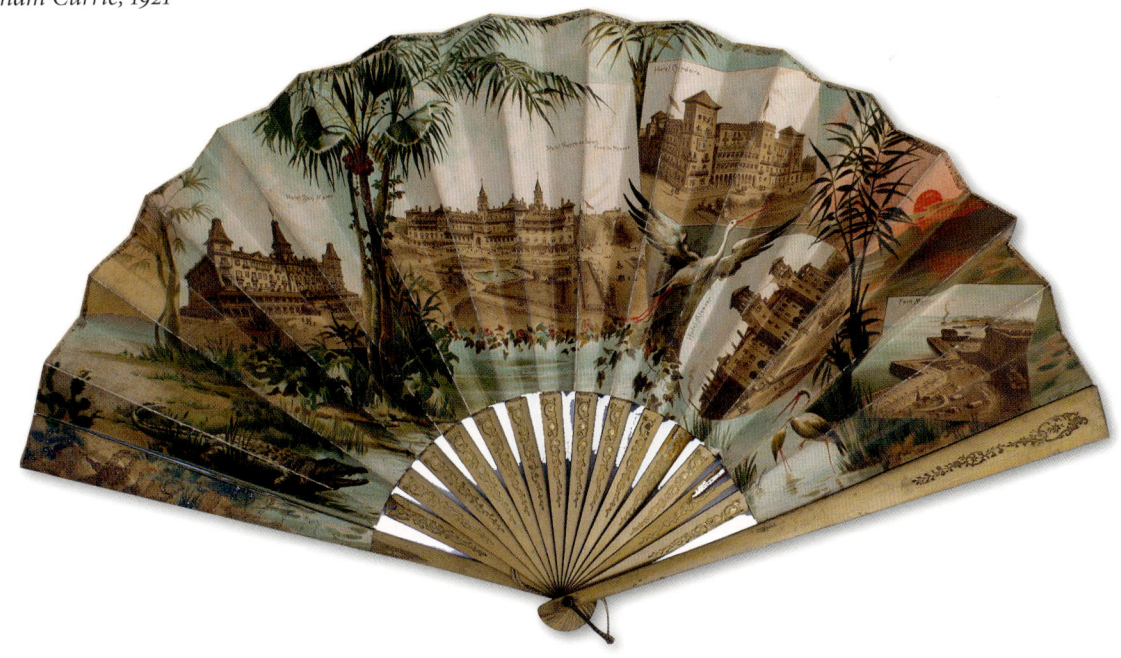

While fans move and cool the air, they also speak a language, suggesting feminine mystique and emotion. Also, the Hampshire Museum Service explains, "fans often represent the most exquisite objects d'art which were the perfect gift for a lady, in an era which cultivated good taste, and connoisseurship of the hand-crafted object."[1] Hand fans represented an elegant and gracious way of life, one especially fitting for the well-heeled who frequented Florida in the late nineteenth and early twentieth century. The fan shown in plate 136 depicts four elegant late nineteenth-century hotels in St. Augustine, better winter residences for the privileged class that Henry Flagler attracted to Florida. It shows too the massive fort, Castillo de San Marcos, with its forty-foot moat and nearly indestructible walls that guarded the first permanent European settlement in the continental United States, as well as the symbolic and omnipresent alligator.

According to the historian Michael Gannon, in 1906 there were 296 automobiles in Florida: 74 in Daytona, 38 in Miami, 17 in Jacksonville, and 15 in Tampa. By 1913, there were 15,000. "Two years later," writes Gannon, "in Governor Trammell's administration, a State Road Department was created and hard-surface paving began. . . . The appearance of the automobile presaged the time, half a century later, when tourism, most of it by automobile, would be the state's leading industry."[2]

Plate 137. Edward "Buk" Ulreich. *Florida Today*, 1939. Fresco, mural. U.S. Post Office, Tallahassee, Florida. Photo courtesy of the U.S. GSA Fine Arts Collection, Washington, D.C.

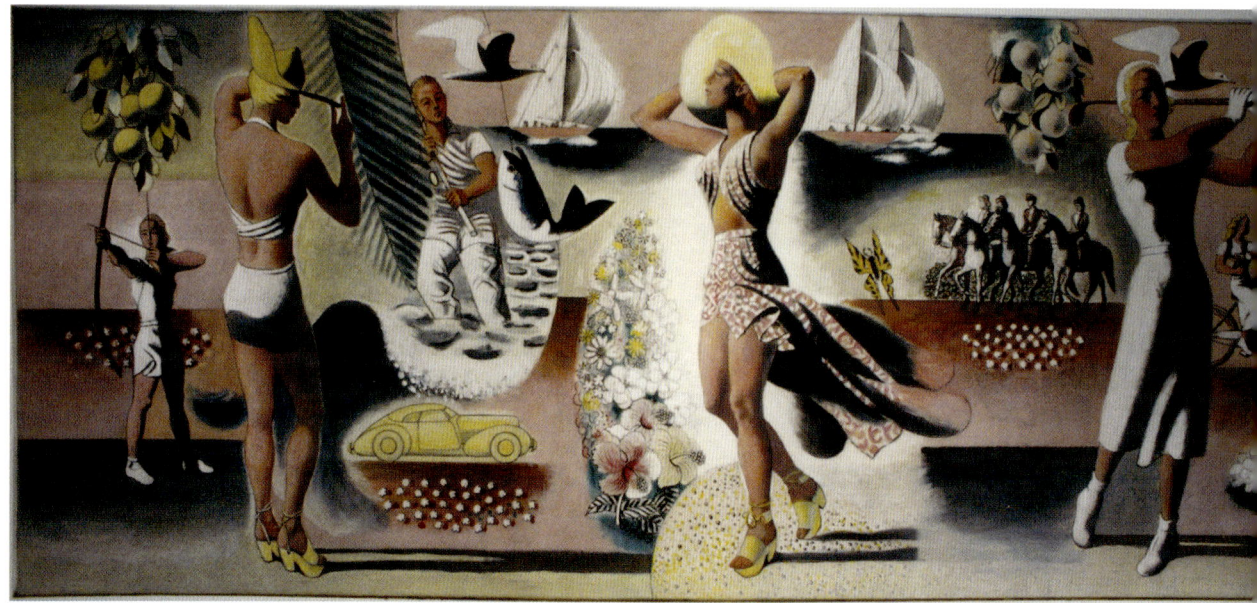

The mural shown in plate 137, painted in 1939 by Edward "Buk" Ulreich through the New Deal's Section of Fine Arts, depicts Florida as a mecca for vacationers and sports enthusiasts. Born in Hungary in 1889, Ulreich grew up in Kansas City and studied at the Kansas City Art Institute and the Pennsylvania Fine Arts Academy. Created for the U.S. courthouse in Tallahassee, *Florida Today* was one of eight scenes painted by Ulreich illustrating Florida's history and culture. It accurately predicts the shift in emphasis from Florida as an exotic and mysterious "lost world" to that of a playground for the rich and famous as well as for the American middle class. In the postwar era of the 1950s, the "Florida vacation" became an American dream, and Florida's identity and economy became ever more closely linked to presenting itself as the destination of choice for millions of tourists each year.

Twentieth-century illustrated travel tracts continued to lure northerners to the subtropics. Even though the steamboat era had passed, the St. Johns River was still a magnet for tourists, and in the 1950s travel literature described the merits of "the inland route to Miami, the St. Johns River Trail." Since most tourists arrived by car, a north-south auto route from the Georgia border to the white sands of Miami Beach provided a pleasant way of getting to the ultimate destination. In between were towns like Green Cove Springs, Palatka, DeLand, Sanford, and Kissimmee where tourists could stop to take in local attractions. As Gary Mormino points out in his book *Land of Sunshine, State of Dreams*, theme parks dotted the state *before* Disney World arrived in the 1960s. Alligator farms, the Fountain of Youth, Silver Springs—the allure of the exotic was still alive even if the means of transportation had changed. In 1950, around 2 million tourists visited Florida; by 1964, that figure had doubled.[3]

With the state's continued growth, brochures informed travelers about points of interest. And, with continuing hype, tourists were enticed by Florida's near-heavenly delights. Baby boomers likely remember the folded advertisements that were placed in racks at hotel and motel lobbies or coffeeshops everywhere. They were colorful and there for the taking, offering a day's adventure to, say, the Miami Seaquarium, Cypress Gardens, or Marineland, where one could witness splashing whales, southern belles, and performing dolphins. . . . An amazed family could even observe frolicking mermaids at Weeki Wachee.

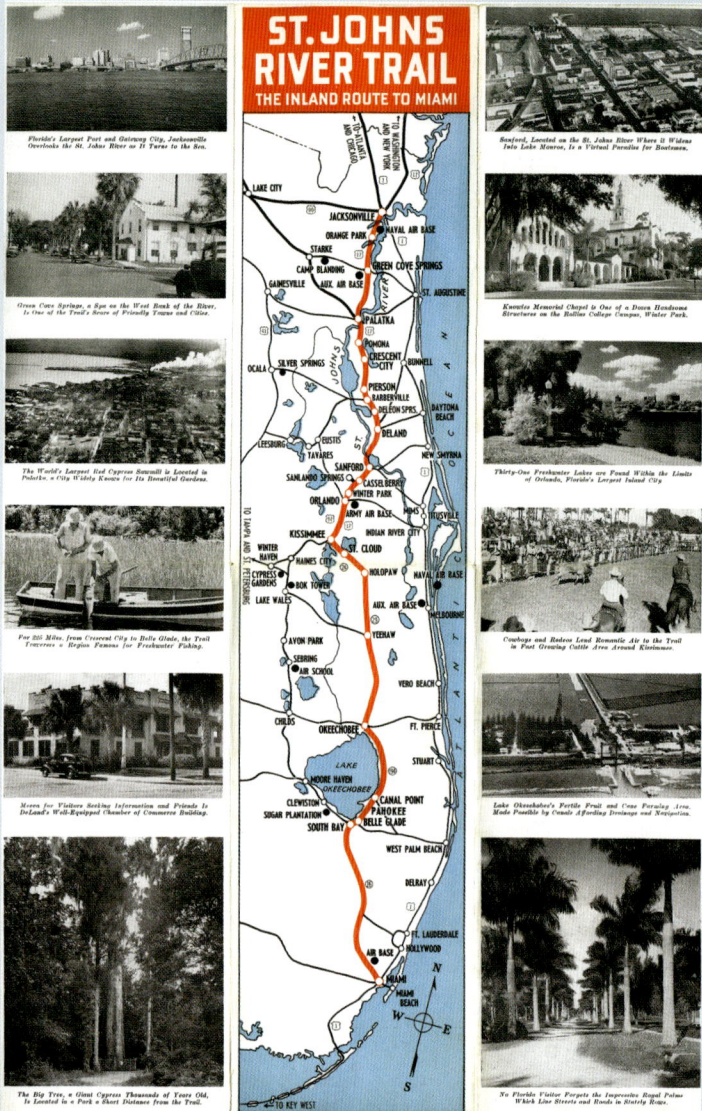

Plate 138. St. Johns River Trail brochure. Published by the St. Johns River Trail Association, n.d. 9 × 4 in. Courtesy of Gary and Teresa Monroe.

This brochure appealed to the ecotourists of the day—those without boats. The car ride from Jacksonville, near the mouth of the St. Johns River, to Miami, which is well below the river's headwaters, is filled with "places to see" and "things to do." Published by the St. Johns River Trail Association, the information describes a bioregion that is a considerably more sedate place than the one created by the efforts at developing a broad economic market. Modern Florida, replete with corporate theme parks and franchised *everything*, is dotted with the homegrown quality heralded by the early tract publications and even modern brochures.

Among the offerings at the Seminole County History Museum is a large, unsigned, hand-painted photograph titled "The Senator," which is also the name of the 127-foot-tall cypress depicted in the photo. The Senator had measured 168 feet until the 1925 hurricane took off its top; lightning rods were attached the next year. With a diameter of 11¼ feet and a circumference of 35 feet, the Senator—in Spring Hammock Preserve's Big Tree Park south of Sanford—is the largest cypress tree in Florida. And, after 3,500 years of life, it is likely the oldest. Early travelers relied on these big trees as landmarks as they traveled on nearby Lake Jesup. These mighty trees fell to the state's growth and development because old cypress heartwood is resistant to decay and infestation.

The Senator has long inspired curious tourists and picnicking families, who gladly leaped log to log to be near it. In 1929, President Coolidge commemorated the tree with a bronze plaque. Regrettably, the plaque and a section of the iron fence that was put around the tree's base as a deterrent to vandals were stolen in 1945. Although the plaque was never recovered, the county replaced the fencing. In 1951, the plaque was re-created and installed. Recent improvements to the park's entry road, which is off busy Highway 17/92 between Longwood and Lake Mary, and the path to the Senator, make a visit here a wonderful respite. The photograph, still in the same condition as it was when placed into the museum's collection, hints at its own and the Senator's survival.

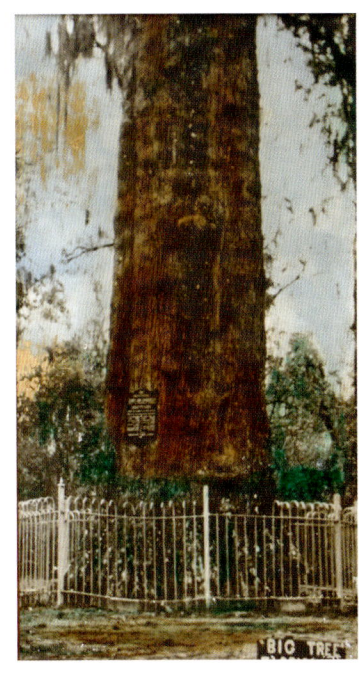

Plate 139. Anonymous. "The Senator," n.d. Hand-tinted gelatin silver print, 67 × 36¾ in. Courtesy of the Museum of Seminole County History.

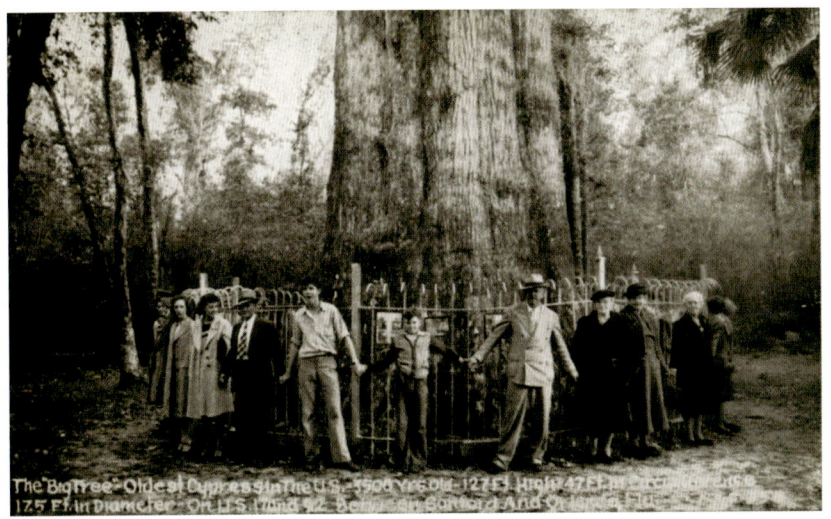

Plate 140. Postcard of tourists around the Senator.

The invention of the glass-bottomed boats at the headwaters of Silver Springs in 1878 boosted tourism to this location. Billed as "Florida's Original Tourist Attraction," Silver Springs differs from the myriad of the state's theme parks that are idea-driven, designed with a master plan and built with gates at which admission was charged from the first day of operation. Silver Springs' draw is the experience of the place itself. And Silver Springs' "place" is beneath the water's surface.

Bruce Mozert's specialty was underwater photography. So passionate was Mozert that he dove with his camera to film the real star of Silver Springs—life underwater. When Mozert once saw a movie cameraman filming through the window of the customary cylindrical tub as it was dragged by a boat, he hurried to the shop to design and build a submersible casing for his camera by shaping sheet metal. He inserted his arm into an automobile's inner tube, attached it to the casing that was housing his camera, and dove into the water to find fresh, responsive vantage points.

His career then blossomed, along with his imagination. As he says, "Everything has a picture in it, a sellable picture. All you got to do is use your imagination."

Mozert came up with all sorts of zany ideas. The success of his underwater photos are partly a result of his discipline and the demands he put on the models: for his underwater photographs the models did not wear scuba equipment nor were air hoses available for them. Mozert explains the models' natural looks in his images: "The girls were trained topside to hold their breath for at least two minutes. They would come up for air and go back down. We would shoot the same scene several times over. Before we would train a girl we would make sure she was a not a smoker. Women who smoked couldn't hold their breaths underwater for more than 30 seconds."[4]

Underwater, a woman cooks on an old stove while putting a wooden spoon to her mouth to sample the dish. Another woman wears a witch's hat as she rides a broomstick—the illusion created by her being suspended in the water makes it look as if she's flying. There's the submerged newsstand where a model shows off a *Post* magazine with the banner: "Eisenhower Elected." Still beneath the surface, Neptune's secretary sits provocatively on the lap of the king of the seas. And to honor secretaries everywhere, one model sits straight while taking dictation from her boss. An archer's

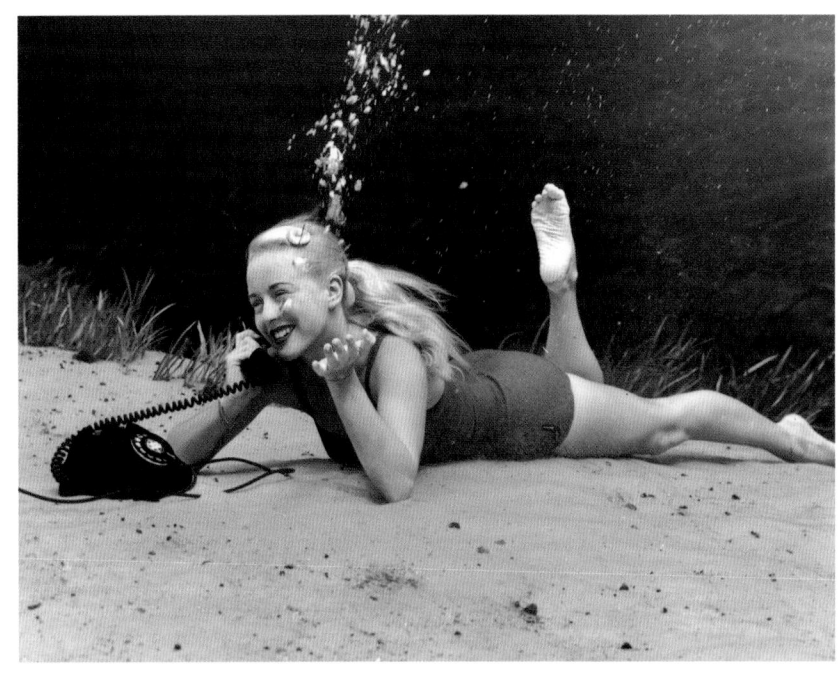

Plates 141 and 142. Bruce Mozert. "Untitled," ca. 1957. Photograph, 8 × 10 in. Courtesy of Gary and Teresa Monroe.

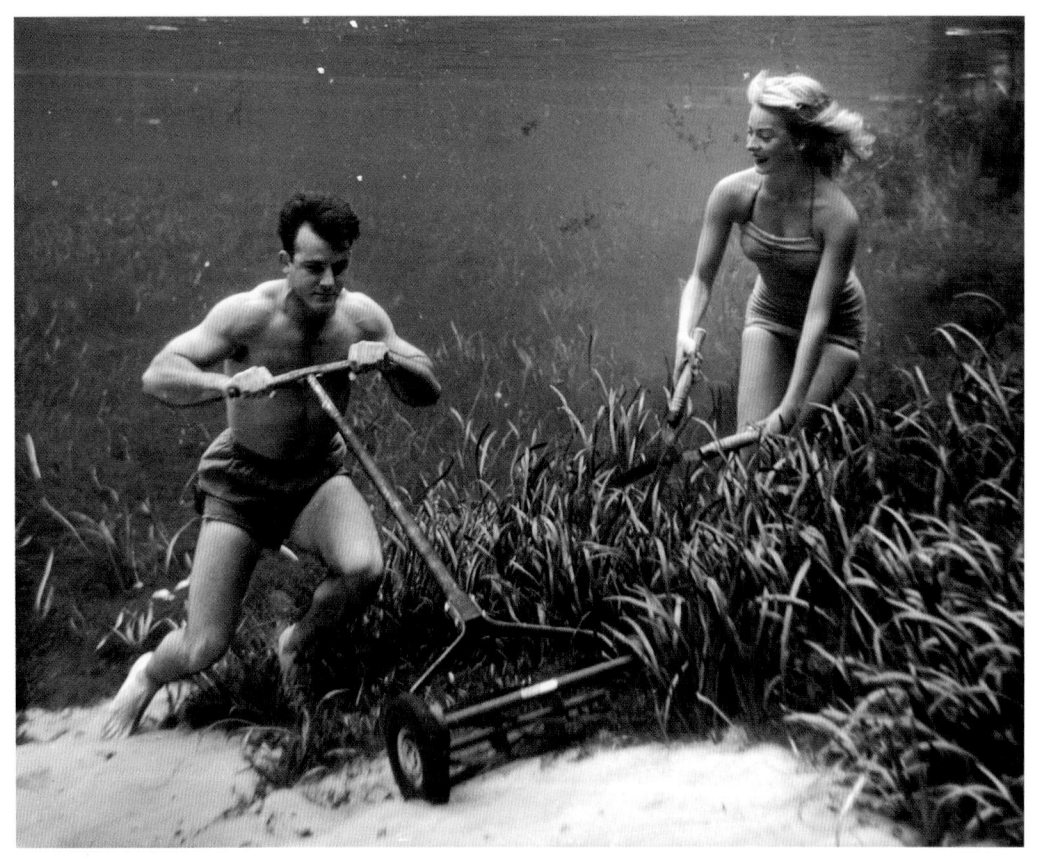

arrow is frozen just before hitting its underwater target. (Mozert also developed underwater lighting gear.) A woman reads a book underwater, wearing large, cheesy sunglasses; another bathes in a bathtub brushing her toes; while still another reclines on a chaise lounge chair as her beau peers through a window complete with an air-conditioning unit. A woman pets a fish, while another sits in an oversized fishing hook, like a paper moon, as "bait," alluring an approaching largemouth bass.

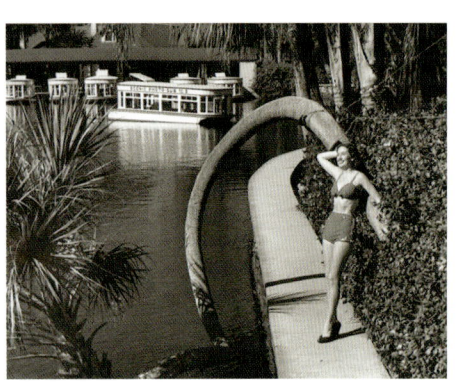

Plate 143. Bruce Mozert. "Untitled," ca. 1957. Photograph, 8 × 10 in. Courtesy of Gary and Teresa Monroe.

Mozert worked on land too, making classically composed pictures of people gazing out at glass-bottomed boats framed by the spring's beautiful foliage. He tricked animals into doing what humans do: a monkey setting a clock's hands, an alligator typing a letter, a squirrel casting a vote in a ballot box while in another picture one is drinking through a straw, a skunk in a flower bed sniffing one of the many flowering plants at Silver Springs. Mostly, though, it was a never-ending stream of beautiful women underwater doing hokey things.

Mozert's attention-getters worked; in 1950, some 800,000 people visited Silver Springs to enjoy the natural wonders of the largest artesian spring in the world. Yet in spite of being placed on the National Register of Historic Places in 1972, within a year attendance began declining because of the completion of I-75—which moved the flow of traffic farther away from Silver Springs than did Highway 441—and the opening of the roaring mouse—all roads led to the Magic Kingdom.

But still, today, as the guide announces that the 72-degree headspring waters are "99.8 percent pure," visitors can peer into the depths while gliding in ever-improved glass-bottomed boats, just as more daring travelers did more than a hundred years ago. Then they rode in a steamboat down from Jacksonville and up the Ocklawaha all the way to Silver Springs by night, bending and turning like the crooked palm tree in the photograph, a bucket of pine knots burning on the bow and lighting the way, discovering Florida.

Publicists were staging scenes to be photographed long before directorial imagery was in art-circle vogue, often shamelessly, and Silver Springs offered everything a publicist could dream of. The publicist was the behind-the-scenes star, orchestrating images for mass consumption and hence increased business.

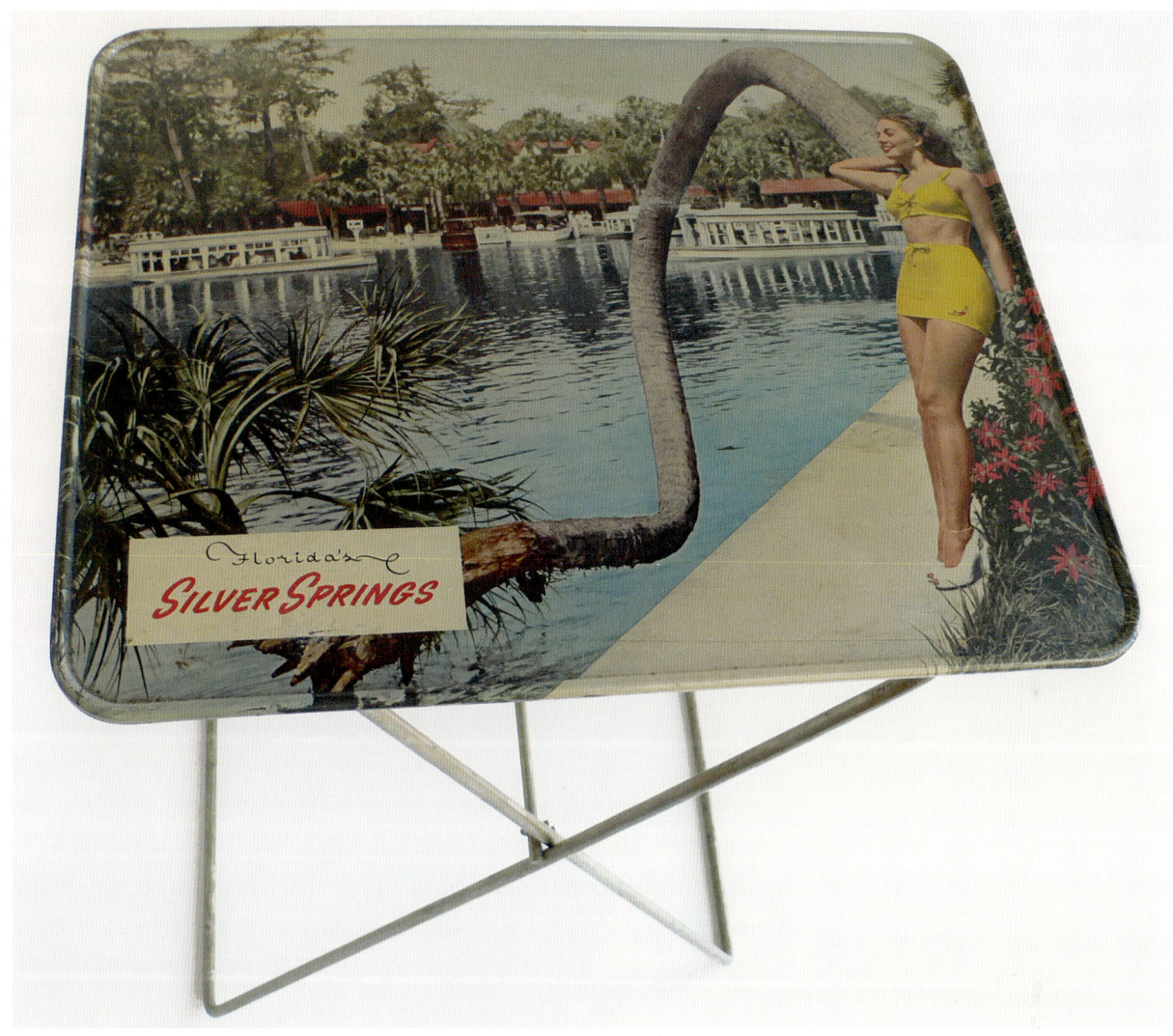

Bruce Mozert had both the imagination and skills to bring forth the most persuasive imagery. For forty-two years at Silver Springs, he took not only the picture that inspired the TV tray pictured here but also countless others. His camera was a compliant witness, making and recording history.

In addition to being a prime tourist attraction in the region, Silver Springs has also served as the backdrop for more than thirty motion pictures, including many Tarzan films and the horror classic *The Creature from the Black Lagoon*.

Plate 144. Bruce Mozert, *Untitled* (Silver Springs TV tray), ca. 1957. Photolithography on metal, 12 × 15 in. Manufactured by Durham Manufacturing Corp., Muncie, Indiana. Courtesy of Gary and Teresa Monroe.

Although she has "always been an artist," favoring the arts to academics, Allison Watson does not portray her art as primarily a commercial venture. In her words, "The urgency to paint existed before the urgency to support myself. I am a professional painter because I love it and that is what I do best, albeit [it is] a difficult way to survive."[5] Watson offers no theoretical treatises about the artist's centrality to contemporary aesthetics, nor does she indulge in lofty statements about her own importance. For Watson, it's all about the land—and making paintings that are appealing enough to be purchased for private collections and public spaces.

Considering her art "refined impressionism, bordering on realism," Watson's relatively tight views direct her to contend with details. At first glance, Watson's paintings may seem like photorealism, but closer inspection reveals that they are optically constructed. One thing's for sure: "I'm good at bark," says the artist about her illusionary powers with acrylics whether exploring the river or the springs and lakes that feed it.

Looking at landscape paintings by Watson and many other contemporary landscapists, one might never guess that the St. Johns River bioregions face severe water shortages and the loss of critical natural habitat due to development. Then again, maybe images that evoke the memory of a more harmonious relationship between man and nature will jar people into recognizing the fragility and importance of the environment and the threat to it posed by industrialization and unhampered development. This response seems most likely to occur when artists paint their remembrances, even if metaphorically, without compromise. Allison Watson's cherished childhood memory that "there was not an evil thing in my world" keeps her laboring to make the images that match her ideals to the point of necessitating that she destroy one in five finished canvases because they just don't measure up.

The painting by Allison Watson titled *On Silver River* depicts the combination of light, shadow, and reflection that is the hallmark of her style. Her love of the land and of that air of mystery recorded in so many visitors' descriptions of the region combine to provide an glimpse of "some Devonian epoch where the green of newly evolved plants and ferns is dominant and mammals are still in cosmic incubation."[6]

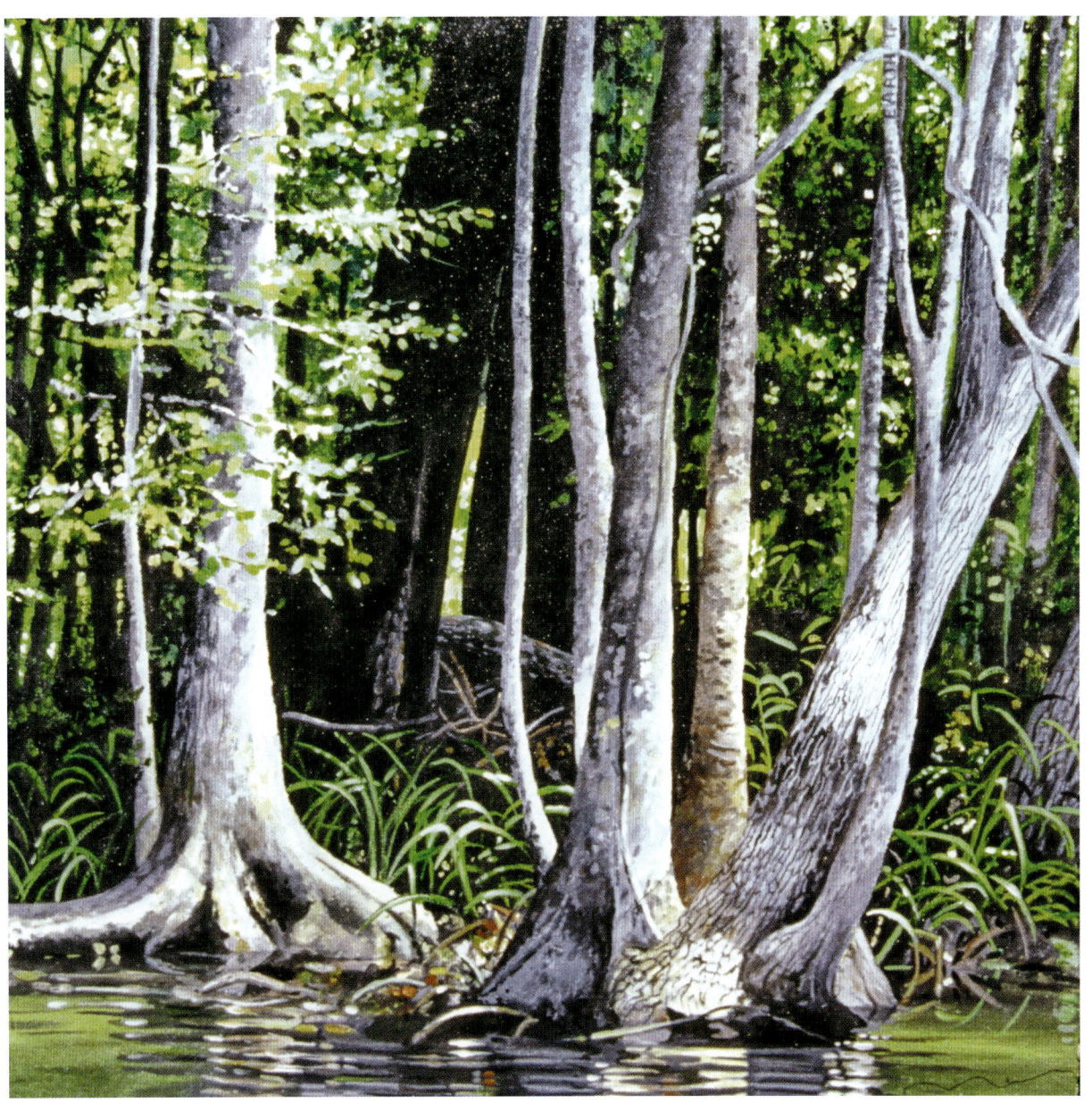

Plate 145. Allison Watson. *On Silver River*, n.d. Acrylic on canvas, 36 × 32 in. Courtesy of the artist.

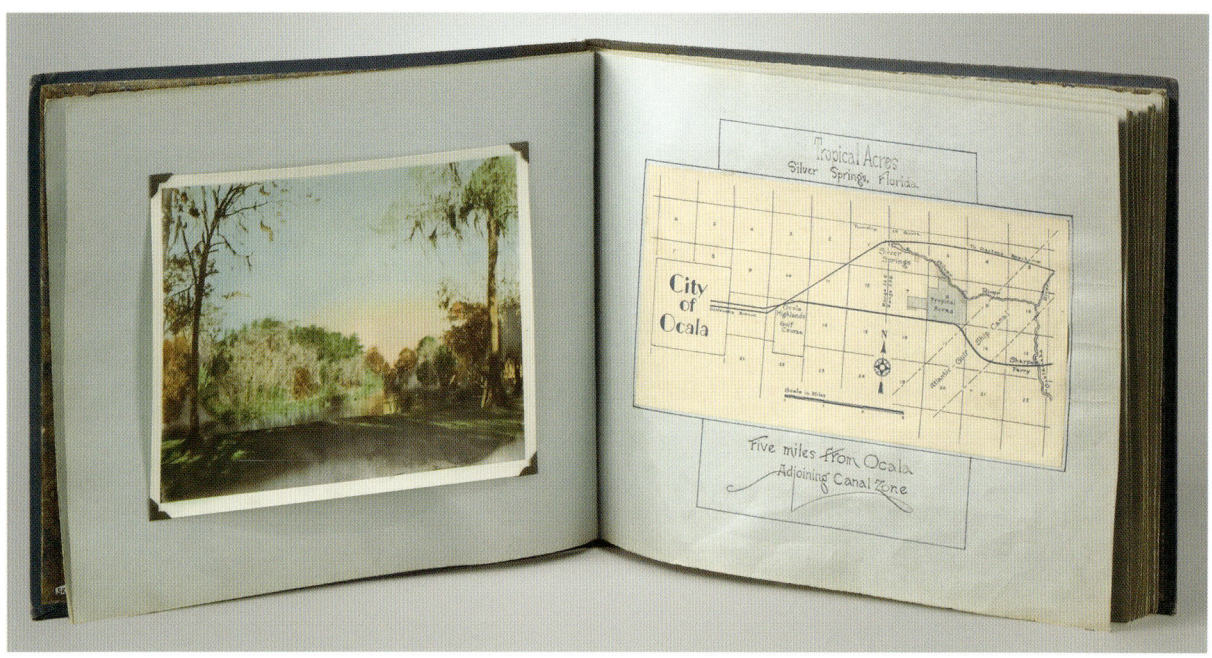

Plate 146. Anonymous. Tropical Acres promotional booklet, ca. 1945. Text and photograph, 12¼ × 15¼ in. Photo by Scott Mitchum. Courtesy of the Silver River Museum.

This booklet, containing tipped-in hand-tinted black-and-white photographs, was made in the 1940s to sell Marion Girdy Tracey's 600-acre property along the Silver River, the run from Silver Springs into the Ocklawaha River. Land-usage proposals included a private hunting preserve, sportsmen's club, golf course, and stock farm. Ed Ball and the Dupont Company bought the land as part of Ball's private collection of springs and properties around Florida. Included in his estate was this property, which the state subsequently acquired to establish the 5,000-acre Silver River State Park. With fourteen natural plant communities that are dotted with springs along nearly twenty miles of river frontage, the park is perfect public space for hiking, canoeing, and camping. Furthermore, the park is home to the Silver River Museum and Environmental Education Center, a pioneer Cracker village and a natural history museum offering hands-on learning for youngsters.

This land could have been sliced, diced, and gated, if not lost entirely to the Cross-Florida Barge Canal, the ill-fated project that proposed connecting the Atlantic Ocean and the Gulf of Mexico, since about a mile of the property is riverfront and identified as part of the canal's route.

Imagine a time before Map Quest or even zip codes. Try to imagine an era when jingles like "See the USA in your Chevrolet" played on your black-and-white television—a time when sunburn and mosquito bites were proof of a summer vacation, when getting there really was half the fun. It may have been enjoyable to plot one's drive, and gizmos like this mileage counter/trip planner made the task easy.

It was a time prior to Interstate travel, and hence a time when tourist attractions were popular, especially mom-and-pop roadside attractions. Maybe stop at the Silver Springs, as suggested on the meter's casing, the attraction that had these meters manufactured, to enjoy "Florida's Underwater Fairyland" from a glass-bottomed boat. One can almost think back and imagine that spinning the dial was as much fun as yelling "Bingo."

It is not surprising that people found a way to gamble with the ever-popular devices by spinning the wheel fast, and whoever came up with the highest number in the distance window won. Charging twenty dollars to replace each of the many broken devices put an end to that illicit activity.

This meter was at a DeLand, Florida, motel, for the use of countless guests. With a spin of the dial, one could know that Detroit is a 1,165-mile drive; it recommends that roads 17, 100, 41, 341, 41, 27, and 25 be taken. Raleigh is 611 miles from DeLand: 17, 1, 301 to 15A is the suggested route. Take 17, 100, 41, 341, and 41 to Chicago, 1,129 miles away. Perhaps an intrepid traveler might spin the dial and go to . . . wherever.

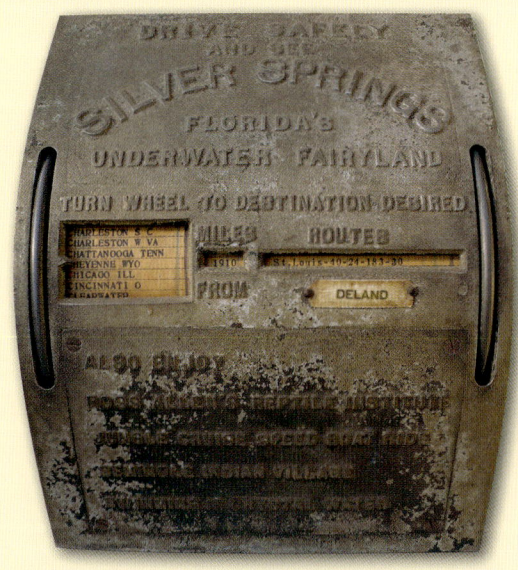

Plate 147. *The Mileage Meter*, n.d., close-up. Paper on cylinder in metal case, 8 × 9 × 8¼ in. Commissioned by Silver Springs. Timely Manufacturing Company, Daytona Beach, Florida. Courtesy of Gary and Teresa Monroe.

Today, mega-highways criss-cross the state, and even most secondary roads have long since been paved. Mark Derr, in *Some Kind of Paradise*, writes: "The state built tens of thousands of miles of roads, counties built roads . . . cities built roads . . . the federal government built roads . . . until Jacksonville to Homestead, the Atlantic coast was a stretch of people broken occasionally by a public beach or a vacant lot."[7] By 1986, nearly 100,000 miles of roads covered the state clogged with 8 million cars as well as those of 20 million-plus tourists.

The Winter Park artist Brenda Hofreiter is a fourth-generation Floridian originally from Miami. She studied painting and drawing at the Crealde School of Art in Winter Park, where she became a fellowship manager. It was during this time that she discovered a passion for painting outdoors directly from the landscape. In 1997, she founded the Plein Air Painters of Central Florida and served as the organization's president for six years. Hofreiter writes: "Although I have had some formal art training, my most profound teacher has been nature itself. My paintings are completed from bare canvas to finished artwork on site. I prefer to work in layers of oil, wet over dry. Paintings are usually begun with a loose drawing in oil on the canvas to formalize placement and composition and followed by a color block in. Working from dark to light, larger shapes are broken into smaller ones and details added until I have said all I wanted to say and the painting is finished."[8] "Whatever painting method I use," Hofreiter continues, "when a painting is successfully completed, I feel as though I have become a part of the lands, and it has become part of me. It is my hope that the resulting paintings share the beauty, peace and serenity that I find in the timeless beauty of the natural world. Their creation has allowed me a greater connection to this time and to these vanishing places."[9]

These days, millions of tourists arrive in Florida each year by airplane. For many of them, Orlando—with its Magic Kingdom and other entertainment venues—is a prime target. However, Disney's extravaganza is not the only tourist destination of choice. The Space Coast also draws its share of visitors, especially when it's time to launch a space shuttle. Just east of the St. Johns National Wildlife Refuge, near the headwaters of the river, lie Cape Canaveral and the Kennedy Space Center, from which the space shuttle leaves the earth and heads out into the larger universe.

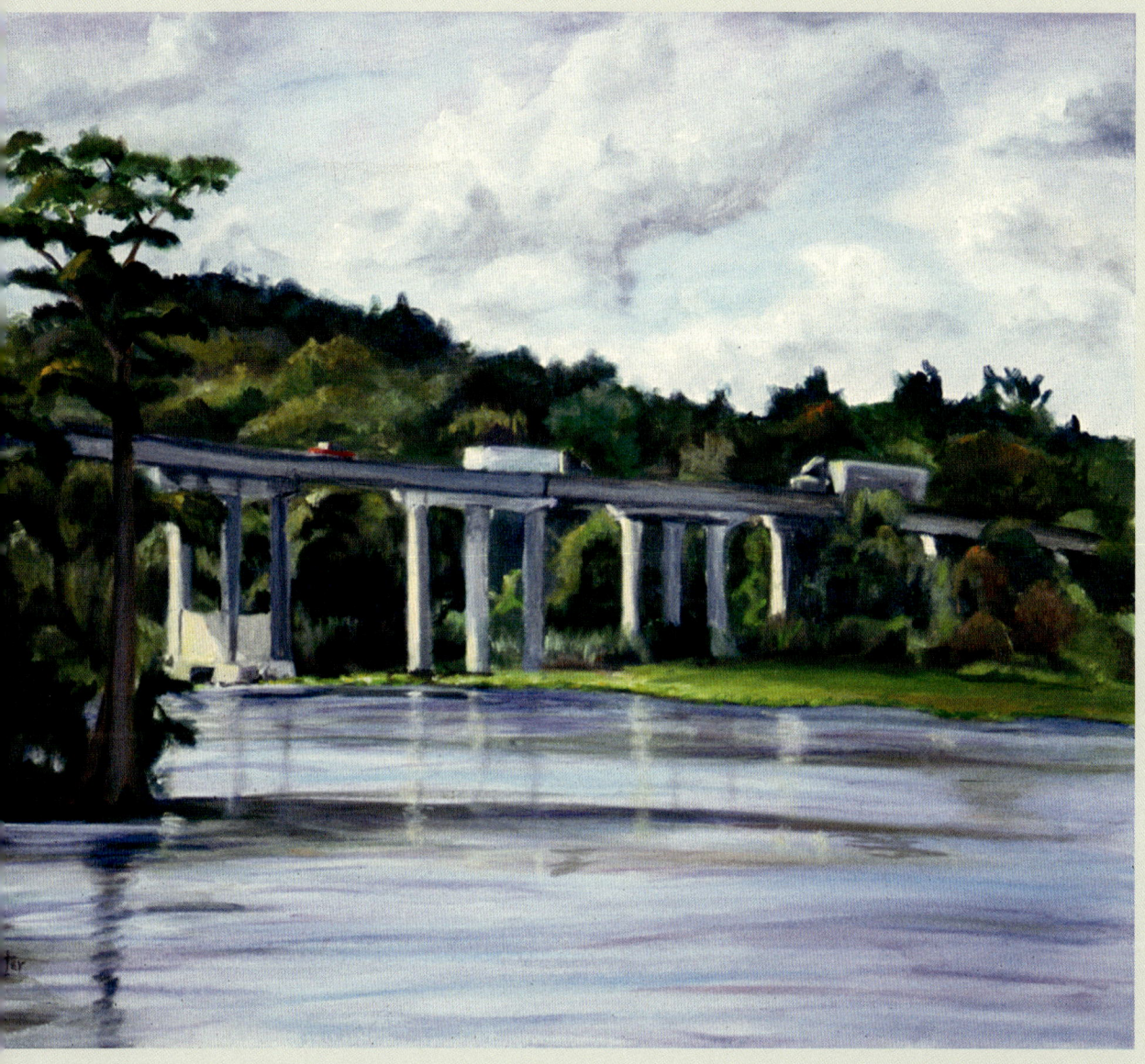

Interstate 4 is the major east-west highway connecting Tampa with Orlando and Daytona. One of the most heavily trafficked roads in a state where heavy traffic is the norm, I-4 crosses the St. Johns River just north of Lake Monroe. In this painting, the Winter Park artist Brenda Hofreiter captures the towering pillars of the I-4 bridge over the St. Johns.

Plate 148. Brenda Hofreiter. *I-4 Bridge over the St. Johns River*, n.d. Oil on canvas, 20 × 24 in. Courtesy of the artist.

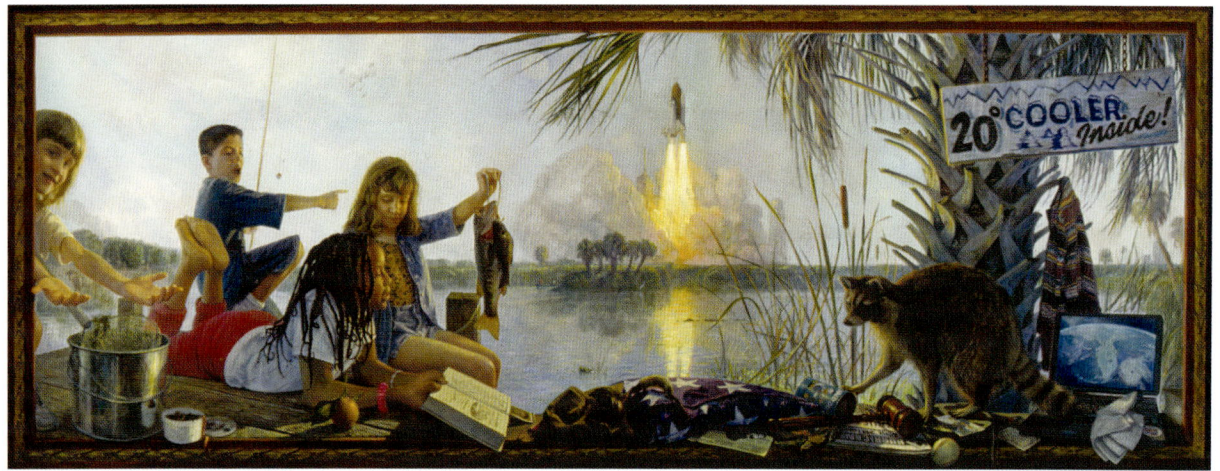

Plate 149. Christopher Still. *A New Age,* **2002. Oil on linen, 48 × 126 in. One of ten paintings by Still commissioned by the Florida House of Representatives, Tallahassee.**

This is the final painting in the series of works that the Florida artist Christopher Still created for the State House of Representatives in Tallahassee. Titled *A New Age,* the painting gives us a view of a space shuttle launch from across the Mosquito Lagoon, just east of the St. Johns National Wildlife Refuge. Four children are seen on the dock—three of them are busy fishing while one little girl reads a book about Florida's history. The painting is filled with historic references—an orange and a can of concentrate, a laptop computer, its screen showing both the shuttle launch and an approaching hurricane, a raccoon and a sabal palm—all icons of Florida's bucolic past and technological present.

A few miles northwest of the launch site is De Leon Springs State Park. Local folklore claims that Ponce de León visited the springs searching for the Fountain of Youth. Whether or not that bit of Florida mythology is true, it *is* true that two Indian dugout canoes recently excavated from the springs were found to be around six thousand years old—among the oldest means of water transport ever discovered in America. It seems ironic that they were found almost in the shadow of the space shuttle launch pad.

10 { Springs Eternal

Water Resources in the St. Johns Region

WATER—WHO WANTS IT, who needs it, who controls it—is fast becoming a major issue in Florida. Water has been central to Florida's allure and has shaped its culture since humans first arrived on the peninsula ten thousand years ago. With twelve thousand miles of rivers and streams, 7,700 lakes, and more than 600 springs, Florida is rich in a resource that no gold can buy. Over the centuries, this precious resource has been treated differently by the many different people who have settled here. For some, it has been a resource to be exploited. For others, it is a gift to be preserved.

The peninsula of Florida contains one of the largest concentrations of freshwater springs in the world. They range in size from the small trickles that can barely be discerned to the huge first-magnitude springs that gush out millions of gallons of water per day. Springs are classified into categories based on how much water they produce in a given amount of time.[1] First-magnitude springs have a flow rate of 100 cubic feet per second or 64.6 million gallons per day. There are seventy-five first-magnitude springs in the continental United States; twenty-seven of these are in Florida.

The existence of so many springs in one area can be attributed to Florida's unique geological makeup. Once a shallow tropical sea, the land that now is Florida was built up over hundreds of thousands of years by the gradual accumulation of limestone. Like the goddess Venus, Florida was born from the sea, rising into the sunlight as geologic forces within the earth's changing crust thrust it upward. Freshwater, falling as tropical rain, was absorbed by the porous limestone, creating an underground reservoir, or aquifer. The aquifer is constantly refilled from falling rain and overflows, rising to form springs.

The greatest number of springs appears in north central Florida, where an annual average rainfall of fifty-three inches keeps the aquifer filled and the

Learning about water is like an exploration to discover how the cosmos works.
—Masaru Emoto, *The Hidden Messages in Water*

When rain falls here, it percolates down through the fine, sandy soils of the ridge, dissolving and enlarging cracks and fissures in the limestone below with its slightly acidic touch. As it does, it creates vast, forever-dark underground rivers and reservoirs, watery veins contained inside the porous limestone "karst," aquifers that supply Floridians with 90 percent of their drinking water. As the weight of the water above—the hydrostatic pressure—builds, the water below seeks faults in the rock where it can escape, surging out through these vents at the bottom of the ride as natural springs.
—Bill Belleville, *River of Lakes*

springs flowing. Because of varying rock structure, vegetation, and climate, each spring is unique. The fifteen-county area that comprises the St. Johns River basin is home to forty-six springs, six of which are first-magnitude.[2]

Springs have had an almost universal appeal throughout history and have attracted people by their beauty as well as their utility. Florida's springs have long been praised for their clarity and their color, and both early explorers and modern visitors have marveled at their extraordinary power and have attributed health-restoring qualities to their mineral-laden water.

Perhaps William Bartram expressed most eloquently the feelings inspired by this amazing natural phenomenon when he wrote: "Behold, for instance, a vast circular expanse before you, the waters of which are so extremely clear as to be absolutely diaphanous or transparent as the ether. . . . But behold yet something far more admirable, see whole armies descending into an abyss, into the mouth of the bubbling fountain; they disappear! Are they gone forever? Is it real? I raise my eyes with terror and astonishment. I look down again to the fountain with anxiety, then behold them as it were emerging from the blue ether of another world. . . . This amazing and delightful scene, though real, appears at first but as a piece of excellent painting; there seems no medium; you imagine the picture to be within a few inches of your eyes, and that you may without the least difficulty touch any one of the fish, or put your finger upon the crocodile's eye, when it really is twenty or thirty feet under water."[3]

One of the great early European myths related to Florida was the Fountain of Youth. The Fountain myth stems from stories associated with the Ponce de León expeditions of 1512–13, first to the island of Bimini, said to be the site of a "fountain of waters that rejuvenated old men,"[4] and later to the east coast of Florida, where Ponce landed near Melbourne Beach on April 2, 1513.

Like many great myths, the Fountain story weaves bits of history with colorful anecdotes and unabashed propaganda. The hero of the story—Ponce de León—is a perfect subject since very little is actually known about him, leaving the field wide open for speculation and embellishment. We know that he was born in Spain, that he accompanied Christopher Columbus on his second expedition to the New World in 1493, and that he served as governor of Puerto Rico from 1509 to 1512. In that year, the aging conquistador received a contract from King Ferdinand of Spain giving him sole rights to the island of Bimini, which Ponce had heard was filled with riches. The next year, he sailed up the uncharted Atlantic coast of Florida and came ashore on April 2 near Cape Canaveral. Attacked by hostile Indians, Ponce withdrew to Puerto Rico.

During a second expedition to colonize Florida's southwest coast, he was fatally wounded and retreated to Cuba, where he died. According to scholars, it's uncertain whether Ponce de León was even aware of the legend of the Fountain of Youth, let alone that it served as his motivation for the Florida adventure, but certainly it makes a good story and has just enough history in it to be palatable. When nineteenth-century writers estimated the locations of Ponce's landfall to be near St. Augustine, the local citizens embraced the myth with gusto, and sometime in the 1880s the town began to celebrate Ponce de León Day each year on April 2, complete with supposedly "historically accurate" reenactments of Ponce's legendary landing and his unsuccessful search for the Fountain that would restore his youthful vitality.

When Thomas Moran visited St. Augustine in 1877 after being commissioned by *Scribner's* magazine to provide illustrations for an article on Fort George Island, the Fountain myth was in full bloom. Several entrepreneurs,

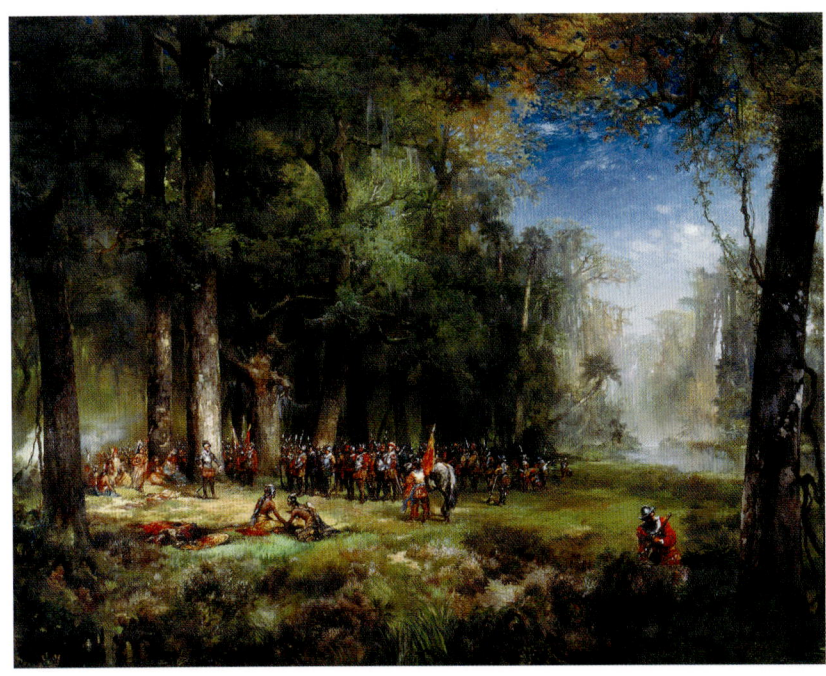

Plate 150. Thomas Moran. *Ponce de León in Florida*, 1878. Oil on canvas, 63 × 115 in. The Cummer Museum of Art and Gardens, Jacksonville, Florida.

smelling a profitable tourist attraction, had staked out potential sites for the mythic spring, including John F. Whitney, who claimed that a stream on his property near Ravenswood was the place. H. H. William's rose garden also became associated with the Fountain. Tourists flocked to the sites to bask in the golden glow of mytho-history.

The enthusiasm for local history and the building wave of tourist-oriented propaganda undoubtedly influenced Moran's decision to begin work on this painting shortly after his return from his Florida assignment. Moran's original intention in creating his *Ponce de León in Florida* (see plate 150) was to sell the work to the U.S. Congress in Washington, D.C., for display in the Capitol. To his chagrin, Congress rejected the painting.[5]

"It's claimed," points out the folk historian Bill Dreggors, that in the early 1500s, "Ponce de León came up the St. Johns River to a huge lake (George), and a ways to another big lake (Dexter), through a creek to another lake (Woodruff), to Spring Garden Run, and then to a big beautiful spring."[6] That became DeLeon Springs. It is likely that, if in fact Ponce de León explored this area in search of the Fountain of Youth, he became ever-hopeful at the run because of its clear running spring water, which was unlike the brown water he had sailed through to that point, water that was darkened due to tannic acids. He would have drunk the water at the springhead, but finding that it did not reverse the aging process, he would have trekked onward.

Before the 1880s, the time when Florida was rediscovered as an American Eden and steamers brought travelers, sportsmen, and "invalids" into the wilds via the St. Johns River, history was of another ilk. Sugar and cotton were cultivated in the region, and Colonel Orlando Rees built a waterwheel to harness the flow to grind his sugar cane and corn at the site that is now

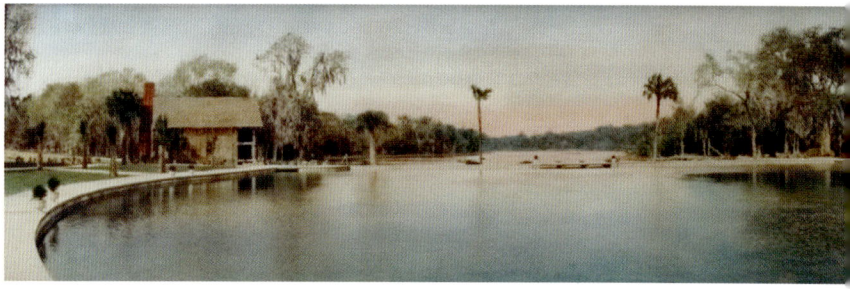

DeLeon Springs. The plantation was sacked during the Second Seminole War (1835–42). Later, Union troops destroyed most of what was rebuilt to hinder the Confederate's milled foods supply flow. As Florida opened up to reveal itself as the Promised Land, the springs had become a winter resort.

The photographer Richard LeSesne was born in Clarksville, Georgia, in 1880 and came to Daytona Beach for health reasons. There he ran his studio from 1903 until his death in 1946. In addition to the staples—postcards to portraits—he documented "the world's most famous beach" and the rise of auto racing, for which the city is best known. His pictures were picked up by the Associated Press wire service and were bought by popular national magazines, including *Life*, and international newspapers.

The man who stands by DeLeon Springs in this photograph by LeSesne appears to be as serene as the surface is tranquil. He may be unaware of the turbulence below as 14 million gallons of water rush through two flows of a limestone cavity daily. Perhaps he is communing with nature, reflecting about life in the God-given wilds that look as they had eight thousand years ago, when Native Americans inhabited the peninsula. He might have come to the springs—as others have done long before—knowing that the water is 68 degrees year-round, and that, as an 1889 an advertisement promised, the springs are "a fountain of youth impregnated with a deliciously healthy combination of soda and sulphur."

LeSesne took this photograph with a cirkut camera, which allows a relatively small camera to transport a long sheet of film that is typically used to record a gathering of people—a class trip or a troop of soldiers or conventioneers, for example. It allows the photographer to work close to the subject and to record a very wide-angle view. The extremely long format

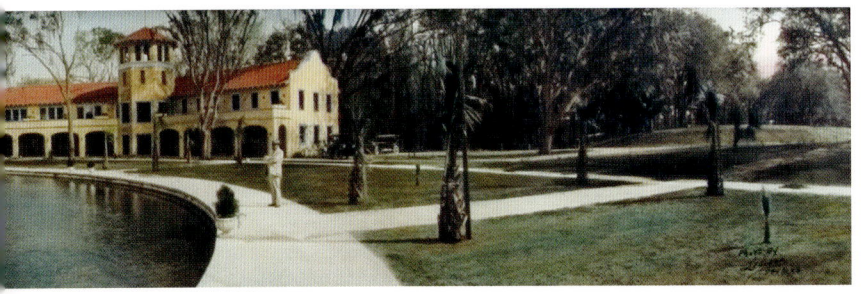

Plate 151. Richard LeSesne. Hand-tinted photograph. Collection of the West Volusia Historical Society, DeLand, Florida.

is perfectly suited for landscapes, too, where a lot of sky and foreground would otherwise diminish the presence of what lies on, near, or in front of the horizon. The panorama, in fact, adds to the calm of the image.

Also adding to the quality of repose is the hand-tinting. This would have been accomplished by LeSesne or by an employee, a "colorist." The dreamy hues support the otherworldly sense of being there, and wondering. Photographs like these were common fare for skilled photographers of the time, when such dedicated workers were a cross between a professional and an alchemist.

The Gainesville artist Margaret Ross Tolbert is an ardent snorkeler. She has been visiting Florida's springs for many years and tries in her massive oil paintings to capture "the experience of being in the Springs." Tolbert writes:

> I often depict them [the springs] as being continuous, from one painting to the next, like the waters of the aquifer, minimizing the differences between them. I am fascinated by the connection between artist and nature. . . . I depict the Springs as singular self-contained units [referencing] the many worlds theory of physics, where there is not one universe, but many, separate and complete, less part of a whole than a whole unto themselves. In fact it is the peculiar reality of the Springs that one limited entry can imply the existence of many others. In the magical structure of the karst rocks with emanations of the aquifer, Springs can simultaneously be discrete and part of a larger whole.[7]

Enter a big disc of light
Fringed with saw-toothed grasses.
Below, a world of tumult with waving plants
Armadas of fish, like tacks sprinkled on the surface
Vaporous breath of grasses; a wedgewood blue horizon
Behind their jagged silhouette. Trajectories of
Looping dives take you in between the gaping caverns.
Grasses shoot out from the vent, an effluent array,
From the center, limestone flakes flung out into the void are
White stars from a dark mouth that blows light into my face.
—*Margaret Ross Tolbert*

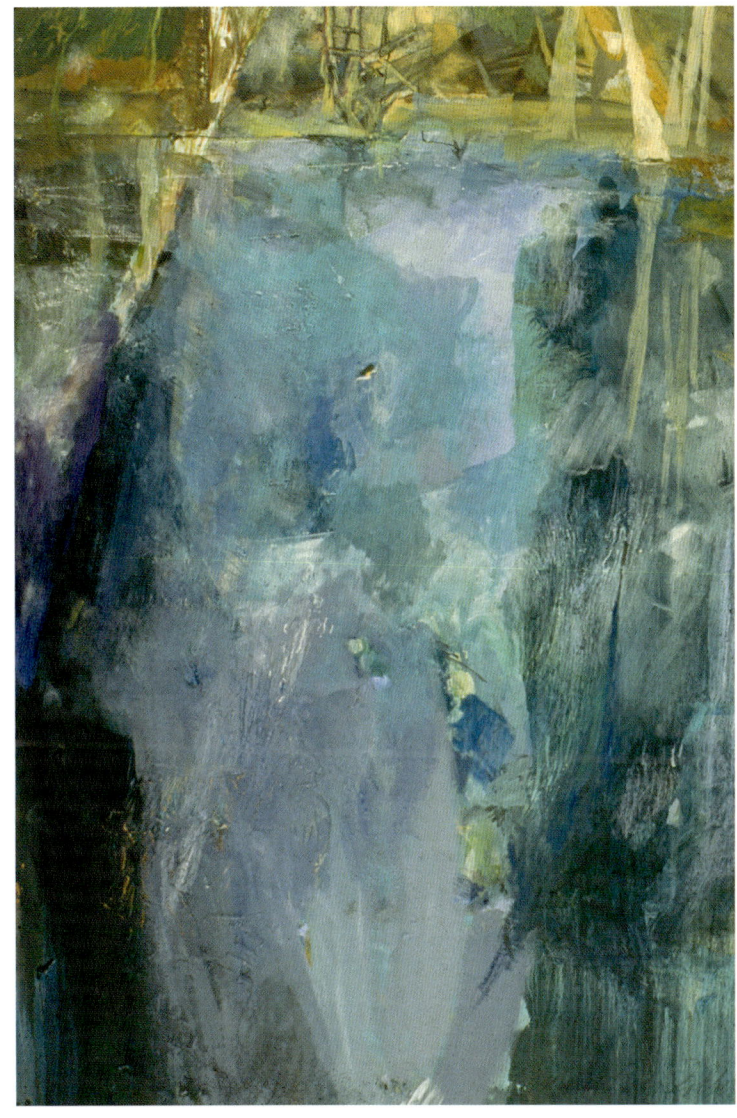

Plate 152. Margaret Tolbert. *Juniper Springs*, 1993. Oil on canvas, 72 × 48 in. Courtesy of the artist.

Part of the cycle of Florida's watery environment is due to the heating and cooling of the oceans that encircle the peninsula. The oceans control the climate, and the climate controls the cycling seasons and the life cycles of the vast numbers of plants and animals that coexist in Florida's diverse ecosystem. One of the most intriguing examples within the Florida ecosystem is the Florida manatee.

Manatees live in Florida at the northernmost fringe of their range. Although these gentle giants may weigh several thousand pounds, they do not have sufficient fat to insulate themselves if the temperature drops below

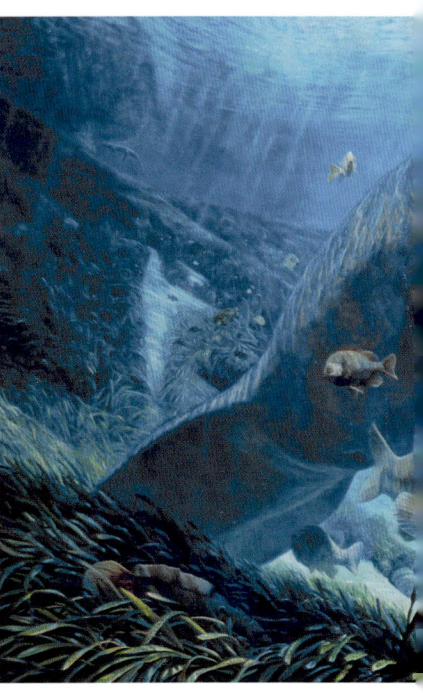

Plate 153. Christopher Still. *The Spring of Life*, 2004. Oil on linen, 56 × 158¼ in. One of ten paintings by Still commissioned by the Florida House of Representatives, Tallahassee.

68 degrees Fahrenheit. The manatee's prehistoric ancestors took refuge in Florida's naturally warm springs, which maintain a constant temperature of about 72 degrees Fahrenheit. Each fall as the ocean temperatures drop, the manatees move inland and journey up Florida's rivers to the springs, ensuring their winter survival.

A close relative of the elephant, manatees were once land animals, waders that lived on grasses and aquatic vegetation. After millions of years, they returned to the ocean. Their front legs became flippers, and their hind limbs evolved into a single large paddle. They have remained air breathers with their nostrils located on the top of their elongated snouts. Because of their large size—adults may reach thirteen feet in length and weigh 3,500 pounds—and their heavy bone structure, manatees are easy targets for reckless boaters. Most adult manatees can be identified by the pattern of scars left on their bodies by boat propellers. Doug Stamm, in *The Springs of Florida*, writes: "Propelled by moving its broad and flat tail in an up-and-down motion, it [the manatee] moves swiftly with effortless agility and grace. . . . The combined use of flippers and tail gives the manatee the ability to perform such hydrobatics as somersaults, half- gainers, head and tail stands, barrel rolls, and upside-down gliding."[8]

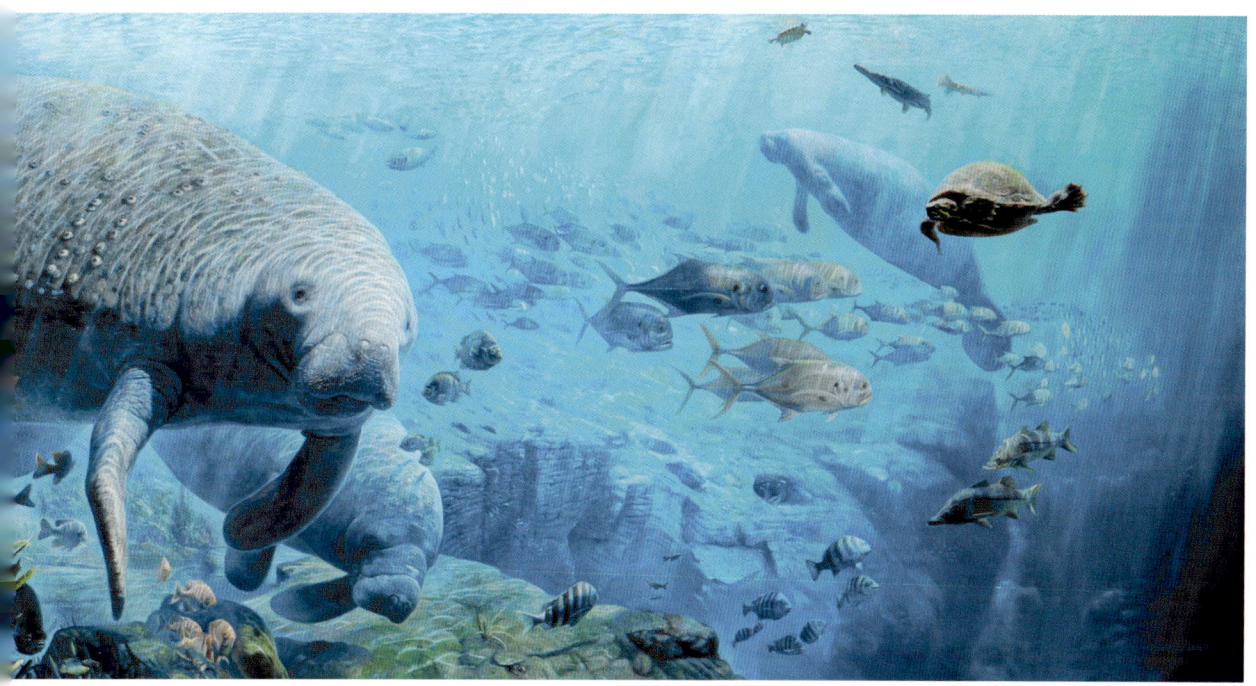

Christopher Still's painting *The Spring of Life* depicts a pair of Florida manatees along with a variety of fish, turtles, and other springs inhabitants, gathering in the unique environment where both fresh- and saltwater fish can be found.

The Florida rancher Sean Sexton sits on the board of the St. Sebastian Water Control District. "Subjects connected to bodies of water are near and dear to me," Sexton writes, "not only as a farmer but as a local decision-maker."[9] About Sexton's concern for the land and its resources, Michael Kemp writes: "Like a piece of flotsam tangled in a net of development, commerce, politics and tourism, Treasure Hammock Ranch is suspended and bound tightly by the modern forces that dominate the southeast coastal plain of 21st century Florida. Still, there is no obvious aspect of the ranch that could not still be from its founding in the early 1940s. Artesian wells, minimal equipment, and pine posts cut from the property, all these define the 600 acres and attest to [the ranch's] plain beginnings. . . . The conscious, spiritual choice has been made to retain this valuable patch of ground and preserve the rooted relationship of man to place. . . . This work speaks directly to our human connection to nature and to art, equal sustenance for our dual nature."[10]

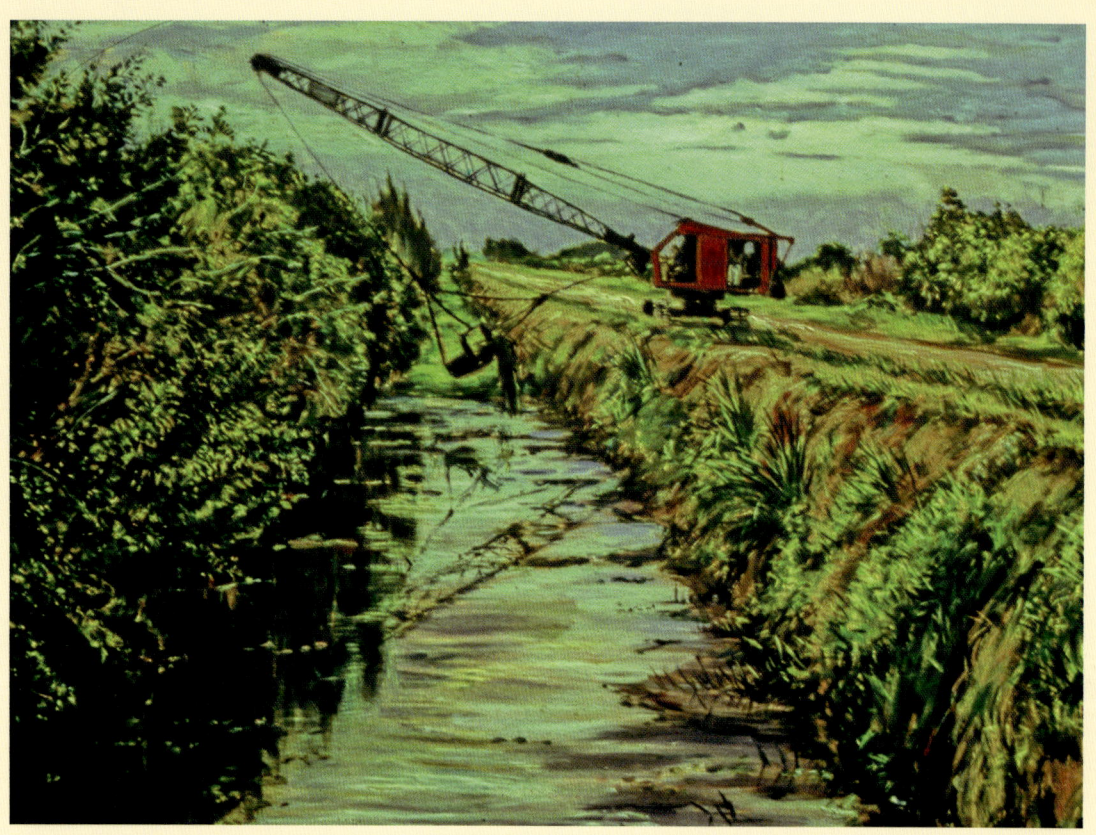

Plate 154. Sean Sexton. *Ditch Cleaning*, 1997. Oil on board, 22 × 30 in. Courtesy of the artist.

In this painting titled *Ditch Cleaning*, Sean Sexton alludes to the ongoing process of canal maintenance that is necessary to keep grazing land from returning to marsh. Intimately familiar with the link between the ranch and its surrounding environment, Sexton contemplates both the impact that man has on the land and the turbulent forces of nature that have always made farming a challenging occupation. Ken Rollins, the director of the Gulf Coast Museum of Art, writes: "Whether on horseback or his trusty tractor, Sean not only carries with him the tools of his trade as a cattle rancher, he is never more than a few feet away from his sketchbook. For more than thirty years, Sean has sketched daily as he tackles the multitude of tasks necessary to manage and maintain a working ranch with 300 head of cattle. His sketchbook journals (now numbering more than 100) are filled with drawings that document his life, his day to day work, and his sensitive observations of nature."[11]

The idea of "improving" Florida's myriad waterways in response to human need or greed has been a preoccupation since the earliest Europeans arrived. Ditching and damming, dredging and draining—humans have been diligently attacking the natural flow of Florida's water for four centuries. One of the most enduring obsessions has been the construction of a waterway shortcut from one coast to the other.

In the late 1500s, Pedro Menéndez de Avilés had already proposed the utility of a cross-Florida waterway to connect the Atlantic with the Gulf of Mexico. Menéndez envisioned a shortcut between Pensacola and St. Augustine that would circumvent the dangerous waters off the Florida Straits and protect Spanish shipping interests from pirates. Menéndez's prescient efforts were never realized, but the idea would remain, an appealing fantasy for those whose goal was commercial exploitation of Florida's vast natural resources.

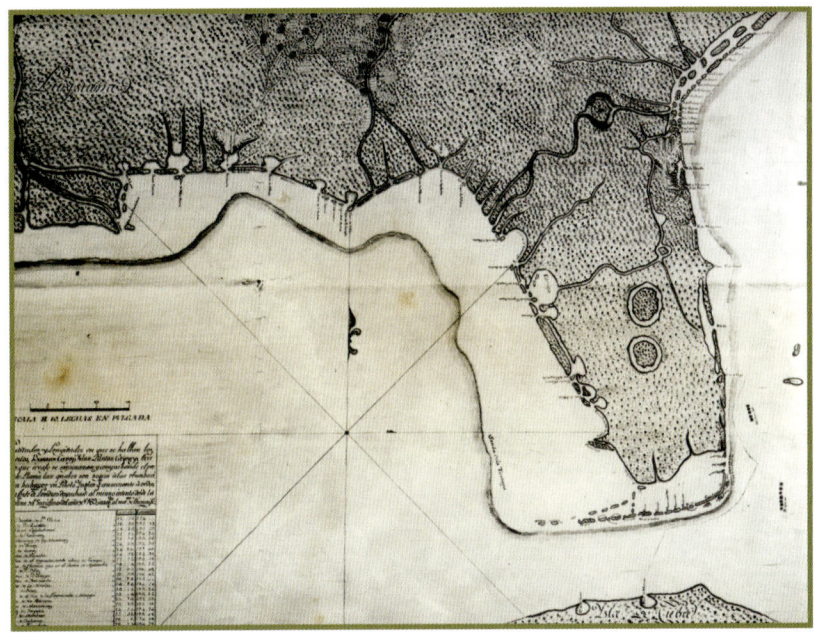

This map, drawn in 1768 by the Spanish cartographer Juan de la Puente, shows the St. Johns River bisecting the peninsula from west to east. This fantasy first appears in a 1565 description of a cross-Florida waterway by Robert Meleneche, and many Spanish, French, and English mapmakers

Plate 155. Juan de la Puente. *Map of Florida*, 1768. Original in Library of Congress. This copy from P. K. Yonge Library of Florida History, University of Florida. Map # RI.1768. 002. 1997. 0176.

continued to show the nonexistent canal for the next two hundred years. Interestingly, the course of the imaginary canal is very close to the route that would be proposed for the Cross-Florida Barge Canal four hundred years later.

After a few tentative sorties in the nineteenth century, technology finally caught up with ambition. The Ocklawaha basin had been steadily degraded during the first half of the twentieth century by careless farming practices that included abolishing wetlands and pouring pesticides and sewage into the area, but the worst was yet to come. In 1963, by a one-vote margin, the U.S. Congress passed legislation authorizing the building of a Cross-Florida Barge Canal. The idea was to create a channel for barges that would save money and time for commercial shipping even though it would also "destroy forty-five of the wildest miles of the Ocklawaha River and twenty-seven thousand acres of river swamp and hydric hammock . . . [with a] canal and lock system that would bisect the Ocala National Forest, curtail the flow in Silver Springs, befoul the Florida Aquifer . . . [and turn] the Ocklawaha and the Withlacoochee rivers into silt-gathering ditches."[12]

In 1964, the U.S. Army Corps of Engineers began construction. By 1968, they had finished the Rodman Dam and Reservoir, destroying nine thousand acres of river and floodplain forest along sixteen miles of the Ocklawaha River. Kevin McCarthy, a professor of English and Florida Studies at the University of Florida, writes: "The proposed Cross Florida Barge Canal was probably the single most dangerous threat to the water resources of the state in the twentieth century. When concerned individuals realized how the canal would threaten the diverse, productive river forest along the Ocklawaha River, they formed the Florida Defenders of the Environment to protect the swamp. Scientists studied the importance of swamps to the environment and concluded that they are necessary for the purification of water and the maintenance of wildlife. . . . A legal challenge by the Environmental Defense Fund and the Florida Defenders of the Environment stopped construction of the canal in 1971, but it took another twenty years, a $2.5 million restudy by the U.S. Corps of Engineers, and public opposition to the Barge Canal to finally ban it in 1990."[13]

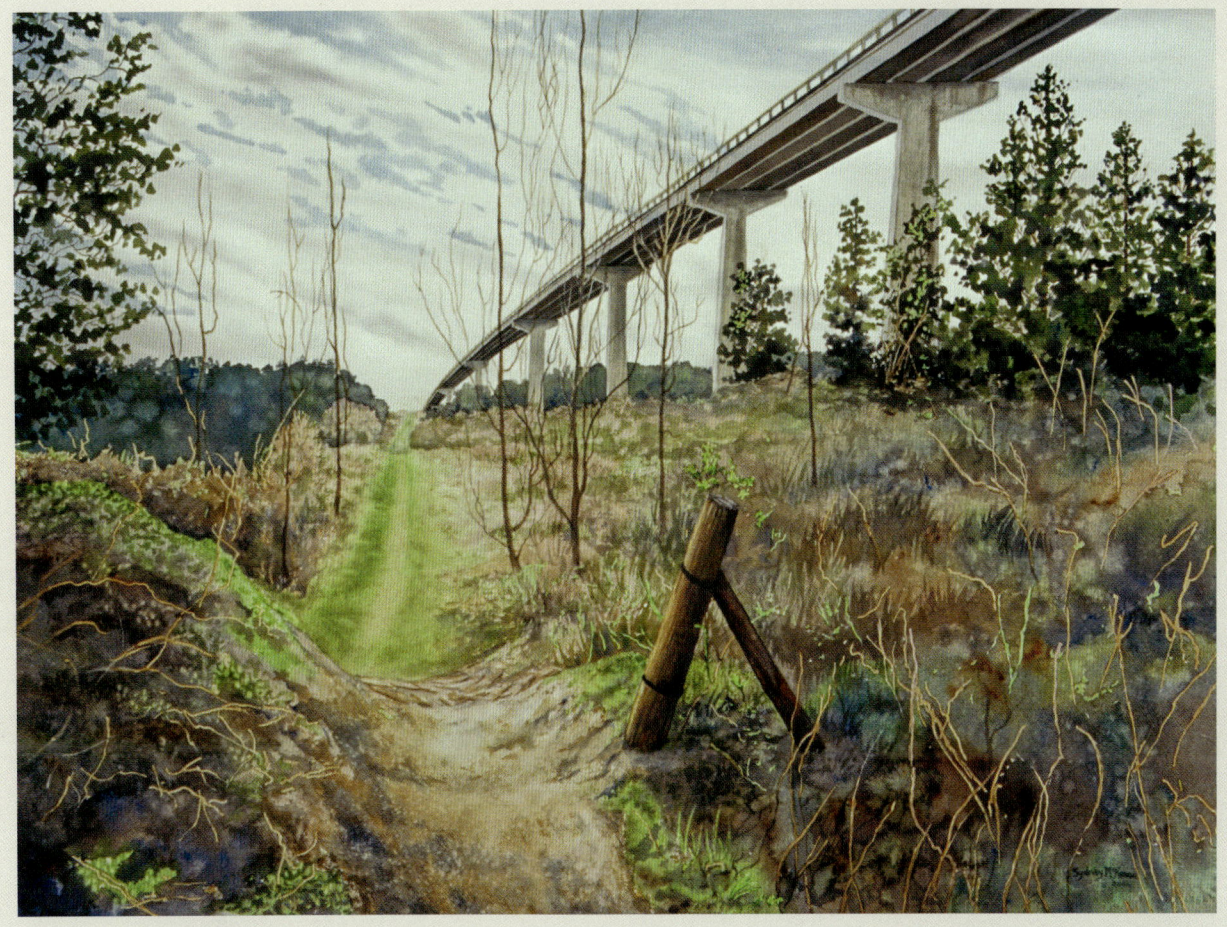

In her watercolor titled *The World Below*, Sydney McKenna depicts the elevated highway that crosses the scars left by the canal construction on S.R. 19 south of Palatka.

Plate 156. Sydney McKenna. *The World Below*, 2000. Watercolor on paper, 22 × 30 in. Courtesy of the artist.

Heidi Edwards came to Florida in 1974. She lived first in the town of Williston near Gainesville and later moved to Irvine in northern Marion County not far from Orange Lake. During the past twenty-five years, she has continued to paint the landscape of the north central region of the state, including scenes along the Ocklawaha River.

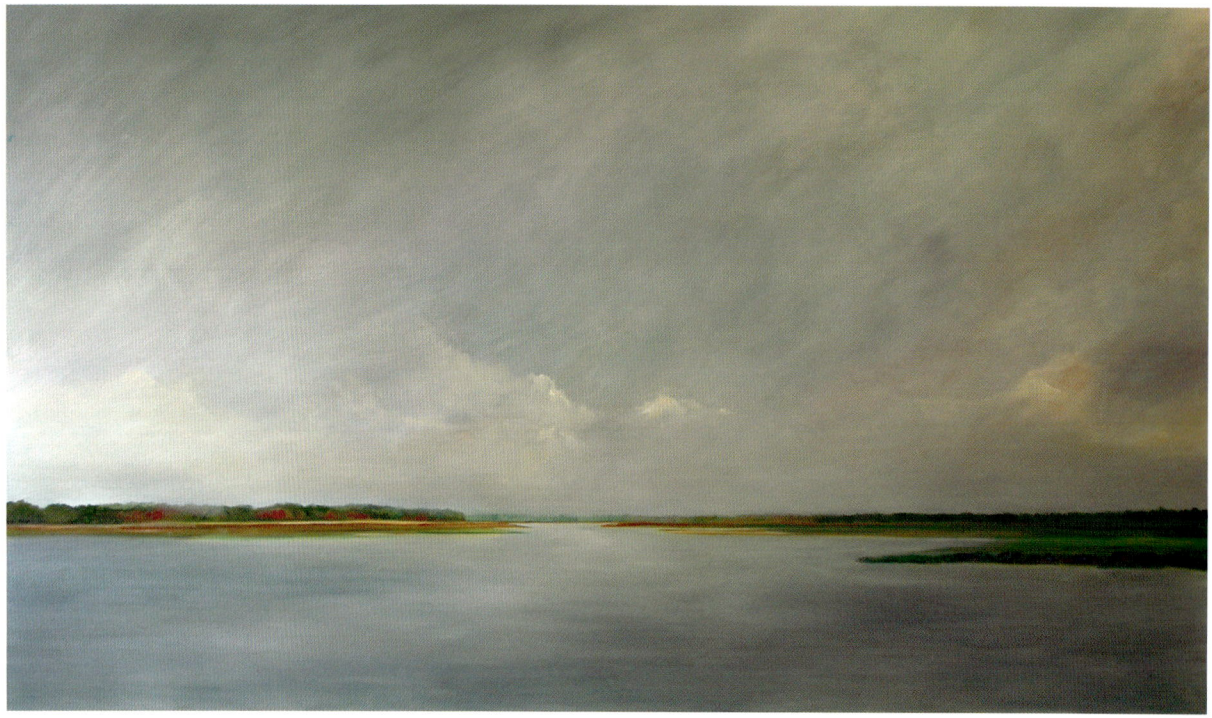

Plate 157. Heidi Edwards. *Rodman Reservoir II*, n.d. Oil on canvas, 46 × 78 in. Courtesy of the artist.

In this painting of Rodman Reservoir, Heidi Edwards concentrates on the elusive beauty of the artificial lake created by the Rodman Dam. In trying to capture the image, she uses wax-based oil bars over an underlying oil base. The liquidity of the pigment reinforces the liquidity of the image. Edwards remains firmly neutral in her depiction of the controversial reservoir. About her painting, she writes: "The landscape is the catalyst for my work. Imagery is only a point of departure, however. My primary subject is color, and the manner in which it becomes atmospheric space. My palette, which juxtaposes low-key and high-key colors, serves not realistic but emotional and decorative ends. . . . My paintings are not intended as social commentary; instead, they are lyrical abstractions—places of the imagination—self portraits of respite and tranquility."[14]

Today, however, sharp differences of opinion exist between those who want to restore the river to its original condition and those who want to keep the dams intact as a sportfishing attraction. Bill Belleville writes: "When the Ocklawaha Basin was first retrofitted, it created its own paradigm, one that existed with little history to guide it. . . . Some sport fishers now covet the vast puddle of 'Lake Ocklawaha' for its great lunker fishing. . . . Although biological studies showed that a revitalized Ocklawaha would actually create a *better* fishery than the artificial lake, legislators right up until the end of the [twentieth] century—grabbing onto the shaky logic of short-term economic loss—refused to destroy Rodman."[15] And so the debate continues.

Modern technology has allowed for the "development" of peninsular Florida in ways that our predecessors could never have imagined. For the first few centuries, Florida's mysterious interior was regarded as a netherworld to be avoided, a huge untamable marsh filled with predatory monsters. As late as the 1890s, steamboat tourists were lured by advertisements promising a glimpse of "savage nature in all its glory." Early European intruders settled on the coast and used the inland rivers for transportation. But as population soared and settlers moved inland, water became more than a resource; it became a nuisance, something to be ditched or drained, altered or subdued. Farmers and cattlemen, engineers and real estate brokers, all have worked together to reclaim dry land from wet, farmland from marsh, subdivision from estuary. As a result, the level of the aquifer is declining, lakes are drying up, springs diminishing. "For the first time in the history of Florida," writes Bill Belleville, "the liquid energy that once shaped us is now being shaped by us. We have taken ownership of *ibi* [water] away from the gods."[16]

Living on a peninsula with abundant bays, rivers, and lakes, we Floridians should set the standard for the nation in thinking deeply about our relationship to water. . . . Preserving the wetlands because we think they are pretty and perhaps even because we enjoy a quasi-religious experience in them . . . does not go far enough. We must change how we think of water, not just how we use it. This will, of course, amount to a change in how we think of ourselves. Our old morality and world view may no longer be viable in the 21st century; we must reexamine, redefine, resituate ourselves. We must come to understand that we do not live in our environment—we live our environment. We do not just drink, wash with, sail on, and swim in water—we live water.
—Ron L. Cooper, "Rethinking Our Place in Nature"

11 { The Western Watershed

Cross Creek and the Ocklawaha River Basin

The extensive Alachua savanna is a level green plain, above fifteen miles over, fifty miles in circumference, and scarcely a tree or bush of any kind to be seen on it. It is encircled with high, sloping hills, covered with waving forests and fragrant Orange groves, rising from an exuberantly fertile soil. The towering magnolia grandiflora and transcendent Palm, stand conspicuous amongst them. At the same time are seen innumerable droves of cattle; the lordly bull, lowing cow, and sleek capricious heifer. The hills and groves re-echo their cheerful, social voices. Herds of sprightly deer, squadrons of the beautiful fleet Siminole horse, flocks of turkeys, civilized communities of the sonorous watchful crane, mix together, appearing happy and contented in the enjoyment of peace.

—William Bartram, *Travels*

THE OCKLAWAHA RIVER BASIN covers nearly six hundred square miles of Alachua, Marion, and Putnam Counties in north central Florida. These three counties lie on the western edge of the St. Johns River Water Management District, connected to the St. Johns River by a network of rivers, creeks, lakes, and marshes that include the Ocklawaha River, Orange Creek, Orange Lake, the River Styx, and Paynes Prairie—William Bartram's Great Alachua Savanna.

In late April 1774, Bartram had the opportunity to explore the westernmost region of the basin. Setting out from Spalding's Lower Store, the trading company located near present-day Palatka, Bartram traveled overland in the company of "four men under the conduct of an old trader, whom Mr. M'Latche had delegated to treat with the Cowkeeper and other chiefs of Cuscowilla, on the subject of re-establishing the trade."[1]

It was during this trip that Bartram explored Paynes Prairie, called by him the "Great Alachua Savanna" and now named for the Seminole war chief King Payne. Now a state preserve, the prairie covers twenty thousand acres of freshwater marsh, oak hammocks, pine flatwoods, swamps, and ponds near Micanopy, Florida, in southern Alachua County. Fed by Sweetwater Branch and the River Styx and connected through Orange Lake to the Ocklawaha River, the prairie is part of the massive western watershed that flows eventually into the St. Johns.

Born in Rochester, New York, the artist Craig Rubadoux moved to Sarasota, Florida, in 1945. An early inspiration was the animals that he saw at the Ringling Brothers and Barnum and Bailey Circus that wintered in Sarasota. He studied art at the Ringling School of Art and Design and then traveled in Europe. Since that time, he has taught at the University of South Florida, Tampa, and at Florida International University, Miami. He has participated in more than seventy exhibitions, including solo shows at the Ringling Museum of Art, the Fort Lauderdale Museum of Art, and the Cornell Fine Arts Museum. His works are in many public and private collections, including the High Museum of Art, Atlanta, and the Museum of Fine Arts, St. Petersburg, Florida.

Rubadoux works primarily on paper or canvas using a variety of media. A commentary on the artist's Web site reads: "Greatly influenced by his environment and a love of nature, Rubadoux's painting style is colorful and fluid. But Rubadoux's paintings are not literal documentations of nature, he seems interested in the essence rather than the facts of nature."[2]

This painting by Craig Rubadoux, *Paynes Prairie Song*, depicts the grand expanse of the savannah dotted with herds of peacefully grazing animals. Many of Rubadoux's lively images depict animals both real and imaginary. "In my work," writes Rubadoux, "I endeavor to express exuberance, the joy of life, a spontaneous celebration. With line and color I try to express the inner energy, the spirit, the essence of life."[3] *Paynes Prairie Song* captures the dramatic scale of a grassy prairie bordered by dense forests, a scene that exists today nearly as it did when William Bartram visited over two hundred years ago.

Plate 158. Craig Rubadoux. *Paynes Prairie Song*, 1992. Oil on canvas, 64 × 120 in. Courtesy of the Alachua County Library.

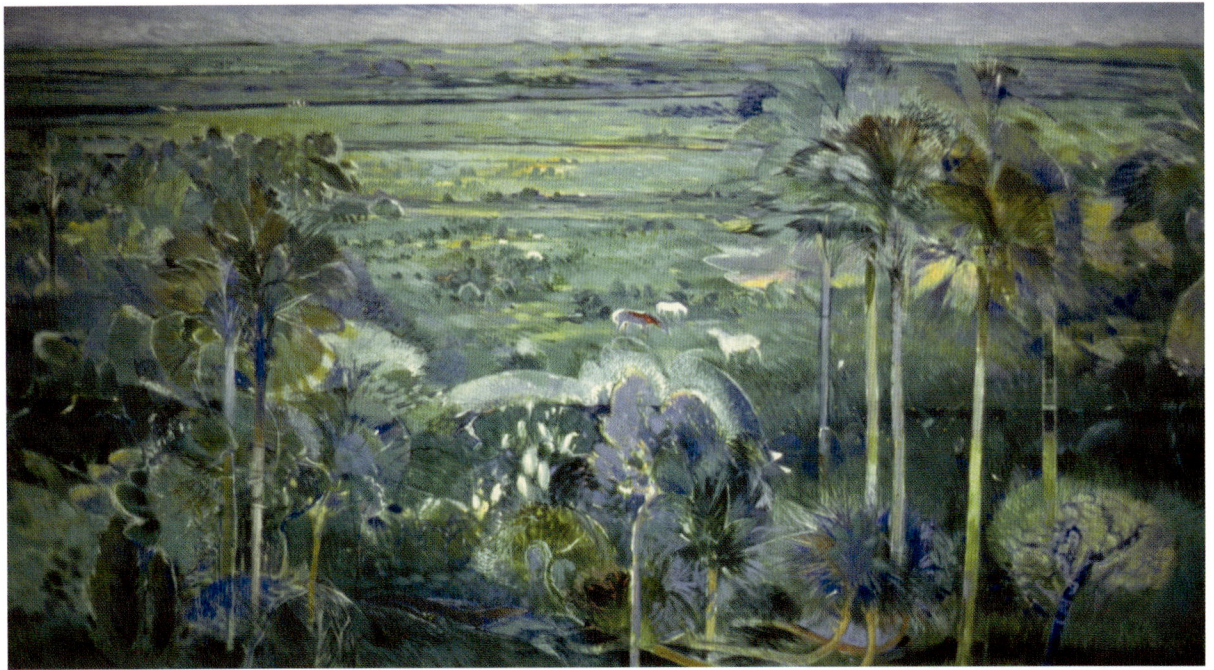

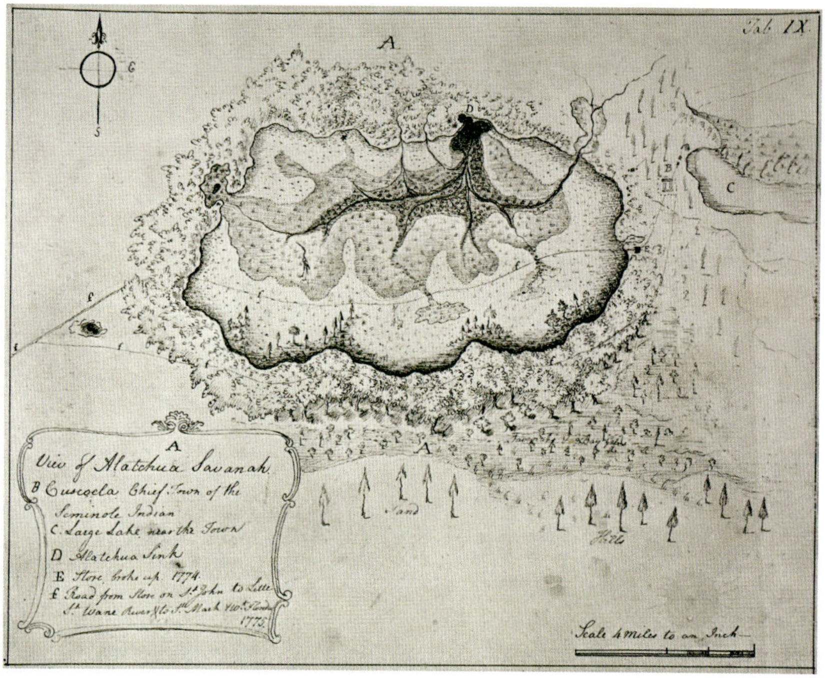

Plate 159. William Bartram. *Map of the Great Alachua Savanna*, ca. 1774. Pen and ink on paper. Original in the Natural History Museum, London. Courtesy of the George Smathers Library Digital Collection, University of Florida.

After giving a glowing description of the savannah itself, Bartram went on to describe his surroundings as twilight neared and the company made camp "on a rising knoll near the verge of the savanna, under some spreading Live Oaks. Dewy evening now came on; the animating breezes, which cooled and tempered the meridian hours of this sultry season, now gently ceased; the glorious sovereign of the day, calling in his bright beaming emanations, left us in his absence to the milder government and protection of the silver queen of night, attended by millions of brilliant luminaries. The thundering alligator had ended his horrifying roar; the silver plumed gannet and stork, the sage and solitary pelican of the wilderness, had already retired to their silent nocturnal habitations in the neighboring forests; the sonorous sandhill cranes, in well-disciplined squadrons, now rising from the earth, mounted aloft in spiral circles, far above the dense atmosphere of the humid plane; they again viewed the glorious sun, and the light of day still gleaming on their polished feathers, they sung their evening hymn, then in a straight line majestically descended, and alighted on the towering Palms or lofty Pines, their secure and peaceful lodging place. All around being still and silent, we repaired to rest."[4]

William Bartram's *Map of the Great Alachua Savanna* is populated with whimsical drawings of frolicking deer, a prowling bear, Cracker cattle, and elegant sandhill cranes.

Curiously—perhaps in deference to his sponsors—Bartram made a prediction that the savanna, "if peopled and cultivated after the manner of the civilized countries of Europe, without crowding or incommoding families, at a moderate estimate, [would] accommodate in the happiest manner, above one hundred thousand human inhabitants, besides millions of domestic animals; and I make no doubt this place will at some future day be one of the most populous and delightful seats on earth."[5]

Bartram was not the only one to envision the savanna as a utopian community. A half century later, Moses Elias Levy, a Sephardic Jew who had purchased a 60,000-acre tract from a Spanish Florida merchant, Fernando de la Maza Arredondo, attempted to establish a community for refugee Jews on the Alachua savanna. He hoped to establish a school for the "education of Hebrew youth of both sexes" that would include "lessons of agriculture."[6] His vision included turning the savanna into a vineyard where fine wines could be produced. Unable to attract recruits to his Florida settlement, Levy eventually gave up his utopian dream and returned to Cuba. His son, David Levy Yulee, went on to become a successful Florida politician.[7]

Today, if you drive south from Gainesville on U.S. Highway 441, it's not unlikely that as you cross Paynes Prairie you will spot a red truck alongside the road and nearby you will see the artist Peter Carolin at work on one of his prairie landscapes. Under the wide-open sky, in blistering heat or frosty cold, Carolin returns again and again to try to capture the essence of his favorite subject. He has compacted his equipment to fit into the back of his truck—a solid-metal easel that can stand up to the wind and hold up to an eight-foot canvas, and a box to hold his paints and brushes. He can set up in a matter of minutes. As he puts it, "Only darkness and mosquitoes take my eyes off the skies."[8] Although most of his paintings include the almost inevitable images of water and palm trees, it is the sky that receives the most attention from the artist. As the well-known saying goes, "Other states have mountains; Florida has clouds."

From tiny popcorn cumulus to magnificent cumulonimbus, Carolin is fascinated by clouds. "I am interested in the color and the structure of

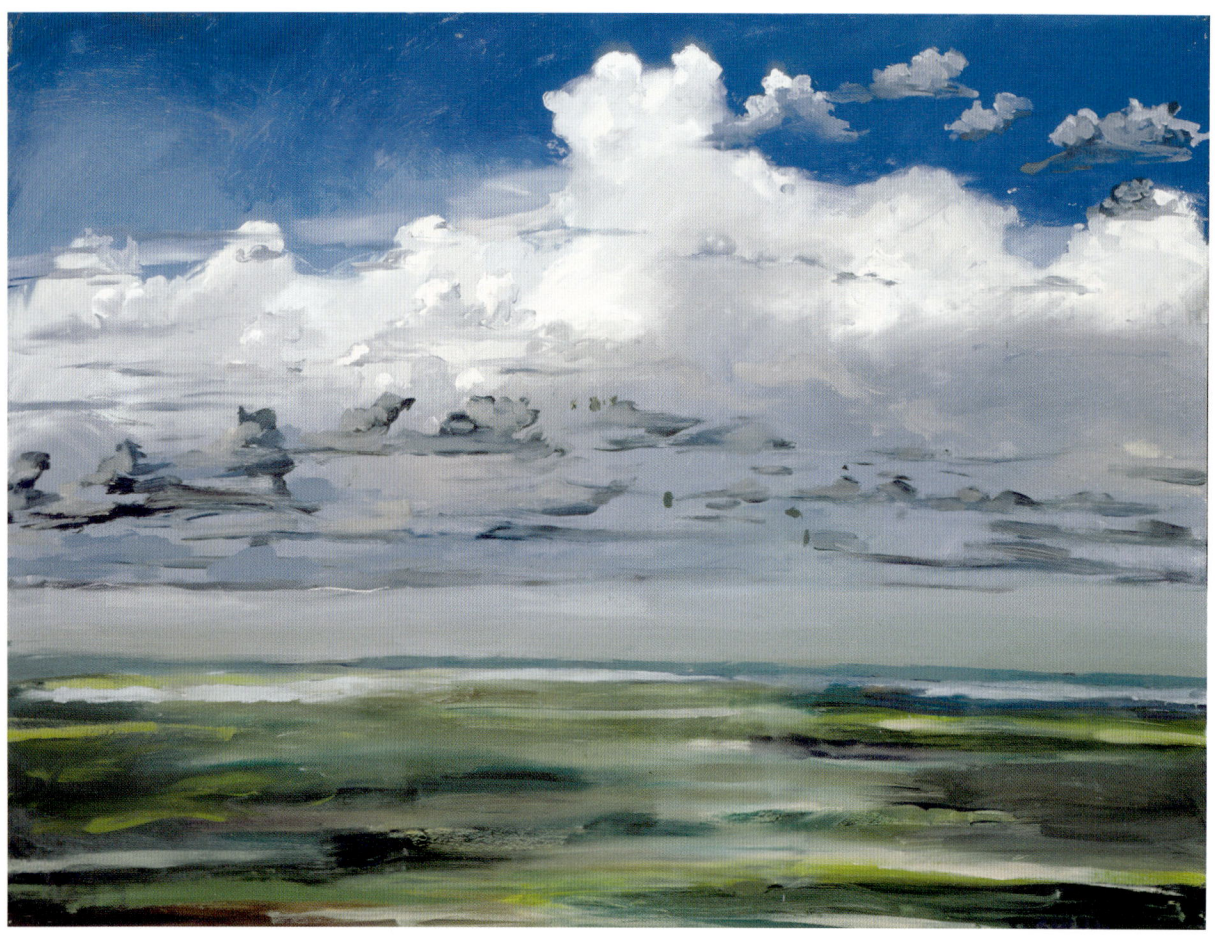

Plate 160. Peter Carolin. *Violet Summer*, 2007. Oil on canvas, 36 × 48 in. Collection of Nancy Lewis.

the clouds," he says. "As the tops of the clouds grow and expand, I enjoy watching the surface puffs and froths avalanche off—but it is a 'floating avalanche,' a cascade in slow motion. . . . I'm interested in capturing that frozen moment before the avalanche falls. Artists are always trying to capture this weird experience, to capture motion in a still image."[9]

To keep track of the changing shapes of the clouds, Carolin keeps a journal of drawings and notes. He draws diagrams of the clouds, breaking them down into geometricized planes, studying the patterns of repetition, the composition of the cloud layers. His studies are reminiscent of the numerous small studies created by the English landscape painter John Constable, who also took delight in the pageantry of the passing clouds.

Carolin received his art training at the University of Notre Dame and later was awarded a master's degree in fine art from the University of Florida.

He has worked as a poster artist for public radio and as a museum exhibition sculptor. A member of the Artist Alliance of North Florida and the Micanopy Community Arts Association, he also taught art in public schools for a number of years. His work is included in private and corporate collections nationally and abroad.

Of his painting *Violet Summer*, Carolin says, "Late afternoon especially affords spectacular ranges and combinations of color." Carolin adds, "They transition from white and fluffy to dark blue-grey and purple as a thunderstorm brews, sometimes glazed by a hazy, golden light. Beauty is gentle and soft here in the St. Johns River basin. Sometimes you feel that time itself is frozen."[10]

Stetson Kennedy, editor of the Federal Writers' Project *Florida: A Guide* and author of *Palmetto Country*, was equally captivated by the subtle beauty of Bartram's Alachua Savanna. In 1995, he wrote this poem to commemorate the prairie's ethereal beauty:

I stand on the rim of the nut-brown bowl
That is Payne's Prairie:
Listen as the cat-squirrel chatters and scolds
The sinking sun.
Clouds in the West
Stretched, gauze-like
On the fingers of the wind,
Dissolve into soft brown rust
And disappear.
The oaks weep crystalline tears
That drip from mossy beards
Into white sand.
A marsh hawk screams,
Swooping after the marsh hare that runs
Trembling under a log.
Flapping white herons
Rise in a long line from the ponds . . .
It is their wings that sing the finale
To the prairie's evening song.
—*Stetson Kennedy*

Cross Creek is a bend in a country road, by land, and the flowing of Lochloosa Lake into Orange Lake, by water.
—Marjorie Kinnan Rawlings, *Cross Creek*

LIKE HER LITERARY FORERUNNER Harriet Beecher Stowe, the author Marjorie Kinnan Rawlings succumbed to the allure of living in a Florida orange grove when she moved to Cross Creek, a tributary of Orange Lake, in 1928. She and her husband, Charles Rawlings, bought seventy-four acres east of Micanopy on the north side of Orange Lake. Charles soon tired of the rural life; although the couple divorced, Marjorie stayed on. Rawlings went on to write movingly about the region and about her "Cracker" neighbors. Her Pulitzer Prize–winning novel *The Yearling* established Rawlings as an important American writer. Ann Rowe, in *The Idea of Florida in the American Literary Imagination*, writes: "Marjorie Rawlings found at Cross Creek something akin to what Thoreau had realized at Walden Pond. Rawlings' Florida . . . was a place where one could live in close accord with nature, attuned to the changes of the seasons, in complete harmony with the surroundings. For Rawlings, life at the orange grove at Cross Creek was as close to an idyllic life as possible on earth. Her Florida of groves, scrub, and rivers was a largely unspoiled paradise."[11]

Rowe also points out that Rawlings frequently used the orange grove as a symbol of enchantment. In *Cross Creek*, for example, Rawlings writes: "Any grove or wood is a fine thing to see. . . . One is now inside the grove, out of one world and in the mysterious heart of another. Enchantment lies in different things for each of us. For me, it is in this: to step out of the bright sunlight into the shade of orange trees; to walk under the arched canopy of their jadelike leaves; to see the long aisle of lichened trunks stretch ahead in a geometric rhythm; to feel the mystery of a seclusion that yet has shafts of light striking through it. This is the essence of an ancient and secret magic. It goes back perhaps to the fairy tales of childhood . . . to all half-luminous places that pleased the imagination as a child. . . . And after long years of spiritual homelessness, of nostalgia, here is that mystic loveliness of childhood."[12] Rawlings continued to write at her grove house for many years before she married her longtime friend Norton Baskin in 1941. Eventually, she moved to St. Augustine, where she died in 1953 at age fifty-seven. She was buried in a small cemetery near Cross Creek in the peace and beauty of the rural Florida that had captured her heart.

The Orlando artist Jackson Walker specializes in painting historic scenes. In his series Legendary Florida, a group of sixteen oil paintings now in the collection of the Museum of Florida Art, DeLand, Walker depicts scenes taken from the pages of Florida's rich and colorful history. A Florida native whose roots go back to pioneering days, Walker was born in Panama City, but as the child of a military family he spent time in Great Britain and many U.S. locations before returning to Florida in 1988 to paint full-time.

Walker immerses himself in three roles: artist, historian, and viewer. He heavily researches the circumstances and personalities of his subjects. "It's a burden to tell big stories," he says, "if the moment is to be recognizable by someone of that era."[13] In fact, Walker spends more time researching than he does at the easel, where he might take four months to complete a painting.

Walker begins by sketching a bird's-eye view of the scene—"like watching a play on a stage from the balcony"—to map things out. Then he sits down below, at the stage level to arrange the composition. Not only does he arc downward to understand the lay of the land, he begins paint-ing the sky to provide a sense of space. He next develops an underpainting to establish the basic composition from which the drama will unfold.

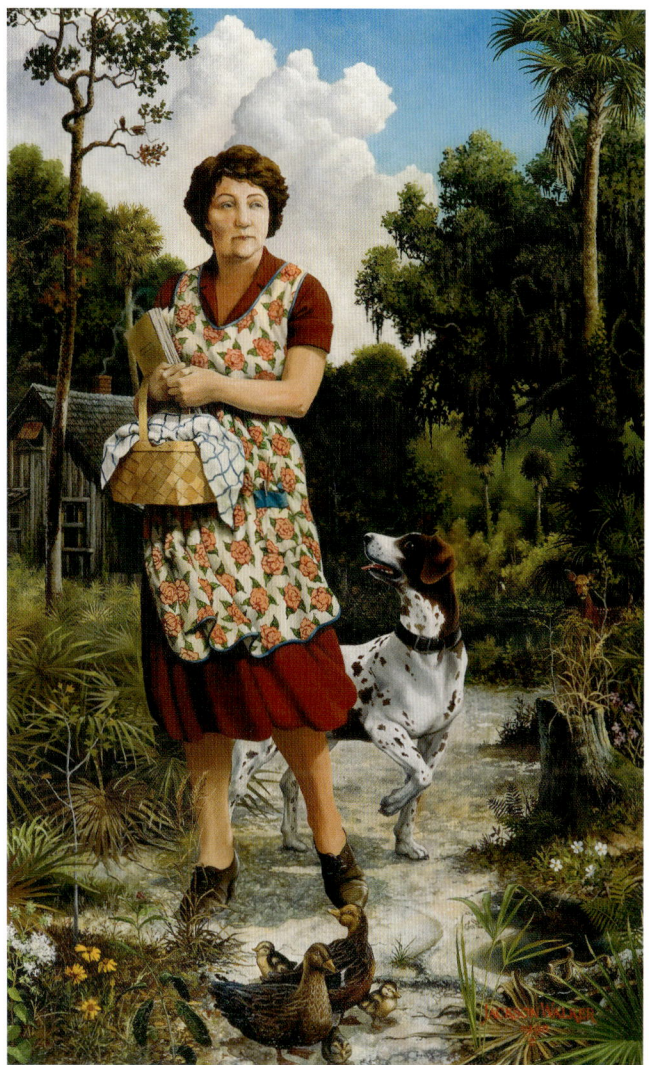

Plate 161. Jackson Walker. *Orange Fritters and a Story, Marjorie Kinnan Rawlings at Cross Creek, 1935*, n.d. Oil on canvas, 36 × 54 in. From the Legendary Florida Collection of the Museum of Florida Art, DeLand, Florida.

Because Jackson Walker carefully researched Rawlings's life at Cross Creek, he was able to include numerous details that give us a snapshot in time, a moment resurrected from history. He portrays the author in the yard of her homestead accompanied by her dog, Moe. She is carrying a basket of orange fritters, a delicacy that was documented in a Cross Creek cookbook written by the local historian Kate Barnes.

In February 1939, Newell Convers Wyeth, his wife, Carolyn, and his youngest son, Andrew, traveled to Cross Creek, Florida, to meet Marjorie Kinnan Rawlings and discuss the illustrations that N.C. was going to do for Marjorie's book *The Yearling*. Wyeth had already established himself as one of the most celebrated illustrators in the world, best known for his illustrations of such classics as *Treasure Island* (1911), *The Adventures of Robin Hood* (1917), and *The Last of the Mohicans* (1919). A native New Englander, N.C. Wyeth had grown up on a farm, attended the Massachusetts Normal Arts School, and studied with illustrator Howard Pyle at his school in Wilmington, Delaware. Wyeth's wife, Carolyn, introduced N.C. to the writing of Henry David Thoreau. After that, Thoreau's *Walden* served "almost as a family Bible."[14]

Wyeth believed that one of his strengths as an illustrator came from his farming background. He was used to observing people at work on the farm—saddling horses, splitting logs, scything a field of hay. He knew how working people moved and what details should be included in a scene to make it believable. He studied and researched the history, the period costumes, and the local landscape before working on any illustrations. Twice during the early years of his career, N.C. traveled to the West to observe the cowboys and Indians who appeared in his illustrations for stories about the "Old West."[15]

It's hardly surprising, then, that when he was given the opportunity to illustrate Rawlings's book, he immediately journeyed to Florida to "get the feel of the place." In a letter to his daughter Ann date February 5, 1939, N.C. wrote: "This is Sunday morning and I'm sitting before the east window of our room. We are on the fifth floor of this modern hotel, which gives me quite a prospect of the town [Ocala, Florida] and the wide rim of the outlaying wilderness called 'the scrub.' . . . Ma is by the north window reading a fascinating article on home cooking and . . . Andy is in the next room doing a watercolor, something based on the notes he made yesterday. . . . 'Marge,' as everyone around here calls Mrs. Rawlings, is not especially interesting nor prepossessing in appearance. She's a bit younger than we expected, and although weather-beaten and tough-fibered looking, she looks not very happy, pretty nervous and at loose ends. . . . But she has given heartily of her time and interest and has put me in contact with just the types of backwoods people I wanted to see, and the experience has been quite thrilling."[16]

N. C. goes on to describe his trek through the "scrub" with his guide, Leonard, and his confrontation with "Old Slewfoot," the bear that played such an impressive role in Rawlings's book. Besides his meeting with the bear, N. C. also had a close encounter with a Florida panther, which he described as "very large, almost as large as a Great Dane."[17] N. C. continued: "Night before last, standing in a swamp with a vast tangle of Bay trees, live oaks, pines, palmettos and heavy vines, all swaying in the night breeze and writhing with the ragged festoons of Spanish moss—and the full moonlight pouring through it all, we listened to the distant shriek, as from a frightened woman, of a panther. It chilled my blood."[18]

Plate 162. Andrew Wyeth. *Showery Day, Florida*, 1939. Watercolor on paper. Private collection. Courtesy of the Andrew Wyeth Foundation, Chadds Ford, Pennsylvania. © Andrew Wyeth.

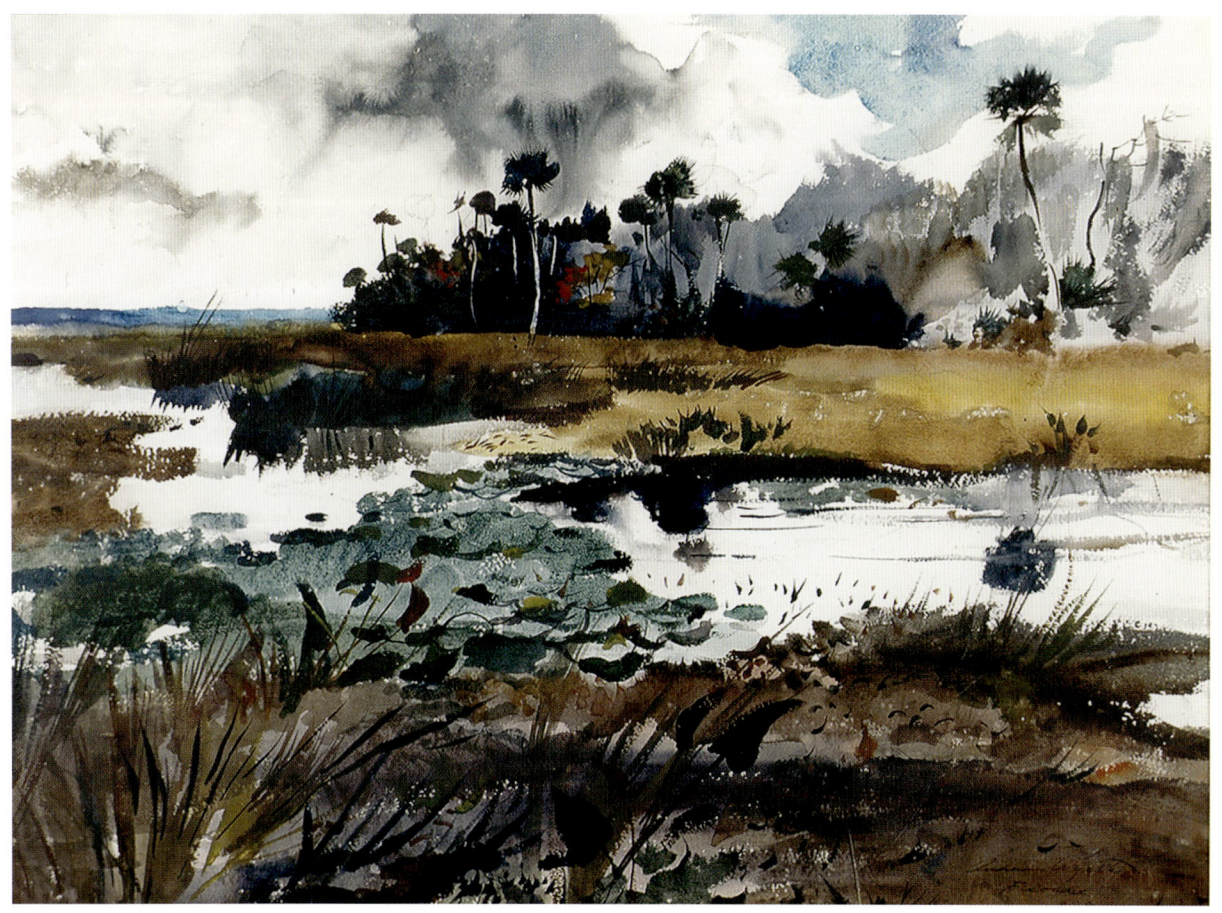

Wyeth ended his letter as follows, "I've seen a number of 'gators' slither into the murky streams and have watched the scuttling of fox squirrels, handsome black animals, have seen a number of deer and caught the glimpse of a bear rolling his way through the scrub. I feel ready to tackle The Yearling in pictures and I wish I were home and at it now."[19]

Andrew Wyeth was still a fledgling artist when he accompanied his parents to Cross Creek in 1939, but his father describes with pride how "Andy made two corking watercolors of inland scenes."[20] One of the paintings, *Near Ocala, Florida*, was likely done looking out the window of the Ocala hotel where the family was staying, while the other, *Showery Day, Florida* (see plate 162), was apparently done near the Rawlings homestead. According to Karen Baumgartner, a curator at the Wyeth Office at Chadds Ford, Pennsylvania, the painting "features an unidentified body of water" that is likely a tributary of Orange Lake.[21] While researching the painting, Historical Resources consultant Murray Laurie came across a letter written by Andrew in 1947 in which he offered to sell a watercolor to Rawlings for $250. He said he had done the painting in 1939 when he was in Florida with his father. Rawlings apparently didn't follow through on the offer. Perhaps the painting was the watercolor titled *Showery Day*.[22]

In 1928, Marjorie Kinnan Rawlings, suffering from the breakup of her first marriage, decided to undertake a pilgrimage on the St. Johns River. She took along her friend, Dessie Smith, and embarked at the S.R. 50 bridge in a wooden eighteen-foot boat for a journey of more than one hundred miles. Like William Bartram before her, Rawlings carefully recorded the sights and sounds of the river—the marshes and channels, the lakes, the springs, the encounters with wildlife. Her notes later formed the basis for "Hyacinth Drift," the next-to-last chapter in *Cross Creek*.

Although they were two women traveling alone in a time when that seemed unconscionably daring, Marjorie and Dessie camped out and lived off the land. The river channel is well marked today, but travelers can still find themselves befuddled by the twists and turns of the river and the maze of smaller creeks and sloughs that branch off from the main channel. Even though they carried maps and a compass, Rawlings and her companion found themselves hopelessly lost on Puzzle Lake, a body of water that the naturalist Bill Belleville calls "a navigational muddle."[23] "It is as if," he writes, "the St. Johns has tired of being confined to a single route and now wants to go virtually anywhere it can."[24] "By standing up in the boat, I could see the rest of the universe," Rawlings wrote, "And the universe was yellow marsh, with a pitiless blue infinity over it, and we were lost at the bottom."[25] After a miserable night spent fighting mosquitoes on a small island of black muck, Rawlings discovered in the morning light a novel solution to her dilemma: watch the water hyacinths.

According to Rawlings, she and Dessie watched a small clump of purple hyacinths float with the slow current, and they followed the drift. "When the river sprawled in confusion, we might shut off the motor and study the floating hyacinths until we caught a swifter pulsing, as though we put our hands close and closer to the river's heart," Rawlings wrote.[26] According to Roger Bull in an article published in the *Jacksonville Times-Union*, Dessie Smith had a different, less romantic recollection. She reported that they found the current not by observing hyacinths, but by tossing a bit of trash into the water and seeing which way it went.[27]

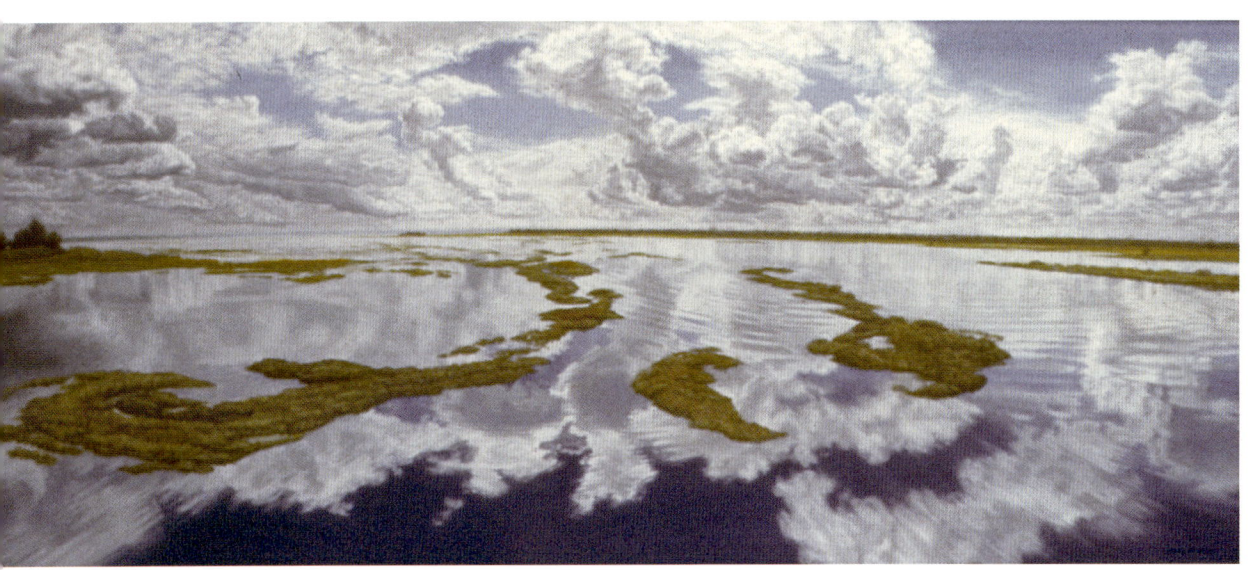

In his painting *Puzzle Lake*, the Orlando artist Hansen Mulford illustrates the twists, turns, mazes, and labyrinths that make Puzzle Lake a navigator's nightmare.

Plate 163. Hansen Mulford. *Puzzle Lake*, 1999. Oil on canvas, 42 × 108 in. Collection of SunTrust, Orlando, Florida.

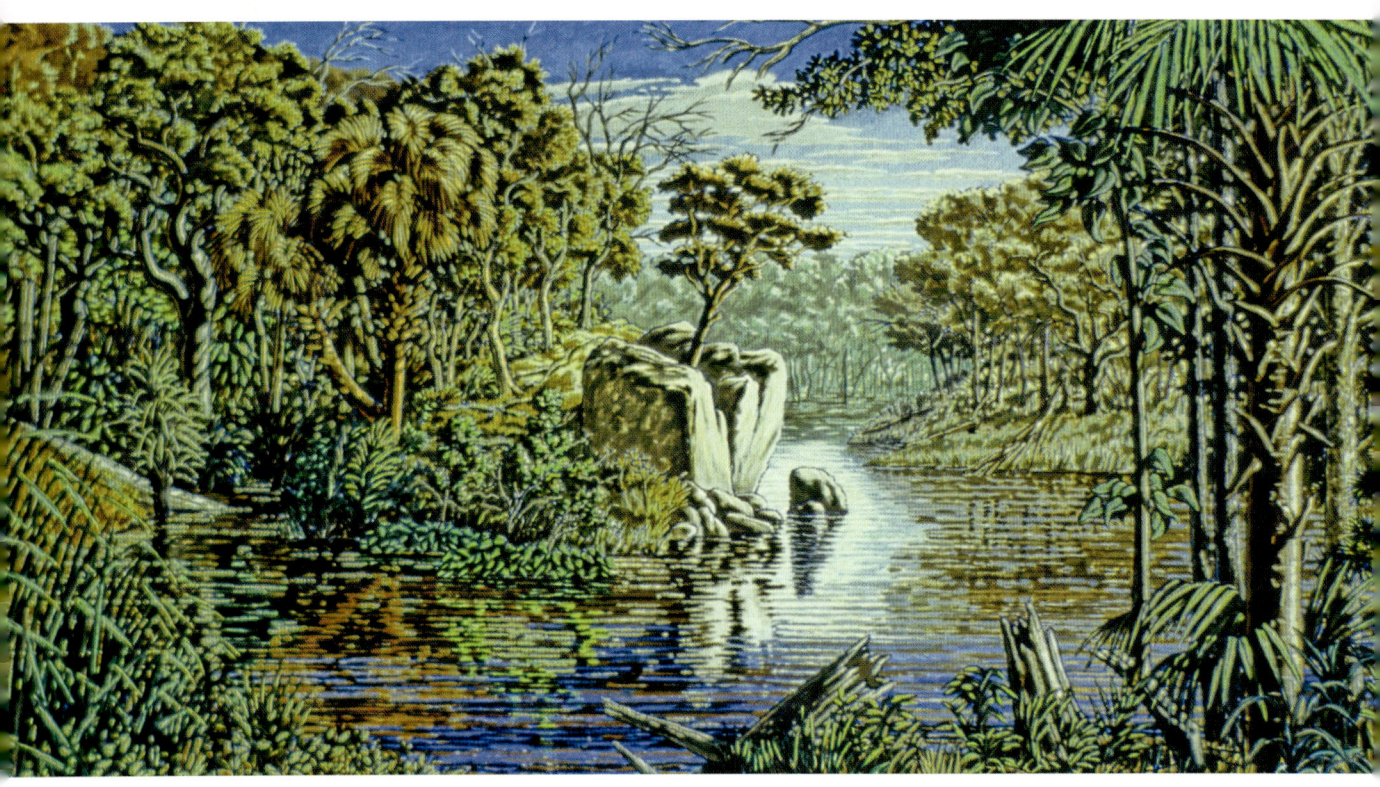

Plate 164. Jerry Cutler. *Florida Waters,* 2002. Oil on linen, 60 × 120 in. Courtesy of the artist.

Jerry Cutler grew up on a dairy farm in rural Wisconsin. Now a professor of art at the University of Florida in Gainesville, Cutler has spent much of the past seventeen years exploring the landscape in his paintings. At first, the paintings focused on the northern environment of his childhood, but over time his work "has become more closely linked to the densely wooded areas found throughout north central Florida."[28] Although his paintings are not "specific locations," Cutler has been influenced by the same brooding, mysterious character of the swamp that can be found in the work of his Romantic predecessors. Experimenting with the form of landscape popularized by the Barbizon school of French painting and the Hudson River school in America, Cutler combines traditional landscape elements with his own personal interpretations of the local environment.

Jerry Cutler's *Florida Waters*, painted in 2002, is a grand example of a combination of influences. Todd Behrens writes: "The forest is a place in which life, growth, decay, death, and rebirth are played out in clear ways. . . . Each [painting] explores the idea of a journey into places both strange and familiar. . . . In *Florida Waters* . . . we stand within the landscape. The patterns of the sky, the eroding bank, and the reflections in the water recall earlier paintings, but the colors of the leaves have a prominent place as well. The cycle of life is clearly presented with a fallen tree in [the] foreground and an intensely colored young tree growing out of the adjacent bank."[29]

In describing his own work, Cutler resorts to poetry to provide a suitable verbal description:

> The afternoon light falls across the ground,
> Slanting and Breaking through the trees,
> Silent shadows muffle the hungry sound,
> And quiet the gnawing greed.
> Sometimes a blaze of paint hovers just above,
> Or a pen scratches down a jagged steep,
> Sometimes a wash of ink descends,
> And the last sweet layers of dusk
> Are Ochre deep.
> —*Jerry Cutler, 1999*

Arnold Mesches moved to Florida in 2003, after spending half his career in Los Angeles and the other half in New York City. Born in Buffalo, New York, Mesches has enjoyed a long and successful career as an artist with over 120 solo exhibitions since 1946, including those at the Pasadena Museum; the Santa Barbara Museum of Art; the Institute of Contemporary Art, Philadelphia; and the Jacksonville Museum of Modern Art. His work is also in numerous public and private collections, including the Albright-Knox Gallery, Buffalo; the Denver Art Museum; the Library of Congress; the National Gallery of Art, Washington, D.C.; and the Metropolitan Museum of Art, to name just a few. He is also a dedicated teacher and has inspired students at Otis/Parsons School, Los Angeles; Rutgers University; New York University; and the University of Florida.

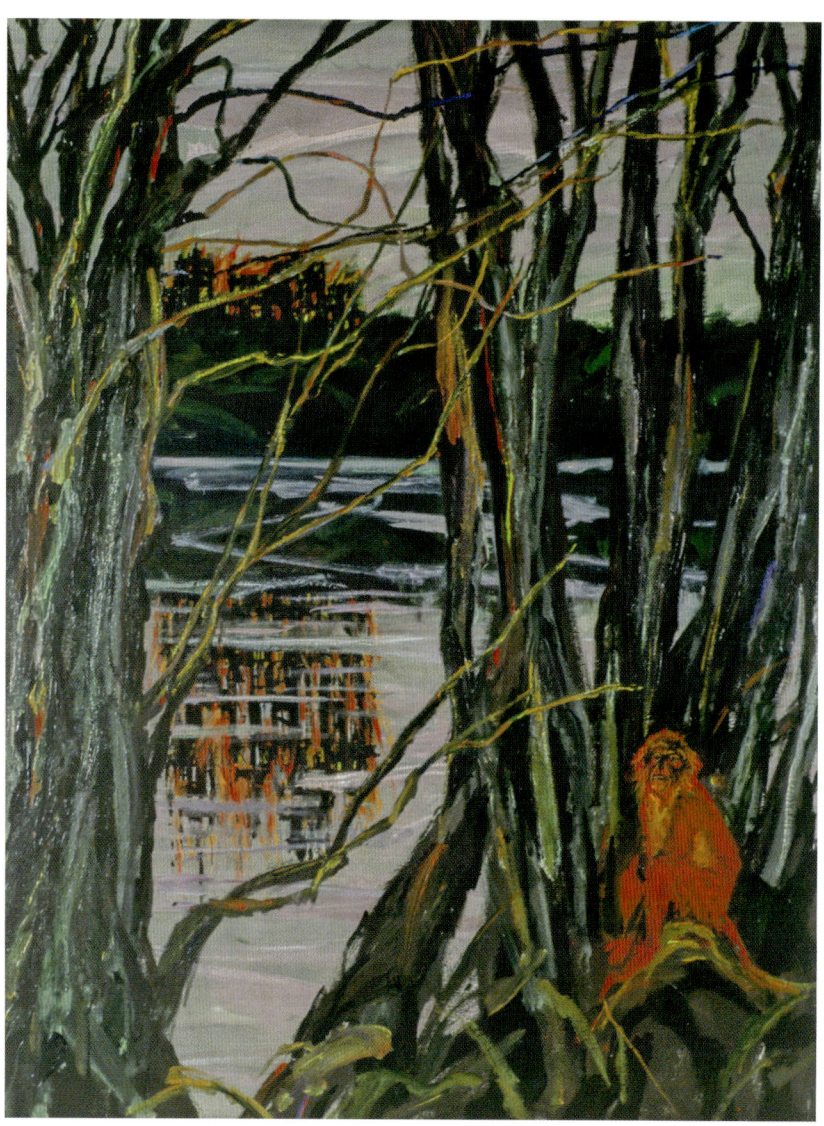

Plate 165. Arnold Mesches. *Fire in the Lake*, 2003. Acrylic on canvas, 66 × 50 in. Courtesy of the artist.

Now a professor of painting at the University of Florida, Arnold Mesches and his partner, author Jill Ciment, live in a remodeled modern-style house on the edge of a lake south of town. The lake, Bivens Arm, is connected through Paynes Prairie to the Orange Lake basin. Although it is in the middle of a populated area, the lake still has a feeling of wilderness. Wildlife— from alligators to turtles to egrets—abounds along the lake's densely foliaged shore and cypress trees, oaks and tangled vines overhang the dark waters. The light changes on the water as the sun and clouds come and go and a rustling in the bushes might be a squirrel—or maybe not. In the painting reproduced here, *Fire in the Lake*, Mesches's powerful imagination introduces a sinister visitor that sits brooding beside the darkening swamp. It is an image that recalls the lessons of art history, turning the "real world" inside out to reveal a heart of darkness.

The critic Eleanor Heartney, in a 1997 article about Mesches in *Art in America*, called the artist "a history painter for our age of amnesia" and went on to say: "But while his works have frequently attacked larger stupidities—the waste of war, the vanity of ambition, the foolishness of the powerful—they have at the same time seemed surprisingly intimate and personal. Mingling with immediately recognizable personages and settings are his cullings from family albums or half-forgotten memories."[30]

In her 1942 semiautobiographical book *Cross Creek*, Marjorie Kinnan Rawlings muses about the ownership of land. What is "property" she asks, and who are the legitimate owners? A person? A bank or lending company? The state? "No man," she states, "should have proprietary rights over land that does not use that land wisely and lovingly." She concludes: "Who owns Cross Creek? The red-birds, I think, more than I, for they will have their nests even in the face of delinquent mortgages. And after I am dead, who am childless, the human ownership of the grove and field and hammock is hypothetical. But a long line of red-birds and whippoorwills and blue-jays and ground doves will descend from the present owners of nests in the orange trees, and their claim will be less subject to dispute than that of any human heirs. Houses are individual and can be owned, like nests, and fought for. But what of the land? It seems to me that the earth may be borrowed but not bought. It may be used, but not owned. It gives itself in response to love and tending, offers its seasonal flowering and fruiting. But we are tenants and not possessors, lovers and not masters. Cross Creek belongs to the wind and the rain, to the sun and the seasons, to the cosmic secrecy of seed, and beyond all, to time."[31]

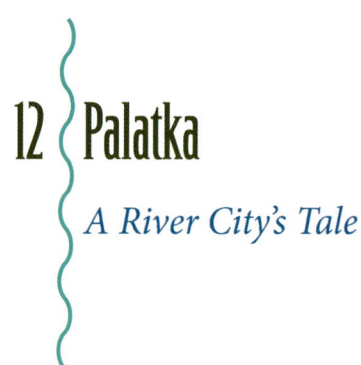

12 { Palatka

A River City's Tale

Palatka is situated on the banks of a beautiful bay of the St. Johns River and is the county seat of Putnam County, so marked by a conspicuous stone structure in the middle of a whole block in the very center of the town. The marked improvements that are everywhere under way, a new sewerage system, miles of new streets paved with vitrified brick, new sidewalks, a river front boulevard, a spacious park with rows of palmetto trees and semi-tropical foliage, a waterworks system that is called free, the opening of a hotel that will accommodate 500 people are all tell tale evidences of Palatka's future greatness.

—*Florida Review,* April 1911

As early as 1655 the Spanish established ranchos in the Palatka area to raise cattle to feed the growing population of St. Augustine. Palatka became a main crossing point on the St. Johns River for cattle herds from the north Florida region being driven to St. Augustine for slaughter. The name "Palatka" is in fact the contraction of a Seminole words meaning "cow crossing."

During the American Revolution, Florida became a haven for British loyalists, and the population swelled as a result. However, when Spain regained control of Florida in 1784, most of the British left, and the population once more declined. But when Florida became a U.S. territory in 1821, development of north Florida increased rapidly, and Palatka, which was the southernmost point on the St. Johns River where large oceangoing vessels could navigate, became an important transportation hub. In 1822, ferry service was established between Palatka and St. Augustine, and the community also was on the main road that connected St. Augustine with Tallahassee and Pensacola.

These early developments were interrupted during the First and Second Seminole Wars. In 1835, the Indians attacked and burned Palatka, and settlers from the entire St. Johns River valley fled to St. Augustine for safety. A military outpost, Fort Shannon, was subsequently built where the town had been. The fort's officers' quarters is still standing and is now the oldest building in Palatka.

By the time the Third Seminole War ended in 1858, settlers were once again pouring into the Florida interior, and Palatka resumed its role as a major transportation hub rivaled only by Jacksonville. Lumber and citrus became the mainstays of the local economy. This period of growth and prosperity was, however, soon interrupted by the outbreak of the Civil War.

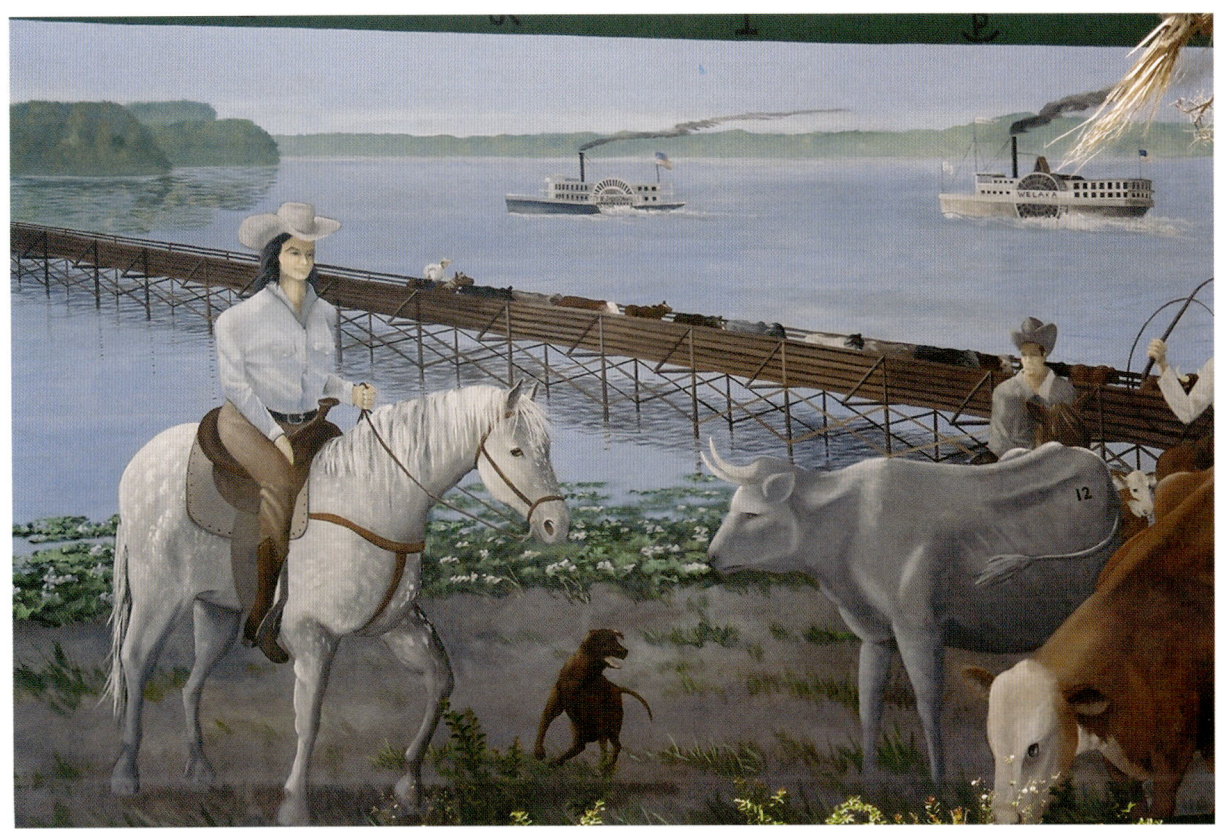

In an effort to celebrate Palatka's colorful history and to help with the revitalization of the downtown area, the Conlee Mural Committee was established to promote an understanding of Palatka's history and to beautify the town with a series of murals created by professional artists. So far, thirty murals have been created in and around Palatka by different artists depicting a variety of scenes from the area's early Indian inhabitants to historic architecture to local flora and fauna. Sponsors for the murals range from individuals to businesses to organizations. Committee members hope to have Palatka designated as the Official Mural City of Northeast Florida. The Spanish established cattle ranches in the Palatka area, and cattle raising remained a major industry well into the twentieth century. This mural shows a cattle drive in progress.

Plate 166. Terry Smith. *Cattle Drive on Paynes Prairie*, 2007. Acrylic on plaster. Courtesy of the Conlee Mural Committee, Inc., Palatka, Florida. Photo by Murray Laurie.

He brought us word that Lt. Reddick said he would go at once to Orange Springs and would not fire on the [Union] gunboat [the USS *Cimarron*]. Still the cannon kept booming over our heads, and women and children were hurrying to escape the burning town [Palatka]. . . . I asked whether anyone had been to beg them not to burn the town, and they told me no man would dare to go to them for he would be taken prisoner. So I said that if there is no man that dares to go I will see what a woman can do.

—Mrs. Boyd, *The River Flows North*

THROUGHOUT THE CIVIL WAR, locations along the St. Johns were the site of frequent skirmishes and attacks. On October 7, 1862, a Federal transport vessel captured a Confederate steamer, the *Governor Milton*, on the river near Enterprise. That same day, the USS *Cimarron* arrived at Palatka. The Union soldiers found the town nearly deserted except for women, children, and the elderly. With the men either away with the army or hiding out in the woods, it was left for the women to plead with the Union soldiers to spare the town. According to the Union commander, Maxwell Woodhull, a group of women headed by "a Mrs. Boyd" begged the force not to shell Palatka. Mrs. Boyd persevered until she gained an audience with the officer in command [Woodhull] and succeeded in convincing him to spare the town.[1] This illustration of the *Governor Milton* on the St. Johns appeared in *Harper's Weekly* in October 1862.

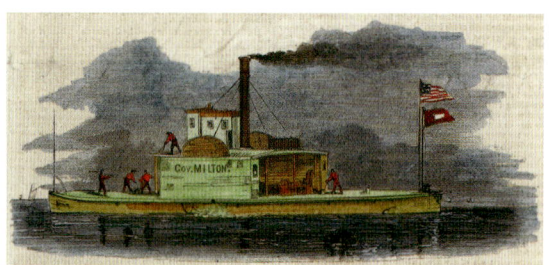

Plate 167. Anonymous. *Rebel Steamer on the St. Johns*. From *Harper's Weekly*, October 7, 1862. Courtesy of the Matheson Museum, Gainesville, Florida.

On May 23 1864, the USS *Columbine*, a Union troop transport, was returning downriver from Volusia to its headquarters in Jacksonville. When it neared Palatka, it was attacked by Confederate troops under the command of Capt. John J. Dickison. Cannon had been placed along the banks in anticipation of the *Columbine*'s approach, and riflemen had been stationed among the cypress trees. The first round struck the boat's wheel chain while another round hit the steam pipe. The ship ran aground, and after a brief battle, the commander of the *Columbine* made the decision to surrender the ship. It was boarded by the Confederates, who found over half the 148 Union troops dead or dying, although a few had made it to shore and returned to St. Augustine. The Confederates, who had suffered no casualties, burned the ship. It was assumed that the *Columbine* had been completely destroyed in the fire or salvaged sometime between 1865 and 1890.

Recently, however, Bill and Sandi Rivers, who live in Keystone Heights, Florida, have challenged the story of the *Columbine*'s demise. Bill Rivers, an accomplished diver, had searched the area near Horse Landing, where the ship supposedly went down, but found no evidence of a wreck. Recalculating the exact location of Horse Landing using early maps, he began exploring a section of the river a mile distant and found the ruins of a wooden vessel. The State of Florida has since made a correction to its file, listing the new information gathered by Bill and Sandi, information that could lead to further investigations of the area.[2]

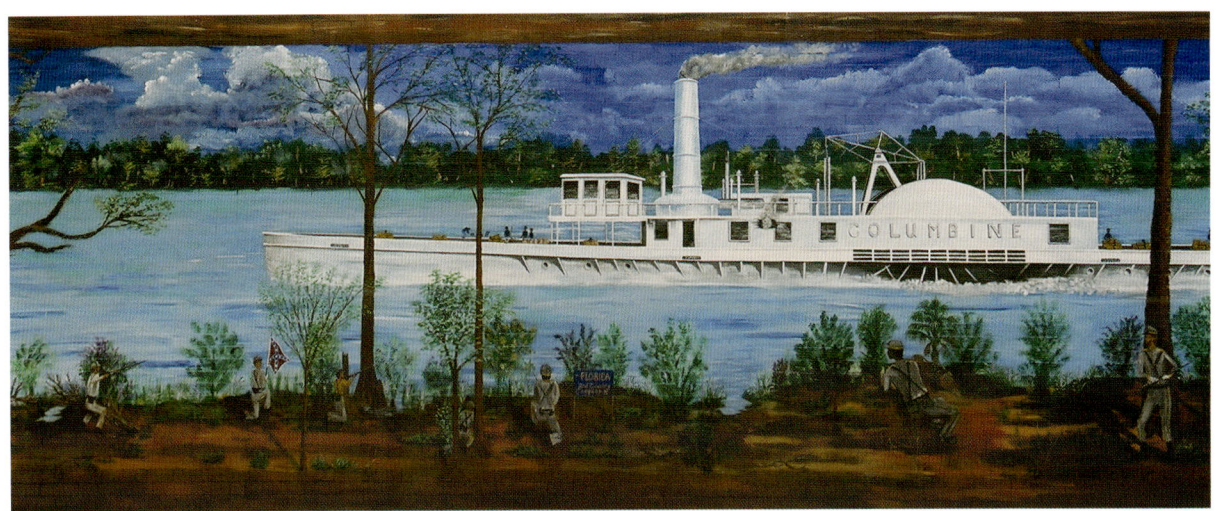

This mural by the Palatka artist Betty Sutliff depicts the *Columbine* steaming downriver near Palatka.

Plate 168. Betty Sutliff. *The Columbine*, 2007. Acrylic on plaster. Courtesy of the Conlee Mural Committee, Inc., Palatka, Florida. Photo by Murray Laurie.

Following the Civil War, tourism became an increasingly important industry in the Palatka area as northern visitors ventured by steamboat into Florida's wild interior. By 1885, seven steamboat lines were based in Palatka, and the wharves extended across the entire riverfront. There were crowds of wintering tourists who enjoyed all of the area's amenities. Brick-lined streets and overhanging magnolia trees added a sense of stately elegance.

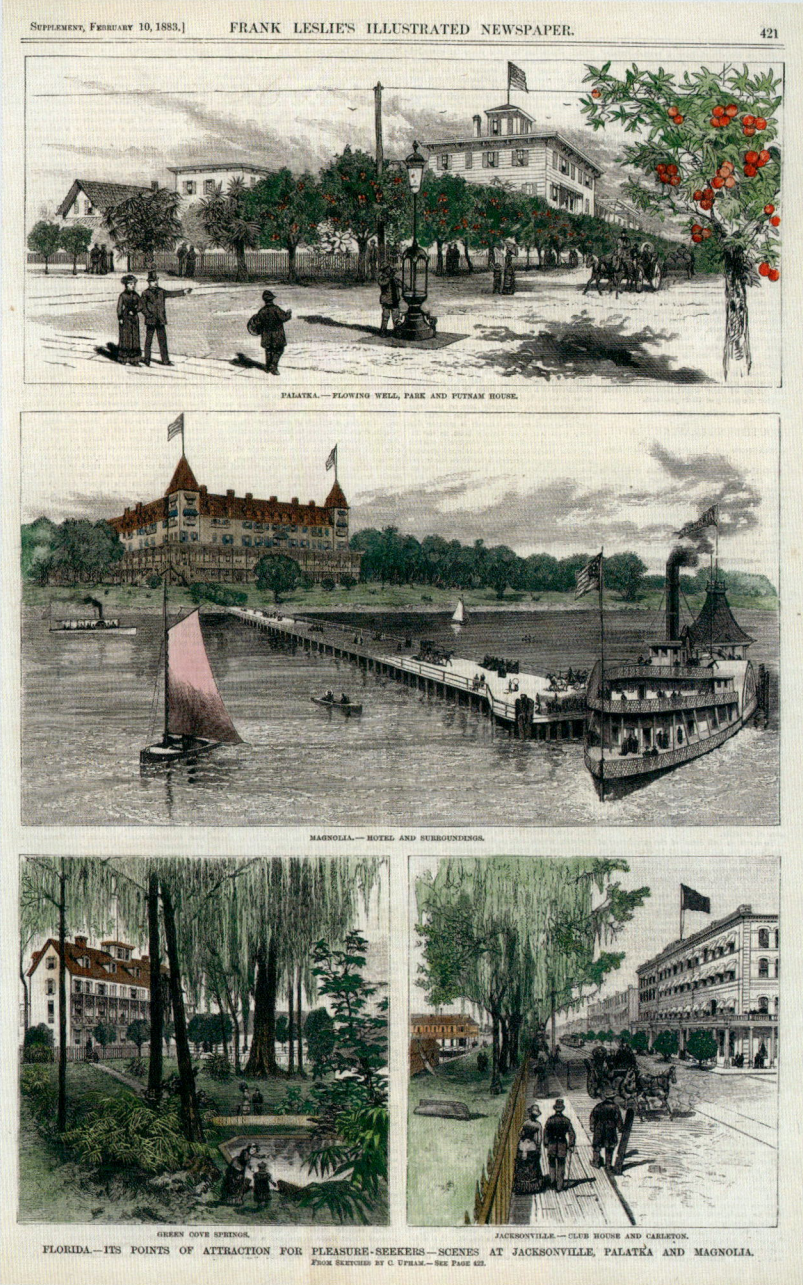

Plate 169. Anonymous. *Jacksonville, Palatka and Magnolia*. From *Frank Leslie's Illustrated Newspaper*, February 10, 1883. Courtesy of the Matheson Museum, Gainesville, Florida

This illustration from *Frank Leslie's Illustrated Newspaper* profiles attractive landmarks in three popular locations along the St. Johns River.

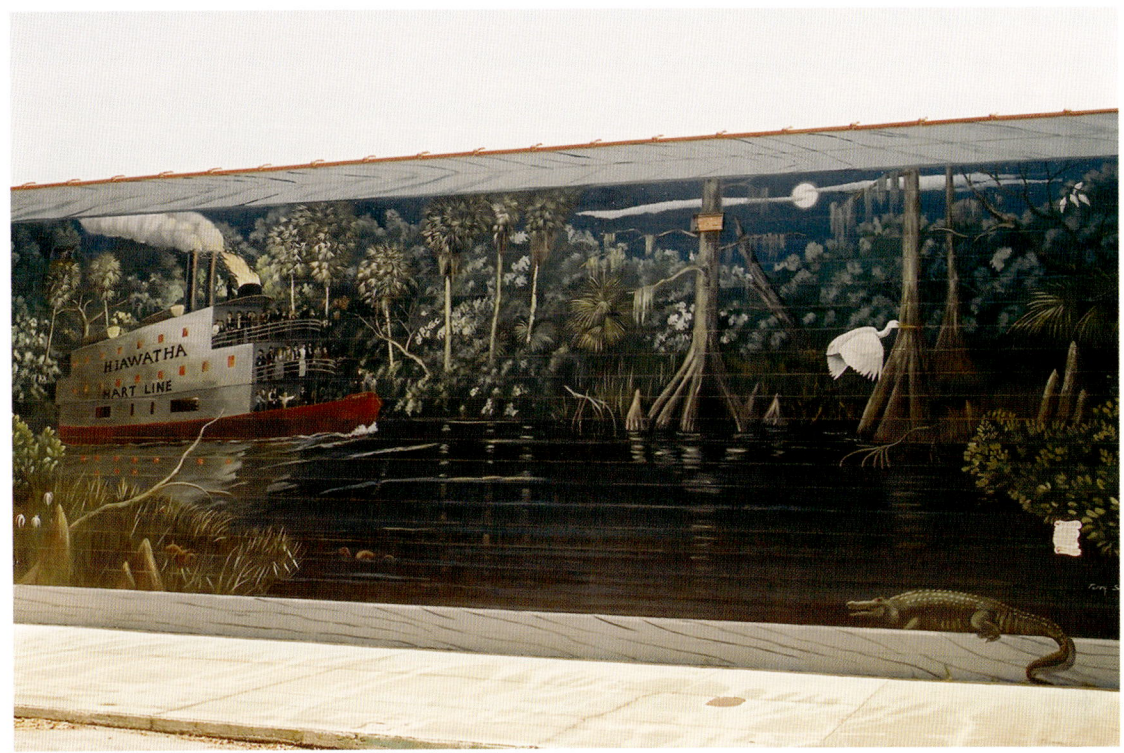

A mural on the wall at the corner of Fifth Street and St. Johns Avenue is titled *Night Passage (Ocklawaha Riverboat).* Painted by artist Terry Smith, the mural depicts a steamboat making its way down the Ocklawaha past a dense jungle of cypress trees and palms. A startled egret crosses the boat's path and gleaming eyes stare from the dark thickets. The steamboat depicted in the mural is the *Hiawatha,* the last steamboat built for the Hart Line. It was a regular on the Ocklawaha River run to Silver Springs for over twenty years. Hart died in 1895, but his brother-in-law took over the business and continued operations for another two decades.[3]

Following a devastating fire that burned much of the downtown area in 1884, grand homes were constructed along the riverfront, and substantial brick buildings were built, giving the town an air of respectability and refinement.

Plate 170. Terry Smith. *Night Passage (Ocklawaha Riverboat),* 2000. Acrylic on plaster, 16 x 40 ft. Courtesy of the Conlee Mural Committee, Inc., Palatka, Florida. Photo by Murray Laurie.

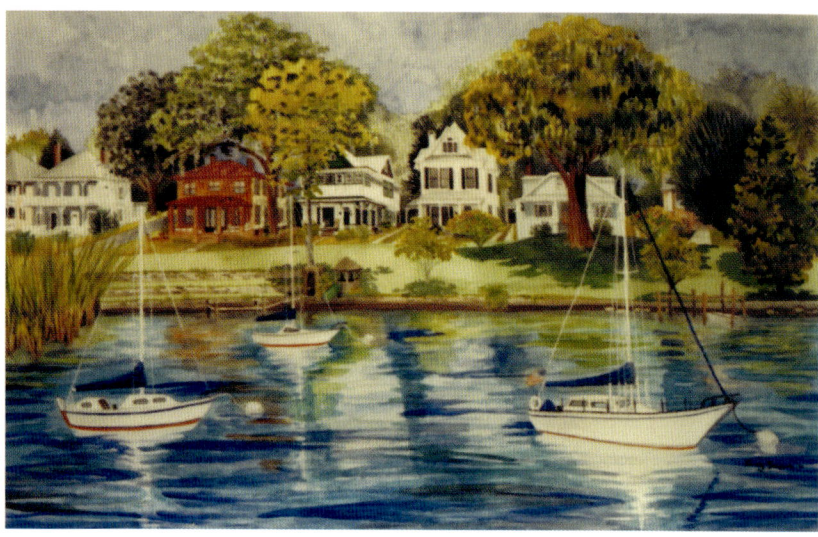

Sustaining the allure to fickle vacationers is tenuous business, with loyalties and trends shifting every few years. It is only the most corporate of theme parks, the ones that analyze market trends and then set out to fulfill them bloodlessly, that seem to thrive today, and they do so far from the banks of the St. Johns.

—Bill Belleville, *River of Lakes*

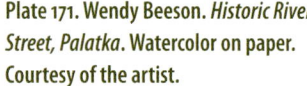

Plate 171. Wendy Beeson. *Historic River Street, Palatka*. Watercolor on paper. Courtesy of the artist.

This painting by the Satsuma artist Wendy Beeson portrays a block of historic houses that were built along River Street facing the St. Johns during the late 1800s, the high point of Palatka's fortunes. Many of the homes have been restored and today are a proud part of the city's cultural and historic heritage.

When the poet Sidney Lanier visited Palatka in 1875 to gather material for a travel guide to Florida, he described it as an "important town . . . containing a population of about fifteen hundred inhabitants. . . . It is a considerable resort for consumptives."[4] He also reported that the town had three hotels, one of which was the Putnam House. By 1890, Palatka had eight first-class hotels, and the Putnam House had five hundred rooms. Winter visitors and residents included President Grover Cleveland and rich industrialists such as James R. Mellon of Pittsburgh, who donated a library to the city.

The Putnam House was a grand hotel and was recommended by Silvia Sunshine in her 1880 book, *Petals Plucked from Sunny Climes*: "The politeness of the servants reminds us of the balmy days of the past, when they were trained for use, and not permitted to roam, like untamed beasts, seeking something which they could kill and eat, or steal, and trade for money."[5] Fresh vegetables were grown on the premises during February, and guests could hunt duck and pose for pictures with their dinners.

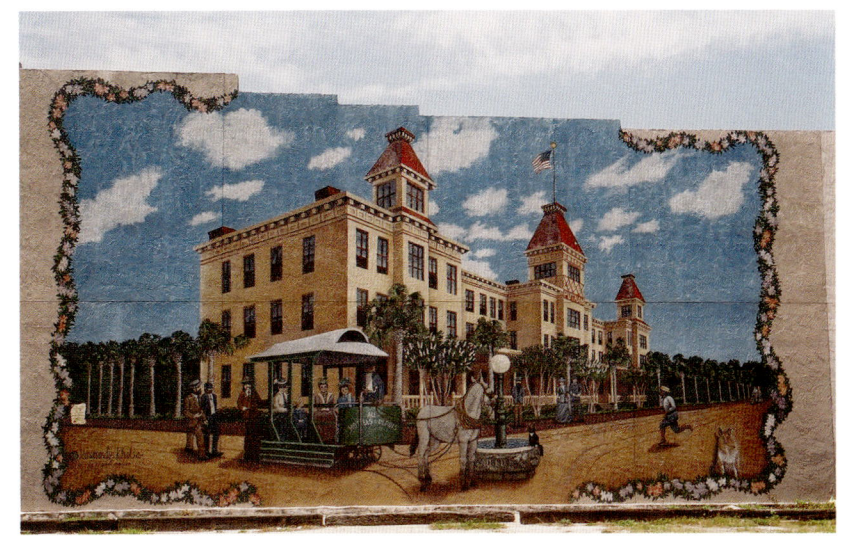

Plate 172. Harimandir Khalsa. *Putnam House Hotel*, 2000. Acrylic on plaster. Courtesy of the Conlee Mural Committee, Inc., Palatka, Florida. Photo by Murray Laurie.

This mural depicts the Putnam House Hotel at the height of its reign.

Palatka was a regal town, second only to Jacksonville, as is indicated by the Putnam Hotel register. The first page of the Putnam House guest book is dated December 17, 1874; the first signature reads "Richard C. Duncan and wife," from Indianapolis. That page shows that guests came from Chicago, New York City, Boston, Jacksonville, Philadelphia, and Fernandina and from towns in Massachusetts and New Jersey. The last entry in the one-inch volume was entered on December 29, 1875. The next page reads "January 1, 1876 . . . See new registry." On December 18, 1875, the word "Hotel" is scratched out, as it is on each following page, and changed to "House," as are the proprietors' names, H. L. Hart and D. F. Larkin, indicating that the hotel had changed hands.

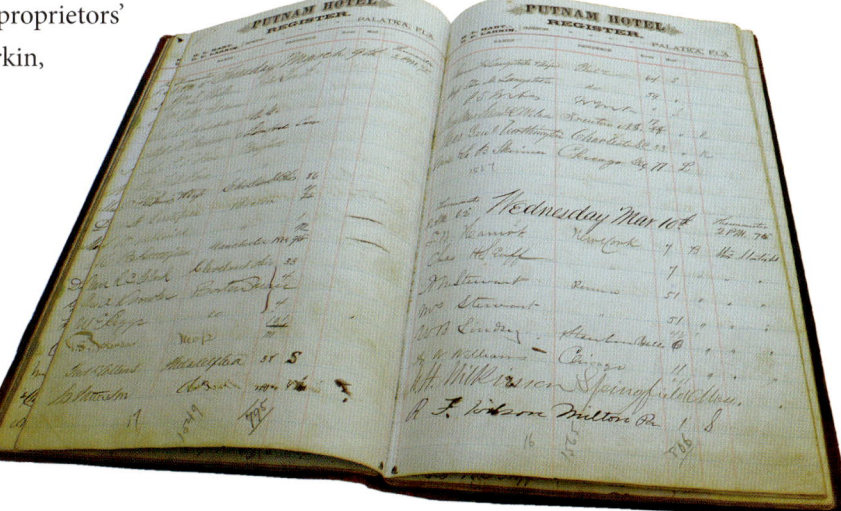

Plate 173. Putnam House Hotel register, ca. 1875. 15⅛ × 10 1/16 × 1 in. Collection of Dan and Tracy McKenna.

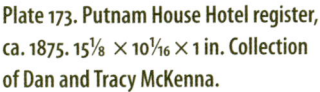

During a celebration on the night of November 7, 1884, sparks from a bon-fire set the town ablaze. The business district was destroyed. Banks, churches, and hotels were lost. Gone was the large and fashionable Putnam House.

The Putnam House was rebuilt in 1885, and it was at that time the most expensive hotel in burgeoning Palatka, with rooms costing four dollars a day. Palatka's hotels traditionally opened in November for wintering tourists and closed with the advent of the inhospitable summers in May. But the freeze of 1890 cast a pall over the tourist trade from which the city did not recuperate. In that year, the Putnam House didn't open until January 10, and it closed in February. And since Flagler's railroad did not network in Palatka, the days of the Gem City of the St. Johns River as a tourist destination were over.

More than a century ago, says a volunteer guide at the city's quiet history center, "All those Yankees would come down. Palatka was the end of the line." Palatka was a steamboat hub, the jumping-off place to explore the remote wilds of Florida's interior until Flagler's railroad began its march to Key West. The city had a meaningful role in the Civil War and a rich history until, as the guide points out, "they found out there was more to Florida, and everything went south."[6]

Tourists, who had previously traveled on the St. Johns and its tributary the Ocklawaha now took the railroad south from Jacksonville to Palm Beach, and the transportation of commodities also shifted from riverboats to railcars. The final blow to the city's economy came in the "great freezes" of 1894–95, which virtually wiped out the citrus industry in the area. Only lumber remained as a viable industry.

Lumber has always been one of the mainstays of Florida's economy, especially in the north, where great stands of pine, cedar, and cypress once grew in seemingly inexhaustible numbers. Throughout the nineteenth century and well into the twentieth, the demand for forest products was insatiable.

The "harvesting" of Florida's forests began with the first European's need for naval stores and shipbuilding materials, but the industry exploded with the development of transportation technology—first the steamboats and then the railroads—that opened up the interior woodlands for exploitation. When Sidney Lanier visited Florida in 1875, he wrote: "The civilization of the pine is that of the timber-cutter and the turpentine distiller. Today they set up their shanties and 'stills,' quickly they cut down or exhaust the trees, tomorrow they are gone leaving a desolate and lonesome land."[7]

With its access by steamboat up the St. Johns River into the interior, Palatka became a center for the logging industry. Resource exploitation brought economic prosperity, at least until the 1930s, when the last of the first-growth trees had been harvested. The Wilson Cypress Company headquartered in Palatka eventually became the world's largest cypress mill, producing 80,000 feet of lumber and 60,000 shingles a day. The mill continued production into midcentury, but deforestation led ultimately to the demise of the operation. Until a recent sale of the property, the Georgia-Pacific Company operated a wood pulp plant in the area.

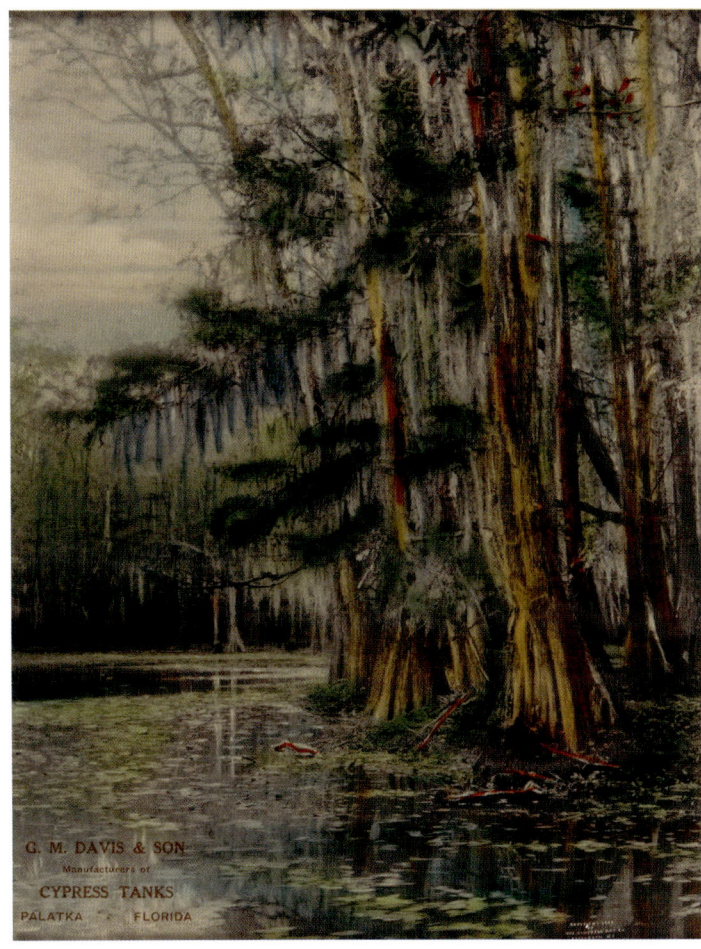

Plate 174. Promotional poster for a Palatka cypress mill. Hand-colored photograph, 9 × 12 in. Collection of John C. Herrmann.

Few species of trees escaped the saw. Live oaks were decimated until the 1860s, when ironclad steamboats began to replace sailing vessels. By that time, however, many of Florida's live oaks were gone. The most abundant tree in the state was the pine, especially the longleaf and slash varieties. The first-growth forests stretched from north Florida to the Okeechobee basin and originally covered 30 million acres. Pines were used for lumber, and their sap was distilled into turpentine and rosin. Cedars, which were extensive throughout the Suwannee River watershed, were used for pencils and cigar boxes. Cypresses, many of them thousands of years old, were used for shingles and shipping crates. Mark Derr writes: "In north and central Florida, narrow-gauge tracks were run into swamps so loggers could cut the cypresses, some up to a dozen feet in diameter, and haul them out. . . . The largest strands of cypress . . . contained some of the oldest trees in North America."[8]

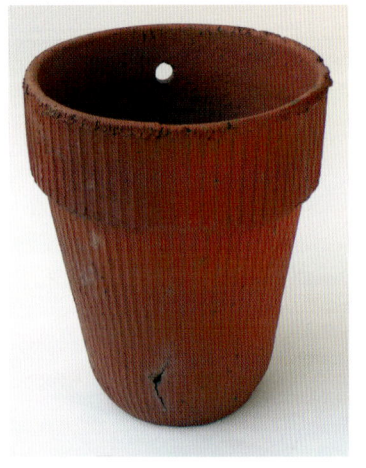

Plate 175. Turpentine collection cup, n.d. Terra cotta, 6⅞ × 5⅝ . Courtesy of Gary and Teresa Monroe.

Turpentine camps had their heyday from the late 1800s through early 1900s, when the product was considered Florida's most important natural resource. Earthenware cups were used for collecting sap from slash and longleaf pine trees to produce turpentine and rosins. The cups were placed at the bottom of the incision to collect the gummy flow. Then crews traveling the forests would gather them and pour the sap into wooden barrels. The barrels were brought to turpentine stills by wagon, often along the river to facilitate transport. There the sap was boiled so that the vapors produced pure spirits of turpentine. Final uses included paint and plastic products, among hundreds of others, including adhesives and perfumes.

Today many of these gum-collection cups are easily mistaken for clay planting pots. It is likely that people at yard sales, for example, walk by them regularly. They would miss the small hole near the rim that allowed the cups to hang by nails on trees, without distinguishing the socially historic artifact from the other common clay pots. Should one be examined by a bargain-hunter it would likely be put down because of chipping that resulted from years of on-the-job handling. Perhaps another similar pot would suffice, or a newer version that is made of plastic instead of clay, made from the product that was extracted from the trees.

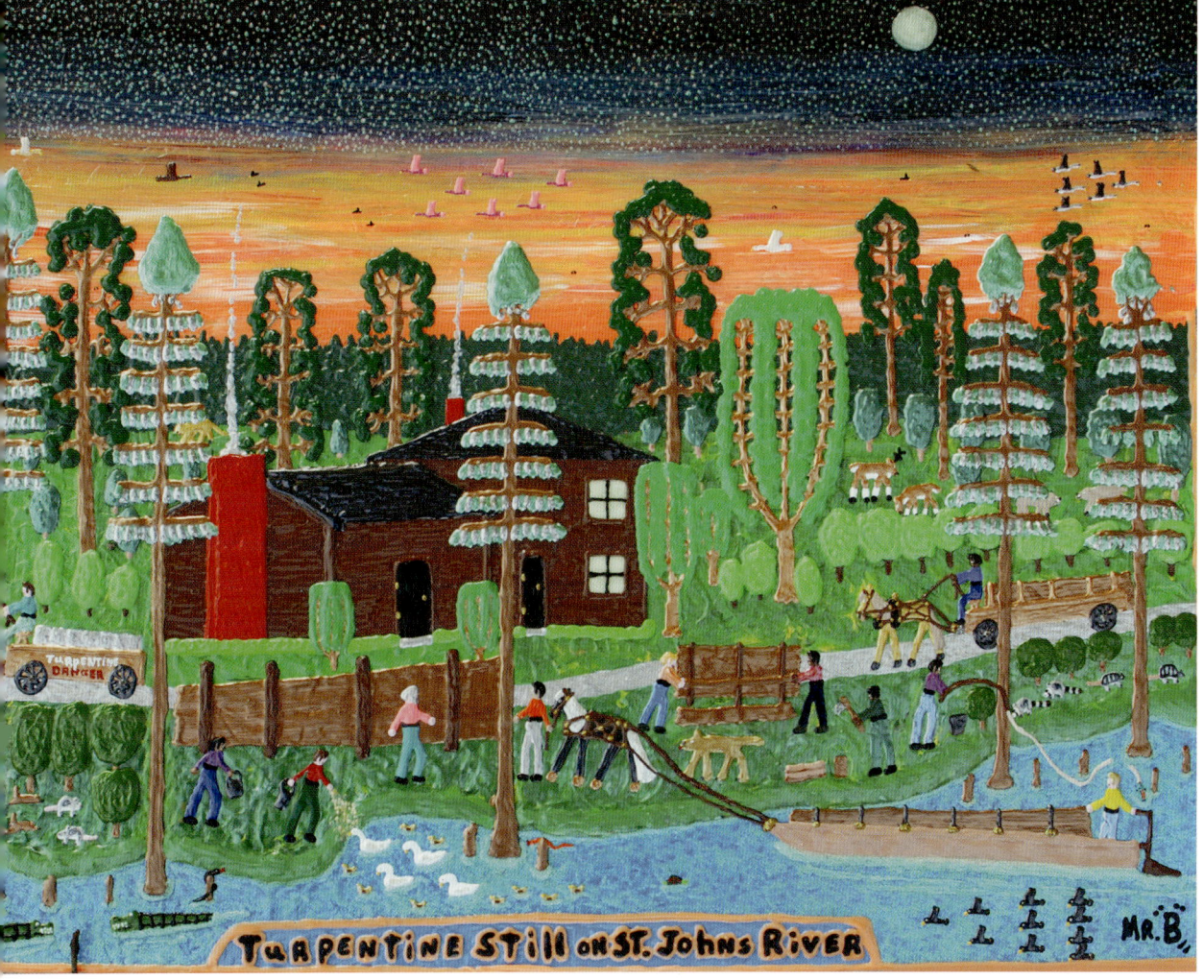

This painting by Jack Beverland, titled *Turpentine Still on St. Johns River*, shows the operation in progress. It's a busy scene made picturesque and lively by Beverland's characteristically fanciful imagination and the inclusion of alligators, ducks, flamingoes, and stylized cypress trees. A close look rewards the viewer with a swarm of details—deer graze in the background, a bear emerges from the trees, rabbits and armadillos caper beneath the bushes. Mr. B's turpentine camp is teeming with life.

Plate 176. Jack Beverland. *Turpentine Still on the St. Johns River, Florida*, 2008. Glow-in-the-dark dimensional fabric paint on canvas, 24 × 32 in. Courtesy of the artist.

These days, all that remains of past turpentine operations are "cat face" scars on the harvested trees from where bark was chipped to induce a drip of resin. North central Florida hunters and hikers who slosh through the swamps might encounter pine forests that had been "cupped" for turpentine. If they are deep enough in the forest, they might encounter a still and even a shack for the Negro workers, called "dippers." Turpentine making was a large-scale operation that required fifty acres to accommodate a "crop" of ten thousand cups. One might recognize cups still remaining on trees. Some might not have been emptied of the last accumulation of pitch when the turpentine gathers vacated a stand for the last time, as it took days for about a pint to fill one of the cups. Maybe a galvanized iron gutter that funnels down into the cup is still intact, with hardened sap. Or perhaps only potsherds of cups remain buried under pine needles, and cat faces eerily smirk in a stand of tapped trees to the unaware.

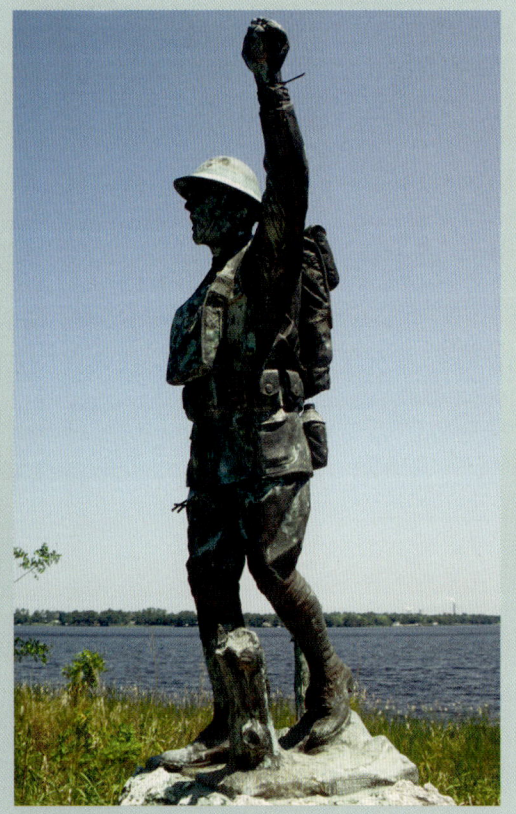

This photograph by Murray Laurie shows a doughboy statue beside the Memorial Bridge that crosses the St. Johns River at Palatka. The Old Memorial Bridge, a bascule-type drawbridge, was demolished in the mid-1970s and replaced by a higher bridge that would allow boat traffic to move freely on the river. Four statues—three of World War I doughboys and one of a sailor—stood on either side of the lift-span of the old bridge. They were removed and placed at either end of the new bridge on the riverbank.

Plate 177. Attributed to E. M. Viquesney. *Doughboy*, ca. 1936. Memorial Bridge, Palatka. Photo courtesy of Murray Laurie.

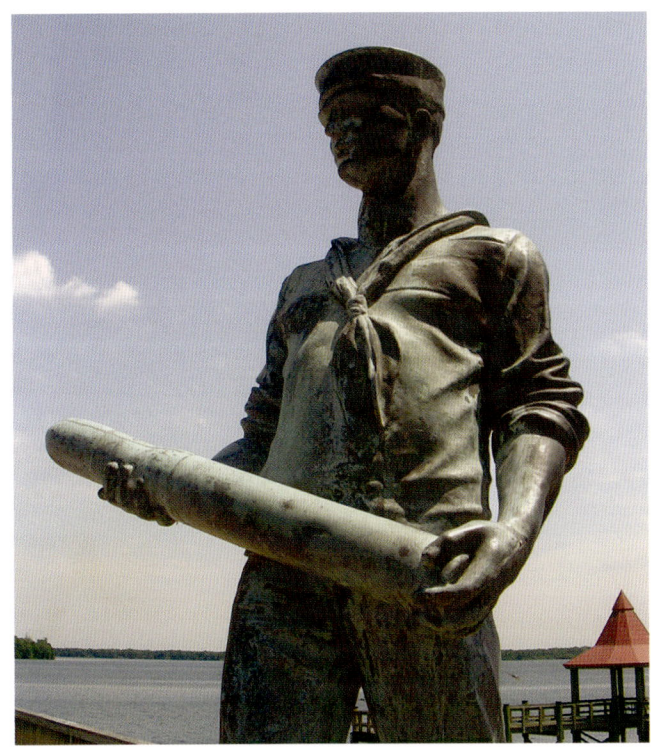

Plate 178. Attributed to E. M. Viquesney, *Sailor*, ca. 1936. Memorial Bridge, Palatka. Photo courtesy of Murray Laurie.

One of the statues shows a sailor holding an artillery shell. This statue was listed in a product brochure printed in 1936 by an artist named E. M. Viquesney that showed the sailor statue and the three others at Palatka as examples of the many World War memorials he had placed around the country. The statues are among several public artworks located throughout the town.[9]

In 1930, with a severe depression gripping the country, T. B. Gillespie of Palatka conceived of a plan to beautify the city while providing much-needed jobs for the local work force. Gillespie thought that an 82-acre site on the southwest side of the city would make a grand park. The land had numerous springs and also a magnificent 120-foot-deep ravine that had been carved by erosion into the native limestone. Gillespie was inspired by gardens that he had seen in South Carolina, and he believed they could be replicated on the Palatka site.

As a road builder and engineer, Gillespie knew that it would be a mammoth undertaking. He also knew it would be costly. Undeterred, he traveled to Washington, D.C., where he applied for a grant through the Works Progress Administration (WPA) to finance the project. He also located a nurseryman in Winter Springs, Florida, and persuaded him to provide seventy-five thousand azalea plants for the sum of ten thousand dollars. At his own expense, he hired the Jacksonville landscape architect Richard Forrester to oversee the garden's development. Forrester trained over one hundred workers to do the labor required for the project.

The springs in the garden area were diverted to the city waterworks located on adjacent property. Yielding 100,000 gallons per day, the springs helped supply the city's water throughout the 1930s.

Although they were initially unenthusiastic about the plan, the citizens of Palatka began to take an interest in the garden and eventually participated in fund-raising projects to complete the transformation. The final result includes a two-mile scenic driveway bordering the ravine, a suspension bridge, footpaths, ponds, and a breathtaking seasonal display of azaleas and other native and subtropical plants. An amphitheater was built that could seat up to three thousand people. For many years, the annual Azalea Festival Beauty Pageant was held in the garden amphitheater.

A 68-foot-high obelisk was erected between the front gates, a memo-

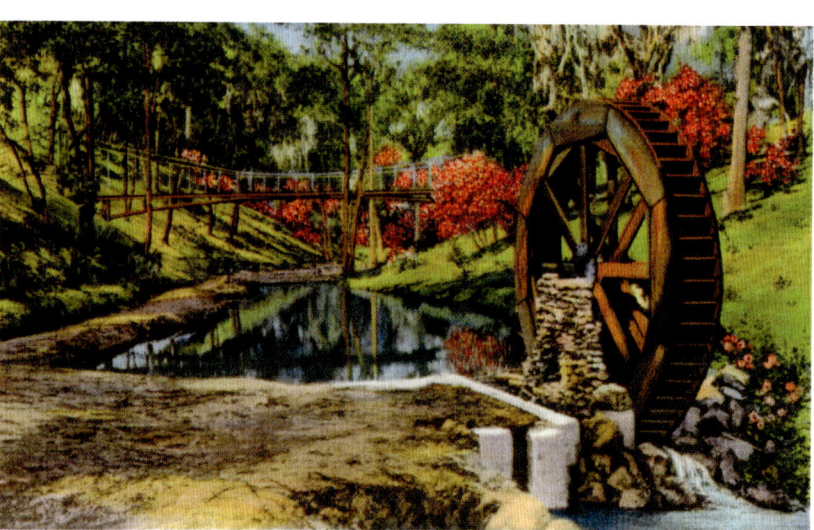

Plate 179. Ravine Gardens, waterwheel. Palatka, Florida. Courtesy of the Florida State Archives of Florida.

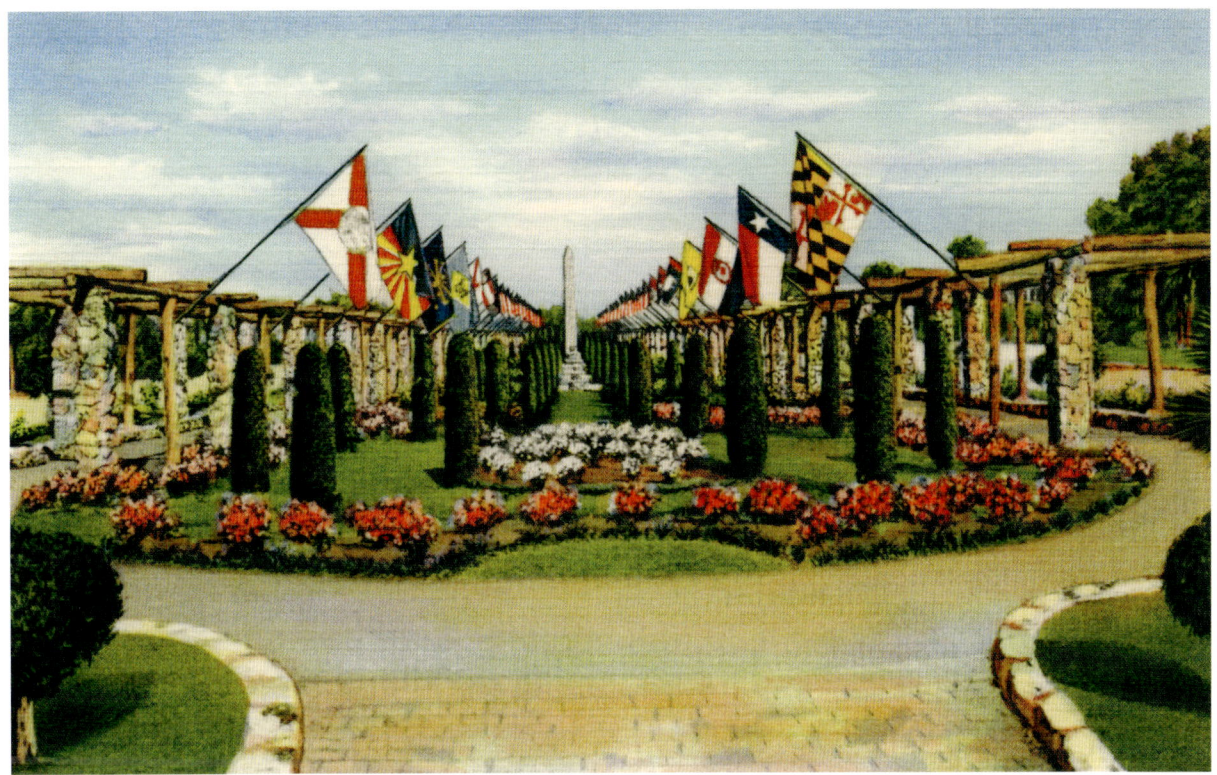

Plate 180. Ravine Gardens, Court of States. Palatka, Florida. Courtesy of the State Archives of Florida.

rial to the spirit of cooperation between the government and the people of Palatka. Inside the gates are two rows of twenty-four rockshafts. Called the Court of States, the flags represent the states of the union.

During the 1950s and 1960s, Ravine Gardens declined due to lack of funding for maintenance. In 1970, the City of Palatka gave title to the park to the Florida State Park Service, which has since managed the property and restored it to its original beauty. The Azalea Festival is once more a highlight of the year, attracting visitors from all over the state.[10]

Highway 17, that heads south parallel to the St. Johns, runs through the one-traffic-light town of Seville about twenty miles south of Palatka. The road has been used less and less frequently since Clarke Garnsey was commissioned to paint murals for the wooden schoolhouse there as part of the Works Progress Administration's program subsidizing artwork in public buildings.

Garnsey likely painted the eight murals in 1936–37, and they were installed in the school auditorium. One expects WPA paintings to evoke class struggle, expressions celebrating the American proletariat à la Thomas Hart Benton, or historical panoramas reminiscent of Diego Rivera. But Garnsey's do neither; they don't even depict Florida. Rather, they show schooners in full mast on the high seas.

Don Emery was the Volusia County director of the project; his pupil-artists included Gladys Butterfield, Catherine "Catto" Eastman, Harold Gore, Marian Heywood, Luther Odom, Isabelle van Dyke, and, of course, Garnsey. The choice of subject matter was, remembers Garnsey, "the result of several informal brainstorming sessions," under Emery's supervision.[11] The team members painted Native Americans, Spanish explorers, historical scenes of local interest, such as the "the First Mail to Volusia County" or imagery of Sanford's once-thriving celery-growing industry. One artist made murals of John Tenniel's illustrations from *Alice in Wonderland*. The young artists took class from 9 a.m. to noon five days a week and painted from 1 to 6 p.m. six days a week, and one Sunday a month. But Garnsey, who had assisted Emery, left the program early. He went to paint in Cuba, and stayed there for a year and a half.

Although the ships in Garnsey's paintings have little relation to any river, the group decided that Garnsey would paint ships of the "types that were known to have plied the waters in that area." Although he researched in the

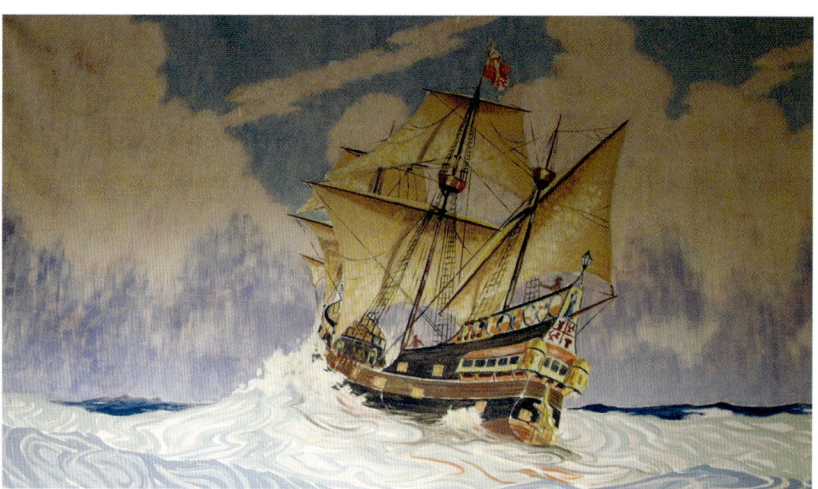

Plate 181. Clarke H. Garnsey, WPA mural in Seville, Florida.

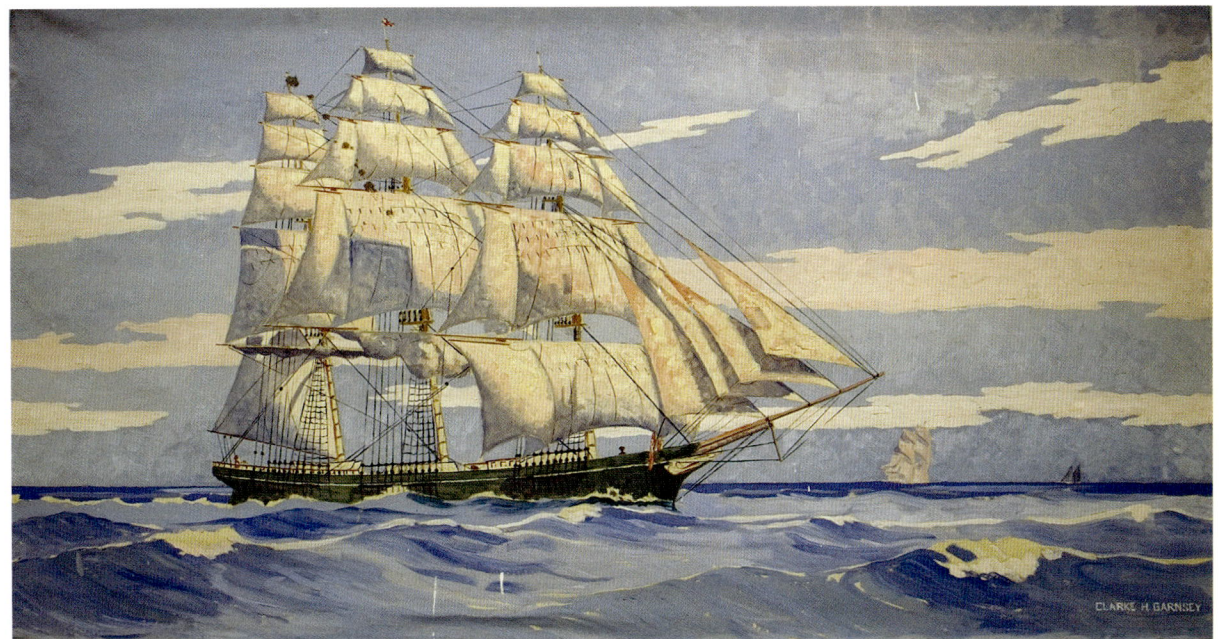

CLARKE H. GARNSEY

local library, the depictions were not specific vessels but characterizations of the tall ships. Their colors and accoutrements are of the artist's fancy.[12]

Plate 182. Clarke H. Garnsey, WPA mural in Seville, Florida.

The Volusia County historian Tom Baskett confirms that, "Schooners did, in fact, come up the St. Johns as far as Palatka—and even further up. For some years, even after the advent of all-steam, or sail-and-steam vessels, they were used for carrying timber from Florida because their holds were so large."[13] They did so until around World War I.

The murals remind Baskett "of things I've seen throughout the interior South and in Midwestern schools, churches, and houses. People often have pictures of far-away things rather than details of familiar places and lives."[14] Romantic and adventurous, the images are most appropriate for young people as they are learning to read, write, and dream, especially in a town lost in time to speedier means of transport than the riverboats had once provided.

Even though Palatka's fortunes dwindled following the decline of the steamboat trade, and the community's cultural dreams remained largely unfulfilled, Palatka has served as a sanctuary for an assortment of artistic personalities. Ernest Kasten is an intriguing example.

Born in 1899 in Vienna, Austria, Kasten received a medical degree from Vienna's College of Medicine and served as a doctor in the Prussian army during World War I. Nothing specific is known about his early training in art, but he was apparently a talented amateur and had even won an award for his paintings while he was still living in Europe. None of his European work has survived, but his later paintings suggest that he was influenced by the artists of the German expressionist movement.

He immigrated to the United States in 1938 and took a position at Providence Hospital in Holyoke, Massachusetts. His wife, a Romanian-born actress named Charlotte Lola Richter, followed him to America the next year. It is likely that the couple were seeking refuge from the Nazi regime that suppressed modern art as "degenerate."

In 1940, the Kastens moved to New York City, where Ernest practiced medicine for over twenty years before retiring to Palatka, Florida, in 1962. It was during the period from 1940 to 1960 that New York became the focus of avant garde art and culture, replacing Paris as the center of the international art world. It was undoubtedly an exciting time in the cultural life of the city, and the Kastens would have had access to the most innovative and provocative art available.

It is not known why Kasten selected Palatka as a retirement destination, although his wife may have had a nephew in the area. The couple bought a modest house and lived simply, relying on income from their extensive investments. According to Robert Torchia, who helped organize the first major exhibition of Kasten's paintings, the couple led an isolated existence in Palatka and were considered by their neighbors to be "eccentrics."[15] Torchia also reports that Ernest Kasten "complained bitterly about his life in the United States and yearned for his native Austria." Kasten died in 1982 at age eighty-two, and his wife died in 1988. The couple were interred together in a mausoleum in the Oak Hill Cemetery in Palatka beneath an inscription that reads, "At last reunited after six years of waiting and lonliness [sic]."[16]

Ernest Kasten painted for himself and did not exhibit or sell his work. He used a variety of materials that included canvas, board, paper, plates, lampshades, and plywood panels. His subjects included landscapes, religious scenes, and narratives, and his style is expressionistic with agitated forms, heavy outlines, rough surface texture, and vivid color. His apparent primitivism is more intentional than imposed, in keeping with the members of Der Blaue Reiter and other German artists who strove for directness and brutal honesty in their work. A Roman Catholic by birth, Kasten often painted religious scenes that are reminiscent of those by Emile Nolde. In his landscapes, Kasten used recurring motifs that reminded him of his native land—mountain ranges, glacial lakes, and roadside shrines.

In his painting *Fantasy Landscape with Patio Umbrella,* Kasten appears to have combined elements derived from his memories of Austria with those that he saw around him in Palatka. In the foreground, we see such familiar Florida motifs as a table with a striped umbrella, a patio, and a semi-tropical garden edged with conch shells. However, across a body of water that may be a river—or perhaps a lake—triangular mountains rise to meet the sky. Only a few of Kasten's paintings refer obviously to Florida—most instead are expressions of his memories and his spiritual struggles. Torchia writes, "Kasten's work constitutes a significant contribution to the cultural history of Florida, but it also has a much broader, universal appeal that commands both our attention and admiration."[17]

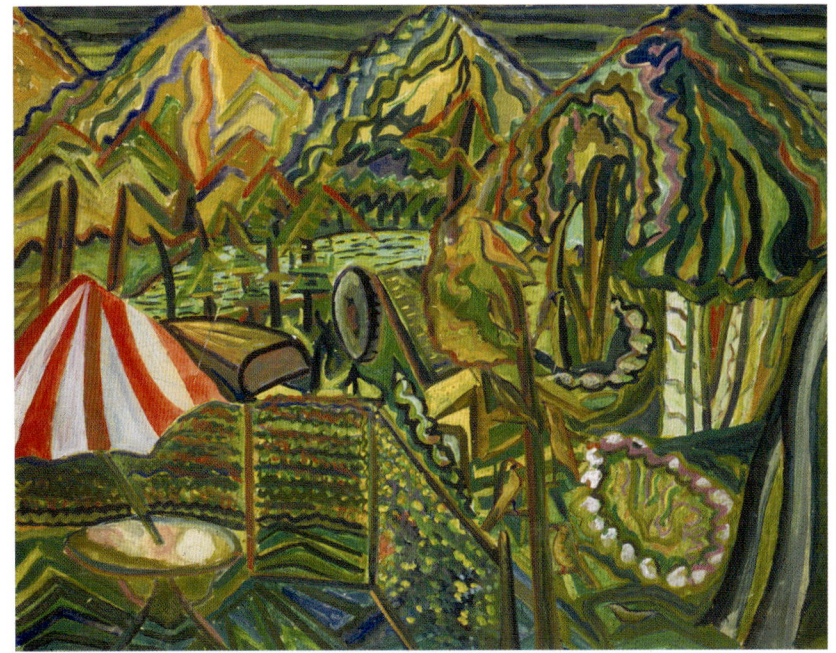

Plate 183. E. C. Kasten. *Fantasy Landscape with Patio Umbrella,* ca. 1970. Oil on wood panel, 20⅛ × 26⅛ in. From the Kasten Collection of David and Susan White.

A few miles north of Palatka on the east side of the St. Johns River is the community of Spuds. The little hamlet is well named since its major industry is growing potatoes, a crop that does well in the sandy soil of the region. However, the area does not exude a sense of prosperity—the miles of potato fields are interspersed with small farmhouses, barns, and groves of slash pine, moss-draped oaks, and saw palmetto. There is a rural charm to the region, but it is not exactly the prosperous "garden spot" that nineteenth-century travel writers envisioned.

It was, however, picturesque enough to capture the attention of several artists, among them Nunzio Vayana (1878–1960), who was born in Castelvetrano, Italy, studied medicine at the University of Rome, and immigrated to the United States in 1903. He settled in Hartford, Connecticut, where he joined the Society of Connecticut Artists and later moved to New York City, where his studio became a hub for artistic dialogue and discussion. In 1920, he founded the Art Center in Ogunquit, Maine, where he served as director for many years.

Vayana came to Florida in 1932 as guest lecturer and featured exhibitor at the St. Augustine Arts Club. St. Augustine, with its picturesque architecture and romantic history, had been a magnet for artists for years. In the late 1800s, hotel tycoon Henry Flagler had provided studio space that attracted a community of artists that included Martin Johnson Heade and other northern landscape painters, but by 1920 the local art scene had diminished to the point that when the painter Heinrich Pfeiffer visited St. Augustine that year, he remarked that the art scene had "just about disappeared" and few professional artists lived in the city. In 1924, the arts received new energy through the founding of the Arts Club "for the purpose of giving men and women of creative mind a place in which to meet and exchange ideas . . . and where they can exhibit the products of their work."[18] Writers, painters, sculptors, and photographers made up the first membership of the club. By 1932, when Vayana made his first visit, the Arts Club had enjoyed nearly a decade of development.

Vayana specialized in painting marine scenes and landscapes, and the Arts Club honored him with an exhibit of approximately one hundred of his paintings. After spending some time in Palm Beach, where he founded the Palm Beach Art Center, Vayana returned to St. Augustine and took up residence. The *St. Augustine Record* extolled Vayana as "an artist and teacher [who] has made an enviable place for himself in the company of his kind, but it is probably in the role of counsel and advocate to promising young men and women that he has made his greatest contribution to American Art."[19]

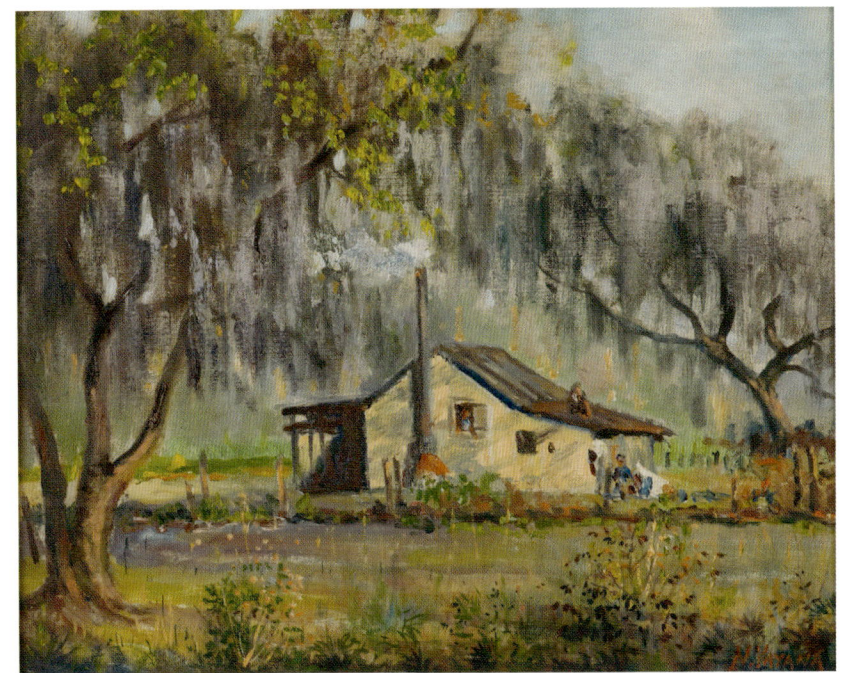

Plate 184. Nunzio Vayana, *Farmhouse in Spuds, Florida*, ca. 1948. Oil on canvas, 16¼ × 20 in. Joseph and Faith Tiberio Collection.

Farmhouse in Spuds was painted in 1948. It shows a small farmhouse set among mossy oaks with several figures going about their chores. When one compares it to earlier paintings of the area, such as John Bunyan Bristol's *On the St. Johns River* (1866), it seems almost as though time has stood still, for the style of the house, the serenity of the scene, and the feeling of rural isolation has a timelessness that indicates the slow pace of change in the rural interior of Florida over time.

Although the Arts Club had changed its name to the St. Augustine Art Association and had, by 1950, attracted more than six hundred members, it was beset by internal conflicts and dissent, and many of the members ultimately withdrew because of the failure of the group to establish a clear identity or attract the participation of well-known arts professionals. Its characterization by the art historian Robert Torchia, a specialist in

American art, as a "Lost Colony" indicates the persistent problems inherent in establishing an artist's settlement in a country that has not supported professional artists to the degree that some other nations have. Today, however, the organization has been revitalized by a new generation of artists and may yet set the stage for an era of creative achievement in the artists' on-again-off-again romance with America's oldest city.

Palatka now has a population of close to eleven thousand and is the county seat of Putnam County. It is the home of St. Johns River Community College and the Florida School of the Arts. Area attractions include Ravine Gardens State Park, the Putnam Historic Museum, the Antebellum Bronson-Mulholland House Museum, the David Browning Railroad Museum, and the nearby Mt. Royal archaeological site. Concrete manufacturing, wood products, vegetable farming, and sportfishing form the basis of the economy.

If you look to the north while crossing the bridge that connects west and east Palatka, you are certain to see the towers of the Seminole Generating Station, a coal-burning electrical generating facility that provides electricity to over 1.5 million people in forty-six Florida counties. The station's water hyperbolic cooling towers are often mistaken for those of a nuclear power plant. At 450 feet tall, the towers are a local landmark and can be seen from miles away.

One of the most unobstructed views of the plant is from the open waters of the St. Johns River. The St. Augustine artist Sydney McKenna made a drawing of the plant from the deck of a boat that was sailing on the St. Johns several miles south of the station. She later produced this oil painting of the station with smoke and water vapor trailing from its dual towers. The wide, dramatic sky, the horizontal lines of the shoreline and dock juxtaposed with the tower's trail of smoke emphasize the expansive view of the river as it widens to a magnificent channel. Once a trickle oozing through marsh grass, the St. Johns is now a flood, wider in spots than the mighty Mississippi.

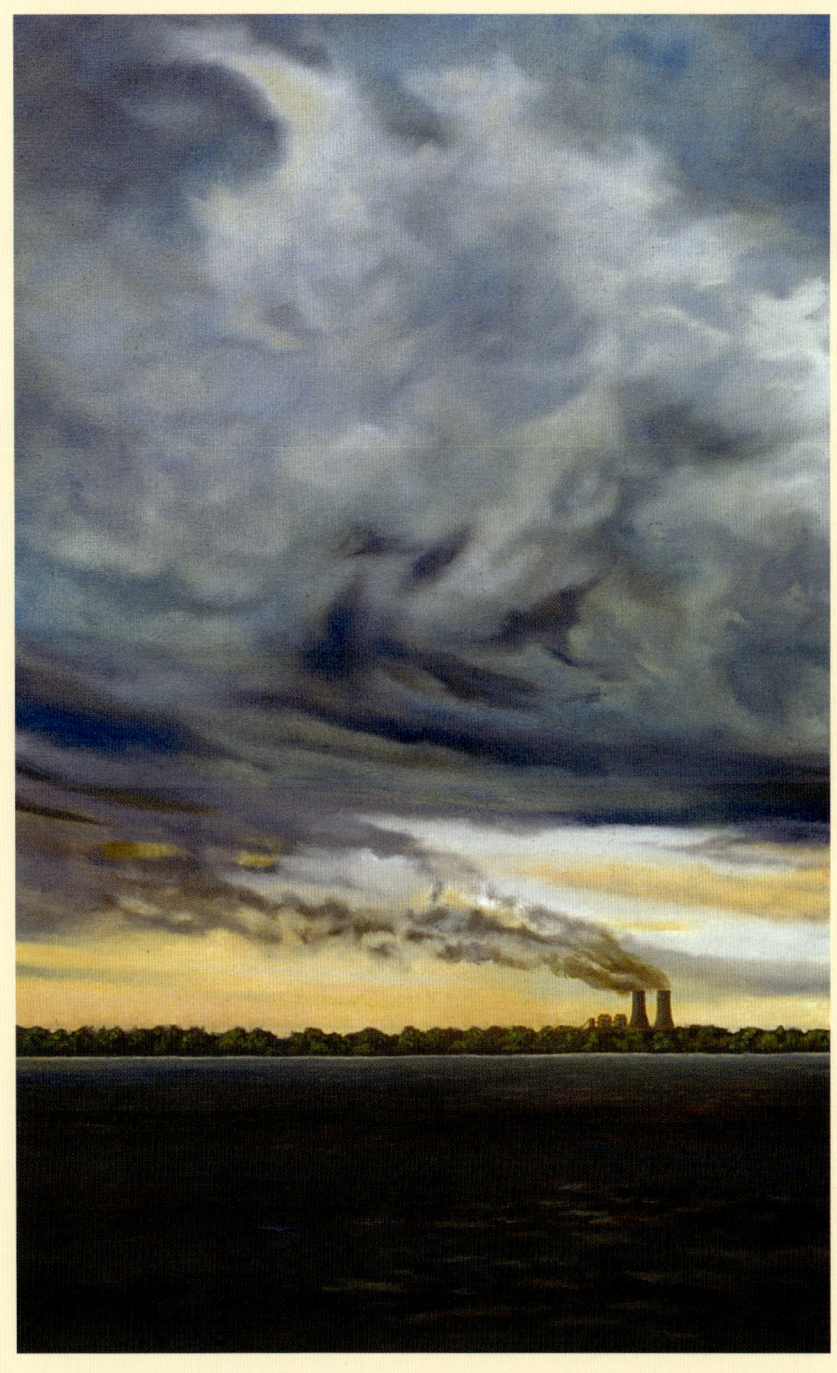

Plate 185. Sydney McKenna. *Seminole Station*, n.d. Oil on canvas, 40 × 25 in. Courtesy of the artist.

13 { From Cowford to Jacksonville

A description of the city [of Jacksonville] in 1855 informs us that it had a population of less than two thousand. Its streets were of deep soft sand, but broad and regular. Fine residences were few, and not much attention was paid to flowers or lawns. Most of the dwellers rooted out the grass so that snakes would be less likely to lurk in the yards. There were two or three groves of oaks and magnolias in the place, and a swamp in which the water was several feet deep in spots. The post office was a little ten by twelve wooden structure in which the postmaster conducted a jewelry business. Two mails arrived each week, one from Savannah, and one from Charleston, both by boat. These boats and a stage twice a week to Tallahassee were the only public conveniences for coming to, or leaving, the city.

—Clifton Johnson, *Highways and Byways of Florida*

JACKSONVILLE MAY HAVE GOTTEN A SLOW START as a major Florida metropolis, but geography made development inevitable. As it nears the end of its long journey toward the coast, the St. Johns River makes a ninety-degree turn before heading out to sea. Long before the arrival of the Europeans, this "bend in the road" had become a rendezvous place for tribal, war, and hunting expeditions. Also, because the river is very wide but not very deep at this spot, it was a natural place to cross the water. The Spanish used the shallows to drive their herds of cattle from one side of the river to the other en route to St. Augustine, hence the early name for the site: Cow Ford.

According to Clifton Johnson in his 1918 book *Highways and Byways of Florida*, it was toward the end of the Second Spanish Period that Lewis Z. Hogans, a settler from the south side of the river, married a Spanish widow who held a grant to two hundred acres of land on the site of the present city.[1] A few years later, a ferry was established to transport people and supplies from one side of the river to the other, and in 1820 an inn was established. In 1833, the town was named in honor of Andrew Jackson, whose success in fighting the Seminoles won him local approval. In 1857, a rail line was built connecting Jacksonville with Alligator, now Lake City.

When Florida became a state in 1845, it was still a largely rural territory dotted with large farms and plantations. The economy was based on cattle and crops—primarily citrus and cotton. The population was approximately 140,000, of whom around 63,000 were African American—mostly slaves. This made Florida a prime candidate for secession at the outset of the Civil War.

When Abraham Lincoln was elected president in November 1860, it took South Carolina only six weeks to decide to secede from the Union. Florida followed in January 1861. By February of that year, Florida and six other southern states had formed the Confederate States of America, and Jefferson Davis of Mississippi was elected president. In April, hostilities erupted at Fort Sumter, South Carolina, and the war began. It would last four years and result in the most casualties in U.S. history.

Its importance as a port city made Jacksonville a target for Union attention, although Confederate troops held the town until March 1862, when Union gunboats arrived and the Confederates retreated to the interior. Throughout the next three years of the conflict, the town was alternately occupied and abandoned by the Federals, and many of the original inhabitants moved away.

Although it was a part of the Confederacy, Florida, as usual, had its own unique role to play during the war years. Although an estimated sixteen thousand Floridians fought in the war, two thousand of those fought on the Union side. In addition, of the many battles fought during the four-year period, only two took place in Florida. Florida's main role was as a provider of goods and materials to support the war effort. The two most important products were cattle, which helped feed the Confederate troops, and salt, an important resource for the army.

With the majority of Florida's eligible men involved in operations to the north, few troops were left behind to defend against Union intrusion. As a result, Union troops occupied and held several towns along the river and also used the St. Johns to transport supplies and personnel. Early in the war, Union commanders realized that holding the river and the ports along the coast would be critical in preventing supplies from reaching the Confederate soldiers to the north. In January 1862, Union troops occupied Cedar Key and cut off the flow of supplies there. In March, a Federal fleet sailed up the St. Johns and captured Jacksonville. In September 1862, Confederate troops established a battery on St. Johns Bluff on the south side of the river to try to stop the movement of Federal troops up the St. Johns.

This picture of the Confederate battery, sketched by H. Van Ingen, appeared in *Harper's Weekly* in 1862.

Plate 186. H. Van Ingen. *Battery on St. Johns Bluff*. From *Harper's Weekly*, October 25, 1862. Courtesy of the Matheson Museum, Gainesville, Florida.

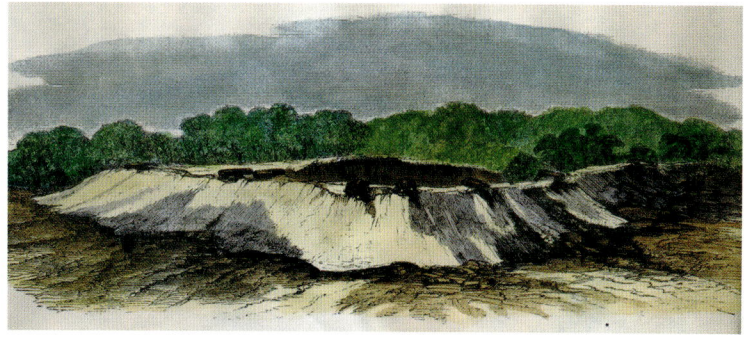

On October 1, 1862, a flotilla of four Union ships arrived at the mouth of the St. Johns and began unloading troops. Six Union gunboats sailed up river toward the bluff while additional Federal troops began marching toward the Confederate position from Mount Pleasant Creek. Realizing they were outmaneuvered, the defenders of the bluff abandoned their position, and when, the next day, the gunboats approached the bluff, they were greeted by silence. The gunboats continued up the river, shelling houses and barns as they passed.[2]

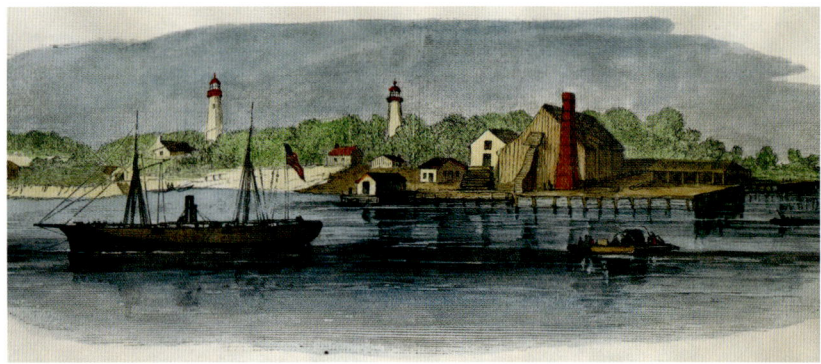

Plate 187. H. Van Ingen. *Mayport Mills*. From *Harper's Weekly,* October 1, 1862. Courtesy of the Matheson Museum, Gainesville, Florida.

This sketch shows Mayport Mills at the mouth of the St. Johns, where the Union troops disembarked to occupy the city of Jacksonville. The Union army used Jacksonville as a hub of operations for blocking shipments of supplies. They also raided the many citrus groves located along the river, destroying the trees and capturing crates of oranges that they shipped to Union troops. In March 1863, the Union forces abandoned Jacksonville after nearly three weeks of fighting as the Confederates tried to retake the town. As they retreated, the Federals set fire to a number of wooden buildings and because of a high wind the whole city was soon in flames.[3]

The Civil War dragged on until April 4, 1865, when the Confederate General Robert E. Lee surrendered to the Union General Ulysses S. Grant at Appomattox, Virginia. With the Confederate forces weakening, southern towns destroyed or captured, and supply lines to the southern troops cut, Florida officially surrendered on April 26, 1865. Union troops took over Tallahassee and immediately raised the United States flag. The war was over. Although Jacksonville's population had diminished during the hostilities—by 1865, only a few hundred residents remained—the stage was set for rapid growth. During the postwar period, the population exploded. As a transportation hub and important port, Jacksonville's destiny was secure.

This illustration published in *Frank Leslie's Illustrated Newspaper* reflects the boom-and-bust atmosphere of Jacksonville in the postwar period. On the one hand, crops such as citrus and tobacco flourished and population soared as the city became an important commercial port. In addition, the postwar tourist trade boomed as curious northerners headed south to see for themselves what had been reported by returning veterans. In 1880, Jacksonville had a resident population of only fifteen thousand, but it boasted forty hotels that, along with dozens of boardinghouses, accommodated some seventy-five thousand visitors annually.[4] On the other hand, there were setbacks such as the yellow fever epidemic that ravaged the city in the 1890s and led to economic hardship, scores of homeless refugees, and the decline of the steamboat industry. Then, in 1901, a disastrous fire ravaged the city, consuming 148 blocks of Jacksonville real estate. This event, however, heralded in an era in which Jacksonville would become one of Florida's three great cities and a center of first the railroad and later the insurance industry.

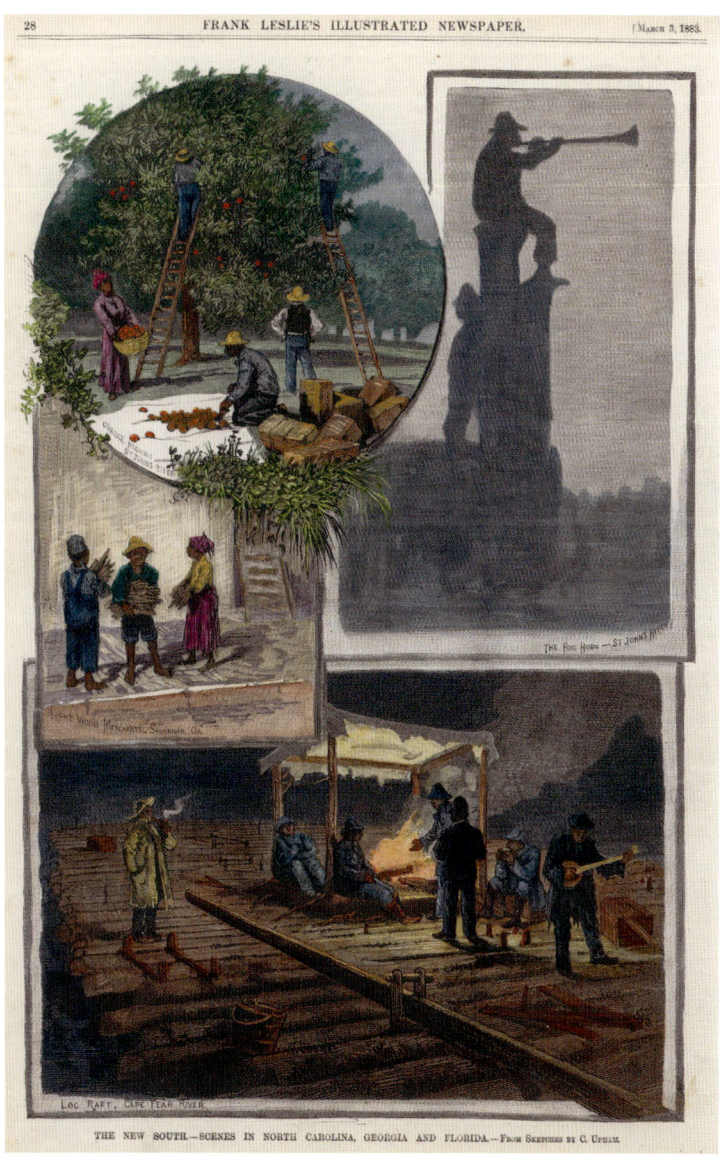

Plate 188. Anonymous. *Scenes of Jacksonville*. From *Frank Leslie's Illustrated Newspaper*, March 1883. Courtesy of the Matheson Museum, Gainesville, Florida.

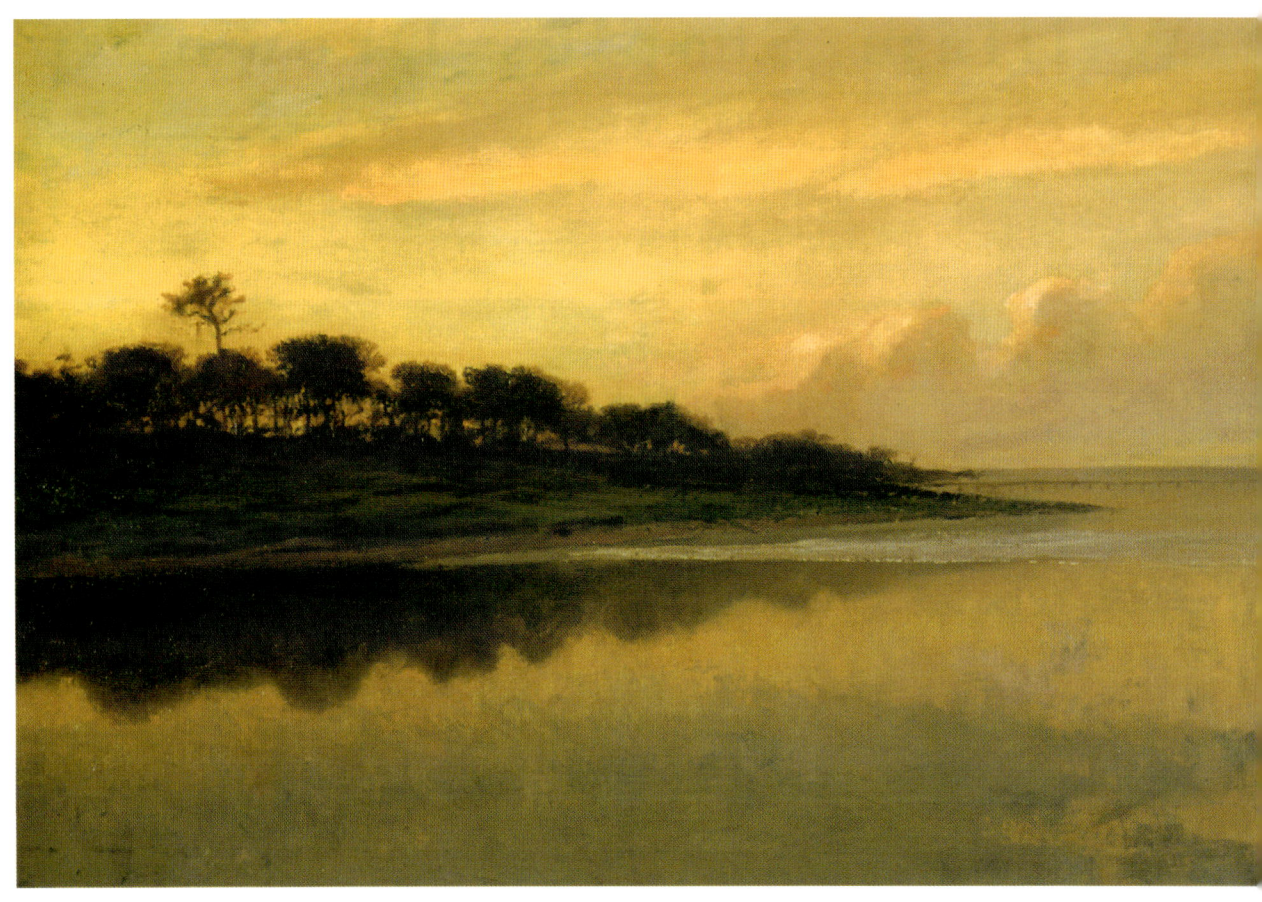

Plate 189. William Morris Hunt. *View of the St. Johns River*, 1874. Oil on canvas, 26 × 40 in. Sam and Robbie Vickers Florida Collection.

One of the most evocative images of the St. Johns was produced by William Morris Hunt, who came to Florida in 1873 to visit his friend, financier John Murray Forbes, who had a home in the Riverside area of Jacksonville. Hunt then took a boat trip up the river to a spa in Magnolia, just north of Green Cove Springs. Leaving behind a failed marriage as well as the memory of a fire that had destroyed his studio and much of his life's work, Hunt seemed to find solace in the quiet beauty of the St. Johns. According to the art critic Henry Adams, before the studio fire Hunt had produced mostly portraits, but once in Florida he began to paint landscapes. "Organized in a series of horizontal planes, and executed in muted colors, these paintings are simpler and broader in execution than earlier American landscapes, but also more emotionally gripping, due to their powerful mood of reverie and loneliness."[5]

William Morris Hunt's immersion in the healing quietude of Nature appears to have revitalized both the artist and his career, for after he returned to New York Hunt he was awarded several exhibitions, including one at the prestigious Museum of Fine Arts in Boston. Initially criticized for their lack of detail, Hunt's paintings are today much admired and are considered to have influenced the work of later artists such as Winslow Homer.

In addition to writing about her adopted Florida home in glowing terms, Harriett Beecher Stowe also brought with her an activist's attitude toward promoting positive change and advancing the cause of education in her new surroundings. She was especially concerned about the education of the former slaves: "My heart is with those poor black people whose cause I have tried to plead in words, and whose welfare I shall seek now to further through religious education."[6] She envisioned the construction of a line of churches along the St. Johns that could serve the small communities that might otherwise not have access to religious instruction. To that end, she contacted the Right Reverend John Freeman Young, then Episcopal bishop of Florida, and outlined her plan. Bishop Young, a dynamic and energetic organizer who led the Episcopal Church in Florida from 1867 to 1885, shared Mrs. Stowe's enthusiasm for expanding congregations within his diocese, and he engaged the help of the New York architect Richard Upjohn, who had designed many large Episcopal churches in the eastern United States, including New York City's Trinity Church (1846). Bishop Young had, in fact, served as assistant rector at Trinity Church earlier in his career.

Upjohn realized that most small parishes, such as those in rural Florida, could not afford to hire architects and purchase expensive materials, yet they wanted to create churches in the Gothic style that conformed to the established tradition and that fit their liturgical and aesthetic needs. Upjohn's solution was to publish plans for a smaller replica of a traditional Gothic style church that could be built by local carpenters using available materials. This architectural variation became known as "Carpenter Gothic" and became popular throughout the country.[7]

Many winter visitors to Florida were familiar with Upjohn's reputation and supported Bishop Young's efforts to build a series of churches based on the celebrated architect's design. In places such as Green Cove Springs, Palatka, Enterprise, and Sanford where popular winter resorts had been established, Carpenter Gothic churches began to appear, often financed by the generous contributions of seasonal guests. Most of the churches followed the design formula suggested by Upjohn, which included lancet windows, board and batten siding, high ceilings, pointed arches, stained-glass windows, shingle-clad steeples, and bell towers.

A number of the Carpenter Gothic churches are still in use today, and even parishes that have outgrown them have often preserved the original chapel to be used for weddings and special services. These charming chapels may not have specifically served the educational purpose initially proposed by Harriet Beecher Stowe, but their grace, style, and architectural integrity have become recognized as a unique part of Florida's history. It is a tribute to Richard Upjohn that so many of the simple wooden churches built according to his designs have endured to become notable Florida historical and religious landmarks.[8]

The Jacksonville artist Bunny Morgan has made it her task to document a number of the Carpenter Gothic churches in a series of watercolors painted over the past five years. Her interest in architectural history is no surprise—she is married to the celebrated architect William Morgan. So far she has painted several of the churches located along the St. Johns River. In this painting, she captures the intimacy and characteristic Gothic style of Fort George Episcopal Church located on Fort George Island near the mouth of the St. Johns.

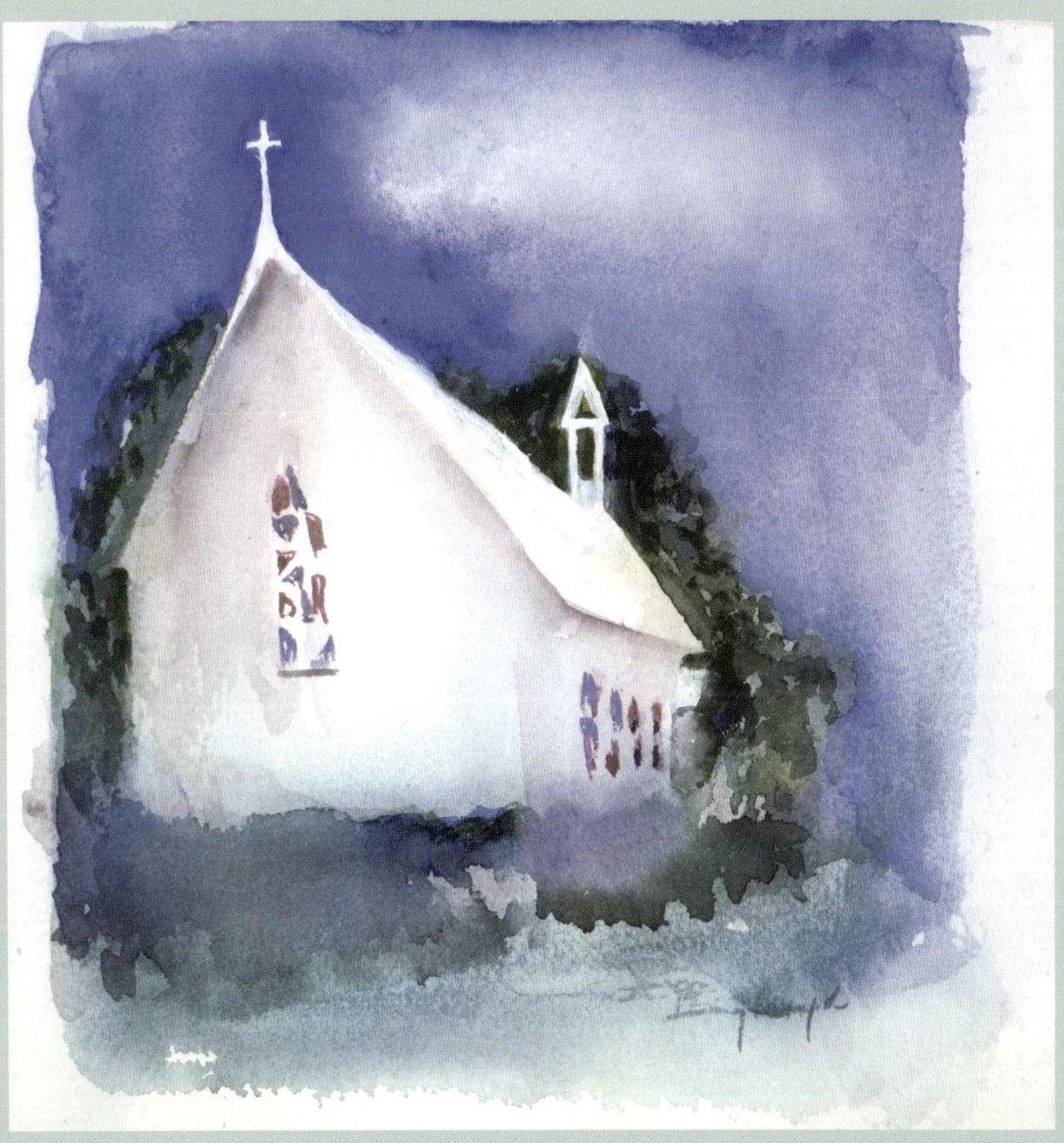

Plate 190. Bunny Morgan. *Fort George Episcopal Church, Fort George Island,* 2004. Watercolor on paper. Courtesy of the artist.

The composer Frederick Delius also had a close connection to the St. Johns River. Born in Bradford, Yorkshire, England, to German parents, young Delius was supposed to go into the family's prosperous wool business, but he rebelled and instead persuaded his father to allow him to move to Florida to oversee the orange plantation at Solano Grove a few miles upstream from Jacksonville on the St. Johns River. Determined to pursue a career in music, Delius soon became involved with the local music community in Jacksonville, where he performed and taught music. Exposed for the first time to African American spirituals, hymns and folk songs, Delius was greatly influenced by them. The peaceful river vistas, the exotic subtropical vegetation, and the songs of the Negro field hands remained with him years after he had returned to Europe. Although he only spent eighteen months in Florida, the experience inspired some of his most memorable compositions, including *Florida Suite* (1886–87) and the opera *Koanga* (1895–97).

Frederick Delius spent a year and a half living on the banks of the St. Johns River, and the sights and sounds of that experience continued to stay

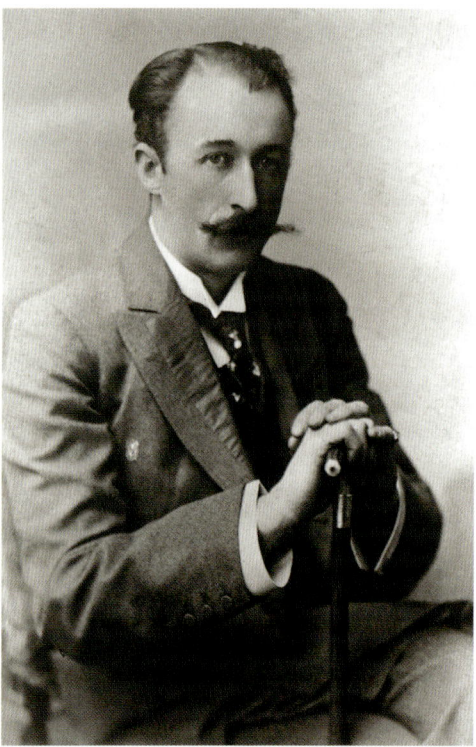

Plate 191. Anonymous. Photograph of Frederick Delius, ca. 1885. Photocopy courtesy of the State Archives of Florida.

in his memory—perhaps in part because they represented the break from his past and the beginning of his musical odyssey.

One of the composer's most memorable works is the opera *Koanga*. The libretto is based on a novel by George Cable. Set on a southern plantation, the story revolves around Koanga, a slave of noble origins who falls in love with Palmyra, a mulatto and half sister to the wife of the plantation owner, Don Jose Martinez. In typical operatic style, the love story of Koanga and Palmyra turns tragic and ends with his death at the hands of Don Jose, and Palmyra's suicide. Most of the music is evocative of the influences Delius absorbed during his Florida stay and the prologue and epilogue of the opera are set in an orange grove.

The Gainesville artist and retired University of Florida art professor John A. O'Connor has often been inspired by musical compositions. Equally enthralled by everything from rhythm and blues to country western to jazz to grand opera, O'Connor has made music and musicians a recurrent theme in his art. Beginning in the early 1980s, O'Connor began to explore the blackboard as a vehicle through which he could manipulate ideas and materials. Calling his method "conceptual realism," O'Connor says that the teaching slate's multiple erasures and transformations trace "a history of approximation." The chalkboard palimpsest refutes fixed reality: What is there? What is missing? What is covered up? O'Connor writes: "My goal is to provoke thought about how we create reality. Humor, paradox, and riddle are aspects of the working process. I am interested in the things the mind thinks it knows, things seen but not apprehended, things perceived but not truly experienced."[9]

One of O'Connor's first blackboard paintings was titled *Othello*. Fascinated with the "black and white" issues and the multiple levels of meaning inherent in the story, O'Connor used the blackboard format to explore the range of passions and the threads of racism and violence that infuse the opera. The next year—1986—O'Connor returned to a musical theme in the painting *Blackboard Jungle*, which paid homage to both the film and the music of Bill Haley and the Comets. In 1989, he painted *Mozart*, in which he explored the life and work of one of his favorite composers, and in 2003 he began a series of "opera blackboards" that included *Arabella* and *La Bohème*.

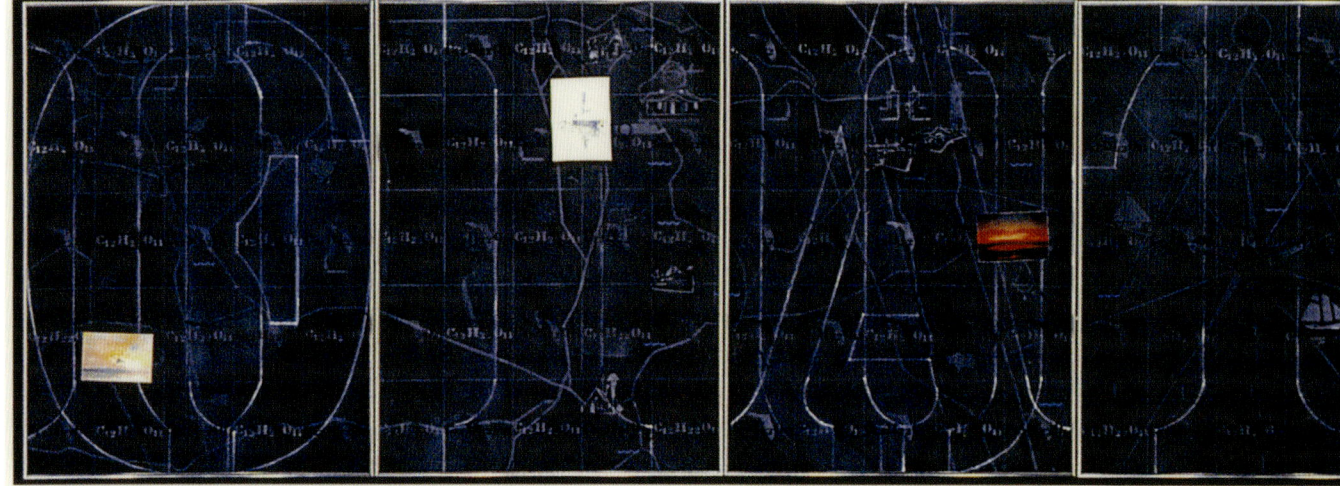

Plate 192. John O'Connor. *Florida Suite*, 2004. Acrylic on Sintra, 48 × 120 in. (four panels, each 40 × 30 in.). Courtesy of the artist.

John O'Connor's *Florida Suite*, painted in 2004, was inspired by one of Delius's earliest compositions. Written in 1886–87, Delius's *Florida Suite* was one of the first works he wrote after leaving Florida and returning to Europe to study at the Leipzig Conservatorium. The beauty and solitude that he had experienced along the St. Johns and the southern musical heritage of spirituals and folk songs were the inspiration for the composition. O'Connor painted his *Suite* in four sections—*Morning, On the River, Evening,* and *Night*—with each panel corresponding to one of the four movements. The painting is unified by a map of the St. Johns River over which O'Connor has added silhouettes of historic buildings, notes about the composer, and postcards of river scenes. O'Connor says: "I tried to select images that would have been there at the time that Delius was living on the river [1884–85] and also indicated on the map the old roads that were there at the time. Despite considerable development in the area, Solano Grove is still today a wild and lonely place, just as it must have been when Delius lived there."[10]

In February 1900, Augusta Savage was born in Green Cove Springs. The seventh of fourteen children and the daughter of a minister, she lived for her first fifteen years on the banks of the St. Johns. It was near the river that she found her first art medium—red clay. She began to use the clay to fashion small animal sculptures, but her father disapproved, calling the creations "graven images" that he said were unreligious. Augusta, however, continued to make little clay sculptures, but did not show them to her father.[11]

In 1915, she moved with her parents to West Palm Beach, where she continued to work in ceramics, making sculptures of animals and people that she sold to people in the neighborhood. When she entered a piece of her work in the county fair, she won a prize and was encouraged to continue her art. She planned to move to Jacksonville and establish herself as an artist, but decided instead to go to New York City. Although she had no money and no family in New York, she managed to win a scholarship to Cooper Union Women's Art School. Her hard work paid off. In 1923, she won a competition to study in France, but unfortunately the scholarship was rescinded when it was learned that she was an African American. This blatantly racist decision did not stop Augusta. She soon won another scholarship award to study at the Royal Academy of Fine Arts in Rome, Italy. Once more, however, she was blocked from her plans because she had no money to make the trip to Italy.

In 1929, she finally realized her dream of studying in Europe when she was awarded the Julius Rosenwald Fellowship to study in Paris for two years. During her stay, she continued her studies and won several awards for her sculpture. Her career was successfully launched, and she returned to New York with enthusiastic plans to do a series of portraits of distinguished African Americans. Her *Head of Dr. Du Bois* was well received, and she went on to numerous successful commissions. She also opened an art school, the Savage School of Arts and Crafts, helped organize the Harlem Artist Guild, and directed the Harlem Community Art Center.[12] In her later years, she focused on teaching and mentoring. One of her most important pupils was Jacob Lawrence, who went on to become a celebrated and successful artist.[13] Augusta Savage, the artist from Green Cove Springs, died in 1962 after a successful international career as a sculptor, teacher, and community leader.

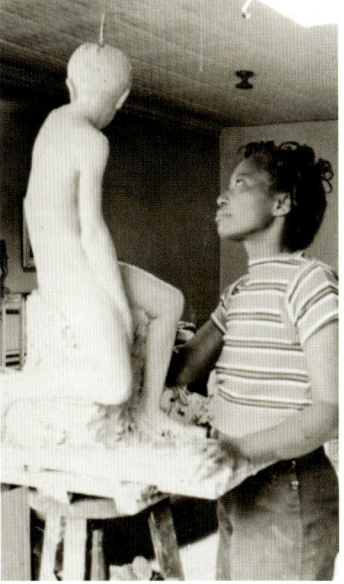

Plate 193. Augusta Savage with her work *Boy on a Stump*. **Photograph courtesy of the Florida Humanities Council.**

In the early years of the twentieth century, New York, not California, was the headquarters of the film industry. Filming in New York, however, was expensive, the climate was cold, and there was a lack of suitable outdoor locations. The moviemakers needed a winter home with exotic scenery. Jacksonville was a logical choice. Following the lead of Kalem Studios, which opened in 1908, other movie studios made Jacksonville their base. Eventually more than thirty film studios opened, including Metro Pictures, later MGM.

Silent films were the order of the day, and Jacksonville studios turned out scores of them, often taking advantage of the local scenery of springs, plantations, and trailing Spanish moss. By 1920, however, many of the major studios had relocated to Southern California, and Hollywood soon eclipsed Jacksonville as the hub of film production.

It was in 1920 that Richard Norman purchased the bankrupt Eagle Film Studios in Arlington just across the St. Johns River from Jacksonville. Norman, who was white, is best known for making silent films starring, and often written by, African Americans. It isn't clear why Norman decided to make films for African American audiences. Black actors in the early years of film-making were usually cast in stereotyped roles or portrayed in degrading ways. Norman, however, was determined to do films that featured black actors in positive ways. Margaret Barlow, in an article in *Florida History and the Arts*, writes: "Besides attracting many accomplished stage actors to perform in his films, Norman featured other talented African Americans of the day. *The Bull Dogger* (1921), a western shot in Oklahoma, gave eastern and southern black audiences an opportunity to see black cowboys in action, including famous rodeo rider Bill Pickett."[14]

Most of Norman's movies are now lost, but his son preserved a number of photographs, posters, and other memorabilia. In addition, the buildings that housed Norman Studios are being restored and may soon house a film history and learning center, part of an Old Arlington, Inc., program to create an ecoheritage area to attract tourists.

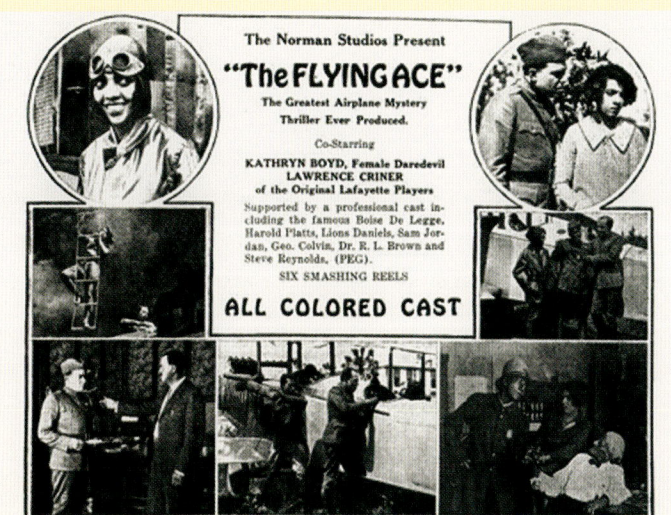

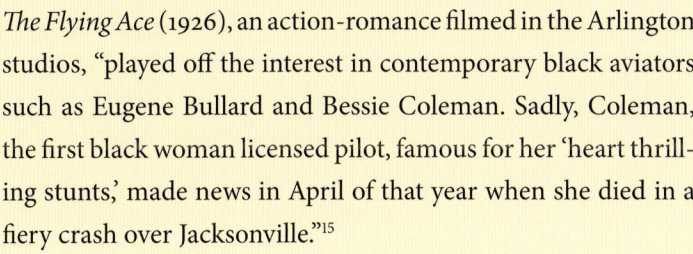

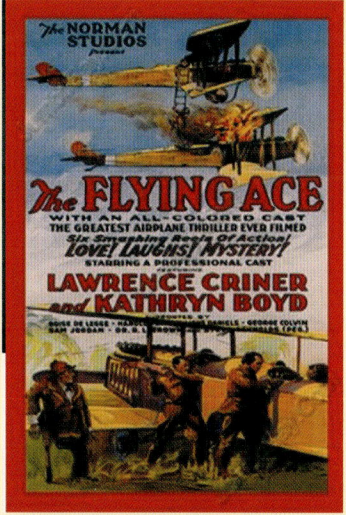

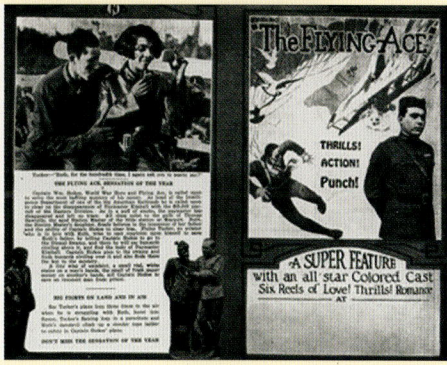

The Flying Ace (1926), an action-romance filmed in the Arlington studios, "played off the interest in contemporary black aviators such as Eugene Bullard and Bessie Coleman. Sadly, Coleman, the first black woman licensed pilot, famous for her 'heart thrilling stunts,' made news in April of that year when she died in a fiery crash over Jacksonville."[15]

Plate 194. Still from the motion picture *The Flying Ace*, produced by Norman Studios, Jacksonville, Florida. Courtesy of the State Archives of Florida.

During World War II, Florida was the site of numerous incidents and skirmishes involving U.S. and foreign warships. In 1941, the Naval Air Station, with auxiliary bases at Mayport and Green Cove Springs, began operations in Jacksonville. Other air-training facilities were also established along the St. Johns at Sanford and Avon Park. Jacksonville's shipyards were filled with activity as cargo ships and other military equipment was constructed. German submarines prowled the coastline looking for targets. Michael Gannon writes: "From Fernandina Beach to the Keys and around into the Gulf, one after another tanker or merchantman, defenseless against the prowling German sea wolves, sank in flames before the helpless gaze of Floridians on their beach-cottage decks and tourists on their hotel balconies."[16]

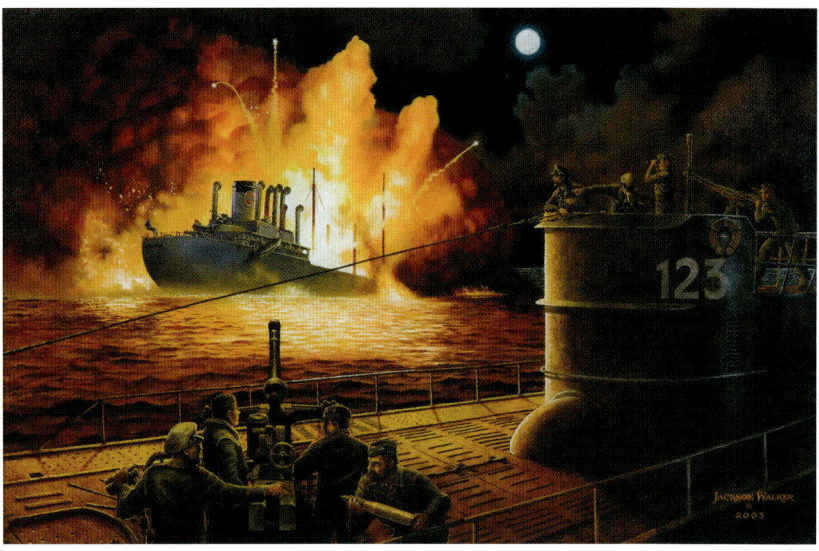

Plate 195. Jackson Walker. *U-123*, 2000. Oil on canvas, 27 × 42 in. From the legendary Florida Collection of The Museum of Florida Art, DeLand, Florida.

The Orlando artist Jackson Walker painted an electrifying image of the sinking of the SS *Gulfamerica* as part of his Legendary Florida series. He recounts an especially memorable incident that took place off the coast of Jacksonville on April 11, 1942: "It was the second year of World War II. The German Submarine force had begun 'Operation Drumbeat'—a large scale plan to attack shipping routes along the eastern seaboard of North America, sinking supply and oil vessels destined for the Allied Forces in Europe. During this time, the oil tanker SS Gulfamerica had set sail from Texas on her maiden voyage laden with oil and petroleum bound for the war. The new ship rounded the tip of Florida and sailed parallel to the east coast, northward. At a point just four miles off Jacksonville, on the night of April 11, U-boat 123 struck the tanker with torpedoes that ignited the fuel into a massive firestorm aboard her. But the ship was slow to sink. The submarine then surfaced and, with her deck gun, began to shoot into the hull to expedite the sinking. U-boat Commander Kapitanleutnant [*sic*] Reinhard Hardigan, prepared to engage the ship but observed the nearness of the shore—there he could see evidence of the well populated coast of Jacksonville. Realizing that if he fired, there was a possibility that overshots could hit the shore, putting civilians at risk. He navigated around the Gulfamerica to a place where his fire would be directed to sea. In doing so, he lost valuable time and was engaged by American warships. The damaged U-123 made a narrow escape back to Europe. The Gulfamerica sank, losing nineteen of her crew, but Hardigan's humane conduct in not firing on the shores of the city was recognized."[17]

Allison Watson's French Huguenot ancestors, the Fatios, came to the Jacksonville area from Vevey, Switzerland, in 1771, when Florida had just become a Royal British province. The family bought land from the Spanish and had plantations along the river from north of Jacksonville to Lake George. Today the National Society of the Colonial Dames of America owns the family home in St. Augustine. Placed on the National Register of Historic Places in 1973, the house is open to the public as a historic museum. Says Watson: "There is a beautiful garden and period furniture, artifacts and probably ghosts of my ancestors. . . . So you can see that the River is more than a fascinating subject for me to paint. My ashes will probably go there."[18]

Plate 196. Allison Watson. *Mystery Oak*, n.d. Acrylic on canvas, 36 × 54 in. Courtesy of the artist.

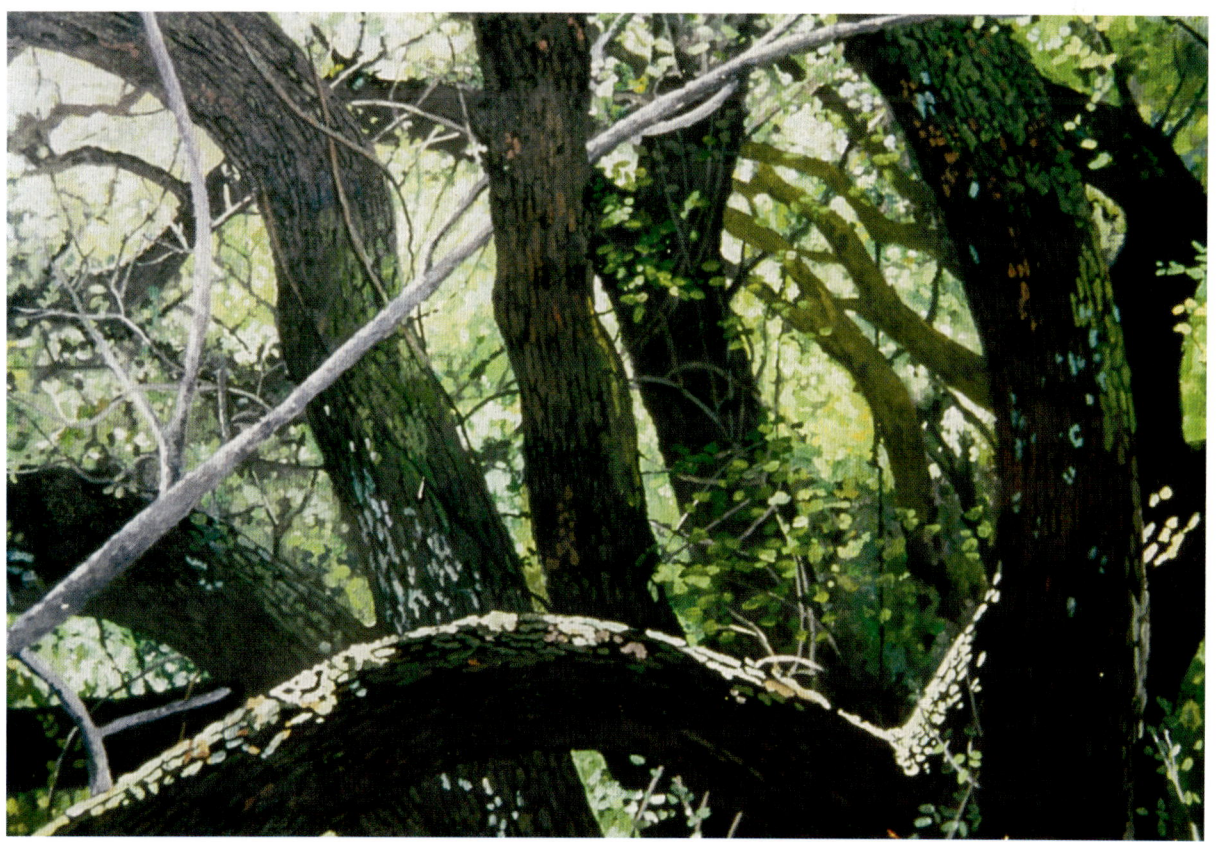

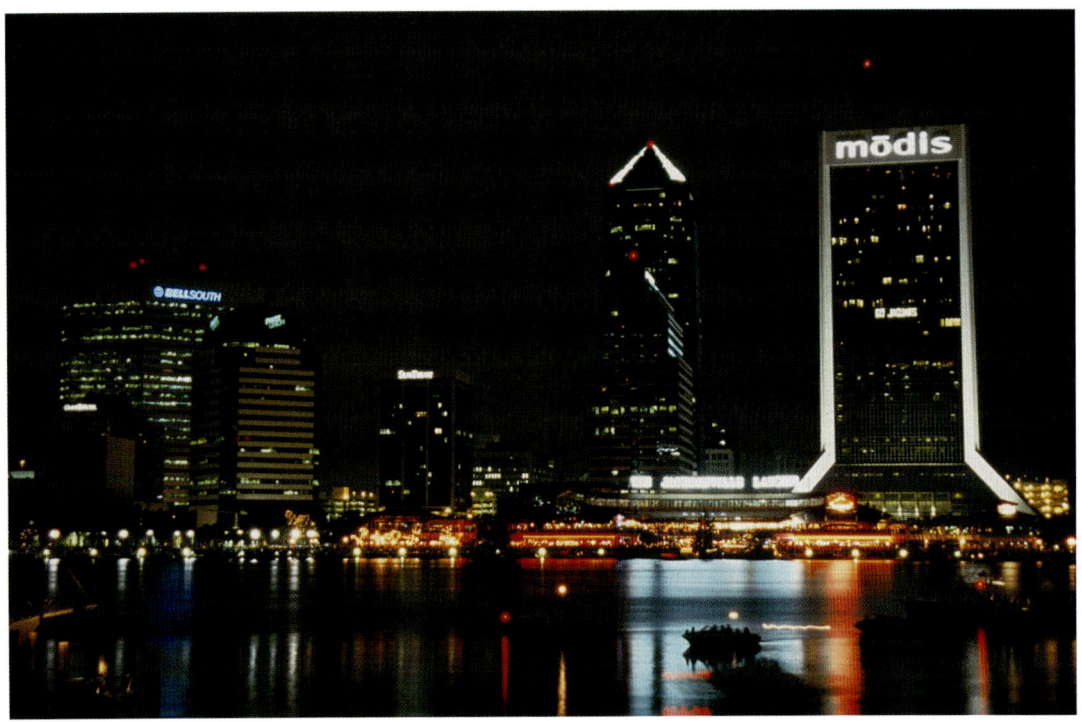

Plate 197. James Johnson. "Jacksonville Skyline: Evening." Color photograph. Courtesy of the artist.

If Allison Watson's images perpetuate the story of Florida's past and the allure of the myth of Xanadu, James Johnson's "Jacksonville Skyline: Evening" shows us that the story of El Dorado is still alive and well. There may not have been any gold in the River May, but there certainly was plenty of money to be made along the noble San Juan. Development opportunities are to the present age what finding gold was to the sixteenth-century entrepreneurs who came to Florida to seek their fortunes.

Johnson's photographs are known to many for providing dramatic images of the Jacksonville area's most alluring landmarks—her bridges, building, boats, and the magical riverscape surrounding them. This photograph of the Jacksonville skyline reveals the mythic power of architecture seen here as a symbol of wealth and authority. Is there a more potent visual symbol for material success than the light-encrusted skyscraper towering over the harbor?

Odd though it may seem, the widest part of the St. Johns is not where the river meets the Atlantic Ocean but farther upriver. By the time the river gets to the city, it is preparing to execute an unlikely maneuver—a 45-degree "dog leg." Bill Belleville writes: "Here the broad St. Johns begins to funnel itself up agilely into the 'Narrows' of Jacksonville, and the bottom is deep—up to seventy feet and more in spots."[19] He goes on to report that Jacksonville, with its six road and railroad bridges, is one of the most bridged cities in Florida. "Bridges helped to define this city," Belleville writes. "Until the Acosta Bridge was in place in 1921, only the Florida East Coast Railroad and ferries carried people and their supplies from one side of the river to the other. Most of Jacksonville's growth was limited to the north side of the river, where the city was originally settled."[20]

Today, the Jacksonville skyline attests to its commercial viability, "a skyscraping tribute to insurance and banking headquarters, hotels, and commercial towers, logos and names claiming territory . . . CSX and Times-Union and Omni. . . . They are all edifices in glass—rectangular and glass, pyramidal and glass, stacked like a stairway and glass, glary even in the winter gray."[21]

Under a cloud-streaked sky, Sydney McKenna captures the profile of the new Cowford, a Sunbelt city illuminated by the golden rays of the late afternoon Florida sun. The city seems to float on the river's surface, a skyline of steel and concrete and glass sandwiched between the river and the sky, as though the river itself had built it and thrust it up from the dark water toward the heavens.

Plate 198. Sydney McKenna. *River City*, **n.d. Oil on canvas, 24 × 48 in. Courtesy of the artist.**

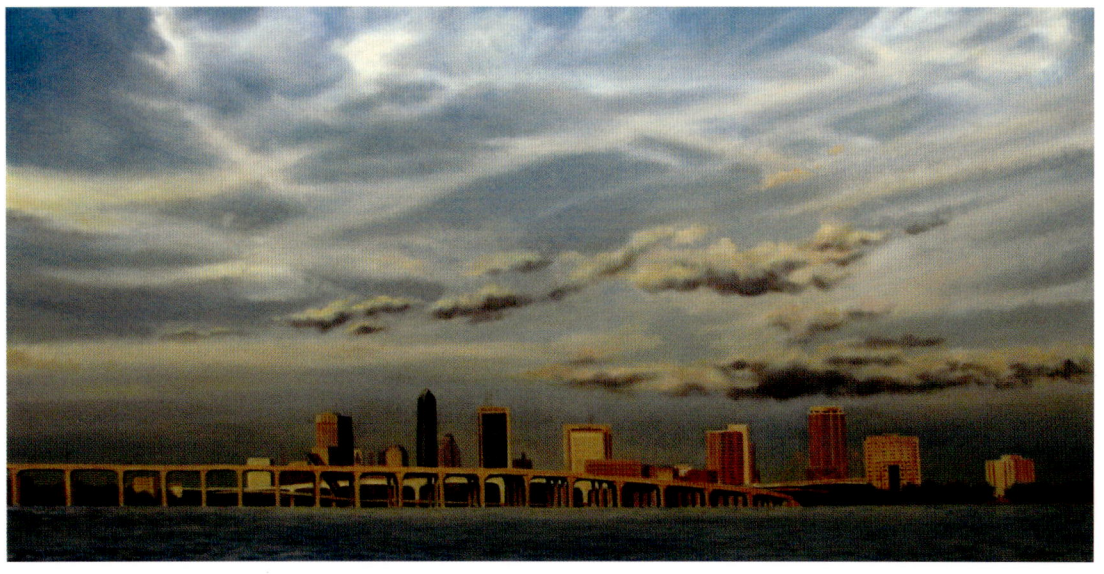

I reach down over the edge of the gunnel and swipe my hand into the cold winter water, bringing my fingers to my lips. Its salt vaguely hints of other tastes, like the ones I stole from inside Croaker Hole and Salt Springs far upriver from here. Those were prehistoric ocean tastes, the remainder of a distant place encapsulated by geology and time and then fed back to me by artesian pressure. I think how this river, despite the ravages against it, still has the capacity to feed each of us with its own memory, if we let it. Just beyond is the place where the whales still come to breach, giant mammals that Le Moyne first drew with their heads out of the water, the same animals I once imagined above my own head, in an ancient Florida lagoon some 310 miles ago. This frothing Atlantic is the beginning of the St. Johns River—as well as its inevitable and timeless end—and I let my heart surge out with it, into the folds of oceanic creation.

—Bill Belleville, *River of Lakes*

IN THE LEXICON OF MYTHOLOGY, the river is a metaphor for life, for the journey. The source is the birth, the Beginning. The destination is union with the sea, the One. The traveler journeys through time and space, following the river's path. There are moments of great beauty and of great danger. There are rapids and shallows, calm and storm, places where you can see ahead for miles and places where you can't see around the next bend. The river is a perfect metaphor for life—perhaps that's why it appears so often as the setting for myth or as the subject of myth itself. Its course reveals a thousand stories and harbors a thousand secrets. It is both open and hidden, revelation and mystery.

The St. Johns River has been our guide on this journey through space and time, through matter and history. Its voice is the soft murmur of serpentine shallows and the raging shout of a Lake George storm. It is a roadmap to our history, a thread that binds together our common heritage—as Floridians and as Americans. As it has shaped our past and molded our present, so too it holds a key to our future, for it is water that will direct our future on this earth, indeed the future of all life. We have heard the river's stories, viewed its images, and learned its rich mythology. Perhaps it is now time to look at the river with new eyes, to peer into the water's dark depths and read our future.

Plate 199. Herman Herzog. *The St. Johns River Entering the Atlantic Ocean*, 1888. Oil on canvas. The Orlando Museum of Art, Orlando, Florida.

Herman Herzog studied painting at the Dusseldorf Academy in Germany, and his European training is evident in the Florida landscapes he painted between 1888 and 1910. An avid sportsman, Herzog painted and sketched many of the state's marshes and creeks, and fishermen were frequent subjects. His style is similar to that of the Hudson River school artists, with an emphasis on the quality of light and the rich textures of the natural landscape. Herzog painted this view of the St. Johns River entering the Atlantic Ocean in 1888.

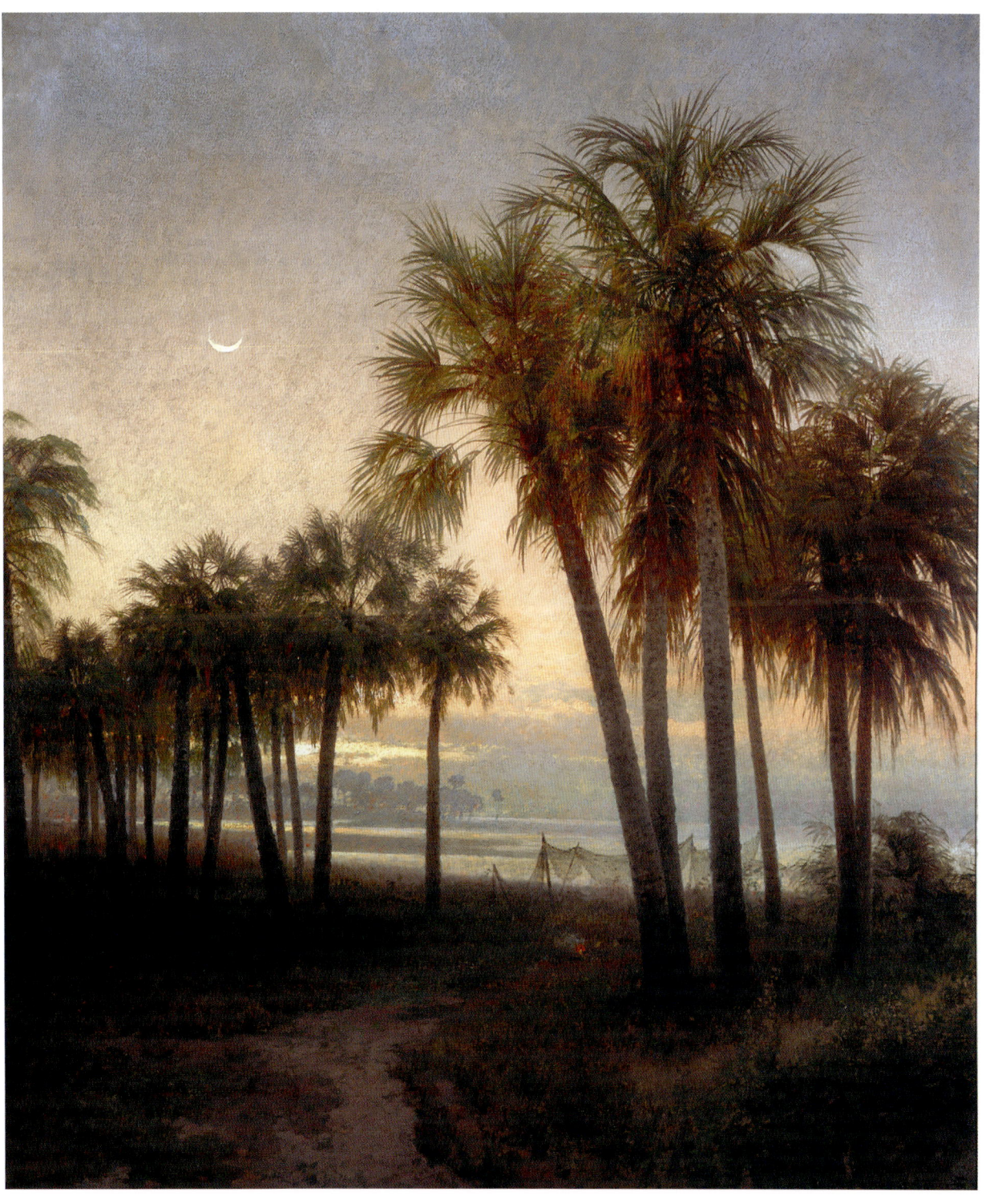

Notes

Front matter

1. Spence Guerin, e-mail, 2007.
2. Ibid.
3. Favis, *Martin Johnson Heade in Florida*, 52.
4. Hansen Mulford, interview by Gary Monroe, 2006.

Introduction

1. Bartram, *Travels* (Van Doren), 163.
2. Ibid., 163.
3. Walker, *The Legendary Florida Series*.
4. Ibid.
5. Ibid.
6. Bartram, *Travels* (Van Doren), 15.
7. Cabell and Hanna, *The St. Johns*, 302.
8. Rawlings, *Cross Creek*.

Chapter 1. First along the River

1. Purdy and Craven, *Indian Art of Ancient Florida*, 13.
2. Brown, *Florida's First People*, 19.
3. Ibid., 22.
4. Ibid., 23.
5. Ibid., 112.
6. Ibid.
7. Thomas Hariot quoted in Lorant, ed., *The New World*, 249.
8. Florida Department of State, Division of Historical Programs, www.myflorida .com.
9. Jad Davenport, "Treasures in the Mud," *Preservation Magazine*, March 29, 2002, www.preservationnation.org.
10. Brown, *Florida's First People*, 114.
11. Ibid., 116.
12. Bartram, *Travels* (Van Doren), 101–2.
13. Milanich, "Early Archaeology on the St. Johns River, Florida," 12.
14. Quigley, e-mail, April 24, 2006.

15. McCarthy, *St. Johns River Guidebook*, 41–42.
16. Larry Moore, interview by Gary Monroe, 2006.
17. Purdy and Craven, *Indian Art of Ancient Florida*, 33.
18. Belleville, *River of Lakes*, 89.
19. Brown, *Florida's First People*, 81.
20. Milanich, *Florida Indians and the Invasion from Europe*, 66.
21. Maury Hurt to Mallory O'Connor, March 17, 2006.
22. Milanich, *Florida Indians and the Invasion from Europe*, 82.
23. Ibid., 84.
24. Archaeologists have recently discovered that, based on the site of the village near DeLand, it's likely that the actual group of people who lived there were the Mayaca Indians, not the Timucua. It could be argued, however, that the type of structure represented in Boswell's painting is accurate because both groups shared many cultural traits.
25. Milanich, *Florida Indians and the Invasion from Europe*, xiv.
26. Ibid., 231.

Chapter 2. The Fourth Part of the World

1. Lorant, ed., *The New World*, 16.
2. Laudonnière quoted ibid., 7.
3. Bennett, *Three Voyages*, 61.
4. Laudonnière in Lawson and Faupel, eds., *A Foothold in Florida,* 18.
5. Lorant, ed., *The New World*, 1.
6. Some scholars, such as the University of Florida archaeologist Jerald Milanich, have gone so far as to question the authenticity of the attribution, pointing out that all of the existing Le Moyne paintings—at least one hundred in various museums and collections—depict "plants, animals, and insects, and none appears to relate to Florida." "The supposition that Le Moyne painted or drew pictures of Florida Indians is based on a note stating that he was being paid by Sir Walter Raleigh to do color illustrations of the French colony in Florida," Milanich continues. "But it is not known if they were ever done and, if so, what happened to them." Nevertheless, Milanich agrees that "we can still enjoy them [the Le Moyne and de Bry images] for what they are: early European portrayals of the Florida Indians" (Milanich quoted in Morris, *Florida's Lost Tribes*, 5, 8, 11).
7. Le Moyne quoted in Lorant, ed., *The New World*, 53.
8. Bennett, *Three Voyages*, 72.
9. Ibid., 7.
10. Milanich quoted in Morris, *Florida's Lost Tribes*, 9.
11. Ibid., 8.
12. Le Moyne qouted in Lorant, ed., *The New World*, 117.
13. Bennett, *Laudonnière and Fort Caroline*, 60.
14. Le Challeux quoted in Lorant, ed., *The New World*, 90.
15. Laudonnière quoted in Lawson and Faupel, eds., *A Foothold in Florida*, 103.
16. Menéndez quoted in Lorant, ed., *The New World*, 27.

17. Lorant, ed., *The New World*, 29.
18. Bennett, *Twelve on the River St. Johns*, 33.
19. Gordon, *Florida's Colonial Architectural History*, 38.
20. Ibid., 38.
21. Ibid., 39.
22. Ibid., 4.
23. Milanich, *Laboring in the Fields of the Lord*, 121.
24. Hann, *A History of the Timucuan Indians and Missions*, 168.
25. Scott Mitchell, interview by Gary Monroe, 2006
26. Hann, *A History of the Timucuan Indians and Missions*, 188.
27. Milanich, *Laboring in the Fields of the Lord*, xiii.
28. Milanich, *Florida Indians and the Invasion from Europe,* xiii.

Chapter 3. The Conquistador's Gift: Cattle, Horses, and Citrus

1. www.Floridacattlemen.org/history.htm.
2. Hann, *A History of the Timucuan Indians and Missions*, 192.
3. Hann, *A History of the Timucuan Indians and Missions*, 193.
4. Akerman, *Florida Cowman: A History of Florida Cattle Raising*, 7.
5. Bartram, *Travels* (Van Doren), 165.
6. Regina Briskey, interview by Mallory O'Connor, May 17, 2006.
7. Akerman, *Florida Cowman: A History of Florida Cattle Raising*, 265.
8. Ste. Claire, "Cracker," 4.
9. Edward King quoted ibid., 53.
10. Ronald W. Haase quoted ibid., 41.
11. Regina Briskey, interview by Mallory O'Connor, May 17, 2006.
12. Deagan and MacMahon, *Fort Mose,* 23.
13. Ibid., 34.
14. Akerman, "America's First Cowmen," 17.
15. Akerman, *Florida Cowman: A History of Florida Cattle Raising*, 131.
16. Zora Neale Hurston quoted in Akerman, "America's First Cowmen," 17.
17. Wolf, www.ecofloridamag.com/archived/ecotour_ranch.htm.
18. Ibid.
19. Sean Sexton to Mallory O'Connor, 2006.
20. Regina Briskey, interview by Mallory O'Connor, May 17, 2006.
21. Piazza, *Sean Sexton: A Pastoral Life Inside/Out*, 2.
22. Ste. Claire, "Cracker," 174.
23. Francis de Castleman quoted in Akerman, "America's First Cowmen," 9.
24. Regina Briskey, interview by Mallory O'Connor, May 17, 2006.
25. Kohen, "Perfume, Postcards and Promises: The Orange in Art and Industry," 33.
26. www.FloridaJuice.com/about_history.php.
27. Mormino, *Land of Sunshine, State of Dreams*, 195.
28. Derr, *Some Kind of Paradise*, 79.
29. Graff, introduction to *Palmetto Leaves*, xiii.
30. Stowe, *Palmetto Leaves*, 145.

31. Ibid., 142.
32. Gannon, ed., *The New History of Florida*, 250.
33. William Cullen Bryant quoted in Mann, *Art in Florida: 1564–1945*, 59.
34. Lanier, *Florida: Its Scenery, Climate and History*, 122.
35. Jim Draper, interview by Gary Monroe, 2006.
36. Ibid.
37. Ibid.
38. Mormino, *Land of Sunshine, State of Dreams*, 196.
39. Emilio Raya, "African-American History through the Arts," www.spfld-museum-of-art.com/catalogue/tanner.html.
40. Ibid.
41. Ibid.
42. Jack Beverland, interview by Gary Monroe, 2006.
43. Florida Citrus Mutual Web site, *Citrus and Vegetable Magazine*, Lakeland, Fla., www.flcitrusmutual.com.
44. Derr, *Some Kind of Paradise*, 387.
45. Thomas E. Cook, "Orlando History Bit: 1983–1989," Florida Heritage Foundation Web site, 2005.
46. Mormino, *Land of Sunshine, State of Dreams*, 205.

Chapter 4. A Parade of Diversities: Colonization and Conflict

1. Bartram, *Travels* (Van Doren), 198.
2. Gannon, *Florida: A Short History*, 23.
3. Ibid.
4. Ibid.
5. Schafer, "Governor James Grant's Villa: A British East Florida Indigo Plantation," 33.
6. Gordon, *Florida's Colonial Architectural History*, 118.
7. Ibid., 121.
8. Cabell and Hanna, *The St. Johns: A Parade of Diversities*, 94.
9. Ibid., 100.
10. Gene Roberds, telephone interview by Mallory O'Connor, April 2007.
11. Ibid.
12. "The Minorcans in Florida," Rootsweb.com.
13. Ibid.
14. Ibid.
15. Libby, ed., *Celebrating Florida: Works of Art from the Vickers Collection*, 52.
16. Ibid.
17. Ibid.
18. "The Minorcans in Florida," Rootsweb.com.
19. James Murphy quoted in Libby, ed., *Celebrating Florida: Works of Art from the Vickers Collection*, 42.
20. Deagan and MacMahon, *Fort Mose*, 9.
21. Ibid., 6.
22. Ibid., 10.

23. Ibid., 11.
24. Jones and McCarthy, *African Americans in Florida*, 13.
25. Ibid., 22.
26. Deagan and MacMahon, *Fort Mose*, 37.
27. Schafer, *Anna Kingsley*, 9.
28. Ibid., 10.
29. Ibid., 11.
30. Ibid., 19.
31. Ibid., 21.
32. Ibid., 24.
33. Ibid., 49.
34. Morris, *Florida's Lost Tribes*, 61.
35. Ibid., 62.
36. Mann, *Art in Florida: 1564–1945*, 40.
37. Dorothy Downs, telephone interview by Mallory O'Connor, January 2008.
38. Gannon, ed., *The New History of Florida*, 187.
39. Ibid., 192.
40. Ibid., 28.
41. Waterbury, *El Escribano* 19 (1982): 30.
42. Christopher Still, *Patriot and Warrior* (brochure for the murals commissioned by the Florida House of Representatives and available to visitors to the Capitol), 2002.
43. Libby, ed., *Celebrating Florida: Works of Art from the Vickers Collection*, 30.
44. Ibid., 31.
45. Cynthia Edmonds, interview by Mallory O'Connor, August 19, 2006.

Chapter 5. Artist-Naturalists in *La Florida*

1. Carr, *A Naturalist in Florida*, 37.
2. Belleville, *River of Lakes*, xxviii.
3. Parrish, *American Curiosity*, 25.
4. Ibid., 8.
5. Some scholars, such as the University of Florida anthropology professor Jerald Milanich, even suggest that Theodore de Bry's engravings of Florida's Timucuan Indians, long thought to have been based on the lost paintings of Jacques Le Moyne, may in fact have been borrowed from the drawings and engravings of Brazilian Indians published by André Thevet and Hans Staden, a German who was shipwrecked on the Atlantic coast of South America in the mid-sixteenth century (Morris, *Florida's Lost Tribes*, 7). If so, the de Bry engravings, which were thought to present a reasonably accurate picture of Timucuan life and culture, will have to be reevaluated.
6. Elsa Conrad, "Biographical References," www.lib.virginia.edu/small/exhibits/gordon/renworld/thevet.html.
7. Pietro Martire d'Anghiera quoted in Parrish, *American Curiosity*, 25.
8. André Thevet quoted in Bennett, *Laudonnière and Fort Caroline*, 32.
9. Parrish, *American Curiosity*, 25.

10. Ibid., 34.

11. www.lib.virginia.edu/small/renwld/Thevet.html.

12. Parrish, *American Curiosity*, 41.

13. Slaughter, *The Natures of John and William Bartram*, xv.

14. Dobrin and Weisser, *Natural Discourse: Toward Ecocomposition*, 69.

15. Slaughter, *The Natures of John and William Bartram*, xvii.

16. Ibid., 118.

17. Bartram, *Travels* (Van Doren), 68.

18. Derr, *Some Kind of Paradise*, 261.

19. Nichols, *Romantic Natural Histories: William Wordsworth, Charles Darwin, and Others*, 19.

20. Parrish, *American Curiosity*, 9.

21. John Bartram to Peter Collinson, August 20, 1753, in J. Bartram, *The Correspondence of John Bartram, 1734–1777*, 354, 387.

22. Sammons, *John and William Bartram: Travelers in Early America*, 30.

23. Slaughter, *The Natures of John and William Bartram*, 231.

24. Ibid.

25. Bartram, *Travels* (Van Doren), 327.

26. Ibid., 327.

27. John Moran, notes provided to Mallory O'Connor, 2006.

28. Bartram, *Travels* (Van Doren), 121.

29. Ibid.

30. Ibid., 201.

31. Ibid., 115.

32. Slaughter, *The Natures of John and William Bartram*, 231.

33. Hope White, interview by Mallory O'Connor, March 2008.

34. Ibid.

35. Ibid.

36. Ibid.

37. Ibid.

38. Reed Pedlow to Mallory O'Connor, November 28, 2006.

39. Bartram, *Travels* (Harper), 118.

40. Reed Pedlow to Mallory O'Connor, November 28, 2006.

41. Ibid.

42. Bartram, *Travels* (Van Doren), 135.

43. Ibid., 135.

44. Ibid., 175.

45. Porter, "Titian Ramsey Peale," 431–44.

46. Ibid.

47. Thomas Say to John Melsheimer, June 10, 1818, in Porter, "Titian Ramsey Peale."

48. Porter, "Titian Ramsey Peale," 13 (citation refers to the unpublished draft).

49. Ibid., 17.

50. Proby, *Audubon in Florida*, xviii.

51. Ibid., xx.

52. Audubon, *The Birds of America*, xii.

53. Audubon quoted in Cabell and Hanna, *The St. Johns: A Parade of Diversities*, 188.
54. Audubon quoted in Proby, *Audubon in Florida*, 315.
55. Audubon quoted in Cabell and Hanna, *The St. Johns: A Parade of Diversities*, 189.
56. Audubon quoted in Proby, *Audubon in Florida*, 127.
57. Ibid., 144.

Chapter 6. A Sportsmen's Paradise: Fishing, Hunting, and Recreation in the St. Johns Region

1. Brown, *Florida's First People*, 114.
2. Bartram, *Travels* (Van Doren), 140–41.
3. Allen, *DeLand Sun News*, 1975.
4. Quoted in Mueller, *Steamboating on the St. Johns*, 83.
5. Tom Baskett, interview by Gary Monroe, 2006.
6. Cikovsky and Kelly, *Winslow Homer*, 254.
7. Hannaway, *Winslow Homer in the Tropics*, 213.
8. Belleville, *River of Lakes*, 43.
9. Frieseke, *Uneventful Reminiscences*, 32.
10. Ibid.
11. Montrose, *Tales from a Florida Fish Camp: And Other Tidbits of Swamp Rat Philosophy*, 3.
12. Ibid., 6.
13. Bull, "Life on the River."
14. *AAA Florida Tourbook*, 134.
15. Harley Strickland, interview by Gary Monroe, 2006.
16. Brian Schanel, interview by Gary Monroe, 2005.
17. Alicia Clark, interview by Gary Monroe, 2005.
18. Ibid.
19. Ibid.
20. Tim Peterson, telephone interview with Mallory O'Connor, March 2008.
21. Peterson, personal communication, 2008.
22. Ibid.
23. Ibid.
24. Ibid.
25. M. O'Connor, notes to *Nate Shiner Memorial Exhibition Catalogue*, 1973.
26. Ibid., 1982.
27. Marcia Tucker in *Nate Shiner*, 1984: 5.
28. Le Moyne in Lorant, ed., *The New World*, 85.
29. Nellie Hayes, notes from a brochure at DeBary Hall, n.d.
30. Tom Baskett, interview by Gary Monroe, 2006.
31. Ibid.
32. Laudonnière quoted in Lorant, ed., *The New World*, 89.
33. Wendy Beeson to Mallory O'Connor, 2006.

Chapter 7. Treasures of Welaka

1. Bettye Reagan to Mallory O'Connor, 2007.
2. Hansen Mulford, interview by Gary Monroe, 2006.
3. Ibid.
4. Belleville, *River of Lakes*, 49.
5. Ibid., 49.
6. Ibid., 52.
7. Ibid., 44.
8. Ibid., 62.
9. Ibid.
10. Susan Mitchell, interview by Gary Monroe, 2006.
11. Christine Mitchell, interview by Gary Monroe, 2005.
12. Ibid.
13. Carl Knickerbocker, interview by Gary Monroe, 2006.
14. Edmund Stowe, notes.
15. Ibid.
16. Wendy Spirduso, interview by Gary Monroe, 2006.
17. Edmund Stowe, notes.
18. Szarkowski, *Looking at Photographs*.
19. Ibid.
20. McCarthy, *St. Johns River Guidebook*, 26.
21. Ibid.
22. Belleville, *River of Lakes*, 70.
23. Tom Sadler, interview by Gary Monroe, 2006.
24. Ibid.
25. Ibid., March 2008.
26. Ibid., 2006.
27. Jim Draper, interview by Gary Monroe, 2006.
28. Ibid.
29. Gannon, ed., *The New History of Florida*, 280.
30. Gilbert Lycan, interview by Gary Monroe, 2005.
31. Belleville, telephone conversation with Mallory O'Connor, 2006.
32. Ibid.
33. Pam Griesinger, interview by Gary Monroe, 2006.
34. Ibid.
35. Ibid.
36. Belleville, *River of Lakes*, 101.
37. McCarthy, *St. Johns River Guidebook*, 51.
38. www.pioneersettlement.org.
39. McCarthy, *St. Johns River Guidebook*, 53.
40. Belleville, *River of Lakes*, 97.
41. Ibid., 104.
42. Ibid.
43. Bartram, *Travels* (Van Doren), 103.
44. Ibid.
45. Rawlings quoted in Belleville, *River of Lakes*, 105.
46. Belleville, *River of Lakes*, 105.

47. Ibid., 107.
48. Sydney McKenna, phone conversation with Mallory O'Connor, September 27, 2006.
49. Ibid.
50. Belleville, *River of Lakes*, 133.
51. David La Cagnina, interview by Mallory O'Connor, 2006.
52. Ibid.

Chapter 8. Searching for Paradise: Tourism in the River Region

1. Derr, *Some Kind of Paradise*, 68.
2. Ibid., 70.
3. Edward King quoted in Favis, *Martin Johnson Heade in Florida*, 3.
4. Ibid.
5. Davidson, "Landscape Icons, Tourism, and Land Development in the Northeast," 4.
6. Ibid., 69.
7. Mueller, *Steamboating on the St. Johns*, 9.
8. Ibid., 11.
9. Ibid., 12.
10. Ibid., 116.
11. Mann, *Art in Florida: 1564–1945*, 97.
12. Davidson, "Landscape Icons, Tourism, and Land Development in the Northeast," 6.
13. Favis, *Martin Johnson Heade in Florida*, 45.
14. Erik Robinson quoted in Libby, ed., *Celebrating Florida: Works of Art from the Vickers Collection*, 58.
15. Abbie Brooks [Silvia Sunshine] in Favis, *Martin Johnson Heade in Florida*, 113.
16. Deborah Pollack, phone conversation with Mallory O'Connor, 2007.
17. Deborah Pollack, quoted in Gary Schwan, "Why Has the Island's First Professional Painter Been Forgotten?" *Palm Beach Post*, August 19, 2007.
18. Ibid.
19. Ibid.
20. Pollack, phone conversation with Mallory O'Connor, 2007.
21. Laura Woodward quoted in Frances Gillmor, *Palm Beach Times*, February 17, 1924, quoted in Gary Schwan, "Why Has the Island's First Professional Painter Been Forgotten?" *Palm Beach Post*, August 19, 2007.
22. Pollack, phone conversation with Mallory O'Connor, 2007.
23. Lanier, *Florida: Its Scenery, Climate and History*, 20.
24. Belleville, *River of Lakes*, 126.
25. Ibid., 127.
26. Margaret H. Watts to Mallory O'Connor, May 2006.
27. Umberto Eco quoted in Mormino, *Land of Sunshine, State of Dreams*, 111.
28. Mueller, *Ocklawaha River Steamboats*, 12.
29. Ibid., 14.
30. Christopher Still, *Patriot and Warrior* (brochure for the murals commissioned by the Florida House of Representatives and available to visitors to the Capitol), 2002.

31. *Harper's New Monthly Magazine*, October 1870.
32. Derr, *Some Kind of Paradise*, 72.
33. Dick Punnett, interview by Gary Monroe, 2006.
34. Ibid.
35. Stowe quoted in D. Miller, "Swamp and Jungle Images and the Modernizing of American Culture," 10.
36. Ibid.
37. Mueller, *Along the St. Johns and Ocklawaha Rivers*, 32.
38. Favis, notes to Mallory O'Connor, 2007.
39. Michael Ivankovich, "Biographical Notes on James Harris," 2002, www.wnut ting.com/books.
40. Ibid.
41. Ibid.
42. Ibid.
43. Larry Roberts, interview by Gary Monroe, 2006.
44. Stowe, *Palmetto Leaves*, 27.

Chapter 9. Tourism Continued: Trains, Planes, and Automobiles

1. Hampshire Museum Services brochure.
2. Gannon, *Florida: A Short History*, 71.
3. Mormino, *Land of Sunshine, State of Dreams*, 93.
4. Bruce Mozert, notes.
5. Allison Watson, interview by Gary Monroe, 2006.
6. Ibid.
7. Derr, *Some Kind of Paradise*, 339.
8. Brenda Hofreiter to Mallory O'Connor, April 2006.
9. Ibid.

Chapter 10. Springs Eternal: Water Resources in the St. Johns Region

1. Stamm, *The Springs of Florida*, 17.
2. Ibid., 16.
3. Bartram, *Travels* (Van Doren), 150.
4. Torchia, *A Florida Legacy: Ponce de León in Florida*, 15.
5. Ibid., 26.
6. Bill Dreggors, interview by Gary Monroe, 2006.
7. Valdés, *Margaret Ross Tolbert: Springs Eternal?*
8. Stamm, *The Springs of Florida*, 58.
9. Sean Sexton, phone conversation with Mallory O'Connor, 2007.
10. Kemp, "Postmodern Cowboy in Florida," 3.
11. Ken Rollins, in *Sean Sexton: A Pastoral Life Inside/Out*, 1.
12. Derr, *Some Kind of Paradise*, 363.
13. McCarthy, *St. Johns River Guidebook*, 76.
14. Libby, ed., *Coast to Coast: The Contemporary Landscape in Florida*, 40.
15. Belleville, *River of Lakes*, 132.
16. Ibid., 13.

1. Bartram, *Travels* (Van Doren), 153.
2. Craig Rubadoux, notes, n.d., www.dabbertgallery.com/artists/Rubadoux.
3. Ibid.
4. Bartram, *Travels* (Van Doren), 167.
5. Bartram, *Travels* (Harper), 251.
6. Monaco, introduction to *A Plan for the Abolition of Slavery*, by Moses E. Levy, xii.
7. Gannon, ed., *The New History of Florida*, 215.
8. Peter Carolin, interview by Mallory O'Connor, September 12, 2007.
9. Ibid.
10. Ibid.
11. Rowe, *The Idea of Florida in the American Literary Imagination*, 108.
12. Rawlings, *Cross Creek*, 7–8.
13. Jackson Walker, phone conversation with Mallory O'Connor, April 2006.
14. Wesley Hromatko, Unitarian Universalist Historical Society Web site, www25 -temp.uua.org/uuhs/duub/listlit.html.
15. Artsedge Web site, Kennedy Center, www.artsedge.org.
16. Betsy James Wyeth, ed., *The Wyeths: The Letters of N. C. Wyeth, 1901–1945*, 781.
17. Ibid., 783.
18. Ibid.
19. Ibid.
20. Ibid., 781.
21. Karen Baumgartner, phone conversation with Mallory O'Connor, October 1, 2006.
22. Murray Laurie, interview by Mallory O'Connor, 2007.
23. Belleville, *River of Lakes*, 33.
24. Ibid.
25. Rawlings quoted ibid., 34.
26. Rawlings, *Cross Creek*, 340.
27. Bull, "Life on the River," 9.
28. Stetson, acknowledgments in *Seeing the Forest: Landscapes by Jerry Cutler*, 1.
29. Behrens, in *Seeing the Forest: Landscapes by Jerry Cutler*, 5.
30. Heartney, "Arnold Mesches at Donahue/Sosinksi."
31. Rawlings, *Cross Creek*, 380.

Chapter 12. Palatka: A River City's Tale

1. Michaels, *The River Flows North*, 102.
2. *Gainesville Sun*, July 1, 2006.
3. Mueller, *Along the St. Johns and Ocklawaha Rivers*, 120.
4. Lanier, *Florida: Its Scenery, Climate and History*, 127.
5. Abbie Brooks [Silvia Sunshine], "Petals Plucked from Sunny Climes," 1880.
6. Volunteer guide at the Palatka History Center, 2006.
7. Lanier, *Florida: Its Scenery, Climate and History*, 76.

8. Derr, *Some Kind of Paradise*, 116.

9. www.worldwar1. com/paltaka.htm.

10. Delzell, *A Historic Tour Guide of Palatka*.

11. Clarke Garnsey, notes to Gary Monroe, 2006.

12. Ibid.

13. Tom Baskett, interview by Gary Monroe, 2006.

14. Ibid.

15. Torchia, *E. C. Kasten: Palatka Expressionist*, 4.

16. Ibid., 5.

17. Ibid., 6.

18. *St. Augustine Record*, Jan. 19, 1924, in Torchia, *Lost Colony: St. Augustine Artists*, 9.

19. *St. Augustine Record*, March 24, 1946, in Torchia, *Lost Colony: St. Augustine Artists*, 112.

Chapter 13. From Cowford to Jacksonville

1. Johnson, *Highways and Byways of Florida* (rpt., New York: Macmillan, 1986).

2. "Florida's Civil War History" Web page, www.flahistory.org.

3. *Exploring Florida* Web site, http://fcit.fsu.edu.

4. Cabell and Hanna, *The St. Johns: A Parade of Diversities*, 245.

5. Libby, ed., *Celebrating Florida: Works of Art from the Vickers Collection*, 48.

6. Cabell and Hanna, *The St. Johns: A Parade of Diversities*, 227.

7. Laurie, "Florida's Carpenter Gothic Churches," 7.

8. Ibid.

9. John O'Connor, *John A. O'Connor: Conceptual Realism*, 15.

10. O'Connor, personal communication, 2005.

11. Jones and McCarthy, *African Americans in Florida*, 66.

12. Ibid., 66–67.

13. *Jacksonville Times-Union*, 2003, 5.

14. Barlow, "The Flying Ace," 2.

15. Ibid.

16. Gannon, *Florida: A Short History*, 105.

17. Walker, *The Legendary Florida Series*.

18. Allison Watson, interview by Gary Monroe, 2006.

19. Belleville, *River of Lakes*, 177.

20. Ibid., 179.

21. Ibid., 180.

Bibliography

Adams, Alto, Jr. *A Florida Cattle Ranch*. Sarasota: Pineapple Press, 1998.

Akerman, Joe A., Jr. "America's First Cowmen." *Forum* 30, no. 1 (Winter 2006): 7–13.

———. *Florida Cowman: A History of Florida Cattle Raising*. Kissimmee, Fla.: Florida Cattlemen's Association, 1976.

Anderson, Lars. *Paynes Prairie: A History of the Great Savanna*. Sarasota: Pineapple Press, 2001.

Audubon, John James. *The Birds of America*. Facsimile reproduction of the 1832 edition. New York: Macmillan, 1937.

Barlow, Margaret. "The Flying Ace." *Florida History and the Arts Magazine* (Winter 2004).

Bartram, John. *The Correspondence of John Bartram, 1734–1777*. Edited by Edmund Berkeley and Dorothy Berkeley. Gainesville: University Press of Florida, 1992.

Bartram, William. *Travels*. Edited by Mark Van Doren. New York: Macy-Masius, 1928.

———. *The Travels of William Bartram*. Edited by Francis Harper. New Haven: Yale University Press, 1958.

Behrens, Todd. *Seeing the Forest: Landscapes by Jerry Cutler*. Exhibition catalog. Lakeland, Fla.: Polk Museum of Art, 2003.

Belleville, Bill. "Our Deep Blue Destiny." *Forum* 25, no. 2 (Summer 2002): 8–13.

———. *River of Lakes*. Athens: University of Georgia Press, 2000.

Bennett, Charles E. *Fort Caroline and Its Leaders*. Pamphlet from the Fort Caroline National Monument.

———. *Laudonnière and Fort Caroline*. 1964. Reprint, Tuscaloosa: University of Alabama Press, 2001.

———, trans. *Three Voyages* By René Laudonnière. 1975. Reprint, Tuscaloosa: University of Alabama Press, 2001.

———. *Twelve on the River St. Johns*. Jacksonville: University of North Florida Press, 1989.

Berkeley, Edmund, and Dorothy Smith Berkeley. *The Life and Travels of John Bartram: From Lake Ontario to the River St. John*. Tallahassee: University Presses of Florida, 1982.

Brown, Robin. *Florida's First People*. Sarasota: Pineapple Press, 1994.

Bull, Roger. "Life on the River." *Florida Times Union*, October 7, 2001.

———. "Our River's Beginnings." *Florida Times Union*, October 7, 2001.

———. "Reflections of Our River." *Florida Times Union*, October 14, 2001.

Burt, Al. *Tropic of Cracker*. Gainesville: University Press of Florida, 1999.

Cabell, Branch, and A. J. Hanna. *The St. Johns: A Parade of Diversities*. New York: Farrar and Rinehart, 1943.

Carr, Archie. *A Naturalist in Florida*. New Haven: Yale University Press, 1994.

Cashin, Edward J. *William Bartram and the American Revolution on the Southern Frontier*. Columbia: University of South Carolina Press, 2000.

Childs, Craig. *The Secret Knowledge of Water*. New York: Little, Brown, 2000.

Cikovsky, Nicolai, Jr., and Franklin Kelly. *Winslow Homer*. Exhibition catalog. New Haven: Yale University Press, 1995.

Cruickshank, Helen G. *John and William Bartram's America*. Greenwich: Devin-Adai, 1957.

———, ed. *Bartram in Florida*. Florida Federation of Garden Clubs, 1986.

Davidson, Gail S. "Landscape Icons, Tourism, and Land Development in the Northeast." In *Frederic Church, Winslow Homer and Thomas Moran: Tourism and the American Landscape*, by Davidson et al. New York: Bulfinch Press, 2006.

Deagan, Kathleen, and Darcie MacMahon. *Fort Mose*. Gainesville: University Press of Florida, 1995.

Delzell, John M. *A Historic Tour Guide of Palatka*. Palatka: Putnam County Historical Society, 1992.

Derr, Mark. *Some Kind of Paradise*. New York: William Morrow, 1989.

Dobrin, Sidney, and Christian R. Weisser. *Natural Discourse: Toward Ecocomposition*. Albany: State University of New York Press, 2002.

Dusenbury, George, and Jane Dusenbury. *How to Retire in Florida*. New York: Harper, 1947.

Favis, Roberta. *Martin Johnson Heade in Florida*. Gainesville: University Press of Florida, 2003.

Fishman, Gail. *Journeys through Paradise*. Gainesville: University Press of Florida, 2000.

Fradkin, Arlene. "Florida Archaeology." Typescript. 2006.

Frieseke, Frederick C. *Uneventful Reminiscences*. New York: Hollis Taggart Galleries, 2001.

Gannon, Michael. *Florida: A Short History*. Gainesville: University Press of Florida, 1993.

———, ed. *The New History of Florida*. Gainesville: University Press of Florida, 1996.

Gordon, Elsbeth. *Florida's Colonial Architectural History*. Gainesville: University Press of Florida, 2002.

Hann, John H. *A History of the Timucuan Indians and Missions*. Gainesville: University Press of Florida, 1996.

Hannaway, Patti. *Winslow Homer in the Tropics*. Richmond, Va.: Westover, n.d.

Hawthorne, Nathanial, ed. *Great American Travel Writings*. London: Octopus Group, 1990.

Heartney, Eleanor. "Arnold Mesches at Donahue/Sosinksi." *Art in America*, September 1, 1997.

———. "The FBI Paintings." *Hanging Loose Press*, 2006.

Hoopes, Donelson F. *Winslow Homer Watercolors*. New York: Watson-Guptill, 1969.

Jay I. Kislak Foundation, Inc. *Myths and Dreams: Exploring the Cultural Legacies of Florida and the Caribbean*. Miami: Jay I. Kislak Foundation, 2000.

Johnson, Clifton. *Highways and Byways of Florida*. New York: Macmillan, 1918.

———. *Highways and Byways of the South*. New York: Macmillan, 1918.

Jones, Maxine D., and Kevin McCarthy. *African Americans in Florida*. Sarasota: Pineapple Press, 1993.

Junker, Patricia. *Winslow Homer, Artist and Angler*. Fort Worth, Tex.: Amon Carter Museum, 2003.

Kemp, Michael. "Postmodern Cowboy in Florida." In *Sean Sexton: A Pastoral Life Inside/Out*. Exhibition catalog. Largo, Fla.: Gulf Coast Museum of Art, 2005.

Kline, Benjamin. *First along the River: A Brief History of the U.S. Environmental Movement*. San Francisco: Acada Books, 1997.

Kohen, Helen, et al. "Perfume, Postcards and Promises: The Orange in Art and Industry." *Journal of Decorative and Propaganda Arts*, ed. Cathy Leff. Miami: Wolfsonian Foundation, 1998.

Lanier, Sidney. *Florida: Its Scenery, Climate and History*. Facsimile reproduction of the 1875 edition with introduction and index by Jerrell H. Scofner. Gainesville: University Press of Florida, 1976.

Lawson, Sarah, and W. John Faupel, eds. *A Foothold in Florida*. Based on a new translation of Laudonnière's *L'Histoire notable de la Floride*. West Sussex, UK: Antique Atlas Publications, 1992.

Laurie, Murray. "Florida's Carpenter Gothic Churches." *Florida Living Magazine*, April 1998, 6–8.

Levy, Moses E. *A Plan for the Abolition of Slavery*. Edited and with an introduction by Chris Monaco. Micanopy, Fla.: Wacahoota Press, 1999.

Libby, Gary R., ed. *Celebrating Florida: Works of Art from the Vickers Collection*. Daytona Beach, Fla.: Museum of Arts and Sciences, 1995.

———, ed. *Coast to Coast: The Contemporary Landscape in Florida*. Daytona Beach, Fla.: Museum of Arts and Sciences, 1999.

Lorant, Stefan, ed. *The New World*. New York: Duell, Sloan and Pearce, 1946.

Lycan, Gilbert. *Stetson University: The First 100 Years*. Exhibition catalog. DeLand, Fla.: Stetson University, n.d.

Matilsky, Barbara C. *Fragile Ecologies*. New York: Rizzoli International, 1992.

Mann, Maybelle. *Art in Florida: 1564–1945*. Sarasota: Pineapple Press, 1999.

McCarthy, Kevin M. *Native Americans in Florida*. Sarasota: Pineapple Press, 1999.

———. *St. Johns River Guidebook*. Sarasota: Pineapple Press, 2004.

McEvilley, Thomas. "Illuminated Manuscripts." *Art in America*, October 2003.

McEwan, James Miller, ed. *Mission San Luis de Apalachee*. Tallahassee: Florida Heritage Publication, 1998.

Merchant, Carolyn. *Reinventing Eden*. New York and London: Routledge, 2004.

Michaels, Brian E. *The River Flows North*. Palatka: Putnam County Archives and Historical Commission, 1976.

Milanich, Jerald T. "Early Archaeology on the St. Johns River, Florida." Paper presented at the Bartram Trail Conference, Gainesville, Fla., October 2001.

———. *Florida Indians and the Invasion from Europe*. Gainesville: University Press of Florida, 1995.

———. *Laboring in the Fields of the Lord*. Washington and London: Smithsonian Institution Press, 1999.

Miller, David C. "Swamp and Jungle Images and the Modernizing of American Culture." In *The Swamp: On the Edge of Eden*, by Miller et al., exhibition catalog. Gainesville: Samuel P. Harn Museum of Art, 2001.

Miller, James J. *An Environmental History of Northeast Florida*. Gainesville: University Press of Florida, 1998.

Monaco, Chris. Introduction to *A Plan for the Abolition of Slavery*, by Moses E. Levy. Micanopy, Fla.: Wacahoota Press, 1999.

Monroe, Gary. *The Highwaymen: Florida's African-American Landscape Painters*. Gainesville: University Press of Florida, 2001.

Montrose, Jack. *Tales from a Florida Fish Camp: And Other Tidbits of Swamp Rat Philosophy*. Sarasota: Pineapple Press, 2003.

Mormino, Gary. *Land of Sunshine, State of Dreams*. Gainesville: University Press of Florida, 2005.

Morris, Theodore. *Florida's Lost Tribes*. Gainesville: University Press of Florida, 2004.

Mueller, Edward A. *Along the St. Johns and Ocklawaha Rivers*. Charleston: Arcadia, 1999.

———. *Ocklawaha River Steamboats*. Jacksonville, Fla.: Mendelson Printing, 1983.

———. *Steamboating on the St. Johns*. Melbourne, Fla.: South Brevard Historical Society, 1980.

Muir, John. *A Thousand-Mile Walk to the Gulf*. Edited by Colin Fletcher. San Francisco: Sierra Club Books, 1991.

Nichols, Ashton, ed. *Romantic Natural Histories: William Wordsworth, Charles Darwin, and Others*. New York: Houghton Mifflin, 2004.

O'Connor, John A. "Artist's Statement." In *John A. O'Connor: Conceptual Realism*, exhibition catalog. Pensacola, Fla.: Pensacola Museum of Art, 2003.

O'Connor, Mallory. *The Great Alachua Savanna: A Visual History of Paynes Prairie*. Exhibition catalog. Gainesville: Santa Fe Gallery, 1997.

———. *Lost Cities of the Ancient Southeast*. Gainesville: University Press of Florida, 1995.

———. Notes to *Nate Shiner Memorial Exhibition Catalogue*. Gainesville, Fla.: printed for Nate Shiner's memorial exhibit, 1984.

O'Sullivan, Maurice, and Jack C. Lane, eds. *The Florida Reader: Visions of Paradise from 1530 to the Present*. Sarasota: Pineapple Press, 1991.

Parrish, Susan Scott. *American Curiosity*. Chapel Hill: University of North Carolina Press, 2006.

Piazza, Kurt. *Sean Sexton: A Pastoral Life Inside/Out*. Exhibition catalog. Largo, Fla.: Gulf Coast Museum of Art, 2005.

Pickard, John B. *Florida's Eden*. Gainesville, Fla.: Maupin House, 1994.

Porter, Charlotte M. "Titian Ramsey Peale." Unpublished draft subsequently published in *Florida Historical Quarterly* (1983): 431–44.

Proby, Kathryn Hall. *Audubon in Florida*. Coral Gables: University of Miami Press, 1974.

Proctor, Sam. *Drawings by Frank Hamilton Taylor*. Exhibition catalog. Gainesville: Samuel P. Harn Museum of Art, 2006.

Purdy, Barbara, with photographs by Roy C. Craven Jr. *Indian Art of Ancient Florida*. Gainesville: University Press of Florida, 1996.

Rawlings, Marjorie Kinnan. *Cross Creek*. New York: Simon and Schuster, 1942.

———. *The Yearling*. New York: Charles Scribner's Sons, 1939.

Ripple, Jeff, and Susan Cerulean. *The Wild Heart of Florida*. Gainesville: University Press of Florida, 1999.

Rivers, Bill, and Sandy Rivers. "The Columbine." *Gainesville Sun*, July 1, 2006.

Rowe, Anne E. *The Idea of Florida in the American Literary Imagination*. Gainesville: University Press of Florida, 1992.

Sammons, Sandra Wallus. *John and William Bartram: Travelers in Early America*. Flagler Beach, Fla.: Ocean, 2004.

Sanders, Brad. *Guide to William Bartram's Travels*. Athens, Ga.: Fevertree Press, 2002.

Schafer, Daniel L. *Anna Kingsley*. St. Augustine, Fla.: St. Augustine Historical Society, 1997.

———. "Governor James Grant's Villa: A British East Florida Indigo Plantation." *El Escribano* 37 (2000). St. Augustine, Fla.: St. Augustine Historical Society.

Stamm, Doug. *The Springs of Florida*. Sarasota: Pineapple Press, 1994.

Slaughter, Thomas P. *The Natures of John and William Bartram*. New York: Vintage, 1996.

Specter, Michael. "The Last Drop." *New Yorker*, October 23, 2006.

Spirduso, Wendy. "Artist E. B. Stowe." *Orlando Sentinel*, n.d.

Ste. Claire, Dana. "Cracker." *Forum* 30, no. 1 (Winter 2006): 4–5.

———. *Cracker: The Cracker Culture in Florida History*. Gainesville: University Press of Florida, 1998.

Stetson, Daniel. Acknowledgments in *Seeing the Forest: Landscapes by Jerry Cutler*. Exhibition catalogue. Lakeland: Polk Museum of Art, 2003.

Stowe, Harriet Beecher. *Palmetto Leaves*. 1873. Facsimile reprint, with an introduction by Mary Graff and Edith Cowles. Gainesville: University Press of Florida, 1968.

Szarkowski, John, ed. *Looking at Photographs*. Exhibition catalog. New York: Museum of Modern Art, 1973.

Torchia, Robert. *E. C. Kasten: Palatka Expressionist*. Exhibition catalog. Tallahassee, Fla.: Museum of Art, 1999.

———. *A Florida Legacy: Ponce de León in Florida*. Exhibition catalog. Jacksonville, Fla.: Cummer Museum of Art and Gardens, 1998.

———. *Lost Colony: The Artists of St. Augustine, 1930–1950*. St. Augustine, Fla.: Lightner Museum, 2001.

Valdés, Karen. *Margaret Ross Tolbert: Springs Eternal?* Exhibition catalog. Largo, Fla.: Gulf Coast Museum of Art, 2003.

Walker, Jackson. *The Legendary Florida Series*. Exhibition program notes. DeLand, Fla.: DeLand Museum of Art, 2006.

Waselkov, Gregory A., and Kathryn E. Braund, eds. *William Bartram on the Southeastern Indians*. Lincoln: University of Nebraska Press, 1995.

Waterbury, Jean Parker. *El Escribano* 19 (1982). St. Augustine, Fla.: St. Augustine Historical Society.

Wilmerding, John. *Audubon, Homer, Whistler and Nineteenth-Century America*. New York: McCall, 1970.

Wilton, Andrew, and Tim Barringer. *American Sublime, Landscape Painting in the United States, 1820–1880*. Exhibition catalog. Princeton, N.J.: Princeton University Press, 2002.

Wissel, Virginia. "Celebrating the Maritime Heritage." *Welcome Magazine*, Winter/Spring 2007, 54–60.

———. "The Sacred Place—Mount Royal." *Welcome Magazine,* Winter/Spring 2007, 32–36.

Wolf, Denise. "Ecotours: A Tour of a Working Florida Cattle Ranch." www.ecofloridamag.com/archived/ecotour_ranch.htm.

Wong, Edie L. Review of *Traveling South: Travel Narratives and the Construction of American Identity*, by John D. Cox. *Biography: An Interdisciplinary Quarterly* (Fall 2006). University of Hawaii Press.

Wright, Leroy. *Saving the St. Johns River*. Indianapolis: Dog Ear Publishing, 2006.

Wyeth, Betsy James, ed. *The Wyeths: The Letters of N.C. Wyeth, 1901–1945*. Boston: Gambit, 1971.

Zeiler, Jill. "Spotlight on Augusta Savage." *Jacksonville Times-Union,* October 5, 2003.

Index

MALLORY O'CONNOR retired in 2005 as an associate professor of art history and the director of the Santa Fe College Art Gallery. Prior to her work at Santa Fe, O'Connor was the visual arts coordinator for the Thomas Center Gallery in Gainesville, Florida. She received her MFA in art history from Ohio University, and is the author of *Lost Cities of the Ancient Southeast* (1995).

GARY MONROE is a professor of fine arts and photography at Daytona State College. His photographs have appeared in exhibitions throughout the state and are published in *Life in South Beach* (1988) and *Florida Dreams* (1993). He is the author of *The Highwaymen: Florida's African American Landscape Painters* (2001), *Harold Newton: The Original Highwayman* (2007), and *Silver Springs: The Underwater Photography of Bruce Mozert* (2008).